THE TROUBLED GIANT

THE TROUBLED GIANT

BRITAIN AMONG THE GREAT POWERS
1916–1939

BY

F. S. NORTHEDGE

*Published for The London School of Economics
and Political Science*

FREDERICK A. PRAEGER, *Publishers*
New York · Washington

BOOKS THAT MATTER

Published in the United States of America in 1966
by Frederick A. Praeger, Inc., Publishers
111 Fourth Avenue, New York, N.Y. 10003

Second printing, 1967

All rights reserved

Copyright © 1966 by F. S. Northedge in London, England
Library of Congress Catalog Card Number: 66–26556

Printed in Great Britain

ἦ πολλὰ βροτοῖς ἔστιν ἰδοῦσιν
γνῶναι· πρὶν ἰδεῖν δ'οὐδεὶς μάντις
τῶν μελλόντων ὅ τι πράξει.

Sophocles, *Ajax*, 1418–20

ERRATA

Page 568, lines 30–35. For the words beginning 'the Germans' and ending 'issue an immediate' substitute the following:

the Germans alleged that his motive was fear that 'his own plans for developing Anglo-Rumanian economic relations' would be nullified by the current German–Rumanian trade talks proceeding in Bucharest. However this may be, the Minister was given a reprimand by Foreign Minister Gafencu and told to issue a

CONTENTS

		PAGE
	Preface	ix
I	The Covenants of War	1
II	The Allied Ascendancy	21
III	The Coming of Bolshevism	46
IV	A Colony of Lepers	65
V	'The Stern but Just Peace'	91
VI	Britain and Islam	125
VII	Enforcement of the Treaty	160
VIII	Negotiating with Russia	197
IX	In Search of Security	223
X	The Making of Locarno	248
XI	New Forces in the Far East	273
XII	Britain and Soviet Communism	303
XIII	Disarmament: the Naval Aspect	327
XIV	The Manchurian Question	348
XV	The World Rearms	368
XVI	The Concert Unrevived	396
XVII	The German Resurgence	426
XVIII	Japan's Challenge in Asia	450
XIX	Man of Peace	481
XX	The Rim of Chaos	511
XXI	The Ides of March	549
XXII	Last Days of Europe	584
XXIII	The Fault in Ourselves	617
	Select Bibliography	631
	Index	643

MAPS

	PAGE
The Peace Settlement	115
The Far East, 1919–39	277
Czechoslovakia, 1938–9	553

NOTE ON ABBREVIATIONS USED IN THIS BOOK

CAB : Cabinet Minutes and Conclusions, *December 1916–October 1922*, and other Cabinet Office papers, Public Record Office.

D.B.F.P. : The series *Documents on British Foreign Policy, 1919–39*, published by H.M. Stationery Office, London.

D.G.F.P. : The series, *Documents on German Foreign Policy, 1918–45*, published by H.M. Stationery Office, London.

F.R.U.S. : The series, *Papers relating to the Foreign Relations of the United States*, published by the United States Department of State, Washington, D.C.

L.N.O.J. : League of Nations; Official Journal.

R.I.I.A. : The Royal Institute of International Affairs, London.

N.B.: Details of sources referred to in footnotes are given in the Select Bibliography at the end of this book. Sources not included in the Bibliography are briefly described in footnotes to the text.

PREFACE

My primary object in writing this book has been to provide within reasonable compass an account of Britain's foreign policy from the middle of the First World War to the outbreak of the Second. The need for such a book is one which any student of modern history or international relations will recognise. British policy during the Second World War has been well described in Sir Llewellyn Woodward's official history and studies of post-1945 policy have recently appeared.[1] The inter-war years, however, so far remain without a historian despite the great volume of source material which has been made available in the last twenty years, though this, owing to the rules governing publication of official British documents, is still regrettably incomplete.

I have chosen to begin this account at the end of 1916, with the formation of the Coalition Government under Lloyd George, because it was at that time that serious moves began for a negotiated end to the war, and these importantly influenced the various governments' attitudes to the eventual settlement. Moreover, the peace negotiations of 1919–23 are incomprehensible except against the background of the military operations and diplomacy of the war's concluding stages. Many things happened in the last two years of the war, notably the Bolshevik Revolution in Russia, the entrance of the United States into the war, the collapse of the Austro-Hungarian Empire, which confronted the British Government with a situation wholly different from what they had expected when they first went to war. It is often forgotten today that in the 1930s Britain was called upon to defend a legal system in Europe, important elements of which had been shaped in the final stages of the First World War without British assistance and in some respects without British approval.

The method adopted in writing this book has been to describe the successive international problems facing British governments and the considerations which influenced the approach of British Ministers to them. In doing so, the aim has been to bring out, in enough detail to show the complexity of these issues but not, it is hoped, so much as to lose the main thread, a

[1] Sir Llewellyn Woodward, *British Foreign Policy in the Second World War*, H.M.S.O., London, 1961; F. S. Northedge, *British Foreign Policy: the process of readjustment, 1945–61*, London, 1962; C. M. Woodhouse, *British Foreign Policy since the Second World War*, London, 1961.

sense of the simultaneity and magnitude of the challenges to the
British international position during these years. Most of the
official British and foreign documents, personal memoirs and
other primary sources made accessible in recent years have been
used, including the Cabinet Minutes and Foreign Office files
for the period December 1916 until October 1922 now available
at the Public Record Office, and heavy reliance has been
placed on the series *Documents on British Foreign Policy, 1919–39*,
published by H.M. Stationery Office. As far as possible,
however, foreign documentary material recently published,
as for instance in the reports of the International Military
Tribunal at Nuremberg, which could not have been in the
hands of the British Government at the time when their decisions
were made, have not been cited, since this work is not so much
international history as a record of strictly British decision-
making. There is also little reference to unpublished sources
such as private correspondence. My belief is that the published
sources now available make possible an understanding of the
essential thread of British policy in this period, and that
what is gained by nuances of interpretation being added
through close study of private papers on particular aspects
may be more than lost through the publication of a complete
study such as this being indefinitely delayed. The chief need
at present is for a reasonably concise study based upon the
massive source material now in print. This need the present
book seeks to satisfy.

This work cannot claim to be an exhaustive account of every
aspect of the vast range of British foreign relations during
twenty-three years; only if it filled many volumes could it do
so. Many problems are treated sketchily; others are omitted,
though the decision to discriminate in this way has always been
carefully considered. As the sub-title indicates, the main emphasis is upon British relations with the family of Great Powers
during a period of mounting pressure on British commitments
and resources throughout the world, pressure which goes far to
explain the fall in Britain's international status since 1945.
This dominant theme of Britain among the Great Powers has
been chosen, partly to give focus to a subject of heroic scope,
partly because reconciliation between the Powers was indeed
the ruling concern of British policy-makers during this period.
If any single axiom has united British Ministers in foreign
policy in the twentieth century it has been the paramount need
for co-existence between the giant Powers of the day. If a label
were attached to British policy in our period it would need to
be: the composition of the greatest Powers.

There is a further object I have had in mind in writing this
book, namely to search for relatively enduring attitudes of mind
behind the daily handling of foreign relations. Admittedly
governments, the British included, act in foreign affairs from
the 'reason of the case', the imperatives, that is, of the deter-
minate situation before them. Each conjuncture of international affairs, too, is *sui generis* and Ministers must deal, not
with general problems, but with particular instances. Nevertheless, within a given country a relatively enduring style of
handling these problems, shaped by material interests, coloured
by traditional habit, cannot but emerge, and governments
facing concrete issues do so with minds to no small extent pre-
determined by such half-articulated premisses. Hence an
attempt is made here to frame a profile of the British style of
foreign policy. In the concluding chapter it is argued that
many of the weaknesses of British policy in this period were due
to the applying of a political style formed in one age to the
problems of another.

I am indebted for generous financial assistance to the
Rockefeller Foundation of New York. I am also grateful to
the London School of Economics for the grant of two terms
leave from teaching for the completion of this book, to my
colleagues at the School who manfully shouldered my teaching
burdens while I was in the library and to Mrs. E. Wilson, of
the School's Geography Department, who drew the maps.

F. S. Northedge

The London School of Economics and Political Science,
January 1966.

CHAPTER I

THE COVENANTS OF WAR

By the end of 1916, after twenty-nine months of the bloodiest war in history, stalemate had arrived in Armageddon, favouring negotiations to end the slaughter and calling into question the covenants to share the spoils which the Allies had been forging between themselves since August 1914. The chief military theatre, that in France and Belgium, had long fallen into the *guerre d'usure* which was the tragic symbol of the 1914–18 conflict, the massive German assault against Verdun and the British attack on the Somme during the summer both petering out with ambiguous results. In the wide Eastern spaces the Russian military machine was grinding to a halt. In July the German Chief of Staff, Falkenhayn, had checked Brusilov's startlingly powerful drive with four armies into Galicia and by December another 350,000 men had been added to Russia's losses. Then came Mackensen's superb thrust through the Carpathians into Rumania, which had joined the Allies in August; by Christmas the greater part of Rumania was under German control, thus prolonging the already overstrained Russian lines by many hundreds of miles. To complete the picture on the Eastern front, Serbia was now *hors de combat*; her army had been cut to shreds by a threefold thrust of German, Austrian and Bulgarian forces in the autumn of 1915, its battered remnants struggling through Albanian passes to the Adriatic in a pitiless winter.

Allied leaders at the close of the 1916 fighting anxiously scanned their superiority of 5 to 3 in manpower on all fronts, almost 14 million men against an estimated enemy figure of little more than 9 millions. They coldly computed that even if four Allied lives had to be given for every three of the enemy, attrition tactics must in the end bring victory. But apart from the willingness of the victims to endure this blood test, the Allied total included 5 million Russians and over half a million Rumanians. The estimated Allied reserve for 1917 consisted of 9 million men, no less than $6\frac{1}{2}$ millions of whom were Russians. On the other side, the Central Powers' operative strength of 9 millions included $5\frac{1}{2}$ million Germans, with their seemingly inexhaustible fighting capacity and clear political ascendancy over their allies. The estimated reserve of the

1

Central Powers for 1917 included 2 million Germans. The stalemating of Russia during the land operations of 1917 thus threw the balance of manpower in Germany's favour. At no time had she less than two-thirds of her strength stationed in the West, and with the retirement of Russia from the war in November was able to exchange 40 refreshed divisions from the East with 40 which had toiled in the West. It is proof of Germany's power to hold the Entente with one hand while extracting her allies from difficulties with the other that in the heat of fierce Allied offensives in 1916 and 1917 German divisions were moved to Galicia and Italy where their intervention was decisive.

On the Allied side, France, having borne the brunt of the struggle for two years with the loss of 2 million men, was near breaking point. The crisis came after the failure of the Nivelle offensive on the Aisne in April 1917, when the French Army seemed too shaken to move again. Haig was so thunderstruck on hearing of mutinies by French officers and men that he dared not commit the facts to paper.[1] This meant that during 1917 Britain must shoulder the main burden; hence the long drain imposed by the Third Battle of Ypres undertaken by Haig to relieve the pressure on the French. The cost was shown at the end of the year when the British Manpower Committee reported that losses on the scale of that year could only be sustained by forcing men out of vital war work at home.[2] To face the crisis in the West in 1918 300,000 men were squeezed into the Army, compared with the 600,000 called for with desperate urgency by Haig. This was the juncture, when her superiority in the West was at its height and before American strength could be felt, at which in the spring of 1917 Germany decided to starve Britain out by unrestricted submarine warfare. Half a million tons of Allied shipping were lost in March, 800,000 tons in April, three times the figure it was thought politic to announce. In the critical month of April Admiral Jellicoe told his American colleagues that losses on this scale would bring Britain to her knees by November.

The year 1917 was thus charged with fate for the British Empire. The power of Germany appeared impregnable, especially after her retirement in March through St. Quentin to the Hindenburg line. Repeated assaults on this bastion brought no visible effect, yet the orthodox plan of 'wearing down' the opponent by lavish doses of Allied blood might not be politically possible for long. The alternative to attrition strategy in

---

[1] A. Duff Cooper, *Haig*, II, p. 114; CAB 23/16. 159 A.
[2] David Lloyd George, *War Memoirs*, V, pp. 2602–3; G.T. 3912 in CAB 24/45.

the West, that of striking at Germany's allies through Italy or the Balkans, was opposed by Allied commanders on the Western front except on conditions enabling them to recall forces sent to these 'sideshows' in emergency. The issue was thrashed out in the Cabinet on 1 May 1917 and ended in the triumph of the Western school.[1] By this time the campaign for 1917 had been in effect determined at the inter-Allied military conference at Chantilly in November 1916, which upheld the primacy of the Western theatre and approved no further action in the Balkans beyond the capture of Monastir.[2] The fact always weighing in favour of Haig's insistence on the priority of the West was that Germany, after all, occupied a central position and could move her forces more easily than the Allies to any point on the circumference of the conflict where she was threatened. Thus, although Greece was brought into the war after the Allies had deposed King Constantine in June 1917, the Salonica expedition made little headway until the end of the war. Yet if Germany was to be defeated where she was strongest, in the West, a degree of strategic unity was needed comparable to that which Germany could impose on her allies. This was achieved only in the teeth of immense resistance: the mutual suspicions of statesmen who had to show that their peoples' efforts were winning a fair share of the victory at no more than a fair share of the cost; the personal rivalries of commanders with armies unprecedented in history at their call; the general reluctance to place the outcome of desperate struggles in one man's hands. Foch's moment was not to come until the final *Kaiserschlacht* in March 1918.

I

The British approach to the politics of the war, as shaped by the Cabinet after its reconstruction under Lloyd George in December 1916, was dominated by the factors which led Britain into the war in the first place. At the same time, the Allies were a coalition, each Power having its own reasons for fighting, its separate aspirations and ideas about the future. These different, often conflicting, aims had to be reflected in British policy if the alliance was to be kept healthy. With some of these allies Britain had entered into engagements, mostly secret, embodying their claims and hers in the event of victory. These Britain was committed to support. But policy had also to be harmonised with the mood of the neutrals; as never before in history, this was a war for the acquisition of moral support on

[1] CAB 23/13. 128 A.
[2] Cyril Falls, *The First World War*, London, 1960, pp. 246–7.

a world scale, and the compulsion to translate purely national interests into universal terms grew as the conflict intensified. Only in this way, it seemed, could the terrifying casualties and sacrifices be justified to one's population, the will of the less resolute elements among the Central Powers undermined, and the inconvenience and illegalities suffered by the neutrals condoned. An additional factor affecting British policy was the fluctuating course of the military events, the immense battles bringing victory now within reach of this side, now of that. Allies retired in defeat, others took their place. These diverse strokes of fortune forced on the British Government revisions of their objects in the war until the country's policy was not much more than a distant relative of what it had been in August 1914.

The administration which defined British attitudes towards the politics of the war at its end was not the same as that which committed the country to the conflict in the first place. The men were different; the war had produced its own war mentality; the political situation at home had changed with striking effect. Asquith, Grey, Churchill, Lloyd George, the men chiefly concerned with foreign affairs in 1914, headed a Liberal majority in the House of Commons whose predominance had been unchallenged since 1906. Foreign policy was still the private business of a few, the leading questions agitating public opinion before the war being severely domestic in character. Even among these few, Britain was still thought of as living in untroubled detachment from Europe, disturbed only lately by German naval and colonial pretensions. There was hardly a public opinion on foreign policy which could be appealed to. A striking demonstration of this was given when Lloyd George's famous Mansion House speech in July 1911 was listened to with interest by his audience of bankers, but with little notice paid to its allusion to Germany.

All this the war altered, possibly for ever. By 1918 Lloyd George, an extraordinary contrast with Asquith in political ethics and capacity to sway the crowds, led an administration which existed by virtue of his having split the Liberal Party and permanently destroyed it as a major force. His foreign policy, being dependent upon Conservative backing, was the external expression of an unnatural alliance between the party of established order and one of its most vehement antagonists. The Prime Minister fought the election of 1918 overawed by this fact, mistrusting his own power of appeal to the country yet captivated by an enlarged electorate sick of war and incited by the more unstable elements to primitive cries for vengeance and compensation. These circumstances tended to force on him—

and no premeditated creed helped him resist them—a catch-penny attitude towards the issues of the war which Asquith scorned and Grey was never required to adopt. This revolution in the climate of British politics between the war's beginning and its end exercised an immeasurable influence on the terms the country demanded for a settlement with Germany, and, what is no less important, on the terms actually imposed.

During the swift movements to battle stations at the end of July 1914, as Russia ranged herself against Austria, Germany against Russia and France against Germany, Britain remained detached. The Cabinet, according to Churchill, was overwhelmingly pacific.

At least three-quarters of its members were determined not to be drawn into a European quarrel, unless Great Britain was herself attacked, which was not likely. Those who were in this mood were inclined to believe, first of all, that Austria and Serbia would not come to blows; secondly, that if they did, Russia would not intervene; thirdly, if Russia intervened, that Germany would not strike; fourthly, they hoped that if Germany struck at Russia, it ought to be possible for France and Germany mutually to neutralise each other without fighting.[1]

Grey went as far, on the morning of 1 August, as to promise Lichnowsky, the German Ambassador, that he would see that Britain remained neutral in the event of a war between Russia and Germany if France was not attacked; the blunder was soon revoked, but revealed his hesitant mind.[2] There followed the unsatisfactory reply from Berlin to the British request for a pledge of respect for Belgian neutrality, French assurances on this point being entirely adequate. Alarm about Belgium on that Saturday was such that in the Cabinet even the 'peace group', led by Lord Morley and John Burns, were persuaded to agree that Germany should be told that the neutrality of Belgium 'does affect feelings in this country—if there was a violation of the neutrality of Belgium by one combatant while the other respected it, it would be extremely difficult to restrain feelings in this country'. This was an unambiguous warning on the sole issue on which the Cabinet were of one mind. Division of opinion remained, however, on the question whether Germany should also be warned at this stage against any attack on the French coasts. Burns resigned on this issue on 2 August

[1] Winston S. Churchill, *The World Crisis, 1911–1914*, I, p. 199.
[2] L. Albertini, *The Origins of the War of 1914*, III, tr. by I. M. Massey, London, 1957, pp. 171, 380–1.

and Morley also felt unable to remain after Grey had been authorised to tell the French Ambassador, Cambon, that maritime protection to France could be relied on. On the same day came news of the German ultimatum to Belgium and in the evening a Cabinet meeting decided that a German infringement of Belgian independence would constitute the *casus belli* for Britain. On the evening of the following day, 3 August, Grey was authorised to ask Germany in the first place not to proceed with the ultimatum to Belgium. This was followed, though not for over twenty-four hours, by the British ultimatum to Berlin at noon on 4 August.

Thus the invasion by Germany of Belgium, calling into question the whole fate of north-western Europe, more than Austria's quarrel with Serbia, more than any sense of obligation towards France, swayed the waverers in the Cabinet during the last days of peace. What the Belgian issue did was to enable Britain to enter the struggle in defence of treaty obligations and as a champion of the weak. 'And what is it that we are fighting for?' asked Asquith in the House on 6 August.

In the first place, to fulfil a solemn international obligation, an obligation which, if it had been entered into between private persons in the ordinary concerns of life, would have been regarded as an obligation not only of law, but of honour, which no self-respecting man could possibly have repudiated. I say, secondly, we are fighting to vindicate the principle, in these days when material force sometimes seems to be the dominant influence and factor in the development of mankind, that small nationalities are not to be crushed in defiance of international good faith, by the arbitrary will of a strong and overmastering Power.[1]

But more earthly considerations loomed behind. As the Cabinet had ruled on 29 July, 'the matter (i.e. of Belgium) if it arises will be rather one of policy than of legal obligation', for the treaty of 1839 gave Britain the right, but not the duty, to defend Belgian neutrality by force of arms.[2] Without a great land army, the security of Britain had depended immemorially on the freedom of the Continent from any single dominant Power. The threat to the European balance for the last quarter-century had come from Germany, allied with the Dual Monarchy. The two counterweights to this combination, France and Russia, united in a military alliance since 1891,

[1] 65 H.C. Deb. 5s. Col. 2079.
[2] J. A. Spender and Cyril Asquith, *The Life of H. H. Asquith, Lord Oxford and Asquith*, II, London, 1932, p. 81.

each nourished formidable grievances against one or other of the Central Powers. For France there was the defeat of 1871, which inaugurated the German Empire. In a revealing reminiscence in 1930 Poincaré, President of the Republic in 1914, remarked of his generation that:

> We said to ourselves: Who knows? A day will come perhaps when Europe in time of peace will undertake a general settlement of the questions which divide her and when we may hope to recover what was taken from us in war. Perhaps also, unfortunately, there will come a day when the German Empire, more and more infected by megalomania, will take it into its head to attack us. Let us remain strong. Let us if possible, have allies. If ever war is declared let us fight it out to victory and let us restore French unity.[1]

Russia on her side had never forgiven Austria for the bitter deception of 1908, when Aerenthal annexed Bosnia and Herzegovina, thus putting the Habsburgs into Turkey's shoes as Russia's antagonist in the Balkans.

Once these two Powers were embroiled with their enemies it might have been a British interest to hold the ring. To neither was she bound by any alliance, defensive or offensive. There was no legal compulsion to fight if France were attacked, although there was a strong opinion in the Foreign Office that this was morally inescapable in view of the decision of the French to concentrate their fleet in the Mediterranean in accordance with the military and naval arrangements agreed to by Grey in writing in 1912. For all his interventionist leanings, Grey insisted that the obligations of the Entente were not the same in 1914 as they had been in 1911.

> The feeling is quite different [he wrote to Bertie in Paris on 31 July] from what it was in the Morocco question, which was a dispute directly involving France. In this case France is being drawn into a dispute which is not hers.[2]

There were two reasons for rejecting neutrality, which might have brought the country into war even had the Schlieffen–Moltke plan never existed. One was the fact that any decisive outcome of a struggle between the two camps could be ruinous for Britain if she had played no part in it. Should the Central Powers prevail, the naval competition would be resumed and,

[1] René Gerin and Raymond Poincaré, *Les Responsabilités de la Guerre*, Paris, 1930, p. 176.

[2] *British Documents on the Origins of the War, 1898–1914*, ed. by G. P. Gooch and Harold Temperley, XI, p. 220.

with Belgian and French ports under German control, in far more menacing form. The idea of the world's greatest land Power, having overcome her enemies on either side, rivalling Britain at sea with such advantages as these in her favour was impossible to contemplate. But even if France and Russia won, the outlook would scarcely be better. These Powers would then be supreme in Europe and the Middle East, which they would be able to remodel at their will, and they were hardly likely to respect the wishes of a country which had stood by in their time of need. Grey received a memorandum from Sir Eyre Crowe drawing attention to this possibility on 31 July:

> The argument [it ran in part] that there is no written bond binding us to France is strictly correct. There is no contractual obligation. But the Entente has been made, strengthened, put to the test and celebrated in a manner justifying the belief that a moral bond was being forged. The whole policy of the Entente can have no meaning if it does not signify that in a just quarrel England would stand by her friends.[1]

More pointedly, Buchanan wrote from St. Petersburg on 2 August:

> I would venture to suggest with all respect that if we do not respond to the [Russian] Emperor's appeal for our support, we shall at the end of this war, whatever be its issue, find ourselves without a friend in Europe, while our Indian Empire will no longer be secure from attack by Russia.[2]

These forebodings were in Grey's mind when he outlined the issues before the country in the House on 3 August.

> I do not believe for a moment [he said] that at the end of this war, even if we stood aside and remained aside, we should be in a position, a material position, to use our force decisively to undo what had happened in the course of the war, to prevent the whole of the West of Europe opposite to us—if that had been the result of the war—falling under the domination of a single Power.[3]

The other argument against attempting to follow a neutral course was that Germany was, after all, a competitor, commercially and imperially. This did not mean that any war against her would be embarked upon to retrieve markets and

---

[1] *British Documents*, XI, pp. 228–9.
[2] *Ibid.*, p. 277.
[3] 65 H.C. Deb. 5s. Cols. 1823–4.

annex colonies. But the future of Germany could never be a matter of indifference to the world's greatest trading nation, with the largest colonial empire in the world. These wider considerations, however, there was no need in those days to bring to the fore. If Germany were overthrown in the end, the dangers implicit in them would be averted without the need for their enrolment in statements of policy. For these reasons early British pronouncements on war aims focused on the wrongs suffered by the invaded nations and kept in the background the rivalry of the two great coalitions growing up over the previous decade. Thus Asquith on 9 November 1914 laid down in a classic speech his four objects of the war: the recovery by Belgium in full measure of 'all and more than all' she had sacrificed: adequate security for France against aggression: the placing of the rights of the smaller nationalities of Europe on unassailable foundations: and the destruction of Prussian military domination. At this date no territorial claims were urged in public, although the French Foreign Minister, Viviani, was saying in December that the provinces torn from France must be joined to her for ever. This demand was not echoed in London, especially as it seemed to rule out a plebiscite. Not until February 1917 was any British pledge given to support the unconditional restitution of Alsace-Lorraine.

II

At the opening of 1915 Britain had no other diplomatic tie with France and Russia arising directly from the war than the Pact of London of 5 September 1914, by which each Ally renounced the idea of a separate peace with the Central Powers. In January 1915 the Pact was made applicable to Turkey, which had entered the war in October. During 1915, however, the territorial claims of the Entente began to take shape in keeping with the changing face of the military operations. On 4 March, allegedly in view of rumours that the Dardanelles expedition was intended to bar Russia from European Turkey, a circular was sent to London and Paris by the Tsarist Foreign Minister, Sazonov, laying claim to Constantinople, the Asiatic Bosphorus, the Sea of Marmara, the Dardanelles and Thrace as far as the Enos–Midia line, as well as the Asiatic littoral between the Sakaria River and a point to be fixed on the Gulf of Ismid, the islands in the Sea of Marmara, and Imbros and Tenedos.[1] There was a breathtaking quality in all this, especially as the Russians were at the time making difficulties

[1] W. W. Gottlieb, *Studies in Secret Diplomacy during the First World War*, p. 92.

for the organisation of an Allied front in the Balkans. Grey
accepted this diplomatic revolution, however, on 12 March, the
Foreign Secretary's reply referring to the Straits as the 'richest
prize of the entire war' and making the acceptance conditional
on the achievement of British aims in Turkey 'and elsewhere'.[1]
The French accepted with less concern in April. By way of
compensation the Tsar agreed to the addition of the central
neutral zone of Persia to the southern sphere of influence in that
country reserved to Britain by the Anglo-Russian Agreement
of 1907, and, secondly, to the recognition of British and French
interests in Asiatic Turkey, to be defined in later agreements.

The arrangements between the three countries to cover the
future of Turkey-in-Asia were embodied in a series of accords
negotiated in Petrograd and London late in 1915 and in the
early part of 1916, the Allied agents concerned being Sazonov,
Paléologue, the French Ambassador in Russia, and Sir Mark
Sykes and Georges Picot, the British and French special pleni-
potentiaries respectively. In all, the compacts comprised three
interlocking groups of understandings. First, on 26 April 1916
France and Russia agreed that in view of the Anglo-French
desire to create an Arab state or confederation of Arab states
in the Middle East, Russia should be allowed to annex the
regions of Erzerum and Trebizond, Van and Bitlis, and thence
up to a point on the Black Sea west of Trebizond, and also an
area of Kurdistan south of Van and Bitlis which for the time
being should be defined only in general terms. Secondly, on
16 May the acquisitions on the one hand and the spheres of
influence on the other in Turkey-in-Asia to be ceded to Britain
and France were determined in London in the so-called
Sykes–Picot Agreement. Under this arrangement the Syrian
coast from a point slightly north of Haifa to a point slightly west
of Mersina was to be under such direct or indirect administration as the French thought fit to arrange with the future Arab
régime in the area, while Britain's share was to be the Haifa–
Acre coastline for use as a naval base, together with southern
Mesopotamia. Palestine was to form an international zone.
The hinterland, consisting of the Syrian towns of Aleppo,
Hama, Homs and Damascus, and Transjordania and northern
Mesopotamia, was to form an independent Arab state or confederation with the French predominant in the north and the
British in the south. The Sykes–Picot Agreement was modified
in December 1918, during a visit of Clemenceau to London,
when he agreed that Mosul should lie within the British sphere
and that Palestine should be under British, not international,

[1] *D.B.F.P.*, First Series, IV, pp. 635–8.

administration. Thirdly, on 23 May 1916 Britain notified Russia that she approved the arrangements concluded between Sazonov and Paléologue in April with respect to Russia's share in the partition of Turkey, and Russian satisfaction with the triangular accords was expressed by Count Benckendorff, the Russian envoy in London, on 1 September.[1]

These proposals for the Middle East, the fruit of traditional interests and the chances of war, were complicated by the arrangements already entered into by Britain with Hussein, Sherif of Mecca, by way of rewarding the Arabs for assistance rendered against Turkey in their revolt of 1916. The plea later canvassed by Arab leaders at the Peace Conference was that the Anglo-Franco-Russian engagements with respect to Turkey were unknown to them when they rose in revolt, and that they remained so until published by the Bolsheviks at the end of 1917. The disingenuousness of this argument is now well established; the purport of the Sykes–Picot Agreement was explained at the time of its negotiation to Muhammed Sherif al-Faruqi, an Arab secret society leader, who was in close touch with Hussein, and in May 1917 Sykes and Picot themselves were in Jedda, where they left no doubt about the agreement named after them. It remains true, nevertheless, that the undertakings respecting the limits of the future Arab state were given to Hussein by Sir Henry McMahon, British High Commissioner at Cairo, several months before the conclusion of the Sykes–Picot Agreement, and that the latter made no reference to these undertakings, apart from the curious phrase that the co-operation of the Arabs 'must be secured'. In July 1915 Hussein, a leader of imagination, craft and ambition, outlined to McMahon his notion of the boundaries of the new Arab state, which were to run from Adana to the western frontier of Persia, thence down to the Gulf, along the Indian Ocean with the exception of Aden, up the Red Sea and across the eastern border of Egypt to the Mediterranean and then up to a point near Mersina. McMahon at first replied that it was premature to talk of boundaries while the Turks remained in possession and still had some Arab support. But under pressure he approved this outline by implication in his fateful letter of 24 October 1915, with the exception of Mersina, Alexandretta and the portions of Syria to the west of Damascus, Homs, Hama and Aleppo, which were not Arab, and with the proviso that the special interests of Britain in the *vilayets* of Basra and Baghdad should be recognised and, more importantly, that Britain could only act in the matter of Arab independence within limits

[1] *D.B.F.P.*, First Series, IV, pp. 241–8.

set by the interests of France. At length, on 1 January 1916, Hussein agreed to resign Beirut and the Syrian coast to the French if the Arabs could raise the question again at the Peace Conference; 'it is impossible,' he said, 'to allow any derogation that gives France or any other Power a span of land in those regions'. He also agreed that the British occupation of southern Mesopotamia should remain for the time being, though compensation was claimed on behalf of the Arab people.[1]

In November 1917 came the declaration associated with Balfour's name favouring a national home for the Jews in Palestine and planting the seeds of the later controversy whether or not Palestine had been included in the promises made to the Arab leaders. It is clear that the need for a 'special régime' in Palestine to provide for the Jews was explained to Hussein by Commander Hogarth, of the Arab Bureau in Cairo, in January 1918, and that Hussein agreed enthusiastically. But this was not understood as implying a Jewish state.

> The King [wrote Hogarth] would not accept an independent Jew state in Palestine, nor was I instructed to warn him that such a state was contemplated by the British. He probably knows little or nothing of the actual or possible economy of Palestine and his ready assent to Jewish settlement there is not worth very much. But I think he appreciates the financial advantages of Arab co-operation with the Jews.[2]

What probably caught the attention of Arab leaders was the reiterated Allied promise of self-determination, rather than any private disclosures of the coloured maps attached to the Sykes–Picot Agreement. Allenby declared to the Emir Feisal in October 1918: 'the Allies are in honour bound to reach a settlement in accordance with the wishes of the peoples concerned'.[3] Likewise, the Anglo-French declaration of 7 November 1918, issued by Allenby as a proclamation in Palestine ran: 'the British and French are at one in encouraging and assisting indigenous governments and administrations in Syria and Mesopotamia and in territories the liberation of which they are engaged in securing—they are concerned to ensure by their support the regular working of governments and administrations freely chosen by the population themselves.'[4] Neverthe-

---

[1] Misc. No. 3 (1939), Cmd. 5957, pp. 12–14.
[2] Misc. No. 4 (1939), Cmd. 5964, p. 5.
[3] *Ibid.*, p. 7.
[4] 145 H.C. Deb. 5s. Col. 36 (25 July 1921).

less, whatever the quarrels in store for the Sultan's heirs in Asia, for Turkey the future looked like being one of imprisonment within a diminishing fraction of the Anatolian heartland. This was an inevitable consequence of war for an empire which had been pronounced a 'sick man' as long ago as 1850. But there is equally no doubt that the dissolution of the Ottoman Empire was more readily acceptable to the Allies because its rulers were non-European. Echoes of Gladstone could be heard in every Entente reference to Turkey during the war. Grey's sensitivity to the charge of imperialism leads him to say in his memoirs that Turkey suffered no more than her due, since by entering the war in spite of the clearest warnings she forfeited all claims to consideration.[1] This is a harsh judgment by the servant of an interested country.

Before these engagements were finalised, their fulfilment had already been made a condition of the satisfaction to be paid to Italy in the eastern Mediterranean in return for her defection from the Triple Alliance. By the Treaty of London between the three Allies and Italy of April 1915 she was recognised as having an interest in the balance of power in the Mediterranean and a right to share in the basin of that sea 'adjacent to the province of Adalia', if Turkey was partitioned after the war. The twelve Dodecanese islands under Ottoman sovereignty were to be annexed to Italy without even that condition. By a further article (XIII) Italy was to receive some compensation on the frontiers of her colonies in Eritrea, Somaliland and Libya if Britain and France extended their colonies in Africa at Germany's expense at the end of the war. But the richest Italian returns on her investment in the hopes of an Allied victory were to come from Austria. These included the Trentino and southern Tirol up to the Brenner Pass, with their population of 250,000 German Austrians; Trieste and all Istria as far as the Quarnero and including, among others, the islands of Cherso and Lussin; and approximately half of Dalmatia, to include Sebenico and the long islands lying athwart the coast. Valona and Saseno islands were to be Italian and there was to be extensive neutralisation of the rest of the coast, thus defending Italy's long eastern maritime frontier which was without a harbour from Brindisi to Venice. Italy was to agree to the setting up of a small autonomous neutral state in central Albania, the foreign relations of which were to be wholly under Roman management.[2] The Italian share in Asia Minor, extending from a point west of Mersina to Smyrna and including

---

[1] *Twenty-Five Years*, II, p. 168.
[2] Misc. No. 7 (1920), Cmd. 671.

all south-west Anatolia, was defined in more detail at an inter-Allied meeting at St. Jean de Maurienne in April 1917.[1]

The Balkans were the subject of still further Allied engagements, concerning some of which there was much doubt afterwards whether they had been entered into at all.   First were the undertakings with regard to Serbia.   On 7 May 1915 Grey gave a conditional guarantee to Supino, the Serbian Minister in London, that Bosnia and Herzegovina, with 'wide access to the Adriatic', would be ceded to Serbia in the event of an Allied victory.   This guarantee was underwritten by the Entente as a whole on 15 August.   As Grey pointed out later, the Entente was under no obligation to act towards Serbia in this way, as she was the assisted country, and Belgrade was in fact expected to yield something in return.   The Allied hope at that time was that if the appetites of Bulgaria could be whetted by a portion of Serbian Macedonia, especially the Monastir district, she might side with the Allies against Turkey.   By August this hope of a favourable Bulgarian intervention was waning, Serbia had driven the Austrians from her borders, and Grey therefore told Supino at the end of the month that if Serbia agreed the Allies could guarantee the eventual freedom and self-determination of Bosnia, Herzegovina, Dalmatia, Slavonia and Croatia.   This involved a conflict with the undertakings reached with Italy in regard to Dalmatia in May, but the Italian Army was at this time at a standstill owing to the strengthening by the Austrian commander Conrad of his position in the Tirol and on the Isonzo after the great Russian rout at Tarnow-Gorlice.   The total destruction of Serbian military power in 1917 threw all these plans for the Balkans into the melting pot once more, though it was clear that an ultimate Allied victory would bring an enlarged Serbia face to face with Italy's Dalmatian aspirations.   There remained also the conflict between Serbian and Rumanian policies.   By an inter-Allied treaty of 16 August 1916 Rumania, in return for her disastrous intervention in the war on the Allied side, acquired a claim to Transylvania up to the Theiss, Bukowina up to the Pruth, and the Banat of Temesvar, the latter being mainly inhabited by Serbs in the west and having large enclaves of Serbs even in the east.

A further disturbing element in the Balkans was Greek territorial ambitions, though these were largely turned towards Asia Minor; they had been vainly stimulated by the Entente time and again in attempts to involve Greece in the war in support of Serbia.   Before Turkey entered the war in October 1914, it was Athens which pressed for war and the Allies who opposed

[1] *D.B.F.P.*, First Series, IV, p. 638.

since they had no wish to provoke Constantinople. Once the die had been cast by Turkey, the tables were turned, Greek zeal cooled and the Allies tried every resource of carrot and stick to revive it. In April 1915 the reward of Smyrna, with its rich and numerous Greek population, was held out to Athens as a bait for a declaration of war against Turkey. When this was refused, Cyprus was offered by Britain but with similar result. When inducements failed, there came the forcible Allied overthrow of the pro-German Greek monarchy in June 1917 and a provisional government under Eleutherios Venizelos at length declared war on Germany and Bulgaria. This gave him the shred of a title to turn up at the Peace Conference with a demand for his pound of flesh in the form of the city of Smyrna.

Finally came certain covenants entered into with the Allies in which the seeds of later conflict were less apparent. On 14 February 1916, for example, the Entente formally undertook to restore Belgian independence after the war and to secure for Belgium an indemnity from the Central Powers. At the other side of the world Japan was all the time quietly making her way as the residuary legatee of the Central Empires in the Far East, the successor of Europe as the dominant influence in China. For Britain, Japanese friendship was a considerable asset in the war, but anxiety lest Japan's actions in the Pacific might alienate the United States, Australia and New Zealand forced Grey to warn Japan against expansion. Nevertheless, the strides made by that country were significant. In May 1915 came the famous Twenty-one Demands on China, many of them modified as a result of American pressure. When these had been accepted by China, Sino-Japanese treaties were concluded on 25 May recognising Japanese interests in Shantung province, Southern Manchuria and Inner Mongolia. These agreements involved no commitment on the part of Britain, except that throughout this period Japan enjoyed British diplomatic support by virtue of the Anglo-Japanese alliance, which had by now been renewed until 1921. On 14 February 1917, however, the Japanese were informed that their claims to German possessions in the Far East north of the equator would be supported in London, if similar British claims south of the equator had the backing of Japan.[1] As early as December 1914 the British Government had stated that they had no intention of withdrawing from German possessions in the Pacific when the war was over.

Such was the complex of promises which Britain had entered

[1] CAB 23/1. 65.

into with the Allies by the closing stages of the war.[1] Among them only those contracted with Russia were totally nullified before the end. After the March revolution in Russia the British Government attempted to secure some revision in the Constantinople agreement from Miliukov, the Foreign Minister in the Provisional Government. But, apart from the specific promise 'to release Poland from her chains', which had in any case been encouraged by the Tsarist régime, neither Prince Lvov nor his successor, Kerensky, showed willingness to forgo Russian claims unless annexations and indemnities were renounced by the Allies as a whole.[2] Then came the Bolshevik seizure of power and the complete disclaimer of territorial gains, which the Leninist Government was in any event in no position to pursue. This allowed Britain to repudiate the Russian agreements. On 5 January 1918, Lloyd George said, 'we do not challenge the maintenance of the Turkish Empire in the homelands of the Turkish race with its capital at Constantinople—the passage between the Mediterranean and the Black Sea being internationalised and neutralised'. A few days later, on 21 January, Curzon spoke: 'we have informed the Persian government that we regard the agreement (of 1907) as being henceforward in suspense.' In other respects the inter-Allied arrangements stood firm by the time the United States entered the war and peace overtures began to be received from the Central Powers. It is in the context of these existing inter-Allied arrangements, together with the political attitudes of Wilson and the American nation, and the peace offers issuing from the Central Powers, that British policy took shape during the period 1916 to 1918.

III

During the first twelve months of the war the United States remained isolated from the political issues of the European conflict, maintaining its preoccupation with domestic questions and inter-American affairs. As late as the eve of President Wilson's re-election in November 1916 Sir Cecil Spring-Rice, the British Ambassador, was reporting from Washington that 'it cannot be too often repeated that the American people are determined to hold aloof if they possibly can, and that the Government cannot take any action of which the great mass of the people do not approve'.[3] Wilson's own view at this time was that the war had become a stalemate. Hence he thought it might be possible

[1] See Foreign Office summary, G.T. 3917 in CAB 24/45.
[2] See below, Chapter III, pp. 51–5.
[3] David Lloyd George, *War Memoirs*, II, p. 673.

for the United States, without intervening militarily, to 'compel peace', as he put it, by prevailing on the belligerents to state conditions which any reasonably detached observer would regard as essential to a lasting peace. These conditions, in his opinion, should include, on the one side, a German renunciation of militarism and, on the other, an Allied disavowal of wholesale annexations and all desire to destroy Germany politically. In return he considered himself able to promise American co-operation in a general policy for maintaining peace.[1] These proposals were sent informally through Colonel House to Paris, Berlin and London, together with Wilson's own suggested terms for peace, in the winter of 1915–16. The House mission may be regarded as the true beginning of active wartime diplomacy. For Britain, it offered an opportunity to explore Wilson's thinking about the war and clarify her own outlook.

The terms for peace which Wilson deemed reasonable were explained by House in London on 14 February 1916, when he met the Prime Minister, Asquith, together with Grey, his most intimate associate in British politics, Balfour and Lloyd George. The restoration of Belgian and Serbian independence naturally headed the list. Alsace-Lorraine should return to France, for which Germany was to be compensated 'outside Europe'. An outlet to the sea should be provided for Russia, although Constantinople was not specified, and guarantees were to be exchanged against the outbreak of wars in the future.[2] There was a sharp contrast between this outline and the provisional German terms handed over by Bernstorff in Washington a year later, immediately before the American breach with Germany, in which Germany demanded the occupation of certain areas of Belgium for security reasons after the war, the cession of several French iron fields, an indemnity from France, and some compensation for Germany's commercial losses during the war. But the House terms were also described as 'preposterously inadequate' by Grey.[3] The points on which the Cabinet in London were unable to satisfy House were the matter of the secret treaties, which were not disclosed to the Americans until after their declaration of war, and the method by which negotiations were to be opened on the breach between Allied demands and the requirements of the Central Powers. The House plan to cover the latter problem was that Wilson should call a conference of the belligerents and, if Germany refused to

---

[1] *The Intimate Papers of Colonel House*, II, pp. 110–11.
[2] *Ibid.*, p. 170, n. 1.
[3] *Op. cit.*, II, p. 131.

attend, the United States, in keeping with a previous undertaking, should enter the war on the Allied side.

Grey was in two minds about this; he feared that if the Allies
hesitated to accept Wilson's offer and found themselves in
military difficulties later on, the President would remain aloof;
at the same time he was conscious of the small prospects of
Allied consent to any American intervention on such conditions. Eventually he agreed to the House plan in a tentative
way on 22 February. Other members of the Cabinet thought
that the United States was more useful as a source of supply
than as an active belligerent and that if she did come into the
war it should be on the submarine issue rather than in the context of the kind of conference described by House. In these
circumstances the Cabinet decided that the time for talking had
not yet arrived. The major objection to the idea of a conference at this stage was that it would without doubt tie the
Allies' hands in the matter of peace terms and, more important,
assign to Wilson a definite voice in the peace settlement.
Moreover, it was doubted whether Wilson could speak for his
country in the matter of making war; such doubts were confirmed when the President later inserted the word 'probably'
into House's promise that America would fight if the proposed
conference failed through no fault of the Allies.[1] With the
rising tension between the United States and Germany over the
sinking of the American vessel *Sussex* in March, Britain distinctly cooled over the conference proposal, for it seemed that
Wilson was steadily drifting into the war without the Allies
needing to commit themselves politically.

It is a peculiarity of total war that, while its spread to wider
areas of the world demands from the belligerents increasingly
confident statements of the justice of their cause, the cost of the
conflict steadily drives up the price which each side insists upon
exacting from the other for a settlement. This occurred in
Britain during the preparations for the offensive on the Somme
in 1916. Walter Hines Page, the American Ambassador in
London, wrote home in June that the British 'won't hear the
word "peace" '—they wanted 'a real victory which will permanently discourage a military dictatorship'.[2] This hardening
mood caused House's reiterated appeals to Grey for a conference
on Wilson's model to be met with various prevarications, the
one Grey especially favoured being that solidarity between the
Allies must not be jeopardised by giving the French the im-

[1] House Papers, II, p. 202.
[2] House Papers, II, p. 257. See also Page's letter to House dated 25 May in
Burton J. Hendrick, *The Life and Letters of Walter H. Page*, II, pp. 157-9.

pression that Britain was tiring of the struggle.[1] This was the time, after all, of Falkenhayn's tremendous onslaughts against Verdun. The French on their side were also impressed by the length of time it had taken Britain, with every nerve strained, to deploy any considerable army in the field, and they considered that the principal military decisions would be reached long before the United States, with its total unpreparedness, could take an effective role. Similar considerations affected British thinking and strengthened Ministers, opposed to Grey, who wished to avail themselves of American supplies without being implicated in Wilson's idealist philosophy, which could be so irritating to a people struggling for its life with an enemy who gave no quarter.

Some of this irritation showed itself after Wilson's speech at a meeting of the American League to Enforce Peace on 27 May 1916.[2] Though the speech marked a distinct movement towards the weakening of isolationist sentiment—'we are participants in the life of the world' was its *motif*—and its tenets of national self-determination, the rights of small states, and the world's right to freedom from aggression sounded unexceptionable enough, the idea of people far from the conflict orating while others were, as they thought, giving their lives for these same ideals served only to vex. Wilson's suspicions of the Allies were characteristically disclosed in his unfortunate phrase 'with the war's objects and causes we are not concerned', which seemed to many even of his own advisers to be more than the position of a neutral required. The irritation resulting from the speech in Britain thus served to aggravate the tension between the Allies and the United States during that summer arising from further Allied interference with American mail for Europe and the blacklisting by Britain of more than 80 American firms for trading with the enemy. When Congress passed a Bill for the construction of new naval vessels for defence against British interference Wilson's advice was, 'let us build a bigger navy than Britain and do what we please'.[3] It was an outburst symbolising the change of attitude towards the Entente which came over Wilson at his re-election; from being sympathetic, House noted, he became obsessed with suspicion of their policies. In part, this was election tactics, but it ran deep in Wilson's mind. The reply was given for Britain by Lloyd George, then War Minister, in an interview with the American journalist Roy Howard on 28 September, setting the

[1] G. M. Trevelyan, *Grey of Fallodon*, London, 1937, p. 318.
[2] Hendrick, *op. cit.*, II, pp. 160–1.
[3] House Papers, II, pp. 316–17.

tone for the future Prime Minister's conception of war strategy. He bluntly told Wilson that he 'wanted no outside interference at this stage'. The outburst was deplored by Grey, Runciman, Lansdowne and McKenna, as 'warning Wilson off the course' and possibly serving to intensify the German submarine campaign as the hopes of an American mediation declined.[1] But by and large it expressed public feelings in Britain about the American bystanders.

[1] Lloyd George, *War Memoirs*, II, p. 856.

CHAPTER II

THE ALLIED ASCENDANCY

I

AT the close of the campaign on land in 1916 debate was resumed in earnest in the Cabinet on the issues of the war. There were two problems to be faced; how to decide whether and when a time had arrived to begin negotiations with Germany on the assumption that a stalemate in the field was inevitable and, if the strategy of the 'knock-out' blow was to be persisted in, how to reply to the impending peace campaign of the Central Powers, with its great emotional appeal to Allied Armies and peoples and to the neutral world. Lord Lansdowne, at that time Minister without Portfolio, replied to Asquith's request for views on these questions by emphasising that the burden of the war would soon be unbearable; 'we are slowly but surely killing off the best of the male population of these islands', he warned.[1] His authority was a formidable one, as he had been Foreign Secretary in 1904, at the time of the making of the Entente with France, and his views were reinforced by those of Runciman, President of the Board of Trade, who foresaw a complete breakdown in shipping before the following summer. Lansdowne with great candour admitted his inability to make any positive suggestions, but said 'we ought at any rate not to discourage any movement, no matter where originating, in favour of an interchange of views as to the possibility of a settlement'.

As against this pessimism, the military advisers, Sir William Robertson, Chief of the Imperial General Staff, and Haig, were confident of victory in 1917, basing themselves on somewhat speculative assumptions concerning the exhaustion German forces must have suffered through the fighting in 1916. It was this sanguine frame of mind which finally disposed Grey, for all his vacillation, against peace talks at this stage. In the wake of these discussions in Cabinet the Prime Minister, Asquith, appeared in the House on 11 October in order to reaffirm the 'well-known Allied aims': they constituted a compact formula, 'adequate reparation for the past and adequate security for the future'.[2] Whatever the precise content to be emptied into this

[1] The Earl of Oxford and Asquith, *Memories and Reflections*, II, p. 142.
[2] 86 H.C. Deb. 5s. Col. 103.

vessel, the words were clearly understood as ending for the time being all immediate hope of peace talks. The differences brought out by these exchanges in the Cabinet contributed very little to the fall of Asquith on 6 December, since the chief dissatisfaction of the rebels, led by Lloyd George, Bonar Law, Curzon and Balfour, was with what they considered to be the lack of vigour shown at the top in the prosecution of the war. But the effects of the accession of Lloyd George and the concentration of supreme power into the hands of his small War Cabinet were to defeat for the time being the Lansdowne school and any allies they had. Such was the situation in which the peace note from Germany of 12 December 1916 was received.

The German note implicitly accepted the indecisiveness of the operations in the West, while claiming that militarily the Central Powers were in the ascendant, and proposed that negotiations for peace should begin. No German terms were specified, however, and only at the conference would the German 'propositions' be disclosed. This was the hiatus in the note which Lloyd George seized upon in the House on 19 December, the day after the note had been formally received through the United States. To enter such a conference, he declared, was 'to put one's head into a noose with the rope end in the hands of Germany'. The only terms possible were those that had been repeatedly stated—'complete restitution, full reparation and effectual guarantees for the future'—and the German note was very far from admitting that the military situation compelled them to accept these.[1] But this did not make it less necessary to give a reasoned reply if only for the purpose of conciliating American opinion. Sir Cecil Spring-Rice reported from Washington that a rejection of the German note out of hand would have adverse effects on American opinion, a view supported by Sir William Wiseman, now the 'confidential intermediary' between Spring-Rice and Colonel House after the decline in personal intimacy between these two.[2] President Wilson himself circulated to the belligerents on the 18th an appeal for 'soundings' in order that the world could be instructed in their real aims; as publicly stated, he said, these aims were virtually the same, and yet the concrete objects of the belligerents had never been stated.[3]

The first public outline given by the Allies of their terms for a settlement appeared in their joint reply of 10 January 1917

[1] 88 H.C. Deb. 5s. Col. 1334. The text of the German note is printed in Misc. No. 38 (1916), Cd. 8406.
[2] Lloyd George, *War Memoirs*, III, pp. 1103–4.
[3] Misc. No. 39 (1916), Cd. 8431.

to Wilson's note. The idea of a League of Nations to ensure peace, provided its constitution was protected by forcible sanctions, was accepted at the outset in view of the primacy it occupied in Wilson's thought. But the prospect of this ever being achieved while Germany was still undefeated in the field was denied. There followed the general objects agreed to by the Allies, which were to be set forth in detail, and 'with all the compensations and equitable indemnities for harm suffered', on the day when actual negotiation began. Belgium, Serbia and Montenegro would have to be restored with indemnification for loss. The invaded territories in France, Russia and Rumania must be evacuated with just reparation, Europe re-organised on the basis of respect for nationalities and guarantees of land and sea frontiers against attack; provinces formerly torn from the Allies should be returned, Italians, Slavs, Rumanians, Czechs and Slovaks 'freed from foreign domination', alien people rescued from Turkish rule, and the Ottoman Empire ex-pelled from Europe.[1] The outstanding feature of the state-ment, however, was its reminder to American opinion that treaty engagements in themselves could not be expected to en-sure security and respect for the integrity of the smaller nations; they would have to be supplemented by appropriate policies. The Allied contention was that the prospect of such policies being adopted in Germany was remote while the existing régime remained.[2] To this point Wilson did not respond until the eve of America's entry into the war. In his 'peace without victory' speech in the Senate on 22 January, for example, he demanded a 'peace between equals', 'an equality of rights' in the relations to be achieved between the belligerents, in the con-viction that if peace was to be based on collective strength or the 'organised major force of mankind', it must in essence be a peace grounded in justice, embodying such ideas as direct out-lets to the sea for all, freedom of the high seas, and disarmament. There was no indication in such utterances of American willing-ness to employ more than the force of exhortation to realise these ideas.

As Wiseman told House, the feeling among the Allies was that the President was making a proposal to enforce arbitration in the future, while they were spending blood and treasure in the present for similar purposes, or at least for purposes which Americans, if they could see the conflict from close quarters, would recognise as akin to their own.[3] The fact that political

---

[1] Misc. No. 5 (1917), Cd. 8468.
[2] Misc. No. 3 (1917), Cd. 8439.
[3] House Papers, II, pp. 423–4.

ideals, no matter how desirable to the onlooker, could not be had for the asking was made clear by the immediate sequel to Wilson's speech. For on 31 January Bernstorff, the German Ambassador in Washington, notified the President of Germany's intention to begin unrestricted submarine warfare. At the same time he gave for the President's personal information a clue to German aims in view of Wilson's statement in his 'peace without victory' speech that Allied aims were more definite than those of the Central Powers. The German Government, Wilson was told, were willing to transfer Upper Alsace to France and to restore Belgian independence, though with economic and strategic conditions in Germany's favour, but demanded certain 'rectifications' of Germany's frontiers, the organisation of a new Polish state for which Russia was chiefly expected to make the sacrifices, and in addition colonies, territorial concessions from France, compensation for the war and a new international law establishing freedom of the seas. From this double communication from Berlin sprang, first, Wilson's decision to break off diplomatic relations with Germany and, after the sinking of more American ships, his declaration on 2 April that a state of war existed between the United States and Germany. But these events did little to modify the President's suspicious attitude towards the Entente. Wiseman, now the British chief of secret service in the United States, explained the mental detachment of most Americans from the war even after the break with Germany; any pronouncement the Allies could make by way of demonstrating that their efforts were likely to benefit the whole world rather than themselves would be intensely gratifying to Wilson. 'Our diplomatic task,' he repeated, 'is to get enormous quantities of supplies from the United States while we have no means of bringing pressure to bear upon them to this end.'[1]

An opportunity was afforded to explain British policy during a visit paid by Balfour, now Foreign Secretary in the reconstructed government, to the United States in April and May, his chief purpose being to give American officials the benefit of British experience in the organisation of national resources for war. Colonel House was reluctant to have war aims discussed with the mission as he feared the effects upon Allied unity if and when differences arose over these aims.[2] Wilson, on the other hand, saw no harm in an exchange of views about war aims provided it was carried on informally. This was done at a meeting between the Foreign Secretary and House on 28 April, when Balfour left with House a map ex-

---

[1] House Papers, III, p. 33.　　[2] Ibid., p. 40.

plaining the secret inter-Allied engagements and outlined the Cabinet's views on Allied desiderata as they stood at that date. The return of Alsace-Lorraine and the unconditional restoration of France, Belgium and Serbia were assumed to warrant no further discussion. The boundaries of an emancipated Poland were sketched and a solution to the problem of a Polish outlet to the sea was suggested in the form of Danzig becoming a free port under Polish sovereignty. Serbia should be allowed to recover Bosnia and Herzegovina but should make certain concessions to Bulgaria on the lines of the first Balkan agreement. Rumania was to be given Bessarabia (though this was contrary to the Allied agreements with Russia), the Banat and Transylvania. Hungary and Bohemia, Balfour was instructed to report, would probably have to be separated from Austria. On the troublesome issue of Constantinople, however, House appears to have understood Balfour as saying that the city should be internationalised, although the agreement of 1915 with Russia was still in force. The liberal revolution in Russia had taken place by then and Balfour may have assumed that the agreement with the Tsarist régime could be revised. Nothing was said as to the future of German colonies and the conversation ignored the Far East, though the inter-Allied arrangements relating to the Middle East appeared to Colonel House to constitute a definite source of future trouble.[1]

Two days later, on 30 April, Balfour met Wilson at the White House; much the same ground was traced as in the meeting with House and the secret treaties were explained again, Wilson making no special issue of them.[2] The probability is that he regarded arrangements to secure permanent peace as more urgent than the treaties, which he considered likely to be swept aside by the force of world opinion when they came up for implementation. Later, on 19 August 1919, he was to tell the Senate Foreign Relations Committee that he knew nothing of the existence of the secret treaties until he arrived in Paris. The most charitable explanation is that Wilson may have confused the agreements between the European Allies with the promises made to Japan in regard to Shantung and German colonies in the Pacific; the Far East, as we have seen, was excluded from the scope of the talks with Balfour. However this may be, the memorandum on the White House talks drawn up by House and Sir Eric Drummond, representing the Foreign Secretary made no mention of specific terms for a settlement, but merely expressed the determination of the United States and the European Allies to continue fighting until the general purposes

[1] House Papers, III, pp. 44-8.   [2] *Ibid.*, pp. 52-3.

referred to by Wilson in his speeches had been attained. The deeper issues between United States and British policies were left untouched for the time being.

In Europe, policy discussions in 1917 arose from four circumstances; the endeavours of the Dual Monarchy to cut its war losses and make a separate peace; Germany's own peace overtures; the pleas for peace of the Pope, Benedict XV; and the revolutionary diplomacy of the Bolshevik leaders after their seizure of power in November. These complex developments failed to effect fundamental changes in the British position, although the first and fourth might have altered the whole face of Europe had the military struggle taken a different course. The sum of their effects was to entrench the conviction of the British Government that the minimum conditions for an acceptable peace were unobtainable short of the total military defeat of Germany and, in particular, of the discrediting in the eyes of the German people of the military cabal who still controlled the main levers of state in Berlin.

On 21 November 1916 the old Austrian Emperor Francis Joseph, whose reign began in 1848, died and was succeeded by his grand nephew Charles. The first address of this young man on his accession contrasted markedly in moderation with the German peace note of December. In keeping with his hankering after an 'Eastern' strategy, Lloyd George promptly sent Sir Francis Hopwood to Scandinavia in February 1917 to see if contacts could be made with Austrian agents there.[1] At the same time the new Emperor's brother-in-law, Prince Sixte of Bourbon Parma, at that time an officer in the Belgian Army, met an emissary of Charles in Switzerland and later, during a secret visit to Vienna in March, Charles himself. The Emperor expressed himself in these talks as agreeable to the eastern frontier demanded by France; he had no objection to the demilitarisation of the left bank of the Rhine, nor to an independent Serbia, in which, however, pan-Serbian societies were to be illegal. There was significantly no mention of Italy, and Charles firmly insisted that the price of Austrian consent to a separate peace was the preservation of the Empire's integrity. At the end of March Prince Sixte saw Poincaré and Cambon in Paris and handed over an autograph letter from Charles which contained these proposals. When the French Premier, Ribot, met Lloyd George in April he explained these developments, along with an Austrian suggestion that Cilicia, the southern coast of Asia Minor, instead of the Trentino, should be awarded to Italy. The two Prime Ministers agreed that the offer could not be kept

[1] Lloyd George, *War Memoirs*, IV, p. 1987.

secret from Rome, but Prince Sixte was adamant in refusing his consent to any disclosure to Italy and Lloyd George was therefore obliged to test Sonnino's opinion at a meeting at St. Jean de Maurienne on 19 April without breaking his promise to the prince.[1] Sonnino turned out to be completely immovable in opposition to any peace with Austria on terms lower than the cession to Italy of the Trentino, Dalmatia and the coastal islands of the Adriatic.[2] After all, he was the statesman chiefly responsible for linking his country's fate with the Allied cause and could not afford to abandon the vast designs he had for Italy.

On this rock the Austrian peace overtures foundered. Prince Sixte himself believed that Austria should settle with Italy at almost whatever cost and advised Charles accordingly; unless the Dual Monarchy retired from the war soon, he thought, it would almost certainly be partitioned as a result of the influence of the United States on Allied policy. But the Italian demands proved impossible to digest in Vienna. Before he could allow the negotiations to fructify, Czernin, Charles' Foreign Minister, wanted definite guarantees for Austrian integrity, and even made the fatal demand that the negotiations be carried on with all of Austria's allies. On the Allied side it was feared, especially in France, that if Italian ambitions in regard to Austria were satisfied she would have no further incentive to remain with the Allies; this possibility was forcefully stated by Paul Cambon at an Anglo-French conference in London at the end of May. As against this, Lloyd George contended that even if Italy left the war the loss to the Allies would probably be outweighed by the advantages of dividing the Central Powers.[3] In the event, however, it was not for the Allies to decide. After the Italian proclamation of a protectorate over Albania in June, the Austrian Government made clear that there was no business to be done with Italy. After seeing Lloyd George for the last time in London on 5 June, Prince Sixte was told by the Quai d'Orsay during a visit to Paris that Sonnino, too, had no intention of negotiating. This was the end of the chapter.

A more hopeful stage began in the explorations with Austria after the great Italian defeat at Caporetto in November. At a meeting of Allied leaders in Paris on 29 November Lloyd George suggested that another attempt be made to take up the Austrian offer and Sonnino and Orlando were hardly in a position, after the Italian reverse, to forbid it. It was agreed that

---

[1] Lloyd George, *War Memoirs*, IV, pp. 2004–6.
[2] CAB 23/16. 391 A.
[3] Lloyd George, *War Memoirs*, IV, p. 2028; CAB 23/16. 159 A, pp. 8–10.

for the time being Britain should act on behalf of the Allies, and
Smuts and Philip Kerr, the Prime Minister's secretary, accordingly went off to Switzerland in December to meet Czernin's
envoy, Mensdorff. At that time the Cabinet were still unwilling to contemplate the breaking up of the Austro-
Hungarian Empire, preferring instead the establishment of a
number of autonomous countries within it, somewhat on the
lines of the British Empire in the days before the Statute of
Westminster.   Now that Russia had fallen some counter-weight
to Germany seemed essential in Central Europe, such as a re-
organised Austria might provide.[1] Smuts, on arriving at the
Swiss rendezvous, found Mensdorff in an accommodating
mood, agreeing to a free Poland, including Galicia but still
linked closely with Austria, and also to a somewhat enlarged
Serbia, similarly connected with Austria.   Even on Italy's postwar position Mensdorff was not entirely deaf to Smuts' suggestions, although there was no moving him in regard to Rumanian
claims to Transylvania.   But there was little or no sign of
readiness to break with Germany; Mensdorff utterly refused to
do more than act as an intermediary between the Allies and
Berlin.   For this, Smuts quickly intervened, the time had not
yet arrived and the talks were brought to an inconclusive end.
Czernin appeared far from satisfied that Germany was unable
to win the war in the end.   Considering the military position—
Caporetto, Haig halted at Ypres, Russia's failure—it was hard
to think otherwise.
   Even in Germany, however, it was evident that moderate
elements existed.   Unfortunately, those who were willing to
scale down German claims on the assumption that the odds
were slowly moving against the Central Powers were not, in
fact, in control of the state machine.   This circumstance determined the character of Allied reactions to German peace
feelers in 1917 and led to the more precise formulation of Allied
aims in January 1918, the idea being to capture the civilian
wing of German politics as soon as the military leadership began
to be discredited.   In July 1917 Michaelis succeeded Bethmann-Hollweg as Chancellor of the Reich and in a speech on
his appointment forthrightly renounced conquests effected by
force and claimed that Germany was fighting solely to defend
her frontiers and the 'vital conditions of the German Empire on
the continent and overseas'.   As the Chancellor was well aware,
recent discussion in some of the Allied countries as to the
desirability of a continued economic offensive against Germany
after the war had aroused intense repugnance, and not only in

[1] Lloyd George, *War Memoirs*, V, p. 2480.

Germany. This enabled Michaelis to claim that, provided peace involved definite guarantees against such treatment, Germany was ready to listen to Allied proposals.

The speech was in reply to the famous Reichstag peace resolution of 19 July, carried by 214 votes to 116, which called for a 'peace of reconciliation' based on freedom of the seas, 'international law organisations' and the renunciation of forced acquisitions of territory and economic warfare. Since this resolution was largely organised by the Catholic Centre Party, it was naturally read in conjunction with the Peace Note circulated by the Pope to all the belligerents on 1 August. In this communication Benedict XV, after stating his responsibility to try to moderate the warring nations, asserted that if the moral suasion of right was to take the place of military force as the arbiter of affairs, the basic requirements of international order must include: the reduction of armaments, arbitration enforced by a sanctions system, 'freedom and community of the seas', the general condonation of damages inflicted during the war and the restitution of all territories, including Germany's colonies, to their former sovereigns. As to the main territorial questions, it was somewhat hopefully expected that once agreement had been reached on the peace principles already stated, the disputed problems could be treated 'in a conciliatory spirit' and with due regard to all interests involved, including the aspirations of the peoples concerned.[1]

The Papal Peace Note was answered by Michaelis in September in terms similar to those of his speech in July and with the same vagueness and generality. Although in a letter to the British Government on 28 September Cardinal Gasparri, speaking for His Holiness, claimed that the German Chancellor had accepted the first two Papal principles (reduction of armaments and compulsory arbitration) all that Michaelis had in fact stated was that these 'would follow' from 'healing the sick body of society by the fortifying moral strength of right'. The rest of the principles were merely described as 'tasks which would then arise'. In reply to the charge of vagueness Michaelis issued a public statement on the same day, 28 September, to the effect that it would be diplomatically inept to tie the hands of negotiators by specific terms given in advance. The reply from Austria to the Pope's Note, dated 20 September, was couched in more fervent language than the German, but was even less precise.[2]

At the same time the German Foreign Office, then under

[1] Misc. No. 7 (1919), Cmd. 261.
[2] Ibid., pp. 12–15.

Baron von Kühlmann, became active in testing the ground for an understanding with the Entente, and with more specific ideas in mind. The German object appeared to be either to define more exactly some basis for an acceptable settlement which could be used by the civilian elements to loosen the hold of the military, or, if that was impossible, to sow dissension among the Allies and perhaps entice one or other of them to defect. For some such reason German offers suddenly took on a more attractive precision, which lasted until the preparations for the final military offensives of March 1918. On 18 September the British Ambassador in Madrid was told that the Germans were inquiring after the Allied terms for a settlement through the Spanish representative in Brussels.[1] At the same time the French were approached through von Lancken, the German Civil Commissioner in Belgium, with appetising promises of Alsace-Lorraine, the restitution of Belgium and Serbia, territorial concessions to Italy, and colonial concessions to Britain.[2] How far all this was an attempt to soften up French morale during the period of recuperation following the mutinies in the French Army was fiercely debated at a meeting of Allied Ambassadors summoned to deal with the German overtures on 8 October. Britain's view at the conference was that the gesture was possibly a sincere one and should be taken up. A telegram on these lines was actually drafted and sent through the usual channels to Berlin, but there was no reply.[3] Instead, on the following day, 9 October, von Kühlmann's 'No! Never!' speech on the subject of Alsace-Lorraine was interpreted in London as meaning that he had been worsted in his struggle with the military masters of Germany.

Nevertheless, the forces demanding a positive and detailed pronouncement on British war aims grew swiftly towards the end of the year. One of these was the publicity which Trotsky, Foreign Commissar in the new Bolshevik régime, was able to secure for the principles of no annexations, no indemnities, and a peace of self-determination, with their strong appeal to the Labour movement. There was also the concern felt by many responsible people lest the financial strain of the war should seriously injure the country after the war was over. Public expression was given to these fears by Lansdowne, now retired from political life. In a letter to the *Telegraph* published on 29 November he boldly argued that the points already in common between the belligerents made a useful discussion feasible.

[1] Lloyd George, *War Memoirs*, IV, p. 2083.
[2] CAB 23/16. 238 A.
[3] CAB 23/16. 239 A, Appendix.

A few days before the letter appeared, Balfour, in explaining why a debate on war aims in the Lords would be untimely, had told Lansdowne that no destruction or dismemberment of the Central Powers was contemplated, apart from the questions of Alsace-Lorraine and Poland; that there was no desire to impose on Germany any form of government contrary to the people's choice; that the government were willing to examine the problems connected with the freedom of the seas; and that there should be some international arrangement for the pacific settlement of disputes as a preventive of future wars.[1]   In one way or another, Lansdowne insisted in his letter, spokesmen of the Central Powers had espoused similar principles themselves. Where Balfour's memorandum had seemed to diverge from the enemy's position, Lansdowne felt that it was debatable, as for instance in the threat of continued economic warfare after the armistice 'if Germany proved unreasonable', and in Balfour's references to a territorial settlement in south-east Europe, which Lansdowne considered should undergo 'suspension of judgment'.[2]   The 'peace letter' evoked inevitable denunciations as treason, but there was no mistaking its challenging tone, which more people might come to echo if the war continued without hope of an early outcome.

Reinforcing these developments was the continuing heavy pressure from the United States for clarification of war aims. As a result of differences between the Allies on how to deal with the Papal peace note, Wilson wrote to House in September that 'we ought to go systematically to work to ascertain as fully and precisely as possible just what the several parties of this war on our side will be inclined to insist upon as part of the final peace arrangements'.[3]   An opportunity for doing this was given by House's visit to Europe in November in charge of the American War Mission.   At first he complained soon after reaching England that Allied war aims had never been made really clear. 'I find it will be useless,' he wrote in his diary after dining with Lloyd George and other British war leaders on 16 November, 'to try to get either the French or British to designate terms.'[4] But when Balfour had brought out his coloured maps once more and suitable explaining had been gone through, House was depressed, not by the absence of clarity in Entente objects, but by what he read as its stark acquisitiveness.   After talking again to Lloyd George and Reading on 20 November, he concluded that Britain meant to retain the German colonies in Africa, an independent Arabia under British suzerainty, a Zionist

[1] Lord Newton, *Lord Lansdowne*, pp. 464–5.   [2] *Ibid.*, p. 467.
[3] House Papers, III, p. 173.   [4] *Ibid.*, p. 238.

Palestine under British or American control, and to work for an independent Armenia and the internationalisation of the Straits. House's view was that any agreement reached between the Allies on such questions could not stand the test of time. What the situation demanded was 'the announcement of general war aims and the formation of an international association for the prevention of future wars'; in other words, the promulgation of the Wilsonian doctrine.[1]

At an inter-Allied conference in Paris at the end of November, House tried, with unenthusiastic British support, to secure the acceptance of a resolution renouncing annexations and aggression and limiting the concrete aims of the Allies to the defeat of militarism. Wilson in approving the terms of the resolution cabled to House on 1 December that the American Congress and people 'would not fight for any selfish aims on the part of any belligerent, with the possible exception of Alsace-Lorraine. Territorial aspirations must be left for the decision of all at the Peace Conference, especially the plans for division of territory such as have been contemplated in Asia Minor'.[2] The House resolution failed, partly through Italian opposition, partly owing to uncertainty as to how 'annexation' was to be interpreted so as not to apply to secessions from the Central Powers of nations with distinct self-consciousness of their own. From this inability of the conference to agree on a statement of war aims repudiating all national advantage from the war sprang the Fourteen Points speech of Wilson the following January. What particularly made it necessary to have some 'logical' statement of Allied war aims, in Wilson's view, was the separate peace talks then being carried on by the Bolsheviks. The Brest-Litovsk negotiations were accompanied by loud and repeated demands from Petrograd to know why the war should continue, and by the publication of the secret treaties to which Tsarist Russia had been a party. These appeared in the *Manchester Guardian* in December.

II

The pronouncements made by President Wilson under the impulse of these feelings brought into the open existing differences between British and American approaches to the problems of a peace settlement, differences which had sufficiently justified an important policy statement by Lloyd George of 5 January 1918, three days before Wilson spoke. In this speech British war aims were set forth in detail for the first

---

[1] House Papers, III, p. 242.
[2] *Ibid.*, p. 288.

time.[1] The difficulty at this stage of wartime diplomacy, as seen in London, was that of reconciling the revolutionary ideal-ism of Wilson with the practical demands of statesmanship as seen from close at hand in Europe. As an example of the problem, the messianic ideals of Wilson expressed themselves in the various demands for a 'just peace'. This would involve the destruction of the German political system and the substitu-tion of a responsible régime. Wilson went as far in his speech to Congress on 4 December 1917 as to say that unless the Germans made this change they would have to be excom-municated after the war. There must be a 'partnership of peoples, not a mere partnership of governments. It might be impossible in such untoward circumstances [that is, if a German military régime remained in power] to admit Germany to the free economic intercourse which must inevitably spring out of the other partnership of a real peace. But there would be no aggression in that.'

Lloyd George renounced any such aim as impracticable in his January speech to Labour delegates at Caxton Hall. 'Our point of view,' he said in this carefully prepared statement, 'is that the adoption of a really democratic constitution by Ger-many would be the most convincing evidence that in her the old spirit of military domination has indeed died in this war, and would make it much easier for us to conclude a broad democratic peace with her. But, after all, that is a question for the German people to decide.' In his Fourteen Points speech three days later Wilson appeared to retract his demand—'neither do we presume to suggest to (Germany) any alteration or modification of her institutions'—but the reason for this was probably to avoid falsifying the claim made earlier in the speech that 'there is no confusion of counsel among the adversaries of the Central Empires'. Although the enforced democratisation of Germany therefore found no place among the Fourteen Points, it remained throughout 1918 a firm conviction of Wilson that his mission included the communication of responsible government to Central Europe. On 4 July, for instance, in a widely celebrated speech at Mount Vernon he gave as ends fought for by the associated peoples 'first, the destruction of every arbitrary power anywhere that can separately, secretly and of its single choice disturb the peace of the world'.

Even greater repugnance was aroused in Britain, especially in official quarters, by the plea for freedom of the seas and open diplomacy (Points I and II). This was increased by the

[1] *British War Aims. Statement by the Prime Minister on January 5, 1918*, H.M.S.O., London, 1918. See also CAB 23/13, 308 A (31 December 1917).

fervour with which the former Point, at least, was welcomed in the replies to Wilson's speech by Hertling for Germany and Czernin for Austria-Hungary on 24 January. Even liberal newspapers like the *Manchester Guardian* and the *Westminster Gazette* were doubtful about the principle of the freedom of the seas, especially when it opened the way, as in Hertling's reply, to the demand for a renunciation of British naval bases, such as Gibraltar and Hong Kong, on the world's sea routes.[1]   As for open diplomacy, Lloyd George's private comment was that it was impossible to give an undertaking that Wilson's rule would be carried out in every case; everything depended on circumstances.

Wilson's insistence in his speech of 8 January that colonial questions and disputed territorial issues should be settled on national principles and with the consent of the people concerned was anticipated in the Prime Minister's statement on 5 January; but when the latter's qualifications were examined, it was seen that he succeeded in leaving unaffected the engagements already contracted. Wilson desired a 'free, open-minded and absolutely impartial adjustment of all colonial claims' (Point V). Lloyd George agreed that 'governments with the consent of the governed must be the basis of any territorial settlement after the war', but he spoke only of this principle in relation to Germany's colonies and ambiguously defined as the ruling consideration to be applied to these the need to place their inhabitants 'under the control of an administration, acceptable to themselves, one of whose main purposes will be to prevent their exploitation'. Again, Wilson called for a sincere welcome to be given to the new Russia into the society of nations under institutions of her own choosing and with assistance of every kind that she might desire and need. Lloyd George welcomed the 'new democracy' of Russia so long as it fought 'side by side' with the Allies, but went on to warn that 'if the present rulers of Russia take action which is independent of their Allies we have no means of intervening to arrest the catastrophe which is assuredly befalling their country'. For the non-Turkish nationalities under Ottoman rule, Wilson demanded an 'absolutely unmolested opportunity for autonomous development' (Point III), and this was paralleled, as was also his insistence on the internationalisation of the Dardanelles, in Lloyd George's admission that Arabia, Armenia, Mesopotamia, Syria and Palestine were 'entitled to recognition of their separate national conditions', but what the exact form of that recognition in each particular case should be

[1] House Papers, III, p. 355.

'need not here be discussed'.   Moreover, in the Prime Minister's recognition that existing treaty arrangements could always
be reconsidered in the light of circumstances there was the
implication that otherwise they remained in force.

On the subject of Italy, the President proposed that her
frontiers should be readjusted 'along clearly recognisable lines
of nationality'.   Lloyd George merely confined himself to expressing satisfaction with the 'legitimate claims of the Italians
for union with those of their own race and tongue'.   This left
unprejudiced the promises made to Italy in 1915, some of which
could not be made to square with the national principle.   Where
the President committed himself to a righting of the wrong done
to France by Prussia in 1871 in the matter of Alsace-Lorraine
(Point VIII), Lloyd George merely promised that Britain would
fight to the last drop of her blood 'for a reconsideration of the
great wrong of 1871'.   Wilson made no mention of reparation
in his speech; Lloyd George demanded compensation for the
devastation of Belgian towns and provinces and for injuries done
in violation of international law, which was no doubt intended
to cover Allied shipping losses, but, with remarkable ability to
see where later controversies would arise, said that this was not
an attempt to shift the cost of war-like operations to the enemy,
'which may or may not be defensible'.   On Poland there was
substantial agreement between the British and American
declarations, although Lloyd George refrained from promising
Poland an access to the sea, which Wilson thought to be
indispensable (Point XIII).   Again, on the need for caution in
regard to any proposal for dismembering the Dual Monarchy,
both statements were at one, the common aim being to keep
the Empire intact as an important future pivot in Europe while
giving opportunity for 'autonomous development', in Wilson's
words (Point X), to the nationalities.

But it was chiefly on postwar organisation that ideas most
strikingly differed, not so much in the published platform
declarations as in the tone of responsible commentary in Britain
and the United States.   It is true that the Prime Minister
ended his speech on 5 January, as befitted his Labour audience,
with a plea for 'some international organisation' after the war.
His own notions, however, were sketchy in the extreme.   The
proposed organisation was dimly referred to as a means 'to limit
the burden of armaments and diminish the probability of war'.
In an address to the Free Churches on 13 March 1918, Lloyd
George spoke derisively of 'phrase-making' by enthusiasts of
international organisation, and said that the 'true apostles of the
League of Nations' were the 'millions of young men in battle

array'. The report of the Phillimore Committee, appointed in February to consider the historical and legal aspects of the proposal for a League of Nations, was forwarded to Colonel House in July to assist him in drawing up a draft Covenant on Wilson's instruction. Some of its articles he used for incorporation in his draft, but his general view was that the British document 'did not at all meet the requirements of the situation'.[1] The principal feature of the Phillimore report was that disputing states should be forced, if other methods failed, to bring their quarrels before an international conference for settlement. Wilson, on the other hand, under the influence of his pan-American experience, demanded precise mutual territorial and political guarantees to be exchanged between the different members of the League. This feature was strongly emphasised in the Fourteen Points speech, in which the case was argued for a general association of nations 'for the purpose of affording mutual guarantees of political independence and territorial integrity to great and small states alike' (Point XIV). In the British view, given by Cecil to House in July, any such guarantees would in effect mean singling out one particular kind of treaty commitment and giving it special force; by implication, the effect might be to weaken other legal obligations.

The reaction of *The Times* to the Fourteen Points speech was that it assumed 'that the reign of righteousness on earth is already within our reach'. This judgment was in keeping with the majority of official opinion in London. The fact that Germany (although not her allies) ultimately laid down her arms on the basis of Wilson's political programme as declared in this speech naturally gave it supreme importance both in wartime diplomacy and in history. It was, however, formulated without consulting the European allies, although its general tenor could have come as no surprise to their leaders. As Lloyd George and Clemenceau told each other when the Supreme War Council at length met to consider armistice terms with Germany, their views on the Fourteen Points had never been sought. Clemenceau's irreverent comment on the Points has become classic. All that the British Prime Minister received on the subject before 8 January was a summary of Wilson's ideas from House when the latter was in London in December. The Fourteen Points therefore represented, not the expression of Allied views, but the breakdown of Allied policy; as such, by a strange irony, they were issued to Germany as the groundwork for the peace.

[1] House Papers, IV, p. 24.

How unco-ordinated Allied policy was at this juncture appeared when the Supreme Council at Versailles on 4 February curtly rejected the German and Austrian replies, both given on 24 January, to the Fourteen Points speech. These, the Council declared, were no real approximation to the moderate conditions laid down by the Allies; and the moral pretensions of the Central Powers, the Council retorted, were already belied by their policy at Brest-Litovsk. This declaration was much criticised in Britain, especially as it drew no distinction between the two replies, although Balfour in a fumbling speech in the Commons on 13 February agreed that the Austrian reply reflected a 'tenderer note, a softer atmosphere'. The Prime Minister himself had opposed making the statement public as he knew how it would ruffle Wilson at this delicate phase of the war. Wilson indeed found it intensely irritating, not because of what it said, with which he was in agreement, but because of its abrupt tone; this he judged to be disheartening to liberal elements in both Germany and Austria.[1] But his hopes of moderate protests from Germany against the Ludendorff spirit faded during the great offensives of the spring. In a speech on the Third Liberty Loan at Baltimore on 6 April he called for 'Force, Force to the utmost, Force without stint or limit'. The dreamer is not seldom converted to limitless force if his dreams are not soon attained.

That summer of 1918 was heavy and stormy with differences between the British and American views on the approaching peace, contrasting with the close accord in the field of battle. Wilson's messianic fury against the German militarists, combined with the demand that politics after the war should take as its starting point the renunciation of self-interest by all countries, victor and vanquished, seemed in Britain to pay no heed to the need for diplomatic flexibility during the war, nor to the legitimate demands of the various allies for changes after its end which would definitely improve their position. What was the war for if the successful were not to find themselves better off at the end? Why should they allow a country which understood nothing of ancient European conflicts to deprive them of these hard-won fruits when victory was in sight? The issue came to the fore in the long-drawn-out question of whether the Japanese should be permitted to land troops at Vladivostok to assist the White Russians and in the whole problem of relations with the new Bolshevik régime.[2] There was also the vexed question whether the Allies should profit economically from Germany's overthrow. In August Balfour

[1] House Papers, III, p. 370.   [2] See below, Chapter IV, p. 69 et seq.

came very near to saying that Britain would retain the German colonies she had overrun in the course of the war. This provoked Solf, the German Colonial Secretary, into saying on 20 August that 'our colonial aim is second to no other war aim of national importance' and that Germany had long won a moral right to be a colonial Power. The fact that, in order to reflect Allied military success in the West, Solf's speech was otherwise exceptionally moderate in tone, renouncing all claim to Belgium and hinting that the Brest-Litovsk treaty was merely provisional, for the moment gave the German position a defensive and innocent air. The result was that the Entente seemed wholly out of line with Wilson's statement in his Mount Vernon speech on 4 July that 'what we seek is the reign of law, based upon the consent of the governed and sustained by the organised opinion of mankind'.

A more serious occasion for dispute between the Cabinet in London and the White House was the issue of postwar trade. An incautious speech by the Prime Minister at a meeting of the National Union of Manufacturers at the end of July, which proposed that German commerce be 'crushed' after the war, touched off a characteristic American outburst against European self-interest and avarice. Wiseman wrote to Reading from Washington on 16 August conveying the President's request for an explanation.[1] Wilson, so Wiseman reported, was increasingly made to feel that the high goals he had set before the Allies were being overshadowed by private interests. His resulting annoyance led him to issue something in the nature of a rebuke during a speech at the Metropolitan Opera House, New York, on 27 September. Notwithstanding the claim Wilson had made, in reply to an Austrian request twelve days before the speech for 'confidential and non-binding discussion on the basic principles for the conclusion of peace', that these had already been stated as far as the United States was concerned, the President once more rehearsed his creed. The basic issue was 'whether the strong were to dominate the weak'; impartial justice must appear 'in every form of the settlement'; a League of Nations must be formed 'under efficacious covenants to see that agreements of peace are fulfilled'.

There then followed, for all the world to see, the basic political divergences between the United States and the European allies, couched in the most challenging terms and under the guise of five concise principles: impartial justice; no special or separate interest not consistent with the common interest of all; no alliances within the common family of the

[1] House Papers, IV, pp. 62–4.

League of Nations; no economic boycott or exclusion except under League supervision and authority; and no further secret treaties. As though to drive home this indirect assault upon the Allies, the war was roundly stated to be 'a people's war, not a statesman's', and the people, Wilson went on, 'were not yet satisfied with what they had been told'.

III

The protracted negotiations preceding the armistice which ultimately determined the positions of the Powers at the Peace Conference began with the first German note to Wilson dispatched on 4 October and received by him on the 7th. This accepted the Fourteen Points as the basis for peace and asked the President to call a conference. The news of this communication reached a meeting of the three European Allies in Paris which was already dealing with the Bulgarian and Turkish situations, and preliminary conditions for an armistice with Germany were outlined there and then. These comprised the immediate evacuation of France, Belgium, Luxembourg and Italy, the retirement of German forces behind the Rhine, the evacuation of Alsace-Lorraine, the Trentino, and Istria, which were not, however, to be immediately occupied by the Allies, the evacuation of Serbia, Montenegro and the Caucasus and of all territory formerly belonging to Russia and Rumania, the ending of submarine warfare and the continuance of the blockade. Although the conference intended that the armistice agreement should not be negotiated by the United States on behalf of the Allies, these terms were forwarded to Wilson for his information through General Tasker Bliss on 8 October. On the same day Marshal Foch in a separate memorandum put forward for the first time his proposal for Allied occupation of two or three bridgeheads of the Rhine within a fortnight of the signing of the armistice and the evacuation by Germany of all the left bank of the Rhine as security for the institution of representative government in that country. These demands were considered by Bonar Law to be tantamount to a demand for unconditional surrender and were opposed by the British Government.[1]

On the following day, 9 October, the terms of Wilson's reply to the first German note were known in Paris, and there was a feeling of satisfaction with his insistence upon a really new régime in Germany, his demand to know whether armistice discussions would relate, as he wished, only to the practical

[1] Lloyd George, *War Memoirs*, VI, p. 3278; CAB 23/8. 484, Appendix.

details of applying the Fourteen Points, and his call for the immediate retirement of German forces from all invaded territory. In general, however, the feeling of the conference was one of suspicion that the fruits of victory were being allowed to escape. At the instance of Lloyd George, the meeting reminded Wilson that it was not enough to secure the mere withdrawal of enemy forces if this meant that they were still to be left intact.[1] This demand for a stronger line to be taken with Germany was reflected in Wilson's reply to a second note from Germany. The latter had been dispatched from Berlin on 12 October, the day after the sinking by a German submarine of the Irish mail-steamer *Leinster*. It was based on the assumption that the European Allies also accepted the Fourteen Points and spoke prevaricatingly of setting up a mixed commission to make arrangements for the evacuation. The effect was a stiffening in Wilson's attitude and on 14 October he forthrightly demanded absolutely satisfactory safeguards and guarantees of the 'present military supremacy' of the Allied armies and the cessation forthwith of inhuman practices by forces of the Central Powers by land and sea.[2]

To this the German Government replied on the 20th, after intense and acrimonious debate, that the conditions of evacuation should, as Wilson insisted, be left to the judgment of the military advisers and that in the future German governments would be responsible to a majority in the Reichstag. On the basis of this note and with the reminder to Germany that he was concerned, not with the future, but with present German governments and that he would ask for surrender, and not negotiations, unless these were democratic, Wilson formally handed the correspondence to the Allies in council on 23 October. They were asked, if they agreed to peace on the terms and principles indicated in the correspondence, to approach their military advisers for recommendations on the measures deemed necessary for enforcing such a peace. Soon after Wilson's second reply to Berlin arrangements had been made to send Colonel House to Paris as the President's special representative at the meetings to frame the pre-armistice agreement. House left the United States on 17 October and arrived at Brest on the 25th.[3]

By such stages the Allied conference, together with the President's envoy, met on 31 October to decide the armistice conditions. In the discussions on the military aspects Haig took the moderate view, as he had when this question came before the

[1] Sir C. E. Callwell, *Field-Marshal Sir Henry Wilson*, II, pp. 134–5.
[2] House Papers, IV, p. 84.   [3] House Papers, IV, pp. 87–8.

Cabinet on 21 October, that the utmost to be expected was the evacuation of invaded territories and the return of Belgian rolling stock and deportees. This was based on the pessimistic view that the German Army was far from defeat, and that if onerous terms were urged on Germany the fighting might continue at least into 1919.[1] In the Cabinet Smuts had sided with this view, believing that Germany should be persuaded to accept lenient terms while the fighting was still going on. Lloyd George and Milner inclined towards the same position.[2] Ranged on the other side was the cogent argument of Sir Henry Wilson, Chief of the Imperial General Staff, supported by Balfour and Bonar Law, that once the fighting had stopped it would be difficult if not impossible to get Allied troops to fight again, and that therefore the strongest guarantees against Germany being in a position to resume the struggle should be demanded once a cease-fire was in contemplation. Both the French and the American military advisers took more extreme views than the British, General Bliss, for instance, pressing for nothing short of the complete disarmament and demobilisation of German forces. The compromise arrived at on 4 November was based on a memorandum by Foch and amounted to a substantial disarmament of German forces in respect of heavy equipment, but it was agreed that total disarmament could not be contemplated in view of the necessity for the authorities to preserve order in a country verging on revolution.[3] Added to this was the consideration urged by Milner against the total deprivation of the Germans of their arms, namely that their assistance might be required against the Bolsheviks.

The discussion of naval terms turned mainly upon the disposal of the German Fleet. Was this to be distributed between the victors or interned for the time being in a neutral port? Not surprisingly, British and French opinion differed in conformity with their differing estimates of the danger of Germany's revival as a naval Power. The French objected to what they called the severity of the British naval advisers on the same ground as Foch's military proposals had been resisted by the British, namely that they would drive the Germans to break off

[1] Lloyd George, *War Memoirs*, VI, p. 3300; CAB 23/14. 489, Appendix II.
[2] CAB 23/8, 490.
[3] In the Armistice agreement (Article 4) Germany was obliged to surrender the following war material:

          5,000 guns
        25,000 machine guns
         3,000 trench mortars
         1,700 fighting and bombing planes.

These final figures represent a slight scaling down of the figures determined by the Supreme Council on 4 November.

negotiations. Foch opposed the interning even of the German battleships, while at the other extreme the Supreme Council's naval committee concluded that the fleet should be surrendered in its entirety and then divided among the Allies. Eventually it was Lloyd George's opinion, acting as a mean between these extremes and backed by the American Admiral Benson, that prevailed. Only the German submarine fleet in this view should be handed over, while the rest of the Navy should be disarmed and interned for the present in a neutral port. Since there was no adequate neutral port available, the fleet was sent to Scapa Flow, where it was scuttled in the following summer by its caretaker crew. This event prompted in France the acid conclusion that while French demands for the military control of Germany had been judged unduly harsh, the British had secured the removal of the greatest threat to their naval predominance at one stroke without themselves being directly implicated.

There remained the question of the political conditions of the armistice. Here the basic problem was to discover whether or how far the Fourteen Points and other principles set forth by Wilson from time to time in his speeches, if accepted as the political basis of the armistice, would handicap the Allies in their later attempts to make secure the legitimate gains of victory. In the light of the greater seriousness attached to the Fourteen Points by the British, violent arguments not unexpectedly arose over Point II, dealing with the freedom of the seas. As soon as House arrived in Paris he was told of stormy sessions held in the British Cabinet on this issue, as well as on that of reparation for losses at sea. For Lloyd George, assent to the principle meant abandoning the power of blockade, without which Britain would be defenceless. The only condition on which the Prime Minister could agree would be if the League of Nations was a reality and nations were no longer required to provide for their own defence. Until the future of the League was clear any Prime Minister consenting to the freedom of the seas would be at once disowned by the British people. Notwithstanding Colonel House's assurance that Point II did not mean the abolition of the blockade, but 'merely a codification of maritime usage that would sanctify the doctrine of the immunity of private property at sea in time of war', Lloyd George remained adamant. The issue threatened to wreck the conference.[1] There was also the question of reparations, which seemed to the Allies insufficiently covered by the Fourteen Points, and inevitably further dissatisfaction arose over terri-

[1] House Papers, IV, p. 170.

torial issues. Lloyd George told House on 29 October that South Africa and Australia must receive a share in German colonies and that Britain would be no more content without protectorates in Mesopotamia and Palestine than the French without a sphere of influence in Syria. What chiefly disturbed House was the Prime Minister's attempt to make the United States an accomplice in all this by suggesting an American trusteeship over Germany's East African territories.

Wilson at once began to fear that his whole philosophy was in danger and risked being elbowed out of the armistice agreement and the peace. The very participation of the United States in the peace settlement, he protested, hung on the acceptance of precisely those points to which objection was being raised in Europe. If these were rejected, he was prepared, on House's advice, to go before Congress and explain the facts of the matter publicly. There was nothing that the Allies feared more than this while Germany was still technically undefeated.[1] So that when House met Lloyd George on the morning of 30 October with the object of reaching an agreement by which the British would seek to influence the French and Italians, the Prime Minister was already more conciliatory. Anglo-American tensions had not been reduced by a threat by Wilson to create the largest Navy in the world and to use it for the protection of the freedom of the seas. Lloyd George therefore agreed with House that a memorandum should be prepared setting out the two Allied reservations on the freedom of the seas and reparations. House found this proposal acceptable as he thought it would imply that the remaining points would be still more binding on the Allies. The memorandum was produced at the Supreme War Council in the afternoon and included in the Council's final statement to Wilson on 4 November which accepted the Fourteen Points with the two reservations.

The adoption, with the reservations mentioned, of the Fourteen Points by the Entente Powers was little less than forced. This was made clear by their reaction to the Points when first announced, by the acrimonious debate about them in the Supreme Council during the elaboration of the pre-Armistice agreement, and above all by Colonel House's belief that righteousness had persisted against great odds. In a private-code message to Wilson on 5 November, the day after the Council's agreement, House wrote that:

we have won a great diplomatic victory—in face of the thoroughly unsympathetic personnel constituting the Entente

[1] House Papers, IV, p. 174.

governments. I doubt whether any other heads of governments with whom we have been dealing realise how far they are now committed to the American peace programme. Both the French Prime Minister and George wanted to make the League of Nations an after-consideration and not—a part of the Peace Conference.[1]

But a victory gained for high principles almost at the pistol point could only be hollow, a victory without peace, to reverse one of Wilson's slogans. The Europeans might well have repeated to themselves Antigone's silent avowal about her lips being bound but not her heart, especially when the author of their capitulation was repudiated at home. On the same day as House's telegram was sent, the American people rejected Wilson's appeal for a Congress to support his ideals and voted overwhelmingly Republican in the House and Senate elections.

The end of the story virtually came with Wilson's fourth and final note to Germany on 5 November announcing that the Allies were willing to make peace on the basis of the Fourteen Points address and subsequent Wilsonian speeches, with the proviso that Point II regarding the freedom of the seas was left for discussion at the Peace Conference and that the restoration of invaded territories (Points VII, VIII, IX) was understood as meaning that compensation would be paid by Germany 'for all the damage done to the civilian population of the Allies and their property by the aggression of Germany by land, by sea and from the air'. Three days passed before the civilian head of the German armistice commission, Erzberger, arrived at Rethondes in Compiègne forest to receive at Foch's hands the conditions drawn up by the Supreme Council. Meanwhile in Germany the government headed by Prince Max was in full retreat before the tide of revolution, then at its height in Stuttgart, Kiel and Munich. On 8 November, when the armistice discussions began in France, the Chancellor warned William II again and again that if he did not abdicate the Social Democrats would probably desert to the extreme left and there would be civil war. On the following day, the day of destiny, William abdicated as Kaiser and King of Prussia, Prince Max resigned and the German republic was proclaimed. At 5.20 a.m. on Monday, 11 November the armistice terms were signed by Erzberger and his colleagues after final protests, especially against the continuance of the blockade, had effected only minor modifications of the agreement. Erzberger's final declaration after the signing ended with the words: 'a nation

[1] Harry R. Rudin, *Armistice, 1918*, p. 283.

of seventy millions of people suffers, but it does not die.' 'Très bien,' said Marshal Foch.[1]

As against the view which became common later that the war should have been carried on until an unconditional surrender could be forced on Germany, there were powerful arguments for an early peace. Almost all the Allied military leaders, including Haig, Pétain and Foch, were in favour of a cease-fire when it came; only General Pershing wished to carry the war into the heart of Germany, and this was because the United States was still untouched by the war weariness hanging over Britain and France. In Britain the difficulties of keeping the Army supplied with manpower, the strikes in industry, the coal shortage, the influenza epidemic, which was killing off 7,000 people a week in November, and the continuing troubles in Ireland made the decision to end the war inescapable. There was also the fear in Britain and France that Germany would turn Bolshevik if not allowed to lay down her arms. It is true that continued fighting might have prevented the legend later concocted in Germany that the Army wanted to fight on, but was betrayed by the civilians. It is, however, a fact of history that it was Ludendorff who at the end of September forced an appeal for peace on a reluctant Prince Max. As this was later ignored by nationalists in Germany, it is probable that any other proof of the conclusiveness of the German defeat would have suffered the same fate.

[1] Rudin, *op. cit.*, p. 383.

CHAPTER III

THE COMING OF BOLSHEVISM

I

DURING the first German onslaughts on France in 1914, in the Loos and Champagne fighting in 1915 and again during Falkenhayn's assault on Verdun in 1916, Russia's contribution went far to retrieve the Allied position. Time and again her forces were thrown, often quixotically, against superior armament, and more with the object of relieving pressure on the Allies than to serve her own strategic needs. Russia's incautious generosity towards the Allies was in fact the reverse side of the medal of the entire inefficiency of the country as an instrument of modern war. Neither administratively nor industrially was she equipped to supply military wants on the scale called for in 1914–18, even had these needs been understood by the Tsarist government. On the eve of the military disasters of 1915 Russian Armies possessed only 60 batteries of artillery, as against an estimated average of 380 German batteries. A total of $6\frac{1}{2}$ million rifles had been adopted as an estimated basis for production in the first three years of the war; 18 millions were found to be required. But perhaps the most fatal of all Russia's failings was the shortage of shell. In the first months of the war she had one shell-factory to every 150 British factories and was producing 35,000 shells a month and using 45,000 a day. Although shell production was estimated to have increased by 1300 per cent in the first nine months of the fighting, as compared with 1900 per cent in Britain, the gap between the supply of war material and the demand at no time came anywhere near to being closed.[1]

Supplies from the outside world might have offset this deficiency had adequate communications existed in the country. The lack of these, together with the sheer magnitude of the eastern front, made it difficult to bring munitions into action, whether produced at home or supplied by the Allies. The Baltic Sea was closed by the Germans. Archangel and Vladivostok, besides being remote from the nearest fighting, were useless during the winter months. The solitary ice-free port of Kola was connected with Petrazavodsk, the northern

[1] Sir Alfred Knox, *With the Russian Army, 1914–1917*, I, London, 1921, pp. 219, 274–5.

terminal of the railway from Petrograd, by the 700-mile long Murman railway. But work on this line was only started in 1915 and it was not opened for through traffic until November 1916, when it was too late to affect Russia's military position.

Added to which were the psychological roots of defeat: ignorance in the Army rank-and-file as to the real issues of the war, leading to bitter feelings against the Entente once the first enthusiasm faded; the naïveté of the Russians in the business of war, as shown by their disclosure of troop movements at decisive moments in the fighting through sending unciphered wireless messages; their strange combination of animal patience with refusal to consider the elementary problems of saving time, life and trouble. The conclusion reached by Sir Alfred Knox, of the British mission with the Russian Army, was that the Russians were 'great, big-hearted children who had thought out nothing and had stumbled half-asleep into a wasp's nest'.[1] It is hardly surprising that such hideous proportions of the $14\frac{1}{2}$ million men called up for military service were lost. In his recollections of the eastern front Hindenburg describes the Germans clearing away mounds of Russian dead before they could find a clear field of fire against further oncoming waves.[2] The weightiest asset of the Russian Army, its vast numbers, tended to militate against mobility and manœuvrability, as the great Russian defeat at Tannenberg in August 1914 showed, and the scale of losses hardened the peasant's heart against continuing the war once the game was evidently lost. The picture at home was no brighter. Rising prices resulting from the diversion of industry to war production made farmers less willing to send their crops to market, while consumption of foodstuffs rose throughout the war owing to the prohibition of the sale of vodka as harmful to the war effort.

The weak and melancholy Tsar and his demented Tsarina ignored all warnings. Early in February 1916 the British Ambassador, Sir George Buchanan, urged Nicholas to work out a policy to remedy the general dissatisfaction. The Tsar's reply was that he would 'think it over'.[3] Eleven months later Buchanan had another audience of the Tsar in which he argued, this time more bluntly, that in every Allied country there would have to be complete solidarity between all classes of the population.[4]

During 1916 an open struggle for power took place between

[1] Knox, *op. cit.*, p. 86.
[2] Paul von Hindenburg, *Out of My Life*, tr. by F. A. Holt, London, 1920, p. 273.
[3] Sir Bernard Pares, *The Fall of the Russian Monarchy*, p. 308.
[4] Sir George Buchanan, *My Mission to Russia and Other Diplomatic Memories*, II, pp. 4, 5, 43-9.

pro-Ally and pro-German forces at the Court, the latter steadily gaining the ascendancy. The focus of this struggle was the conflict between Sazonov, the Foreign Minister and architect of Russia's alignment with the Entente, and the shallow and corrupt Sturmer. On 2 February, to everyone's surprise and to none more than that of the Prime Minister, Goremykin, Sturmer was appointed by the Tsar as head of the government. There followed in July the intriguing of Sazonov himself out of office, his portfolio as Foreign Minister being also given to Sturmer.[1] Buchanan at once cabled Nicholas advising him to reconsider Sturmer's elevation. There was no immediate result, but in November Sturmer was dismissed, over the Tsarina's protests, in favour of the able and firmly anti-German Minister, Trepov. The Foreign Office passed into the hands of Pokrovsky. He too was pro-Ally, although it was chiefly his financial experience which recommended him to the Tsar. Events were to show, however, that although the Tsarina had been defeated over Sturmer, she was able to ensure that there would be no change in his policies. More important for the morale in the Army was the dismissal of the able and popular War Minister, Polivanov, in April 1916 on account of his alleged hostility towards Rasputin, the Tsarina's protégé and reputed lover. He was replaced by the bewildered Shuvayev, who tearfully protested his insufficiency to fill the post when he saw Knox for the first time.[2] When Buchanan wrote home to a friend in October he reported a definite increase in anti-Ally propaganda in influential circles in Russia throughout the year.[3]

Russia's military plight was viewed with alarm in London, not merely because of its effects on the whole Eastern position, but owing to its depressing impact on the financial standing of the Entente in the United States. Lloyd George, consistently with his Eastern strategic ideas, was one of the first to perceive this. In September 1916, when still Minister of Munitions, he proposed that the Chief of the Imperial General Staff, Sir William Robertson, together with Lord Reading, should visit Russia to inquire as to her requirements and co-ordinate her military operations with those of the Western Allies. Some effort in the same direction had been made in May, when Viviani, the French Minister of Justice, and Albert Thomas, Minister of Munitions, had gone to Russia, though without much result.[4] In the event Robertson refused to go since he

[1] F. A. Golder, *Documents of Russian History 1914–1917*, p. 105.
[2] Pares, *op. cit.*, p. 327.
[3] David Lloyd George, *War Memoirs*, II, p. 775.
[4] Maurice Paléologue, *An Ambassador's Memoirs*, tr. by F. A. Holt, II, p. 261.

feared, not unreasonably, that Lloyd George was intriguing to oust him from his post. Russia's position was then taken up at an Allied political conference in Paris on 15 and 16 November 1916, at which Lloyd George pressed once more the case for diverting supplies to the East. Since the conference was unable to reach a conclusion without first-hand knowledge of the facts, it was decided to send a high-level mission to Petrograd. Various postponements of the plan, however, proved fatal. The French, after their mission in May, were unhopeful and were not easily persuaded to send authoritative representatives; later the mission's departure was delayed by the Russians. Eventually the delegation sailed from Oban on 21 January and arrived in Petrograd on the 29th. The conference itself occupied the first three weeks in February and the mission returned to Scapa Flow on 6 March, a few days before the Revolution swept away the monarchy.

The Petrograd conference should have provided the leaders of the British delegation, Lord Milner, a member of the War Cabinet, Lord Revelstoke, and Sir Henry Wilson, with clues to the condition of the country. Anguished cries were heard outside the conference room from moderate members of the Duma, men like Chelnikov, Prince Lvov and Maklakov. Inside the conference it was virtually impossible to deal in a confidential way with the real authors of Russia's policy. According to Sir George Buchanan, only in the technical commissions dealing with transport and munitions was any useful work accomplished, and the effects of this came too late to arrest the spreading decay in the Russian Army. Yet, in spite of indications that the régime was near catastrophe, no immediate upheaval seems to have been anticipated by the mission's leaders or by the Ambassador on the eve of the bread riots of 11–12 March (27–28 February by the old Russian calendar) which ushered in the Republic. Milner told the Cabinet on his return that there was a good deal of exaggeration in the talk about revolution and especially about the alleged disloyalty of the Army. He considered that the 'root cause, even of the domestic discontent, is dissatisfaction with the course of the war and bitter resentment of the mismanagement—for which the Government is held responsible—that has been the cause of so many failures'.[1] A junior member of the British party, David Davies, M.P., was one of the few Western visitors to foresee the imminent uprising, and another was Sir Walter Layton.[2] Even when the rioting

[1] G 131, CAB 21/42.
[2] Lloyd George in his account of the mission ungenerously omits to mention Davies; *War Memoirs*, III, p. 1587. For Davies' report, see G 137, CAB 21/42.

in Petrograd had actually begun Buchanan was reporting to London that the trouble would probably blow over. With greater pessimism about the enterprise, the chief French delegate, Doumergue, used the occasion mainly to seize from Nicholas II an endorsement of his country's claim to the left bank of the Rhine. This realism about the mission contrasted strangely with Doumergue's illusion that the Tsar's act would bind his successor.

II

The March Revolution, when it occurred, was regarded in Britain as a protest against Tsarist mismanagement of the war, rather than against the war itself. On 15 March Bonar Law told the House that 'all our information leads us to believe that the movement is not in any sense directed towards an effort to secure peace, but, on the contrary, the discontent—is not against the Government for carrying on the war, but against it for not carrying on the war with that efficiency and with that energy which the people expect'.[1] A few days later the Prime Minister said he was confident 'that these events—will result not in any confusion or slackening, but in an even closer and more effective co-operation between the Russian people and its Allies'.[2] Demoralisation in the Russian Army was pervasive, but it was not impossible that new leadership might enable the country to remain in the field as a military force to be reckoned with, a stone wall if no longer a steam-roller. When it became clear that even this was doubtful and that, in the words of Pétain, the Russian Army would disintegrate if it tried to move at all, the Allies began to press the Provisional Government to strengthen discipline in the ranks and harass the enemy. The unsuccessful Brusilov offensive undertaken in response to these appeals ended in the fall of Prince Lvov and the advent of Alexander Kerensky as chief Minister on 16 July.

Allied pressure was resumed, Buchanan telling Kerensky straightforwardly in August that the Allies would send no more guns unless the Commander-in-Chief was given authority to restore discipline at the front. Italy took a hand, intimating that Japan would be permitted to act as she pleased in Siberia if the Provisional Government contemplated a separate peace. Only a month before the Bolshevik seizure of power, Buchanan, along with his French and Italian colleagues, saw Kerensky, Tereschenko, the Foreign Minister, and Konovalov and read them an angry note on the need for urgent prosecution of the war. The inflamed Kerensky retorted by charging the Allies

[1] 91 H.C. Deb. 5s. Col. 1421.   [2] *Ibid.*, Col. 1537 (19 March).

with dilatoriness in sending supplies, adroitly seizing upon Lloyd George's old complaint. The truth was that while the uprising in March had united a wide variety of discontents against the régime, the strongest emotive force behind it was the sufferings of primitively equipped peasant masses in conditions of mechanised war. Once the will to return home had hardened in them only one or other of two remedies was available to Ministers: either to restore discipline by an efficient dictatorship until enough success was won in the field to dispel the fatalism of the Tsarist order, or to apply for an armistice. Kerensky was prepared for neither alternative.

Besides at first affording hopes of a Russian military revival, the March Revolution was welcomed in Britain as helping to remove a patently reactionary element on the Allied side. Bonar Law was able to say in welcoming the revolution in the Commons on 22 March that 'we cannot forget that one of the issues, and the greatest of all the issues of the war, is whether or not free institutions can survive against the onslaught of military despotism, and we cannot but rejoice in the hope that in the final stages of the world conflict all the Allied Powers will be under the direction of Governments which represent their peoples'.[1] The events of March also inspired the warmest relief in radical quarters, appearing like the first streaks of dawn after a long night, thus facilitating the task Lloyd George had set himself of reconciling Labour to the war programme. At the same time the fact that the Provisional Government was appealing to the principles of self-determination and an unimperialistic peace gave the British Government a cue for suggesting a revision of the secret treaties with Russia, for these agreements both ran against the grain of Britain's traditional diplomatic aims and gave Allied policy a distinct annexationist colour. Hence in a note of 8 June the British Cabinet joined in the Provisional Government's acceptance of Wilsonian principles and said that the arrangements already reached with Russia were consistent with these standards; but, if the Provisional Government wished, Britain was prepared 'to examine and if need be to revise these arrangements'.[2]

Nevertheless, liberal fervour released by the fall of Tsarism brought its own problems. A new spirit might be infused into Russia's peasant millions. Equally the revolutionary tide might carry them to the point at which discipline or restrictions of any kind were unbearable. Moreover, in Britain, contrary to first appearances, the Russian turmoil tended, as time went on, to widen the rift between the War Cabinet and the various

[1] 91 H.C. Deb. 5s. Col. 2086.   [2] Misc. No. 10 (1917), Cd. 8587, p. 5.

shades of Labour dissent. In its proclamation of 27 March the Provisional Government denied that the new order in Russia aimed 'at dominating other nations, at depriving them of their national patrimony or at occupying by force foreign territories'. This was the signal for Labour critics of the British Government to press for a liberalisation of Allied war aims. In a debate in the Commons on 16 May Philip Snowden moved for a British declaration in similar terms and argued that the Allied note of 10 January was now obsolete, 'a child of undemocratic diplomacy', which he said had served only to stiffen the resistance of the German people. Lees-Smith, following in support, agreed that the 'original obligations of honour', as for instance the evacuation of enemy occupied territory, should remain, but insisted that such further objects as the annexation of Constantinople and Germany's colonies, and even France's recovery of Alsace-Lorraine, were negotiable. It was not difficult for government spokesmen to explain in reply that the Russian slogan 'no annexations, no indemnities' assumed that the world after the war could remain in all essentials the same as it had been in 1914, whatever the Allies did. Moreover, as Lord Robert Cecil pointed out in the debate, many changes demanded by the Allies could not be described as annexation, such as the reconstitution of Poland and the satisfaction of Italy's national claims. Only in one respect, said Cecil, with a pertinent reference to Russia's own position, was the Allied note of January in need of revision. This was the demand for the 'thrusting out of Europe of the Ottoman Empire as decidedly foreign to Western civilisation'. When MacDonald's turn came he admitted that the word 'annexation' required to be read 'in the Russian sense'. By it Russia meant that she wanted no annexation 'as practised by the Tsar'. But he agreed that the dissolution of an 'artificial state' such as Austria-Hungary would not be annexationist but an attempt 'to join nationalities together'.[1] Nevertheless, the new Russia could not promulgate declarations in these terms without deepening suspicion on the Left as to the entire Entente objects in the war. While Ministers in London and Paris were indignant that the Provisional Government, having lost thousands of square miles of Russian territory, were acting magnanimously at their allies' expense, Labour in both countries settled upon the Russian slogans as offering a short cut to the end of the slaughter.

The three months given to the intense Kerensky were of necessity spent, not in attempting to scale down Allied war aims, which the rising distrust between Russia and the West in

[1] 93 H.C. Deb. 5s. Cols. 1625–1740.

any case rendered impossible, but in seeking to hold the balance between the military-conservative faction, on the one hand, and the Bolsheviks on the other. The former, under their new leader, General Kornilov, saw no salvation short of restoration of discipline at the front. The Bolsheviks, with or without collusion with the German High Command, were bent on a separate peace. In this conflict the British Government saw their interest as lying with the Right, but their refusal to desert the ambiguous Kerensky foreshadowed later contradictions of policy after November. In any event the Russian military disasters of July, together with the Bolshevik uprising in that month, made the attempt to exercise any kind of control from outside more and more dubious. The blunt truth which London, taking its cue from the Milner mission in February, had evaded for so long was at length harshly stated by Knox, the British Military Attaché, in reporting on the July offensives: 'the Revolution has been a protest against the burdens of the war, and not a protest, as the English Press at first tried to pretend, against the half-hearted way in which the late government prosecuted the war.' Knox thought that the Russians would gladly have the Tsar back again if he could give them peace. On 4 August he wrote that the country was 'moving straight to ruin as things stand at present'. On the same day Buchanan was writing to the Foreign Office that the time had come 'to tell the Government frankly that, while we will continue to do all that is possible to relieve the pressure on their front by pushing our offensive, we expect her in return to concentrate all her energies on the re-organisation of her armies and to re-establish discipline both at the front and in the rear'. This advice was adopted at an inter-Allied meeting in London on 7 August at which a reproving note to Russia was drawn up by Albert Thomas.[1] Three days later Buchanan, acting on instructions from this conference, saw Kerensky and warned him that unless General Kornilov, who had succeeded Brusilov as Commander-in-Chief on 5 August, was authorised to restore discipline in the Army, no more guns would be forthcoming from the Allies. The early benignity towards the Provisional Government now gave way to brusque commands.

Obstinately but faithfully Kerensky refused to play the only card that would have stolen the game from Lenin, an application for a separate peace. He regarded the war effort as a stage in the liberalisation of Russia. He realised that in any case the continuance of the war was at once the basis of the Coalition Government and the condition of Allied support.

[1] Lloyd George, *War Memoirs*, V, p. 2560.

Yet he was a Socialist and saw that to authorise the Army leaders to rebuild the armed forces was to destroy the revolution. His assumption that the Russian masses could be persuaded, like the majority of Socialists in the West, to regard the war as a defence of the Fatherland and at the same time a means for improving their own condition was false. For it implied that a war begun under Tsarist auspices and mismanaged by Tsarist Ministers could be transformed into a crusade for democratic Socialism. The Russian people had never been privy to the reasons for the war. No representative of theirs had been consulted about it. In their eyes it was now merely an encumbrance from the past which had cost them dear.

The Cabinet in London were strongly urged by Knox on 7 September, on his return from Russia, to break with Kerensky on grounds of his failure to check the drift towards anarchy, and to switch their support to Kornilov as the best man in sight on the Russian scene.[1] The necessity to choose between the two became urgent two days later, when Buchanan and Noulens, who had now succeeded Paléologue as French Ambassador, were called to the Foreign Ministry and told that Kerensky and the Commander-in-Chief had quarrelled on the issues of military discipline and the restoration of the death penalty in the Army. This was one consequence of the capture of Riga by German troops on 3 September, which opened up the entire Russian industrial north-west to the enemy. On 10 September Kornilov, thinking his moment of destiny had arrived, came out in open revolt and proclaimed himself 'Dictator of all Russia'. In this rift at the Russian summit the government in Britain took up a neutral position, largely owing to the known disapproval of the United States for any policy savouring of interference in the revolution. Hence on 12 September the Cabinet decided that any action they took in the crisis would have to be through the recognised leader, Kerensky, who was accordingly urged to make it up with the General.[2] The wisdom of this choice was shown by the failure of the Kornilov rebellion owing to resistance by mutinous troops. But it was clear that if Kerensky, having rejected Kornilov's strong-arm methods, sought to keep Russia in the war he would risk losing whatever influence over the revolution he still had. There was little he could do when presented with a collective Allied note on 9 October (in which the United States did not join) calling for the immediate reorganisation of Russia's war effort, except to protest his intention of resuming the fighting in the spring while

[1] CAB 23/4. 229.
[2] Lloyd George, *op. cit.*, V, p. 2564; CAB 23/4. 231.

complaining about delays in Allied supplies to Russia. When the Provisional Government was finally thrust aside by the Bolsheviks a month later it had already been effectively written off in London.

Had Russia been prepared for modern warfare in 1914, had the monarchy been even moderately intelligent and honest and the Duma taken into its confidence, the appalling losses might not have occurred which, by November 1917, had eaten away the natural patriotism of the ordinary soldier. Once this loyalty had melted neither Kornilov's old-fashioned military discipline nor Kerensky's reformism could keep Russia in the war. Had support for the war existed among the masses of the country in the summer of 1917 on anything like the same scale as in other Allied nations, the Bolsheviks would probably have remained no more than an irritating fringe of defeatists. On the other hand, Kerensky's own account of the fall of the Provisional Government ascribes it in the main to lack of Allied sympathy for its Wilsonian programme and weakness of Allied material support.[1] But it is doubtful whether any general adoption of the slogan 'no annexations, no indemnities' by the Allies, even had they been talked into accepting it, could have prevailed much against Russia's war weariness in her last summer of the war. The news in mid-October that an inter-Allied conference on war aims would at length meet in Paris on 10 November was a relief to the Russian Premier, but there was little likelihood of it achieving anything dramatic. In London Bonar Law told the Commons that it was not war aims but the conduct of the war that was the subject of the meeting. As for Allied material support for Russia, at hardly any time did confidence exist in London or Paris in the willingness or power of Russia to resume the war effectively. In any event such confidence would have had to overcome the reluctance of military commanders on the Western front to see supplies diverted at the time of the Nivelle offensive and Passchendaele.

III

The momentous events of 7 and 8 November 1917, when key points in the Russian capital were seized by forces of the Soviet, followed by the arrest of the Provisional Government and the formation of the Bolshevik-dominated Workmen's and Peasants' Government, at first received little notice from the British Government. Lenin, it was felt, could not last long and there had been more than one abortive uprising in the unfolding of the revolution since the monarchy fell. Whatever the out-

[1] *La Révolution Russe, 1917,* Paris, 1928, *passim.*

come of the struggle for power in Russia, there was little hope of any resumption of activity on the Eastern front, and this was the aspect dominating the attitude of London. As Knox wrote at the end of November, 'the bulk of the Russian army refuses to continue'.[1]

The Bolsheviks themselves were unknown to governing circles in Britain. *The Times* perplexedly referred to them as 'maximalists' or 'anarchists', an outcrop of Russia's disordered mind and history. To Balfour, the British Foreign Secretary, they were 'dangerous dreamers' with 'crazy' ideas. When they talked about foreign policy the Bolsheviks spoke Wilson's language in working-class accents, and hence could easily be confused with the many pacifist and revolutionary groups which came to life in the winter of 1917–18. But whereas Kerensky on the eve of his fall was telling a representative of the Associated Press that Russia would not quit the war, the Bolshevik manifesto demanded an immediate armistice on all fronts in order that these principles might be negotiated with the Central Powers. Nevertheless, Russia was a vast, unpredictable country. It was hard to believe that these new, wild men, with their wild ideas, could bring it wholly under their control.

The Cabinet in London did not seriously take stock of the situation until 22 November, when it was merely decided to avoid any gesture which tended to strengthen anti-Allied feeling in Russia.[2] At a meeting four days later comfort was drawn from reports showing that only the industrial workers were really behind the Bolsheviks. The peasants, forming some four-fifths of the country's total population, were said to be either hostile or indifferent. Large areas of Russia were known to be beyond Lenin's writ, more particularly the Don basin, the Ukraine, Siberia and the Caucasus, regions which included the foremost granaries and oilfields.[3] By this time Trotsky, the new Foreign Minister, had circulated to the Allied Ambassadors in Petrograd on 21 November a note calling for an immediate armistice on all fronts and enclosing a manifesto of 8 November indicating the lines Bolshevik policy would follow when peace talks were opened. Buchanan described Trotsky's demand as an 'insolent communication' which he claimed had been received nineteen hours after the Commander-in-Chief, the ill-fated Dukhonin, had been instructed to open *pour-parlers* with the Central Powers for a truce.[4] Although this delay may perhaps have prevented the Allies from dealing adequately with

[1] Lloyd George, *op. cit.*, V, p. 2566.   [2] CAB 23/4. 280.
[3] Lloyd George, *op. cit.*, V, p. 2567.
[4] Sir George Buchanan, *op. cit.*, II, pp. 225–9.

the note, the intention of the Bolsheviks to press for an immediate general peace was widely known on the eve of their seizure of power. In the event Dukhonin refused to obey Trotsky's order, for which he paid with his life at his soldiers' hands and the German High Command was not approached until 26 November.[1]

Cecil in a statement on 23 November and Balfour in the Commons on 26 November said that the government could not reply to Trotsky's appeal for a general armistice and would regard any one-sided Russian move as a breach of the undertaking by the Allies severally in September 1914 not to conclude a separate peace. But in the Cabinet serious attention had to be given to the risk that Allied unfriendliness towards the new régime might drive Russia into the arms of Germany, and not only for the duration of the war. A Russo-German alliance, wrote Buchanan from Petrograd on 27 November, would constitute a perpetual menace to Europe, and to Britain in particular. He considered that Russia should be released from any further obligations towards the Allies in order to cut the ground from under the prevailing Russian bitterness towards Britain and France. He sharply dissented from the warning given by the three Allied Military Attachés to Dukhonin on 22 November, during Dukhonin's last twenty-four hours as Commander-in-Chief, which threatened 'most serious consequences' (understood to mean giving Japan a free hand in Siberia) in the event of a separate peace being concluded. This ultimatum Buchanan condemned as an 'ill-advised step which has done us any amount of harm'.[2]

The argument for caution on the part of the Entente was subjected to severe strain by the Bolshevik's cavalier treatment of the secret engagements of the war. These had already been declared void, as contrary to national freedom, in the Bolshevik statement on international policy on 8 November. Then came the publication of the first collection of treaties on 23 November, the aim evidently being to strengthen the appeal for a general peace. Nevertheless the fear of a Russo-German entente prevented the Cabinet in London from deciding to back Kaledin, the organiser of the Don Cossacks against the Leninists, when a case for doing so was made at a meeting on 29 November. There was greater sympathy for Buchanan's opinion that use should be made of every possible friction between the Bolsheviks and the Germans. Support for the Whites, at least for the time being, was inconsistent with this strategy. At the same

---

[1] J. W. Wheeler-Bennett, *Brest–Litovsk: the forgotten peace*, p. 75.
[2] CAB 23/4. 286.

time it was somewhat hopefully considered worthwhile approaching the Bolsheviks for an agreed revision of the secret
treaties, partly to discourage any further disclosures and partly
to facilitate peace overtures towards Turkey, to whose territory
the agreements with Russia chiefly related.[1] Accordingly,
Lloyd George reported at an Allied meeting in Paris on
30 November Buchanan's view that Russia should be released
from the Pact of London and proposed that the Allies' Ambassadors in Russia should separately tell the Bolsheviks that
their governments were ready to discuss war aims. To this
Clemenceau and Orlando adamantly objected and the conference concluded that the British proposal should be made
dependent upon Russia having a stable government, which was
in effect to relegate it to limbo. On the same day Trotsky told
the Allied Embassies that a truce was imminent on the Eastern
front and asked if they desired to take part in the truce negotiations, which were to begin on 2 December. There was no
reply.

It was the assumption of British policy that it was fully consistent with the sacred principle of non-intervention in the
revolution to give aid and encouragement to Russians who
wished to continue fighting should the Bolsheviks be really set
on peace. This conception of the revolution as essentially a
struggle between domestic political factions in Russia and one
which could be isolated from international events, underlay a
Cabinet discussion on 9 December. By this time a Russian
delegation led by Joffe, subsequently the first Bolshevik Ambassador to Germany, had arrived in Brest-Litovsk to begin
armistice negotiations on 3 December, although the armistice
agreement itself was not signed until 15 December. Balfour
had prepared a paper on the Russian position for the Cabinet
meeting, which he hoped would offset the strong views among
his colleagues that support should be given to Kaledin. He
began with the premise that 'no policy would be more fatal than
to give the Russians a motive for welcoming into their midst
German officials and German soldiers as deliverers'. On this
ground he opposed the Cabinet's refusal to repatriate the interned Bolshevik leaders Chicherin and Petrov: 'it is to our
advantage,' he wrote, 'as long as possible to avoid an open
breach.' But opposing opinions were expressed. It was felt to
be vital to prevent the Bolsheviks giving aid to Germany. How,
it was asked, could Russia's resources, such as wheat from the
Ukraine and oil from the Caucasus, be kept safe from German
control except by organising such local forces as were willing

[1] CAB 23/4. 286.

to defend them? In the prevailing political situation within Russia, these forces could not be other than anti-Bolshevik. By such reasoning the Cabinet arrived at the self-contradictory decision not to interfere in the course of the revolution and at the same time to strive to keep Russia in the war, or at least to influence the impending peace talks between the Bolsheviks and the Central Powers in the Allies' favour.[1]

The best means of insuring against the two dangers, firstly that Germany might acquire control of Russia's resources and secondly that the Allies might be isolated from the Bolsheviks in the event of Lenin's régime proving permanent, were explored again by the Cabinet on 21 December, the eve of the Brest parleys.[2] The outcome of this discussion was a memorandum taken the next day by Milner and Cecil to a meeting with the French in Paris. The argument of the paper was that unofficial contact with the Bolsheviks should be maintained now that the official Allied missions had retired to Vologda, in order to prevent Russian military equipment from falling into German hands for use in the coming spring offensives in the West and thus possibly deciding the whole issue of the war. At the same time it was recommended that financial assistance should be given to any forces in Russia, more particularly in the Ukraine, which were willing to continue to fight against Germany. Two days later, on 23 December, this course was approved by Clemenceau and his Foreign Minister, Pichon, at the Paris conference, and the resulting Milner–Clemenceau agreement marked the beginning of organised Anglo-French intervention in Russia's internal affairs, however stoutly the name was denied on the British side. By the terms of this agreement France was to 'direct her activity' north of the Black Sea 'against the enemy', while Britain was to concentrate south-east of the Black Sea 'against the Turks'. The ostensible idea inspiring the latter arrangement was that of combining Armenia with Georgia to form an independent state in the hope that this would forestall a great Turanian state coming into existence 'extending from Constantinople to China'. The imaginativeness of the scheme was combined with a more earthy British resolve to secure possession of Mesopotamia at all costs after the fighting. The zones of Entente influence in southern Russia were defined in the document as follows: to Britain, the Don Cossack territory, the Caucasus, Armenia, Georgia, Turkestan in Central Asia; to France, Bessarabia (in order to prevent the Bolsheviks forcing an entrance into Rumania), the Ukraine and the Crimea.[3]

[1] CAB 23/4. 295.   [2] *Ibid.*, 304.
[3] *D.B.F.P.*, First Series, III, pp. 369–70; CAB 23/4. 306, Appendix.

This agreement, however, did not imply any abandonment of the policy of keeping the lines open to the Bolsheviks and of preparing to intervene should their power crumble, a dual object to be followed during the long negotiations at Brest. This attitude was to some extent justified by the fluctuating course of the talks, the drift of which neither party sought to conceal, as differences appeared among the Bolsheviks, on their side, and the Central Powers, on theirs, on the conditions of a settlement. This development took some time to become clear. At first the Russians were agreed on the tactic of dragging out the conference in order to use it as a sounding board for world revolutionary propaganda. Their initial assumption was that, with the advent of the revolutionary storm, a treaty would never have to be signed with the existing rulers of the Central Powers. The representatives of those Powers, on their side, Kühlmann and Czernin, the German and Austrian Foreign Ministers respectively, desired simply to sign a peace as soon as possible, the German because the High Command wanted their hands free for a final great assault in the West, and the Austrian because of the desperate food shortage at home. These conflicting purposes of the two sides looked for one moment as though they were to be reconciled on Christmas day, when Czernin on behalf of the Quadruple Alliance gave an astonishingly mild rejoinder to Joffe's schedule of demands: these included the evacuation of occupied territory without forcible appropriations, the restoration of independence to nations deprived of it during the war, self-determination for hitherto dependent nations, no war indemnities or economic boycotts, and the settlement of colonial problems in terms of national freedom. The Austrian Foreign Minister's reply made a show of accepting the slogan of no annexations and no indemnities, but not that of self-determination for nations not yet sovereign. His basic condition, in any case, was that these terms should first be accepted by all the Allies.

As the Central Powers were thus seeking to insure themselves against threats to their territorial integrity from the Western Allies, the Brest talks were broken off and the Allies given until 8 January to decide whether they wished to associate themselves with the modified Joffe proposals. Accordingly Trotsky made 'one last appeal' to the Allies on 28 December to send representatives to Brest if they wished to secure themselves against the effects of a Russian separate peace. Trotsky's declaration left no doubt that support could not be looked for from the Bolsheviks for changes in the map in the Allies' favour. Indeed the Bolsheviks were demanding immediate self-determination for peoples within the Allied states and colonies. In effect the Allies were thus offered a choice between universal self-determination, as required by the Bolsheviks, and limited self-determination as approved by Czernin. The latter conception was understood to apply only to territories occupied during the war, other annexations, as for instance Alsace-Lorraine, being 'sanctioned by historical prescription'. It was not made clear what the Bolshevik position would be in the event of the Allies joining the talks on the basis of an acceptance of the Central Powers' conception of self-determination. But that the Bolsheviks regarded the talks merely as a prelude to revolutionary upsurges in all the belligerent countries was apparent in Trotsky's conclusion:

> in these negotiations, with the condition that there should be complete publicity, the Russian delegation would continue to defend the programme of international socialistic democracy as opposed to the imperialistic programmes of the Governments, Allied and enemy alike. The success of our programme will depend upon the degree in which the will of the imperialistic class will be paralysed by the work of the revolutionary proletariat in every country.

These words were regarded in London as scarcely an invitation to a serious discussion. Consequently the only Allied reply given to Trotsky, apart from Wilson's sympathetic allusion to the new régime in Russia in his Fourteen Points speech on 8 January, was Lloyd George's warning of 5 January, given at a Labour and Trade Union conference, when he said that the only real issue was whether Russia was going to surrender to Germany. There could be no sympathy for her in Britain if she did, the Prime Minister went on, whatever approval there might be for the principle of self-determination in general terms.

Hence, Christmas of 1917 marked the apex of Bolshevik revolutionary optimism and the deepest abyss so far between the Bolsheviks and the Allies. The gulf was dug still deeper when the Bolsheviks dissolved the Constituent Assembly on 19 January, thus finally burying all liberal hopes aroused in Britain by the March Revolution. However, with the stiffening of the German attitude at the end of December over the question of self-determination for Poland and the Baltic States, which Germany said had already seceded from Russia, the question began to be asked once more whether the Bolsheviks might even yet fight on the Allied side. On his arrival in Brest to conduct the Russian case on 7 January Trotsky declared that he would accept no peace which was not 'just and democratic', but, after interminable debates with Kühlmann on the meaning of self-determination, he was bluntly confronted with the demand that he should recognise the Social Revolutionary régime in Kiev which was seeking autonomy under German encouragement and a separate peace. On 18 January Trotsky therefore returned from Brest to report to the Third Congress of Soviets on this serious turn of events, taking with him Hoffmann's map, which reserved Poland, Lithuania, western Latvia, Riga and the Moon Sound islands for Germany. There it was that, in opposition to Lenin, he won approval for his refusal to accept any peace with the Central Powers which involved the denial of announced Bolshevik principles, and yet to do so without continuing the war. Trotsky's formula, 'no war, no peace', was at length agreed to by Lenin with immense reluctance in order to save the Central Committee of the party from the folly of Bukharin's motion in favour of a revolutionary war.[1]

When the Commissar for Foreign Affairs returned to the talks at Brest ten days later he took with him a mandate to press for nothing short of a democratic peace, within the Russian meaning of the term. With him went a delegation of Ukrainian Bolsheviks and, with a chorus of approval from these, he denounced the Social Revolutionaries of Kiev as unrepresentative. By 12 February the Bolsheviks had actually driven the German-sponsored Rada from Kiev, although by this time these non-Bolshevik Ukrainian nationalists had signed a treaty with the Central Powers under which they virtually surrendered the material resources of the country and ensured permanent German and Austrian predominance there. From this moment, and especially after Trotsky's dramatic declaration of refusal either to sign the treaty or to fight, the German Supreme Command, which had insisted upon the treaty with the Ukraine being signed, seriously began to force the Bolsheviks away from debate and towards surrender. On 18 February the Germans declared that the armistice was expired and five days later military operations against unresisting Russian forces were resumed, a step rendered all the more necessary through the Ukrainian Rada's failure to fulfil the obligations under the treaty they had signed with Germany to provision the Central Powers. Enormous tracts of Russia were absorbed in this resumed German drive, the line finally coming to rest along the towns Narva, Pskov, Polotsk, Orsha and Mogilev, while in the south the Bolsheviks were driven from the Ukraine and the Rada was re-established in Kiev. By 24 February the Central

[1] J. W. Wheeler-Bennett, *op. cit.*, p. 193.

Committee of the Bolsheviks and the Central Executive Committee of the Soviets had no alternative but to abandon the myth of an impending revolution in Germany and swallow the bitter opinion Lenin had urged from the outset, namely that Russia must give way. The Russian delegation left for Brest for the last time on the same day and signed the treaty without much serious scrutiny of its terms on 3 March. Consistently with British and French views of the Brest deliberations, General Hoffmann's boot was the only serious reality.

The Allies' coolness towards Trotsky's appeal of 28 December arose partly from the assumption that, even in the event of a Russian capitulation, her resources could not be made immediately available to the Central Powers. Knox gave the Cabinet his reassuring view that it would take Germany at least six months to satisfy all her requirements from southern Russia and thus nullify the blockade. Nevertheless, when Ludendorff began to force the Bolsheviks under the yoke, the attempt to make contact with the latter was resumed in London, albeit half-heartedly. Some encouragement had been given by Trotsky. On 24 January, for instance, two days after the Central Committee had voted on the 'no war, no peace' resolution, he sent for the French Military Attaché, Sadoul, and showed him General Hoffmann's map. Hence, at a Cabinet meeting in London on 7 February, Lloyd George urged that Lockhart, described as a 'recognised intermediary', should tell the Bolshevik leaders that no interference with the social aims of the revolution was intended and that if they broke off the talks and resumed the military struggle they would have Allied support.[1] In this he overruled objections to relations with the Bolsheviks raised by the Italian Government, who were afraid that Allied acceptance of Trotsky's principles of peace would rob them of their war gains. However, an ill-timed Soviet decree published on the very next day, which repudiated Russia's state debts, had a chilling effect on the prospects of recognition of the Bolsheviks.

The unofficial Allied agents in Russia, Lockhart, formerly British Consul-General in Moscow, Sadoul, of the French military mission, and Raymond Robins, of the American Red Cross, found themselves promising help to Lenin if the talks with the Central Powers were broken off or, after 3 March, if the treaty was not ratified: yet they were unable in the event to guarantee it owing to the distrust which had now grown up between the Allies and the Bolsheviks. The nearest that Robins went to securing an undertaking from the United States

[1] Lloyd George, *op. cit.*, V, pp. 2591–5.

was a letter to this effect from the American Ambassador Francis, who also prepared a draft urging this course on the State Department. But neither letter was sent.[1] On 5 March, two days after the Bolsheviks had signed the treaty after having declined the appointment of commissions for the detailed examination of its terms, Trotsky saw Robins and said he would defeat ratification in the Central Committee of the Party if Allied and American help against Germany was forthcoming, so destructive of Russian independence did he consider its terms to be. Lenin also agreed to oppose ratification if the United States gave an encouraging reply to Trotsky's inquiry. A possible explanation of their attitude was that they feared that the treaty might be rejected by the Central Committee since its terms were far more crushing than those proposed by the Central Powers before the German advance was resumed, or that Germany might nevertheless continue her military inroads into Russia notwithstanding the treaty. Trotsky's and Lenin's messages were passed on by Robins to Lockhart, who promptly cabled Lloyd George for authority to say that the proposed Japanese intervention in Siberia would be shelved and the Soviets helped materially to resume fighting against Germany. Lockhart himself saw Trotsky on 5 March and was told that the Congress of Soviets would break the armistice, but only if Japan was restrained. This, the desperate Lockhart reported, was the last chance to undo the Brest peace.

Neither from Britain nor from the United States, however, did a word of encouragement come. Kamenev's mission to Britain in late February to ascertain the conditions of Allied assistance to Russia ended in fiasco. His luggage was searched by Government officials and a cheque for £5,000 taken from him. The French refused to allow him to land in their country. Hence on 13 March Robins was forced to tell Lenin that he had had no reaction from home to the Bolshevik inquiry, and on the same day the United States State Department in a message to the American Ambassador made no mention of the Trotsky proposal, although Francis had specifically asked for guidance on this. The final page of the Brest chapter was written in Moscow on the evening of 16 March, when Lenin was told by Robins that neither he nor Lockhart, who had remained in Petrograd as he thought ratification was now inevitable, had heard from their governments. Before rising to address the all-Russian Congress of Soviets he said to the bitterly disappointed Robins, 'I shall speak for the peace. It will be ratified.'

[1] C. K. Cumming and W. W. Pettit, *Russian–American Relations, 1917–1920*, New York, 1920, pp. 65–7.

CHAPTER IV

A COLONY OF LEPERS

I

LENIN and Trotsky trusted the Allies no more than they did the Central Powers. Even their insistence that during the armistice the Central Powers should move no troops to the West other than those already in transit arose from a doctrinaire wish not to distinguish between foes rather than from any desire to assist the Allies.[1] Nor could they have goaded their Army into fighting had they wished, or achieved anything with their exhausted forces had they fought. 'Give me an army of 100,000 men,' Lenin told the Bukharinites, whose stomach turned at the Brest peace, 'an army which will not tremble before the enemy, and I will not sign this peace. Can you raise an army? Can you give me anything but prattle and the drawing up of pasteboard figures?'[2] On no condition was Lenin prepared to rely on the Allies for military aid: 'as long as there is no intensification of the class struggle in Germany and England leading towards the social revolution,' he wrote, 'the Russian Revolution must seek the most favourable conditions for its existence, relying as little as possible either on the English or German Governments. The Russian Revolution must adopt a neutral attitude towards both imperialistic camps, and this is only possible by coming out of the war.'[3] While these views held, the Allies were reluctant to throw good money after bad into a country which was neither willing nor able to use it for the intended purposes.

After the assassination of the Communist leaders Volodarsky and Uritsky and the attempt on Lenin's life in August, the outbreak of terror, Red and White, dissipated any tendencies for an accommodation with the Bolsheviks. The British agents in Petrograd, Woodhouse and the ill-fated Cromie, reported to Balfour on 19 August that the Bolshevik position was becoming rapidly untenable. On the same day Sir Esmé Howard from Stockholm gave details of the arrest of British subjects in Moscow and the raiding of the British consulate; acts intended, Howard thought, to provide the Bolsheviks with hostages in the

[1] E. H. Carr, *The Bolshevik Revolution, 1917–1923*, III, p. 28.
[2] J. W. Wheeler-Bennett, *op. cit.*, p. 260.
[3] *Pravda*, 23 February 1918; also M. Philips Price, *My Reminiscences of the Russian Revolution*, London, 1921, pp. 245–6.

event of their fall.   On 6 September the Netherlands Minister
in Petrograd, who looked after British interest after the sacking
of the British Embassy, wrote that the Bolsheviks 'realise that
the game is up and have entered on a course of crime and
madness—the Bolsheviks have burned their boats and are now
ready for any wickedness'.   Lockhart himself, after his expulsion from Russia on a charge of conspiring to unseat the régime,
wrote to the Foreign Office on 18 November that the Bolsheviks
had 'established a rule of force and oppression unequalled in
history'.   Kimens, the British Vice-Consul in Petrograd, reported two days later that central authority was collapsing in
Russia and 'every province was a state within a state'.[1]   Such
prophecies of Communist downfall reached London every day.
It was hard to assign exact weights to the factors on the other
side: Bolshevik tenacity and discipline; the unrivalled insight
and leadership of Lenin; Russian patriotism and sullen resistance towards attempts to control the country from outside.

Once the idea of feeding Russian hostility towards the
Draconian peace by promises of military support had been
rejected, it remained for the Allies first to denounce the Brest
treaty and then to try to frustrate it by organising resistance
within Russia to the enjoyment by the Central Powers of their
immense gains.   A beginning was made at an Allied meeting
in London on 16 March summoned to review Brest-Litovsk.
The 'most mordant pen in Europe', that of Clemenceau, was
recruited to draft a retort which, while breaking with the Bolsheviks, reaffirmed the determination to continue fighting 'in
order to finish once for all with this policy of plunder'.[2]   But
even at the outset the more sinister notion of allowing Germany
to compensate herself in the East for what she was being asked
to forgo to the Allies in the West was involved in intervention.[3]
Hopes of a negotiated settlement with Kühlmann on some such
lines had continued throughout the winter of 1917–18.[4]   But
intervention in Russia was a halting thing, stumbling on through
stops and starts, and this pro-German element in it, if it ever
existed at all in any strength, faded in the spring with the bitter
struggles against the *Kaiserschlacht*.

Allied intervention originated in the stresses of war.   Balfour,
defending the proposed Japanese landing in Siberia, said in the
House of Commons on 14 March, the day on which debate on
the ratification of the Brest treaty began in the Congress of

[1] Cmd. 8, April 1919, *A Collection of Reports on Bolshevism in Russia.*
[2] Lloyd George, *op. cit.*, V, p. 2596.
[3] E. H. Carr, *op. cit.*, III, p. 23, especially note 6.
[4] See above, Chapter II, p. 29, *et seq.*

Soviets, that Russia was 'derelict upon the waters' and there was 'now nothing to prevent her falling a prey to the German malady'.[1] Initially intervention was an attempt to unmake the Brest treaty and followed logically from the statement of the Supreme Council on 18 March repudiating the treaty. How to stop Germany and Turkey reaching the Caspian oilfields; how to prevent stocks of Allied military stores in Murmansk, Archangel and Vladivostok from falling into enemy hands; how to re-form an anti-German front in Russia, or at least to enable anti-German elements to make their escape to the West: these were the questions to which Allied intervention was a confused reply. Thereafter it wavered between two extreme and equally impracticable policies: an attempt, if possible with German co-operation, to unseat the Bolsheviks and install a régime more favourable to Russian and foreign property-owners, and the more limited object of setting Germans and Russians at each other's throats wherever possible and disengaging Allied forces the moment the fighting in Europe ended.

The hopes of a limited intervention, with the assistance of the Bolsheviks themselves, rose and fell in inverse ratio to the temperature of the Russo-German relations. By a curious irony, at the moment when Allied help was most acceptable to Lenin the British Government were cool; when the British Government were beginning to warm to the possibility, the Bolshevik *rapprochement* with Germany was just beginning. During the last week of February, when the Bolsheviks were stunned by the new German terms, Lockhart feverishly pressed London to offer help and to drop the idea of Japanese intervention in Siberia. On 2 March, as a result of a misinterpretation of a telegram from Brest, Trotsky urged the Murmansk Soviet to fight on and co-operate with the Allies. An understanding with the Soviet was actually reached by the British naval representative, Admiral Kemp, under which the Soviet turned over to him the local naval force, consisting of three destroyers, to protect the coast against German U-boats. Even after Brest-Litovsk Lockhart continued to appeal for support of the Bolsheviks in case they refused to ratify the treaty. The reply given by Balfour strangely echoed the advice tendered by Lenin to his followers: 'an army cannot be made of fine words'. Lockhart persisted, in the teeth of news from home that his policy was undermining confidence in him in official quarters. He reported a conversation he had had with Chicherin in which the Foreign Minister said that German demands were exciting resentment in Russia and that the present was the moment for

[1] 104 H.C. Deb. 5s. Cols. 549–52.

a demonstration of Allied sympathy.[1] Lockhart was brusquely answered by the Foreign Office that he misunderstood British policy. Returning to the charge again on 10 March he claimed that the Russian working class was 'the only section that had an interest in opposing the Germans'. On this Balfour marginally commented that Lockhart was failing to convince the Russian leaders that Britain had no intention of intervening in their affairs.[2]

Towards the middle of the following month a sudden change occurred in the British attitude, caused in part by the severe fighting on the Western front, in part by the alarm caused in Moscow by the movement of German troops towards the city to suppress the Right Social Revolutionaries and the pro-war wing of the Bolsheviks, who were seeking to destroy the German-sponsored régime in the Ukraine. Lockhart found to his puzzlement a long dispatch from Balfour in which, after having been kept in the dark as to London's attitude for three months, he was told that 'if you can indeed persuade Trotsky to resist German penetration, you will have earned the gratitude of your country and of all humanity'.[3] The Cabinet went as far on 22 April as agreeing to send Smuts to Kola to talk with Trotsky about the possibility of his using the army he was building up to resist the Germans with the help of Allied subsidies, though this proposal was never implemented.[4] A few days later, on the 25th, Balfour was proposing to the United States an inter-Allied expedition to Russia in collaboration with the Leninists:

> Trotsky, at least, has for some time shown signs of recognising that co-operation with the Allies is the only hope of freeing Russia from the Germans—He has now definitely asked for a statement of the help which the Allies could give, and of the guarantees which they would furnish—The British Government are of opinion that the Allies should avail themselves of this opportunity to offer Allied intervention against Germany, accompanied by a suitable declaration of disinterestedness, and by proper guarantees as to the evacuation of Russian territory.[5]

With the sending of Allied military missions to Murmansk, Archangel and Vladivostok, however, this phase of co-operation with the Bolsheviks against German forces came to an end.

---

[1] R. H. Bruce Lockhart, *Memoirs of a British Agent*, p. 243.
[2] Blanche Dugdale, *Arthur James Balfour*, II, pp. 258–9.
[3] Lockhart, *op. cit.*, pp. 274–5.
[4] Louis Fischer, *The Soviets in World Affairs*, I, p. 99; CAB 23/14. 396 A.
[5] James Bunyan, *Intervention, Civil War and Communism in Russia, April–December 1918*, pp. 73–4; CAB 23/14. 409 A, p. 86.

At the end of May, at a meeting in Vologda, Noulens, the French Ambassador, the 'only Allied representative who knows his own mind', as Lockhart described him, and the French Military Attaché, Lavergne, advocated intervention if necessary against the Bolsheviks.　To this Lockhart at length consented and in doing so cast away his entrée to the Bolshevik leaders.　'I had now identified myself,' he decided, 'with a movement which, whatever its original object, was to be directed, not against Germany, but against the *de facto* government of Russia.'[1]　On 7 May Lloyd George, apparently without consulting Lockhart, sent to Russia as his secret service agent the international adventurer, Sydney Reilly, a Jew from Odessa, whose object was nothing short of the organisation of a *coup* against the Council of People's Commissars.　While this deterioration of Allied relations with the Communists was proceeding, Russia and Germany were coming closer together, as symbolised in the armistice signed by Russia and the Ukraine on 12 June, an event which led to the slackening of German military pressure on Russia.　There were three factors which conduced to this growing Russo-German intimacy: the Allied plan for Japanese intervention in Siberia, which had been maturing since at least the beginning of the year; the outbreak of fighting between Bolshevik forces and Czech war prisoners at various points on the Trans-Siberian railway; and the touch-and-go position of the Bolsheviks at home between July and September, as they wrestled for supremacy with the anti-German Social Revolutionaries.

As early as November 1917 the British Government had taken steps to secure the situation in Eastern Siberia should the revolution take on a distinctly anti-Entente complexion.　At some time in that month Colonel Ward, commanding the 25th battalion of the Middlesex Regiment in Hong Kong, received orders to hold himself and his men in readiness for an unknown destination, which Colonel Ward believed to be Vladivostok.[2]　During this period the Japanese Government were alarmed about the possibility of a Russian separate peace, which might have the effect of admitting German forces to Russia's Far Eastern provinces, whence they would be able to punish Japan for her seizure of German possessions in the Far East.　They therefore suggested to the Allies that they be permitted to send troops to Siberia on condition that the intervention be exclusively Japanese, that Japan's paramount interest in China be recognised and that she received exclusive mining, timber

[1] Lockhart, *op. cit.*, pp. 284–7.
[2] John Ward, *With the 'Die-Hards' in Siberia*, N.Y., 1920, p. 1.

and fishing concessions in Siberia. Britain was favourably disposed to the general principle of intervention in Siberia. Balfour in the House of Commons on 14 March 1918 underlined a former statement by Cecil to the effect that the intention of the expedition was to prevent the 'Germanisation' of Siberia, and gave as reasons for the project the need to recover the vast stores belonging to the Allies which lay derelict in the port and environs of Vladivostok, and to put an end to the arming of German and Austrian war prisoners in Siberia who might later be sent to the Western front.[1]

Neither object sounded convincing. The real cause of the accumulation of war stores at Vladivostok was the bottlenecks along the Trans-Siberian railway, especially at Tomsk, and it was unlikely that the Germans, in the revolutionary tumult in Russia in 1918, could have remedied these obstructions even had they wished to move the supplies westwards from the port. As for the scare of an enemy army being recruited from the war prisoners, reports by two agents sent to Siberia by Lockhart and Robins, Captain Webster, of the American Red Cross, and Captain Hicks, of the British mission in Moscow, showed that this was without foundation. 'After seeing the armed prisoners,' they reported on 26 April, 'we feel there is no danger to the Allied cause through them.' The Allied Consuls in Siberia had given contrary reports, they said, owing to their being unanimously anti-Bolshevik in sympathy.[2]

From the outset, however, the British Government was opposed to any unilateral action by Japan, as Balfour told the Japanese Ambassador in London as early as 26 December.[3] Their reason was fear of United States disapproval, especially at a time when it was essential to have American sympathy for general intervention in the Russian revolution. Hence, in view of the fact that the two companies stationed in Hong Kong were the sole British forces in the area, the War Cabinet decided to ask for an American contingent.[4] No definite answer was given to this request and in the first few days of January 1918 an Anglo-Japanese naval force proceeded alone to Vladivostok, with the ostensible object of protecting foreign nationals in the port. The British note to the United States was followed on 10 January by an appeal to the same quarter from France for more extensive inroads into Siberia. The French note drew a negative response from Secretary of State Lansing, who held

[1] 104 H.C. Deb. 5s. Cols. 549–50.
[2] Cumming and Pettit, op, cit. pp. 177–84.
[3] George F. Kennan, Soviet–American Relations, 1917–1920, I, Russia Leaves the War, p. 312.
[4] CAB 23/4. 294 (7 December 1917).

that intervention would have the effect of alienating Russian opinion against the war aims of the Allies.[1] By this time, however, the Japanese demand for an intervention carried out by themselves alone was much stronger, so that on 28 January a further British approach was made to the State Department to give its blessing to the Siberian expedition, which however this time suggested that Japan act as mandatory for the Allies with no thought of annexation or further control.[2] The reply to this came as a blunt American rejection on the grounds that it would certainly arouse bitter opposition among the Russian people and cause them to rally round their present government.[3]

Nevertheless, pressure on Wilson continued unremittingly both from the Allies and from his own military advisers, culminating on 27 February in a visit to the President by Lord Reading, the British Ambassador, who plainly warned that Japan contemplated action on her own although, in the absence of Allied support, she lacked the means to achieve the object of the exercise. This urging sufficed to evoke a Presidential message on 1 March dissociating the United States from the proposed expedition but raising no objection to it. The message was shown to the British and French envoys the same day. The handwashing nature of Wilson's attitude, however, met with strong objections from his *entourage*, especially from Colonel House, and the message was replaced by a further note on 5 March, in which the wisdom of the project was described as 'most questionable' and fear was expressed that the whole action 'might play into the hands of the enemies of Russia, and particularly of the enemies of the Russian revolution, for which the Government of the United States entertains the greatest sympathy'.[4]

Pressure for the Siberian expedition was then suspended to cover the period of the ratification of the Brest treaty, but again on 17 March the Supreme War Council, at its meeting to consider the effects of the treaty, took up the question and decided to ask once more for Wilson's consent to the expedition. Wilson remained adamant, however, and limited British and Japanese forces were landed on Russian territory on 5 April from the warships sent to Vladivostok, Japanese troops for the defence of their nationals, British troops to give an inter-Allied colour to the landing.[5] But the plan for large-scale intervention in Siberia continued to mark time. At a Cabinet meeting in London on 19 June the Chief of the Imperial General Staff, Sir Henry

[1] *F.R.U.S.*, *1918, Russia*, II, p. 29.
[2] *Ibid.*, pp. 35–6.   [3] *Ibid.*, pp. 41–2.
[4] *F.R.U.S.*, *1918, Russia*, II, pp. 67–8.
[5] Lloyd George, *op. cit.*, VI, p. 3178.

Wilson, backed by Milner, pressed for a Japanese intervention, as he had throughout the spring, on the grounds that otherwise British forces then at Pechenga, Murmansk and Archangel would be driven into the sea. The Prime Minister hung back and another telegram urging American support, this time in the name of the Imperial War Cabinet, was sent to President Wilson on the following day.[1] Again the question was conconsidered in Cabinet on 16 July, three months after the formation of an anti-Bolshevik Far Eastern Government at Chita with Japanese support and with Admiral Kolchak as Minister of War. Balfour, who had been hostile to the Siberian proposal from the beginning, continued to report United States opposition, but, according to Sir Henry Wilson, the Premier and Cecil knew that the President was weakening.[2] On the next day it was known that the White House provisionally consented to the operation in Siberia. By 15 August American troops were entering Vladivostok to join the British, French and Japanese forces which had been landed two weeks earlier. The political consequence of this hard-won intervention came a month later, on 22 September, when a Provisional All-Russian Government was brought into being as the leading anti-Bolshevik centre by a conference held at Ufa.

What had in the end swayed Wilson was the outbreak of fighting between the Bolsheviks and a force of Czech prisoners captured from the Austro-Hungarian armies by the Russians before the Bolsheviks sued for peace. At the end of 1917 these Czech soldiers were distributed along the whole length of the Trans-Siberian railway, slowly making their way to Vladivostok, whence they hoped to make their escape from Russia. Apart from the role they were destined to play in securing Czech independence, their experiences decisively influenced relations in mid-1918 between the Bolsheviks and the Western Powers, for the growing fear of the Bolsheviks that the Czech legion was being manipulated from the outside as a means of destroying the revolution drove a final wedge between Lenin and the Allies.

Winston Churchill, then Minister for Munitions, first grasped the possibility of employing the Czech force, numbering some 50,000 men, in his plans to wipe the Bolsheviks off the map. He wrote to Benes on 1 April advising him to allow the men to remain in Siberia, where, in co-operation with the anti-Bolshevik leader Semyonov, they could be of greater use to the Allies in helping to re-establish an Eastern front than if they

---

[1] Sir C. E. Callwell, *Field-Marshal Sir Henry Wilson*, II, p. 109.
[2] Callwell, *op. cit.*, p. 116.

made the long journey by sea to France.[1] In any event it was doubtful whether shipping was available for the latter course. Balfour and Cecil wrote to Benes to the same effect in May; since Allied landings at the northern ports and at Vladivostok were contemplated for July and August, they argued that the Czechs, by striking at the Bolsheviks from the east, could create a diversion to cover these operations. At first Benes refused and in doing so was supported by the French, Pichon insisting on the priority of Western needs at an Anglo-French conference in London on 28 May.[2] Ultimately, however, both he and Masaryk were won over by the promise of British support for Czech independence at the Peace Conference if they agreed to use their forces as the British wished.[3] What hastened their decision was the unexpected turn of events in Siberia on 14 May, when a Czech soldier was accidently injured by an object thrown from a train carrying Hungarian war prisoners. The Czechs were already angered over an arrangement, which they appear to have misunderstood, between Trotsky and General Lavergne, the French Military Attaché in Russia, for speeding their departure from the country through Archangel, and the incident led to fighting. Certain Czech soldiers were arrested by the local Soviet, only to be released a few days later after an attack on the jail by their comrades.

The Bolsheviks and Czechs were now open enemies. Chicherin, Trotsky's successor as Commissar for Foreign Affairs, told the Allies that Russia was no longer a belligerent and could not tolerate the presence of independent armies on her territory.[4] On 25 May Trotsky, after ordering the local Soviets along the Trans-Siberian line to de-train the Czechs and draft them into the Red Army, cabled an order to shoot all armed Czechs on the spot. This was the signal for a general Czech uprising. Forces of the Legion seized Novo-Nikolaevsk and Cheliabinsk on 26 May, Penza two days later, Omsk on 7 June and Samara on 8 June. It was under the cover of these operations that the anti-Leninist Social Revolutionary Government recruited from the former Constituent Assembly was able to establish itself at Samara.[5] What made the situation critical for the Bolsheviks was an uprising by the Left Social Revolutionaries in Moscow in the first days of July. During the ensuing weeks until the middle of September it was touch and go with the Soviet régime.

[1] Eduard Benes, *Der Aufstand der Nationen*, Berlin, 1928, pp. 465–6.
[2] Lloyd George, *op. cit.*, VI, p. 3184.
[3] Louis Fischer, *op. cit.*, I, p. 114.
[4] Cumming and Pettit, *op. cit.*, pp. 224–6.
[5] W. H. Chamberlin, *The Russian Revolution*, II, pp. 14–15.

Once the Czechs were in open conflict with the Bolsheviks, the need to help extricate them was welcomed by interventionists in London as a means for overcoming any misgivings about the Siberian enterprise. But for all the blend of adventure and dubious politics in the Czech exploit, the military contribution it made to the White cause was not in the long run impressive, and this mainly owing to the failure of the Whites to unite. The Directory established at Omsk by the State Conference at Ufa in September lived a precarious and divided life under the shadow of a military dictatorship.[1] The original Allied plan was that Archangel, which was occupied by British forces on 2 August and made the seat of a moderate conservative government under N. Chaikovsky, should act as a base for an expedition to be sent up the Dvina to join hands with the Czechs as they advanced from Kazan. But the heavy demands for men in France meant that less than 1,200 British troops could be landed at Archangel, and their progress along the Dvina was held up by Trotsky's forces. By the middle of September the Bolsheviks had reached Kazan, which fell to them on the 18th. It was their first victory in the Civil War. In the following weeks the basin of the middle Volga was cleared of White forces and the Czechs fell back to the Urals. Thence they made their way singly and in small parties to Allied-held Vladivostok; before they arrived they had marred their prestige by handing over Kolchak, who surrendered to them on 1 January 1920, to the authorities at Irkutsk by whom he was executed. By the time they reached Europe the Central Powers had surrendered.

Apart from the northern ports and Vladivostok there were were three more points at which British forces were engaged in support of the anti-Bolsheviks in the period between the May days on the Western front and the meeting of the Peace Conference in Paris at the end of 1918. The first was the Caucasus and Transcaspia, the area where Russia meets the Middle East. Major-General L. C. Dunsterville was sent from Baghdad up to Enzeli, in Persia, in January with instructions to prevent the Turks reaching the oil wells of Baku and joining hands with the Germans pushing south-west through the Ukraine. In July he crossed the Caspian at the request of the Mussafatists, the moderate Tartar nationalists, who had ousted the Bolshevik Soviet from Baku. But this footing in the Caucasus was held for less than a month, as on 14 September Turkish forces pressed forwards and succeeded in driving 'Dunsterforce' back into Persia.[2] The Caspian Sea, however, remained under British

[1] Chamberlin, *op. cit.*, pp. 20–1.
[2] L. C. Dunsterville, *The Adventures of Dunsterforce*, London, 1920, Chap. XVII.

control and the Turks were unable to use the oil wells as they were out of the war within six weeks.[1] At the same time General Malleson's Anglo-Indian detachment seized and held Russia's Transcaspian provinces. After the Turkish surrender British forces returned to Baku on 16 November and crossed to Batum on the Black Sea on the 23rd.

The second and third theatres of anti-Bolshevik operations under British protection were respectively in the north-west and the south. In the former a British squadron was put ashore at Reval on 12 December and equipped Estonian forces with arms for use against the Bolsheviks. In the south there was a joint Anglo-French movement to support the Whites from the Black Sea after the expulsion of the Turks from those waters. In this area the French had the greater interest, both on account of the Milner–Clemenceau agreement of December 1917 and owing to their desire to immunise Eastern Europe, later to form a pillar of the French security system, from Communist influence. Towards the end of the war with Germany Clemenceau and Foch, in their anxiety to deal with the Bolshevik problem before the demobilisation of Allied forces, pressed on with a grand design for creating a strong anti-Bolshevik wedge extending from the Baltic to the Crimea. On 27 October Clemenceau wrote to General Franchet d'Esperey, the Allied Commander-in-Chief in the Balkans, that the 'main line of the plan of action which should be adopted is not only to continue the struggle against the Central Powers, but also to bring about the encirclement of Bolshevism and to provoke its downfall'. Immediately after the mutiny in the German Navy on 8 November he wrote to Lloyd George urging that the war in Europe be finished because the 'Bolsheviks, not the Boche' were the enemy. The next move was to call a conference of anti-Bolsheviks to plan the campaign in the south. This was held at Jassy in Rumania under French sponsorship between 17 and 24 November with the question of 'aid to Russia in the struggle against the Bolsheviks' as the chief item on the agenda, and appointed Denikin as head of the whole counter-revolutionary movement in southern Russia. On 17 December French forces landed at Odessa and before long the entire Ukrainian coast of the Black Sea was held by twelve thousand French troops.

II

Thus, when the Conference to frame a peace settlement with the Central Powers met in Paris at the end of the year, Bolshevik Russia, though it had surmounted its greatest crisis of the

[1] Lloyd George, *op. cit.*, VI, pp. 3193–6.

summer, was isolated within a ring of enemies, foreign and domestic, at every point of the compass except for the cold desert regions of the extreme north and north-east. In the east was the Japanese-protected régime at Chita, invulnerable for the time being through its remoteness. There was the central hub of anti-Bolshevik power at Omsk, where on 18 November Kolchak, the Minister of War, had arrested his colleagues with the connivance of the Allies and given himself the title of Supreme Ruler of Russia. His chief source of supply for muni-tions was Britain, who also clothed and fed his troops and provided many of his officers. In the Ukraine, Denikin was the spearhead of the French penetration. The forces against Moscow in the north-west were the new Baltic states and Fin-land, bitterly hostile to the Leninist order and threatening Petrograd and the island defences of the city in the Baltic. In the far north the Murmansk-Archangel régime relied upon British and United States support.

The British Cabinet was divided on how best to deal with a situation of British military involvement in Russia which had grown, almost absent-mindedly, out of the exigencies of war. Churchill pressed with furious energy for material and financial support for the Whites with the object of obliterating the Red government, giving the Russian people freedom to chose their rulers and satisfying foreign holders of Russian property. He was backed by Birkenhead, Montagu, Curzon and, with much vacillation, by Milner. At the other extreme stood the Prime Minister, Balfour and Cecil. Lloyd George was anxious to cut British losses in Russia; campaigning in distant theatres, he knew, would not be tolerated now that the war with Germany was ended. As the soldiers stood about, waiting for de-mobilisation tickets, restlessness grew and mutinies at Folke-stone and Dover on 3 January alarmed Wilson, the Chief of the Imperial General Staff, who nevertheless continued to back Churchill's dream.[1] Economic recovery also began to dom-inate the Premier's mind and with extraordinary adroitness he switched from the technique of the 'knock-out-blow' to the re-vival of the world's channels of trade. Above all, he grasped the quicksand quality of Russia, characterising it as a 'morass', a country 'easy to get into but difficult to get out of'. His instincts ran against the Churchill school which, he felt in his bones, led towards a bottomless pit.[2]

In Paris the Allies differed in their views of the Russian problem. President Wilson never lost his vague admiration

[1] Callwell, op. cit., II, pp. 160–1.
[2] CAB 23/8. 511 (10 December 1918).

for the Russian Revolution or his suspicion that intervention was a mere pretext for Great Power imperialism. But the Russian miasma was painful to contemplate; he was apt to let the situation drift, toying with ideas of recognising the Leninists, then realising that the Russian Revolution was not intended, like the American Revolution, to defend property, but to destroy it. In any case his real business in Paris was to get the European politicians to accept his League of Nations with the least concession to their cupidity. As for the Italians, the difficulties of exacting the fulfilment of Entente promises to Italy left Orlando with comparatively little time for Russia; he sided with British or French views according as Italian preoccupations dictated. It was the French who pushed intervention most strongly towards its logical conclusion. In the light of their treatment of the heavy French investments in Russia, Clemenceau regarded the Bolsheviks as beyond the pale. He vehemently opposed inviting them to Paris as though they were a 'colony of lepers', in Lloyd George's words, setting himself, as his major objective, the Foch plan for a concerted attack on the Soviets from all directions under the supervision of the Peace Conference, and, as his minor objective, the utmost assistance to the successor states emerging on Russia's western borders in their efforts to extend themselves at Russia's expense.

But neither British nor French exponents of intervention on the grand pattern were able to point to the means by which the policy was to be carried on. The most revealing moment came when Lloyd George asked his colleagues in the Supreme Council on 21 January whether they could provide the 150,000 troops to serve in Russia which the military advisers had said were essential if intervention was to succeed. There was a succession of negatives in reply.[1]   Henceforward it was evident that Allied intervention would be limited to the supply of arms, money and sympathy to the Whites and that soon the White régimes would have to stand on their own feet. As for the British Empire, there was an even firmer refusal of military aid from Dominion representatives, and the idea of fighting in Russia was so distasteful in England that Lloyd George told a meeting of the four leaders of the Council on 16 January that 'if a military enterprise is started against the Bolsheviks that would make England Bolshevik and there would be a Soviet in London'.[2]   The position was also rapidly deteriorating in Ireland. Sir Henry Wilson noted in his diary on 17 January that guns and tanks were needed there if anywhere.[3]

[1] Cumming and Pettit, op. cit., pp. 289–96.
[2] Ibid., p. 287.   [3] Callwell, op. cit., II, p. 164.

There was no lack of approaches by the Bolsheviks to the Allies for a peace settlement.   In the early days of intervention, on 5 August, the Council of People's Commissars wrote to the American Chargé d'Affaires in Russia, De Witt Poole, asking him to use his influence with the United States Government to bring about a settlement.   There followed a scurrilous letter from Chicherin, the Foreign Minister, to President Wilson on 24 October.   In a curious effort to pull Wilson's leg, Chicherin proposed that the League of Nations should be based on the 'expropriation of the capitalists of all countries'.   'In your country,' he went on, 'banking and industry are in the hands of such a small group of capitalists that, as your personal friend, Colonel Robins, assured us, it would be enough to arrest twenty heads of capitalist cliques and to transfer to the masses the control by which, by characteristic capitalist methods, they have come to power, to destroy the principal source of new wars.'[1] As the collapse of the Central Powers became imminent, this bantering tone changed and the Soviet note of 3 November, addressed to all the Allied governments, and the resolution passed by the Sixth Congress of Soviets on 7 November were serious offers of terms for diplomatic relations, though couched in Communist idiom which failed to clarify what the government really intended.   On 24 December, in a 'Christmas message' from Litvinov to Wilson, which was read out at the opening session of the Peace Conference, there came a surprising change.   The Bolsheviks were apparently now ready to discuss a peace settlement on the basis of three concessions, each of which was intended to undermine the case of further Allied intervention.   Firstly, an amnesty and 'freedom from interference' were promised to the 'Russian friends of the Allies'. Secondly, in order to facilitate assistance from the outside world to repair war damage in Russia, 'should an understanding with the Allies be arrived at, the Soviet Government would be willing to reconsider some of its decrees affecting the financial obligations of Russia towards other countries without infringing the cardinal principles of its economic and financial policy'. Thirdly, there was an undertaking to desist from carrying on propaganda in Allied countries.[2]

With the object of clarifying these offers, Wilson sent William H. Buckler, special assistant in the United States Embassy in London, to talk with Litvinov in Stockholm.[3]   The Bolsheviks, however, refused to give more details until they were told the

[1] J. Degras, *Soviet Documents on Foreign Policy*, I, pp. 112–20.
[2] Cumming and Pettit, *op. cit.*, pp. 270–3.
[3] *F.R.U.S., 1919, Russia*, p. 4.

exact footing on which they stood in relation to the Peace Conference.[1]   On 10 January Litvinov and Vorovsky explained to
Dr. Meyer, a Norwegian lawyer who agreed to act for Wilson,
that it was impossible to be more precise until the Allies had
formulated their own agreed demands; the Paris Conference
was referred back to the offer of 24 December as evidence as to
the sincerity of Bolshevik intentions.[2]   In the meantime, on
3 January 1919, Lloyd George circulated to the other four
major delegations an *aide mémoire* proposing that the Bolshevik
and other authorities in Russia be asked to conclude a truce and
send representatives to Paris.[3]

The Prime Minister's suggestion was to declare a 'truce of
God' between all belligerent parties in Russia so that they could
send agents to the Peace Conference 'to give, so to speak, an
account of themselves'.[4]   At a further meeting on 21 January
it was decided to summon all the contending parties in Russia
to be represented at a conference on the island of Prinkipo in the
Sea of Marmara, to meet on 15 February, since Clemenceau
could not bear Marxist untouchables in Paris.   Some opposition came from the British General Staff, who considered that
positions already won in Russia should not be lightly abandoned.   Sir Henry Wilson was ready to quit Omsk, Archangel
and Murmansk, but insisted that the British position should be
strengthened on the line Batu, Baku, Krasnovodsk and Merv.[5]
But this was not sufficient to deter the Prime Minister, and the
message was sent.   The White authorities soon received it as
their agents were already in Paris; Sazonov, the former Tsarist
Foreign Minister, now acted for Kolchak's régime at Omsk
while Chaikovsky represented Archangel and other White
centres.   With characteristic distaste for the Bolsheviks, no invitation to the Prinkipo meeting was sent either to Petrograd
or to Moscow.   Had it not been for a wireless announcement
of the Conference proposal from Paris the régime would never
have heard of it.[6]

It was the Bolsheviks nevertheless who took up the proposal,
while the White groups in Siberia, Archangel and southern
Russia remained silent themselves on the assumption that
Clemenceau's reluctance to accept the plan betokened further
French support.[7]   Chicherin's reply to Paris on 4 February de-
veloped the offer made by Litvinov in his Christmas message

[1] *Ibid.*, pp. 15–17.   [2] Degras, *op. cit.*, I, pp. 133–5.
[3] *F.R.U.S.*, *1919, Russia*, pp. 2–3.   [4] *Ibid.*, pp. 10–14.
[5] Callwell, *op. cit.*, II, p. 167.   [6] Louis Fischer, *op. cit.*, I, p. 167.
[7] On 21 February, after the date fixed for the Prinkipo meeting, it was reported
that Chaikovsky, the President of the North Russian Government, had agreed to
participate; cf. Cumming and Pettit, *op. cit.*, p. 305, n. 1.

and specified what was expected of the Allies in return. The Bolshevik authorities were willing to recognise Russia's financial obligations to creditors who were nationals of the Allied Powers. The interest on these loans was to be guaranteed by payments in raw materials. Timber, mining and other concessions would also be forthcoming, so long as these did not conflict with the 'economic and social order of Russia'. On their side the Allies must undertake to abstain from 'annexationist policies', defined as the maintenance of Allied arms or forces assisted by the Allies in former territories of the Tsar, with the exception of Poland and Finland. Lenin was ready to enter into negotiations on the basis of such conditions with the Allied Powers or with 'any Russian political groups'.[1] However, in the event the terms passed into limbo since 15 February, the date fixed for the Prinkipo meeting, came and went without signs of acceptance from Kolchak or the others.

In the latter half of February and in March debate between the advocates and opponents of intervention went forward at Paris, reflecting the changing fortunes of the conflict in Russia and the course of European politics. Pressures in favour of the total disengagement of Allied forces from Russia were coming inexorably to a head, however, and piecemeal decisions were made for the withdrawal of British and French troops. On 12 February Sir Henry Wilson noted in his diary that the Cabinet showed no disposition to approve warlike operations against the Bolsheviks.[2] By the end of the month even Foch was agreed on evacuation; he had no confidence in either Kolchak or Denikin. Churchill went over to Paris on 18 February, while the Prime Minister was in London dealing with labour unrest, and canvassed support for a general invasion of Bolshevik territory with German co-operation. But even Sir Henry Wilson demurred and hoped for little beyond the promise of some support against Bolshevism to the border states.[3] The Premier opposed any unlimited support and insisted that Russian agreement was essential to further intervention: 'it is an outrage on every British principle of freedom that we should use foreign armies to force upon Russia a Government which is repugnant to its people.'[4]

A month later the Supreme Council had before them a statement of Leninist peace terms which dealt with some of the questions begged in the Bolshevik reply to the Prinkipo pro-

[1] Degras, op. cit., I, pp. 137–9.
[2] Callwell, op. cit., II, p. 169.
[3] Ibid., p. 171.
[4] Winston S. Churchill, The World Crisis: the Aftermath, p. 175.

posal. This message had been brought back by William C. Bullitt, a personal agent of Colonel House, who had gone to Russia after the failure of the Prinkipo plan. This time Lenin and Chicherin agreed to recognise all the *de facto* governments on Russian soil until the people concerned freely decided upon régimes of their own choice; to disarm provided that their rivals in Russia did likewise; to recognise Russia's financial obligations; and to give an amnesty to all anti-Soviet factions. All this was conditional upon the Allied blockade of Russia being lifted and non-Russian troops being withdrawn from the country after the signing of the agreement. The demand of 4 February that the Allies should give no further help against Bolshevism was repeated.[1]

At first Lloyd George appeared to regard this offer as affording a basis for settling the Russian imbroglio. On 25 March he drew up his memorandum at Fontainebleau on the principles of peace with Germany. The means of defeating Bolshevism were in his opinion to be found in the reduction of war passions, the return to peaceful trade and industry, and in disarmament. He admitted the destructive purposes of the Leninists, but 'somehow or other they seem to have managed to keep their hold upon the masses of the Russian people, and what is much more significant, they have succeeded in creating a large army which is apparently well directed and well disciplined—it is the only army that believes that it has any cause to fight for'.[2] These considerations he repeated on the following day at a meeting of the four leaders.[3] But powerful sectors of British opinion were opposed to any peace with Bolshevism. *The Times* denounced such deals without qualification. Warning telegrams from M.P.'s came to Paris in shoals. The result was that the following day, 10 April, the last day set by the Bolsheviks for the acceptance of the Bullitt offer, was allowed to pass without response.

In the House of Commons on 16 April, to the surprise of those who knew of these contacts with the Bolsheviks, Lloyd George referred slightingly to the Bullitt mission and even denied that overtures from the Bolsheviks had been received. The basic conditions of British policy in this important speech were said to be three in number. First, the 'volcano'-like character of the Russian Revolution, which was still 'in fierce eruption', made it impossible for the government to do more than 'provide security for those who are dwelling on its

---

[1] *F.R.U.S.*, *1919, Russia*, pp. 77–80.
[2] Cmd. 1614 (1922).
[3] Paul Mantoux (ed.), *Les délibérations du Conseil des quatre*, I, p. 28.

remotest and most accessible slopes and arrest the devastating flow of lava, so that it shall not scorch other lands'. Secondly, there was the complexity and fluidity of events in Russia, which 'does not justify us in committing this country to a gigantic military enterprise in order to improve the conditions in Russia'. But, thirdly, there were the moral obligations of the Allies to the armies of Kolchak and Denikin, raised 'at our instigation' and 'largely at our expense', so that the Germans should not have access to Russia's natural resources and thus defeat the blockade. It was out of the question to say to these, now that their purpose had been served, 'thank you very much, now the Bolsheviks can cut your throats'. The immediate problem was to 'arrest the flow of lava', that is, to organise a containment of Bolshevism in the territories bordering Russia, especially Poland, Czechoslovakia and Rumania. As to the future, there were signs that Russia was emerging from the trouble; 'when that time comes, when she is more sane, calm and normal, we shall make peace with Russia—we have had quite enough bloodshed'. It was in accordance with this policy of provisioning the Whites and organising containment in the border regions that the decision had been taken a month previously to withdraw British forces from the Arctic territories as soon as possible.[1]

Lloyd George's defection in this speech from the movement for making contact with the Bolsheviks has been attributed to his vacillating temperament, the burdens of the Peace Conference, or his realisation that Bullitt's report was intended for Wilson and that the President was hostile to it.[2] But important events were taking place at this time which swung the scales towards the interventionist argument. On 21 March occurred the Bela Kun *coup* in Budapest, which created a Soviet régime in that city on 5 April. Bavaria, true to the prophecies of the Prime Minister but serving only to excite criticism of his Russian policy, was in Communist ferment. On 9 April the Central Executive Committee of the Soviet Communist Party welcomed these developments in terms recalling the language of 1792: 'no efforts of the imperialists of Europe and America to crush the first steps of the Communist revolution can henceforth save them from the ultimate triumph of Communism.' Meanwhile, Kolchak's forces were savouring a striking success. Their victories of 6 March had driven Communist troops reeling back towards the Volga and during April and May there were hopes in Paris of the imminent fall of Moscow. More-

[1] 114 H.C. Deb. 5s. Cols. 2939–46.
[2] Thomas Jones, *A Diary with Letters, 1931–1950*, p. 172.

over, by 7 May the German peace treaty had been completed at Paris and was in the hands of Brockdorff-Rantzau. Contrary to expectations, it was not at once rejected and there was thus a feeling that the Allies' hands were now free to deal with the Bolsheviks.

Kolchak's improved position strengthened President Wilson's fear that he would create a military dictatorship over all Russia, and the Supreme Council was therefore pressed by Washington to define the conditions on which the Allies were supporting him. Lloyd George's secretary, Philip Kerr, was asked to draft a dispatch to Omsk, which was then adopted by the Council and forwarded on 26 May. It laid down six conditions, to be put into effect 'as soon as (the Omsk authorities) reach Moscow'. These were intended to secure the fulfilment of the aims of Allied policy in Russia, which were defined as 'to restore peace within Russia by enabling the Russian people to resume control of their own affairs through the instrumentality of a freely elected Constituent Assembly and to restore peace along its frontiers by arranging for the settlement of disputes in regard to the boundaries of the Russian state, and its relations with its neighbours through the peaceful arbitration of the League of Nations'.[1] At a meeting of the Council on 24 May the Prime Minister reported that the conditions had been read to a delegation of trade unionists in Britain, who had 'been satisfied on the whole'.[2]

By the time Kolchak had replied to this note the military tide was beginning to turn against him. On 3 June, the day on which the Council of Four received news that the Omsk leader had made a speech going far to meet the Allies' conditions, it was rumoured in Paris that his star was waning.[3] On the same day Curzon, in charge of the Foreign Office in London, heard from Robertson, the British consul in Vladivostok, that Kolchak was definitely falling back, that the Omsk régime was unsatisfactory and peasant discontent increasing.[4] A further complicating factor was the issue of former Tsarist territories in Europe. The Bolsheviks had more than once announced their willingness to see this periphery flake away if such be the will of the inhabitants, and it was not likely that opinion in Britain would be satisfied with anything less from the Whites. Yet the position of the latter on this issue was decidedly equivocal. Sazonov, Kolchak's Foreign Minister, was reported on 3 June as urging rejection of the Allied note of 26 May on this ground.[5]

[1] D.B.F.P., First Series, III, pp. 331–2.   [2] Ibid., p. 314.
[3] Mantoux, op. cit., II, pp. 286–7.   [4] D.B.F.P., First Series, III, pp. 339–40.
[5] Mantoux, II, p. 287.

It was only on the evasive condition that the Constituent Assembly should decide the question of self-determination for the border nations that Kolchak ultimately accepted the Allies' conditions.[1]   Curzon was obliged to tell Nabokov, Kolchak's Chargé d'Affaires in London, on 11 June that 'in refusing to accept the Constituent Assembly of 1917 and in making difficulties about Finland, Kolchak did not understand the pressure on the Allies to stop helping him and the danger of having to desert him unless he complied'.   On the following day the Council of Four accepted Kolchak's reply.   He confirmed the independence of Poland, but left to the Constituent Assembly the settlement of Russia's future frontiers, including those with Finland. An undertaking was given that there would be no return to the régime existing in Russia before the March Revolution.[2]   But the tide was running against him.   On the very next day, 13 June, he was driven back to the Urals and the Supreme Council's letter of acknowledgement was cold in tone.   Curzon wrote to Eliot in Vladivostok on 21 June asking him to convey to the admiral the dislike entertained towards him and his régime in Britain.   He should therefore be careful 'as to the wording of the proclamations issued by him from time to time'.[3]

With the decline of Kolchak's military prospects the divisions in the forces operating against the Bolsheviks came into the open.   Finnish forces under Mannerheim were moving against Petrograd in June with British sympathy and to the great consternation of the Russian Whites.   The British recognition of independent Finland on 6 May drew the strongest protest from Denikin on the 30th.   On 12 June an Estonian delegation asked Balfour for recognition of Estonian independence, to which Balfour replied that the consent of a future Russian government would be required.   The Estonians therefore switched their petition on 17 June to the Supreme Council, which also had to entertain similar representations from leaders claiming to speak in the name of Azerbaijan, Georgia, Latvia, Northern Caucasus, White Russia and the Ukraine.   Again the petitions were referred to the future Constituent Assembly, in accordance with the Council's agreement with Kolchak. Curzon urged that an agreement be reached between Kolchak's Political Committee, already in Paris, and the border nationalities, but Balfour replied that there was 'too little common ground between the parties to make success a reasonable possibility'.[4]   There were also signs of cleavage between the

[1] *D.B.F.P.*, First Series, III, pp. 362–4.   [2] *Ibid.*, pp. 376–7.
[3] *Ibid.*, pp. 393–4.   [4] *Ibid.*, pp. 409–11.

communities seceding from Russia; Poland and Rumania for example planned to partition the Ukraine between themselves. This evoked some of Lloyd George's most outspoken rhetoric against the imperialism of small nations. The Poles were even rebuked by Wilson, but a disturbing rumour began to circulate at the end of June that if pressed too hard on the question of the border nations, Kolchak might throw in his lot with the Germans and the Japanese, and hence that Poland's friendship might be needed should this fear be realised.[1] These cross purposes, together with the withdrawal of Italy from Allied intervention on 3 July, the White collapse in Siberia and the evidence of corruption and administrative malpractices in the White régimes, brought to the fore once again for the British Government the question of whether and how the Bolsheviks could be approached. Hoare, writing from Archangel, was forthright in his condemnation of the Whites on 24 July: 'it is painful to admit the failure of our policy but failure is evident and absolute.' At a meeting a few days later the Cabinet decided to quit northern Russia altogether, to restrict British efforts in Siberia to the provision of small missions and to help Denikin as much as possible.[2]

Yet abhorrence at the idea of leaving the Whites to their fate remained strong. In a memorandum drawn up on Cabinet instructions on 25 July Curzon exhibited all the self-contradictions in Allied policy. The opening paragraphs had a distinct anti-White colouring, attention being drawn to the more conciliatory measures of the Leninists in recent months, while the Whites were blamed for the 'unwieldy bureaucracy at Omsk and gross mismanagement of public affairs generally'. But once the Supreme Council had given its trust to Kolchak, Curzon went on, it was impossible to withdraw it. For the Allies to adopt a policy of siding with the Soviet Government would be disastrous, as the effects would be 'that we should forfeit our good name with all our friends in Russia for many years to come—play the game of the Soviet Government and ultimately lose our whole hand in the country to Germany, who is only waiting to derive advantage from the uncertainties of Allied policy'. The assumption behind this conclusion was that, whatever the outcome of the Civil War, organised anti-Bolshevik factions would continue to exist in Russia, either in office or in opposition, and it was important to have their goodwill.[3]

[1] *D.B.F.P.*, First Series, III, p. 402.
[2] Callwell, *op. cit.*, II, p. 207; CAB 23/11. 601 (29 July 1919).
[3] *D.B.F.P.*, First Series, III, pp. 438–44.

The policy of supporting the Whites therefore continued. But to all intents the Cabinet were waiting for the final collapse of White resistance before they could decently withdraw from Russia. It was now evident that no White general, Kolchak perhaps least of all, could take Moscow and set up the freely elected Constituent Assembly from which the Allies' desiderata were supposed to flow. By October the Red Army was thrusting deep into Siberia and Kolchak himself was captured and shot on 7 February 1920. By September 1920 the forces of Yudenich were no longer a serious threat to the Soviet state and in November Wrangel, Denikin's successor in the south, was thrust back into the cul-de-sac of the Crimea. What remained for Britain was to try to ensure that the Caucasus at least should be in hands amenable to British influence.

The difficulty was, as Curzon wrote to Balfour on 12 August, that the Chief of the Imperial General Staff wanted an immediate withdrawal, as the troops were impatient for demobilisation, and the whole position was thus in danger of being lost.[1] On 14 August he wrote again to Balfour, this time to report that the Menshevik Government in Georgia, set up after the surrender of Turkey, were offering Britain a lease of the coaling station at Batum, and that it was difficult to accept the offer without arousing envy among the other Allies.[2] It was impossible, however, to recognise the governments of Georgia and Azerbaijan until the middle of January 1920, since the consent of Denikin, the chief surviving anti-Bolshevik force in the south of Russia, had to be obtained, and by the beginning of 1920 his authority was virtually at an end. In March all but two British battalions were withdrawn from the Caucasus and these were stationed in Batum. A month later the Red Army entered Baku and established an autonomous Soviet republic in Azerbaijan. This led to the decision of the Allies at the San Remo conference on 23 April to evacuate Batum, in spite of Curzon's vigorous arguments to the contrary. The Caucasian episode at least served to demonstrate that however much moral distaste for the Communists influenced the British Cabinet, the permanent features of Anglo-Russian rivalry were not lost to view.

III

The Civil War in effect ended in November 1920, with the defeat of the last White force in the Crimea, and with it Allied intervention in Russia, except for the Japanese-sponsored opera-

[1] *D.B.F.P.*, First Series, III, pp. 482–4.
[2] *Ibid.*, p. 490.

tions in the Far Eastern territories. The Russo-Polish war, however, requires some notice on account of its close connection with the internal struggle in Russia. Moreover, the Polish war exemplified the complicated impulses behind both British and Soviet policy. Once Polish forces began to retire in June, Lloyd George, with one of his acts of personal diplomacy, at once promised British assistance should Polish independence be definitely threatened. This undertaking was given at the Spa Conference of the Supreme Council on 10 July.[1] The next day Britain warned Moscow against crossing the provisional Polish frontier, which hence came to be called the 'Curzon line', and this the British Government committed themselves to defend. At the same time they demanded that Bolshevik representatives be sent to London to discuss a settlement.[2] On the 20th Curzon repeated this warning in the strongest terms, the Premier refusing to consider seriously an 'impudent' message from Chicherin, the Soviet Foreign Minister, received on 18 July which demanded the unconditional ending of Allied aid to Denikin and the exclusion of Britain and France from any Soviet–Polish peace talks. Little thought was given, however, to the forces that would be available on the Allied side should the Prime Minister's gauntlet be taken up.

On 25 July a British mission consisting of Lord D'Abernon, Sir Maurice Hankey and Sir Percy Redcliffe arrived in Warsaw, together with a delegation from France, to organise the defences of the capital. At home there was strong Trade Union opposition to military assistance being given to the Poles, but a grave and threatening situation had been reached and Lloyd George, having committed himself with scant premeditation, now inclined to the French view of the seriousness of the Red Army's progress. On 8 August he met Millerand, Foch and Berthelot at Lympne and agreed to help the Poles should the Soviet–Polish peace talks at Minsk on 10 and 11 August end in failure through no fault of the Poles.[3] On 10 August he was able to tell the House of Commons in jubilation that Kamenev, who was in London to assist the Anglo-Soviet trade discussions, had proposed peace terms to the Premier which the government thought to be acceptable. The Bolsheviks, he reported, would be satisfied with a frontier even less favourable to themselves than the Curzon line. But Kamenev, it transpired, had played a trick on the anxious Prime Minister in omitting to say that the Bolsheviks were

---

[1] CAB 23/22. 41 (20), Appendix II.
[2] *Ibid.*, Appendix I.
[3] CAB 23/22. 46 (20), App. II and III.

demanding that the Poles concur in the creation of a Polish proletarian militia of 200,000 men, which would have meant putting the country in charge of Communists. The Russian terms also stipulated a limited nationalisation of the land in Poland under cover of compensation to war victims. Not until the end of August, when the Red Army was being driven back from Poland, did Chicherin inform Britain that Russia was prepared to waive the demand for an armed militia. It was on this understanding that the talks which had been broken off at Minsk were resumed, this time at Riga, on 20 September. An armistice and preliminary peace treaty were signed on 12 October and the definitive treaty fixing the Soviet–Polish frontier on March 18 of the following year.

Britain thus came near to war on the issue of an independent Poland. Yet the expansionist propensities of the Polish leader, Marshal Pilsudski, aroused the strongest repugnance in London, the Marshal being severely rebuked for his territorial appetite by the leaders of the British delegation at the Peace Conference. A similar scene was enacted at the Spa Conference in July 1920 when Grabski, the Polish Foreign Minister, was denounced in the roundest terms for his government's advance into the Ukraine. The fear that Poland might acquire more territory than she could conveniently digest and thus become a prey to one or other of her neighbour great Powers impelled the Cabinet to desire a Soviet–Polish settlement on strictly ethnographical lines. There was also the feeling in London that France was infecting her protégé with her own anti-Germanism. This could not but end disastrously, if not at once then when Germany and Russia had resumed once more the full plenitude of their strength.[1]

On the Bolshevik side, the Polish war represented a tension point between the revolutionary and the nationalistic urges actuating Soviet foreign policy. On 9 July 1920 Narkomindel, the Foreign Trade Department of the Soviet Government, issued a statement on the trade talks which had taken place in London between Krassin and British Ministers between 23 May and 7 June.

> Only peace negotiations [it ran] can put an end to hostile relations between Russia and England. The Soviet Government agrees to review the basis of its entire foreign policy and in particular to refrain from taking part in any hostile measures or activities directed against Britain if a similar undertaking is given by the British Government with the

[1] Mantoux, *op. cit.*, I, p. 48.

requisite guarantees for its strict execution, embodied in a
special treaty.[1]

Yet at this very moment a surge of messianic fervour swept the
Red Army to the gates of Warsaw, where the hopes of a world
social upheaval were refreshed. The price of this was the
suspension of the trade talks in London and the impetus given
to the belief in the West that conciliatory gestures by Moscow
were merely tactics for advancing a larger revolutionary
strategy. Between the limits of peaceful trade and of revolutionary war Soviet policy in the Polish conflict thus wavered,
while in Britain the opponents of a war of liberation against
Russia and the advocates of the policy of merely containing
Bolshevism similarly disputed the course of British action.

The conflict between Left and Right which subsequently
characterised European international affairs had the effect of
making relations between Russia and the Allies in the period
covered by this chapter look like the opening round of this
conflict. Allied hostility towards the Bolsheviks, Allied intervention in the Civil War and support for the Whites tended to
be construed later as the first reaction of capitalism to the
'spectre haunting Europe'. There is much to support this
view. But prejudice against the social ideas of the Communist
Revolution in Russia was not the only, or even the major, force
governing British attitudes. The March Revolution, which
came subsequently to be regarded as a kind of prelude to November, a brief interim between Tsarism and Leninism, was
widely conceived in Britain as a true emancipation of Russia.
The thoroughness with which it was thrust aside by Lenin embittered British opinion, which at first saw in Kolchak and other
White leaders the means for resurrecting the régime of the Provisional Government. Moreover the Bolsheviks, even in their
most conciliatory moods, left no room for doubt that their
mission was to draw the whole world down into the same chaos
that overwhelmed their own country after their seizure of
power. There was accordingly intense alarm in Britain, much
more than distaste for the political conceptions of the Bolsheviks, which were in any case not well understood.

The most unfortunate aspect of the Russian Revolution, as an
event presented to the makers of British foreign policy, was that
it took place in the course of a war in which Russia was utterly
defeated and compelled to make peace with the Central
Powers. This act appeared as treachery in British eyes and
a hand was extended to any forces in Russia willing and able

[1] Degras, *op. cit.*, I, pp. 191–4.

to resume the struggle, or at least to prevent the enjoyment by the Central Powers of the effects of a cease-fire on one of their most important fronts.   Even so, British policy was the reverse of consistent or uniform.   It was divided within itself because actions initiated to further certain purposes became ends in themselves and continued when the original object had become irrelevant or had been abandoned.   It was responsive to personalities, to changes in the public frame of mind, and to events in the world situation as a whole, in which the Bolshevik problem was only one part.

The policy of the Soviet authorities was no less mixed in origins and haunted with self-contradictions.   Instead of a simple repetition in the non-Russian world of the Bolshevik upsurge there was a rapacious Germany to make peace with, which showed little sign of succumbing to proletarian insurrection.   There were the Allied Powers, in Lenin's view not a whit less rapacious, but victorious in the war, rich, advanced, and surprisingly resistant to Communist sedition.   There were relations to be established with countries which could help Russia during the reconstruction period; yet these agreed to do so only on conditions of freedom from Communist interference, which meant surrender by the Bolsheviks of the world revolutionary thesis.   Lenin's eventual solution was to reject the notion that all imperialist states were alike and to play off one against the other, to rule them, or to secure the effects of ruling them, by dividing them.   Such a policy unfortunately gave no clue to which country was to be cultivated and which held at bay at any one time; it had the drawback that, if announced too openly, it might provoke a union of non-Communist states to forestall the destructive rivalries between themselves which Lenin sought.   The failure of the Communist Revolution either to disappear from Russia, as Britain and her allies hoped, or to spread beyond Russia's borders, as they feared, meant that neither the Bolsheviks among themselves, nor the Allies among themselves, could agree on what its place should be in future world politics.   On this ambiguous note the next phase was to open, the fight of the Communists for diplomatic recognition.

CHAPTER V

'THE STERN BUT JUST PEACE'

BRITISH politics on the eve of the Peace Conference were dominated by the General Election on 14 December 1918. The Coalition Government justified an immediate appeal to the electorate partly on grounds of the age of the House of Commons (it had sat since 1910), partly in terms of the need for a mandate for reconstruction. This reasoning was clearly influenced by a desire to capitalise on the general feeling of relief with the ending of the war and uncertainty as to how the new electorate, now including women for the first time, would vote. There was also Lloyd George's curious tendency to underestimate his actual authority in the country; at best he forecast a majority of 150 seats whereas the margin gained was 262.[1] These circumstances explain the resort to the 'coupon', that is, the supporting letter given by government Whips to M.P.s who had voted with the government in the Maurice Debate in May 1918, and the crude appeal, voiced more by backbenchers than by Ministers, to the immediate Armistice Night emotions of thankfulness and greed.

In its results the Election effected a shift in the political balance which explains, though its influence should not be overstated, some of the more demagogic features of the peace treaties. The Asquithian Liberals were reduced to 33 seats, the leader himself being defeated, and Labour, with 49 seats, replaced them as the official opposition. Thus Lloyd George seemed to have become a prisoner of the Right. In the Debate on the Address on 11 and 12 February he singled out the themes of foreign policy on which he assumed public opinion to be clamorous: first, punishment of the war makers; second, reparations; third, a League of Nations. The tone of the new House was set by the Brigadier Page-Crofts, the Horatio Bottomleys, the Lieutenant-Colonel Walter Guinnesses, with their cries for full indemnities, no truck with Bolshevism or Pacificism, colonies to hand to the faithful Dominions, a quick peace, and, an incongruous item in the list, the fulfilment of the government's no-conscription pledge.[2]

---

[1] *Lord Riddell's Intimate Diary of the Peace Conference and After, 1918–1923*, p. 4.
[2] 112 H.C. Deb. 5s. Col. 70 *et seq.*

The 1918 Parliament was certainly one of the most insular and ignorant in British history.   Yet this very fact enabled the British delegation at the Paris Peace Conference to negotiate to the accompaniment of strident clamour from home on a few sensational issues but with substantial interference on hardly any of the main problems.   On issues such as the Rhineland, the Saar, Germany's eastern frontiers, and the settlement of Italy's claims the Prime Minister was left with almost complete freedom to decide, largely because Parliament had no positive opinion to offer.   It is an extraordinary fact that the Anglo-French Treaty, signed at the same time as the treaty with Germany and committing Britain to defend France against unprovoked aggression by Germany, was hurried through its second reading in the early hours of 22 July 1919 with little or no informed criticism from any quarter.   Its revolutionary significance was barely grasped.

Behind Parliamentary clamour for German money and the Kaiser's head lay more subtle undertones, foreshadowing the great retreat of British sentiment on the peace settlement which startled and shocked Britain's continental partners in mid-1919. Behind the demand for a smash-and-grab peace lurked the hope that its wounds would heal quickly enough to work no lasting harm on international trade.   Along with the call for tough action against the Bolsheviks was the quieter, more persistent plea for demobilisation and cuts in military spending. Above all, running through the Parliamentary session was worry over industrial unrest, eventually dwarfing the cries to search Germany's pockets.   More often than not Conservative harping on the need 'to strengthen the Government's hands' on the reparation issue reflected the fear that Communism was making headway among the working classes and needed to be headed off by anti-German or anti-Leninist diversions.   When Lloyd George returned from Paris to address the House on 16 April he sensed these undertones, choosing to mollify Members with pleas that 'we want no more bloodshed' and the statement that 'the world wants to get back quickly to work .... the enormous expenditures of war should be cut down ruthlessly and as soon as possible.   That is why peace is necessary.'   The debate had opened with a solid front of 370 government supporters instigated by Lord Northcliffe to warn the British delegation in Paris by telegram against any weakening on the reparation issue.   It languished in the early evening and the House was counted out.[1]

[1] 114 H.C. Deb. 5s. Col. 3022.

I

The Paris Peace Conference formally opened in plenary session on 18 January 1919. The question on which the British Government, mindful of election promises, demanded the earliest decision was that of compensation for Allied losses during the war. The statement of principle however was followed by technical questionings never fully answered. Most experts agreed that Germany's capacity to pay, when account was taken of the effects of the war and the territorial and other changes to be imposed by the treaty, was less than the cost of the war to the Allies, and less than the most conservative estimates of that damage. But how much less, and how the transfer of reparation payments was likely to affect the economy of the receiving states, were questions beyond the economic techniques of the day. Lloyd George's committee of financial and business advisers reported on 1 December 1918 in terms capable of warming the greediest heart.[1] The committee computed the total cost of the war to the Allies as £24,000 million, on which it was stated that the enemy Powers would be able to pay £1,200 million in annual interest in the form of cash, goods and securities and by means of a funding loan when normal conditions had been restored in the paying countries.[2] The Allies would receive in all from Germany under this scheme some £40,000 million in damages and indemnities. Both Lloyd George and an expert committee set up in the Treasury and including J. M. Keynes dismissed this arithmetic as 'devoid of commonsense'. The Treasury experts contemplated a sum of approximately £2,000 million as being within Germany's capacity to pay. On the other hand, first reports of French reparation demands, characterised by the British Foreign Office as 'fantastic', inclined the British delegation to maintain rather than reduce their initial estimates.[3]

Besides the question of estimating Germany's capacity to pay there was also the problem of reconciling any claim to the full cost of the war with the pre-Armistice agreements on the basis of which Germany had laid down her arms, and the diplomatic problem, with its vistas of sordid wrangling, of allocating the profits among the Allies. Subtle connections existed between the two issues. The European Allies at their Paris meeting on

[1] Its members were: W. M. Hughes, the Australian Prime Minister; Walter Long, a moderate Conservative; W. A. S. Hewins, an economist; Lord Cunliffe, the Governor of the Bank of England; and the Hon. Herbert Gibbs, of the firm Anthony Gibbs and Sons.

[2] David Lloyd George, *The Truth about Reparations and War Debts*, pp. 12–13.

[3] David Hunter Miller, *My Diary at the Conference of Paris*, I, p. 31.

31 October 1918, called to review the correspondence between Wilson and the German Government, had insisted that the 'restoration' specified in the section of the Fourteen Points dealing with the invaded regions must include 'compensation for all the loss and damage done to the civilian population of the Allies and their property as a result of German aggression by land, sea and from the air'.   But was this reservation to cover indemnities in the sense of a penal fine to be exacted from the defeated in addition to the civilian damages sustained by the Allied peoples, to which it seemed at first sight to be restricted? Lloyd George brushed aside this distinction as 'a matter of purely academic interest'.[1]   His reasoning, now departing from the legal grounds on which he based the general case for reparation, was that in any event Germany's capacity to pay would be exhausted long before the bill for reparation alone had been met, and hence that if the terms of the pre-Armistice agreement were strictly followed, Britain would receive little except on account of losses of merchant ships and windows broken in Zeppelin raids.   By the same token the Dominions would receive even less.

From the first President Wilson set his face against the inclusion of indemnities, firmly backing his experts' refusal to sanction the exaction of the full costs of the war.   Deadlock ensued on this at the Reparation Commission's first meeting and, when the matter was referred back to the Supreme Council, Wilson cabled from his ship, in which he left for a visit to the United States on 14 February, his continuing support for his experts. Thus the battle for the full costs of the war was lost, but the ingenious device invented by the British delegation for including in the Allied claims the outlays on war pensions and separation allowances finally divided the President from his experts owing to his desire to complete the main conditions of the peace with all speed.[2]   The British asked whether compensation for a ruined chimney was to rank higher than payment for a lost life or a pension for a blinded or wounded soldier.   In a memorandum drawn up by General Smuts on 31 March, which the Four at Paris agreed, it was argued that the Allied reservation in the note to Wilson of November 1918 virtually meant the abandonment of the limitation of compensation to the invaded territories.   Smuts' conclusion was that

While direct war expenditure (such as the payment and equipment of soldiers, the cost of rifles, guns and ordnance and

[1] Lloyd George, *op. cit.*, p. 17.
[2] P. M. Burnett, *Reparations at the Paris Peace Conference*, I, p. vii.

all similar expenditures) could not be recovered from the Germans, yet disablement pensions to discharged soldiers, or pensions to widows and orphans or separation allowances paid to their wives and children during the period of their military service are all items representing compensation to members of the civilian population for damage sustained by them, for which the German Government are liable.[1]

This casuistry found its way into the Reparation Section (VIII) of the German Treaty. There it was admitted that this category of compensation did not precisely fall under the reservation of the pre-Armistice agreement, but formed the celebrated Annex I, which was supplementary to the category of civilian damages cited in the pre-Armistice agreement.

The Smuts formula represented a triumph for the British theory of reparation, the first of a series of triumphs. It was agreed to by Wilson partly because of the moderation in which the British attitude to reparation at the Conference was couched, contrasting with the monotonous French cry *que l'Allemagne paye d'abord*, partly because of the thoroughness with which the British team always prepared the detailed bill of their demand. The British Prime Minister, once the principle of including war pensions and separation allowances had been won, adroitly gained Wilson's good opinion by ridiculing the vast, shadowy estimates of French reconstruction costs presented to the Council of Four by the French financial expert Loucheur, and by his warnings, to which he would always resort when the other Allies presented inconvenient claims, of the effects on German revolutionary opinion of a harsh peace.[2]

To round off the British victory, after weeks of inquiry by experts into the principles on which the bill for damages and Germany's capacity to pay should be based, the decision was made in deference to the Prime Minister not to include a total figure for reparation in the text of the treaty. This was to be left to an inter-Allied Reparation Commission to determine. Here it was Wilson who stood chiefly against the British view, on the ground that the proposal meant leaving the Germans with undefined liabilities and hindering the revival of international finance. The Prime Minister pointed out in reply that the inclusion of any rational figure, even if one could be agreed amid the turmoil of the Conference, would probably

[1] Bernard M. Baruch, *The Making of the Reparation and Economic Sections of the Treaty*, pp. 29–32.
[2] Paul Mantoux (ed.), *Les délibérations du Conseil des quatre*, I, pp. 24–34. See also CAB 23/9. 536.

shock Allied opinion by its moderation as much as it outraged enemy opinion by its magnitude. The effect of this decision, however statesmanlike, was that all the efforts of the Conference to draw up a bill of demands, to estimate German ability to pay and portion out the yield among the Allies, came to nothing. Only the categories and bases of reparation were agreed to.

The second British means for effecting the enemy's punishment, mirroring the naïveté of popular thought, was the call for the legal prosecution of the German leaders. 'This question,' Lloyd George told the Council of Four, 'along with that of reparation, interests British public opinion most of all—we shall be unable to sign the treaty unless it is solved.'[1] But it was easier to shout for the Kaiser's blood than to answer objections to a judicial process for shedding it. In 1815 Napoleon had simply been hurried off to St. Helena by administrative decision and as an act of policy. Such a method was felt in 1919 to be out of keeping with the times; in any case it would have robbed the victors of the public exhibition they had paid a high price to see. In a paper drawn up in November 1918 for the Imperial War Committee by the then Sir F. E. Smith, the Attorney-General, a plausible legal basis for the trial was devised. The prosecution of individuals for breaches of international law, it was conceded, was unprecedented, but not more so than the magnitude of the offence. The trial might provide the world with new principles of law to deter future régimes from aggression. And so on.[2] The Imperial War Committee had given the proposal a mixed reception when it was first considered on 20 November, but was carried off its feet by Smith's brilliant exposition.[3] Nevertheless there was weighty opinion on the other side. Viscount Bryce in a Lords debate on the German Treaty in July 1919 considered the absence of precedent to be fatal. He also believed the trial would make the ex-Emperor a sympathetic figure among the neutrals.[4] A sweeping indictment of the whole enterprise came from Lord Buckmaster, who condemned it as alien to English law.

> To ask an English judge (he said) to sit and administer a law he does not know, by a procedure which is not defined, in a Court where he has no control, and to inflict a punishment

[1] Mantoux, *op. cit.*, I, p. 192.
[2] Lloyd George, *The Truth About the Peace Treaties*, I, 1938, pp. 102–13.
[3] Lord Hankey, *Politics, Trials and Errors*, Oxford, 1950, p. 1.
[4] 35 H.L. Deb. 5s. Cols. 1010–11 (24 July 1919).

which is anticipated by everybody as a result of his labours, is to ask him to do a work which in my humble judgment he is not fitted to discharge.[1]

These doubts were reflected in the report of the Inter-Allied Commission in Paris appointed to consider the question, which rejected the principle of criminal prosecution. Taking his cue from this, Wilson rehearsed a catalogue of objections to the trials, to each of which Lloyd George replied with characteristic vigour and with Clemenceau as his coadjutor. Would the trial not make the Kaiser a martyr in the eyes of the world? The Prime Minister was more afraid of History's reproach against the Allies for weakness.[2] Could the Allies properly act as judges in their own cause? The Premier replied that this might apply to France and Belgium, but Britain and the United States, who would also be represented on the proposed tribunal of five members, had come into the war as impartial arbiters and to secure international justice.[3] As for the complaint of lack of precedents, Clemenceau's reply was that the Allies were making precedents; a beginning with the Rule of Law had to be made somewhere.[4]

Wilson found an ally in the Italian Prime Minister, Orlando. The conception of criminal responsibility, Orlando asserted at a meeting of the Four on 8 April, was not a part of international law as then known; it certainly could not be created, with retroactive effect, merely by *fiat* of the Conference. He doubted whether a distinction could be drawn between the responsibility of a people and that of its leaders, and he regarded the lack of precedent as an insuperable difficulty. Orlando's intervention (which was not upheld by his legal advisers) was decisive, since it led to the acceptance of the Commission's view that international law should not be the principal basis for the trial, and that international morality should be the main indictment. Notwithstanding Lloyd George's determination to secure a legal footing for the procedure, it was accepted, with extraordinary candour, that legality should apply solely to the form in which the trial was to be held; it would be a moral examination in a legal setting.

The public arraignment under Article 227 against the German ex-Emperor (ran the Allied Reply to the German Observations on the Treaty) had not a juridical character as regards its substance, but only in its form. The ex-Emperor is arraigned as a matter of high international policy, as the

[1] 35 H.L. Deb. 5s. Col. 1023.
[2] Mantoux, I, p. 123.
[3] *Ibid.*, p. 122.
[4] *Ibid.*, p. 191.

minimum of what is demanded for a supreme offence against international morality, the sanctity of treaties and the essential rules of justice. The Allied and Associated Powers have desired that judicial forms, a judicial procedure and a properly constituted tribunal should be set up in order to assure to the accused full rights and liberties in regard to his defence and in order that the judgment should be of the most solemn judicial character.[1]

The demand for the trial of William II for criminal breaches of international law and by a 'solemn tribunal composed of the best legal minds of the day' thus petered out as a self-inculpating charge-sheet which ran together political, legal and moral offences. Whether any body of judges could ever have been assembled to pass on such an indictment was fortunately never put to the test. As for the lesser war criminals, the Dominions' Prime Ministers contended that these should be named in the treaty along with William. But the most that could be done was to promise to submit to Germany a suitable list later on. Eventually the refusal of Holland to extradite the ex-Emperor made it absurd to attempt to prosecute his assistants, and the trial was dropped. Only a few minor war criminals were tried by the German Supreme Court in Leipzig in 1920, the Allies having by that time wearied of the whole business, which they asked the Germans to take out of their hands.

II

British views on the territorial problems arising from the peace settlement with Germany were shaped by two imperatives; the need to fulfil undertakings assumed during the war for the righting of old wrongs or for future security, and on the other hand fear that if these objects were pressed too far, a spirit of revenge would be provoked in Germany which would hamper European enconomic recovery and perhaps open the floodgates to Communism.[2] Britain's position in 1919 was compared by a Foreign Office official to that of a departmental store 'which has fallen on difficult times, mainly but not entirely owing to the fact that the territory which it serves has been devastated by some disaster'.

[1] The Treaty of Peace between the Allied and Associated Powers and Germany, Foreign Office, 1925, pp. 316–17.
[2] The settlement of the Italian and Japanese claims at the Conference and the distribution of Germany's colonies raised no fundamental questions for Britain and are not dealt with in this account. The attempt to compensate Italy in Anatolia by the abortive Treaty of Sèvres and Japan's claims at Germany's expense in China are discussed in Chapters VI and XI respectively.

If the directors of the store are wise, they will spend as much time upon helping to revive the general prosperity of the community as they will upon their ruined affairs. For only when its customers have money in their pockets can the store recapture its prosperity.[1]

This commercial mentality, mistrustful of territorial disturbances, worked throughout the Peace Conference in uneasy partnership with the spirit of maintaining Britain's alliances. Once British claims against Germany had been satisfied, especially in regard to the German Fleet and merchant marine, the former German colonies and reparation, it made the British feel comfortably far-sighted and generous to counsel fair play.

The British notion of themselves, in the Prime Minister's words, as 'impartial arbiters, forgetful of the passions of war' was evident in their attitude even to the most legitimate of French territorial claims, the restoration of Alsace-Lorraine. Not only did the government reject out of hand France's claim for the frontier of 1790, which would have included the basin of the Saar in an enlarged Alsace-Lorraine,[2] but in their wartime references to the territory they spoke with purposeful ambiguity. While President Wilson explained to the French Foreign Minister, Pichon, that in the Fourteen Points he meant by 'redress of the wrong of 1871' the complete restitution of the provinces as they were before the Prussian invasion, Lloyd George, in his declaration of 5 January 1918, limited himself to a 'reconsideration' of the annexation of 1871, for which, however, Britain would 'stand by French democracy to the death'.[3] The Liberal and Labour wings of British opinion even believed that the two provinces should not be handed over without some indication of local wishes in the matter, 'an insultingly illegitimate solution' in the French viewpoint.[4] To be sure, these hesitations were silenced when the Conference began. But no more than the frontier of 1815 was conceded.

The enlarged Alsace-Lorraine which France claimed in her agreement with Russia of February 1917, and of which Balfour said that Britain had never had official cognisance, included the basin of the Saar. To this claim the French returned at the Conference. Their position on the Saar basin was compounded of the nostalgia of Clemenceau, who claimed to see the past not in terms of hundreds, but of thousands of years, and the sombre

---

[1] Sir Arthur Willert, *Aspects of British foreign policy*, p. 5.
[2] Balfour in the House of Commons, 19 December 1917 and 16 May 1918; 100 H.C. Deb. 5s. Col. 2017; *Ibid.*, 106, Col. 579.
[3] *Papers Respecting Negotiations for an Anglo-French Pact*, Cmd. 2169 (1924), p. 8.
[4] André Tardieu, *La Paix*, p. 264.

economic forecasting of Tardieu and the French Finance
Minister, Klotz. The systematic destruction of the coal mines
in the Nord and Pas-de-Calais areas was estimated to have
robbed France of 20 million tons of coal annually. If this
figure was added to the pre-war deficit, supplemented by the
new coal requirements resulting from the passing of Alsace-
Lorraine under French sovereignty, something like 50 million
tons would have to be imported every year. As Germany
alone was in a position to supply these imports, the resulting
condition of dependence on that country would not only be
humiliating for France, but would enable Germany to fix
French industrial prices and thus 'dominate her policies'.[1] If,
in order to avoid this, the entire coal basin were to be brought
under French ownership, a special administrative régime would
be needed so as to rule out German interference with the
management of the mines. The administrative area contemplated would require to be wider than that area of the Saar
which was made over to Prussia in 1815 in order to block
France from the East. The frontier of 1814, however, which
was already claimed on grounds of history and national pride,
would have given France only part, and the less economically
important part, of the coal basin. Hence the Tardieu memorandum presented to the Council of Four in March 1918 took
the form of a threefold demand: the restitution to France of the
territory south of the 1814 frontier, territory which, it was
claimed, was 'wrested by force' from France in 1815; a special
political administration for the territories of the mineral and
industrial basin north of this frontier; and full French ownership of the mines in the two zones.[2]

When the French case was outlined to the Four by Tardieu
and the French financial adviser, Loucheur, on the morning
of 28 March Wilson was tired and succumbing to influenza.
His reception by Congressmen when he returned home to explain the Covenant of the League of Nations had depressed and
embittered him. He was angry with his deputy, House, for
what he suspected to be the latter's attempt to take the Conference into his own hands during Wilson's absence and to finalise
the territorial sections. This fact set him all the more against
the French Saar claim since House had accepted the 1814
frontier, with certain enlargements, as 'suitable compensation
for the destruction of the coal mines of Lens and Valenciennes'.[3]
All this chagrin Wilson vented on the French advocates. The
Conference as he had understood it was falling to pieces. He

[1] Tardieu, *op. cit.*, p. 286.   [2] *Ibid.*, pp. 279–89.
[3] House Papers, IV, p. 398.

would consent to no more than the handing over to French
ownership of the mining properties of the Saar.   Once exceptions began to be made on historical or strategic grounds to the
moral basis of the treaty, the efforts for a better world might as
well be given up.

> The map of Europe [he went on] is covered, I well know,
> by ancient injustices, not all of which can be repaired.   What
> justice demands is that France should be compensated for
> what is due to her through the loss of her coal mines and that
> the whole region be given the necessary guarantees for the
> free exploitation of its coal.   If we do that, we can hardly
> reasonably expect to do more.[1]

Wilson therefore proposed merely to compensate France out of
the Saar mines until French mines had been restored, but
would not hear of the separation of the area from German
sovereignty.

Between these two intractable positions, the American and
the French, no alternative was left to the British delegation except to act as mediators, suggesting modifications not so much
with an eye to the real needs of the Saar, but in order to prevent
a breach between the protagonists.   Lloyd George perceived
that there was no moving the President in his main position that
German sovereignty in the Saar must not be expressly terminated, and that the Saarlanders should be assured a free
choice, without undue French interference, at the end of the
15-year period.   He therefore consented to join the President
in urging the latter's proposal on the French Premier, who was
able to secure only a few concessions in return.   Instead of a
mere Court of Arbitration there was to be an international commission of the Saar, to be appointed by the League of Nations.
The League was to govern and not merely administer the
territory.[2]   No elections to the Reichstag would be held in the
territory.   On the basis of this agreement the committee of
three worked all night on 9–10 April, and produced a draft
Statute for the Saar on the next day.   This provided for the
surrender of the mines to France under full ownership and the
transfer of the government of the territory to the League of
Nations, which would then entrust it to a commission of five.
There was to be a customs union between France and the Saar.
At the end of fifteen years the people of the Saar would be asked
in a plebiscite conducted by the League to declare whether they
wished to remain under German sovereignty, to be annexed to

[1] Mantoux, I, p. 69.   [2] Ibid., p. 210.

France or to stay under the League régime.[1] The Statute was adopted in main outline by the Council on 10 April thus ending a dispute which threatened to dissolve the Conference. The British had taken a mediatory role intended to assure as many concessions to France as were consistent with the kind of treaty the enemy would sign, while at the same time avoiding at all costs a retirement by the United States into isolation.

The Saar was a conflict of national interest, that of France, against moral principle, but there was in the issue of the western frontier of Germany and its relation to the river Rhine a clash of the national interests of Britain and France, as visualised in both countries through the spectrum of history and encrusted mental habit. The protagonists in the two conflicts were also different. Over the Saar, Clemenceau's opponent was Wilson, with the British Prime Minister conciliating now one, now the other. Over the Rhine frontier, Lloyd George was Clemenceau's adversary, with Wilson inclining to the British view, although cautiously pro-French on occasion. Moreover, the Rhine question extended throughout the entire life of the Conference, and was left by the British and French on 28 June, when Germany signed the treaty, with the greatest misgivings on both sides. Because the military occupation of the Rhine provinces which the treaty provided was at once a pledge for the payment of reparation and a measure of national security for France, it was deeply enmeshed with the financial and military provisions of the settlement. Since this occupation was to be reduced by five-year stages, it foreshadowed inter-Allied frictions long after the Peace Conference had closed. In addition, the fact that the treaty gave the Allies the right of continuing or resuming the military occupation of the west bank and bridge-heads of the Rhine as long as reparation went unpaid added to the uncertainties of the future, especially in British eyes. Above all, the frictions between Britain and France engendered by the left bank question, British mistrust of French imperialism and French lack of confidence in British understanding of strategic realities, acted as the solvents of the Franco-British accord, an accord which, with the eventual defection from the peace settlement of the United States, alone stood against the military revival of Germany.

The handling of the French Rhine policy at the Conference was marred by ill-tempered differences between the chief military adviser, Foch, and the Prime Minister, Clemenceau, ably supported by André Tardieu. Foch was not always in agreement with himself in what he demanded for French security.

[1] This became Section IV of Part III of the Treaty.

In his note to the Allies on 27 November 1918, he contended that the German inhabitants of the west bank should be definitely 'included in the French military establishment', whereas in his principal statement to the Allied Council on 10 January 1919 he limited himself to the permanent occupation of the Rhineland, pending agreement on a suitable political status for the inhabitants. But at all times he was more extreme than Clemenceau who desired above all to avoid the collision with Wilson over the Rhine which the Foch doctrine would have certainly involved. Clemenceau could fight Wilson over the Saar since the British sympathised, if intermittently, with the French claim. But on the Rhine, where every British sentiment ran against France, it would have been fatal to the French case to alienate Wilson. By restraining attacks in the Paris press on Wilson and by special efforts of conciliation towards Colonel House, Clemenceau sought to secure the American ear for France's Rhine attitude. The response, however, was hesitant. House was not averse to an independent Rhenish Republic, but was severely warned by Wilson not to commit himself too far until the President reached Europe.[1]

These doubtful American reactions alongside the known British resistance both to severing the Rhineland from Germany and to a prolonged Allied military occupation of the territory, evidently decided Clemenceau to throw in his lot with Foch and to state the maximum French demand. Tardieu's memorandum for the Conference on 26 February, prepared under the Prime Minister's guidance, led off with the premiss: 'what happened in 1914 was possible only for one reason; Germany, because of her mastery over offensive preparations made by her on the left bank of the river, thought herself capable of crushing the democracies, France and Belgium, before the latter could receive the aid of the overseas democracies, Britain, the Dominions and the United States.' The logic of the paper rolled on; first, 'a common guarantee against the recurrence of any sudden attack from Germany is necessary'; second, 'this guarantee cannot be completely assured, either by the limitation or the suppression of Germany's military power or by the proposed clauses of the Covenant of the League of Nations'; thirdly, this guarantee can be found 'only in the fixation at the Rhine of the western frontier of Germany and in the occupation of the bridges by an international force'. There followed at the end two appendices, one being 'an outline of a political system applicable to an independent Rhineland', and the other 'a

[1] House Papers, IV, pp. 345–6, 368, n. 2.

study of the economic results of its independence, both on the
left bank of the Rhine and in Germany itself'.[1]

Serious discussion of the Rhineland proposal began early in
March. Wilson was absent in America; House still inclined
to see elements of strength in the French plan, while the British
confessed themselves astounded that the French failed to admit
that German disarmament, the creation of the League and, if
necessary, the demilitarisation of the left bank provided adequate guarantees for their safety. Tardieu's exposition before
a committee consisting of himself, Philip Kerr and the American
expert, Dr. Mezes, on 11 and 12 March opened up the conflict.
'As my explanation proceeds [he wrote afterwards] I become
conscious of the psychological barrier—I am offered a strengthening of the disarmament clauses. I am offered a reinforcement of those dealing with demilitarisation. As soon as I return to the question of occupation, opposition becomes more
marked.'[2] Kerr gave the substance of the British delegation's
case in reply:

> England [he said] is equally opposed both to a permanent
> Army and to the use of British troops outside of English
> territory. Furthermore, occupation tends to create a nation-
> alist irritation not only on the left bank of the Rhine but
> throughout all Germany—Do we agree to the creation of an
> independent state on the left bank of the Rhine?—If, after a
> longer or shorter period, this independent state asserts its will
> to reunite with Germany what shall we do?—If local con-
> flicts occur, whither will they lead? If war results from these
> conflicts, neither England nor her Dominions will have that
> deep feeling of solidarity with France which animated them
> in the last war.[3]

There was insight in this. How could the pacifically minded
English, with their feeling of boredom with far-off squabbles, be
expected to defend a settlement which, if the French had their
way, would have been imposed on them almost as much as it
was imposed on Germany?

Tardieu's reply, that if the British public did not yet understand that their most important frontier was now on the Rhine,
it was the 'duty of the British Government' to make it understand, might have been more effective had it been addressed to
a Prime Minister willing and able to lead his electorate. The
French, however, intended to do more than argue. 'To ask us
to give up occupation is like asking England and the United

---

[1] Tardieu, *op. cit.*, pp. 165–84.
[2] *Ibid.*, pp. 190–1.   [3] *Ibid.*, pp. 191–2.

States to sink their fleet of battleships,' Tardieu went on, 'we refuse. We insist upon our demand.' The French draft of the Rhineland articles, presented to the Council on 12 March, accordingly envisaged the western frontier of Germany as lying along the Rhine, with German sovereignty over the left bank definitely surrendered. The line of the Rhine was to be occupied by an inter-Allied force under a mandate from the League of Nations. Demilitarisation was to be enforced within a zone 50 kilometres wide on the right bank. The left bank, except of course for Alsace-Lorraine, was to constitute one or more independent states under the protection of the League of Nations.[1]

The revolutionary offer to France of a guarantee pact against unprovoked German aggression which was made on 14 March as a means of solving the impasse was the greatest achievement of the personal diplomacy of the British Prime Minister and the American President. Neither the American Congress, nor the British Parliament, nor the public opinion in either country, appears to have been consulted beforehand. There is no evidence, either, that before March 14 the British or American Governments contemplated a pledge they had consistently re- fused to give in the past.[2] The offer was, however, conditional upon implementation by both guarantors: thus Britain was assured that she would not be alone in her obligation to defend France. Moreover, the British delegation believed that the other guarantees of the treaty, German disarmament, the Rhine Army of occupation and the League, would be sufficient in themselves without the need arising for the pact to be invoked. The original British conception was that of a stop-gap insurance policy, which could be surrendered when the world returned to 'normality' after the postwar upheavals. The preamble of the original British draft began: 'Whereas there is a danger that the stipulations relating to the left bank of the Rhine, contained in the Treaty of Paris—may not, at first, provide adequate security and protection to the French Republic.'[3] The French were able to secure an amendment of this by pointing out that the disparity between French and German manpower, which the Conference was being asked to counterbalance, was no mere postwar affair. The British, however, were successful in securing the rejection of the French provision, after this had been approved by Wilson, by which the pledge was to continue in force 'until it is considered by *all* the signatory Powers that

[1] Tardieu, *op. cit.*, pp. 194–5.
[2] Lloyd George raised the possibility in the Cabinet on 4 March but said Wilson would not hear of it; CAB 23/15. 541A.
[3] Tardieu, *op. cit.*, p. 230.

the League of Nations itself affords sufficient protection'. On British insistence it was provided that the League Council should decide, if necessary, by majority.[1] Thus the British notion of the pact as a provisional measure was pressed home.

But what if the pact was not ratified by one or other of the parties, as in fact was to happen when the United States Senate refused to agree? Clemenceau, with this possibility in mind, secured from Wilson his assent to the final paragraph of Article 429 of the treaty, which read: 'if at that date [that is, at the end of the fifteen-year period of occupation] the guarantees against an unprovoked aggression by Germany are not considered sufficient by the Allied and Associated Governments, the evacuation of the occupying troops may be delayed to the extent regarded as necessary for the purpose of obtaining the required guarantee.' It was a bird, or rather a few feathers, held firmly in the hand while the flock in the bush made ready to depart.

Lloyd George denied in the House of Commons in the debate on the treaty on 21 July that the offer of the two pacts was made as a means of inducing the French to abandon their claim to the left bank of the Rhine. Such a claim, he said, the French had never put forward.[2] Although the French Premier never seems officially to have asked for the annexation of the left bank, a meeting of Clemenceau, Foreign Minister Pichon, Tardieu and Loucheur, at the French War Office on 15 March certainly agreed that the offer was conditional upon the suggestion of a separate Rhineland state being dropped from the French case. It remained to be seen whether the demand for an army occupation would have to be dropped as well.[3] The French reply accepting the offer on 17 March asked for certain supplements to the proposed pacts, in particular a confirmation of the French right to re-occupy the Rhine bridgeheads, comprising a radius of 50 kilometres, if Germany refused to carry out the military conditions of the Treaty. They then promptly insisted upon an inter-Allied Rhineland force, with, it was ambiguously stated, 'this immediate and lasting result, the separation of the left bank from the German Reich and Zollverein'.[4]

Demilitarisation of the two zones and of the entire left bank and a 50-kilometre strip on the right bank having been agreed to, debate centred on the question of occupation, which the British and American leaders clearly regarded as having been disposed of, along with the proposed Rhenish Republic, by the offer of the guarantee pacts. Lloyd George's Fontainebleau memorandum of 25 March harped on the unsettling effects of

[1] *Ibid.*, pp. 231–2.   [2] 118 H.C. Deb. 5s. Col. 1127.
[3] Tardieu, *op. cit.*, pp. 195–6.   [4] *Ibid.*, pp. 197–200.

occupation. In the Council he repeated, after the manner of a refrain: 'you must fully understand the state of mind of the British public. It is afraid to do anything whatever which might repeat the mistake Germany committed in annexing Alsace-Lorraine.' Wilson for his part in a note on 12 April rehearsed the American and British demilitarisation proposals as representing 'the maximum of what I myself deem necessary for the safety of France or possible on the part of the United States'.[1] The isolation of France was complete. None of the other military advisers of the Allies supported Foch when he was called upon by Clemenceau to defend the French case before the Council of Four. The King of the Belgians, who came before the Council on 4 April, opposed an extended occupation.[2] The deadlock on the issue coincided with the climax in the Saar question and together they comprised the great April crisis of the Conference.

Nevertheless, it was the Anglo-Saxon Powers who relented on the occupation issue, so firmly was the French position held and so real the danger of the collapse of the French Government if more ammunition against their policy at the Conference was placed in the hands of assailants at home. On 20 April Wilson at length accepted the principle of an extended period of Allied occupation of the left bank and the Rhine bridgeheads. He was followed two days later by Lloyd George, protesting to the last against the cost of occupation forces to the British taxpayer, the potentialities of military occupation for breeding international ill-will, and the length of the proposed occupation, which was to be 15 years for the southern section of the Rhineland, ten years for the middle and five years for the northern zone.[3] It was an uneasy compromise, and no sooner had the bargain been struck on 22 April than forces on both sides began to move against it. In France the Foch party was intoxicated by an article in *Le Matin* on 18 April, said to have been written by the Marshal himself, in which the entire proposed conditions of peace in their bearing on the problem of French security were attacked. Then came Foch's bitter public assault on the temporary character of the occupation, launched at the plenary session of the Conference on 6 May. But the greatest blow against the compromise of 22 April came from the British.

Towards the end of May alarm seized the British delegation lest the Germans refuse to sign the treaty, which had been presented to their representatives on 7 May, and lest revolution break out in force across the Rhine. Either contingency might postpone peace indefinitely, involving Britain in incalculable

[1] Tardieu, *op. cit.*, p. 202.   [2] *Ibid.*, p. 204.   [3] *F.R.U.S.*, *1919*, V, p. 112.

military commitments at the very moment when public clamour for demobilisation was rapidly becoming even more strident than that for reparation or the Kaiser's head. On 29 May in the Council of Four Lloyd George confessed that he had had second thoughts about the project for the military occupation of the Rhineland; this he now judged to be both excessively costly and provocative to Germany. He also attacked it on the ground that, the stronger Germany became with the passing years, the more the army of occupation, in accordance with the agreed schedule, would be reduced. But the most powerful British assault came on 2 June, when the Prime Minister reported that, after holding four meetings with such members of the Imperial War Cabinet as could be got together in Paris, a widespread revolt had come to his attention against the harshness of the treaty. Too many Germans were being included in Poland; the settlement of the Saar question offended against the sacred principle of self-determination; Germany should be admitted into the League of Nations 'if she showed a disposition to carry out the treaty'; and so on. Above all, the Cabinet refused to accept the suggestion of an army of occupation in the Rhineland. It was ridiculous, they said, to keep an Allied Army 200,000 strong on German territory at a time when German forces had been reduced by the treaty to half that number. It was also unnecessary after the offer of a guarantee pact to France.[1]

It was soon clear, however, that while France might agree to inconsiderable territorial readjustments in Germany's favour, there would be no yielding on the occupation. Had Clemenceau been forced to return to his people without it, it is almost certain that he would have been disowned. British pressure therefore moved from the question of the principle of occupation to the demand for a Civilian High Commission of the Rhine, which it was thought might deal more understandingly with the inevitable disputes as they arose between Allied soldiers and the local German population. Britain also pressed for reductions in the size of the contemplated occupation forces. The Rhineland Commission of the Conference reported favourably on the former proposal on 13 June and the Council adopted it over Foch's objection.[2] The utmost achieved by way of limiting the size of the occupying forces, however, was an agreement that, when German disarmament was definitely completed, these forces should be reduced to 150,000 men. A further proposal that the Rhineland convention, the legal basis for the occupation, should be limited in duration to two or three

[1] *F.R.U.S., 1919*, V, pp. 139–42, 144.   [2] *Ibid.*, VI, pp. 377 ff.

years in the first instance, to give Germany time in which to establish her good faith, broke down in the face of French resistance. The French had gone as far as they could; they would go no more.

Of all the compromises effected in the Paris negotiations the Rhineland agreement was the most unhappy. British delegates were struck by the burning sincerity of the French arguments but dreaded tension between the occupying army and the local population such as might ignite again the old Franco-German feud which had cost Europe and British prosperity so dear. France, or rather that part of French opinion which Clemenceau was always seeking to satisfy on the matter of the security offered by the treaty, remained in a cruel dilemma: unless the moment was seized to cripple Germany and destroy her power to invade France, the race against German strength would be lost; and yet the crippling of Germany was vetoed by allies whose goodwill France would need in the hour of Germany's revival. This was not all; in unfolding her plight as she saw it to the British at the Paris Conference France could not but fill them, 'in their island, behind the rampart of the sea', with the greatest forebodings as to the future of Franco-German relations. In these relations the British were now implicated as never before.

III

The Franco-British conflict at the Conference on the Rhineland was reproduced in the settlement of Germany's eastern boundaries. The British had been led to support the rebirth of Poland, not by faith in self-determination, but by the force of events. Up to the signing of the treaty of Brest-Litovsk in March 1918 the British Government regarded the Polish question either as an internal Russian issue or as an aspect of the general European balance of power. On 22 March 1917, Lord Hugh Cecil said in the Commons, 'I do not suppose that the question before the Peace Conference will be any question of Home Rule for Poland—I do not suppose that this country will dictate to Russia what form of Home Rule is to be given to Poland and I am quite sure that Russia will not dictate to us what form of Home Rule should be given to Ireland.[1]' On 26 March, a few days after Cecil's statement, Balfour reported to the Imperial War Cabinet on a discussion he had had with Roman Dmowski, the Polish leader, who had approached the Foreign Secretary on the subject of an Allied declaration on Poland:

[1] 91 H.C. Deb. 5s. Col. 2125.

Personally, from a selfish western point of view, I would rather that Poland was autonomous under the Russians, because if you made an absolutely independent Poland lying between Russia and the Central states, you cut off Russia altogether from the west. Russia ceases to be a factor in western politics, or almost ceases. She will be largely divided from Austria by Rumania. She will be divided from Germany by the new Polish state and she will not be coterminous with any of the belligerents. And if Germany has designs on the future of France or the west, I think she will be protected by this new state from any action on the part of Russia and I am not at all sure that this is to the interests of western civilisation.[1]

With the retirement of Russia from the war and the clarification by Germany of her purposes in eastern Europe at Brest-Litovsk, the British view was brought more into line with Wilson's declaration to the United States Senate on 22 January 1917, when he formally adopted the policy of favouring the reconstitution of Poland. Hence Lloyd George's war aims speech of 5 January 1918 included references to 'an independent Poland, comprising all those genuinely Polish who desire to form part of it' as an 'urgent necessity for the stability of western Europe'. The suggestion of a plebiscite in these words, however, did not pass unnoticed, no more than the omission of any reference to an outlet to the sea for Poland and the emphasis on Polish independence as a requirement of European peace, rather than a moral necessity in itself. The British attitude to the Poles remained circumspect and ungenerous. When in the last days of the war Haig discussed with the Cabinet the conditions for a cease-fire, Lloyd George bluntly stated that 'we cannot expect the British to go on sacrificing their lives for the Poles'.[2] During the discussion between the Allies in Paris on the proposed Armistice terms Balfour 'listened with anxiety' to Pichon, the French Foreign Minister, arguing the case for a German retirement to the Polish frontier of 1772, and would agree to no more than the frontier of August 1914, thus leaving the Poles to recover the province of Poznan (Posen) for themselves.[3] Lloyd George firmly opposed the representation at Paris of the Polish National Committee, which had been formed at Lausanne in August 1917, on the ground that the new Poland owed its existence entirely to the efforts of the Allies, and that during the war most of the Poles had been on

[1] *F.R.U.S.*, *The Lansing Papers*, II, p. 19 *et seq.*
[2] *The Private Papers of Douglas Haig, 1914–1919*, ed. Robert Blake, p. 334.
[3] S. Terrail, *Les négociations secrètes et les quatre armistices*, p. 247.

the opposite side of the fighting line. 'The task of the Parisian treaty-makers,' he frankly admitted, 'was not to decide what in fairness should be given to the liberated nationalities, but what in common honesty should be freed from their clutches when they overstepped the bounds of self-determination.'[1]

These attitudes characterised most senior members of the British group at Paris. Balfour, as we have seen, had been persuaded to support the reconstitution of Poland only with the greatest reluctance. He kept to the end the view he expressed in a memorandum for the Cabinet in November 1916 on the 'Peace Settlement in Europe', in which he voiced his fear 'that the new Poland will suffer from the diseases through which the old Poland perished'.[2] General Smuts, when the British attitude towards the work of the Commission on Polish affairs was being formulated in March 1919, gave way to his strong pro-German feelings in a letter to the Prime Minister: 'instead of dismembering and destroying Germany, she ought in a measure to be taken into the scope of our policy and be made responsible for part of the burden which is clearly too heavy for us to bear. Are we going to defend Poland and Bohemia as we have defended the Ukraine against the Bolsheviks?—we cannot save Europe without the co-operation of Germany.'[3] In a final attempt to persuade the Premier to try to secure a revision of the eastern settlement, he said in June: 'Poland is a historic failure and always will be a failure, and in this treaty we are trying to reverse the verdict of history.'[4] Smuts, it will be recalled, was the author of the suggestion that the mandates system should apply to the successor states, which in his view were all too immature, while the former German colonies should be annexed outright. Again, the opinion of J. M. Keynes was that, without prosperous and orderly neighbours, Poland was 'an economic impossibility with no industry but Jew-baiting'.[5]

But this mistrust of small nations was chiefly concentrated in the person of the head of the British delegation, the Prime Minister, and was chiefly directed against Poland. While he acquiesced without a murmur in the inclusion of three million Sudeten Germans in the new Czechoslovakia, every possible argument was urged against the incorporation of Germans in the new Poland. 'Poland must be given a corridor to Danzig,' he wrote, 'but this must be drawn irrespective of strategic or transportation considerations so as to embrace the smallest

[1] *The Truth about the Peace Treaties*, I, p. 91.
[2] Blanche Dugdale, *Arthur James Balfour*, II, p. 437.
[3] Sarah Gertrude Millin, *General Smuts*, II, p. 210.
[4] *Ibid.*, p. 237.
[5] *The Economic Consequences of the Peace*, London, 1920, p. 273.

possible number of Germans.'[1]   His outbursts against Polish
territorial claims provided many of the dramatic moments of
the Conference.   'The Poles had no idea of organisation,' he
said, 'they had no capacity to direct or govern.   The Premier
was a pianist: the President an idealist without any practical
ideas.'[2]   Later, when Paderewski exclaimed that Poland would
'lose faith in the Allies if a plebiscite were forced in Upper
Silesia', the Prime Minister retorted, 'Poland has won her freedom, not by her own exertions, but by the blood of others; and
not only has she no gratitude but she says she loses faith in the
people who won her freedom.'[3]

If there was prejudice and ignorance on the British side, the
Poles exhibited a strange blindness to the tragic discouragements surrounding the birth of the new state.   Clemenceau's
view was that Poland should not merely be re-born, but should
be formed into a buffer between Germany and Russia.[4]   To
this conception the Polish leaders lent themselves, forgetting
that a buffer state must abjure policies of alienating its neighbours.   While the Conference was at work in Paris, the Poles
were at war with the Czechs for the prize of Teschen; neither
side heeded the Conference's plea for an orderly determination
of the frontier.   The Poles also fought against independent
Ukrainian forces for the possession of Eastern Galicia, rejected
the armistice proposals of the commission of the Supreme
Council and began a major offensive in Eastern Galicia on
14 May 1919 with the aim of bringing that territory under their
control whatever the views of the Council might be.   Instead
of seeking to make allies of the White authorities in the Ukraine,
their military incursion seemed designed to drive these groups
into the arms of the Bolsheviks.   Instead of endeavouring to
show that a free Poland was in Germany's interest as well as
their own (and in some sense it was), the Poles, by incorporating
German irredenta in their territory, were driving permanent
wedges between themselves and Germany, a Power with whom,
for good or ill, they were obliged to live as neighbours.   Lloyd
George let no occasion pass without prophesying that the
Corridor and Danzig, if determined as Poland willed, would
provide the starting points of the Second World War.[5]

The application of self-determination to the settlement of the
German–Polish frontier by the Supreme Council, which began
so promisingly for the Poles, demonstrated the force of British
influence in the making of the peace settlement even in the

---

[1] *The Fontainebleau Memorandum*, Cmd. 1614 (1922), p. 8.
[2] *F.R.U.S.*, *1919*, IV, p. 414.   [3] *Ibid.*, VI, p. 197.
[4] *Ibid.*, VI, p. 142.   [5] Mantoux, I, p. 112.

regions beyond the limits of recognised British immediate
interests.   The Polish case for a territorial restoration to the
position before the first partition of 1772 and for the constitution of Koenigsberg and its surroundings into an independent
German state was presented by Dmowski to a sympathetic
Council of Ten on 29 January.[1]   The Commission on Polish
Affairs, appointed by the Council on 12 February, recommended a reduction of the Polish claim in the west by one-third
and proposed a plebiscite in the Regierungsbezirk of Allenstein,
but definitely awarded Danzig to Poland, together with two
railway lines from Warsaw to the Baltic Sea.   The report was
unanimous, the British representative, Sir Esmé Howard, having
identified himself on all material points with Robert Lord, the
American.   The hostility of the British Ministers to the Danzig
proposal, however, was common knowledge long before the
Commission reported.[2]   When the report was considered by
the Council of Four on 12 March, Lloyd George was the only
member of the Council to criticise it, beginning with an objection to the proposal to draw a frontier to suit the convenience of
transportation and closing with his usual fear that the Germans
might refuse to sign the treaty, this time on the ground that two
millions of their countrymen would be lost in Poland.[3]   The
report was accordingly sent back to the Commission for reconsideration, only to be endorsed again without change of
substance.   On 22 March when the question came before the
Council for the second time, the Prime Minister decided to hold
his fire for the time being, and merely thanked the Commission
for their impartial findings.   These he accepted on condition
that the Council reserved the right to review them when the
'total effect of all these provisions' came up for reconsideration.
He repeated his fears of a German refusal to sign.[4]

The principal British attack on the Danzig proposal was reserved for the Fontainebleau memorandum, drawn up by the
Prime Minister and his intimates on 25 March, in which he laid
down the entire British philosophy of a lenient treatment of
Germany, though largely at the expense of France and her
friends, the successor states.   Placing the Commission's proposals for Poland within this setting, he went on:

> I cannot imagine any greater cause for future war than
> that the German people, who have proved themselves one of
> the most powerful and vigorous races of the world, should be
> surrounded by a number of small States, many of them con-

[1] *F.R.U.S., 1919*, III, p. 773.   [2] House Papers, IV, p. 345.
[3] *F.R.U.S., 1919*, IV, p. 414.   [4] *F.R.U.S., 1919*, IV, p. 449.

sisting of peoples who have never previously set up a stable government for themselves, but each containing large masses of Germans clamouring for reunion with their native land. The proposals of the Polish Commission that 2,100,000 Germans should be placed under the control of a people of different religion and which has never proved its ability for self-government throughout its history must, in any judgment, sooner or later lead to a new war in the east of Europe.[1]

The moderation of this paper was calculated to appeal especially to President Wilson, who was at that very moment passing through one of his worst crises with the French over the Saar question. At the decisive meeting of the Council on the afternoon of 1 April the President showed the effects that the Prime Minister's subtle eloquence had had. He outlined four possible solutions for Danzig: Free City status; two different types of cession of the port and city to Poland; and a Danzig assigned to Poland, but possessing an autonomous status under the protection of the League of Nations. When Lloyd George expressed a preference for either the first or the fourth of these solutions, Wilson went on to outline a scheme for a Free State of Danzig under a High Commissioner appointed by the League. Marienwerder, which the Prime Minister wished to award to Germany, was to have its future determined by plebiscite. In answer to an expression of doubt by Clemenceau whether Germany could ever be appeased by concessions, Lloyd George replied that it was not a question of the German attitude to the settlement, but of the future attitude of Allied public opinion. 'What I ask,' he said, 'is that we might not put into the peace treaty the provisions for which we would not be ready to declare war. France will fight tomorrow for Alsace—but would we carry out a war for Danzig?'

In a second British assault against the Polish settlement at the beginning of June, Lloyd George used much the same arguments in his demand for a plebiscite in Upper Silesia as he had over the Corridor and Danzig, namely that British soldiers might refuse to fight the Germans any more if a plebiscite were not held.[2] As he had himself frankly admitted earlier, he was most interested in getting Germany's signature; even if a plebiscite in Upper Silesia made no difference to the ultimate destination of the territory, he would favour it if it enabled Germany to sign.[3] In the face of such an attitude the arguments of Paderewski that western Silesia, which was agricultural, would probably vote for Germany owing to the influence

---

[1] Cmd. 1614 (1922), p. 3.   [2] F.R.U.S., 1919, VI, p. 303.   [3] Ibid., pp. 148–9.

THE PEACE SETTLEMENT

of the Catholic clergy, while the eastern mining sections would vote Polish, a result which would place Poland's mining areas in a strategically insecure position on the frontier, made no headway.[1] The only question in the British mind was whether a plebiscite would satisfy Germany that she was receiving justice, and hence encourage her to accept the treaty. Wilson pointed out that the Fourteen Points did not commit the Allies to holding plebiscites in 'indisputably Polish areas'; nevertheless he assented to the establishment of an international commission for the impartial supervision of the vote.[2] It was agreed on 11 June, on the recommendation of the Polish Commission, that the plebiscite should be held after one or two years, in order to allow the backward political mentality of the people in the western areas to become more advanced, Upper Silesia being governed in the meantime, not by Poland, but by an international commission of four.[3] Besides the concession of a plebiscite in Upper Silesia, rectifications of the proposed Polish–German frontier were effected in the Guhrau-Militsch and Schneidemuhl-Konitz regions in deference to the Prime Minister's fears of an adverse German reaction to the draft treaty.

IV

It remains to refer to the least controversial and, in later British opinion, the most fruitful part of the Conference's work, the drafting of the League Covenant. A permanent international body intended to place barriers in the way of aggressive nations was widely demanded by British public opinion in the last two years of the war; all vocal opinion welcomed the League, Labour leaders and Opposition Liberals warmly, Conservatives rather less so.[4] It was manifest that Wilson regarded the League as the most important aspect of the Conference's work. He was resolved to make the Covenant an integral part of the treaties; he welcomed the idea of leaving to the League the role of arbiter in many acute issues on which the Conference was unable to agree. In those days it was confidently believed that the United States would remain an active party in Europe, and the League was a means for making that participation agreeable in American eyes. Moreover, through a League of Nations satisfaction might be given to the wishes of the Dominions Governments, of which the Conference was never left in doubt, to rank as sovereign states.

[1] *F.R.U.S., 1919*, VI, p. 191.   [2] *Ibid.*, p. 154.   [3] *Ibid.*, p. 311.
[4] H. R. Winkler, 'The Development of the League of Nations Idea in Great Britain, 1914–1919', *Journal of Modern History*, XX, No. 2, 1948, pp. 95–112.

The League idea was all the more acceptable to British Ministers in 1919 in that it was by no means a revolutionary conception, at least in its less extreme formulations. The report of the Phillimore committee, appointed by Balfour early in 1917, which provided for inquiry and delay before a signatory went to war and for a form of financial, economic and military sanctions, represented little more than an institutionalisation of diplomatic practice as it stood in 1914. No permanent organ was envisaged in the report; 'its Conference was the diplomatic group in a particular capital which came together when they were convened in times of stress'.[1] The Government at no time put forward a plan of their own, but accepted in principle the Cecil Plan of November 1918 and the Phillimore report as outlining the general principles of a recurrent conference of the Powers, procedures for inquiry and delay, and a possible system of sanctions. To agree, whether hopefully or resignedly, to the further step of creating permanent bodies for consultation, was inevitable, provided no radical change of diplomatic method or real sacrifice of interest was intended.

The material issues before British delegates at Paris, as far as the shaping of the Covenant was concerned, were two: how to avoid obligations being built into that document which might handicap the pursuit of British objects in the postwar world, and how to adapt the Covenant to the work of improving provisions of peace treaties which British officials considered either undesirable or positively dangerous. These ends were attained, partly by restraining the smaller Powers, who wanted greater representation on the Council,[2] but mainly by supporting the Americans against the French wish to make the League into a superforce for crystallising the *status quo* created by the Conference. Britain and the Dominions, with their detached attitude towards European politics and their belief in conciliation rather than enforcement, looked askance at the whole idea of the League as a super-national police force for the enforcement of the treaties.

The general emphasis of the comments and actions of the Dominions leaders at the Peace Conference [writes Miss Carter] was upon preserving long-cherished rights of individual decision. Over and beyond this stood their conception of a League through which wars might be prevented by the provision of means for the pacific settlement of disputes—

[1] David Hunter Miller, *The drafting of the Covenant*, I, p. 10.
[2] Miller, *op. cit.*, I, p. 161.

Canadian leaders in particular opposed League guarantees of rigid territorial arrangements lest they bottle up resentment to the point where the explosion of war became inevitable— 'Security from war' was a platform on which all Dominions could meet, but geographical position was to lead to different interpretations of its meaning in specific cases.[1]

It was impossible to prevent the incorporation in the Covenant of the Wilsonian principle of guarantees of territorial integrity and political independence, although these figured neither in the Phillimore report, nor in the final Foreign Office memorandum of November 1918, nor in the Cecil draft.   Later Cecil wrote: 'Article 10 [embodying the guarantees] led to considerable discussion.   I for one objected to it on the ground that it seemed to crystallise for all time the actual position which then existed.   Eventually it was agreed to, subject to a provision for the pacific modification of the *status quo*, which became Article 19 of the Covenant.'[2]   But it was at least possible to oppose the French demand for an international force to implement the guarantee.   Any such force might have removed from Britain the control of her fleet, which might be required at any time for purposes beyond the scope of the League, and it would have implied the use of British contingents to uphold treaty obligations entered upon by the British Government at the Conference with the greatest misgiving.   'A League of Nations,' said Winston Churchill at Dundee in November 1918, 'is no substitute for the British fleet.'   *The Times* followed on 11 December with the words: 'one thing is clear.   This war could not have been won for civilisation but for British sea power.   There can therefore be no question, so far as this country is concerned, of diminishing the sharpness of the weapon that has given us victory in this war.'[3]

So far from Britain being willing to surrender control of her means of defence to an international organ, the aim was, if anything, to make the League an instrument for achieving the general disarmament which British public opinion believed to be the true prerequisite of peace, provided that disarmament did not deprive the British Empire of the wherewithal for protecting its widely-scattered interests.   In the British delegation G. N. Barnes was alone in favouring the formation within the League of the nucleus of an international force.   But if the Covenant was not to be implemented through an international force, what means of enforcement remained?   The most im-

[1] Gwendolen Carter, *The British Commonwealth and International Security*, p. 9.
[2] *A Great Experiment*, p. 77.
[3] Quoted in R. S. Baker, *Woodrow Wilson and World Settlement*, I, p. 381.

portant sanction, British Ministers felt, was the rising public
belief that war had become a defective instrument of foreign
policy, and should never be resorted to without a careful examination, carried out in full public view, of the actual issues
involved.   This was the conclusion reached by Cecil in his
defence of the Covenant in the Commons in July:

> The great weapon we rely upon is public opinion, and if
> we are wrong about it, the whole thing is wrong.   When
> these questions come up before the Council, they will be
> discussed and considered in public, and when, as a result of
> that discussion, it appears clear that one side is right and the
> other side is wrong, you will get the whole weight of public
> opinion behind the one side, and you will find, I think, that
> the nation that is in the wrong will not persist in the course
> which has been publicly and overwhelmingly condemned . . .
> the Council . . . will be able to do everything if it acts honestly
> and fairly and if its members are animated by a desire to
> make the thing work, provided the cases which come before
> it are clear on one side or the other.   If they are not clear,
> then it is evident that international action would be out of
> place.[1]

The extreme caution qualifying the hopes of even this most optimistic Ministerial advocate of the League is clear.   Yet it
needed very little experience of international affairs to appreciate that issues in which one side is wholly and patently right
and the other wholly and patently wrong occur rarely, if
ever.

In the official British contribution to the making of the
League there was little of an assumption (as was sometimes later
made by League champions) that the fundamentals of international relations were being re-cast.   Cecil himself always
stressed the conservative character of the new institution; he
told the Conference on 14 February 1919 that what was sought
was 'to devise some really effective means of preserving the
peace of the world consistently with the least possible interference with national sovereignty'.[2]   In his more irresponsible
asides the Prime Minister referred to the organisation as a harmless gesture towards American idealism which did not effect the
main work of the Conference.   He told an intimate shortly
after the first outline of the Covenant had been approved by
the Commission, 'Wilson has gone back home with a bundle of
assignats.   I have returned with a pocketful of sovereigns in the

[1] 118 H.C. Deb. 5s. Cols. 992–3 (21 July).
[2] Cecil, *op. cit.*, p. 97.

shape of the German colonies, Mesopotamia, etc. Everyone to his taste.'[1]   At best the League, by bringing international disputes into the light of day, might serve to reduce the incentives to war, and no country had a greater interest in peace than Britain.   'Society,' said Lloyd George in the Commons in July, 'with all its organisations has not stopped every crime.   What it does is that it makes crime difficult or unsuccessful, and that is what the League of Nations will do.'[2]   But the British focus was in essence not upon the League as a possible preventive of war; certainly there was little official support for a coercive system of sanctions.   The conception on which all parties in Britain were able to unite was not that of the League as a peace-enforcing machinery, but as a means for revising those parts of the treaty with Germany on which the Cabinet at the close of the Conference had the greatest reservations.   The League was to be, if anything, an instrument of justice and pacification, and this as between France and Germany, rather than between Britain and the rest of the world.   The Prime Minister repeatedly harked back to this theme.   'We are setting up machinery capable of readjusting and correcting mistakes,' he said in his speech in the Commons on 16 April.[3]   Similarly, when he finally commended the treaty to Parliament in July: 'where (the treaty) is not perfect, I look forward to the organisation of the League of Nations to remedy, to repair and to redress—the League of Nations will be there as a Court of Appeal to readjust crudities, irregularities, injustices.'[4]   This view was warmly acclaimed by Government backbenchers and Opposition leaders.   Lieutenant-Colonel Murray described the League as an 'antiseptic to some of the wounds which the treaty has inflicted'.[5]   Clynes, the Labour leader, also approved the League as capable of dealing with the blemishes of the treaty. He quoted the unanimous resolution of the Southport Conference of the Labour Party, which called for: 'Germany's speedy admission to the League of Nations and the immediate revision by the League of the present provisions of the treaty, which are inconsistent with the statements made on behalf of the Allied Governments when the Armistice was made.'[6]

This British attitude towards the new League of Nations foreshadowed the failures to come.   In the act of debating the League framework, both at the Paris Conference and in the Parliaments of the several Allied Powers, an advertisement was

---

[1] Lord Riddell, op. cit., p. 24.
[2] 117 H.C. Deb. 5s. Col. 1227 (3 July 1919).
[3] 114 H.C. Deb. 5s. Col. 2937.   [4] 118 ibid., Col. 1054 (21 July).
[5] Ibid., Col. 1023.   [6] Ibid., Col. 959.

given to the world, not only that the peacemakers, the chief forces behind the League, differed as to the justice of the peace settlement, but that certain specific differences as to this settlement existed. France and the successor states wished to use the League machinery principally to enforce their gains from the Peace Conference, including those on which British opinion had mental reservations. Britain, on her side, made it known that not only was she withholding from the League the force for maintaining the peace settlement, but that she would use that institution to revise those parts of the peace settlement of which she disapproved. At the same time, the League's work of revision was not thought in Britain to refer especially to the British gains from the Conference. The vindictiveness of the treaty lay not in what was done in Samoa or Tanganyika, but on the Rhine and in Danzig. From the outset the League was thus condemned to serve, not as the jailor of the vanquished nations, as these nations represented it to be, but as the symbol of Allied discord. The circumstances of its birth provided the fulcrum on which the discontented could shake the world.

V

Some of the most serious criticisms of the Versailles Treaty were voiced by government spokesmen themselves, and even more (although of an opposite kind) by government supporters in Parliament.[1] In all his subsequent defences of the treaty Lloyd George unconsciously implied, if he did not say, that he saw much force in such strictures as those of General Smuts on the 'harshness' of the treaty. It was a 'stern but just peace': 'I ask anyone,' he reiterated, 'to point out in respect of any of these main conditions a single act of injustice.'[2] Any oppression of Germany which lingered after his efforts to moderate the treaty in Paris would be softened, he said, by time and the healing influence of the League. This self-reproach (which was far from the mood of Coalition back-bench M.P.s) set the tone of Opposition Liberal and Labour objections, though these were muted on the whole, the feeling of the House of Commons being one of qualified satisfaction. The general acquiescence of the British Parliament in the work of Paris was reflected in the fact that the Second Reading of the Treaty of Peace Bill occupied no more than one day each in Lords and Commons, as compared with the several weeks' discussion in the French

[1] See B. Ling, *Parliaments and the Peace Treaty*, unpub., London Ph.D. thesis, 1938, p. 41.
[2] 117 H.C. Deb. 5s. Col. 1214 *et seq.* (3 July).

Chambers.[1]   It was left to government backbenchers to express residual frustration over the reparation clauses.

The relative accord between Government and Opposition supporters in the views they took of the German treaty is perhaps paradoxical considering that government policy during the Paris negotiations had been predominantly conservative in spirit, and often negative in practice.   As was often complained later, no sign was shown in the British delegation of any resolve to break with the past and to set the pace towards a new order in world affairs.   However much Lloyd George and other British leaders may have distantly sympathised with President Wilson, they would apply their hands to no kind of revolution in international policy.   Once the chief British claims had been satisfied, their desire was to heal the wounds of war, to oppose far-reaching alterations in the law of Europe, to return to normal.   British policy was negative in that much of it (more than Keynes ever saw) was taken up with frustrating the demands of other allies for far-reaching movements of frontiers or transfers of resources.   Neither did British negotiators bring forward constructive ideas, with the possible exception of the Mandatory régime and the international organisation of labour, to which world opinion might rally, and on which future international relations might be based.   They failed, it had been argued, to mobilise behind peace-making notions which looked to the future and not to the past.   The creation of the League of Nations is hardly an exception to this, for the British conception of the League was deeply coloured by tradition.

But were such ideas to hand for embodying in British policy, given that the Parliamentary majority behind the government had agreed?   Two such ideas have been suggested: the one that Britain might have directed the Paris statesmen towards 'food, coal and transport', the Keynesian trinity, or in other words the reconstruction of the European economy, rather than trafficking in frontiers and national gains and losses;[2] the other being that Britain should have grasped the opportunities offered by the creation of the League to lead the world towards the final renunciation of force as a means of national advantage. The former criticism supposes that, in the mood of postwar Europe, economic wants counted for more with nations and

[1] Of the 175 M.P.s present on 21 July (the number itself is significant) only 5 voted against the Bill. In the final vote in the French Chamber of Deputies on 2 October, 53 voted against, there were 72 abstentions and 20 Deputies were absent. The French Senate ratified the treaty on 11 October with 4 abstentions.

[2] In the famous words of *The Economic Consequences of the Peace*, 1920, p, 211: 'it is an extraordinary fact that the fundamental economic problem of a Europe starving and disintegrating before their eyes, was the one question in which it was impossible to arouse the interest of the Four'.

their leaders than national pride and security, and that a freely functioning world economy, promptly restored to its feet in 1919, would never have suffered the collapse of 1929, which in fact precipitated the world into the tensions of the 1930s. But the criticism falls to the ground chiefly because it could have made no headway against the Rhine policy and other such requirements of the French. Lloyd George's Fontainebleau paper was indeed couched in Keynesian terms, but it had little effect upon the French, except to strengthen their conviction that the British were hypocrites who, from a safe remove, chided others for their nervousness.

The other criticism, that Britain made no fundamental breach with traditional diplomacy in 1919, and that, had she done so, her example would have been infectious, is equally unsound. It was not any British lack of faith in the League which persuaded the American Senate against joining that institution. Once America had failed to join, European members were, if anything, more confident, not less, that their old defences, their armed forces and alliances, must be kept in good repair. Had Britain surrendered her fleet to the League, as the French urged, it would have been used to defend a settlement to which many, and perhaps most, British champions of the League seriously objected. The League Council, had it disposed of its own forces in the conditions of the 1920s, would probably have been either as deadlocked as the United Nations Security Council after 1945, or would have acted as the policeman of the *status quo*. The old world, which these critics repudiated, would have been even more confirmed by a British determination to assign real powers to the League. It must be remembered that British dissatisfaction with the peace of 1919 was shared by few other original Members of the League.

A much more valid ground of criticism of British policy at the peace negotiations was the unwillingness of Ministers to face, or at least make clear to the country, the new balance of international forces which had emerged by 1919. Of the two policies open to Britain, the arming of the League and the return to traditional practice, the former was largely ruled out by the state of public and Parliamentary opinion, as well as by inter-Allied disagreements on the peace which an armed League was to defend. But the traditional politics which Britain was free to play in 1914 had disappeared for ever by 1919. New factors had entered the international scene, especially the revolutionary unsettlement in eastern Europe and the permanent disparity in strength between France and Germany. The idea that Britain, after imposing a penal fine on Germany, could retire and carp at a safe distance at French efforts to come to terms with the new situation was disastrous.

Time and again during the Peace Conference Lloyd George had insisted that a peace treaty lasts as long as the peoples of the signatory states feel confidence in its adequacy to the times. This confidence can only result from the public's knowledge of what is required to maintain peace in the circumstances of the day. The British Government of 1919, so far from helping to create this confidence by familiarising the country with the changed conditions of the world, lent themselves to that whittling away of the treaties which marked the route to the retreats of the 1930s.

CHAPTER VI

BRITAIN AND ISLAM

THE new Turkey, the tough successor to the old Ottoman state, was the last enemy with which the Allies made peace. The making of the settlement occupied no less than four and a half years, from the Armistice of Mudros, signed on 30 October 1918, until the final signature of the peace at Lausanne on 24 July 1923. During these years the shaping of the settlement in the Near and Middle East underwent many vicissitudes. On the Anglo-French partnership it placed immense strains, paralleled by discords between the two countries over the application of the Treaty of Versailles in Europe. It helped to destroy the Coalition Government in Britain; it drove British public opinion into injured isolationism. Yet the settlement eventually reached at Lausanne after many months of negotiation has endured to this day, except for the peaceful modification of the Convention of the Straits effected at Montreux in 1936.

The explanation for this lies partly in the nature of the Kemalist revolution in Turkey, which swept away the Sultanate and Caliphate and forced the Allies to revise the catastrophic Treaty of Sèvres, which they had attempted to impose on Constantinople. But there was also the fact that the Lausanne settlement, for all its appearance of being a Turkish victory over Entente imperialism, in effect secured the chief desiderata of Great Britain. It provided for the freedom of naval access through the Straits for which Britain pressed, as against the Bolshevik allies of Kemal; it ended—not by its terms, but by reason of the reformed policy of Turkey—the old tragedy of persecution of the non-Turkish minorities under the régime of the Porte; and it secured the promise at least of British influence with the new Arab states, thereby assuring British communications with India and the Far East and facilitating access to the oil on which British naval power now depended. By the time this chapter in British foreign policy had ended the main features of the postwar world had shaped themselves. The tumult and shouting of 1918–19 had died away. The nations were attempting to make the best of the world they had made, or had seen made on their behalf.

The Turkish revolution of 1920–1 dramatically upset the

125

expectations of the Allies and ranged them against each other, France conspiring with the new Turkey against England, England with Venizelist Greece against France. But it was not only this which delayed the settlement. There was also the protracted failure of the United States to undertake a mandate in the Near East, which President Wilson had half-promised and to which Lloyd George had looked as a possible means for securing a friendly influence either at the Straits or in Anatolia, without Britain herself incurring the expense and odium of establishing herself in either region. There was the pressure of Central European questions at the Paris Peace Conference, questions in which, after all, the interests of Britain and France were more deeply engaged than they were in the Near and Middle East. There was the well-nigh intractable problem of Bolshevist Russia, whose policy disturbed the position in the Black Sea and at the Straits. Above all, there was the great variety of countries, and self-appointed representatives of countries-to-be, which had some sort of stake in the settlement, and which were able to refer to promises of influence or territory in the area which had been hastily made to them by the belligerents in the course of the war. In 1918 the whole area later covered by the Lausanne Treaty and the Middle Eastern mandates was a labyrinth of conflicting claims, backed by more or less vague engagements entered into by the Allies.[1] These claims required to be equilibrated or neutralised one against the other before the Turkish settlement was effected. Kemalist military force and tortuous Allied diplomacy made this possible.

I

The first phase of the negotiations dealing with the Near and Middle East, from the Mudros armistice of 30 October 1918 to the signing of the Treaty of Sèvres on 10 August 1920, formed a chapter in Anglo-French discord. At hardly any period between the end of the First World War and the beginning of the Second did the temperature of relations between Britain and France drop to a lower point. The differences between the two countries at the Peace Conference over German and East European questions have been described in the previous chapter. These differences formed the background of the intense mutual distrust and suspicion excited by the problems of the Near East settlement.

The quarrel which sprang up between Britain and France over the arrangements for the armistice of Mudros, by which

<hr>

[1] See above, Chapter I, pp. 9–15.

Turkey capitulated, exemplified the tension. Although technically the French commanded Allied forces in the Mediterranean, it was a British officer, Admiral Calthorpe, in charge of British naval contingents in the Mediterranean, who hastened to Mudros on 11 October 1918. There he dictated to the Turks armistice terms giving naval control of the Straits to Britain. On the day on which these terms were signed, 30 October, a heated quarrel broke out between Lloyd George and Clemenceau in London over the refusal of Calthorpe to co-operate with Admiral Amet, representing France, in accepting the Turkish surrender. The customary inter-Allied charges of infidelity towards the alliance and of seizing advantages while the other was busy elsewhere were heard on the French side, and of failure to contribute an equal share to the defeat of Turkey on the British.[1]

It was the Syrian question, however, which drove the two countries to the verge of rupture. The French sought the fulfilment of the Sykes–Picot Agreement, but they aspired beyond it to an extension of French control far into the interior of Syria, if necessary in the guise of a mandate, if possible without one. Against this stood the determination of the Emir Feisal, who for the moment held the allegiance of the Syrian notables, not to accept French tutelage on any conditions. In his formal memoranda to the Peace Conference of 1 and 29 January 1919 Feisal asked for the independence of all Arabic Asia from the Alexandretta line south to the Indian Ocean. This broad zone included Syria, Iraq, Jezirah, Hejaz, the Nejd and the Yemen.[2] The British delegation were reluctant to alienate France, but lost no opportunity to point up the moral of the smooth relations Britain enjoyed with the Arabs as compared with those of France. Lord Milner, then Colonial Secretary, wrote to Lloyd George on 8 March 1919 of a conversation he had had on the subject of Syria with the French Prime Minister:

> I told Clemenceau quite frankly that, while we were dissatisfied with the Sykes–Picot scheme which he had himself recognised the necessity of radically altering, we had no desire to play the French out of Syria and to try to get Syria for ourselves. Our interest was confined to an extended Mesopotamia, to Palestine and to a good connection between them. The Syrian difficulty was not our doing, but was due to the fact that the French had unfortunately fallen foul of

[1] Lloyd George, *War Memoirs*, VI, pp. 3313–15.
[2] David Hunter Miller, *Diary*, IV, pp. 297–300.

the Arabs.   This put us in a very awkward position, as we were friends with the French, but also friends with the Arabs who had fought gallantly on our side against the Turks and contributed materially to our victory.   It was—entirely in our interest that the French and the Arabs should get on better terms with one another.[1]

Inconclusive discussions on the Syrian question took place at the Peace Conference in Paris in March and May 1919.[2] Lansing, the United States Secretary of State, encouraged by Lord Allenby's insistence that the Syrian Arabs could not stomach the French as mandatories, eventually proposed a mission of inquiry to discover the wishes of the local population of Syria.   At first Clemenceau appeared to agree, provided the inquiry covered Palestine, Mesopotamia and other parts of the old Turkey in addition to Syria;   then he refused to join in the project.   As it would have been improper for Britain to participate in view of French objections, the commission was selected by Wilson alone, his choice falling upon Dr. Henry C. King, President of Oberlin College, and Charles R. Crane. The report of the inquiry, which was to hand at the end of August, when Wilson had returned home, was much of a fore-gone conclusion, and as such had no effect on the outcome of the Syrian negotiations.   The commissioners reported that there was no support in Syria for any form of French control; the consensus of opinion was that if a mandate for Syria, in-cluding Palestine, was decided, pending the time when an Arab state or confederation could stand on its own feet, it should be entrusted to the United States or alternatively Britain.[3]

Anti-French tendencies among the Arabs were confirmed by information coming into the hands of the Foreign Office in London.   Lieutenant-Colonel Cornwallis, the British Deputy Chief Political Officer at Damascus, wrote on 16 May 1919: 'the Arab politicians have only two convictions; firstly, that they want independence and secondly that they do not want France.   Anti-French feeling is surprisingly strong amongst the people who count and it is very doubtful whether Feisal would be permitted to bring about a *rapprochement* even if he wanted to.'[4]   The Emir Feisal himself saw the two American commissioners on 3 July and said that he attributed this feeling against France to abhorrence at their ideas on colonial govern-

[1] Lloyd George, *The Truth about the Peace Treaties*, II, p. 1046.
[2] *F.R.U.S., 1919, The Paris Peace Conference*, V, p. 112 ff.
[3] The text of the Report was published in *Editor and Publisher* (New York), 2 December 1922, and reprinted in George Antonius, *The Arab Awakening*, London, 1938, pp. 443–58.
[4] *D.B.F.P.*, First Series, IV, pp. 263–6.

ment, as practised in Algiers and Tunis, fear that French rule meant the exploitation of Syrian markets and manpower in French interest, and the bad impression produced by French administration when he was in Europe.[1] Later the same year Colonel Meinertzhagen, a British officer in Cairo, wrote to Curzon about a talk he had had with Feisal. The Emir had 'reaffirmed the policy of a united Syria to the absolute exclusion of France and everything French. He and his people would fight on these points. . . . At the first sign of the Peace Conference handing Syria over to France our political influence over the Arabs and Feisal will disappear.' He added that Feisal's ultimate object was 'an Arab Federation embracing Mesopotamia and a Jewish Palestine, all under a British mandate'.[2]

No one in official quarters in Britain seriously objected to French tutelage over Syria. Britain was disinterested, as Ministers repeatedly told the French. But their unwillingness to make this clear beyond doubt to British officers and agents with the occupation forces in the country argues a certain British *Schadenfreude* in contemplating French unpopularity with the Arabs. However, since the British Government had decided that they wanted no part in the mandate for Syria, the next step, in the absence of a general settlement with Turkey, which the hesitations of the United States ruled out for the time being, was to withdraw British forces from Syria and Cilicia and to encourage Feisal and the French to come to an agreement on the future régime in those areas. Feisal had already reached an accommodation of sorts with Clemenceau before he left Paris in April 1919. In an exchange of letters with the Arab leader the French Prime Minister had agreed to an independent Syrian federation, but made clear that France would expect to provide assistance in the constitution of the Arab state and the restoration of order.[3] However, the formidable reception accorded to Feisal by the Syrian nobles on his return ruled out co-operation with France on the basis of this agreement.

Throughout the summer of 1919 rumours reached the Peace Conference that British officers were rousing the Sherifian forces of the Hedjaz against the French and supplying them with arms. Meanwhile the date when British forces must withdraw from the contested areas approached. On 13 September Lloyd George sent to Clemenceau an *aide-mémoire*, which was placed before the Supreme Council on 15 September.

[1] *D.B.F.P.*, First Series, IV, pp. 311–13.   [2] *Ibid.*, pp. 382–3.
[3] *Ibid.*, pp. 252–3.

This proposed that the retirement of British troops from Syria and Cilicia should commence almost at once and be completed by 1 November.   The occupied area west of the Sykes–Picot line, that is, west of the line Damascus–Hama–Homs–Aleppo, together with Cilicia, was to pass under French military control, while Arab forces were to take over the rest of Syria.[1]   The news of this arrangement created consternation among the Arab leaders as it seemed to imply a separation of the Syrian Arabs, who would come under French orders, from those who would enjoy a semblance of independence.   The British Government therefore invited Feisal to London in order to discuss the implications of the proposed British withdrawal at meetings at 10 Downing Street on 19 and 23 September. But the absence of the French made it impossible to decide what the situation would be when the British left.   The French Government liked the *aide-mémoire* no more than the Arabs, for it seemed to close to them the door to eastern Syria.   In this mood they refused to accept Lloyd George's invitation to send General Gouraud, the newly appointed High Commissioner for France in Syria and Commander-in-Chief of the Army of the Levant, to the Downing Street conference, arguing that changes in the system of occupation raised political issues which it was not for generals to decide.

Mounting tension against British policy in France, fed by the suspicion that Britain considered Feisal to be her special protégé, led to a violent outburst from Clemenceau on 14 October.   In this tirade he denounced the British Government for complicating affairs for France in the Middle East.   Four days later the challenging, self-exculpating riposte came from Lloyd George which he knew so well how to deliver.   For the first time the dispute emerged from formal exchanges in Foreign Ministers' chambers and the backbiting of soldiers in the East and became a duel at the summit.   In an extended and strong defence of British policy, the Prime Minister said that its object was not to drive the French from Syria, but to make possible an understanding between them and Feisal.   Hence the suggestion that Feisal should call on Clemenceau in Paris on his way home from the Downing Street meetings.

The British Government [Lloyd George continued, in that officious vein which gave point to the French complaint that Britain took too much on her shoulders] are so impressed with the importance of bringing about an understanding between the Arabs and the French that they did not communicate

---

[1] *D.B.F.P.*, First Series, I, pp. 700–1; IV, p. 384.

[Clemenceau's] message to the Emir Feisal in the somewhat insulting form in which it reached them. . . . As it is the desire of the British Government that France shall exercise the mandatory power it is clearly of the utmost importance that the French Government should spare no pains to establish a friendly understanding with the Emir Feisal and the Arab population of Syria.[1]

Feisal's visit to Paris to interview Clemenceau proved as in-conclusive as had all earlier discussions with the French. Not until the end of the year was agreement reached between them on the principle of a French mandate for Syria. This recog-nised the right of Arabic-speaking Syrians to form an indepen-dent nation with the advice and guidance of the French. France was authorised to defend Syria against threats to its independence and, at the request of the Syrian Government, was to appoint councillors, administrators and advisers to control certain branches of the administration. She was to have priority in the raising of loans and financing of the government of Syria generally and the right to appoint French officials to represent Syria abroad.[2] The agreement left un-settled the two problems of the nature of the autonomous regions to be created within the Syrian federation and the question of a Parliament for Syria. Nevertheless, the Syrian question was now clearly an issue between the French and the Arabs, for it was evident that Feisal was only in partial control of the more extreme sections of Syrian opinion. To all intents the Peace Conference had divested itself of the problem. As far back as 30 January 1919 it had declared that

> The Allied and Associated Powers are agreed that Ar-menia, Syria, Mesopotamia and Kurdistan, Palestine and Arabia must be completely severed from the Turkish Empire. This is without prejudice to the other parts of the Turkish Empire.[3]

At the San Remo Conference of the Allied Powers which drew up the Treaty of Sèvres in April 1920 it was finally decided to allocate the Arab mandates on the basis of the Arab boundaries as these had been settled between the Allies during the war. The League of Nations, which had only just been created, was not consulted since these questions were conceived as part of the peace settlement and therefore a responsibility of the Allied

[1] D.B.F.P., First Series, IV, pp. 479–89.
[2] Ibid., pp. 625–7.
[3] Miller, Diary, XIV, pp. 130–1.

Powers alone. Britain accepted the mandates for Mesopotamia and Palestine, France those for Syria and Lebanon. The substitution of civil for military administration was carried out subsequent to and as a consequence of these arrangements.[1]

By the time the San Remo Conference met Feisal had been elected King of Syria by an Arab Congress meeting at Damascus on 10 March. He at once repudiated and never thereafter accepted the conclusions of the San Remo Conference. The Arab Congress which hoisted him, not altogether willingly, into the throne proclaimed 'the complete independence of Syria within its natural boundaries from Mount Sinai to the Taurus, and from the Syrian desert to the sea, without any protectorate, mandate or any form of foreign interference'.[2] In May, Feisal, for whom Lloyd George had sought representation at San Remo, definitely rejected the French mandate. From that point the descent to catastrophe was swift. General Gouraud, on behalf of the government in Paris, issued an ultimatum to Feisal on 14 July demanding acceptance of the French mandate and the punishment of those who resisted the French occupation. After a second ultimatum to the same effect, French forces entered Damascus on 25 July 1920. Feisal was forced to leave the country. The fact that this Arab leader who had so defied the French was promptly created King of Iraq by a Congress of Iraqi nobles with the full approval of the British did not endear Britain to France.

France was handicapped during the Syrian negotiations by lack of local military power; her forces in the area numbered no more than a few thousands. Along the Lebanese coast, however, France's naval control provided a lever to raise her terms in the bargaining for shares in the oil potentialities of upper Mesopotamia.[3] The so-called Long–Berenger Agreement, concluded on 9 April 1919, gave France a 20 per cent share in the Turkish Petroleum Company, which had been formed with mainly British capital for the exploitation of the wells of the Mosul region. With the development of Anglo-French tension in Syria French attitudes stiffened and Britain was refused permission to construct the railway line to the Levant coast through the French mandate for the building and maintenance of a pipeline for the conveyance of Mosul oil. The agreement was

---

[1] J. de V. Loder, *The Truth about Mesopotamia, Palestine, and Syria*, London, 1923, p. 140. *D.B.F.P.*, First Series, VIII, pp. 176–7.

[2] Leonard Stein, *Syria*, London, 1926, p. 26 *et seq.*

[3] The rising importance of oil from the Middle East to Britain at this time is reflected in the fact that, whereas in 1914–18 Britain obtained more than 80 per cent of her total petroleum requirements from the U.S.A. and only 4 per cent from Persia and Mesopotamia, by 1924 the former figure had fallen to 40 per cent and the latter had risen to 27 per cent (*The Economist*, 9 May 1925).

therefore cancelled by Lloyd George on 21 May. The fact that the Prime Minister claimed to have heard of the agreement only 'casually' may be read as an indication of the haphazard diplomacy of the times. By the end of 1919, when an understanding of sorts seemed to have been arrived at between Feisal and the French, Anglo-French relations markedly improved, and the effects were registered in a revised agreement, concluded on 21 December and signed by Berenger for France and Hamar Greenwood for Britain. This raised the French share to 25 per cent and gave Britain the right to build a pipeline and supporting railway line through Syria.[1] The agreement was confirmed in a further accord, which settled the general relations between British and French oil interests in other parts of the world as well, signed by Phillippe Berthelot and Sir John Cadman at the San Remo Conference on 24 April 1920.[2] The agreement relating to Mosul, however, was a case of counting the chickens before they had hatched, since events were to prove that Mosul was far from being securely in British hands. It was not in fact made over to Iraq until 1926.[3]

II

The British Government hoped that the United States would accept a mandate for Constantinople and the Straits, or for the contemplated independent state of Armenia, envisaged in 1919 as Europe's atonement for the Ottoman massacres of the past. The choice of the United States was arrived at by eliminating alternatives. In Lloyd George's view, Russia would have suited Britain's book better, and this would have been in accordance with the Sykes–Picot Agreement. But the Bolsheviks had changed the whole picture. A second best, he thought, though in this he collided with Curzon, would be Greece, since she would always be too weak at sea to close the Straits against the Allies. But there were unsurmountable objections to having the Greeks as mandatories at Constantinople, not least from Italy. An Italian mandate would similarly have to be imposed upon Greece. The rivalry between Britain and France in the Near East ruled out the possibility of the permanent patronage of either country at the Straits. This left the United States, the claims of which were strong on

---

[1] *D.B.F.P.*, First Series, IV, pp. 1114–17.

[2] Cmd. 675 (1920): *Agreement regarding petroleum relating to Rumania, Asia Minor, the territories of the old Russian Empire, Galicia, the French colonies and British Crown colonies.* M. Berthelot was Director of Political and Economic Affairs at the French Foreign Ministry; Sir John Cadman was the Director in charge of H.M. Petroleum Department.

[3] See below, p. 155.

account of its reputation for impartiality and lively concern for minority peoples.[1]

President Wilson seemed to approve the suggestion of an American mandate over some portion of Turkey when it was raised at the Peace Conference; it appealed to his idealism. He assented on 14 May 1919 to the decision of the Council of Four to approve a United States mandate over Armenia and the Straits, subject to the Senate's consent. But the prospects of the latter condition being fulfilled quickly faded. Wilson found scepticism towards American participation in the League of Nations awaiting him when he returned home in February 1919. Hence, on his final return to the United States from Paris in June, after the signing of the Versailles Treaty by German representatives, he concentrated his campaign on securing approval for the ratification of that treaty, since this would have made America a member of the League. Little was said about an American mandate in Asia Minor. Even if this strategy had not been followed, the almost insuperable task of persuading the Congress to accept oversea responsibilities, especially after its experience in the Philippines, was rendered futile by Wilson's paralytic stroke on 25 September. Temperamentally an autocrat, he had trained no disciple to carry on the fight. Colonel House he now excluded from his presence.[2] On the basis of reports that the President's stroke was a temporary nervous breakdown from which there might be a recovery in a few weeks, Lloyd George continued to place his hopes in an American mandate, rejecting Curzon's repeated appeals for an immediate peace with Turkey. In this the Prime Minister's judgment failed him.

Even before Wilson's illness Lindsay, the British Minister in Washington, was writing to Curzon on 16 August that the Versailles Treaty was due to come before the Senate in October and that it was most unlikely that a mandate over Turkey would be accepted.[3] On 22 October Lord Grey of Fallodon, who had failed in his efforts to interview Wilson on the mandate during his official mission to the United States, wrote to the Foreign Secretary to say that the United States Secretary of State had confirmed that there was 'no chance whatever' of Congress authorising the acceptance of mandates for Constantinople.[4] Hopes continued to linger in London, however, until finally eclipsed on 19 March of the following year, when the

[1] Lloyd George, *The Truth About the Peace Treaties*, II, pp. 1258–60.
[2] Wilson now regarded House as too pro-British: *D.B.F.P.*, First Series, V, p. 1022, n. 4.
[3] *Ibid*, IV, p. 730.
[4] *Ibid*, pp. 842–3.

Versailles Treaty failed to command the constitutional majority in the Senate. The United States thereupon withdrew from the Supreme Council. All that remained were sad strictures from Wilson's sick bed on the Allied proposals for the Turkish settlement. In his letter of 24 March he ruled out the prospect of American commitments either in Armenia or elsewhere. He was willing and able to act only as an arbitrator in the settlement of the frontiers of the new Armenia.[1]

Meanwhile the position of the Allies in Turkey steadily deteriorated. Curzon, with his strong interest in a prompt Eastern settlement, pressed for the separation from Turkey of its European territory, but otherwise argued for a compact Anatolia securely under Turkish control.[2] This policy was substantiated by the news reaching London of stiffening Turkish resistance and the weakening of the Sultan's authority in the face of growing nationalist forces in Anatolia. The rallying of these forces around Kemal Pasha, whom the Sultan's government had unwittingly dispatched to northern Anatolia as a military inspector, had been chiefly inspired by the landing of Greek forces at Smyrna in May 1919, to which the Supreme Council had consented as a means of forestalling independent armed action in Asia Minor by Italy.

The Kemalists were fully prepared to accept Allied military supremacy and come to terms with it. But the Greeks they regarded as their inferiors in all the arts of war, government and civilisation; under no circumstances would they bow to the creation of an independent Greek enclave at Smyrna, especially one which showed no sign of being limited to the immediate environs of the city. Admiral Webb was writing from Constantinople to Sir Eyre Crowe in Paris on 17 August that 'the one thing that is quite certain is that the worst day's work for his country which Venizelos ever did was when he induced the Supreme Council to allow Greek troops into Smyrna to "pacify" the place—the only *possible* hope for comparative peace and tranquillity in the future between the two races is the withdrawal of Greek troops . . . from Asia Minor and a return to the *status quo*'.[3] The consequences of such advice being ignored were felt in October, when the government at Constantinople fell and a new administration with Ali Riza Pasha as Grand Vizier was formed. The new régime was described as a compromise between the party of the Sultan and the party of Kemal. Kemal himself, in a forceful telegram to

---

[1] Lloyd George, *The Truth*, II, pp. 1296–1300; *F.R.U.S.*, 1920, III, pp. 750–3·
[2] The Earl of Ronaldshay, *The Life of Lord Curzon*, III, pp. 262–71.
[3] *D.B.F.P.*, First Series, IV, pp. 733–4.

Constantinople, demanded immediate elections, to be held under the supervision of the Nationalists, and the arrest and trial of certain members of the former government, including the Grand Vizier, the Minister of War and two successive Ministers of the Interior, and certain provincial governors.

Curzon received an alarming analysis of the impact of these events from Admiral de Robeck at Constantinople on 10 October.

> Thus was effected [the message ran] another of those minor revolutions which have occurred at intervals in Constantinople since 1908. Power has passed from a party which, however anxious to save as much as possible of the Empire, saw salvation in submission to, and collaboration with, the Entente authorities, to a party whose avowed object is to contest any attempt on the part of the Entente to impair the integrity and independence of Turkey and who in their programme have made it quite clear that their 'Turkey' comprises as a minimum all territory not occupied at the time of the armistice, while leaving it vague in how much more of the old Turkish Empire they hope to uphold the rights of the Caliphate and the Sultanate.[1]

The Kemalists were quick to note that Allied military power in Turkey was dwindling, and that such of it as remained was diminished by Anglo-French discords on such issues as that of the nationality of the Supreme Allied Commander. British troops were leaving Samsun in the north and gradually being reduced in the Caucasus. A similar retirement from southeastern Kurdistan was in prospect. The British withdrawal from Syria and Cilicia had been agreed in September and was to be completed by 1 November. There were moreover unmistakable signs in Britain, France and Italy, if not yet in Greece, that the seemingly endless military service was becoming intolerable, the men wanting to return home and savour the new world in peace. For the Allies the tide was ebbing.

The main feature of an Anglo-French meeting at the Foreign Office on 22 December was the disclosure of the difference of views between Britain and France on the future site of the Turkish capital and the centre of Turkish political life. Lloyd George hankered after the expulsion of the Sultan from Constantinople. He reverted to the well-worn argument that the Turks were an alien element in a Europe they had misgoverned, and that Constantinople and the surrounding areas contained

[1] *Ibid.*, p. 805.

more non-Turkish than Turkish people. He borrowed the
historical argument supplied by Curzon that Constantinople,
so far from being one of the ancient capitals of Islam, had not
been the seat of the Caliph for more than four hundred years.
The Prime Minister's solution was that some form of international control of the capital should be combined with generous
compensation to the Greeks out of Turkish territory in Europe.
The French, on the other hand, were influenced by their heavy
financial stake in the old Ottoman Empire; the most effective
way of protecting this, they considered, was to hold the Sultan
close at hand in Europe, where he was more amenable to Allied
control than if he were in the heart of Asia Minor. This issue
was left unsettled, while four primary axioms for the settlement
were agreed. These were, first, that Ottoman militarism
should be suppressed once and for all; secondly, that the Straits
should be permanently neutralised; thirdly, that the Armenian desire for an independent state should be gratified;
and fourthly, that all connections should be severed between
Turkey, on the one hand, and Syria and the other Arab states,
on the other. The discussion then moved to the subject of an
arrangement for protecting French financial interests in return
for French agreement to a form of internationalisation for the
Straits. These were to be regulated by an international
council with Britain and France alternately providing the chairman. The banks of the Dardanelles and the Bosphorus were
to be neutralised. Constantinople itself was to form a separate,
perpetually neutralised and internationally protected state.
In Asiatic Turkey there was to be a scheme of direct financial
control exercised by the Allies over the economy of the country
as a whole, accompanied by complete disarmament. Italy
was to withdraw her forces while receiving economic concessions in Anatolia. Substantial transfers to Greece of territory
in Eastern Thrace and the Smyrna *vilayet* were contemplated.
Separate development for Armenia remained a pious hope
throughout the meeting, though its scattered population and
fierce political factionalism were the worst of omens.

Had the decisions of the Foreign Office meeting been adhered
to there would have been two parts of Turkey; 'the one' [to
use Curzon's description] 'was to be an area taken from the
Turks and governed by an international body. The other was
to be an area left under the sovereignty of the Turks but subject
in certain respects, that is, finance and gendarmerie, to international supervision.'[1] But opposition at once sprang up in the
Cabinet against any plan for expelling the Turks from Europe,

[1] *D.B.F.P.*, First Series, IV, p. 957.

the War Office and India Office providing the strongest pressure for a Turkish Constantinople. The military advisers felt that control of the Sultan and his Ministers would be easier if they remained in the old capital, whereas in Anatolia they would be accessible to the influence of the Nationalists. This was a powerful argument swaying Lloyd George away from Curzon's side, although he was later to claim that this change of position was in deference to French and Italian views.[1] In a debate in the House of Commons on 26 February 1920 he explained the new position:

> I ask my Noble Friend [Lord Robert Cecil] if he were an Armenian would he feel more secure if he knew that the Sultan and his Ministers were overlooked by a British garrison and that out in the Bosphorus the British ships were within reach of them than if he were at Konia, hundreds of miles across the Taurus mountains from the nearest Allied garrison and the sea with its great British ships and its guns out of sight and out of mind.[2]

Joined with this appeal to the practical aspect of applying force—always the starting-point of policy in Lloyd George's mind—was the unceasing pressure from the India Office and the Government of India in favour of maintaining Constantinople as the Turkish capital. On the eve of Kemal's destruction of the Caliphate it was argued that if a Christian Constantinople were created and the clock set back to 1453 the allegiance of 80 million Indian Moslems towards the Crown would be undermined. The argument never appealed to the Prime Minister. Curzon made fun of it. But the Secretary of State for India, Edward Montagu, was a power in the Cabinet; the sentiment which had so often in the previous century roused Ministers to a fever of anxiety over Russian movements towards India was lively still. But by far the largest objection to the project for driving the Turks from Europe was that it was impossible to decide, in that event, what the future status of Constantinople and the Straits would be. It was easy enough to paste the slogan 'internationalisation' over inter-Allied suspicions, jealousies, fears, but when the problems of devising a form of international administration,

[1] Lloyd George, *The Truth*, II, pp. 1270–2. In this passage Lloyd George argues as though France had changed her position on the question of Constantinople before the meeting of the London Conference on 12 February 1920. In fact at the Foreign Office meeting on 22 December she had given way to Britain. Since by February Britain had come to accept Constantinople as the Turkish capital France merely reverted to her previous stand.

[2] 125 H.C. Deb 5s. Col. 1969.

which had never worked elsewhere, were faced, there was an immediate recoil. Bonar Law explained the difficulties in the House on 25 February 1920,

> I can tell the House that when we tried to put it in black and white it was the contemplation of what such an international state would mean that made us decide that at least was impossible. It was not really commonsense. It has been tried in many cases. Can anyone point to a single instance where this kind of joint dominion had succeeded? And can one find a case less difficult than that of Egypt, in which this joint control nearly brought us to war?[1]

To these questions no answer came.

Curzon took up the struggle against the Montagu faction in an able paper on the future of Constantinople dated 4 January 1920. It was wrong to believe, he said, that the Foreign Office plan for an independent state of Constantinople would so outrage the Turks that on no circumstances would they sign such a peace. The main strength of the plan was that it made secure an integral Turkish Anatolia. 'Our object was,' he continued, 'if possible, to free the Turkish Dominions in Asia Minor from the Greeks or Italian or any other foreign territorial encroachment, but to place his Government under so much of foreign financial and administrative control as to ensure that he should not repeat there the outrageous misgovernment of which he has for centuries been guilty in Europe'.[2] He was supported by the Prime Minister and Balfour, but the victory of the India Office came in the Cabinet two days later.[3] Accordingly Montagu was invited to prepare the proposals of the British Government for the forthcoming meeting with the French. By a remarkable act of humiliation Curzon was only allowed to see the Montagu draft at the suggestion of Hankey.[4]

The paper which resulted from the Cabinet discussion on 6 February was prepared jointly by the India Office and the Military Section of the British delegation to the Peace Conference. It opened by accepting the four principles already agreed at the Foreign Office meeting with the French in December. Five more were added. Armenia was to be definitely constituted as an independent state, the question of its boundaries being reserved for the time being. The national

[1] 125 H.C. Deb. 5s. Col. 2054.
[2] D.B.F.P., First Series, IV, pp. 992–1000.
[3] H. Nicolson, Curzon: the last phase, p. 113; CAB 23/20. 1 (20).
[4] D.B.F.P., ibid., pp. 1037–42.

aspirations of the Arabs, including the Syrians, were to be given satisfaction. Article 292 of the Treaty of Versailles was to apply to Turkey.[1] No reparations were to be claimed from Turkey in view of her bankrupt condition.[2] Turkey was to be left with a foothold in Europe, but the status of Adrianople was left undecided. The Montagu draft then went on to propose a permanent Allied force to safeguard the neutrality of the Straits and an inter-Allied commission for the control of Turkish finance. Smyrna was to be a free port, though whether under Turkish or Greek sovereignty was left open.[3] Finally, Italy, as in the conclusions of the Foreign Office meeting the previous December, was to be compensated with economic rights in southern Anatolia for the withdrawal of Italian forces, which was insisted upon. The Dodecanese, however, were to be annexed to Greece.[4]

The Montagu draft represented the main position of the British Government in the so-called First London Conference of the Supreme Council which opened on 12 February 1920, the object of the Conference being to prepare recommendations on the settlement of Turkey. There was general agreement at the outset that no purpose would be served by waiting further for news of the American attitude on the question of a mandate in the Near East. The principle of the retention of Constantinople by the Turks was then approved, Lloyd George affecting to believe that it was pressure from Allies which had induced him to accept that principle, whereas it had been settled on other grounds in the Cabinet on 6 January.[5] Discussion then passed to the subject of the control of the Straits. It was agreed that the waterway should be neutralised and managed by an international body the members of which would be appointed by Britain, France and, if American opinion was agreeable, the United States. The most heated argument, however, sprang from the proposed French scheme for the creation of an Inter-Allied Commission to take over the entire control of the financial life of Turkey. The Prime Minister, supported to-

[1] Article 292 ran: Germany recognises that all treaties, conventions, or arrangements which she concluded with Russia, or with any State or Governments of which the territory previously formed a part of Russia, or with Rumania, before 1 August 1914, or after that date until the coming into force of the present Treaty, are and remain abrogated.
  The effect of this proposal of the draft was that pre-war German concessions in the old Ottoman Empire would fall into the hands of the Entente Powers.
[2] The Foreign Office disagreed with this.
[3] In Lord Curzon's rejoinder to the Montagu draft it was proposed that Smyrna should remain under Turkish sovereignty, but with a 'predominantly Greek régime' and on a free city basis.
[4] For the text of the Montagu draft see *D.B.F.P.*, First Series, IV, pp. 1037–42.
[5] Lloyd George, *The Truth*, II, pp. 1271–2; Ronaldshay, *op. cit.*, III, p. 270.

wards the end of the discussion by the Italian Premier, Nitti, argued that any such scheme was impracticable; it would amount, he said, to governing the country from the outside, involving the Allies in wholly indefinite commitments.[1]   Nevertheless, the proposal was adhered to until the framing of the Treaty of Sèvres.

During the First London Conference an event occurred which showed how unreal these various plans were.   This was the serious defeat inflicted on the French Army at Marash, the largest city in Cilicia, by a force of some 30,000 regular Turkish troops, who were believed to be acting at the instigation, if not under the direct orders, of Kemal.   The Marash affair threw into the melting pot the discussions at the London Conference. It accelerated the decline in Italian interest in Anatolia and turned the Italian Government's face, once more, towards the Adriatic.   It was the forerunner of the crucial Franklin-Bouillon Agreement between the French and the Kemalists which, a year later, dramatically changed the whole picture in the Near East. Above all, the reverse at Marash showed up the illusion behind Allied policy, namely that the Kemalists were a disorganised group of brigands who could soon be brought to heel if Allied pressure was brought to bear at Constantinople.

'It may be asked,' the Prime Minister later wrote in his memoirs of the Peace Conference, 'why, in the face of this formidable Nationalist movement, the Allies did not pause in their schemes for the partition of Turkey?'[2]   It may indeed.   He himself, however, gives no clear answer to the question, apart from stating the opinion that, had he received Allied backing and support from his own people, Venizelos would have been fully capable of holding Smyrna and its hinterland against the Kemalists.   However that may be, when the Allies finally met at San Remo in April 1920 to draft what was supposed to be the definitive peace treaty with Turkey, they found a situation even more disadvantageous than it had been at the London Conference in February.   Yet the peace treaty emerging from their labours was drawn up as though Mustapha Kemal and the passions he aroused among his countrymen had never existed.   It was believed that a distinct concession was being made to Turkey when Constantinople was allowed to remain the capital, protected by a belt of European territory extending only as far as the Chatalja lines.   The rest of Turkey-in-Europe,

---

[1] *D.B.F.P.*, First Series, VII, pp. 56–60, 86–98.
[2] *The Truth*, II, p. 1292.   For warnings of the consequences of attempting to enforce the proposals on Turkey see the message of the British High Commissioner at Constantinople, 10 March 1920: *D.B.F.P.*, First Series, VII, p. 500.

along with the Aegean islands of Imbros and Tenedos, was handed to Greece. What Venizelos had asked for in Thrace the previous year was now granted. The Straits, however, and its shores, together with the islands in the Aegean Sea confronting the mouth of the Dardanelles, were perpetually neutralised and placed under an International Commission charged to secure the free navigation for ships of all countries, except as the Council of the League of Nations might otherwise decree. Having thus made a qualified concession in the matter of Constantinople, the Allies felt that they were at liberty to partition Anatolia. An independent Armenia was to be created, its frontiers in the *vilayets* of Trebizond, Erzerum, Van and Bitlis to be determined by the arbitration of President Wilson. The decision to create the state of Armenia was taken despite the fact that the Armenian population of Erzerum had been seriously reduced by massacre from the estimated 160,000 of pre-war days, when the Turkish population of the district was acknowledged to be 360,000, and although the Allies' military advisers reported that the Armenians did not command sufficient military strength to capture and hold Erzerum against the Turks.[1]

As for Smyrna, the port and a large area of the hinterland were placed temporarily under Greek control, the option being given to the inhabitants of the *vilayet* to pass under Greek sovereignty by referendum after five years. Kurdistan was accorded local autonomy, with the right to vote for secession from Turkey within twelve months. The loss of the Arab communities to Turkey was confirmed and their future status as mandatories recognised. Hedjaz was to become an independent state. Turkey renounced all rights over Egypt, the Sudan and Libya, and recognised the British protectorate of 1914 over Egypt and that of France over Tunis and Morocco. To underline the total defeat of Turkey and the vast problems of reconstruction which it faced, the proposed Financial Commission representing the Allied Powers was charged with the task of controlling the entire finances of the country, of supervising its budget, approving government spending, ensuring the servicing of its external debt and applying such surplus as might remain to pay the costs of the army of occupation and the war indemnity. To complete the reduction of the defeated country to client status, the Capitulatory régime, under which in pre-war times certain states enjoyed extra-territorial juridical and other rights for their nationals in Turkish territories, was not only

---

[1] Lloyd George, *The Truth*, II, p. 1306. For Foch's opinion see *D.B.F.P.*, First Series, VIII, p. 122.

confirmed, but extended to all the Allied Powers.[1]   It was a peace of humiliation.

The draft of the treaty was presented to the Sultan's representatives on 24 April 1920 and signed by them on 10 August. It is an extraordinary fact that Lloyd George, who constantly pressed for moderation in the shaping of the peace treaty with Germany, should have approved this vindictive agreement despite the military position in the Near East in early 1920.   In August 1922, when the Sèvres Treaty was in ruins, he sought to pin responsibility for its collapse on the Commission of the Peace Conference, as though this was independent of the governments: 'we never interfered with that Commission,' he said.[2]   Later he came to regard the Sèvres Treaty as just and workable.[3]   But that he supported it in April 1920 there can be no doubt.   The most unreal element in the Treaty of Sèvres, the proposal to create an independent Armenia, Lloyd George did indeed riddle with criticism at the San Remo Conference, on the ground that only Allied military power could make Armenia, especially the Great Armenia envisaged in the Sèvres Treaty, a practical proposition.[4]   The Allies, everyone knew, were quite unwilling to provide any such power.   Yet Lloyd George agreed to the creation of a paper Armenian state when a British veto could have prevented it.

The explanation for the Premier's loss of realism when he left European affairs and dealt with the Near East lies partly in his total lack of sympathy for the Turks or Turkey, in which in all probability Turkey's frustration of his own plans to defeat Germany from the east and south-east played its part.   A second factor was the absence of the vital economic interests in that region which made for moderation in the British attitude towards defeated Germany.   Such British economic interests as there were in Turkey, when the Arabs had seceded, lay in transit into the Black Sea through the Straits rather than in the economy of Anatolian Turkey itself; these interests were not injured by harshness towards the Turks.   Also at work was the Prime Minister's vision of Greek and Italian enterprise, no doubt under British naval protection, repairing Turkey's ravages in Asia.   The pipe-dream of an Anatolia turned into

---

[1] Treaty Series No. II (1920).   Treaty of Peace with Turkey signed at Sèvres, 10 August 1920, Cmd. 964.

[2] 157 H.C. Deb. 5s. Col. 1999 (4 August).

[3] *The Truth*, II, p.1358: 'In substance the modified plan of Sèvres was sound, and if carried out would have conduced to the well-being of the millions to be liberated by its terms for ever from Turkish rule.'

[4] Lloyd George, *The Truth*, II, p. 1333; *D.B.F.P.*, First Series, VIII, pp. 139–40. At the San Remo Conference Lloyd George still hoped that the United States would accept a mandate for Armenia.

a vineyard by Greek and Italian hands unable to drive poverty from their own countries, excited him while in London Bonar Law, Stanley Baldwin and the Conservative ranks reckoned up the cost.

III

Even before the Sultan's representatives signed the Treaty of Sèvres in August 1920, the Allies had tried to crush the Turkish nationalist revolution, but they did so in Constantinople, not in Anatolia, where the heart of the revolution lay. They had made known their willingness to recognise the Nationalist Assembly, which had adopted the National Pact, provided it met at Constantinople and was presided over by the Sultan Mehmed IV. Contrary to Kemal's advice, the majority of the deputies left Ankara for Constantinople in accordance with the Allies' suggestion on 11 January and in the old capital a newly elected Parliament met, with strong Kemalist represen-tation. 'The Allies,' Churchill wrote, 'were loyal to the prin-ciple of representative government; accordingly the Turks had voted. Unhappily they had almost all of them voted the wrong way. The new Chamber was pre-ponderantly Nationa-list, or, it might be said, Kemalist.'[1] The Allies replied first by demanding the resignation of the Minister of War and of the Chief of the General Staff. Then, when the new Turkish Parlia-ment adopted the National Pact on 28 January, Constantinople was occupied on 16 March by British, French and Italian forces, several of the Nationalist deputies were arrested, and the Grand Vizier, Ferid Pasha, was argued into forming a more compliant Cabinet. At the end of April the Nationalist Parliamentarians who had escaped when the blow fell on Constantinople in March joined forces with those who had remained behind in Ankara with Kemal to form a new National Assembly beyond the reach of the Entente. From this moment the seat of power in Turkey definitely shifted to the interior.

At the meeting of the Council at Hythe in June the Greek Premier, then in the high noon of his influence, offered the Allies some 90,000 Greeks to repel the Kemalists.[2] The offer was accepted and on 22 June the Greek Army left Smyrna bound for the Straits. Contrary to all forecasts by British and French military advisers, they routed the Turks at the first engagement and then pushed on to make contact with the Bri-tish contingent on the Ismid line. For Lloyd George it was a moment of triumph: 'I believe,' he said in the House of Com-

[1] *The World Crisis*, V, *The aftermath*, p. 375.
[2] *D.B.F.P.*, First Series, VIII, pp. 307–8; CAB 23/22. 53 (20), Appendix III.

mons on 23 June, 'that we shall be able to establish authority
in these areas.'[1]   But if the summer saw the zenith of Greek
power in Asia Minor, the extraordinary political events of the
winter ran together like opening words in some final chapter
in the Greek tragedy.   The first of these events was the death
of the young Greek king, Alexander, from sceptic poisoning
after having been bitten by a pet monkey on 2 October.
Venizelos then allowed his political acumen to desert him
when he decided the form of a plebiscite to be held on 5
December in which the Greeks were simply asked to declare
whether they wished to see the return to the throne of ex-King
Constantine, then in exile, whom the Allies had dethroned for
his pro-Germanism in 1917.   The plebiscite was overwhelmingly in favour of Constantine's return.   By this time Venizelos
had himself been overwhelmingly defeated at a General Election held on 14 November and had at once resigned amid what
looked like the ruins of his eastern policy.   Contrary, however,
to the apparent war-weariness inspiring the Greek voters, Constantine had no interest in ending the war with Turkey; instead he decided to pursue the campaign in the following spring
with greater vigour.   The result was total failure.

Although Lloyd George announced that the ex-King's return would make no difference as far as Britain was concerned,
it was clear that support for Greece in Asia Minor would be
hard to defend with British opinion so long as Greece was ruled
by a brother-in-law of the ex-Kaiser.   'In England,' Churchill
wrote, 'the feeling was not resentment, but a total extinction
of sympathy or even interest.'[2]   In France and Italy the feelings
were even stronger and were intensified by the discovery that
the British Prime Minister, reluctantly but firmly, continued
his support of the Greek Government.   These Allies now saw
the folly of complicating further their relations with Kemal
merely to give satisfaction to Constantine in his Anatolian esca-
pades.   At the end of December rumours spread of a separate
agreement between Rome and Ankara.   On 3 May the House
of Commons was told that such a treaty had existed since 24
April; it provided, in return for an Italian undertaking not to
support Greece further, for the favourable consideration of
Italian applications for concessions to build railways, mines
and public works in Turkey.[3]   It was the first open crack in the
Western Alliance.

By far the most dangerous threat, however, to the British

[1]   130 H.C. Deb. 5s. Col. 2260.
[2]   *The aftermath*, p. 388.
[3]   153 H.C. Deb. 5s. Cols. 1344–6.

diplomatic position after Constantine's return to Greece was the French movement for a separate peace with the Turkish Nationalists. The French were not encumbered by phil-hellenism. They realised that, if Kemal was to be crushed, it could not be with French force, and hence that Britain and Greece would be the beneficiaries. As early as September 1919, at the height of the Anglo-French tension over Syria, Georges Picot had gone to Sivas to talk with the Nationalists on behalf of the French Government. Again, in the latter part of 1920, General Gouraud, whom the French Government had sent to pacify Syria, offered to surrender to the Kemalists certain oil-bearing areas of northern Syria in which Britain was interested. At last on 20 October 1921 these efforts bore fruit in the form of an agreement concluded between Franklin-Bouillon, a French Deputy and one-time Chairman of the Foreign Affairs Committee of the French Chamber, and Yous-souf Kemal Bey, the Foreign Minister in the Kemalist ad-ministration in Ankara. The agreement bore every sign of being a separate peace, and was therefore contrary to the still unratified Treaty of Sèvres. France agreed to evacuate Cilicia and to retrocede to Turkey a tract of territory in north-ern Syria amounting to 10,000 square miles, which had been entrusted to her by the San Remo Conference as part of the Syrian mandate. In a note annexed to the agreement Yous-souf Kemal Bey indicated that France was to receive in return concessions for the exploitation of iron, silver, chrome and other minerals in the new Turkey and permission for French capi-talists to acquire an interest in Turkish banks, forts, waterways and railways.[1]

What the Franklin-Bouillon Agreement and Curzon's pro-test against it demonstrated was that the Anglo-French solid-arity essential to any settlement with the Kemalists which was to serve the long-term interests of the Western Powers would not be forthcoming. This conclusion was further underlined by the negotiations during 1921 for an armistice in the Greco-Turkish war, to be followed by modification of the Sèvres Treaty. The first attempt in this direction was made at the London Conference in February 1921 attended by represen-tatives from Greece and from Sultanate and Kemalist Turkey, as well as from the Allied Powers.[2] The Conference was a total failure largely because Lloyd George, exulting at the

---

[1] Turkey No. 2 (1921). Dispatch from H.M. Ambassador at Paris enclosing the Franco-Turkish Agreement signed at Angora on 20 October 1921, Cmd. 1556.

[2] The Kemalists appeared at the Conference as members of the Constantinople Delegation. The position of the latter was presented by Bekir Samy Bey, the chief spokesman of Ankara.

Greek victories of the previous summer, was unwilling to set a limit to Greek advances and seek an immediate peace with the Kemalists on the basis that the Greeks should not be encouraged to attempt the total defeat of Turkey.   'The Prime Minister,' wrote Curzon, 'is as convinced a Venizelist and phil-hellene as ever, and uses all the advantages of his position as chairman in that direction.'[1]   The only significant achievement of the meetings at St. James's Palace was to bring the French Premier and Kemal's representatives together for talks on the evacuation of Cilicia.   'We were not long in coming to an agreement,' said Briand in the Chamber of Deputies on 16 March.[2]   In a letter to the Prime Minister on 22 February, after the Conference had ended, Churchill warned that it was 'a fearful responsibility to let loose the Greeks and re-open the war'.[3]   But Churchill's proposal for ending the deadlock, namely that the Turks be asked to accept peace terms which included the evacuation of Smyrna by the Greeks, was ruled out by the extent of the Greek military successes of the summer.

Curzon recognized that the Allies, by their repeated promises of territorial compensation to Greece, had assumed distinct moral obligations to Athens; yet, as he explained to the Imperial Conference in London on 22 June, the Kemalists had created a body of national sentiment and military strength which appealed to the eviction of the Greeks from Smyrna as the basis of national unity.[4]   There was no peace for Kemal as long as Greek control existed in the city.   By autumn moreover the strain of the fighting was being felt in Athens; Greece was maintaining 200,000 troops in Asia Minor at a cost of £250,000 a week.   In his search to alleviate the strain, the ill-fated Greek Prime Minister, Gounaris, determined to visit London, accompanied by his Foreign Minister, Baltazzis, in order to impress the British Government with the consequences of the Greeks having to retire for want of supplies.[5]

The Gounaris visit was seized upon by Curzon as an opportunity to press for modifications of the Treaty of Sèvres to satisfy the Kemalists.   First he secured Cabinet approval for a meeting of the British, French and Italian Foreign Ministers in mid-January 1922 to discuss revision of the Sèvres Treaty.[6]

---

[1] Ronaldshay, *op. cit.*, III, pp. 277–8.

[2] H. H. Cumming, *Franco-British Rivalry in the Post-War Near East*, London, 1938, p. 137.

[3] W. S. Churchill, *The aftermath*, p. 395.

[4] Ronaldshay, *op. cit.*, p. 278.

[5] Gounaris was executed in Athens on 28 November.

[6] CAB 23/27. 93 (21), Appendix.

This plan was however given no chance to work. Instead the Cannes Conference of the Supreme Council took place in January. Here Lloyd George offered Briand the Treaty of Guarantee which the French had been pressing upon Britain for so long, together with an undertaking to prevail upon the Greeks to withdraw from Smyrna, failing which they would lose all British support. In return the French were asked to stand at Britain's side in presenting a revised Treaty of Sèvres to the Turks. For a moment the omens were set fair for Briand's acceptance. But the accumulated dislike in France towards the Prime Minister for the opposition the French had endured at his hands since November 1918 at every point of the compass was suddenly discharged in their reaction to a press photograph of a game of golf at Cannes, in which Lloyd George was seen acting the teacher and Briand the fool. Briand fell from power. His successor, the unbending Poincaré, when visited by Curzon in Paris on 16 January, was in no hurry to see the Turkish imbroglio settled. He said he would reply to Curzon's proposals, only later and in writing.[1] It was not until 22 March that an Allied meeting could be collected together in Paris.

The conclusions of the discussion were that Greek forces should retire from Anatolia under Allied military supervision, that a new code for the protection of minorities in Turkey should be drawn up, its execution being entrusted to the League of Nations; the League should be asked to co-operate in finding a solution to the Armenian question consistent with Armenian aspirations for a national home; the shores of the Straits were to be dimilitarised and the Gallipoli peninsula as far as Rodosto on the Sea of Marmara occupied by Allied forces; and an international commission was to be created to supervise the Straits. Constantinople would remain Turkish but encircled by a demilitarised zone of considerable depth while Eastern Thrace was to be Greek. Military service in Turkey was to be on a voluntary basis and strictly limited. The Capitulations were to remain in a revised form. These recommendations were accepted by the Greek Government, although doubt was expressed whether they could be enforced against Greek public opinion. This question, however, was never put to the test since the proposal for a truce on this basis was rejected by Ankara on the ground that, before any armistice came into effect, the Greek evacuation of Asia Minor should be completed, the Nationalists suggesting four months for this operation. The British Prime Minister, supported by the House of Commons, agreed with the Greeks that to accept such terms meant giving

---

[1] Ronaldshay, *op. cit.*, III, pp. 281–3; CAB 23/29. 2 (22).

up the Greek population of western Anatolia to massacre if Greek troops dwindled week by week before the cease-fire was actually effective. 'The Greeks,' Lloyd George said, 'could not retire and leave 500,000 of their nationals to the mercy of the Turks without guarantees against a recurrence of the Pontus massacres.'[1]

Outraged by a French suggestion in July that the Allies should not make negotiations on the basis of the Paris conclusions dependent upon Turkish consent to an armistice, King Constantine determined to play for the highest stakes; he withdrew two of his divisions from the Smyrna region and disembarked them at Rodosto on the Sea of Marmara with the object of seizing Constantinople from under the noses of the Allies. This move had two far-reaching consequences, separate but often confused. The first was Kemal's decision to seize his opportunity and strike at the denuded Greek position at Smyrna on 18 August. Within little more than a week the Greeks were in flight, and in early September scenes of destruction were enacted in the city unexampled even in Turkish history. The second consequence of the Greek king's decision was the announcement by the Allies, which they had no option but to make, that they would oppose the seizure of Constantinople by force. Lloyd George was moved by this statement, whether through loyalty to the Greeks in their moment of crisis or through incautiousness, to make a speech in the House of Commons on 4 August which was so heartening to Athens that portions of it were published by the Greek High Command as an Order of the Day.

There are even suggestions [the Prime Minister said], not altogether without foundation, that the Kemalist forces are being re-equipped from Europe. The Greeks, under other conditions, would have been entitled to blockade the coast of Asia Minor. Had it been any other belligerent, they would have been entitled to search ships, and to prevent arms going to the Kemalists. They are not allowed to do that . . . on the contrary, one of the unfairnesses of the situation is that they are driven, by the position we occupy there, into not giving a fair field and no favour to fight the issue out. Peace the Kemalists will not have, because they say we will not give them satisfactory armistice terms; but we are not allowing the Greeks to wage the war with their full strength. We cannot allow that sort of thing to go on indefinitely.[2]

[1] 157 H.C. Deb. 5s. Cols. 2001–2 (4 August 1922).
[2] *Ibid.*, Col. 2004.

The speech has been variously interpreted as due to Lloyd George's 'evil genius'[1] or to his sense of fair play as between Greeks and Turks.[2]   In any event it probably came too late to provoke the Turkish offensive, launched fourteen days later and probably in preparation at the time when the speech was made.   But it certainly served to publicise the rift in Allied attitudes through which the diplomatic pressure of the Kemalists poured.   The French were unprepared to back the Greek venture.   So were the Italians.   Although the Opposition at Westminster applauded the Prime Minister's declaration, the seizure of Constantinople by the Greeks, at which Lloyd George seemed to be conniving, could only be tolerated if the Allies had agreed to abandon entirely their responsibility for peace with Turkey.   The Prime Minister acknowledged this fact in another passage of the same speech.   'They were our troops,' he said, 'who overthrew the Turks, and therefore the responsibility for the establishment of peace in Turkey must be our responsibility.   We cannot abrogate the predominance which has been made by the sacrifice of our own people.'[3]

During the Parliamentary recess the Prime Minister's allusion to the Allies' responsibility was put to the test.   Flushed with their triumph at Smyrna, Kemal's troops swept up to the Straits, while excited reports reached the Cabinet that it was their object, not merely to send the Greeks packing from Asia Minor, but to liberate all former Turkish territory, Thrace, Gallipoli and the old capital itself, from Allied control.   On 15 September a Cabinet meeting decided to inform the Dominions of the state affairs had reached, to strengthen the single British battalion at Chanak, which stood on the shores of the Dardanelles well inside the neutral zone, and to use all military and naval force available in the area to defend this zone against Kemalist incursions.   When the meeting was over, Curzon, believing the situation was well in hand and assuming from Poincaré's telegram of the 14th that the Cabinet had full support from France, retired to his house at Hackwood.   The position in London was left in less restrained hands.   On the following day, Saturday, 16 September, Churchill, who had consistently opposed the Prime Minister's Greek policy, nevertheless wished to reaffirm the Allied position at the Straits:

I found myself in this business [he wrote afterwards] with a small group of resolute men: the Prime Minister, Lord Balfour, Mr. Austen Chamberlain, Lord Birkenhead, Sir

[1] Ronaldshay, op. cit., III, p. 298.
[2] Nicolson, op. cit., p. 270.
[3] 157 H.C. Deb. 5s. Col. 2002.

Laming Worthington-Evans. .... We made common cause. The Government might break up and we might be relieved of our burden. The nation might not support us: they could find others to advise them. The Press might howl, the Allies might bolt. We intended to force the Turk to a negotiated peace before he should set foot in Europe.[1]

From this conclave issued a *communiqué*, drafted in characteristic style by Churchill. It set out the position, enlarged on the dangers of a Turkish incursion into Europe which would have nullified the effects of the war, and called on the Allies for support. Curzon, who read the statement in a Sunday newspaper, denounced it as a 'flamboyant manifesto'. He said it would, forthwith and fatally, alienate France and Italy.[2] But the fault lay not in the *communiqué's* tone but in its timing. It was immediately published and read in the capitals of the Dominions before the British appeal to them for support, which the Cabinet had drafted the previous day and to which the text of the *communiqué* referred, had had time to be deciphered. It was this, together with the unwillingness of Canada in particular to be involved in the Near East, which made the Chanak crisis a classic episode in the history of the independence of the Dominions from British foreign policy.[3] Curzon had also correctly gauged French reactions. After expostulating in the Cabinet on Monday, 18 September, against what he called the alarmist tone of the *communiqué*, Curzon crossed to France and was met with the news that on the previous day Poincaré had given orders for the withdrawal of the French contingent which had been moved to Chanak to support the small British force there. Poincaré made clear in his talk with Curzon on 20 September that he was unwilling to risk French lives merely in order to further Lloyd George's Turkish policy. From that position he could not be moved. The sole agreement to be reached with the French concerned the terms of a proposed armistice to be sent to Kemal. This invitation to armistice talks at Mudania was sent to Ankara on the evening of the same day, 23 September.[4]

There can be no doubt that the Cabinet in London would have committed all the force they could muster to repel a Kemalist attack had one been launched. 'It was not a bluff,' wrote Lloyd George many years later. 'I certainly meant to fight and I was certain we should win.'[5] The British garrison,

[1] W. S. Churchill, *The aftermath*, pp. 423–4.
[2] Ronaldshay, *op. cit.*, III, p. 302.
[3] Gwendolen Carter, *The British Commonwealth and International Security*, pp. 84–9.
[4] CAB 21/241. File No. 18/J/130.   [5] *The Truth*, II, p. 1350.

though slender, was merely a shield force and, since British ships held the maritime approaches to the Straits from the Aegean, could soon have been strengthened. The Turkish forces, even with the estimated 80,000 men released from Cilicia by the Franklin-Bouillon Agreement of the previous October, were in all respects inferior to such British troops as could have been assembled within a few days. At the same time, what the consequences of an open war between Britain and the new Turkey could be no one could tell. Opinion in Britain would probably have soon rallied round the government had war broken out. In letters to *The Times* and *Daily Express* on 7 October, a day spent by Curzon in Paris attempting to persuade Poincaré that Britain was deadly serious, the Conservative leader, Bonar Law, attacked the meddlesome policy which he considered had brought about the Chanak crisis; but he left no doubt that the challenge would be met resolutely whatever the government in office. 'When the Greek forces were annihilated in Asia Minor and driven into the sea at Smyrna,' he wrote, 'it seems to me certain that, unless a decisive warning had been issued, the Turks, flushed with victory, would have attempted to enter Constantinople and cross into Thrace.'[1] But whether British opinion at large, four years after the ending of Armageddon in Europe, would have readily taken up arms against the Turks in order to keep Thrace in Greek hands is another question.

The situation required strong nerve. The Turks demanded that they should be allowed to occupy Eastern Thrace; they were supported in this by the French. Only hard bargaining between Curzon and Poincaré in Paris on 6 and 7 October broke this front. At last, in the early hours of 7 October, Poincaré agreed to a formula under which the Greeks would retire to the line of the Maritza and Eastern Thrace would be occupied by the Allies for one month pending its final restoration to Turkey. This understanding provided the basis for the Convention of Mudania, signed by the Turks on 11 October.[2] The Franco-Turkish axis had, for the present, been broken, but not so completely as to dissipate the mutual Anglo-French suspicions which accompanied all the shifts and changes of the subsequent peacemaking.

Before a conference to negotiate the final terms of a settlement with Turkey could meet, the Lloyd George Coalition had fallen. At a celebrated meeting at the Carlton Club on Thursday, 19 October, Bonar Law and Stanley Baldwin led a

---

[1] Robert Blake, *The Unknown Prime Minister*, London, 1955, p. 447.
[2] Ronaldshay, *op. cit.*, III, pp. 310–11.

majority of Conservatives in the decision to break with the Prime Minister. The latter handed in his resignation on the same day and a wholly Conservative administration was formed with Bonar Law as Prime Minister, which was confirmed at a General Election on 15 November. Curzon, after playing a somewhat ambiguous role in the comings and goings among Unionist leaders preceding the decisive meeting on the 19th, remained in office and carried on as Foreign Secretary in the new régime, the 'Cabinet of the Second Eleven'. It was the combination of Irish and domestic questions which ruined the Coalition, but the Near Eastern crisis played its part. The traditional Tory respect for the Turks was one factor. More important, the Conservative rebels against Lloyd George correctly appraised the mood of weariness which had spread through the country. This was the theme dominating the Conservative manifesto at the General Election, bringing relief after the wide-ranging diplomacy of Britain's wartime leader. 'The crying need of the nation at the moment,' it ran, 'is that we should have tranquillity and stability both at home and abroad so that free scope should be given to the initiative and enterprise of our citizens, for it is in that way far more than by any action of the Government that we can hope to recover from the economic and social results of the war.'[1] Conservatives thus renounced the imperialistic adventures of the Liberal statesman. If the ensuing Treaty of Lausanne, which closed the chapter, was for France a 'peace of lassitude',[2] it was perhaps even more so for Britain.

IV

The peace conference at Lausanne formally opened on 20 November 1922. The three main achievements of the chief British delegate, Curzon, concerned the régime of the Straits, the minorities question and Mosul. With the exception of the first, these were qualified successes, especially in regard to minorities. Nevertheless, against the background of September, they were remarkable. Owing to Curzon's work in isolating the Turks from the Bolsheviks, the Soviet proposal on the Straits found no support; it would have closed the Straits to foreign warships and permitted Turkey to militarise them. This formula was vigorously opposed by the Rumanian delegation on behalf of the Little Entente, the members of which would have been left alone in the Black Sea to face Soviet military power had the Soviet proposal been adopted. The British counter-proposal derived from the principle that never

[1] Blake, *op. cit.*, p. 466.   [2] Cumming, *op. cit.*, p. 187.

again should Turkey be able to bar the Straits against Allied naval power or interfere with Allied communications through the eastern Mediterranean. Its essence was that merchant ships should enjoy freedom of transit in peace, and in war if flying under a neutral flag and if Turkey was a belligerent; that naval vessels should enjoy freedom of transit in peacetime, except that their stay in the Straits should be limited in duration and their number at any one time restricted to the size of the total forces of any one Black Sea naval Power; that warships should enjoy the same freedom in war as in peace if Turkey were neutral, but that if she were a belligerent freedom of transit should exist only for neutral warships; and that zones on both shores of the Straits should be demilitarised and a Mixed Commission, possibly under Turkish chairmanship, should guarantee passage and supervise technical services. The Turks had committed themselves by the National Pact to accept any solution for the Straits which the Conference approved; they therefore accepted the British proposal on condition that the Straits territory received an international guarantee. When the Conference resumed in April, however, they substituted for this proviso the abolition of the Capitulations, which the Conference accepted. In effect this meant that the British Navy gained at Lausanne what foreign, especially French, businessmen lost.

On the second question, that of the minority peoples, it was abundantly clear that the old dream of an independent Armenia, an autonomous Kurdistan, and a self-governing Smyrna, had now to be abandoned. There was no point in struggling further against the National Pact. The utmost to be secured was the rejection of a proposal that the Turks should simply verbally undertake to respect the rights of the Greeks, the Armenians, Nestorians, Assyrian Christians, Jews and other non-Turkish peoples. At least Turkey agreed to join the League of Nations (thus incidentally isolating herself even further from the Bolsheviks), a step intended to bring her minorities under the surveillance of that organisation. The idea of a permanent League Commission in Constantinople with power to report on Turkish treatment of the minorities, however, was more than the Kemalist heirs of the Sultan could endure.

But it was on the third issue, that of the future of the *vilayet* of Mosul, that Curzon fought hardest, his main concern being with the oil resources of the area, the strategical disadvantage to Britain's position in Iraq if Mosul remained in Turkish hands, and the possible loss of face if the district were ceded. The struggle began with an agreement to differ over the legal position, since the Turks had never accepted, and could not be persuaded to accept, either the Sykes–Picot Agreement of 1916, which purported to assign Mosul to the French sphere, nor the revision of that agreement effected in December 1918, when the French agreed to recognise it as part of the British mandate for Mesopotamia.[1] Curzon then had little difficulty in establishing the folly of Ismet Pasha's suggestion for holding a plebiscite in the area, with its population of drifting nomads. He was, however, unable to impose his own proposal to refer the question to the League Council. Under a compromise reached on 4 February, twelve months of Anglo-Turkish negotiations on the subject were provided for. If these failed, the British plan for submitting the dispute to the League would come into effect. This formula, with the twelve-month period reduced to one of nine months, was accepted at the resumed Conference on 26 June and written into the text of the Lausanne Treaty. The question was not finally resolved until 1926. The Anglo-Turkish talks were duly held; there was discussion in the League Council and a decision by the Permanent Court. Finally a treaty concluded by Britain and Turkey on 5 June 1926 recognised Mosul as lying within the borders of Iraq. The eventual Turko-Iraqi frontier, as it stands today, is practically identical with that proposed by Curzon at the Lausanne Conference.[2]

These were solid achievements, and the British delegation ran risks to secure them. But on the question of the future geographical shape of Turkey the Kemalists frustrated all Allied plans for partitioning Anatolia. The peninsula was freed from enclaves of Greek and Italian occupation or spheres of influence; the Straits, though demilitarised, were assured to Turkish sovereignty. Constantinople remained in Turkish hands, as did Gallipoli. At the Conference Ismet Pasha fought hard on behalf of a plebiscite in Western Thrace, which had been ceded to Bulgaria after the Balkan Wars of 1912 and 1913 and which came into Allied hands by the Treaty of Neuilly of 27 November 1919.[3] In this he was unsuccessful, but Eastern Thrace, which had been handed to Greece by the Sèvres Treaty of 1920, was returned to Turkey. The European frontier of Turkey, with a demilitarised zone on either side, now ran, as in 1914, along the Maritza River, then followed the old boundary to the Black Sea, leaving Adrianople within Turkey. Only the Demotika area, which in 1915 Turkey was compelled

---

[1] See above, p. 10.   [2] Nicolson, *op. cit.*, *p.* 340, n. 1.
[3] See Ismet Pasha's statement on 23 November 1922: Turkey No. 1 (1923), Lausanne Conference on Near Eastern Affairs, 1922–3, Cmd. 1814 (1923), pp. 41–8.

by Germany to cede to Bulgaria, along with Karagatch, was lost. Thus, territorially the National Pact was fulfilled and the nightmare of the secession of Armenia, Smyrna, Kurdistan, Adalia, Cilicia, ended. Imbros and Tenedos, guarding the mouth of the Straits and awarded to Greece at Sèvres, were restored to Turkey, and these islands, together with those confirmed to Greece, that is, Mitylene, Chios, Samos and Nikaria, were to be demilitarised.

The Conference was broken off on 4 February, when for all practical purposes the principal British objects had been attained. The French delegate, Bompard, had made a final effort to persuade Ismet Pasha to accept the economic and judicial proposals of the Allies as integral parts of the draft treaty. In doing so he as much as admitted that the policy of encouraging the Turks in their unwillingness to sign was not always to France's advantage. Bompard's efforts failed, however, and the Conference adjourned. When the resumption took place at Lausanne on 23 April agreement had already been reached in principle on the abolition of the Capitulations, as required by the National Pact of 1920. The only question was that of the form of judicial protection for foreigners in Turkey. The Allies suggested a panel of foreign counsellors to advise the Turks on their legal system and in some cases actually to sit in Turkish courts. This was rejected as inconsistent with Turkish sovereignty. The most that the Turks would agree to was the appointment of a number of foreign jurists to serve for a period of not more than five years in the Turkish Ministry of Justice, for the purpose of advising on legislation and hearing complaints from resident foreigners; they were to have no part in the administration of Turkish law. This was the sole remnant of foreign legal control which remained after the passing of the régime of the Capitulations.[1] In much the same way, the old machinery of a foreign-dominated Council for ensuring the payment of the Ottoman public debt was swept away. Henceforward Turkey was to have charge of the administration of her own revenues without external interference. The residue of the Ottoman debt was distributed between Turkey herself and the successor states of the old empire. The former Council, in effect the agency for the economic government of Turkey from the outside, was now to hold its sessions in Paris. Turkey thus re-entered into the enjoyment of her sovereign financial rights.[2]

[1] H. N. Howard, *The Partition of Turkey*, p. 307.
[2] Treaty Series No. 16 (1923). Treaty of Peace with Turkey, Cmd. 1929 (1923), pp. 35–45.

Judgment on the settlement varied. The first phase at Lausanne was described in one French newspaper as 'le triomphe de Lord Curzon' and in an English newspaper as the 'failure of Lord Curzon'.[1] The completed Treaty evoked similar conflicting judgments. Churchill called it a 'peace of mutual respect', Lloyd George a 'rout'.[2] The fact was that Turkey under the Kemalist revolution had been transformed into a compact, proud national state, in no mood for a peace which gratified the economic imperialism of the Allies. As Ronald McNeill, the Under-Secretary of State at the Foreign Office, said in the House of Commons during an adjournment debate on 2 August 1923, 'we were no longer in a position at Lausanne to dictate peace. We had to negotiate a peace with the Turks on an equal footing, discussing every clause and line in the same way as we discuss Bills in this House.'[3] As against a united, unyielding Turkey the Allied front, strained by the emergence of the new Arab states and the Ruhr crisis in Europe, crumbled at points where it should have been firm. In the words of Joseph Grew, the American observer, 'instead of pooling their interests for the greater good of the greater number, each Power went into the Conference with its own individual interests paramount to any other consideration, each suspicious of his neighbour, and none willing to adopt a comprehensive plan and to stick to it through thick and thin'.[4] Yet these very conditions contained the seeds of permanence in the settlement. Simply because the Lausanne Treaty was signed when the enemy had recovered his strength and the war-welded solidarity of the Allies was dissipated, the agreement proved more enduring than any other of the peace settlements.

V

The handling of British foreign policy throughout the many phases of the Near Eastern settlement is easy to criticise, as for instance the attempt to enforce an old-fashioned scheme of partition on an Asian state as it passed through the rejuvenation effected by modern nationalism. But the difficulties facing Britain should not be ignored. For neither Britain nor France was the Near East the major theatre of diplomacy at this time. It served rather as the receptacle for the effects of the greater Anglo-French struggle concerning the implementation of the Versailles Treaty in Europe. At the same time there were

[1] Nicolson, p. 349.
[2] *The aftermath*, p. 437; *The Truth*, II, p. 1361.
[3] 167 H.C. Deb. 5s. Col. 1847.
[4] Joseph C. Grew, *Turbulent Era*, I, p. 570.

distracting domestic questions, such as the Irish Treaty negotiations, the unemployment problem, the increasing discomfort of
the Conservatives with their position in the Coalition.   There
were the tensions between the Foreign Office, on one side, and
the India Office and War Office, on the other, with the Prime
Minister on occasion flitting between the two.   Nor did the
curious relation between Lloyd George and Curzon make for
coherence or firmness in foreign policy.   The Prime Minister
dreamed his dreams of a revived Near East, mixing progressive
Liberalism with blindness to Asian sentiment.   From time to
time he would sweep into the fray with devastating effect,
leaving the Foreign Secretary to tidy up afterwards.   Curzon
had his mastery of the history, geography and psychology of the
East, but this was backed by little understanding of the revolutionary effect of Western ideas on political thought in those
regions.   Even when he saw further than his Cabinet colleagues (and more often than not he did), his native self-mis-
trust would, at decisive moments, drive him to echo their views.
Curzon never understood when he should resign and was unable to employ at critical junctures the threat of resignation.
Added to all this was the wavering, mistrustful attitude of
France, the unwillingness of the United States to do more
(except in the matter of oil concessions) than exhort from afar,
the unsteady politics of Greece, the wild, eloquent casuistry of
the Armenians, the temptations afforded to Britain by Arab
flattery.   There were many reasons, including the devastating
fates moving in the history of the Levantine world, why British
policy at this period was neither very consistent nor very wise.
    Yet, despite the retreat represented by Lausanne, British
diplomacy in the area suffered little permanent damage.   The
Kemalist revolution neither petered out, nor did it turn into
an aggressive military dictatorship.   Instead it made of Turkey
a stable, reformed but essentially conservative state.   There was
no revanchism, no implacable hatred of the peacemakers.
British ships could come and go in the Levant and through the
Straits without hindrance from Ankara.   The British position
in Egypt, in Cyprus, in Palestine and the Arab mandates was
not complicated by Turkish irredentism.   The book of Pan-
Turkism was closed.   British relations with France, too, settled down after Lausanne; at least they were freed from the
angry collisions and confrontations of the years immediately
following the Mudros armistice. With France's southern
neighbour, Italy, British relations were easily re-shaped after
the coming of the Mussolini régime; Sonnino's visions of an
Italian Anatolia were soon forgotten.   The same was true for

Anglo-Greek relations, the loss of Eastern Thrace and Smyrna leaving no deep scar. The Armenian and Kurdish secessionists were left to nourish thoughts of perfidious Albion, but, in the harsh world of politics, this could be of little real consequence. In any event Kemal himself violently broke with the Ottoman tradition of mistreating the minorities. What Allied supervision could never have effected was freely conceded in the declaration on minorities drawn up and signed on behalf of the new régime in Turkey by Ismet Pasha on 24 July 1923.

CHAPTER VII

ENFORCEMENT OF THE TREATY

I

The dominant factor in the European situation after the 1919 Peace Conference was the French conviction, strongest among ultra-nationalists but affecting opinion of every shade, of having been betrayed by their allies and hence of the necessity to reinsure against future German aggression by forceful action. Under pressure from Britain, supported by the United States, Clemenceau had abandoned the demand for a separate German Rhineland during the peace negotiations; for this he earned, from Foch, the terrible hostility of that symbol of French resistance, and, from the Allies, an agreement to a fifteen-year occupation of the western Rhineland, together with the Rhine bridgeheads, and the promise of British and American assistance in the event of unprovoked German aggression. In French eyes neither Allied offer was fitting compensation. By the time the military occupation had ended a new generation would have grown up in Germany which would have either forgotten the 1918 defeat or been instructed that it was not irreversible. Moreover, the paper character of the British and American guarantees was made brutally clear by the refusal of the United States Senate to co-operate further with the Entente in enforcing the treaties. In November 1919 the Senate passed a resolution reserving the American position on Article X of the League Covenant; Lord Curzon at the Foreign Office observed that this seemed to rule out ratification of the American guarantee to France, and hence the British obligation, which was conditional upon it, too.[1] This became an accomplished fact in the following March when the Versailles Treaty received its *coup de grâce* in the Senate.

Undisguised relief was expressed in Britain at the American withdrawal from the guarantee. Britain, Curzon told the Belgian Ambassador in London in September 1919, had never been enthusiastic about the guarantee; the government could not regard it as warranted by the European situation.[2] In France, too, relief was felt at the American action though for a different reason. The field was now considered free of 'Wilsonian obstacles'; the time had arrived for France to make

[1] *D.B.F.P.*, First Series, V, p. 799.   [2] *Ibid.*, p. 490.

the most of her alliance with England.[1] During December 1919 French pressure in London for the more effective coercion of Germany built up. While Lloyd George was demanding the fixing of a definite sum for German reparations so as to restore Germany's credit in the world money markets, the French were grappling with the task of assessing the damage inflicted in their north-eastern departments. Their most immediate difficulty, however, was the coal shortage. It was estimated in Paris that even with the Saar production added to her own output the destruction of mines in the Pas de Calais area and the decimation of miners' ranks during the war had reduced France's coal supplies from an annual figure of 40 million tons in 1913 to some 22 million tons in 1920. In anticipation of this decline provision had been made in the treaty for the delivery by Germany of annual amounts of coal to France, Belgium and Italy. In the French case the coal deliveries were to consist of 7 million tons a year for ten years and in addition, for a period not exceeding ten years, annual amounts equal to the difference between the pre-war and the postwar output of coal from the Nord and Pas de Calais mines.[2] These deliveries were hard to exact from Germany and the French concluded that German ill-will was the only explanation.

Britain not merely had nothing to gain from tightening the screw on Germany; she stood to lose from deliveries of German coal at pithead prices in inflated German currency. The British coal industry had enough competitors in the world as it was. Besides, the government were not satisfied that the failure in coal deliveries was Germany's fault. All coal production, Lloyd George argued, had been affected by the war and the German miner was not encouraged by food, housing and clothing shortages to produce more. The British Chargé d'Affaires in Berlin, Lord Kilmarnock, supported this view when he wrote to Curzon in January 1920 that:

> As the price of defeat and in expiation of their past crimes, the German people may be forced to make bricks without straw—they cannot make them without clay. If my judgment is correct, we have before us now the spectacle of a people beaten in war, torn by revolution, physically exhausted, suffering from privation and nervous strain, dependent, sometimes almost despairingly, but still capable of an effort and on the whole willing to make that effort if it sees the slightest chance of success.

[1] *D.B.F.P.*, First Series, V, p. 918.   [2] *Ibid.*, pp. 823–4.

The question, Kilmarnock concluded, was whether the Allies could do anything to encourage the German people to think that their efforts would not be disappointed. The dispatch was favourably minuted by Lord Hardinge at the Foreign Office and initialled by Curzon.[1]

British Ministers feared a Communist revolt in Germany or some understanding between the pariah nations, Germany and Russia, if the Versailles yoke was pressed too hard. In a forceful memorandum circulated to the Cabinet in February 1920 the General Staff urged that concessions be made to Berlin to strengthen the government's position against Bolshevism. They proposed the retention of a German army of up to 200,000 men throughout 1920, whereas the Supreme Council had decided in August 1919 that the following April should be the last date for reducing the Reichswehr to the 100,000 men prescribed by the treaty; the *Sicherheitspolizei* (Security Police) should be maintained at a maximum strength of 60,000 men for internal order and control of the frontiers; Germany should be given a foreign loan to help her industry to its feet and German war criminals should be handed over to German or neutral courts so as to avoid forcing on German officers the humiliation of having to hand over their colleagues to the Allies.[2] Alarming news also reached London that an agreement had been signed by Berlin with the Russian Bolsheviks, at first merely for the exchange of prisoners of war, but subsequently for the dispatch to Russia of German technicians and chemists to work in Soviet laboratories. Lord Kilmarnock was told by a member of the British military mission in Berlin that the factor driving Germany into the arms of Russia was the Allies' demand for the extradition of German war criminals.[3]

But the incident which virtually destroyed the Allied front and opened a breach in Anglo-French relations not effectively closed until the Locarno agreements was the Kapp putsch in Germany, carried out in the night of 12–13 March 1920, and the resulting Spartacist uprising in the Ruhr in protest against the return of militarism to Germany. Rumour had it in Germany that Kilmarnock was implicated in the putsch; this he strenuously denied by recalling the four or five occasions on which he had previously warned the German Government of the dangers of a *coup* by the Right. Nevertheless, the Chargé d'Affaires' first accounts of the *coup* undoubtedly spoke as though Kapp, as pretended Chancellor, and General von Lutt-

[1] *D.B.F.P.*, First Series, IX, pp. 25–8.
[2] *Ibid.*, pp. 40–6.   [3] *Ibid.*, pp. 81–3.

witz, as pretended Minister of Defence, were gradually con- solidating their position. This might have satisfied the British Government's desire to have a strong régime in Berlin to seal off the country from penetration by the Left. But in the event the Kapp putsch failed to find support in the rest of Germany. The country west of the Elbe was uniformly hostile and in the Ruhr a quasi-Soviet authority was set up, with an army esti- mated at 40,000 men, to take up the struggle against Kapp should he show signs of succeeding. South Germany was almost equally unsympathetic. The Kapp régime fell on 17 March and the Bauer Government, which had fled to Stuttgart, resumed an uncertain hold over the country. In the course of doing so it applied to the Allies for permission to send into the Ruhr, which had been neutralised by articles 42–4 of the treaty, forces up to a limit of 200,000 men to suppress the workers' régime. This request presented the Entente with its greatest challenge before the Ruhr crisis of 1923.

The weakness of the Allied agencies of co-operation became at once clear. The Supreme Council, sitting in London, went one way, British influence predominating, while the Conference of Ambassadors in Paris to all intents surrendered to France. At the Ambassadors' Conference on 17 March, the day the Kapp régime fell, Millerand, acting as chairman, reported that the German Government had approached Nollet, of the French military mission in Berlin, for leave to send troops into the neutral zone to put down the anti-Kapp disturbances. Mil- lerand saw this request as a challenge to the whole Versailles system; he favoured an expedition into the Ruhr by the Allies to keep order.[1] This was opposed by Derby with the support of his Italian colleague, Count Longare, on the following day. Millerand appeared to accept this, but insisted, and persuaded the Conference to agree, that the German request be refused.[2] Since Derby was then informed that the decision was at vari- ance with British views expressed on the same day at the Su- preme Council (where Cambon had had no instructions from his own government), a strong argument broke out at the Ambassadors' Conference on 19 March. It was clear that Millerand was propelled by the formidable Foch, who saw an opportunity to achieve the subjugation of a Prime Minister which he had failed to accomplish with Clemenceau.

Beware! [Foch cried] you are in a very dangerous posi- tion and you must look at it closely. We are today faced

[1] *D.B.F.P.*, First Series, IX, pp. 158–60.
[2] *Ibid.*, pp. 170–80.

with the fact that German disarmament does not exist; that the German demobilisation does not exist. Are you going to remain in that position? . . . Let us consider the matter and see what measures are to be taken.[1]

In order to circumvent Derby Millerand resorted to a ruse. On 21 March he agreed at the Conference to let German troops enter the Ruhr but only if the area of Allied military occupation was extended, though not necessarily into the Ruhr.[2] However, he left Cambon in London uncertain how far he was insisting on this proviso. There was therefore alarm in London at the end of the month when reports appeared in the French Press that Millerand had seen the German Chargé d'Affaires in Paris and told him that if further German troops entered the Ruhr, Allied (some newspapers said French) forces would occupy Frankfurt and Darmstadt. Curzon at once saw Cambon, who knew nothing of the line his Prime Minister was taking, and remonstrated with him on French arrogance in speaking for the Allies as a whole.[3] But this did not prevent Millerand summoning Goppert, the head of the German Peace Conference delegation, on the following day and telling him that France agreed to the German action provided Germany consented to an Allied occupation of five more Rhineland towns if the Ruhr was not evacuated in two or three weeks. Then, after Millerand's permission for Germany to enter the Ruhr had been announced by the German Chancellor in the Reichstag, the French Prime Minister withdrew it again.[4] These convolutions were brutally terminated on 6 April, when French forces entered Darmstadt and Frankfurt in fulfilment of a design long cherished by extremist Parliamentary opinion in Paris.

Bonar Law, in the absence of Lloyd George, who was on his way to the Council's meeting at San Remo, explained to Cambon the dilemma in which Britain was placed: either she must dissociate herself from this measure, thus dealing Allied unity a heavy blow just as talks were about to open on the best means of securing from Germany assurances regarding fulfilment of the treaty, or she must be considered as approving the French action. All this was quite apart from the danger of incidents occuring in the newly occupied towns which might provide further incentives to political extremism in Germany.[5] Millerand showed little sign of contrition; on the contrary he was able to dictate terms to Britain, protesting that unless she

---

[1] *Ibid.*, p. 201.   [2] *Ibid.*, VII, pp. 214–15.
[3] *D.B.F.P.*, First Series, IX, pp. 276–8.   [4] *Ibid.*, p. 285.
[5] *Ibid.*, pp. 321–2; CAB 23/21. 18 (20).

accepted the wording of the statement he proposed to make in the Chamber of Deputies on 13 April he would not join Lloyd George at San Remo on 16 April. Since Lloyd George was most anxious to obtain French support at San Remo for his proposal for a direct approach to Germany, this was a threat of consequence. In Millerand's long statement in Parliament there was no suggestion of apology, merely an assurance that in future France would only act in accordance with the Allies. Bonar Law, in his own statement on the incident in the Commons, plainly wished to hush the matter up in the hope that a new course would be initiated at San Remo.

> As the House is aware [he said] a difference which His Majesty's Government greatly deplore has arisen between the British and French Governments, but the exchange of notes which has taken place between London and Paris justifies the belief that both Governments recognise more than ever the necessity of maintaining intimate and cordial agreement for the settlement of the grave questions confronting them in Germany and elsewhere. The approaching Conference of the heads of the Allied Governments will no doubt serve to confirm and consolidate a complete understanding between the Governments.[1]

For the moment Britain was satisfied with Millerand's promise to withdraw his forces as soon as the excess German troops above the 17,000 men which the Supreme Council had sanctioned for the neutral zone the previous August had left the Ruhr.

The talks at San Remo between 18 and 26 April 1920 were principally concerned with finalising the draft Turkish peace treaty to be signed at Sèvres.[2] Nevertheless they provided Lloyd George with an opportunity to expound his new policy towards Germany. The state of undeclared war in Europe could not go on for ever; the time had come for a new method. 'It was necessary,' Lloyd George said, 'to find out from the Germans what proposals they had for fulfilling their obligations. Germany should be made to state what she meant to do . . . [she] needed to be pulled together by the Allies.'[3] He was unimpressed by paper figures drawn up by the Reparation Commission, which did not face the question of how the German Government was to raise such sums of money or secure their transfer to the Allies. He preferred trying to get the

[1] 127 H.C. Deb. 5s. Col. 1382 (12 April 1920).
[2] See above, Chapter VI, p. 141.
[3] D.B.F.P., First Series, VIII, p. 193.

Germans to measure up to the facts and see what they were able to do in the circumstances.

He would like [he said] to invite the Germans to Paris and put to them a regular questionnaire in regard to reparations, disarmament, coal, etc., and press them on each point as to what they could do and demand explanations. He would insist on definite and clear promises of the fulfilment of their obligations. If they could not fulfil them the Allies would have to confer, but before any action was taken he would have to be in a position to show the British public that everything within reason had been done to avoid it. It was easier to enter Germany than to leave it.[1]

Millerand was not averse to this proposal, provided that any such conference was to be for the purpose of hearing explanations from the Germans, with a view to obtaining an 'integral execution' of the treaty, rather than for compromising with them. But he insisted that the Allies should concert together the demands they intended to make and agree in advance what they should do in the event that the German representatives refused. In the declaration issued to Germany at the close of the San Remo meeting the threat was therefore held out that if Germany continued her failure to carry out the treaty the Allies would, in a carefully negotiated phrase, 'take all measures, even to the extent, if necessary, of an occupation of German territory, which will have the effect of securing the execution of the treaty'. It was insisted, however, that the Allied Powers had no intention of annexing German territory. If Germany wished to avoid coercion, the statement ran, her leading Ministers should attend a meeting of Allied governments in order to present precise explanations and proposals concerning her failure to disarm, destroy totally her war materials, provide the agreed coal deliveries and fulfil her other obligations with respect to reparations and the cost of Allied occupation forces.[2] On Germany's reply to this offer would depend the Allies' attitude to the request from the German Minister of War on 20 April that Germany should for the time being be permitted to retain in the Reichswehr twice the number of men allowed by the treaty.

Lloyd George reported back to the House of Commons on the San Remo meetings with his usual optimism. The storm with France over the Ruhr incident had passed; it had been

[1] *D.B.F.P.*, First Series, VIII, p. 8.
[2] Protocols and Correspondence between the Supreme Council and the Conference of Ambassadors and the German Government and the German Peace Delegation between 10 January 1920 and 17 July 1920, Cmd. 1325 (1921), p. 94.

merely a difference of opinion about policing the Ruhr and restoring order. He then stated his identity of view with France in a manner which left in doubt just what practical agreement there was; 'We made it quite clear that on questions of disarmament, reparations and such matters, we certainly would not merely discuss with them the best methods of enforcing them but would take any action which could be agreed upon by the Allies.' He went on to disclose the total differences between London and Paris on Germany's mental attitude towards the Versailles Treaty in saying that 'we know perfectly well that in her present condition [Germany] cannot pay. She cannot maintain life decently. We want to see that Germany really acknowledges her liability and is thinking about the best method of liquidating it.'[1] Only a few days before making this statement the Prime Minister had heard Millerand say at the San Remo Conference that the difference between himself and Lloyd George and Nitti was that the last two Allied leaders believed in the good faith of Germany and he did not.[2]

If Lloyd George really believed in German good faith his confidence was severely tested during the inter-Allied negotiations on a common position to be adopted at the meeting with the Germans. At a two-day meeting at Hythe on 15–16 May the Prime Minister expressed to Millerand his concern at the slow rate of German disarmament. It was agreed that in the longer interval now arranged before the Spa meeting (this was to have been on 25 May, but in view of the German national elections on 6 June it was deferred until 21 June) the French Government should prepare a list of the Allies' requirements on which Germany was defaulting, and that Britain should see and approve the document before it was forwarded to the German Government.[3] At a second meeting with Millerand at Hythe on 20 June Lloyd George complained about the 15,000 guns said to be still lying about in Germany. 'It was very important,' he said, having undergone one of his lightning changes of mood, 'to create the necessary atmosphere of alarm on the part of Germany in order to induce her to put forward reasonable proposals in regard to reparation and not such proposals as would not even form a basis of negotiations.'[4] The Prime Ministers decided that when they met at Boulogne on the next day, where Belgian, Italian and Japanese representatives would join them, the military advisers should be asked to draw up proposals for accelerating German disarmament.

At the first meeting of the two-day Allied conference at

---

[1] 128 H.C. Deb. 5s. Cols. 1462–6.   [2] *D.B.F.P.*, First Series, VIII, p. 17.
[3] *D.B.F.P.*, First Series, VIII, p. 258.   [4] *Ibid.*, p. 311.

Boulogne Lloyd George said that the time had come when the Germans 'must be made to hear the crack of the whip'.[1] Toughness was all the more necessary in view of the outcome of the national elections in Germany on 6 June.   Both Right and Left extremists had won decisive accretions of strength. The Majority Socialists had lost some 55 seats and the Democrats 30 seats to these sections.   Heavy gains were registered by the extremist Independent Socialists, the Nationalists and the Right-wing Deutsche Volkspartei.   It was evident that the Right would wield predominant influence in the Reichstag and would well be placed either to dictate to or render powerless any German delegation which went to Spa.   The British Rhineland Commissioner, Arnold Robertson, wrote to the Foreign Office on 9 June:

> I earnestly hope that His Majesty's Government will realise that it is not France but the British Empire which is the ultimate goal of Prussian ambition, now as before the war.   They feel that they can overrun France in a few weeks and then will come our turn.   That that is the basic thought which in the future, as in the present and in the past, will guide the policy of the Prussian Right, whether Deutsche Nationale or the less extreme Deutsche Volkspartei I have no doubt at all.   France and we must stick together![2]

The existing British mood thus enabled three strong notes to be sent to Germany as the outcome of the Boulogne meetings. The first was a peremptory demand that the German Army should be forthwith reduced from its present level of 200,000 men, a figure which should have been reached on 10 April and had only just been attained, to the figure of 100,000 demanded by the treaty; and that the *Sicherheitspolizei*, a distinctly paramilitary formation, should be disbanded within three months. The second note complained about German commercial policy, which was alleged to be discriminatory against Allied trade and thus contrary to the treaty.   The third rejected a German plea of 4 June that the government be allowed to retain an army of 200,000 men after the expiry date of 10 July on the ground that the Allies in their note to Germany from San Remo had appeared to leave the question open until the Spa Conference.[3]

But as July approached, the date of the Spa meeting having again been postponed until 5 July at Britain's request, little

[1] *Ibid.*, p. 357.
[2] *D.B.F.P.*, First Series, IX, pp. 538–40.
[3] Cmd. 1325, pp. 150–4.

sign of co-operativeness appeared from Germany. By the end of June the government had made no preparation for the conference. Kilmarnock wrote from Berlin a few days before the Spa talks began that the Germans would refuse all demands on the ground that they were impossible to fulfil.[1] When the long-awaited Spa Conference finally opened on 5 July it was at once clear that the Chancellor, Dr. Fehrenbach, his Foreign and Finance Ministers, Simons and Wirth, and General von Seeckt were in no mood for concessions. They flatly claimed that, owing to the political unrest in Germany and the presence in that country of 2 million rifles which the authorities were unable to trace, no date could be set for the reduction of the Reichswehr to the treaty figure of 100,000 men. They admitted that no arrests had yet been made of German war criminals, although the Allies had forwarded a list of 900 names in February which had been reduced to 45 in May, on the ground that inadequate charges had been made out to justify making arrests. An insolent speech by the coal magnate Stinnes held out no improvement in coal deliveries to the Allies so long as the miners were impoverished and uncertainty existed as to the Upper Silesian minefields. Lloyd George complained bitterly about the 'Teutonic obstinacy' shown by the German delegation and expressed alarm at the German Government's powerlessness to deal with the explosive situation created by the widespread possession by civilians of old army weapons. But he was quick to find reasons for letting the German delegates down lightly if only they would repudiate the awful Stinnes. This the Chancellor and Foreign Minister readily did, alleging that they had no knowledge of the tone he was going to adopt.

Lloyd George said the German Government could not be expected to do the impossible; he favoured requiring them to issue a proclamation ordering the surrender of arms by the civil population and fixing appropriate penalties. The reduction of the Reichswehr should be deferred until 1 January 1921. Millerand, at a private inter-Allied meeting, raised strong objection to this and insisted that an interim reduction to 150,000 men should be effected by 1 October and that, if the Allied commissions of control reported at any time before 1 January 1921 that the reduction of effectives and materials was not proceeding according to this schedule, the Allies should reserve the right to occupy further German territory, including the Ruhr. To this formula Lloyd George, after much hesitation, consented, provided that any Allied troops eventually sent to

[1] *D.B.F.P.*, First Series, IX, p. 573.

the Ruhr kept well away from the mining villages. He also agreed to an occupation of the Ruhr in the event that Germany failed to carry out the new agreement on coal deliveries which the German delegates were compelled to accept at Spa, since a Ruhr occupation had already been contemplated in the conclusions of the San Remo Conference. The new coal agreement stipulated that as from 1 August 1920 Germany should deliver two million tons of coal monthly to the Allies, to be credited to her reparation account, for a trial period of six months. This was twice the figure originally suggested by the Germans at Spa although the French pointed out that it was a mere 60 per cent of the figure decided in the treaty. A concession was made to Germany's difficulties, however, by an undertaking that the Ally which received the coal should pay Germany a premium of five gold marks per ton for the purchase of foodstuffs for the miners. The British Prime Minister also made clear that he would only agree to the sanction of the Ruhr occupation being included in the Spa protocols on conditions. The occupation must end as soon as any coal deficiencies were made good; all the Allies should participate in it; no negro troops should be included in the occupation forces; at all costs the occupation should keep clear of the towns and villages. That the Prime Minister did however accept the principle of the Ruhr occupation did not strengthen the British position in the Ruhr crisis of 1923.

Lloyd George, in a private interview with Dr. Simons, which incidentally infringed the rule that the Allied leaders should not discuss separately with the Germans, confided that the last thing Britain wanted was an occupation of the Ruhr; it would have deplorable consequences. He had always favoured a prosperous, integral Germany; but a military party existed in France and Britain was not without anti-German elements. It was vital for Germany to make the best of her circumstances, if only to prevent Millerand's fall. The interview led to the German delegation's acceptance of the three protocols of Spa, dealing with disarmament, coal deliveries and war criminals; the reparation issue as a whole was simply set aside.[1] But it could not but leave on the German leaders' minds the impression that, if the agreed sanction, the Ruhr occupation, ever had

[1] For the discussions at the Spa Conference see *D.B.F.P.*, First Series, VIII, Chapter VIII. The text of the Spa Protocols are published in Cmd. 1325 of 1921, pp. 171–3 and pp. 175–6. The Protocol on War Criminals provided that the Attorney-General of the Court at Leipzig, where it had been agreed that the trials should be held, should confer with the Attorney-General of England and the Ministers of Justice of the other Allied Powers on the preparation of the legal basis for the trials.

to be applied, Britain would find it difficult if not impossible to consent to it.

What Lloyd George wanted above all else in the relations of France and Germany was tranquillity. For him the punishment of Germany was not only undesirable as involving the risk of driving her into Russia's arms, but because only in extreme cases of German intransigence was it possible to defend it in the House of Commons. Thus he seized the opportunity in a speech on 21 July of assuring the House that the time of troubles with Germany was largely over. The German Government were making a real effort to pay the indemnity. The men he had met at Spa, especially Fehrenbach and Simons, had made up their minds to do their utmost to carry out the treaty.[1] Spa had made life possible for Germany while keeping the treaty as valid as on the day when it was signed. Pragmatic politics, Lloyd George felt, had been vindicated.

II

The ruin of Germany could never be a part of British policy. The sense of fair play, the European balance of power, economic logic were all against it; nor did the enforcement of the treaty, in British eyes, require it. British Ministers looked back to the Treaty of Frankfurt in 1871, the last great European peace treaty, in which they saw the origins of the war in 1914. Germany had taken Alsace-Lorraine from France. Britain did not wish to see France make a similar mistake. The only encouraging thing about the Frankfurt Treaty was that Prussia made her indemnity modest; she did not attempt to crush France in the act of exacting it; and France was allowed to reestablish her credit in the world money markets in order to pay it. In 1920 France was seen by Britain as pursuing two incompatible objects: the ruining and humbling of Germany and the fulfilment of the German debt. How was it possible to have golden eggs and roast goose at the same time?

The British talked of Germany as potentially rational while the French had an equally simple picture of the eternal enemy. Germany was neither; she was a chaos of conflicting forces, the more extreme of which drew the middle mass towards themselves. Alongside Fehrenbach, Simons and Wirth were unrepentant militarists like Ludendorff, still dreaming of a revived garrison state which would, however, avoid the Kaiser's mistake of being on the opposite side from Britain. In July 1920 Ludendorff proposed to Kilmarnock through his agent, Captain Rechberg, a fantastic scheme for an Anglo-French–

[1] 132 H.C. Deb. 5s. Cols. 487–96.

German alliance against Bolshevist Russia; Germany would provide an army of a million and a half men, to be munitioned by the Entente and under the command of Ludendorff and Hoffmann, the negotiator of Brest–Litovsk. In the meantime the Versailles Treaty would be conveniently suspended.[1] In August Ludendorff added further conditions to his 'offer'; the treaty should be scrapped, not merely suspended, and the left bank of the Rhine freed of occupation troops. This was Potsdam bombination too unreal to be reckoned with.

But the open defiance of the Allies by Bavaria, which armed and subsidised its *Einwohnerwehren*, the supposedly peaceful militia which the German leader at Spa had agreed to disband at once, was more serious. Shooting competitions organised in Bavaria by the militia were to all intents military festivals. At a competition held in Munich in September 1920, 70,000 *Einwohnerwehren* from all over the state attended, 'the flower of Bavarian manhood', and were addressed by the Bavarian Prime Minister, Herr von Kahr, who ended his speech by saying that they were a united people of brothers and would not separate 'whatever the danger and stress of the times'.[2] General Bingham, the British representative on the Allied military control commission, said that the majority of Bavarians regarded Berlin and the north as likely to turn Communist; they were determined to retain sufficient force to keep Communism out of Bavaria.[3] With Soviet armies in Poland threatening Germany's eastern frontiers and the marching and training of extreme nationalists and revolutionaries within the country, the ordinary German was hard put to find a middle ground from which he could support a government dedicated to producing a 'good Germany' for the Allies.

Lloyd George concluded that the political turmoil in Germany would only be aggravated by insistence on strict implementation of her obligations.[4] At Spa it had been decided to set aside the problem of fixing the total of German indemnity: this was to be examined, in the light of German capacity to pay, by an expert conference representing Belgium, Britain, France and Italy to meet at Geneva in August. This was what Lloyd George had always hankered after, imagining that experts were more likely to be moderate in their estimates than the highly political French members of the Reparation Commission. But the French sought to postpone the meeting of the expert committee in order that the issue might be prejudged by a prior verdict of the Reparation Commission, which was obliged by

[1] *D.B.F.P.*, First Series, X, pp. 277–8. [2] *Ibid.*, pp. 393–4.
[3] *Ibid.*, p. 465. [4] See CAB 23/23. 80 (20).

the treaty to report not later than 1 May 1921. Lloyd George complained bitterly about Millerand's prevarication on this score when he met the Italian Prime Minister privately at Lucerne on 22–23 August. He proposed that British and Italian financiers, together with Belgian, if they would join, should combine to exert their influence against France at the experts' meeting and thus impose their views. Lloyd George complained again, this time to Delacroix, when he met the Belgian Prime Minister in London in October 1920, receiving in return an assurance that Belgium would not follow France into the Ruhr, if, as Lloyd George expected, the expert committee issued a pessimistic report on German capacity to pay and the French tried to take matters into their own hands. Delacroix thought it unlikely that the French would march without Belgium.[1] At length, at an inter-Allied meeting at 10 Downing Street on 4 December the French consented that the expert meeting should assemble at Brussels on 13 December with German colleagues in attendance.

While thus preparing the ground against the French, Lloyd George also resorted to surreptitious diplomacy in order to bring home to the Germans that it was up to them to forestall a crisis by fulfilling the Spa contracts with respect to disarmament, war criminals and coal deliveries. At the Lucerne meeting with Giolitti in August he secured a promise of Italian co-operation in a secret approach to Berlin on these lines. The instrument of this manœuvre on the British side was Kilmarnock, who was asked by Curzon on 18 September to tell the German Government that the British and Italian governments would not approve further occupation of German territory unless they were convinced that it was required by the treaty, and that was mainly up to Germany.[2] Kilmarnock was not to inform his French colleague about this message; he was told that it was a 'friendly warning' to the Germans if they wished to avoid the sanctions threatened at Spa.

The warning was duly handed in but failed to produce effect. After the Brussels expert conference had met on 13 December Dr. Simons told the French that Germany would show more energy in the matter of disarmament if France was more accommodating in regard to reparations at Brussels. The French Ambassador in London, de Fleuriau, told Sir Eyre Crowe that this statement had produced a bad impression in France; it falsified Germany's plea that she was doing all she could to disarm.[3] Nor did Lloyd George's intrigue succeed

[1] *D.B.F.P.*, First Series, VIII, pp. 792–4.
[2] *D.B.F.P.*, First Series, X, p. 304.   [3] *Ibid.*, pp. 477–8.

against the French. At the expert meeting in Brussels, which was continued in Paris in January 1921, the French representative refused to accept the British proposal for fixing a sum to cover Germany's total liabilities. Britain contended that Germany's financial credit, on which her ability to meet her reparation debt ultimately depended, could not be restored until the full extent of her liabilities were known; whereas France objected to making any final estimate of German capacity to pay while the German economy had not yet fully recovered from the war. The French therefore proposed a provisional solution based on a scheme of German payments of 3 milliard gold marks for each of the succeeding five years. Since this scheme seemed to be acceptable to the German experts, who were troubled by the effects on opinion at home of the adoption of any conceivable total, the committee at length approved it on 18 January.[1]

But the British Prime Minister was not to be beaten. At an inter-Allied Ministerial conference in Paris at the end of January he rejected the experts' proposals as not constituting a final solution. It was not, he said, a question of fidelity to the treaty, but one of how the money was to be raised in Germany, and how it was to be transferred abroad. Before the war, he argued, Germany sold 10 milliard marks' worth of goods to the rest of the world, using the proceeds to pay for essential imports and raw materials. She still had to live in order to be able to pay her way and she must not ruin her trade competitors through developing an excessive trade surplus. 'She must pay her indemnity,' he said, 'in such a way as not to damage the industries of the Allied countries and it is a very difficult problem to find means for exacting an indemnity in a way which will not injure the industries, the essential industries, the vital industries of France, of Great Britain, of Italy and of Belgium.' Here was the permanent core of the British argument throughout the years of discussion on reparation. 'You are injuring your debtor and a debtor is a person you ought to cherish.' The slump of 1921 gave added power to the argument. It could not appeal to the French, who had little genuine interest in international trade and were in any case enjoying boom conditions. But the argument had force outside Europe. 'The British Ambassador from America, whom I met last night,' the Prime Minister ended, 'told me that America was convinced that the fact that there was no settlement of the indemnity question with Germany was having

[1] Report on the work of the Reparation Commission, H.M.S.O., London, 1923, p. 27; CAB 23/24. 3 (21).

a very injurious effect upon trade, commerce and industry throughout the world.'[1] In January 1921 this was a mere debating point, but its significance was growing.

After many days' discussion the Paris conference agreed to submit to Germany the following proposal for a schedule of payments:

1921–3   2 milliard gold marks per annum
1923–6   3 milliard gold marks per annum
1926–9   4 milliard gold marks per annum
1929–32 5 milliard gold marks per annum
1932–63 5 milliard gold marks per annum

Payments were thus to be extended over 42 years and Germany's total payment would be 226 milliard gold marks, as compared with the 269 milliard proposed at the Boulogne meeting of the Allies in June 1920. In addition, Germany was to pay the Allies 12 per cent of the value of her exports each year, thus relating the scale of her reparation payments to the ups and downs of her prosperity and the volume of international business in the world as a whole. From the German point of view, however, the fixing of a proportion of earnings from exports to go into the Allies' pockets meant that the harder the Germans worked the heavier the reparation yoke would be.

Partly for this reason and also because of the unanticipated size of the Paris annuities, the proposals provoked an instantaneous outburst in Germany, which boded ill for a meeting arranged with German Government leaders in London for 1–14 March. Lloyd George became so apprehensive that he gave a warning to Germany in the Debate on the Address on 18 February that her delegates must talk seriously when they came to London in a fortnight's time.

> It will be my first duty [he said] to insist that Germany shall carry out the essential parts of the treaty which I think at present she has failed to carry out. She has not taxed herself up to the limit of her capacity. She has not taxed herself up to the level of the Allies. . . . It is not that Germany is too poor to meet these demands. We shall not be convinced that she is until she has imposed upon her people charges which we are entitled to expect.[2]

But this did not prevent Dr. Simons, at the first session of the London meeting on 1 March, bluntly rejecting the proposals the Supreme Council had agreed at Paris. Instead he

[1] Lloyd George, *The Truth about Reparations and War Debts*, p. 50.
[2] 138 H.C. Deb. 5s. Col. 468.

suggested an interim solution which followed only the first five years of the Paris schedule; that is, Germany should pay 2 milliard gold marks (£100 million) for the first two years and 3 milliards for the next three (£150 million), with only the vaguest outline for the remaining 42 years. He assented to the 12 per cent levy on German exports embodied in the Paris proposals but only on two conditions: that the Allies should extend to Germany the most favoured nation treatment they had gained from her by article 264 of the Versailles Treaty, and that the Simons offer should in any case be voided if the plebiscite in Upper Silesia voted all or part of the territory to Poland.[1]

The British Prime Minister refused to listen to Simons' detailed exposition; the mere outline was enough. The Allies broke off the talks and went into conference among themselves on the measures to be applied to bring Germany into a more amenable mood. On 3 March the German delegation was summoned to hear a forceful indictment from Lloyd George of their bad faith in regard to their treaty obligations. He warned Germany that unless she adhered to the Paris proposals within four days, or made an equivalent offer, military and economic sanctions would be enforced against her. After this outburst negotiations continued for a time in a more business-like way, but the French had now warmed to the idea of clinching the reparation problem once and for all. They were as adamant in demanding the Paris schedule as the Germans were regretful in their protests of inability to fulfil it. With the inevitable breakdown of the talks the Allies resorted to the sanction of the occupation of Düsseldorf, Duisburg and Ruhrort. 'We do not consider,' said Lloyd George in the Commons on the eve of this reprisal, 'that £100 million rising to £150 million, plus 12 per cent of the exports, is something which is beyond the capacity of 55 million industrious people.'[2] Lloyd George's policy of attempting to bring France and Germany together on an agreed reparation settlement had clearly failed. It remained only to try to impose an Allied formula by force.

At an Allied conference in London from 29 April to 5 May consideration was given to the report of the Reparation Commission on Germany's total liability for the categories of damage specified in Chapter VIII of the treaty. The report had been issued on 27 April, four days before the final date set in the treaty for the completion of this part of the Commission's work, and fixed the capital liability at 132 milliard gold marks,

---

[1] Carl Bergmann, *The History of Reparations*, pp. 67–8.
[2] 139 H.C. Deb. 5s. Col. 133 (7 March 1921); CAB 23/24. 11 (21).

or £6,600 million.   Briefly, the terms of settlement, which came
to be known as the London Schedule of Payments, were as
follows: the total of 132 milliard marks, less any sums Germany
had to her credit in the reparation account, plus the Belgian
war debt, was split up into three parts, to be paid for by the
issue of three series of bonds.   'A' bonds, to the value of 12
milliard marks, were to be prepared and issued by 1 July 1921.
Germany was to pay 5 per cent interest and 1 per cent towards
amortisation on these.   'B' bonds, to the value of 38 milliard
marks, to be created and delivered by 1 November 1921, had
similar arrangements as to interest and sinking fund.   The
total of 'A' and 'B' bonds together was thus 50 milliard marks,
or approximately £2,500 million at the rate of exchange officially prevailing in May 1921.   This sum compared with the
30 milliards proposed as a total settlement by Dr. Simons at the
London conference in March, but was in fact almost precisely
the figure suggested by the German delegation at the Peace
Conference in 1919.   The service on these bonds was to be
borne by Germany through annual payments of 2 milliard
gold marks each, together with 26 per cent of the annual value
of her exports.   The two taken together were estimated in a
normal year to amount to 3 milliard marks or the 6 per cent
service and amortisation charge on the two series of bonds.

The rest of the reparation debt, representing 82 milliard
marks, was to be covered by 'C' bonds.   These were to be deposited with the Reparation Commission by 1 November but
were not to be issued unless the Commission was satisfied that
Germany's financial position was able to bear it.   If issued, the
rate of interest and amortisation was to be the same as for the
'A' and 'B' bonds.   No serious suggestion was ever made,
except at the London reparations conference held in mid-
December 1922,[1] that this portion of the German debt should
be called on.   The London Schedule therefore may be said to
have relieved Germany of well over a half of the debt which
the Reparation Commission, acting strictly within the terms of
a treaty Germany had signed, had determined; in effect the
Schedule bound her to pay a sum which she had declared at
Paris in 1919 to be within her capacity.[2]   This did not mean
that the Commission's report and the London Schedule were
easily accepted by Germany.   A new German Government
with Wirth as Chancellor only assented on 11 May under the
threat of Allied force, notwithstanding the fact that Bergmann,

[1] See below, p. 184.
[2] *Documents Relative to the Amount of Payments to be effected by Germany under the Reparations Account*, H.M.S.O., 1922.

the leading German official accredited to the Reparation Commission, considered that a rejection would be illogical in view of previous estimates by Germany of her capacity to pay.[1]

Further, the combined effects of German efforts to procure the foreign exchange needed for her payments, the gains of currency speculators afforded by Germany's regular demands for foreign currency, and the incompetent management of the German budget induced the first symptoms of a precipitate collapse of the mark.   The curve of its flight was from a value of 62.30 to the dollar in May 1921 to 84.31 in August, thence to 104.91 in September and to below 260 in November.   By August it was clear to J. M. Keynes and by the end of the year to most other people that Germany would be in no position to meet her reparation bill for the early months of 1922.   Wirth's brilliant Foreign Minister, Rathenau, went to see Lloyd George in London on 14 December in the hope of inducing some sympathy in Britain.   The Prime Minister took to Rathenau and thought he had made out his case.   They discussed the possibility of the payment being reduced to 500 million marks in cash for 1922, though with a continuance of payments in kind in full.   The Reparation Commission was unable to reach an agreement on this when it met at the end of December, but at the Cannes Conference (6–13 January 1922) there was some discussion of a reduction of the money payments for 1922 to some 750 million marks.   Unfortunately relations between Lloyd George and Rathenau were now strained owing to a foolish remark made by the Foreign Minister in the Reichstag.[2] A solution on some such lines was, however, chiefly blocked by the tragi-comic circumstances of Briand's fall from power in the middle of the Cannes Conference.   He made way for the unrelenting Poincaré, who had already sharpened his claws against Germany during his service as French member and president of the Reparation Commission.   Poincaré's opinions on anything to do with Germany were compared by Lloyd George to those of a Salvation Army captain about the devil.[3] When Rathenau, 'the prophet in a tail-coat', was mercilessly shot in the streets of Berlin later in the year a French journal greeted the news with the absurd words 'one German less'.

All that could be patched up after Briand's fall was a temporary moratorium and this was not arranged, after the hardest bargaining with France, until 21 March.   German payments for that year were to total 720 million marks in cash and twice

[1] Bergmann, op. cit., p. 77; CAB 23/25. 38 (21).
[2] The story is told by Viscount D'Abernon, An Ambassador of Peace, I, p. 40.
[3] The Truth about Reparations and War Debts, p. 66.

that amount in kind, but this partial suspension was made dependent upon Germany's carrying out the necessary financial measures to put her house in order.   To which the German Government replied that it was impossible for her to do so without a substantial foreign loan.   A committee of international bankers was set to study the prospects of a loan but reported on 10 June that there was little chance of money being raised on the scale required without some revision of Germany's capital debt first.   Meantime, the inflation went on, the government printing increasing amounts of money to meet increasing deficits.   The mark, which had stood at 317 to the dollar in June, exchanged at more than 1,000 to the dollar in August, over 7,000 in November and 7,589 by the end of 1922.   Precisely what Lloyd George had predicted time and again to Millerand, Briand, Poincaré, if Germany was forced to pay more than her system could stand, was coming about.   But this had little effect on Poincaré.   In a definitive and characteristic speech at Bar-le-duc on 24 April he made no concessions to German difficulties, claiming the bond up to the last ounce. The relief granted to Germany in March nevertheless proved quite inadequate and on 12 July 1922 the government formally applied for a total suspension of cash payments to cover not only the current year but the following two years as well. This drastic application formed the subject of an Allied conference in London from 7 to 14 August.

III

By this time the reparation issue had become entangled with the settlement of inter-Allied war debts.   In the British view the debts, together with reparation obligations, had become a vast financial incubus on the world economy, requiring a single slate-clearing operation.   But war-devastated France wanted a reparation settlement before she could consider paying her own debts, and American public opinion, with its conception of war loans as a purely business affair and its growing delusion that they had dragged the United States into the war, wanted the debts repaid whatever the reparation settlement.   In March 1921 the U.S. Secretary of Treasury, A. W. Mellon, began moves for a settlement of the debt issue.   In the following February Congress passed the Debt Funding Act setting up a commission of five members under Mellon's chairmanship. It was laid down that repayment of American war loans by the Allies should be completed in not more than 25 years and that interest should be reckoned at not less than 4.25 per cent. The Commission then asked for offers for the settlement of outstanding debts on this basis and the British Government felt obliged to set about developing an official debt policy towards its own allies. The outcome of this was the Balfour Note of 1 August 1922.

Although the note was signed by Balfour, in phrasing and spirit it was the work of the Prime Minister. Addressed to the representatives in London of France, Italy, the Serb–Croat –Slovene state, Rumania, Portugal and Greece, it pointed out that Britain would never have raised the debt issue had it not been for the American demand for the funding and repayment of the British debt. The optimum solution, the note went on, was the cancellation of all inter-Allied debts and reparations as well. Britain favoured such a remedy even though financially she stood to lose a great deal. Apart from her share of reparations, she was owed by the Allies some £3,400 million and herself owed the United States only about a quarter of that sum, that is, about £850 million, exclusive of interest accrued on the debt to America since 1919. In the absence of any such general renunciation of debts, however, Britain could fairly expect from her allies and, by way of reparations, from Germany, as much as, but not more than, what she had to pay America. Hence the allies were asked 'to make arrangements for dealing to the best of their ability' with their obligations to Britain, it being understood that these need not in total exceed the ultimate funded British debt to the United States.[1]

This was on the face of it a generous proposal. Yet the Balfour Note, issued less than a week before the opening of the London Conference summoned to deal with the German appeal for a moratorium, is said to have done more than anything to harden feeling in France in favour of strong action against Germany, even in quarters previously hostile to the notion of a Ruhr occupation.[2] First, Britain, in calling on France and the other Allies to make arrangements to pay their bill, appeared to make no allowance for their capacity to pay similar to that which her Ministers were always pleading for in Germany's case. France, regarding herself as the victim of unprovoked aggression by Germany, saw no reason why Germany's postwar weakness should be held to mitigate her financial obligations and France's weakness should not mitigate hers. Secondly, the implication of the note was that the less Britain could extract from Germany by way of reparations the more she would have to extract from France by way of debt

---

[1] Misc. No. 5 (1922), Cmd. 1737.
[2] Sir Andrew McFadyean, *Reparation Reviewed*, p. 43.

repayment, and hence the less France was able to meet her needs from German reparations the heavier on her would lie the burden of debt to Britain. At the same time the note seemed to carry to Germany the disloyal advertisement that reparations would be unnecessary in a rational world if former warriors showed a decent generosity after the conflict. In his reply to the Balfour Note on 1 September Poincaré therefore insisted that Germany's fulfilment of her reparation obligation, and accordingly the need for the Allies to stand together in forcing Germany to comply, came before anything else.

> As far as France is concerned [wrote Poincaré] there can be no question for her of contemplating any settlement of the debts she contracted during the war, so long as the outlay made by her for the reconstruction of her devastated regions has not been covered by Germany directly, or by means of a transaction which would allow her to mobilise as soon as possible an adequate portion of her debt.[1]

Hence the London Conference opened in August at the flashpoint of tension in Anglo-French affairs. After Lloyd George had expressed regret that the meeting had not been postponed until the Reparation Commission reported on the German request for a moratorium, Poincaré's turn came to depict the plight of France. Morally and politically, he said, she was at the end of her tether. The unfinished work of reconstruction could not be held up; yet increases in taxation were out of the question. Any moratorium granted to Germany must therefore be of shortest duration and on the strictest conditions. The latter he defined as the extension of Germany's customs line to the east of the occupied areas, so as to put the Allies in a position to increase their tax on German foreign trade; the handing over to the Allies of German state mines and forests as well as certain chemical factories capable of manufacturing poison gases; and the control of all German customs by the inter-Allied Committee of Guarantees in Berlin which had been created under the London Schedule of Payments to supervise its execution.[2] To this Lloyd George protested that all the Allies were suffering from the war, not France alone. Under inflationary conditions, he said, coming to the crux of the matter, the question was not one of collecting German money but of securing its transfer into currencies worth something to the Allies. The essence of the problem, as always in the British

---

[1] Lloyd George, *op. cit.*, p. 115.
[2] Misc. No. 16 (1922). Minutes of the London Conference on Reparations, August 1922, Cmd. 2258, pp. 5–12.

view, was German capacity to pay; of this only experts were at all qualified to judge. Lloyd George proposed the subjection of Poincaré's ideas to expert examination to see whether they would produce the cash.[1] Poincaré at length agreed to yet another expert committee, but only on condition that the French representative should be Seydoux, the French Finance Minister, and that France should not be regarded as committed to the principle of a moratorium without conditions.

In the expert committee, which promptly met under the chairmanship of the British representative, Sir Robert Horne, the Anglo-French conflict as to the effectiveness of the guarantees proposed by Poincaré reproduced itself afresh. Ranging themselves against Seydoux, the British, Italian, Japanese and even Belgian delegates considered that the drawbacks attached to the suggested guarantees would be far greater than the value of any proceeds which might be realised; the proceeds themselves might well turn out to be paper currency impossible to transfer across Germany's borders.[2] Not surprisingly the draft prepared by the British delegation on the conditions to be attached to the grant of a moratorium fell far short of Poincaré's call for the immediate surrender to the Allies of German state mines and forests. The draft led off with a strong charge against Germany for failing to deliver in full the coal and timber deliveries ordered by the Reparation Commission, and deplored the unsatisfactory German record for cash payments in 1922. As to guarantees for the future, however, the draft went little beyond the existing arrangements by which the Reparation Commission and the Committee of Guarantees were authorised to limit the German floating debt and the provision by which Germany was compelled to hand over to the Committee of Guarantees gold or foreign currencies equivalent to 26 per cent of the value of German exports. From the French viewpoint the significant articles of the draft were 7 and 8; in these Germany was warned that if she failed to fulfil her timber delivery requirements the Reparation Commission 'would consider' the establishment by application of article 248 of the treaty of a supervision over the state forests, and similarly for the state mines in the event of a German default in respect to coal deliveries.[3]

The difficulty about these articles for the French was that, as Poincaré explained, they deferred the taking over of the forests and mines to an indefinite future date, and the decision whether a default had occurred was left to the Reparation Commission to decide. Poincaré insisted that this was an

---

[1] Cmd. 2258, p. 21.   [2] Ibid., p. 35.   [3] Ibid., pp. 67–8.

issue for the Allied governments and went on to develop the French conception of the Commission as an agent of the governments, with which the British never agreed. Lloyd George, on the other hand, believed that action should proceed only on the basis of facts as declared by a Reparation Commission playing the role of an impartial arbiter, notwithstanding its composition.

In view of these fundamental differences on the conditions of a moratorium all that remained was for the Conference to decide in what manner it should part. Lloyd George favoured an adjournment until Allied delegates had returned from the United States, where they were discussing debt questions. In the meantime the question of German payments should be left to the Reparation Commission. Realising that this formula implied a surreptitious linking of reparations with war debts, which France firmly opposed, Poincaré refused to accept it as a basis for adjournment. He suggested that they should merely retire in a friendly way and each party should 'reflect separately on the situation'.[1] On these terms the meeting broke up on 14 August.

Lloyd George's prophecy that it was the financial plight of Germany rather than the moral or legal rights of the Allies which would ultimately govern the reparation settlement was validated when talks between the Allies began again in the winter. The deterioration of the mark broke the co-operative Wirth government in November and the task of stabilisation was now taken up by Dr. Cuno. Cuno's first task was to consider the report of a group of international financial experts summoned by the German Government to prepare a plan for monetary stability; this was accepted by the new administration which communicated its proposals based on the report on 14 November. Beginning with the premise that stabilising the mark was impossible without foreign co-operation, the argument was that Germany should be relieved of all reparation payments in cash or kind for three or four years, except for deliveries to the devastated areas. To stabilise the mark Germany proposed to create a fund of one milliard gold marks, to be made up of 500 million marks contributed by the Reichsbank and a similar sum in the form of credits from foreign banks. When these measures had preceded far enough the government would raise an internal gold loan. There followed a list of suggested internal reforms for cutting down government spending and increasing the revenue.[2] The Reparation Commission

[1] Cmd. 2258, p. 103.
[2] Misc. No. 3 (1923). Inter-Allied Conferences on Reparations and Inter-Allied Debts. Reports and Secretaries' Notes of Conversations, Cmd. 1812, pp. 3–17.

was asked to take the necessary measures by way of granting the moratorium and calling a conference of international financiers to make arrangements for the proposed foreign credit.

The new British Government under Bonar Law, who had succeeded Lloyd George in October, felt that a preliminary Allied meeting was necessary to consider these proposals before 15 January 1923, on which date it had been agreed that the Reparation Commission should give its views on the conditions for a moratorium. This preliminary meeting was held in London from 9 to 11 December. It was at once evident when the Conference began that the Balfour Note of 1 August was still a strong irritant to the French. Poincaré complained bitterly that France was expected to settle her debts to Britain while she was unable to raise an internal loan owing to the unsatisfactory prospects of getting further German reparations. He therefore returned to the principle of the full reparation debt as drawn up by the Reparation Commission in April 1921 and proposed that the 'C' bonds, which had never been seriously considered as a definite part of the German debt, should be used to pay off inter-Allied obligations. In the meantime he stood firm on his refusal to concede any moratorium without strict 'gages' of a character which, if necessary, the Allies could exploit themselves.[1] The trouble about this, Bonar Law replied, was that if the German debt was fixed at such a high figure that there was no prospect of it ever being paid the 'C' bonds would at once become valueless. His own view was that there was no solution to the Allies' difficulties unless some arrangement were made for putting their debts on a reasonable basis and fixing the German debt at a level which would persuade the financial world that Germany was likely to become and remain solvent.[2] Both the British and French Prime Ministers, however, agreed in rejecting the German scheme for internal and external loans designed partly for stabilisation, partly for reparation, purposes.

By the time the Conference resumed in Paris on 2 January the mood of France had worsened owing in the main to two characteristically maladroit acts of German diplomacy. On the day before the meeting in Paris, that is, on 1 January, the German Ambassador to France, Dr. Mayer, had seen Poincaré and shown him a conciliatory plan for a reparations settlement, which however lacked in even greater degree the quality the French missed in the German plan presented to the London Conference: precision. On the same day the German Ambassador in Washington had seen Hughes, the Secretary of

[1] Cmd. 1812, p. 27.   [2] Ibid., p. 35.

State, and put to him a suggestion for a non-aggression pact between Britain, France, Germany and Italy, under which these countries would pledge themselves for a generation not to make war upon one another without first putting the question to a popular vote.[1] The idea behind this scheme, the French thought, was to put them in the wrong if and when they sought to apply forcible sanctions in the Ruhr. Adding fuel to French indignation at these German moves was the action of the British representative on the Reparation Commission, Sir John Bradbury. He had crowned two years' dissent from French reparations policy by standing out from the otherwise unanimous decision of the Commission to declare Germany in default in respect of timber deliveries. He had then gone on to prevent a similar decision on coal deliveries by insisting that the Commission should await the outcome of the inter-Allied meetings in Paris before reaching a final position. French opinion was therefore hostile from the start to the British plan presented to the Conference by Bonar Law in the hope of avoiding a total breach with the French.

The essence of the plan was that Germany should be afforded four years' freedom from reparation obligations, except for certain deliveries in kind, in order to put her house in order. A new schedule of payments was proposed, based on a total liability of £2,500 million, as compared with the £6,600 million proposed by the Reparation Commission the previous year. This should be cleared off by German annuities of £100 million (2 milliard gold marks) for ten years immediately following the end of the moratorium, rising to £166 million (3.32 milliard gold marks) thereafter. The payments were to be made in the form of two series of bonds at 5 per cent and redeemable at call by the German Government. Apart from certain payments due from the reparation account to Britain and France, all inter-Allied debts were to be written off, except that interest payments on the second of the proposed series of reparation bonds were to be placed in a pool for distribution to Allied debtors of the United States in proportion to their indebtedness. The guarantee of German co-operation proposed in the British plan was an arrangement for the supervision of Germany's finance until such time as she was regularly discharging her obligations. This supervision was to be effected by a Foreign Finance Council sitting in Berlin and consisting of appointees of the four Allies together with an American member and a representative of a neutral European nation. The German Finance Minister, who was to act as the ex-officio

[1] Cmd. 1812, p. 69.

chairman without a vote except when there was an equality of votes, would be required to act on the Council's advice in all matters affecting currency legislation, budgetary matters, Treasury administration and financial controls.[1]

Poincaré criticised the British plan on three grounds. He said that it virtually abrogated the Versailles Treaty and the legislation which had been enacted in many countries in connection with it. Secondly, the British were proposing a four-year moratorium during which time Germany would be wholly outside the scope of Allied control and in the French view there was no power in the world which could force her to pay after such a lapse of time; France, Poincaré continued, had whittled down her demand for guarantees but could not give up the irreducible minimum for which she was now asking. Thirdly, the British programme amounted to a restoration within a short time of German hegemony throughout Europe and the world. Under favourable circumstances the German debt would be amortised in the British plan after 15 years, thus leaving Germany as the only country in the world without an external debt.[2] These objections to the British plan were repeated by M. Theunis, for Belgium, who added the further condemnation that the plan would put Belgium in the front rank of sacrifice.[3] It was also significant that, for the first time, the Italian position, as expressed by the Foreign Minister, the Marquess della Torretta, was ranged at France's side in opposition to Britain.[4]

At the final meeting of the Paris Conference in the late afternoon of 4 January the differences between the British standpoint and that of her allies were not unfairly stated by Poincaré in the following words:

> Great Britain, on the one hand, thought that it was necessary to try and restore German credit in order to obtain reparations and that the restoration of credit required a certain liberty of action for Germany and a moratorium during which recourse to pledges and sanctions must be avoided. France, Italy and Belgium, on the other hand, thought that if Germany was in a difficult situation it was through her own fault that Germany was not solvent, but that she would only yield to pressure. If then it was necessary to accord a moratorium it should be accompanied by the seizure of certain pledges which, if suitably chosen, should not affect German credit.[5]

[1] Cmd. 1812, pp. 112–19.   [2] Ibid., pp. 121–4.   [3] Ibid., pp. 132–7.
[4] Ibid., pp. 154–7.   [5] Ibid., pp. 188–9.

The pledges the French Prime Minister referred to had been closely defined in a French paper laid down on 2 January, when the Conference began. They comprised a levy of foreign securities on the basis of German exports coming from the occupied territories and the Ruhr basin; the seizure of customs houses in these two areas; and a tax on coal workings in the Ruhr and the occupied lands. If the German Government failed to co-operate, the penalties specified in the paper were the immediate occupation of the whole of the Ruhr basin, together with Essen and Rochum, and the establishment of the customs barrier east of this newly occupied territory.[1] Bonar Law said that if this programme were carried into effect it would have a disastrous effect on the economic situation in Europe; he therefore declined to take part in or accept any responsibility for the French programme.[2]

IV

The occupation of the Ruhr which France and Belgium, hesitantly supported by Italy, embarked upon on 11 January 1923 marked the culmination of the division between Britain and her continental allies on the German problem which had been widening since the treaty was signed. It is unnecessary to dwell on the factors which had led to it: the differences in national psychology and historical experience which caused Britain to consider the reparation question in terms of general world pacification and reconstruction after the war, while French and Belgian views were dominated by the strategical necessity to guard the Rhine against a fresh German incursion.

In October 1923, when the German Government had formally ended passive resistance, Curzon summed up French policy at the Imperial Conference by saying that it was productive of no good results and was leading to disaster and ruin.[3] The French Government disagreed with this pessimism; the decision to occupy the Ruhr, they claimed, had been fully justified. This was no mere face-saving statement. They judged the occupation, as they judged every other incident in the reparation issue, from a different angle from that of Britain. They were less interested in the payment of reparations than in producing in Germany a mood of acquiescence. This they judged had been attained when passive resistance ceased in

[1] Cmd. 1812, pp. 105–8.
[2] *Ibid.*, p. 194.
[3] *Imperial Conference, 1923.* Appendices to the Summary of Proceedings, Cmd. 1988, p. 40.

September. 'It was no wise a question,' the French Ambassador told Curzon on 30 July, 'of seeking the immediate and total payment of reparations; we knew very well that the exploitation of the Ruhr by the Allies would not in itself procure the necessary sums, even if the German Government in conformity with the Treaty of Peace had allowed us to take the coal and collect the taxes which we had resolved to levy (in the Ruhr).' Passive resistance, the Count de Saint-Aulaire admitted, had prevented Poincaré's pledges from being productive, but what the French wanted was nothing so material as reparations; it was something psychological, namely a German frame of mind.

What we wanted [he said] was, first and foremost, to create in Germany, by a seizure of pledges and by coercion, the will to pay; it was to cause such inconvenience in the economic and political organisation of the Reich that it would prefer the execution of the Treaty of Peace to this inconvenience; it was to obtain what we have not obtained for four years, i.e. the recognition by Germany of her obligations, not from the general and theoretical point of view, but from the practical point of view.[1]

The British had only on rare occasions doubted German will to pay; the question in British eyes, as always, was a practical one: was the German economy strong enough to raise the necessary funds and transfer them into foreign currencies? Could the Allied countries receive these payments without ruining their export industries or suffering an increase in unemployment? Hence in his note to the Allies of 20 July proposing conditions for drawing a decent veil over the Ruhr catastrophe, Curzon returned to the British position at the Paris Conference: in order to obtain from Germany the payments the Allies were entitled to receive German external credit must be re-established, the mark must be stabilised, the budget balanced and productivity in German industry encouraged.[2] His conditions for an evacuation of the Ruhr therefore suggested the creation of yet another body of impartial experts to advise the Allied governments and the Commission on German capacity to pay and the economic sureties to be demanded from Germany by way of guarantees. The necessary impartiality, the Foreign Secretary explained, was to be assured by the inclusion of an American member, who could no doubt be ex-

---

[1] Misc. No. 5 (1923). Correspondence with the Allied Governments respecting Reparation Payments by Germany, Cmd. 1943, p. 28.
[2] *Ibid.*, p. 19.

pected to strengthen Britain's hand against any future French demand for physical penalties.[1]

In a further note of 11 August Curzon dealt forcefully with the objection France and Belgium had raised, namely that they could not permit negotiations to begin until passive resistance had ended. Britain, Curzon said, had never raised the question of the legality of the occupation before, but their opinion was that the occupation was not a sanction authorised by the treaty and so they could not agree that German resistance was illegal. Curzon then defended the British principles for a settlement. An impartial body to assess German capacity to pay was necessary, he said, because the Reparation Commission had become in practice 'an instrument of Franco-Belgian policy alone'. It was desirable that the new body's findings should be freely acceptable by Germany because 'an understanding freely entered into because acknowledged to be just and reasonable stands, in practice, on a different footing and offers better prospects of faithful execution, than an engagement subscribed under the compulsion of an ultimatum, and protested against at the very moment of signature as beyond the signatory's capacity to make good'.[2] To accommodate the argument to French ears, Curzon added another proposal for an inter-Allied debt settlement intended to make Britain look fully as interested in German reparations as any of her allies. This was that Britain would only expect from her debtors and from Germany enough to pay to the United States the £710 million debt which had been funded by negotiations in Washington resulting in the agreement of 18 June.[3] This offer, like that made by Bonar Law at the Paris Conference, represented the writing off of a considerable proportion of British foreign assets, but did not conciliate France and Belgium towards the Curzon debt formula. In any case they were waiting for passive resistance in the Ruhr to end before beginning talks on the reparation question as a whole.

The liquidation of the Ruhr crisis was the work of an inter-Allied conference which met at the Foreign Office in London on 16 July 1924 and which was joined by a German delegation led by the Chancellor, Dr. Marx, and Stresemann, his Foreign Minister, on 5 August. The Final Protocol signed by the conference on 16 August included four agreements, one between the Reparation Commission and Germany, two between the

[1] *Ibid.*, pp. 21–2.
[2] *Ibid.*, pp. 48–61.
[3] American Debt. Arrangements for the funding of the British debt to the United States of America, Cmd. 1912 (1923).

Allies and Germany and a fourth between the Allies themselves.[1] These agreements put into effect the report issued on 9 April by an expert committee, known as the Dawes committee after its American chairman, General Dawes, which the Reparation Commission had appointed the previous November. The Commission had at the same time appointed a second committee under the chairmanship of Reginald McKenna to inquire into foreign assets owned by German nationals and the means by which they could be repatriated for footing Germany's bills, but this committee made no significant contribution to the reparation settlement.

The Dawes committee was not asked to concern itself primarily with reparations; its task was rather the pragmatic one of inquiring into the means of bringing stability into the German economic system and balancing the budget. The assumption was, as British Ministers had always contended, that the first question was to measure the productive capacity of Germany and mark out the financial controls required, given that she had reparation obligations on roughly the scale of the Schedule of Payments of 1921. The committee did not attempt to form an estimate of the total German debt, but accepted the standard annuity of the 1921 Schedule, that is, approximately £125 million or 2.5 milliard gold marks. The committee proposed that this level should be attained after a partial moratorium of four years during which period Germany would pay reduced annuities ranging from £50 million to £87.5 million. The report did not, however, accept the traditional British view that the Germans should be left to themselves to work out what resources they could earmark for producing the necessary revenues. It recommended that the standard annuities should be specifically financed partly from budget revenues, partly from railway bonds and industrial debentures, partly from taxes on tobacco, alcohol, sugar and beer, and partly from customs duties. To secure these levies a group of agencies should be established representing a greater inroad into the management of the German economic system than ever previously contemplated by the Allies.

Germany still assumed full responsibility for raising the money in Germany, but the problem of transfer, which had dogged all previous discussion on the reparation issue, was left to the Allies. There was to be created a Transfer Committee composed of bankers whose function it would be to devise means of transferring the mark payments received from Ger-

---

[1] Misc. No. 17 (1924). Proceedings of the London Reparation Conference, July and August 1924, Cmd. 2270, p. 322 ff.

many without endangering the German currency. In order to provide Germany with the initial financial basis for launching the plan the Republic, as the British had always urged, should be granted a reparation loan valued at 800 million gold marks, or £40 million. It was this loan proposal which provided an opening for bringing to an end the Ruhr occupation. The Dawes committee, while declaring that questions of military occupation were not within its terms of reference, nevertheless insisted that the success of the plan would depend upon economic unity being restored to Germany. Its forecasts of German ability to pay the specified annuities were

> based on the assumption that economic activity will be unhampered and unaffected by any foreign organisation other than the controls herein provided ... existing measures, in so far as they hamper that activity, will be withdrawn or sufficiently modified as soon as Germany has put into execution the plan recommended and .... will not be reimposed except in the case of flagrant failure to fulfil the conditions accepted by common agreement.[1]

This meant that the banking world, especially British bankers, who would be expected to arrange the credit, would require satisfaction in the form of assurances that the events of 11 January 1923 would not be repeated.

The key phrase in the inter-Allied agreement signed on 16 August which satisfied the bankers was only arrived at after the London Conference had passed its greatest crisis. It stated that 'when the Reparation Commission is debating on any point relating to the (Dawes) Report ... a citizen of the United States of America appointed as provided below shall take part in the discussions and shall vote'. This American member was to be chosen by unanimous vote of the Commission or, in cases where unanimity was wanting, by the President of the Permanent Court at The Hague. When the Commission had to decide whether Germany had committed a default in respect of her obligations either under the Versailles Treaty or under the expert's recommendations, it could do so on a mere majority vote, but any member who had taken part in the vote, including the American citizen, could appeal against the Commission's decision to an arbitral board consisting of three persons nominated for five years either by unanimous decision of the Commission or by the President of the Permanent Court. To bolt the door further against arbitrary punitive measures against

---

[1] Report of the Dawes Committee, Cmd. 2105 (1924), p.13.

Germany, no sanctions could be imposed in connection with any alleged German default unless this fell within the definition laid down in the report of the Dawes committee. Thus Germany's territorial integrity and economic sovereignty were protected against future Poincarism in two ways: firstly through dissenting Allies being given an appeal to arbitration, which Bonar Law would have been relieved to have at the Paris Conference in January 1923, and secondly through the change in the balance of forces in the Reparation Commission towards greater impartiality.

British Ministers, Lloyd George, Bonar Law, Curzon, had repeatedly insisted that the exaction of reparations was not a trial of strength between France and Germany; it was part of the total world economic problem of the 1920s, to which there was no solution short of stability in its leading European component, Germany. Blindness to this fact was for them a form of sinning against the light. But, if France persisted in this sin, American financial circles could hardly continue to do so. The fall in American wheat prices in 1922 and 1923 brought United States opinion face to face with the economic *malaise* of Europe, while Wilson's high idealism had failed to interest it in Europe's diplomacy.

The United States Secretary of State, Charles Evans Hughes, in an address at New Haven on 29 December 1922, accordingly asked why they should not 'invite men of the highest authority in finance ... men of such prestige, experience and honour that their agreement upon the amount to be paid, and upon a financial plan for working out the payments, would be accepted throughout the world as the most authoritative expression obtainable'. This appeal, the true origins of the Dawes committee, had already been rejected by France when privately suggested by the Secretary of State.[1] Hence the throwing open to the public of the proposal at New Haven. After the end of German passive resistance in September 1923 President Coolidge let it be known that the Hughes offer was still available. By this time American interest had been stimulated by the generous arrangement for funding the British war debt which had been signed in June; it was believed that the only obstacle to an equally successful liquidation of all war debts owed to the United States was the reparation tangle. Later in October Hughes went as far as to warn France through her Chargé d'Affaires in Washington that if she let slip this opportunity of ending her policy of coercion she would forfeit the sympathy of the United States. This warning was the

[1] *F.R.U.S., 1922*, II, pp. 128, 175, 182.

immediate forerunner of the decision of the Reparation Commission on 30 November to appoint the Dawes committee.
At the London Conference in July 1924 an American delegation
led by the Ambassador, Kellogg, participated throughout.
They were in no sense on the same footing as the other delegations and could not commit the United States to the final
protocols, but they made known that there would be no objection
to an American national joining the Reparation Commission, as
provided in the protocols, and acting as Agent-General for
reparation payments under the plan.

But possibly the greatest satisfaction in Britain with the outcome of the London Conference was caused by the fact of
German agreement to the settlement, offering as it did some
assurance that Germany's obligations would not be later represented by nationalist firebrands as dictates of ruthless con-
querors.   This principle had been the consistent thread in
British reparation policy since Versailles.   Its embodiment in
the London protocols was in some respects a personal triumph
for Ramsay MacDonald, who acted as chairman of the London
Conference by virtue of the formation of the first Labour
Government after the British general election in November
1923.   Whatever the later effects of time on MacDonald's
mind and personality, he fitted into the international scene in
1924 like a long-lost key.   MacDonald was without the conspiratorial tendencies of Lloyd George, which had embittered
the French and led the Germans into the illusion that they
would always have British support no matter now badly they
behaved.   He was also free from the grandeur that was Lord
Curzon.   Whereas Curzon had ruled the Lausanne Conference
the previous year from the clouds, lecturing the Turks as though
they were undergraduates, MacDonald set the German delegation immediately at their ease when they arrived on 5 August
and gently led the Conference step by step to a set of compromises between the reports of the three committees of the Conference and the German delegation's objections.   To be sure,
Marx and Stresemann were denied what they had chiefly come
to London to ask: the withdrawal of the French from the
Ruhr.   That was not to come until twelve months after the
end of the Conference, but henceforward they were assured
that there would be no futher interference with German economic self-government throughout the Reich.   Moreover, at
every point at which disputes might arise in the carrying out
of the Dawes plan between Germany and either the Reparation
Commission or the Transfer Committee provision was made for
arbitration, and Germany was given an equal voice with the

Commission or the Committee, as the case might be, in choosing the arbitrators.[1]

The Dawes plan came into operation on 31 October 1924 and ran an untroubled course until it was superseded by the less fortunate Young plan of 1930. General Dawes himself once said that it was the Ruhr occupation which had made the preparation of the Dawes plan possible.[2] While the British felt that this was true in the sense that for every remedy there has to be a preceding disease, the remark could be more properly taken as meaning that the Ruhr occupation by the summer of 1924, had demonstrated, not perhaps to the politician in Paris, but to France of the provinces and countryside that Poincaré's policy could in the end reduce Germany to submission but only at the cost of his own country's ruin. The consequence was the defeat of Poincaré at the French elections in May and his resignation on 1 June, followed by that of his coadjutor, President Millerand, on 11 June. Poincaré's successor, the Radical Socialist Herriot, was still so much under the influence of the extreme Germanophobes in France that he was forced to take with him to the London Conference what was to all intents a Poincarist brief. Nevertheless, when Herriot left the conference on 9 August for a week-end of struggle with his Cabinet in Paris, he succeeded in imposing his principle that the occupation should be used as an economic rather than military pawn in the Dawes settlement. That week-end signalled the death of Poincarism.

Even more importantly, the Franco-Belgian action in the Ruhr also made clear that unilateral action against Germany could only throw western Europe into a chaos which held no profit for anybody, except perhaps the Communists, and would ultimately drive the Entente to a point from which there was no return save through open conflict. The signs were clear enough. In the British note of 11 August 1923 a warning never before uttered by London was given, when Curzon wrote that 'separate action may be required in order to hasten a settlement which cannot be much longer delayed without the gravest consequences to the recovery of trade and the peace of the world'.[3] This was followed by a series of threats to France which the Foreign Secretary communicated through Lord Crewe, at the Ambassadors' Conference, when Curzon had the Foreign Office to himself during Baldwin's election campaign. It was made clear on 19 November that if France persisted in her pro-

[1] Cmd. 2270, pp. 226, 334.
[2] McFadyean, *op. cit.*, p. 86.
[3] Cmd. 1943, p. 61.

posal for restoring Allied military control over the whole of Germany Britain would take her leave of all inter-Allied agencies and commissions for German affairs.[1] This British attitude of increasing toughness culminated in an uncompromising rejection of France's policy of fostering separatism in the Bavarian Palatinate, a natural sequence to the Ruhr occupation. Basing himself on investigations carried out by the British Consul-General in Munich in the teeth of French opposition, the Under-Secretary for Foreign Affairs, Ronald McNeill, made the British view of separatism abundantly clear in a statement in the House of Commons in January 1924. Three quarters of the Separatists, he said, came from outside the Palatinate and signatures assenting to a separate Palatinate, obtained in a number of cases under threat, could by no means justify the idea that the majority of the peasants favoured an autonomous government.[2] Thus the Ruhr occupation, by forcing an intolerable breach in the Allied front, made possible, as well as necessary, the Dawes solution. Anglo-French relations had come to a point in January 1923 at which it was essential to take one look over the precipice before the decision to live could really begin to work its way.

As compared with the change of government in France, the coming of MacDonald's first Labour Cabinet in Britain had relatively little effect on the resolution of the reparations question. The factors of a settlement with Germany were already present when MacDonald took over the Foreign Office together with the premiership; in particular the firmness shown by Curzon in November 1923 had done much to sober France.[3] As we have seen, the main principles of the Dawes settlement were closely in line with ideas which had guided British Ministers throughout the reparations crisis. Moreover, MacDonald, was fortunate in that he never had to resort to the threats from which Curzon did not shrink, since France's mood had already altered by the time the London Conference met. MacDonald's principal assets were patience and order. He urged on the French that the Conference on the Dawes plan should be the first of three meetings, the two later meetings to deal with security and inter-Allied debts respectively. This meant that the reparations issue, in its fearsome complexity, could at least be isolated from anxieties on other matters, which had tended to blind the French mind to the economic realities of the European situation. Again, during the London

---

[1] George Glasgow, *MacDonald as Diplomatist*, pp. 14–15.
[2] 169 H.C. Deb. 5s. Cols. 485–6 (21 January 1924).
[3] See Glasgow, *op. cit.*, Chapter I.

Conference itself, MacDonald set the pattern of one step at a time, leading the French and German delegates insensibly into the acceptance of a total structure which might have repelled or frightened had it been presented to them whole.

Above all, MacDonald's genial, imprecise patience and optimism carried through an operation so vast that few of its implications could be exactly foreseen and so imponderable that each representative in London had to take it largely on faith. The fact was that, by 1924, realism, calculation, caution, had got Europe into the worst impasse it had seen since 1914; a certain benignant vagueness was not felt to be out of place. MacDonald told the Conference, which was his diplomatic masterpiece, that he was there as a businessman, and wanted to deal with the agenda in a business spirit. But the truth was that, for a brief period, he symbolised a hunger for new approaches, for more faith, after the arid experiments of the previous four years.

CHAPTER VIII

NEGOTIATING WITH RUSSIA

I

WITH the return of world war in 1939 British opinion tended to conclude that Hitler had been allowed to disturb the peace by the failure of Britain, France and Russia to concert their policies.[1] This was true, though it assumed that states can bury their quarrels before a common enemy has openly taken up a position against them. Anglo-French differences during the 1920s, as we have seen, were real enough; they were partly the result of differences in national psychology, partly of different national interests, which step by step ranged the two countries on opposite sides. It is a fallacy of post-1945 'realism' to think that states disagree because of conflicting interests only, as it was a fallacy of pre-1939 'idealism' to think that they do so for psychological reasons only. In the case of British relations with Russia, had interest alone counted the two countries should have joined together in defence of peace during the whole inter-war period. They had fought as allies in the two previous great European wars; they were to do so again as from June 1941. Instead, prejudice and fear on both sides prevented common interests from resulting in common policies.

On any showing Britain and Russia in the 1920s were deeply concerned with the maintenance of peace, Britain because of her general interest in political stability and trade, Russia because internal unsettlement and economic reconstruction necessitated security from external attack. Both countries, moreover, stood to gain from a *rational* application of the peace settlement. Britain, no more than Russia, wanted Versailles restrictively enforced on Germany, yet she, like Russia, profited from the existence of a barrier of independent states, provided their ambitions were limited, on Germany's eastern frontier. Soviet Russia's leaders, though they loudly denounced the peace treaties as the quintessence of capitalist greed, had no strong revanchist feelings, except in regard to Rumanian

---

[1] This was strikingly shown in the approval given to Etienne Mantoux's book, *The Carthaginian Peace*, published in Britain in 1946 and, among many other popular books of the same kind, to Ambassador Davies' *Mission to Moscow*, published in 1942.

Bessarabia, and had as sound reasons for making friends with the East European successor states as these had with Russia. The Soviets welcomed Kemalist Turkey, which Britain grew to accept. Both Russia and Britain had an interest in a peaceful issue to the conflict between the Chinese nationalist revolution and the rights of foreign Powers and in curbing Japanese ambitions in East Asia.

Economic realities too, as distinct from economic theories, should have brought them together, had material advantage been the sole yardstick. Russia desperately needed the capital equipment which Britain, with her massive unemployment, could have supplied, though the possibilities in this direction were far less than British Communists pretended. Although in the early years Russia lacked the means to pay for such supplies, her economic progress and hence her capacity to refund loans from Britain would have been accelerated by the national security which good relations with Britain would have gone far to ensure. Yet, despite this basis of rational common interest, Anglo-Soviet relations in the 1920s staggered from one angry diplomatic note and threat of rupture to another. Soviet spokesmen denounced Britain as the chief instigator, with France, of a forthcoming attack on Russia. British governments called the Bolsheviks servants of the devil, with the one redeeming virtue that they would soon be driven from the country they had ruined.

The most important reason for this *contretemps* on the Russian side was the ingrained xenophobia and persecution complex of the Bolshevik leaders. Harold Laski once compared this mentality to that of a 'secret battalion making war by night in an unknown country against an encircling and merciless enemy'. These attitudes were held in varying degrees by all Russia's leaders, reflecting in part their personal insecurity in a revolutionary state newly emerged from civil war, in part their doctrinal conviction of the inevitability of war between Russia and the capitalist West. The natural focus of these attitudes was Britain, in Marxist eyes the most advanced example of capitalist imperialism and the strongest pillar of the international Establishment. On the British side, the most important immediate reason for continuous strained relations was not so much the horror aroused in British ruling circles by the Russian Revolution and its social programme as the re-awakening by the Revolution of old fears of Russian intrigue against the British Empire, especially in Asia. Though the apocalyptic raptures of the Bolsheviks stirred the deepest loathing in men like Churchill and Lord Birkenhead, no British Government had ever taken the offensive, in arms or even words, against a foreign revolutionary régime unless it clearly threatened British or Imperial security. This was precisely Pitt's position during the last great revolutionary upheaval in Europe, the French Revolution of 1789. While ideologists like Burke would have made war against France to avenge Louis XVI and his family, there was no serious prospect of this as long as the revolutionaries left the Low Countries alone. The same was true *mutatis mutandis* of the reactions of the war-weary British to the Russian Revolution.

As we have seen in a previous chapter, British assistance to White forces during the Russian civil war of 1918–20 was not anti-Communist in origin, though the more vocal interventionists in Britain wished it had been and the Bolsheviks accordingly assumed that it was.[1] British Ministers knew far too little about Communism to wish to turn aside from their life-and-death struggle with Germany to crush it. In the first instance British intervention was intended to keep Russia in the war, or, if that was impossible, to prevent Germany profiting from Russia's collapse. When the war with Germany ended Lloyd George had no desire to continue supporting the Whites, even if the mood of British servicemen and the public at large had allowed him to do so. At the Peace Conference he was even more active than Wilson in trying to bring the Bolsheviks into the settlement. Likewise, Britain's guarantee to Poland in July 1920, which brought her to the brink of war with Russia, was not a defiance of Bolshevism but a desperate attempt to uphold the authority of the Allies. After all, the Allies had fought with Germany partly to re-create Poland; they could hardly allow Russia, who had capitulated to Germany, to destroy it. After the treaty of Riga in March 1921, which established a Russo-Polish frontier more unfavourable to Russia than the 'Curzon' line proposed by Britain in the previous year, fear of Communism remained a running theme of Anglo-Soviet affairs but was not the prime cause of the estrangement.

The challenge presented by Soviet Russia and Communist propaganda to the British position in Asia was more formidable, or so it seemed to the British Minister mainly concerned with it, Curzon, who became Foreign Secretary in October 1919. Curzon, a specialist on Persia and former Viceroy of India, was at home with Asian, unhappy with European, affairs; to defend the outposts of the Empire in Asia was his most cherished dream. As it happened, Curzon's fellow Minister in Russia, Chicherin, had been in Tsarist times head of the Asiatic section

[1] See above, Chapter IV.

of the Foreign Office. The Soviet Government, however, turned to Asia, not so much as unconscious heirs of the Tsars but in order to gain a field of attack on Western imperialism, one which became increasingly important as the outlook for revolution in Europe dimmed. By the winter of 1920 it was becoming clear to all but hardened doctrinaires of the Third International that European capitalism was not fundamentally shaken by the war. The Soviet régime in Hungary of 1919 was crushed, so were the disturbances in Germany of that year. When the next great opportunity for Communist revolution in Germany, in September 1923, came and went, it was clear that the alternative strategy to world revolution, namely that of using the differences between the capitalist states so as to prevent them leaguing together in war against Russia, must be tried. The most successful example of this policy was the common cause made with the other pariah state, Weimar Germany, and expressed in the Rapallo treaty of April 1922.

The significance of the Rapallo agreement was that it was essentially a compact between Bolshevism, on one side, and the German Right and the Army, on the other. The leaders of the Third International optimistically assumed that when the German revolution came the Army would be dissuaded by their Russian connection from coming to the assistance of the Weimar Republic. But this did not alter the fact that Rapallo signified a switch in Soviet policy from fomenting revolution in Germany to cultivating that country against the Entente. In somewhat the same way the Soviet appeal to Asian nationalism, although it excited intense alarm in British governing circles, already conscious of the disturbing effects of the war on Western power in Asia, meant, not the pursuit of Communist revolution, since no Marxist after 1920 could regard Persia or Turkey as ripe for proletarian revolt, but the weakening of Britain, regarded as the head of the capitalist conspiracy against Russia. In the case of Asia, however, it was less easy to distinguish the two strategies. When Western influence was expelled, it would not be easy to forecast the direction to be taken by social forces in Asian countries, whereas in western Europe capitalism was reasserting its grip.

II

Soviet attacks on the British position in Asia centred on the four countries which had served as the crossroads of British and Russian policies in the nineteenth century; Afghanistan, China, Persia and Turkey. While the main object was apparently to excite anti-British attitudes in the governments of these states, attempts by the Soviet authorities to stir up revolutionary feelings among the workers and peasants of Asia generally were soon abandoned, both as ineffective in themselves and offensive to the Asian governments which Moscow was seeking to influence. The most notable expression of these efforts was the First (and only) Congress of Peoples of the East held in Baku in September 1920, at which Zinoviev, the director of the Third International, founded in March the previous year, called for a *Jihad*, or Holy War, against British imperialism.[1] At the same time a Propaganda School was founded at Tashkent for training promising young Asians for careers as propagandists and revolutionaries when they returned home. Similar Soviet endeavours were the foundation of the Institute of Oriental Studies in the autumn of 1920 for the provision of instruction 'for those preparing themselves for practical activity in the East or in connection with the East' and the founding of a Communist University of Toilers in the East by the Central Executive Committee of the Russian Communist Party in April 1921. These activities were a constant source of complaint by the British Government after the conclusion, in March 1921, of the Anglo-Russian trade agreement, with its mutual renunciation of interference in the other country's affairs. The Soviet Government on the other hand were clearly anxious to reduce them in the interests of developing commercial relations with the capitalist states. Hence the winter of 1920–1 marked the highest peak of activity on this level of direct appeal to the revolutionary forces in Asia.[2]

Afghanistan, with its sensitive proximity to India, had been a bone of contention between Russia and Britain throughout the later nineteenth century, its capital, Kabul, being the headquarters of intrigue and counter-intrigue on both sides. After the Second Afghan War in 1878–9 the country was made a British protectorate with a British resident at Kabul. By an Anglo-Russian agreement signed at St. Petersburg in August 1907 and known as the Nicolson–Isvolsky treaty, Russia agreed to conduct all her relations with Afghanistan through Britain and to send no more agents of her own to Kabul. This agreement was no longer considered binding by the Soviet Government and when the reforming Emir of Afghanistan, Amanullah, denounced his treaty with Britain and instigated armed incursions across the frontier with India in May 1919 his actions were loudly applauded by the Soviets.[3] Matters took a turn

[1] W. H. Chamberlin, *The Russian Revolution*, II, pp. 392–3.
[2] E. H. Carr, *The Bolshevik Revolution, 1917–1923*, III, pp. 260–8, 289.
[3] Papers regarding hostilities with Afghanistan, Cmd. 324 (1919), p. 18.

for the worse in February 1921, when Russia concluded a treaty with the Emir which recognised Afghan independence, notwithstanding the Anglo-Russian agreement of 1907, and authorised the opening of five Soviet consulates in the country. Britain followed suit on 22 November by abolishing her special privileges in Kabul and acknowledging Afghan independence, whereupon Lenin dispatched a letter to the Emir on 27 November proposing an increase in Soviet-Afghan trade the object of which, Lenin said, was that of 'furthering the struggle with the most rapacious imperialist government on earth—Britain'. Lenin also offered military assistance, though Russia at that time had little to spare, and spiced the offer with promises of territorial concessions.[1]

In China the Anglo-Russian conflict took on a much more dangerous edge owing to the highly explosive character of the Chinese nationalist revolution. From the moment when the Chinese delegation returned in disgust from the Paris Peace Conference in 1919, having refused to sign the German treaty owing to its provision for surrendering to Japan former German rights in China, Russia began to tempt China with offers to retrocede Tsarist rights. This culminated in an agreement reached on 14 March 1924 between the Foreign Minister of the Peking Government, C. T. Wang, and Leo Karakhan, the Soviet Vice-Commissar for Far Eastern affairs, which embodied Chinese recognition of the Soviet régime. At the same time the Soviet Government were making contacts with the rebel Kuomintang authorities. As a result of talks between the Soviet representative, Adolf Joffe, and Dr. Sun Yat-sen in Shanghai in January 1923 a Soviet political and military mission under the general direction of Michael Borodin arrived in China in September accredited to the Kuomintang. During the mission's sojourn in China, Britain and Russia were openly ranged against each other, Russia seeking through Borodin to drive out all foreign influence from China, as a prelude to the communising of the country, while Britain strove to drive a wedge between the Kuomintang and Moscow by adopting a conciliatory position on the unequal treaties question.[2]

There is little doubt that the Conservative Government's decision to terminate diplomatic relations with Soviet Russia in May 1927 was more inspired by experience of Soviet intrigue against Britain during the troubles in China in 1925–7 than by any other single issue. Fortunately for Britain a sharp change in Soviet policy towards China took place in 1927 and played

[1] Louis Fischer, *The Soviets in World Affairs*, I, p. 286; CAB 23/27. 88 (21).
[2] See below, Chapter XI.

into Britain's hands. This was the decision to cease colla-
borating with the Kuomintang Right on the basis of the mutual
non-interference agreement of 1923 and to embark upon an
active policy of communising China, which created a breach
between Moscow and Nanking such as the British Government
had been seeking. The withdrawal of the Borodin mission
on Kuomintang insistence and the persecution of the Chinese
Communists by Chiang Kai-shek closed this phase of Anglo-
Soviet conflict, Britain and Russia remaining distant from each
other, though not actively hostile, during the Sino-Soviet
struggle in Manchuria in 1929 and the Japanese conquest of
Manchuria in 1931–2. In a wider sense the recall of the Borodin mission also ended for the time being the forward policy of
promoting world revolution on the part of Russia's rulers.
Borodin's failure entrenched the policy of Socialism in One
Country.

The same pattern of initial success, followed by retreat, in
the Soviet policy of appealing to Asian nationalism against
Britain was seen in the case of Persia. This country, like many
others in Asia which accepted Russian tenders of help in their
struggles with Britain, had had recent experience at first hand
of British military force and was seeking to free itself from that
force. In the spring of 1918, after Russia's military collapse,
British troops occupied northern Persia, which had been assigned to Russia by the Anglo-Russian agreement of 1907, and
thus held both north and south at the time of the armistices in
1918. At the end of the European war the Persian Government approached Britain to abrogate the 1907 agreement,
which the Bolsheviks had already denounced, in order to release
themselves from all foreign troops. Since it was held in London that the occupation of northern Persia was essential to
the help Britain was furnishing to White forces across the
Caspian Sea in Russia this proposal went unheeded. Instead
Lord Curzon, thinking of Persia, as he did of almost all Asian
countries, as part of the '*glacis* of India', hastened to conclude
an agreement with the Persian Foreign Minister in London on
9 August 1919, while British troops remained as an inducement.
The basis of the agreement was a virtual British monopoly of
financial assistance to Persia, as well as of munitions supplies
and expert advisers.[1] Since this treaty would, in Russia's
eyes, have afforded Britain a permanent foothold from which
to launch attacks on the Soviets, the Bolsheviks made it their
object to frustrate Curzon's design. According to a Soviet
statement issued on 30 August, 'the Russian people stretch out

[1] Persia No. 1 (1919), Cmd. 300.

to you, oppressed masses of Persia, their brotherly hand; the hour is near when we will indeed be in a position to complete together with you our task of struggle against all robbers and oppressors, great and small, the origin of your untold sufferings'.[1] This was the kind of language which normally emanated, with little effect, from the Soviet capital but in Persia's case it was followed by action as soon as Russia, with the withdrawal of British troops from northern Persia, could move. In May 1920 Red Army forces were landed at the Persian port of Enzeli on the Caspian and a Soviet-type authority was established at Resht which lasted until October 1921.

This Soviet move alienated Persian opinion but was not entirely unwelcome to the new force in Persian politics, Riza Khan, who had forced the Shah to make him Minister of War and Commander-in-Chief in February 1920 and subsequently Prime Minister. The presence of Russian forces in the north enabled the Persian national assembly, the Majlis, at the instance of Riza Khan, at first to temporarise and then flatly to refuse to ratify Curzon's treaty of 1919. By July 1921 Curzon was admitting to a 'feeling of disappointment, almost of despair' at the turn of events in Persia.[2] In place of the British treaty the Persian Government concluded an agreement with Russia on 26 February 1921. This included the highly contentious article 5 which gave Russia authority to send troops into the country should any third state 'intend to pursue a policy of transgression in Persian territory or to make Persian territory a base for military attacks against Russia' and as a result Persia was unable to remove the resulting danger to the Soviet frontier.[3] While the Soviets thus appeared to triumph over Curzon, however, the Persian authorities had little further use for Russia after she had served their purposes against Britain. The Soviet régime was driven out of northern Persia and Riza Khan looked elsewhere for his advisers.

The same Soviet policy of giving aid and encouragement to Asian nationalism against Britain, with almost the same results, was followed in relation to Turkey. Both here and in Persia, as distinct from Afghanistan and China, Russia had direct security interests of her own to defend in addition to her general desire to weaken Britain's imperial position. Since Kemal clearly renounced the pan-Turanian traditions of the Ottoman Porte and wished to confine the Turkish nation strictly

[1] Jane Degras (ed.), *Soviet Documents on Foreign Policy*, I, pp. 161–4.
[2] 46 H.L. Deb. 5s. Col. 16 (26 July 1921).
[3] *Soviet Treaty Series* (ed. Leonard Shapiro), The Georgetown University Press, Washington, D.C., I, 1950, pp. 92–4.

to the Anatolian heartland, a bargain with the Soviets evidently could be struck.   Shortly after Kemal put himself at the head of the nationalist revolt against the Sultan in August 1919 the Soviet Foreign Minister, Chicherin, addressed an appeal to the workers and peasants of Turkey on 13 September calling upon them to combine with Russia and 'drive off the European robbers and destroy and make powerless those within the country who are accustomed to building their happiness upon your misfortune'.[1]   The settlement of frontier differences with Kemal, however, did not prove easy.   During the discussions on a pact between Moscow and the Turkish nationalists Kemal at first demanded Batum, which his troops had entered in March 1921 during the disorders which followed the fall of a Menshevik local authority.   When the Soviet–Turkish treaty was signed on 16 March Kemal agreed to restore Batum but received in return Kars and Ardahan, the old claims of the Tsars against Constantinople.   Russia also agreed to abolish her rights under the Capitulatory régime in Turkey.   The resulting accord between Moscow and Ankara, though anxiously watched by the Kemalists because of its potentially revolutionary effects in Turkey, was highly inconvenient to Britain.   It was a prime condition for the success of Kemal's operations against Greece, whom Britain was backing, that he should be secure on his northern front.   It was not, however, until the major Greek defeat at the Sakaria river in September 1921 that a Soviet general, Frunze, was sent to Ankara to arrange for military assistance from Russia.

As the peace conference to revise the abortive treaty of Sèvres with Turkey of 1920 approached Russia's demand for representation was stepped up, her purpose being to secure a strong and friendly Turkey which would bolt the door of the Straits against the navies of hostile capitalist Powers, especially Britain.   The first opening shot in the campaign was fired by Karakhan in a note to Britain on 13 September 1922, in which he protested against the opening of the Straits to Greek warships by the Allies.   The legal status of the Black Sea and of access into it, Karakhan said, was a matter for the riparian states alone, and if the Entente purported to make a peace with the Turkish nationalists which decided the future of the Straits, Russia would not be bound by it.[2]   The British reply was a statement issued three days later maintaining that Britain, France and Italy were the Powers with the greatest interest in

[1] Degras, *op. cit.*, I, pp. 164–7.
[2] The text of Karakhan's note was published in the *Manchester Guardian* on 23 September 1922.

the Straits.[1] This strangely unhistorical declaration was vigorously rebutted by Chicherin in notes to Britain and Italy on 19 October, a week after the Mudania armistice between the Allies and Turkey had fixed the Near Eastern Conference for December at Lausanne. Russia, Chicherin said, would not tolerate being excluded from the Conference in the same way as she had been excluded from the Washington Conference on the Far East since she was the only country in Europe to have recognised the Kemalist régime in Turkey.[2] Britain eventually agreed to Soviet representation at Lausanne, but only during the proceedings on the future of the Straits. Thus, although the Conference opened on 20 November it was not until 4 December, at the ninth meeting of the Territorial and Military Commission, that a delegation led by Chicherin and Vorovsky representing Russia, the Ukraine and Georgia was allowed to put in an appearance.

At Lausanne the Russians, while describing themselves as champions of the sovereign rights of all Black Sea Powers, were chiefly concerned to block the Straits against the passage of Allied warships on offensive operations against southern Soviet Russia. The Black Sea, Chicherin contended, was essential to the economic life and security of Russia. Before the war, he said, 70 per cent of Russia's corn exports were shipped through that sea and the Sea of Azov, and by the armistice of Mudros with Turkey in 1918 the Allies were able to enter the Black Sea without hindrance and occupy the Russian towns of Odessa, Nikolaeev, Kherson and Sebastopol.[3] The Foreign Minister's efforts to pass Russia off as the general guardian of the Black Sea states were soon rendered vain when the Bulgarian, Greek and Rumanian delegates made clear their unwillingness to be dominated by the Soviet navy. The isolation of Russia was completed by Curzon's sarcastic exposure of the hollowness of Chicherin's expression of concern for Turkish sovereignty.[4] Chicherin energetically protested against the British principles of opening the Straits to foreign warships and demilitarising the shores of the Straits, and against the Allies' decision to give the League of Nations authority to appoint a commission, none of whose members at that time recognised the Soviet régime, to supervise the Straits convention. All this Chicherin denounced as 'violations of the sovereignty and independence of Turkey'. But the Turks had little stomach for further fighting, and if Curzon's ultimatum of 4 February 1923 was to be rejected and the war with the Allies resumed

---

[1] *The Times*, 18 September 1922. [2] Degras, *op. cit.*, I, pp. 339–40.
[3] Turkey No. 1 (1923), Cmd. 1814, p. 130. [4] *Ibid.*, p. 133.

little military aid could be expected from Russia. Moreover, for the Kemalists, though demilitarisation was a bitter pill to swallow, national sentiment had largely shifted from Constantinople to the home of the revolution, Anatolia. Accordingly the refusal of the leader of the Kemalist delegates, Ismet Pasha, to accept Chicherin's definition of Turkish policy on the Straits left Soviet intentions in Turkey frustrated.

When the Lausanne Conference resumed in April the Turks submitted to the British demands and the leading Soviet delegate, Jordansky, who had been sent to replace the assassinated Vorovsky, failed to maintain their resistance even to demilitarisation. Jordansky eventually signed the Straits convention at Rome on 14 August, three weeks after the Lausanne treaty was signed by the states which had participated in the whole proceedings. Eventually Russia refused to enter the commission created to supervise the new Straits régime and even failed to ratify the convention. Nevertheless, the negotiations on the Straits had some advantage for her. Lausanne represented the first effective international conference attended by the Soviets and the Straits convention was the first multilateral treaty to bear the name of the revolutionary régime.[1]

III

These hostile encounters with Russia at the points of contact between her border provinces in Asia and the outposts of the British Empire provided the chief background to Anglo-Soviet frictions in the 1920s. The fact that the British Foreign Secretary of the time, Curzon, was at once the personal embodiment of the class system the Bolsheviks meant to destroy and an unwavering adherent of Britain's imperial mission in Asia served only to embitter the conflict. Chicherin once said that where Lloyd George realised that he was living in the twentieth century, 'though he had not always the courage to make the necessary deductions', Curzon was 'determined that if this is not the nineteenth century he will behave as if it were'.[2] These traditional Anglo-Russian conflicts in Asia were moreover overlaid with ideological tensions with which they were so closely mingled as to be almost indistinguishable. Soviet efforts to inspire social insurrection in Asian nationalist states soon petered out since the only condition of diplomatic accord with such countries as Kemal's Turkey and Riza Khan's Persia was non-interference in their internal affairs. Nevertheless, the fact that Russia's alliance with Asian nationalism was often

[1] Louis Fischer, *op. cit.*, I, pp. 409–12.
[2] In an interview given to the *Manchester Guardian*, 19 February 1923.

draped in revolutionary language made her support for Asian resistance to British policies all the more obnoxious in London.

In general, however, Soviet policy towards Britain and other western capitalist states at this time tended to be sharply disputed between the Left and Right wings of Soviet government, the Right wishing to tone down the revolutionary appeal to working-class opinion outside Russia's borders so long as Russia needed western trade and financial assistance, while the Left considered that Russia's survival in a hostile world could not be assured unless the Communist revolution spread. While the Soviet threat to British interests in Asia was unmistakable in that it tended to represent an agreement between these two wings of Soviet government, the tension between the Bolshevik Right and Left over foreign policy generally served to confuse British thought as to the best way of dealing with the Russian Revolution as it entered a more stable phase.

Soviet leaders accepted, though with reluctance, Lenin's advice that the failure of postwar Communist revolutions in Europe and the danger of an Allied invasion of Russia during the Russo-Polish war imposed a policy of coming to terms with capitalism in order to split the enemy. The exploiting of capitalist 'contradictions' replaced the policy of frontal attack on the capitalist citadel. As Lenin described it during the Soviet debate on the offer of concessions to foreign firms in November 1920, the fundamental rule was:

> To exploit the contradictions and the antagonisms between the two Imperialisms (that is, the European and the American), between the two systems of capitalist states, inciting them one against the other. ... At present we are between two enemies. If neither of them is to win, we must manage to dispose our forces in such a way that they fall on each other. ... But as soon as we are strong enough to fight the whole of capitalism we shall take it on by the neck.[1]

But if the revolutionary struggle was only temporarily relegated to the background as a time-buying tactic, the instruments of revolutionary struggle must be kept sharp. In any case, leaders reared on Marxist categories and bent on the re-education of their country in Marxist thought could hardly lay aside the language and expectations of revolution merely at the bidding of national expediency.

Hence, side by side with the movement from War Communism to the controlled private enterprise of the New Economic Policy, introduced in March 1921, went the continued develop-

[1] Degras, *op. cit.*, I, pp. 221–2.

ment of the Third International. Although the third Congress of the Third International met in Moscow in July 1921 in distinctly chastened mood after the decisive revolutionary failures in Germany and Hungary two years before, there was no question as to the continuance of the Comintern. The practitioners of peaceful co-existence, trade and diplomatic relations with the outside world, chiefly concentrated in the Foreign Ministry and the Foreign Trade departments (Narkomindel), were merely in theory applying a contemporary phase of a world revolutionary strategy, while Zinoviev and the Comintern were concerned with long-term aspects. Nevertheless, considerable frictions and confusions sprang up between the two voices. These confusions were heightened by the fact that during the critical period from 1922 to 1924, when Russia's diplomatic contacts with the outside world were being formed, Lenin, who had guided the Bolsheviks through the perplexities and doctrinal revisions accompanying the failure of Communism in Europe, was desperately ill after the attempt on his life in 1922 and died in January 1924. This meant that the almost impossible effort to ride the two horses of peaceful co-existence and world revolution in a single harness had to be carried on in the midst of bitter rivalries as to the succession. Not until 1927, with the casting into the wilderness of Trotsky, the symbol of the world revolutionary theme, did the issue reach a point of stability.

The British Prime Minister chiefly concerned with the early phases of this Soviet adjustment to postwar realities, Lloyd George, had, almost from the outset, sought to come to terms with the Bolshevik upheaval in Russia.[1] Apart from a natural sneaking regard for the classless aspirations of the Leninists, stability in Europe meant for him reconciliation between the great established Powers, to which the ambitions of the smaller states should take a definitely second place. Deeply shocked by the territorial appetite of Poland's leaders, he grasped at every opportunity during the Russo-Polish conflict for a settlement with Russia which would open the way to economic reconstruction in eastern Europe. These main themes were reflected in the government's pronouncements on foreign policy at the end of 1919 and throughout 1920. The King's Speech at the closing of Parliament on 23 December 1919 dwelt on the 'grave economic position of a large part of Europe', which demanded 'measures of relief and reconstruction which can only be undertaken as a result of joint action by all nations'.[2]

---

[1] See above, Chapter IV.
[2] State Papers, Vol. 112, 1919, p. 677.

When Parliament reassembled in February 1920 the Speech again referred to the 'vast regions of eastern Europe without whose contributions to world supplies the cost of living could not be reduced or general prosperity restored'.[1] At the close of the 1920 Parliament on 23 December the Prime Minister, through the King's Speech, returned to the same theme, with the expression of hope that trade would shortly be resumed with Russia and that this would lead to an era of peace 'greatly needed by the suffering peoples of East Europe'. At the same time a further rebuke was administered to Poland. She was told to settle her differences with her neighbours and to devote herself to 'producing internal stability and the task of economic reconstruction'.[2]

Lloyd George's Russian policy came under fire from militant anti-Communists in the Coalition Cabinet, led by Churchill, who persisted after the failure of intervention in blackening Russia's name with British opinion. But Lloyd George's most serious clash was with Curzon. Curzon never wavered from his view of the Soviet régime, expressed at the Imperial Conference in June 1921, as 'this deplorable Government'. The only change in his opinion before his retirement from the Foreign Office in 1923 was that Bolshevism was becoming more stable 'because everybody or agency that could dispute its strength has been destroyed'.[3] Curzon was in one sense a more formidable critic of Lloyd George's line with Russia than Churchill or Birkenhead in that he had the kind of expert knowledge of Middle Eastern and Asian affairs which generally commanded the Prime Minister's respect. Had not Lloyd George regarded Curzon as a pompous menial always willing to sacrifice his genuine opinion for the charms of office, he might have been more moved by Curzon's alarm at Soviet intrigue against British interests in Asia, especially since Russia opposed Lloyd George's Turkish policy which Curzon himself frowned upon. Since the Prime Minister declined to take his Foreign Secretary to the vital encounter with a Soviet delegation at Genoa in April 1922, Curzon had no alternative but to unburden himself to his Conservative colleagues. Fearing 'some disastrous agreement with the Russian Government', he wrote to Austen Chamberlain on 13 May that the assurances given by the Russians at Genoa ignored the political conditions of Anglo-Soviet relations required by the Conservatives, especially the strengthening of the undertaking to refrain from

[1] State Papers, Vol. 113, 1920, p. 12.
[2] *Ibid.*, Vol. 112, p. 250.
[3] The Earl of Ronaldshay, *The Life of Lord Curzon*, III, p. 295.

propaganda in the trade agreement of 1921 and a promise to stop Soviet aid to Kemal. 'To have dealings with such people,' Curzon wrote, 'is bad at all times. . . . But to do it in the conditions described in order to scrape something out of Genoa would be the nadir of humiliation.'[1]

But these murmurings against the policy of welcoming Russia's offers of trade as a means of diverting Bolshevism into peaceful channels hardly affected Lloyd George's optimism, despite the failure at Genoa. On returning from the conference he told the House of Commons that:

> whatever we thought about the Soviet Government . . . some arrangement with Russia was necessary in order to save the misery in Russia itself, necessary in order to enable Russia to make her contribution to the needs of the world, necessary to enable Russia to help in the swelling of that volume of trade upon which so many people depend for their daily bread, necessary in order to give a sense of stability.[2]

There could hardly be a more characteristic example of Lloyd George's belief, by no means personal to himself, that if it were not for the wild fanatics in both Britain and Russia solid business could be done between the two countries which was the only sure basis for peace.

After the first British agreement with the Bolshevik régime, which was signed at Copenhagen on 12 February 1920 and dealt with the exchange of prisoners-of-war,[3] the British terms for a trade agreement were laid down in a government statement on 1 July, following meetings in London from 31 May until 7 June between the Soviet Foreign Trade Minister, Krassin, and British trade officials. The two central principles in this statement were mutual abstention from propaganda and interference in each other's affairs and the recognition in principle by Russia of her obligations to repay war loans and compensation for nationalised properties, though Britain was not asking for immediate repayment.[4] Although these conditions were accepted in a Soviet reply on 7 July, the talks were interrupted, first by the British ultimatum to Russia on 11 July, during the Russo-Polish war, and subsequently by what the Prime Minister described as 'Russian interference in British affairs'.[5] When the talks were resumed in December the British Government insisted upon a stronger wording of the

[1] Ronaldshay, *op. cit.*, III, p. 297.
[2] 154 H.C. Deb. 5s. Col. 1457 (22 May 1922).
[3] Russia No. 1 (1920), Cmd. 587.
[4] *The Times*, 13 July 1920.
[5] 133 H.C. Deb. 5s. Col. 351.

proposed political preamble to the trade agreement. But by this time a new factor had entered into the situation, namely objections from Paris. French citizens had lost more through Bolshevik repudiation of Tsarist loans than the nationals of any other country. France was more interested than Britain in strengthening the successor states of East Europe against both Germany and Russia and had less to gain from the revival of European trade. What made French objections particularly important for Britain was the need for French support against Kemalist Turkey.

In a note to Britain on 25 November 1920 the French Government tried to secure some co-ordination in British and French measures for assessing and presenting their claims in respect of foreign confiscated property in Russia and Entente loans to that country. They took their stand on the note sent to Moscow by the Allies and six neutral countries in February 1918 which declared that Soviet decrees ending all former Russian financial obligations to the rest of the world were null and void, and on an international conference held in Paris on 10–12 June 1920, which a British delegation attended and which unanimously voted in favour of common action in the matter of claims against Soviet Russia. The November note then went on to propose an international agreement based on the principles of Soviet responsibility for Tsarist obligations and Soviet reparation for damage inflicted upon foreign rights as they existed in August 1914, together with the creation of an international commission to portion out the Russian debt as between the former Russian territories, some of which were now separate states.[1] These 'suggestions' were ignored by Britain. Lloyd George maintained that the resumption of trading with Russia could not be left until every detail of the claims controversy had been settled to the satisfaction of all the many claimants. He did tell the Commons on 22 March 1921, however, that French financial claims would receive British support 'when there is a general discussion with a view to establishing peace between Russia and the Western Powers'.[2]

Since France refused to relax her demand for a debt settlement before any agreement with Russia was reached, the Premier decided that Britain was free to conclude her own trade pact with Russia. This was effected when a bargain was struck with Krassin on 16 March 1921, which was described as a 'preliminary agreement' pending the conclusion of a general treaty with Russia. The trade agreement was a form

[1] Russia No. 2 (1921), Cmd. 1456, pp. 3–7.
[2] 139 H.C. Deb. 5s. Cc. 2508.

of *de facto* recognition of the Soviet régime in that, by article 4, each side was authorised to nominate from among their nationals persons to carry out the agreement in the territory of the other. By article 5 these official agents were granted immunity from arrest and search and permitted to communicate with their governments through sealed bags like diplomatic representatives.[1]

The French Government formally lodged a protest with Britain against the trade agreement on 6 April. They expressed particular concern about article 9, which prevented Britain seizing goods from Russia which were 'not identifiable as the property of the British Government'.[2] France argued that this might imply a valid sale of property rightfully belonging to Frenchmen which Russia had stolen and later exported to Britain under the trade agreement. In a further note of 24 May the French Government referred to the case of *Venesta Ltd*. vs. *Krassin*, in which three English judges held that since Britain had accorded *de facto* recognition to the Soviet régime by the trade agreement, properties claimed by the Soviet Government were legally their possessions.[3] In the British reply to these complaints, which Lord Hardinge, the British Ambassador in Paris, handed in on 14 June, the French November 'suggestions' were dismissed as 'too vague to be regarded as a basis for detailed procedure', and it was somewhat disingenuously argued that article 9 of the trade agreement 'did not prevent foreigners from using English courts to secure the restitution of their property'. But, the British note ran, unless France was prepared to come to a reasonable settlement with Russia on the claims and counter-claims issue, Britain had no alternative but to make what terms she could with Moscow, without however prejudicing the claims question. The note then qualified the statement of support for French claims which Lloyd George had made in March by saying that Britain would continue to support French claims 'so long as there is a reasonable chance of obtaining French co-operation in the general treaty between Russia and such of the Western Powers as are willing to negotiate with Russia'.[4]

The trade agreement secured one of the principal British desiderata in that Russia gave a pledge to refrain from 'hostile acts and propaganda', together with an additional undertaking not to encourage India or Afghanistan in 'hostile action'

[1] Cmd. 1207 (1921).
[2] Cmd. 1456, pp. 13–14.
[3] *Ibid.*, pp. 15–17.
[4] *Ibid.*, pp. 19–20.

against Britain.   By article 12 it was agreed that infringement of this or any other undertaking in the agreement would invalidate it, though each side agreed that the other should be given an opportunity to furnish explanations or remedy grievances if any such infringement was alleged.   The declaration in the agreement which provided for recognition by Russia of British claims in respect of loans to the Tsar and properties sequestrated by the Soviets and, by Britain, of Soviet counterclaims relating to damages inflicted by British forces during the intervention was less satisfactory.   It was merely stated that these claims and counter-claims would be 'equitably dealt with' in the forthcoming general treaty.   Lloyd George defended this shelving of the problem in a Commons debate on the agreement on 22 March by emphasising the urgency laid by British traders on the normalising of trade with Russia and by insisting that the government did not intend 'to forgo any of these claims'.   Concern was expressed in the debate lest the reference in the agreement to the Soviet undertaking in principle to pay compensation to 'private persons who have supplied goods and services to Russia for which they have not been paid' ruled out compensation in respect of confiscated private property, war-debts and loans to the Tsarist authorities.   Lloyd George denied that it did and pinned his faith to the new mood in Russia which he thought was symbolised by NEP.   To Major Barnett, the most outspoken critic of the agreement in the House, he said that 'by and by' he would find Lenin 'is a man after his own heart if he does a little business with him'.[1]

This simple-minded, essentially British assumption was soon belied, and during the next two years the effort to negotiate the general treaty with Russia to which the trade agreement was supposed to be an introduction ran into the sands.   The foremost reasons for this were, on the Russian side, the firm refusal to grant the kind of assurances without which Western states felt that they had no confidence against further confiscations, and, on the side of the west European states, the refusal to grant the credits and loans without which Russia claimed that she could not satisfy her external obligations. This deadlock might have been resolved had there existed a general climate of trust between Russia and the West.   Since the Russians were firmly convinced that an attack from the West was inevitable sooner or later and Western statesmen could not believe that the Soviet system would survive or, if it did, that it would prove either peaceful or honest, this condition was never in sight.

[1] 139 H.C. Deb. 5s. Col. 2511.

IV

Lloyd George's dream of a European economic conference to heal the breach between Russia and the West and to satisfy the hopes of British businessmen seeking concessions in Russia, such as Urquhart, chairman of the Russo-Asiatic Company, and Sir Henry Deterding, was agreed to by France at Cannes in January 1922. This was, however, only at the price of the fall of the Briand Cabinet and the drawing up of such agenda for the conference as made an advance along the lines preferred by Lloyd George almost impossible. Three conditions were inserted, largely through French pressure, into a resolution agreed to at Cannes which favoured 'a united effort by the stronger Powers to remedy the paralysis of the European system'. The first was that foreign investors in Russia and other countries should enjoy respect for their property and other rights and the full fruits of their enterprise; the second required recognition of all public debts and compensation for the confiscation or withholding of foreign properties; and the third insisted that all countries (though it was principally Russia which was meant) should give a formal undertaking to refrain from propaganda subversive of order in other states. No indication was given as to what Russia could expect to receive, except for diplomatic recognition, if she met these conditions, even though she could hardly do so without going back on many of the most fundamental axioms of the Revolution.[1]

Chicherin set little store by the Genoa Conference, which met on this basis on 10 April. He regarded it chiefly as a means for entering into diplomatic contact with the various countries represented and believed that the West had been deluded by NEP into thinking that the Revolution had gone into reverse.[2] He therefore lost no time at Genoa in answering that there was no prospect of repaying war debts, which in any case would have to be written down, or meeting the 'just claims' of foreign property-owners without considerable external financial help. Even so, none of these obligations could be assumed without *de jure* recognition from the Powers concerned. In a letter to Lloyd George on 20 April Chicherin entirely set aside the pre-1914 financial obligations of Russia and although these commitments were assumed, with heavy qualifications, in a Soviet statement of 24 April, this was balanced by further limitations in the concessions to owners of confiscated properties.

[1] Resolutions adopted by the Supreme Council at Cannes, January 1922, as the basis of the Genoa Conference, Cmd. 1621 (1922).
[2] Louis Fischer, *op. cit.*, I, p. 333; CAB 23/29. 21 (22), Appendix I.

The latter were to have their possessions restored only in so far as this was consistent with the 'social and economic system and the fundamental laws of the Russian Republic' and only, save for some minor exceptions, in the form of leases or concessions.[1] The principal case of the claimant states in reply was presented in the form of a memorandum of 2 May on which the French delegation deferred its approval. This began with an outline for a plan for an international investment consortium with an initial capital of £20 million, with which Russia could expect to deal, and then listed the requirements the Soviets would have to accept. They were not to interfere in other countries' internal affairs or act against the *status quo*; they must suppress attempts on their territory to assist revolutionary movements abroad and use their influence to help in restoring peace in Asia Minor while adopting a neutral position between Greece and Turkey. Moreover, Russia was to recognise all debts contracted by the Tsarist régime and the Provisional Government, though no claim would be pressed for the time being. Russian counter-claims were not admitted. It was also laid down that in order to encourage the resumption of foreign economic activity in Russia, the Soviet Government was to pledge itself to restore or compensate foreign interests for loss or damage through the confiscation or withholding of their property. Finally, Russia was to take all necessary measures for the future protection of foreigners and their property in Russia.[2]

This tough bill of demands, which could only have been accepted by a Soviet Government which had either repudiated Marxism root and branch or was in such straits that any terms of foreign aid would have been admissible, was rendered wholly unconvincing by the fact that, owing to American non-participation and German coolness, the international consortium, practically the sole inducement offered in return, was never likely to see daylight. The decision to put the demands forward reflected, not any rational hope that they would be accepted, but the bitter reactions of the Allies to the diplomatic *coup* of 16 April, when the German and Soviet delegates made their trip to Rapallo to conclude the treaty the draft of which had already been approved in Berlin before the Genoa Conference assembled. The Rapallo treaty, besides arousing the suspicion that it contained secret military clauses, involved the mutual renunciation of financial claims by the parties. Since these claims formed part of the subject under discussion at

---

[1] Papers relating to International Economic Conference, Genoa, April–May 1922, Cmd. 1667, pp. 25–6.
[2] Cmd. 1667, pp. 28–37.

Genoa, the Allies joined in an indignant letter to the German delegation on 18 April accusing them of dealing with the Russians on the matters in dispute behind the back of the Conference and ending with the request that they should take no further part in the work of the Conference on the conditions of a settlement with Russia. But since by article 3 of the Rapallo treaty Russia committed herself not to satisfy claims arising from any Soviet legislation which infringed foreign rights, while Germany on her side agreed to drop such claims on behalf of her own nationals, the rest of the Russian part of the Genoa Conference had little point. No one felt more embittered than Lloyd George, who had fought so hard for the economic conference and had manœuvred the French into accepting it, if on impossible terms. All that remained to him was the melancholy satisfaction of knowing that he had been right to publish, on the eve of the Genoa meetings, his famous Fontainebleau memorandum of 25 March 1919, in which he had warned France at the Peace Conference that unduly harsh treatment of Germany and Russia would only have the effect of driving them into each other's arms.[1]

The Soviet reply of 11 May to the memorandum was equally tough. Deriding the inviting Powers for throwing away the concessions with which the Russians tried to whet the appetite of foreign business, Chicherin rebutted the memorandum at every point with a mordant pen. The absence of any mention of a direct loan to Russia was singled out for special mention, since Russia's capacity to meet any of her obligations was said to be dependent upon the receipt of assistance, while the consortium scheme, which was regarded merely as a means for helping foreigners to trade with Russia, was dismissed as irrelevant. It was denied that Russia could be held responsible for war debts since she had not shared in the spoils of victory and in any case, the Soviet note went on, her counter-claims arising from the civil war and Allied intervention would have to be set alongside any such liabilities. It was flatly denied that Russia had any obligation to restore confiscated property or offer compensation. As for the requirements in the memorandum of 2 May respecting political conditions, especially the undertaking not to assist foreign revolutionary movements and not to stir up trouble for the Allies in Asia Minor, these were dismissed with even greater contempt. The purport of the reply was clear: Russia was prepared neither to tolerate private trading between foreign and Soviet concerns on her territory or operations by foreign businesses, except on a purely

[1] Peace Conference (Paris), 1919, Cmd. 1614 (1922).

temporary basis, nor would she commit herself to repay debts or compensate foreign property owners, unless these liabilities were exactly matched by Soviet counter-claims, without substantial loans from foreign governments the servicing and repayment of which would relegate the payment of old claims to the infinite future.[1]

'How many trade unions,' Lloyd George asked the House of Commons on 25 May, 'would have invested their funds on the strength of that document?', referring to the Soviet statement of 11 May.[2] For the moment his attempt to mediate between France and Russia, while bringing back some prospects for British business, had failed. The Soviets had found a friend in Germany and were beginning to resume a position in European affairs which would before long bring them the diplomatic recognition the Genoa Conference offered only at a heavy price. Two years later Moscow was offering a prize to the first country (after the Baltic states, Germany and Poland, which had already entered into diplomatic relations) to accord diplomatic recognition. But the prize, a minor trade concession, was very different from what the Genoa Powers demanded. A further influence militating against Genoa was the attitude of the United States. The Harding administration's view of the Soviet régime was that it could not be seriously regarded as a responsible government and that Russian interests, as for instance at the Washington Conference on the Far East in 1921–2, should in the meantime be held as a 'moral trust' by the civilised nations.[3] No American support was therefore forthcoming for schemes of financial assistance to Russia. Moreover, the United States forbade a solution to which Lloyd George's mind had been turning at Genoa, namely the grant by Russia of concessions to such countries as were willing to make separate terms with her. American oil interests were entirely opposed to this, with the result that British business groups felt less enthusiastic about Genoa. In addition, French misgivings about Russia had been to some extent borne out by the signing of the Rapallo treaty, and although it was open to Lloyd George to express through Curzon in February 1922 his disgust with Poincaré's efforts to destroy the Genoa Conference in advance, by the summer French support was required against the mounting threat of Kemal at the Straits.[4]

---

[1] Cmd. 1667, pp. 38–47.   [2] 154 H.C. Deb. 5s. Col. 1464.
[3] C. C. Hyde, 'Charles Evans Hughes', in *The American Secretaries of State and their Diplomacy* (ed. S. F. Bemis), New York, 1929, p. 281.
[4] Misc. No. 6 (1922). Correspondence between H.M. Government and the French Government respecting the Genoa Conference, Cmd. 1742.

The result was that when an experts' meeting assembled at The Hague in July 1922 in order to carry discussion further on the Soviet memorandum of 11 May the British Government suddenly swung round towards the French position. The British delegate, Lloyd-Graeme, told Litvinov, the Soviet deputy Foreign Minister, that there was no prospect of British credits to finance reconstruction in Russia without definite assurances of Russian economic efficiency and probity. He also supported the French demand for the full restitution of confiscated property, even though at Genoa the Prime Minister had been prepared to accept a diluted form of compensation. Litvinov, at a plenary session of The Hague Conference which he had specially summoned, appeared to drop the demand for credits, but Britain was now cooling towards the idea of dealing with Russia in view of pressures from the United States (though no American representative was present) in favour of the Open Door in Russia and against the grant of one-sided concessions. When the Conference passed a resolution recommending governments not to help their nationals acquire property which formerly belonged to other foreigners and had been confiscated by Russia, the avenues through which Britain might have entered into an agreement with Russia seemed closed.

The ways of the two countries were in fact moving apart. Things were gradually on the mend in Russia after the disastrous famine of 1921 and the argument for help from the West at almost any cost was losing its force. On her side, Britain was moving into the crisis in the Near East which almost brought war with Kemal in September. With both France and Russia openly or secretly backing Kemal there was no reason for risking the support of the French on behalf of the hypothetical friendship of the Russians, especially when Chicherin had made quite clear at Genoa that Soviet–Turkish relations were no business of other countries.

Meanwhile the underlying acerbity in Anglo-Soviet affairs had been steadily rising to the surface from the moment when the trade agreement was signed in March 1921. The two main themes of British complaints, of which Curzon was the ready voice, were Soviet activities against Britain in Asia and the Soviet Government's refusal to admit responsibility for propaganda issuing from the headquarters of the Third International in Moscow. On 7 September 1921 Curzon sent Hodgson, the British agent in Moscow, a record of the 'most flagrant violations of the 1921 agreement' at the end of which Soviet Ministers were charged with complicity in the Third International's campaign against British interests. Some of these charges had that comic-opera quality which often crept into British allegations against Russia, such as the references to activities of a Dr. Hafiz in Kabul who was allegedly receiving money from Moscow in order to manufacture smokeless bombs for throwing against the ramparts of the British Empire in India. On a more serious level, the Soviet Government were accused of trying to prevent Turkey from coming to an agreement with the Entente and of agreeing to pay a million roubles a year to Afghanistan to stir up the Waziristan tribes against Indian frontier posts. Curzon branded all these activities as breaches of the trade agreement and asked for assurances that they cease.[1]   The Soviet reply was given by Litvinov, who said that the charges of anti-British activities by Russia in Afghanistan, India and Turkey were 'either unfounded or based on false information or forgeries'. He then reiterated the standard Soviet argument on the propaganda of the Third International:

> The mere facts of the Third International having for obvious reasons chosen Russia as the seat of its executive committee as the only land which allows full freedom to the spreading of Communist ideas and personal freedom to Communists, and of some members of the Soviet Government in their individual capacity belonging to the executive committee, give no more justification for identifying the Third International with the Russian Government than that the Second International, having its seat in Brussels and counting among the members of its executive committee M. Vandervelde, a Belgian Minister, gave justification for rendering identical the Second International with the Belgian Government.[2]

If this was the position and Britain really had no redress when Soviet Ministers chose to summon the discontented of the world to rebel from the tribunal of the Third International rather than from that of the Kremlin, the commitment to refrain from propaganda in the trade agreement seemed to have little value.
Curzon retorted through Hodgson on 2 November that the leaders of each department of the Soviet system were the same.[3]   The argument was, however, clearly fruitless and the Foreign Secretary took up a new theme in January, namely irregularities in the administration of Soviet criminal law, none of which however, even if established, could be easily related to the trade agreement. On 3 January Curzon asked Hodgson

[1] Russia No. 3 (1927), Cmd. 2895, pp. 4–12.
[2] *Ibid.*, p. 13.   [3] *Ibid.*, pp. 17–20.

to inquire into the case of C. F. Davison, a British subject who had been executed two years before on what the Foreign Secretary described as 'trumped-up evidence' of fraud in the supply of food to Soviet institutions. In March Weinstein gave the *tu quoque* of the Soviet Government by accusing British troops in Russia during the civil war of having executed in September 1918 twenty-six Bolshevik commissars captured at Baku by joint British and White forces.[1] A year later Curzon was appealing for a postponement of the execution of Butkevich, a Roman Catholic priest condemned to death for espionage by the Praesidium of the Soviet Supreme Executive Committee. This intercession evoked a reply in such violent terms from Weinstein, with accusations of 'barbarous and inhuman treatment' of political prisoners in Ireland by their British captors, that Hodgson refused to receive it.

The carrying out of the sentence on Butkevich and the imposition of a long term of imprisonment by the Soviet authorities on Archbishop Cieplak at the end of March finally led to an ultimatum from Curzon on 2 May. In Curzon's magisterial style this summed up the sheet of British charges, added new complaints about British trawlers having been molested outside Soviet territorial waters, demanded compensation for the execution of Davison and the indemnification of a Mrs. Stan Harding, a British journalist arrested in Russia on espionage charges in the summer of 1920, and insisted upon the recall of the Soviet agents Raskolnikov and Shumiatsky, who had been sent to Afghanistan and Persia respectively for allegedly agitational purposes. The Curzon note ended by threatening the denunciation of the trade agreement within ten days if the British demands were not met and the two notes of Weinstein withdrawn.[2] The ultimatum seemed all the more ominous to Russia in that it was almost immediately followed by the assassination on 10 May of the Soviet delegate at the adjourned Lausanne conference, Vorovsky. Hence in the exchange of letters between the two governments which continued until the middle of June the characteristic charges and counter-charges were repeated in a new atmosphere of bitterness. Russia offered concessions on all the main British demands, however, although she demanded strict reciprocity in the proposed undertakings to refrain from hostile actions against each other. On this inconclusive note the correspondence petered out in June without the trade agreement having been affected.[3]

[1] Russia No. 1 (1923), Cmd. 1846, p. 7.
[2] Russia No. 2 (1923), Cmd. 1869, pp. 6–13.
[3] Russia No. 4 (1923), Cmd. 1890, pp. 9–14.

Curzon's various expostulations, culminating in the May ultimatum, perhaps served to clear the air, although at the end of the year Chicherin, in an interview given to a British newspaper, was accusing Britain of attempting to destroy Afghanistan's independence with the same anti-Soviet intent as had inspired Curzon to destroy the barrier of the Straits at Lausanne.[1] What these angry exchanges were proving was that the basis of Anglo-Soviet relations was likely to remain unsound so long as complaints had to be handled through intermediaries and at a distance.

[1] *Manchester Guardian*, 24 December 1923.

CHAPTER IX

IN SEARCH OF SECURITY

I

THE essence of Anglo-French differences over German reparations was that British politicians saw reparations as a contractual liability arising from an engagement, the Versailles Treaty, the legality of much of which they doubted, whereas for French governments reparations were an aspect of Franco-German power relations. Poincaré stated only the more extreme version of the French position in saying that the aim of reparation policy should be to force Germany's will, to make her submit to a treaty won at hideous cost in French blood.[1] This was not merely contrary to British notions of fair play; it was a mixture of business with politics horrifying to the British mind. In British eyes, the problem of European security was distinct from reparations. The Dawes plan, as Britain saw it, expressed this distinction; it provided a solution for a financial problem in financial terms.

The security problem however remained. Its central component, apart from the withdrawal of the United States from territorial engagements in Europe, was the rapid contraction of British interest in maintaining the peace settlement in its entirety, since many of its details had become abhorrent to British opinion. Troubles in Ireland, Egypt, India and the long-drawn-out settlement with Turkey, together with British isolationism and unwillingness to act 'as policemen for the world', meant that British forces would not be available to protect all elements in the *status quo* signed and sealed at Versailles. This was in accord with the advanced opinion which believed in the new order under the League of Nations. It often went unnoticed that this opinion was at the same time calling for a stronger League Covenant, which would almost certainly have required increases in British military commitments throughout the world.

The French realised these inconsistencies of British thought. The conclusion they drew was that arrangements for their own security must be proportionately more dependable, and their voice in Allied security policies greater. The country which,

[1] Cmd. 1943 (1923). Correspondence with the Allied Governments respecting Reparation Payments by Germany, p. 28.

in a strictly military sense, had lost the war thus came to be left with the main role, for a few years at least, in preserving victory. The security apparatus constructed by France for fulfilling this role comprised three elements: the maintenance of her panoply of war, behind which was a devious resistance to all-round disarmament; the formation of a defensive *glacis* on Germany's eastern frontiers from France's allies, Poland and the states of the Little Entente, Czechoslovakia, Yugoslavia and Rumania;[1] and an attempt to secure from Britain a pledge of military assistance should German aggression recur, an event which few Frenchmen doubted. To each of these expedients Britain turned a suspicious face.

The interdependence of these elements in French security policy was explained by the French Ambassador in London, the Count de Saint-Aulaire, when he explored the ground for an Anglo-French pact in a talk with the British Foreign Secretary, Curzon, at the Foreign Office on 5 December 1921. The defensive alliance the French were proposing was to cover not merely direct attacks by Germany across British and French frontiers (the only British frontiers in question being those of India), but 'indirect' attacks in the form of aggression against France's allies in eastern Europe. Such aggression, however indirect in inception, 'would presently develop', according to the Count de Saint-Aulaire, 'into a direct attack upon France'. The consideration Britain was to receive from signing such an alliance, apart from French support for Germany's admission into the League and French co-operation in plans 'to reconstruct the shattered fabric of the Russian State', both of which were British aspirations, was the reduction in French land armaments for which Britain had been pleading during the previous two years. In reply Curzon foreshadowed all the later difficulties in the effort to breathe life into the idea of an Anglo-French security pact. The main objection was to the 'enormous undefined responsibilities' implicit in the French scheme, which were enough to frighten Parliament out of its wits. If Britain were ever to enter into any such arrangement, which on the face of it had far greater advantages for France, her price must be some prior settlement of the outstanding political issues between the two countries, such as those in Morocco and Egypt.[2]

[1] The Franco-Polish treaty of mutual defence was signed on 19 February 1921. Poland was linked by treaty with Rumania on 3 March 1921 and the Little Entente was completed by a Rumanian-Yugoslav treaty of 7 June 1921; see A. J. Toynbee, *Survey of International Affairs, 1924*, p. 5.

[2] France No. 1 (1924). Papers respecting negotiations for an Anglo-French Pact, Cmd. 2169, pp. 109–12.

The state of French armaments again provided the starting point for an exchange of views on the pact between Lloyd George and the French Prime Minister, Briand, in London on 21 December. Britain had been disturbed by the French delegation's attitude at the Washington Naval Conference, which had opened on 12 November, and especially by French reserves in the matter of submarines. Briand himself had said in the French Chamber on 23 November that he wanted to erase suspicions aroused by the Washington meetings by a 'positive alliance' with Britain.[1] Unfolding the idea to Lloyd George at the December talks Briand spoke of a 'very broad alliance' to guarantee each other's interests in all parts of the world; this would provide a nucleus around which would be built a general organisation, eventually to include Germany, for keeping the peace and buttressing the League Covenant. But it was clearly security in Europe which interested Briand most since he defined as one of the alliance's main objects the discouragement of German military designs on Poland and Russia. It was precisely this aspect of the proposal which most disquieted the British. Lloyd George said that there would probably be a majority in Parliament for a plain guarantee to France in case of invasion, but the British people were not much interested in Germany's eastern frontiers. Giving vent to his characteristic views of East Europe, Lloyd George went on:

> They would not be ready to be involved in quarrels which might arise regarding Poland or Danzig or Upper Silesia. On the contrary, there was a general reluctance to get mixed up in these questions in any way. The British people felt that the populations in that quarter of Europe were unstable and excitable; they might start fighting at any time and the rights and wrongs of the dispute might be very hard to disentangle.[2]

These initial differences came even more into view in the discussions between the two Prime Ministers at the conference held at Cannes by the Supreme Council in January 1922.[3] While Lloyd George's conception of the pact was limited in one sense, it ranged far and wide in another. The limitation was the geographical restriction of the British version of the pact to French soil, which Britain was prepared to guarantee

---

[1] France, Ministère des Affaires Étrangères, *Documents diplomatiques relatifs aux négociations concernant les garanties de sécurité contre une agression de l'Allemagne*, Paris, 1924, p. 251.

[2] Cmd. 2169, pp. 112–13.

[3] For the circumstances in which the Cannes Conference met see above, Chapter VIII, p. 215.

against unprovoked aggression by Germany.   But the political conditions attached to the offer covered virtually the whole extent of Anglo-French differences as they had come to light since the armistice.   These were in effect to be settled according to the British view.   France was to agree to naval talks for avoiding competition in shipbuilding, which was to be under-stood as bringing to an end the French submarine programme. France was also asked to agree to an economic conference, to which Russia was to be invited, where the general European reconstruction essential to economic recovery in Britain was to be undertaken.   There must also be absolute agreement be-tween the two countries on Allied policy in the Near East. The only reference in the British draft to German obligations, other than that of respecting French territory, was that the Allies should consult together in the event of a breach of the demilitarisation of the Rhineland or of any infringement by Germany of the military, naval or air clauses of the Versailles Treaty.[1]

Briand's reply largely ignored the wide-ranging British de-mand for a prior settlement of all Anglo-French differences and concentrated on the question dominating French thoughts: security.   Instead of the unilateral British guarantee to France envisaged by Lloyd George, the French Premier insisted on a bilateral pact on the grounds that this would bring home in Berlin the identity between the two allies, and because Britain was no longer safe against modern methods of attack.   Briand further proposed that Britain should come to France's aid, not merely in the event of a German attack on French soil, but in case of any German violation of the disarmament provisions of the Versailles Treaty, and especially of the articles relating to the demilitarisation of the Rhineland.   The Briand draft then went on to bind Britain and France to consult together should anything occur likely to disturb European security and to arrange for a convention between General Staffs, so as to give effect to the undertakings contained in the pact.   The con-vention, Briand added, and one can imagine him smiling to himself as he did so, would help them to settle the question of competitive armaments, which was proving so close to the British heart.[2]

The Briand Cabinet fell before British reactions to the French proposals could be fully tested.   But the draft of the proposed treaty drawn up by Briand's successor, Poincaré, and handed to Curzon by the French Ambassador on 26 January

[1] Cmd. 2169, pp. 114–20, 127–8; CAB 23/29. 1 (22), for Cabinet discussion.
[2] Cmd. 2169, pp. 121–6.

closely followed Briand's lines. The chief difference was that the general undertaking to consult together in the Briand version was more directly related to the 'general order of things set up under the treaties of peace of which (Britain and France) are signatories'.[1] This was merely to underline the points on which Briand had lost the confidence of the French Chamber. Poincaré further proposed that the duration of the pact should be thirty years, not ten as proposed by Lloyd George during the talks at Cannes.

Provisional British views on the draft were dealt with by Curzon at the same interview with the Ambassador. He said that the government would consider the proposal for making the pact bilateral in a friendly spirit, if it was a matter of French *amour-propre*; Germany, like Britain, the implication ran, was too sensible to be impressed by mere paper declarations. But the idea of extending the pact to cover a guarantee of the demilitarisation of the Rhineland was unacceptable to British opinion because it was inconsistent with the 'new theory' that 'the old policy of rival groupings of Great Powers was to disappear and to be replaced by a concord of the nations'. At no price would Britain consent to an Anglo-French hegemony in Europe since it would be contrary to the principles of general reconciliation inherent in the League Covenant. Nor was Curzon attracted by the French conception of the pact as the nucleus of a general European association, which must have the result of ossifying the established order of affairs along with all the grievances it provoked. Curzon also spoke disdainfully of the French wish for a permanent *entente* between the General Staffs of the two countries, which he thought had no practical significance and only the questionable moral purpose of putting fear into Germany. He deprecated the implied undertaking in article 4 of the French draft to safeguard the general order of things set up by the peace treaties, which jarred on the British concern to limit commitments in Europe. The thirty years' duration of the pact was also far too long in the Foreign Secretary's view, though the British Cabinet might be willing to consider fifteen years provided a good case could be made out.[2]

On 1 February Curzon drew up a careful paper on the British attitude towards the Poincaré proposals. In this he raised no objection to the pact having a reciprocal character, but could not relinquish his belief that only French pride made this necessary. He adhered to the words 'soil of France',

---

[1] Cmd. 2169, p. 131. Article 4 of the Poincaré draft.
[2] *Ibid.*, pp. 131–6.

rather than 'France', as the subject of the British side of the guarantee, since only the actual crossing of the French frontier would seem to British opinion sufficient reason for going to war against Germany again. He rejected the proposal to make any German violation of the Rhineland articles of the Versailles Treaty the *casus foederis* of the pact, especially if the alliance were to be for fifteen or twenty years, that is, longer than the Allied occupation of the Rhineland under the Treaty. British public opinion was never likely to regard German territory on the left bank of the Rhine in the same light as actual French soil. Moreover, any joint undertaking by Britain and France to guarantee the execution of a treaty to which many other states were signatory would be tantamount to bisecting Europe into hostile combinations similar to those which had led to war in 1914, to say nothing of running the risk of driving Germany into Russia's arms.

Curzon then went on to reject once again the French principle of an *entente constante* between the two General Staffs, partly because it might give the impression (which the French wanted it to give) that the two countries were more closely tied by mutual military guarantees than was the case, and partly because the definition of the obligations undertaken in the pact might slip more and more out of civilian hands into those of the military. The nightmare of an escalation into war through military arrangements moving automatically towards hostilities never, after 1914, ceased to haunt the British imagination. Curzon admitted that in the pre-war Entente, as from the Algeciras Conference in 1906, military and naval conversations had been authorised by the two governments, but argued that there was no written agreement to hold them.[1] He conceded that under the pact similar talks would probably continue, and Germany would hear of them and be just as much impressed with the reality of the Anglo-French pact as if the talks were provided for in the pact or in a separate exchange of notes on the signature of the pact. Then came the Foreign Secretary's expected rejection of the article in the French draft committing the two governments to act together on all questions likely to endanger the general order of things set up under the peace treaties. The article was objectionable in Britain because it sought to make Britain and France the arbiters of all European disputes in a manner inconsistent with the principles of multilateral settlements of the League Covenant. Britain could not act as the auxiliary of France in the defence of the territorial

---

[1] Curzon evidently played down the exchange of letters on the subject between Sir Edward Grey and Paul Cambon in September 1912.

status quo and in circumstances in which it was clear that, in the patrolling of the Continent, French forces would have the greater part to play. Curzon was willing, however, to extend the duration of the pact to fifteen years to coincide with the period of Allied occupation of the Rhineland.[1]

By this time Poincaré's impact on Anglo-French relations was making itself felt and support in Britain for a pact with France, at no time very great, began to dwindle. The Government were therefore obliged to return to Lloyd George's insistence at Cannes that, if there were to be a pact for making France more secure, it must be merely one element in a general settlement of outstanding issues. Curzon told the French Ambassador bluntly on 19 March 1922 that the time would come to talk about the pact and submit proposals to Parliament when the British Government were able to report progress with Anglo-French discords; the most important of these were Turkey, on which an Allied conference was about to meet, economic reconstruction issues, to be considered at the Genoa Conference in April, and Tangier, where the French were proving difficult.[2] On 30 May, after the failure of the Genoa talks and when Balfour was in charge of the Foreign Office during Curzon's illness, the Count de Saint-Aulaire returned Poincaré's answer. The French Prime Minister denied that agreement on the pact was conditional on the settlement of these general issues; at the same time he made clear that the Anglo-French alliance was conceived in Paris as no more than the axis of a wider and much grander European combination, the intention of which was plainly to realise Poincaré's dream of a *Pax Gallica* embracing all Europe.[3] Poincaré showed his understanding of the British position when he told the British Ambassador in Paris, Lord Hardinge, in June that the pact in the limited form preferred by Britain was of no importance to him since Britain, in her own interest, would always come to the assistance of France and Belgium if German aggression took place whether there was a pact or not. Britain was giving nothing and expected obedience in all things from France in return.[4] Poincaré returned to the theme of political conditions for the pact when he wrote to Balfour on 3 July, a month before the disastrous reparations conference in London in August. All that Lloyd George had meant at Cannes, he said, in linking European economic reconstruction with the negotiation of the pact was that France should consent to the calling of the Genoa Conference. This the French had done, but they could hardly be

---

[1] Cmd. 2169, pp. 154–62.
[2] *Ibid.*, p. 163.
[3] *Ibid.*, p. 164.
[4] *Ibid.*, pp. 166–7.

held to account for the results of the Conference.[1]   On this, however, according to the British Government, more than one opinion was possible.

The Anglo-French breach on reparations at the London Conference in August and the resulting Ruhr crisis of January 1923, when the Entente lay in ruins, ended all serious talk about a security pact.   From time to time during the angry exchanges on the Ruhr crisis London appealed for a resumption of the discussions on security, thereby hoping to manœuvre the French into a retreat from the Ruhr policy.   Poincaré's reply was that he was ready to renew discussion of the pact, but that guarantees against new aggression could not deprive France of her right to reparations, especially when it was doubtful whether the guarantees, as defined by Britain, would prove effective.[2] In a debate in the Chamber of Deputies on 23 November Poincaré returned to the insistent French claim that no guarantee pact was satisfactory to France without a firm military convention.   France did not wish to run the risk of having 'certain measures of disarmament' imposed upon her without receiving in return 'definite compensating securities'.[3]

The failure of the bilateral pact was thus the outcome partly of basic differences in British and French attitudes towards European security, differences in which geographical position, history, national character played their parts, and partly of the larger Anglo-French conflicts of the postwar period, which formed an angry backcloth to the exchanges.   As far as security was concerned, Britain believed that this was not attainable without the free acceptance by the defeated countries of the arrangements imposed on them in 1919, and this obviously required some modification in those features of the 1919 arrangements which it was unreasonable to hope that the defeated could accept.   This did not rule out British guarantees of French and Belgian territory, and even British co-operation with France in enforcing the indispensable parts of the treaties, for such span of time as peace should not be fully secure.   The French, for their part, never believed in the free acceptance by Germany of the treaties, unless the latter were so amended as virtually to destroy the Allied ascendancy.   The numerical superiority of Germany over France, together with German inbred militarism, made a future German attack on the Versailles restrictions in either east or west probable if not inevitable. The only circumstance which might deter it was a strong mili-

---

[1] Cmd. 2169, p. 170.
[2] *Ibid.*, p. 174.
[3] *Documents diplomatiques*, pp. 253–4.

tary alliance of all the states with an interest in the *status quo*.
To these differences on the approach to security were added
the confusions resulting from the conflicts of British and French
policies at every point at which they intersected on the globe.

II

The security pact negotiations with France were exacer-
bated by discords which culminated in the Ruhr crisis and the
bitter outcries in Britain against France's separatist Rhineland
policy.   But over and above the state of Anglo-French relations
were factors in Britain's world position and outlook which ensured that her participation in schemes of security should always
be limited to particular and well-defined areas of conflict.
Foremost among these factors was the overwhelming British
desire after the war for relief from foreign commitments and
involvement in foreign quarrels.   The desire engendered its
own illusions, among them the belief that the world was exhausted with strife and would readily lay aside its weapons if a
genuine lead were given.   Disarmament, especially of the great
continental land armies, seemed the greatest single need of the
time and everything should be done to avoid arousing dormant
hatreds and jealousies.

Secondly, there was the constant awareness in British political
circles that the confederation of the Great Powers, through
which British policy had worked in the nineteenth century, was
dangerously incomplete through ruptures effected by the war.
Ramsay MacDonald referred, as Lloyd George and Bonar Law
had done so in other circumstances, to the 'menacing vacant
chair' reserved for Germany when he appeared as Prime
Minister and Foreign Secretary at the League Assembly in
September 1924.   But there were at least two more, those of
the United States and Russia.   Without the complete company
of the Great Powers British Governments feared that the burden
of keeping the peace would fall heavily on their own shoulders,
and that the rival coalitions of pre-war days would shape themselves again, this time in the form of League Powers ranged
against Powers outside the League.   If the vacant chairs were
to be filled, commitments entered into by the active Powers
must be limited lest burdensome undertakings deter the out-
siders from knocking on the door.

But a third factor also imposed restraint: the current changes
in the character of the British Empire.   The days when Empire
foreign policy was made in London belonged to history.   The
Dominions, as the embarrassing independence they had shown
at the Peace Conference and their separate membership of the

League made clear, were no longer to be regarded as falling automatically behind Britain whatever she should decide.   Yet, once it was admitted that in Canada, Australia, New Zealand and South Africa foreign policy must command the broad assent of the people, the natural isolationism of British public opinion after 1918 was magnified at least four times.   If the quarrels of Europe seemed flat and unprofitable in London or Manchester, there was even more reason why they should do so thousands of miles away in Ottawa or Melbourne, Auckland or Cape Town.   British Governments were at liberty to enter security engagements with European Powers without binding the Dominions; this was their intention had the security pact with France been pressed to a conclusion.   Nevertheless, they could never enter such engagements without seriously con- sidering whether action to fulfil them, should the need arise, would command general sympathy in the Dominions.   The Chanak episode in September 1922 showed that a British Government might find itself in an advanced position from which it might call to the Dominions for aid and call in vain.[1]

Such considerations governed British attitudes towards the efforts of the first League Assemblies to strengthen the peace- enforcement machinery of the Covenant.   These efforts were unsuccessful, however strenuously League apologists argued then and since that something was saved from the wreck. Their unsuccess reflected, on the one hand, France's inability to concede the disarmament which Britain demanded unless the Covenant were made foolproof against aggression and, on the other, the refusal of Britain to help provide the necessary sanctions against aggression unless the motives for war were first removed by the fulfilment of the disarmament under- takings of the Covenant and Part V of the Versailles Treaty relating to Germany's military status.   Disarmament thus came to provide a common ground on which Labour and Con- servative ideas on foreign policy could meet in Britain in the 1920s.   So long as France and her anti-German allies remained armed the Right in Britain refused to take seriously the various proposals for general security within the League.   So long as such schemes seemed to require from Britain an increase in military commitments they were discouraging to Labour. Hence the identity of view for all practical purposes between the first Labour Government and the Baldwin Cabinet towards the Draft Treaty of Mutual Assistance and the Geneva Protocol.

The origins of these two supplements to the League Covenant

[1] For the attitude of the Dominions in the Near East crisis of 1922 see above, Chapter VI, p. 151.

are well known. The Temporary Mixed Commission on armaments created by the League Council in February 1921 did not take long to conclude that the disarmament undertakings in article 8 of the Covenant were unlikely to be carried out so long as the security system provided by the Covenant failed to provide a reliable substitute for national armaments. There were many risks to be faced by countries relying on the League for protection. The Council might be undecided on the merits of a dispute, perhaps through the veto of one of its permanent representatives, and hence the parties would be free, by reason of one of the Covenant's famous 'gaps', to go to war. Economic and financial sanctions might prove insufficient to deter a resolute and strong aggressor and distant countries, such as Canada, which had already disinterested themselves in the European *status quo*, might refuse to take action even when the Council was agreed. Or, if economic sanctions failed to restrain the aggressor and the Council appealed for military force, League Members might be afraid to run the risk of retaliation by assisting victims of attack in disputes in which they themselves were not directly involved. These possibilities made essential the construction of a tougher machinery of security than the Covenant as it stood if Members were to feel safe enough to disarm.

The result was the Draft Treaty of Mutual Assistance drawn up in the Temporary Mixed Commission largely through the efforts of the British and French delegates, Viscount Cecil and Colonel Réquin, and submitted for approval to the Fourth League Assembly in September 1923. The discussion in the Assembly aroused such differences of view that it was decided not to adopt the document but to submit it to Member governments for their observations. Although the Draft Treaty was described by its champions as an implementation of the Covenant in fact it extended Covenant undertakings which were already proving more than any Members were willing to fulfil. For example, where the Covenant article 16 pledged Members to assist one another in reducing the economic and other losses arising from the application of sanctions, in the Draft Treaty this mutual assistance was, by article 2, to be confined to signatories which had complied with the disarmament provisions of the treaty. These committed signatories to inform the Council of the arms reductions they considered justified in view of the security afforded by the treaty, to co-operate with the Council in the preparation of a general plan of disarmament, and to carry out within two years the reductions specified in the general plan after this had been agreed to by the governments

concerned.   These provisions gave a sharper edge to the disarmament undertakings of the Covenant as defined in article 8.

But the most far-reaching advance on the Covenant proposed
in the Draft Treaty was the strengthening of the Council's
authority.   In the Covenant the Council was intended to be
little more than a conciliating organ whose reports on disputes
were authoritative guides to Members in the discharge of their
obligations and whose views on military sanctions had only the
force of recommendations.   In the Draft Treaty, however, the
Council was given authority almost equal to that of the Security
Council under the United Nations Charter of 1945.   By article
4 the Council was authorised to decide within four days of the
outbreak of hostilities which of the signatory states was the
object of aggression and whether it qualified for assistance under
the treaty.   The Council was also to decide the form of assistance to the victim of aggression and the economic sanctions
to be applied against the aggressor and to name the states whose
co-operation was required.   Above all, the Council was
authorised to decide, and not merely, as in the Covenant, to
recommend, the armed forces which signatories were to furnish
in fulfilment of the scheme of mutual assistance, although it was
provided that no state would be expected to co-operate in military sanctions in a continent other than that in which it was situated. These provisions gave the Council a directive function which
had never been contemplated, except by the French, in 1919.[1]

The Draft Treaty was the work of individuals rather than
government delegates and therefore Britain was in no way
bound by it when the time came to send to the League the
official British reply.   Moreover, the Conservative Party, of
whose international views Cecil was an untypical representative, was worsted in the general election held on 6 December
1923 and the first Labour Government, heavily relying on
Liberal support, was formed under Ramsay MacDonald on 22
January 1924.   It is a striking testimony to the continuity of
British views on foreign affairs at this time that MacDonald,
who had been expelled from a Lossiemouth golf club for his
anti-war position in 1915, should not merely have led a British
Government in 1924 but should have continued in all essentials
the main lines of British policy.   MacDonald said of his visit
to the Fifth League Assembly that he came away from Geneva
'fully convinced that peace was possible, fully convinced that
the change that had to be made was not a great big somersault.

[1] For the text of the Draft Treaty see League of Nations Official Journal, Special
Supplement No. 16. Records of the Fourth Assembly. Minutes of the Third Committee, Geneva, 1923, pp. 153–5.

... After very intimate conversations and a very thorough exploration of the problems, I came to the conclusion that the alteration that was required was the very smallest fraction of a change in the angle of vision.'[1] This conservatism arose partly from MacDonald's concern to correct any impression that Labour's rule would reverse the order of nature and partly from his own detachment from many of the idealistic sentiments moving the party he led. But its most important basis was the fact that Labour's antagonism to militarism and military coalitions was fully shared, for different reasons, by the Conservatives. The Left continued to indentify the Right with policies of force; but it was owing to their rejection of policies of force that the Conservatives had broken with Lloyd George in October 1922 and it was for the same reason that they could make no progress with the French towards a mutual security pact. In a statement published in the *Daily Herald* immediately after a European tour he had made in the autumn of 1923 MacDonald spoke in accents which Bonar Law, Baldwin, Curzon, no less than Lloyd George, would have not found hard to echo:

Europe is getting sick of Napoleonism. Therefore, my general conclusion is that whilst in Governments there may be no change, whilst vain men gain some reputation from vociferous sections in their own States from empty triumphs, the general mind turns away from them and looks for other voices and other leading. Things have been allowed to go so far wrong that they cannot be righted in a day; wisdom will be frowned on at first as hostility by some Governments perhaps; but the supreme need of Europe now is that the Liberal elements in all the nations should be drawn together, should be made to live, and should get a lead in a comprehensive policy of pacification and reconstruction.[2]

Pacification and reconstruction in MacDonald's mind fell into two parts: reparations and security. The first culminated in the London Conference in July and August and occupied the first half of his brief spell of office. As to security, he agreed with the new French Premier, Herriot, in talks held in London on 21 and 22 June to co-operate in devising solutions 'through the League of Nations or otherwise' and 'to continue consideration of the question until the problem of general security can be finally solved'.[3] Although this implied a common Anglo-French approach to the problem after the Dawes plan had been

[1] 185 H.C. Deb. 5s. Col. 1582 (24 June 1925).
[2] Quoted in George Glasgow, *MacDonald as Diplomatist*, p. 25.
[3] Misc. No. 12 (1924). Franco-British Memorandum of July 9, 1924, Cmd, 2191, p. 5.

agreed, MacDonald expressed himself on the Draft Treaty of
Mutual Assistance in a letter to the League Secretary-General
on 5 July, eleven days before the London Conference on the
Dawes plan met.

MacDonald's reply singled out the weak features of the Draft
Treaty as a formula for general security, but in doing so made
clear that any British Government, of Right or Left, would
have the greatest difficulty in accepting any universal scheme
going far beyond the Covenant. As a particular formula, the
Draft Treaty was criticised in MacDonald's letter because it
called on the League Council to decide within four days on the
identity of the aggressor; four days, in the British view, was too
short for the Council's examination of a complex issue, but
probably too long for the victim of aggression to survive for
the purpose of being assisted at the end of that period. But
it was when MacDonald went on to discuss the nature of the
assistance provided in the treaty that the virtual impractica-
bility of any general scheme of security, given the existing
premises of national policy, became apparent. If states are
to rely on such general guarantees so as to feel able to reduce
their armaments, he argued, assistance in emergencies must be
immediate and effective. Economic sanctions might prove too
weak a weapon and military sanctions, if they were to have
speedy results, would have to be pre-arranged. In the nature
of things all the states of the world, or even the large number
required to make a success of the Draft Treaty, could not concert together to meet in advance all the various situations in
which one of their number might attack another, nor could there
be any real assurance that, if they did, the promised assistance
would be automatically forthcoming if the need arose. As
MacDonald said in a passage exposing the self-contradictions
implicit in schemes of general security:

> The possibility will always exist that the States most
> favourably situated for providing the necessary force may at
> a given moment not be in a position to do so, owing to com-
> mitments elsewhere, the state of public opinion, or the politi-
> cal condition of the country at the time. The appointment
> of the higher command will itself involve delay. The Coun-
> cil will have great difficulty in reaching a unanimous decision,
> for no nation places its troops under a foreign command
> without very careful consideration. A system which in-
> volves prolonged delays before the first step in bringing mili-
> tary pressure to bear on an aggressor nation can be taken does
> not reach that standard of effectiveness which is essential.

There were three ways in which it was proposed in the Draft Treaty that these difficulties in mustering immediate force against aggression should be overcome; to each of these the Labour Prime Minister and, it seems safe to say, British public opinion behind him, were hostile. In the first place, while in the longer term the climate of security produced by the treaty would no doubt make disarmament less uninviting, the immediate need was to keep adequate armed force held in readiness by states party to the treaty. As MacDonald pointed out, this might involve an increase in British naval power and similar increases in the armed strength of other signatories. This would place a Prime Minister at odds with the Conservative Opposition over the Singapore base in a strange position and would not strengthen British Governments in their efforts to get the French to disarm. Secondly, the treaty provided for 'partial agreements' among signatories for self-defence by way of implementing regionally the general mutual assistance afforded by the treaty. But this was contrary to the British aversion to military alliances, especially prevalent in the rank and file of the Labour Party, and since the obvious partners of Britain in any such agreements in western Europe were France and Belgium, the treaty seemed to lead back into the cul-de-sac of the Anglo-French pact talks. Thirdly, as we have seen, the treaty greatly magnified the League Council's authority to call for economic and military action by signatories in restraint of aggression. For MacDonald to consent to such a reform of the League was not merely to confirm the charges that Labour intended to hand over the Royal Navy to foreigners; it was to reverse at one stroke the policy of opposition to an international army which Britain had consistently followed since the drafting of the Covenant. It was unthinkable that such a change could be effected by a minority government in precarious enjoyment of power.[1]

Yet in spite of MacDonald's rejection of the Draft Treaty, he was committed by the agreement with Herriot in June to continue the search for the ideal formula. Such was his personal appeal that when he decided to attend the Fifth League Assembly in September 1924, along with Herriot, his action against the Draft Treaty, and especially the form in which it was couched, were forgotten. The event was thought to herald a new dawn for mankind. MacDonald was met with much the same kind of fervour with which a war-weary Europe greeted

---

[1] Misc. No. 13 (1924). Correspondence between H.M.G. and the League of Nations respecting the proposed Treaty of Mutual Assistance, Cmd. 2200, pp. 10–14.

Wilson in 1919; he was the superman who was going 'to get Europe out of the mess'.[1] He came with a great diplomatic triumph behind him, the ending of the Ruhr crisis and the launching of the Dawes plan based on American sympathy and Franco-German accord. He had recognised Soviet Russia. He led the British Labour Party, which was satisfactory to those who wanted revision of the peace treaties, yet he had expressly dissociated himself from revision, thus pleasing France and the successor states, when his Home Secretary Arthur Henderson, had attacked the Versailles Treaty at his by-election in Burnley.[2] In that blissful dawn there was little difficulty in believing that MacDonald might bring together a France which had turned away from Poincarism and a Germany in which Stresemann had worked the miracle of abandoning passive resistance, and might, on the basis of their reconciliation, build a security system strong enough to deter the covetous and encourage the fearful to disarm.

But on this supreme occasion MacDonald might well have used King Arthur's words as Tennyson visualised them: 'Comfort thyself, what comfort is in me?' He knew that the government's minority position would never warrant radical commitments to the League by Britain. He knew that even if Germany entered the League, as he insisted, the concert of Powers would still be incomplete without Russia and the United States, and the stronger the League became as a peace-enforcing agency the less the likelihood of these two being willing to join. The most that could be done, MacDonald knew, was to heighten the incentives towards peaceful settlements, to identify those who feared or refused peaceful settlements, while the sanctions machinery must mark time until perhaps there was a change of mind in Russia or the United States.

Hence MacDonald's speech to the Assembly on 4 September concentrated on three themes: the danger of military alliances, the need for expanding the League's membership and improving methods of abitrating international disputes. Military alliances, said MacDonald, in the exact spirit of his predecessors, were a 'grain of mustard seed' which grows 'until at last the tree produced from it overshadows the whole of the heavens and we shall be back in exactly the military position in which we found ourselves in 1914'. The last thing Britain could afford was to side with one group against another, especially if the former included new states in east and south-east Europe about which Britain knew little and among the latter

[1] H. M. Swanwick, *I Have Been Young*, London, 1935, p. 388.
[2] Mary Agnes Hamilton, *Arthur Henderson*, pp. 238–40.

was the United States without whose support or benevolent neutrality British naval or military action was out of the question. But if peace could not be enforced, the frictions menacing it could be arbitrated away. The most significant passage in the Prime Minister's speech came when he said:

> The only method by which we can secure, the only method by which we can approximate to an accurate attribution of responsibility for aggression is arbitration. . . . The test is, Are you willing to arbitrate? The test is, Are you willing to explain? The test is, Will you come before us and tell us what you propose to do? The test is, Will you expose your commitment? Are you afraid of the world? . . . Such is the test, the only test.[1]

MacDonald's speech encouraged the Assembly to vote without opposition the famous two-part resolution moved by the British and French delegations from which the Geneva Protocol for the pacific settlement of international disputes was born. The first part instructed the Assembly's Third Committee, dealing with disarmament, to 'examine the obligations in the Covenant in relation to guarantees of security which a resort to arbitration and a reduction of armaments may require'. The second asked the First Committee, concerned with legal and constitutional issues, to consider the possibilities of amending the articles in the League Covenant relating to the peaceful settlement of disputes and, secondly, to 'examine within what limits the terms of article 36 (2) of the Statute of the Permanent Court of International Justice might be rendered more precise and thereby facilitate the more general acceptance of the clause'.[2]

III

Thus the next stage in the strengthening of the Covenant, the Geneva Protocol, was begun on Britain's initiative and on lines suggested by a British Prime Minister. France was ready to follow, even to the point of agreeing to Germany's admission into the League. But she expected her reward in the form of a positive British commitment to act against a state which

---

[1] *League of Nations Official Journal.* Special Supplement No. 23, Records of the Fifth Assembly. Plenary Meetings, pp. 41–3.

[2] Article 36, the so-called Optional Clause, allowed signatories of the Statute to assume obligations to refer disputes compulsorily to the Court on a reciprocal basis. MacDonald told the Assembly in his opening speech that Britain contemplated signing the Optional Clause but not until it had been drafted 'in the most specific form possible'. The clause was actually signed on Britain's behalf by the second Labour Government in 1929. See Misc. No. 8 (1929). Permanent Court of International Justice. Declaration made on behalf of H.M.G. at the time of the signature of the Optional Clause, Cmd. 3421.

refused to arbitrate or accept the results of arbitration. 'Arbitration,' said Herriot, 'is essential, but it is not sufficient. It is a means, but not an end. It does not entirely fulfil the intentions of article 8 of the Covenant, which are security and disarmament. We in France regard these three terms—arbitration, security and disarmament—as inseparable.'[1] It was little comfort to France to find that, after the resulting Protocol had been drafted by the two committees and generally endorsed by the Assembly on 2 October, the MacDonald Government fell from power on an issue irrelevant to the Genevan debate. The succeeding administration formed by Baldwin did no more than administer the *coup de grâce* to the scheme of general security to which it is probable, judging from MacDonald's speech in September, that the Labour leader himself would have objected.

The Geneva Protocol resembled the Draft Treaty in some respects. It too was a pact of mutual non-aggression, a pledge of mutual assistance, although in the Protocol this assistance was not limited to states which had disarmed, and an expedient to speed disarmament. The Protocol stipulated that a world disarmament conference would meet on 16 June 1925 in Geneva and the Protocol was not to come into force until a disarmament plan had been adopted by the conference; it could moreover be declared void by the League Council if the disarmament plan was not carried out within a period to be fixed by the Council. The novel feature of the Protocol was its complicated system for the settlement of every conceivable dispute and its precise definition of aggression. Peaceful settlements were to be ensured, first, through acceptance by all signatories of the Optional Clause of the Statute of the Permanent Court, though without prejudice to their right to make reservations compatible with the clause. Further, by article 4 the League Council was to try to persuade the parties to any dispute to refer it to a court of law or to arbitration. If the parties failed to agree, the dispute could be referred to arbitration at the request of one of the parties, the Council being authorised to finalise this procedure if necessary. But if neither party asked for arbitration the Council could take charge of the dispute; if it failed to reach an agreed report (in which case it would be left to all concerned, under the Covenant, to act as they thought fit) the dispute automatically went to arbitration. The parties agreed in advance to carry out in good faith judicial sentences or arbitral awards and any state which failed in this undertaking and resorted to war was, by the definition of the Pro-

[1] Records of the Fifth Assembly. Plenary Meetings, p. 52.

tocol, an aggressor. The Council was authorised, in the event of aggression thus defined, to call upon signatories to apply sanctions and they would be afforded belligerent rights if involved in war when carrying out the Council's decisions.

In contrast with the Draft Treaty, the duty of signatories to comply with the Council's call for sanctions was strictly limited. Signatories were bound by article 11 (2) to co-operate 'loyally and effectively' in support, but no state was expected to do more than its geographical situation and 'its particular situation as regards armaments' allowed. This meant that a disarmed country, like Germany under the Versailles Treaty, would still have a part to play, proportionately to its resources, under the Protocol. More importantly, though the Council, somewhat similarly to the Security Council under article 43 of the United Nations Charter, was authorised to receive undertakings in advance as to the armed support of the Covenant and Protocol which signatories would be prepared to offer in emergencies, it was entirely open to a state to decide for itself how much or how little of a contribution it felt able to make under this head.[1] This disposed of the foolish rumour of the time in Britain that the Protocol meant the automatic surrender of the Navy to the League.

It was largely in deference to British fears of military commitments that the Protocol placed the lightest possible obligation on signatories in the matter of enforcement. Henderson reiterated that under the Protocol 'neither the Permanent Court nor the Council of the League have any control whatsoever over the forces of any particular country'.[2] The British delegation on its return from the Fifth Assembly further assured a nervous public opinion that the 'Draft Treaty tended towards the realisation of the idea of the League as a "super-State"; the Protocol respects the principle of national sovereignty'.[3] These reminders that it was the arbitration rather than the security in the Protocol which chiefly interested Britain were what prompted the French to ask Henderson what the phrase 'loyal and effective' co-operation in article 11 really meant, and caused them not to be fully reassured by his reply that 'it means we shall knock them on the head'.[4] They could not forget that, at a meeting of British and French delegates on Sunday, 7 September, before the two committees seriously set to

[1] The fullest and most authoritative exposition of the Protocol is the book by P. J. Noel-Baker, *The Geneva Protocol*, in which the text is printed in Annex VIII.
[2] 182 H.C. Deb. 5s. Col. 302 (24 March 1925).
[3] Misc. No. 21 (1924). League of Nations, Fifth Assembly, Report of the British Delegates, Cmd. 2289, p. 9.
[4] Mary Agnes Hamilton, *op. cit.*, p. 247.

work, Lord Parmoor insisted that whatever else the phrase meant it did not mean that Britain could commit herself in advance to supply given forces.[1]

Nevertheless it was precisely the coercive aspect of the Protocol which most disturbed the Dominions. Since the government formed by Baldwin in November needed time to adjust to office the decisive discussion of the Protocol was postponed at Britain's request until the meeting of the League Council in March 1925. The government hoped that it might be possible to hold a meeting of Dominions Prime Ministers in London in March in order to arrive at a common position before the Council met. This proved impossible for most of the Premiers and an exchange of views by cable had to be substituted. The tone was set for this by Baldwin himself in a message to the Governors-General of the Dominions on 19 December 1924, when he said that the Protocol involved submission even of vital interests to compulsory arbitration, sanctions 'of the most drastic character' and a possible breach with the United States.[2] The Dominions found that this echoed their own fears. The South African Prime Minister regarded the Protocol as a 'political alliance' which might deter such countries as the United States from joining the League and embroil South Africa in matters in which she had no direct concern. The New Zealand Premier, Massey, objected that the Protocol would place his country's immigration laws under the jurisdiction of a world court 'consisting mainly of foreigners'. He pointed out that MacDonald's criticism of the Draft Treaty, namely that it conferred no advantage 'sufficient to compensate the world for the immense complication of international relations which it would create', applied in equal measure to the Protocol. Canadian objections naturally turned largely on the difficulty of enforcing sanctions when the United States was neither a member of the League nor a likely signatory of the Protocol; in other respects, however, the Canadian reply was more conciliatory than those of the other Dominions, which may have been due in part to the fact that Sir Robert Borden, the Canadian Prime Minister during the war and at the Peace Conference, was a supporter of the Protocol.[3]

The judgment of Australia resembled the general tone of the replies in placing more emphasis on the fostering of confidence than on the organisation of force and argued that the latter was

---

[1] Lord Parmoor, *A Retrospect*, p. 235.
[2] Protocol for the Pacific Settlement of International Disputes. Correspondence relating to the position of the Dominions, Cmd. 2458 (1925), p. 6.
[3] Lord Parmoor, *op. cit.*, p. 262, on Borden's opinion.

too prominent in the Protocol. The possible effects of compulsory arbitration on the White Australia policy, however, were chiefly in that government's mind. Article 10 of the Protocol defined as a partial test of aggression the resort to hostilities in disregard of an arbitral award which recognised that the dispute arose out of a matter which by international law fell within the domestic jurisdiction of the state attacked, but the belligerent state would not be an aggressor if it had already submitted the question to the Council or Assembly of the League under article 11 of the Covenant. This, in the Australian view, provided an Asian country such as Japan with immunity from the charge of aggression in case of hostilities with Australia, provided that it had already raised the White Australia policy before the League without receiving satisfaction. In the case of the Irish Free State, however, the local interest which it was feared might be jeopardised by the Protocol was not immigration control but the campaign against Northern Ireland. In a speech in the Dail on 13 May 1925 the Irish Minister for External Affairs said that the intention of the framers of the Protocol appeared to be to exclude from pacific settlement disputes regarding existing territorial divisions and this detracted from the instrument's value; 'it may in time become apparent that present boundaries are in some cases unsuitable and provocative of ill-will'. The bias of the Baldwin Government against the Protocol was thus reinforced from within the Empire on grounds respectable and otherwise.[1]

It may be argued that Britain might nevertheless have signed the Protocol, following the example of France and a handful of other states which signed before leaving Geneva, and on the same basis as she had intended signing the abortive Anglo-French security pact and as she was to sign the Locarno guarantee treaty, namely without committing the Dominions but leaving them free to adhere if they chose. She might have calculated that if she was ever at war with an aggressor as defined by the Protocol the Dominions would none the less come to her aid out of loyalty or common interest. There was an important difference, however, between the Anglo-French proposal for a pact and the Locarno guarantee on one side and the Protocol on the other. If Britain were ever to be at war again in western Europe, for instance in defence of France, she would be fighting for her own life and that would be abundantly clear to the Dominions. But through the Protocol she might be involved in conflicts which neither British opinion nor opinion in

[1] Cmd. 2548.

the Empire could regard as having as their issue the life or death of Britain. Another possibility was that the Protocol, had it struck London as relevant to the needs of the times, might have been subscribed to by Britain in the hope of persuading the Dominions to accept it later on. So far from encouraging the Dominions to take a more far-sighted view, however, the Baldwin Cabinet put the negative words into their mouths it wanted to hear.

This was not due to hasty or preconceived ideas on the Protocol or any want of careful examination. The new Foreign Secretary, Austen Chamberlain, advised Baldwin as early as 25 November 1924 'to get some idea of the lines on which we ought to move' before the Dominions were approached.[1] According to Curzon, speaking in the House of Lords shortly before his death in March 1925, the examination of the Protocol by the Cabinet, the Committee of Imperial Defence and the Government Departments concerned continued throughout the winter, meetings being held sometimes twice or thrice a week.[2] During this scrutiny it became clear that the whole design of the Protocol was contrary to the approach to foreign policy to which Britain, by every inclination and interest, was committed and which she had followed at least since the French Revolution. It was above all on this ground, the inherent incongruity of the Protocol with British practice, that it does not seem to have been considered necessary to hold any high-level meeting with the French on the subject before Chamberlain saw Herriot in Paris on 7 March, on his way to the League Council in Geneva. There he told Herriot of the negative British decision, but was so alarmed by French fears as to security that he at once asked Baldwin to authorise him to put up to Herriot some alternative arrangement.[3]

Chamberlain's assault on the Protocol was in effect its death warrant as there could be no life for it without Britain. The argument was outlined in Chamberlain's speech to the League Council on 12 March, ending with the suggestion of 'special arrangements to meet special needs' which was the first public intimation of the Cabinet's acceptance of the principle of the Rhine pact. The speech was based on the two cardinal tenets informing British policy since the end of the war; firstly, that only commitments on the Continent of the most restricted scope were acceptable to British opinion and the Dominions govern-

---

[1] Sir Charles Petrie, *The Life and Letters of the Rt. Hon. Sir Austen Chamberlain*, II, pp. 253–4.
[2] 60 H.L. Deb. 5s. Col. 374 (3 March 1925).
[3] Petrie, *op. cit.*, p. 263.

ments, and, secondly, that nothing should be done to delay the rebuilding of the concert of Great Powers. As Chamberlain later wrote, 'only in the case where her interests are immediately at stake and where her own safety must be directly affected by the result of any change has Great Britain ever consented to bind herself beforehand to specific engagements on the continent of Europe'. As for the second of these axioms, Chamberlain went on, 'Britain's role, as interpreted by successive governments, has been, whilst remaining faithful to old friendships, to seek a reconciliation with former enemies, to act as a link between the Great Powers. . . . Above all, it has been the endeavour of British statesmen to prevent Europe falling back into two hostile camps.'[1]

Against this mental background, traditionalist, disregardful of the shrinking geographical scope of world politics, yet sensitive to the postwar mood of Britain, the speech falls into place alongside MacDonald's criticism of the Draft Treaty as a tight, yet indefinite, security system within an international community from which some of the greatest Powers, and especially the United States, were still absent. Whereas Britain desired old grievances to fade, the Protocol seemed to propose means for awakening them and for defining responsibilities in the event of a breakdown in their peaceful settlement when awakened. Britain wanted the world to drop into the same obliviousness to war and feuds between the nations as she had herself; the Protocol seemed busily to organise forces against the day of their return. The old British counsel to Europe to live like good neighbours and cease counting the possibilities of quarrelling again was re-stated.

> Such catastrophes [as war] belong to the pathology of international life, not to its normal condition. It is not wholesome for the ordinary man to be always brooding over the possibility of some severe surgical operation; nor is it wise for societies to pursue a similar course.

There were of course 'extreme cases' in which the existing League provision for conciliation might fail to work; but there was little point in looking for trouble. The Protocol, Chamberlain said, multiplied offences but did nothing to strengthen remedies.[2]

MacDonald, the former Prime Minister, whose words had

---

[1] Austen Chamberlain in the symposium, *The Foreign Policy of the Powers*, by Jules Cambon and others, New York, 1935, pp. 65–6.

[2] Misc. No. 5 (1925). Statement by the Rt. Hon. Austen Chamberlain on behalf of H.M.G. to the Council of the League of Nations, Cmd. 2368.

inspired the Protocol, bitterly complained to Chamberlain on 18 November 1924, when it was already clear that the Protocol would probably not survive with the new government; no new obligations were imposed on Britain, he said, it was merely a case of tightening up old ones and making them more precise and specific.[1] But MacDonald himself, even if his government had not fallen as soon as it did, would have had the greatest difficulty in ratifying the Protocol in its essential form. He was insistent, when the British delegates at the Fifth League Assembly wished to sign the Protocol there and then, that they should not do so.[2] To commit Britain to such far-reaching general obligations in the face of the unanimous opposition of the Dominions and with a minority government was too much for the cautious MacDonald. In the House of Commons in February 1924, before the rejection of the Draft Treaty, he said he wanted to enlarge the League's membership, not to provide bigger forces for collective security, but 'to lend moral weight to (the League's) judgment of right and wrong'.[3] In a letter to Poincaré on 21 February he wrote that later decades might see universal disarmament and universal abitration, but that in the meantime confidence must be created, as for instance by the establishment between certain states of 'bands of neutralised territory under mutual or even collective guarantee and supervision', a hint of Locarno rather than the Protocol.[4] Even in his pamphlet *Protocol or Pact*, published after leaving office, when it was not unnatural to overstate his willingness to move forward within the League, MacDonald doubted the practicability of sanctions: 'I have never regarded these powers as being of any importance, except in so far as their presence on paper is a harmless drug to soothe nerves.'[5] The warmest tribute MacDonald ever paid to the Protocol came when he made the qualified statement in the Commons on 24 March 1925 that:

> I know that there are serious problems in this Protocol, but I maintain that it is a splendid foundation for consideration, and for negotiation for change, and it is in that spirit and conception that I am sorry on account of the attitudes which the Foreign Secretary has taken at Geneva. It will come again. There will be no security except on those lines. Not in those words and not in those clauses but on those lines.[6]

[1] Petrie, *op. cit.*, II, p. 252.
[2] Lord Parmoor, *op. cit.*, p. 253.
[3] 169 H.C. Deb. 5s. Cols. 772–3 (12 February).
[4] Published in *The Times*, 3 March 1924.
[5] Published by the Labour Party, 1925 (?), p. 5.
[6] 182 H.C. Deb. 5s. Col. 345.

Nor was there a majority in the Labour Cabinet in favour of the Protocol. Henderson, with his passionate belief in the instrument for which he had toiled unceasingly, was angry with MacDonald for not being allowed to sign on the spot.[1] On returning to London he threw himself into the task of converting the Cabinet to his own views, but, according to Josiah Wedgwood, then Chancellor of the Duchy of Lancaster, did not quite succeed.[2] Wedgwood himself was against ratification, so were Snowden and Ponsonby. Haldane, the Lord Chancellor, thought that MacDonald had not really worked out the implications of his Geneva policy, especially its effects on defence; the Navy, he considered, was uneasy about it.[3] Lord Parmoor, who had played a role at Geneva only second to that of Henderson, was naturally a supporter of the Protocol, but even he was disturbed by the Dominions' attitude. In a Lords Debate on the Draft Treaty in July 1924 he had asked Cecil, one of its authors, whether it was possible 'to conceive the idea of separating Dominion opinion from that of the Mother Country on a matter of this kind'.[4] Moreover, when the contribution which Britain, the greatest naval Power in the League, would be expected to make in execution of the sanctions in the Protocol became clearer, it was equally doubtful whether ratification would have had the support of the Labour Party in Parliament or the country, though conference votes of vague approval were easy to pass. The stress which MacDonald and, no less, the Baldwin Cabinet continued to lay on conciliation suited the mood of Left as well as Right.

[1] Mary Agnes Hamilton, *op. cit.*, p. 250.
[2] *Memoirs*, p. 184.
[3] Sir Frederick Maurice, *Haldane, 1915–1928*, II, London, 1939, p. 167.
[4] 58 H.L. Deb. 5s. Col. 971 (24 July).

CHAPTER X

THE MAKING OF LOCARNO

I

As Austen Chamberlain was well aware, the French never considered even the Geneva Protocol adequate unless reinforced by additional arrangements for continental security similar to those which Briand had urged on Lloyd George in December 1921. European governments, Chamberlain said in the House of Commons in March 1925, thinking especially of France and her allies, regarded the Protocol as 'something which must be followed, as it had been preceded, by special, subsidiary or complementary alliances and agreements'.[1] He returned to the theme in June. France, he said then, had never accepted the Protocol in full discharge of the undertaking given by MacDonald to Herriot twelve months previously, that European security, after a reparations settlement, was the next item on the agenda; the Protocol was merely 'an instalment towards it.'[2] During the Commons debate on the Protocol in March the Foreign Secretary even questioned the sincerity of the seventeen countries, including France, which had signed but not yet ratified the Protocol. The allegation was backed by Lloyd George who described the Protocol as a 'booby trap for Britain baited with arbitration'.[3]

But if France and her friends never seriously intended to subject issues like Silesia or the Rhineland occupation to arbitration and if her purpose in accepting the Protocol was merely to find yet another route to a British guarantee, could not Britain explore once more the possibilities of a guarantee without undertaking the wider commitments of the Protocol? For a Conservative Government nervous of innovation there was a precedent in the Anglo-American guarantee of 1919 and Lloyd George's offer at Cannes. Chamberlain, from the day he entered the Foreign Office, began to cast around for a safe alternative to the Protocol.

Guarantees had never been popular with Parliamentary or public opinion; they suggested the coalitions of pre-war years, which, substituting cause for effect, the British held responsible

[1] 181 H.C. Deb. 5s. Col. 310 (24 March 1925).
[2] 185 H.C. Deb. 5s. Col. 1558 (24 June 1925).
[3] 181 H.C. Deb. 5s. Col. 333.

for the catastrophe. MacDonald had rejected the Draft Treaty partly because it envisaged partial alliances involving rigid postures; we want a policy, he said, which will not 'tie itself up to the present moment, when there is so much formative, unknown and undiscoverable ... in Europe and the world'.[1] The Ruhr crisis had shown the paths into which Britain might be led through a French alliance. But this very danger, Chamberlain contended, made some such pact essential. Britain could not disinterest herself in Europe. The failure of the Anglo-American guarantee of 1919 had resulted in a network of alliances between France, Poland and the Little Entente which Liberal and Labour opinion considered the chief threat to peace. 'We are involved,' Chamberlain went on, 'whether we like it or not, and the question for us to consider is within what limits, upon what principles and for what purposes we can undertake fresh obligations.'[2] Early in 1925 he therefore set the Central European Department of the Foreign Office to work on the means for meeting France's security fears. The outcome was a memorandum dated 20 February and circulated immediately to the Cabinet urging a defensive pact with France.

The proposal ran into strong criticism from such influential members of Baldwin's Cabinet as Balfour, Birkenhead, Curzon, Churchill. Any such pact, they thought, would throw Germany wholly into Russia's arms, consolidating the Rapallo Treaty of April 1922. Churchill, as Chancellor of the Exchequer, had a further grievance against France arising from her position on inter-Allied war debts.[3] Chamberlain was therefore forced to fall back on a proposal for a multilateral pact to cover the *status quo* in western Europe which had reached him under conditions of great secrecy from Berlin on 20 January. Its receipt filled Chamberlain with suspicion. The proposal struck him as a device for separating Britain from France; its secrecy suggested intrigue. Later he came to trust Stresemann, the German Foreign Minister who made the suggestion, and on examination the idea seemed to have merits about it. It was without the complexion of a military alliance against a third party which most disturbed the Opposition, yet it seemed to meet Herriot's fears, which had so impressed Chamberlain. It held out the possibility of separating Germany from Russia. It had the appeal of limited commitments central to Chamberlain's conception of Britain

[1] *Ibid.*, 185 Col. 1583–4 (24 June 1925).   [2] *Ibid.*, Col. 1561.
[3] An account of the memorandum and the Cabinet discussion is given in D'Abernon, *An Ambassador of Peace*, III, p. 155.

as being at once the focus of Empire and inextricably tied to Europe.

On 5 March, shortly before his departure for Geneva to deliver the death blow to the Protocol, Chamberlain admitted that a proposal had come from Germany. The government, he said, were contemplating a regional security arrangement in Europe and behind them was the authority of Lord Grey, who had said in a speech the previous evening that British public opinion must recognise that the one thing it could do to help the European situation was to make some firm offer to promote European security in which the Empire could join.[1] In Paris two days later Chamberlain found the French Prime Minister, Herriot, in a despondent mood after reading an unfavourable report by the Inter-Allied Commission of Control on German disarmament in the demilitarised zone. The Foreign Secretary at once cabled Baldwin asking for authority to say that Britain agreed to join a west European security pact. The Prime Minister called an informal meeting of Ministers but objections were again voiced by Churchill, Birkenhead and Amery, this time, it seems, even to the multilateral Rhine pact proposed by Germany.[2] Chamberlain was therefore without firm Cabinet instructions when he rejected the Protocol at the League Council on 12 March. On the same day he wrote to Sir Eyre Crowe, permanent head of the Foreign Office, who had been present at the informal Cabinet meeting, bitterly complaining of the Cabinet's indecision. On returning to London, however, he found that the misgivings about the pact had temporarily subsided and he was able to write to Lord Crewe, the British Ambassador in Paris, that the outlook was set fair again.[3] But the road to Locarno was never easy. As late as 18 March, six days before he explained the proposed pact in the Commons, it was again rejected in the Cabinet by a majority led by Churchill.[4]

If the German suggestion was hard for Britain to adopt, it was harder for Stresemann to make. A similar offer, with the same purpose of forestalling the formation of an Anglo-French front, had been made in December 1922 by the German Chancellor, Dr. Cuno, to the United States Secretary of State, Charles Evans Hughes, at that time interesting himself in the prospects for American intervention in the reparation deadlock.[5] The idea was that the British, French, German and

[1] 181 H.C. Deb. 5s. Col. 714.
[2] Petrie, *op. cit.*, II, p. 264.
[3] *Ibid.*
[4] Antonina Vallentin, *Stresemann*, tr. by Eric Sutton, p. 175.
[5] See above, Chapter VII, pp. 184–5.

Italian governments should make a pledge to the United States not to wage war between themselves for a generation unless a popular plebiscite decided otherwise.   In the prevailing French mood Poincaré had no difficulty in pouring contempt on the idea and Bonar Law could only agree with him at the Supreme Council to reject the Cuno offer.   The suggestion of a generation for the duration of the pact (which Cuno later withdrew) seemed merely to confirm French allegations that in 1940 or 1950 Germany would be ready to avenge the Versailles peace, and the idea was appalling that the German people, whom the French held responsible for war in 1914, should be asked when they next wanted to commit aggression.   There was moreover little hope of American willingness to receive the undertaking or guarantee it.

Yet Cuno repeated the offer, again without success, in the following May.   Five months later Stresemann, during his Hundred Days as Chancellor (13 August–23 November 1923), made the offer once again, this time without Cuno's unacceptable conditions.   In a speech at Stuttgart he said that 'if the nations interested in the Rhine ever confer in order to secure to each other for a fixed period the integrity of the present territorial rights, Germany will always be prepared to join them, to prevent the danger of renewed clashes and renewed bloodshed and loss of national strength'.[1]   For the third time the offer was rejected by Poincaré.

Stresemann needed immense courage to persist.   A pact based on the free acceptance of the *status quo* in the west would mean at least a partial abandonment of the German campaign against Versailles which was common ground to all German politicians.   Coupled, as a west European pact must be, with Germany's entrance into the League, it all but meant German acquiescence in the peace treaty system as a whole, of which the League had come to be the guardian and which had as its premise the attribution to Germany of guilt for the war.   It was true that even if Germany accepted the *status quo* in the west, including the cession of Alsace-Lorraine, the demilitarisation of the Rhineland and the Allied occupation, this did not extend, in Stresemann's mind, to the acceptance of Germany's eastern frontiers of 1919 and certainly not to the Upper Silesian solution imposed by the Allies in October 1921.   Nevertheless, Germany could not return to the comity of nations without some pledge not to try to revise the eastern settlement by force. As a League Member she would have the resources of article 19 available to her by way of peaceful change.   But no one

[1] Edgar Stern-Rubarth, *Three Men Tried*, p. 75.

seriously imagined that France, Poland or Czechoslovakia would peacefully allow any substantial return of the lost German lands in the east.

Above all, the Stresemann offer and Germany's entry into the League would slacken the bonds developed since 1918 between Germany and Russia; indeed this was one of the attractions which the British Government saw in the Stresemann offer. For German nationalists and the Reichswehr the common interests of Germany and Russia were too real to risk injuring them through an illusory reconciliation with old enemies in the west. Germany's determination to revise her eastern frontiers could not be realised without Soviet help. Germany received support from Russia against the Versailles system, which the Bolsheviks hated for their own reasons. The link with Russia allowed the Reichswehr to renew its strength through illicit co-operation with Soviet military establishments under the aegis of the Rapallo Treaty.[1] What had the Allies to offer to offset this eastern interest?

Stresemann himself was no perfect instrument for a policy of *status quo* in the west. For Allied public opinion even his appearance, the bald crown and Prussian 'bull neck', the strident voice, aroused mistrust, fitting the standard wartime picture of the Teuton enemy. The respects in which Stresemann did not conform to the image, his lofty intelligence, cultivated rhetoric and diplomatic finesse, only served to reinforce suspicion. Inside Germany, though far enough to the Right not to be mistaken for a weak internationalist, he rarely won affection or trust, even in times of great triumphs. Always compelled to maintain a coalition of political forces behind him, he was judged an opportunist and in Berlin cabarets they sang: 'Stresemann der mal links kann und mal recht kann.' His aim, to keep the Right loyal to the Weimar Republic, often involved attacks on the Left, such as the suppression of the Leftist Saxon state government in October 1923, when Stresemann was Chancellor, and the winning from the Allies of successive alleviations of the Versailles system.

Stresemann's political education had centred on two vital experiences: the discovery that Imperial Germany was incapable of winning the war it had so confidently embarked upon in 1914, and the Franco-Belgian invasion of the Ruhr. The former taught him that a strong army was not enough; the diplomatic situation has to be managed so that one does not have to use an army, or that one uses it, if one must, with

[1] Gerald Freund, *Unholy Alliance. Russian–German Relations from the Treaty of Brest-Litovsk to the Treaty of Berlin*, London, 1957, pp. 124–5.

greatest effect.[1]   The second showed that while Germany was outside the comity of nations she was exposed to military force against which her disarmed state gave her no redress.   Thus the greater part of Stresemann's life was spent in teaching Germany the need to swallow pride, to admit defeat and avoid fighting old battles again, in order to win vantage points for national revival.   Only extraordinary persuasive powers and conspicuous patriotism helped Stresemann to survive, even literally, after his decision as Chancellor to end passive resistance in the Ruhr without compensation in September 1923. He could claim a month later that he was the best hated man in Germany.   'No German Foreign Minister,' he wrote, 'was able to pursue a popular policy because there was always so serious a discrepancy between the high tension of national feeling and any practicable policy.'[2]

It is beside the point to inquire whether Stresemann was 'sincere' in making the Rhine pact offer and in the later golden summer of his relations with Briand.   Stresemann sought the reconstruction of Germany as a Great Power, the same object which Hardenberg and Stein had set themselves when they revived Prussia from enslavement by Napoleon.   If Germany was to be free she must come to terms with France, since while disarmed and suspect she had no means of dealing with French force.   'Our task,' said Stresemann in the Reichstag in April 1923, 'is resolutely to support the State as now existing . . . to rally to its defence and to support its leadership, and then by a policy of national good sense and by the concentration of all our forces, to secure for ourselves a future—a future that will be more grateful to contemplate'.[3]   Stresemann did not differ from German Nationalists in his view of the Versailles Treaty and the War Guilt clause.   In a letter to the ex-Crown Prince written on 7 September 1925 he wrote that his prime aim was 'to get this stranglehold off our necks', that is, to free German soil from foreign troops.   His subsequent aims, he said, were to solve the reparation issue in a sense tolerable to Germany, protect the ten or twelve million Germans living under the foreign yoke, recover Danzig and the Corridor and revise the frontier in Upper Silesia.[4]   But, even if it hurt German sentiment to admit it, the road to revival lay through Paris, with London's sympathetic help.   The security pact proposal of January 1925 was a step towards that goal.   To the Secretary

[1] Stresemann's disillusionment with the Imperial régime is discussed in Vallentin, *Stresemann*, pp. 10–2.
[2] Eric Sutton (ed.), *Gustav Stresemann. His Diaries, Letters and Papers*, I, p. 224.
[3] Sutton, *op. cit.*, I, pp. 61–2.
[4] *Ibid.*, II, p. xi.

of State, Ago von Maltzan, a protagonist of the Eastern School of German foreign policy, Stresemann wrote on 7 April 1925 that 'our security offer was undoubtedly correct. It secured the Rhineland against the French policy of aggression, split the Entente and opened new prospects for the East'.[1] But would German public opinion co-operate, especially since Stresemann's policy towards the Allies had not, even at the London Reparations Conference in 1924, produced the evacuation of the Ruhr? Would further rebuffs from the Allies, like those of 1922 and 1923, ruin his party and himself and drive Germany finally into the hands of the Eastern School with the result of consolidating the Allies against Germany?

Stresemann's guide in approaching the Allies was the 'Lord Protector of Germany', in other words the British Ambassador in Berlin, Lord D'Abernon, aptly known as *praeceptor Germaniae*. D'Abernon was a financial expert sent to Germany by Lloyd George to help deal with the monetary chaos and reparations. Unlike most of Lloyd George's choices, he was orthodox in every fibre. His advice to Germany on inflation was simply to hold up the printing presses and try strict balancing of the accounts. The Dawes plan and the introduction of the Rentenmark appealed to him as wholly in the spirit of Threadneedle Street. By the same token D'Abernon wrote off the Russian Revolution as a primeval darkness with which no respectable country like Germany could sympathise. He considered the German delegation at Genoa had been 'stampeded' into the Rapallo Treaty, which 'no dominant section' of Germany really desired.[2] Nevertheless, he realised that Russo-German relations followed an inverse course to Germany's relations with the Allies, and that the Allied decision to grant the greater part of Upper Silesia to Poland in October 1921 had played a part in the genesis of Rapallo.[3]

Germany's future, he urged, lay with the West and she should make her contribution to pacification as soon as possible. This was in Britain's interest too. If Germany was permanently alienated from the West the result could only be either Communism, flooding into Europe through the Soviet–German alliance, or the division of Germany with a militaristic France left as the lord and master. In a characteristic passage D'Abernon wrote:

The essential interest of England is to prevent the breaking up of Germany. As long as Germany is a coherent whole,

[1] Sutton, *op. cit.*, p. xiv, n. 3.
[2] D'Abernon, *An Ambassador of Peace*, I, p. 303.
[3] Freund, *op. cit.*, p. 91.

there is more or less a balance of power in Europe . . . Many of the arguments which were valid in 1914 against Germany are valid today against France. Indeed this is an under-statement, for then the Triple Alliance was balanced by the Russo-French Alliance; today France and the Smaller En-tente is balanced by nothing. Anyone who supposes that a French Government dominating the Continent as Napoleon dominated it after Tilsit will remain friendly to England must be a poor judge of national psychology . . . Desiring the maintenance of the Anglo-French Entente, I am com-pelled to desire the existence of a strong Germany.[1]

For D'Abernon the war had been a terrible mistake; Britain and Germany had fought on the wrong sides. Like English soldiers in the Crimean War who cried 'Those damned French-men!' whenever they saw the enemy, D'Abernon regarded Bonapartism as the greatest danger of the 1920s. That these illusions were shared by the great majority of Parliamentary opinion in England, especially on the Left, was shown by the doubts expressed about an Anglo-French security pact. It was Chamberlain who proved to be out of touch with this opinion and was compelled to accept, as an alternative to a French alliance, the multilateral west European pact which D'Abernon had got into the habit, with Carl von Schubert, the successor to Maltzan at the German Foreign Office, of calling 'the baby' (*Das Kind*).[2]

II

The German proposal, forwarded in the first instance to London on D'Abernon's advice on 20 January, was actually intended for France. France alone was able to decide its fate; she stood in the same relation to the pact as Britain had stood in relation to the Protocol. The purpose of sounding London first was ostensibly to seek British advice on the manner of making an approach to France. The unstated reason no doubt was at the earliest possible moment to try to head Chamberlain off from a renewal of the Cannes guarantee to France. Suspecting that this might be the case, the Foreign Secretary was not at once convinced. After some delay, long enough to make Stresemann seriously consider withdrawing the offer, he told the German Ambassador that France should be drawn into the talks and that the proposal should go to Paris. There it was dispatched on 9 February and the interim French

[1] D'Abernon, *op. cit.*, II, London, 1929, pp. 238–9.
[2] Maltzan was later killed in an airplane accident in 1927 while on his way to take charge of the German Embassy in Washington.

reply stated that the German suggestion would have to be put to the Allies and agreement reached by them on a system of security 'within the framework of the Treaty of Versailles'. With these two defensive bastions raised France prepared for the coming struggle.

The German offer, now formally before the British and French Governments, was paraphrased by Chamberlain in the House of Commons on 24 March to mean that:

> Germany is prepared to guarantee voluntarily what hitherto she has accepted under the compulsion of the Treaty, that is, the *status quo* in the West; that she is prepared to eliminate, not merely from the West, but from the East, she is prepared absolutely to abandon, any idea of recourse to war for the purpose of changing the Treaty boundaries of Europe.   She may be unwilling or she may be unable to make the same renunciation of the hopes and aspirations that some day by friendly arrangement or mutual agreement a modification may be introduced into the East which she is prepared to make in regard to any modification in the West.[1]

In its actual terms the offer was a reformulation of the Cuno suggestion of 1922 for a mutual renunciation of war by the Powers 'interested in the Rhine' for a lengthy period, coupled with a comprehensive abitration treaty.   To these was to be added a pact guaranteeing the *status quo* on the Rhine.   This would involve an undertaking to respect the territorial status on the Rhine, including the demilitarisation provided for in articles 42 and 43 of the Versailles Treaty and a joint and individual guarantee of the fulfilment of this undertaking.   The pact was to be supplemented by arbitration treaties between Germany and such states as were willing to enter into such treaties with her.   As though to appeal to the public opinion in Britain and France which had looked hopefully to the Geneva Protocol, the memorandum ended by referring to the proposed pact as a step towards a world convention for the pacific settlement of international disputes.[2]

The proposal contained dangers for France.   Apart from the vagueness as to how the guarantee would be implemented should the undertakings be violated, the distinction drawn between the eastern and western borders of Germany, and the omission of any guarantee of the former, were full of dangerous implications for France's allies situated between Germany and

---

[1] 182 H.C. Deb. 5s. Col. 318.
[2] Misc. No. 7 (1925). Papers respecting the proposals for a pact of security, Cmd. 2435, pp. 3–4.

Russia. The proposed renunciation of force for the revision of Germany's eastern frontiers would have no sanction behind it and the German Government were clearly not agreed on what it meant. When Chamberlain said in the Commons on 24 March that Germany meant to pledge herself not to resort to force in the east, he was afterwards told by Sthamer, the German Ambassador, who had been in the gallery, that no such inference could be drawn; Chamberlain was so angry that he threatened to return to the Chamber and speak against the offer. Later it turned out that Sthamer was either without instructions on the point or had misread his instructions. But even if such a pledge were given by the present German Government, what help would France and her allies receive from Britain if it was infringed by a later German Government? Moreover, would the Rhine pact operate so as to prevent France coming to the aid of her allies in the east if they were at war with Germany? France had always insisted on the interdependence of security in east and west. She could not understand the British conception of limited commitments; containing an expansive military state like Germany on one side only meant forcing her to break out on the other.

Yet the German proposal undoubtedly had its attractions for France. In the first two years of the League France had opposed German membership as giving Berlin a certificate of respectability. But the League had become a pillar of the *status quo* and Germany's membership would commit her to attempt revision, if at all, by canvassing votes in a League electorate heavily pre-disposed to the existing order. Moreover, Chamberlain was demanding that Germany must come to Geneva as an equal, with the same rights and obligations as other League Members. In the correspondence between Berlin and Geneva on German membership of the League at the end of 1924 the German Government had claimed that, as a disarmed state, the Republic should be excluded from the obligations of article 16, the sanctions article of the Covenant, since she had no means of defence against an aggressor. But Chamberlain would have none of this, and thus Germany, seated as an equal on the League Council between Britain and France, might have to play the part of a policeman of the existing order instead of plotting dark conspiracies with Russia. Perhaps also as trade between Germany and the successor states grew, grievances arising out of the frontier would gradually fade. So Briand confided to Chamberlain.[1]

But the factor chiefly moving France to take a serious view

[1] Petrie, *op. cit.*, II, p. 268.

of the Stresemann note was that the Rhine pact was proving the only condition on which Britain would underwrite French security. The Draft Treaty and Geneva Protocol had been defeated by British isolationism. There was no going back to the offer made by Lloyd George at Cannes. Germany had been given an equal place in the provisions for arbitration in the Dawes plan; the time for treating her as an outcast had gone. British opinion was astonished that Stresemann was able to go as far as he did in freely undertaking to accept the Versailles solution in the west. Lloyd George could hardly believe his ears when he heard it from Chamberlain.[1] It was most unlikely that, once Britain had warmed to the opportunity for replacing consent for force as the basis of the treaty, she would return to coercion. Moreover, the events of the last few years had led more and more people, especially in the United States, to conclude that Britain had been right and France wrong; stubborn French attitudes now might alienate even more. Britain had been right about reparations; French policy led to the Ruhr. Britain had followed her dream of disarmament to the Washington Conference; France seemed to be holding up the development of the Washington example. Britain's policy of finding a place for Germany in the scheme of things suited the American mood and American finance was too vital for Europe for this mood to be ignored. Britain stood on a pinnacle of diplomatic influence and could afford to dictate to France. As Chamberlain said with some arrogance:

> The British Empire, detached from Europe by its Dominions, linked to Europe by these islands, can do what no other nation on the face of the earth can do, and from east and west alike there comes to me the cry that, after all, it is in the hands of the British Empire and if they will that there shall be no war there will be no war.[2]

Chamberlain claimed that he loved France like a woman, but, if so, he was no believer in the equality of sexes. In the struggle which ensued on the terms of a reply to the German offer he adopted towards the French almost the tone used by Clemenceau to the German delegation at Paris in May 1919. When he talked with the French Ambassador, de Fleuriau, in May about the French draft reply in order to secure 'supplementary information' to assist in briefing the Cabinet, his tone was superior. The French, he said, should not presume to speak in the name of the Allies, even though before long

[1] 182 H.C. Deb. 5s. Col. 318 (24 March 1925).
[2] Ibid., Col. 322.

Chamberlain was insisting on re-writing the French reply in order to safeguard the British position. He objected to the French desire to place the proposed guarantees 'within the framework of the Treaty of Versailles'. He questioned the French on the use of the word 'arbitration' for the settlement of issues arising out of the proposed pact, even though the word had originally been suggested in the Stresemann note. He was anxious not to rule out conciliation through the League Council as a means of modifying the more provocative legal rights of France against Germany under the treaties. He insisted on provision being made for the fullest possible exploration of peaceful methods before coercive action was taken if the contemplated agreements were infringed. But Chamberlain's most serious doubts arose from the proposal in the French draft that all signatories of the pact should 'jointly and severally' guarantee all the abitration treaties which Germany might sign with her neighbours under the plan, and that this guarantee should be on precisely the same footing as the guarantee of the frontiers between Germany, on one side, and France and Belgium, on the other.[1] No one could suggest such a thing to Britain if he had read his history since the war.

The French were therefore obliged to abandon efforts to inveigle Britain into acting as guarantor of all the abitration treaties. All they wanted, they said in replying to Chamberlain on 22 May, was to leave the Allies free, if they wished, to come to the assistance of countries in conflict with Germany after arbitration had failed. None the less Chamberlain pressed his advantage in a note to France of 28 May which should stand as a perfect example of the insular disdain of a Britain conscious, as Chamberlain said, of her power to make or break. The note, giving the Cabinet's conclusions on the French draft, began by reiterating that any new British obligation must be 'specific and limited to the maintenance of the existing territorial arrangement on the western frontier of Germany'. Britain could play no part in guaranteeing arbitration treaties between Germany and states other than the actual signatories of the Rhine pact. While she was willing 'in principle and subject to a careful examination of the actual terms ultimately proposed' to guarantee arbitration treaties between the other pact signatories, that is, Belgium, France, Germany and Italy, the guarantee would only be implemented coercively where the defaulting state had been allowed to refer the point at issue to conciliation as an alternative to arbitration in the strictly legal sense (thus permitting Germany, for

[1] Cmd. 2435, pp. 11–13.

example, to appeal for equity in a moral sense) and when the aggrieved party had not itself refused arbitration or failed to carry out an arbitral award. Even so, force would only be used in the area covered by the Rhine pact. This was indeed to tilt the scales against France and Belgium, though these were still regarded in Britain as the innocent victims in 1914. For these countries, according to Chamberlain's note, to receive assistance from Britain in the event of a German failure to observe the arbitration treaties they must themselves have a completely clean record in the matter of arbitration, and a conciliation organ, such as the League Council on which Britain had a permanent vote, must have unanimously condemned Germany, France presumably not having a vote as the issue would come under the heading of peaceful settlements. Chamberlain then went on to re-write the French reply 'in such a way as to confine it to such a statement of policy as (the British Government) believe is common to both countries'. Still, the reply must be sent in France's name, referring only collectively to the Allies on points with which Germany could not quarrel. That France would find herself alone if she quibbled too much was hinted at in the Foreign Secretary's substitution of the words 'French Government' for 'Allied Governments', as the quarter to which the German reply should be sent.[1]

Briand, now the French Foreign Minister in the Painlevé Government formed on 16 April, told a press conference that he had no alternative but to accept the British amendments.[2] Nevertheless, he must have enjoyed re-stating some of Chamberlain's words in his own retort to Britain, with the added implication that it was precisely the mentality behind them which bred in the British such a misty unconcern for realities.

> We realise that in present circumstances the fact that the constituent elements of the British Empire are scattered throughout the world leads His Majesty's Government to limit their undertakings on the European continent to those which they consider essential, even when their interests are indistinguishable from those of the Continental Powers.

But France had her pride. The French Government, Briand continued, 'consider that their anxiety to maintain the general peace and the liberty of all the nations of Europe as well as the exigencies of their own national defence preclude them from limiting their preoccupations to solicitude for their security alone'. France could not allow the proposed Rhine pact to

[1] Cmd. 2435, pp. 18–28.
[2] George Glasgow, *From Dawes to Locarno*, p. 61.

stand in the way of her coming to the assistance of her allies on Germany's eastern borders, to whom on the British admission she was free to offer her guarantee. She meant to reserve her action 'in the case of a violation of an eventual arbitration treaty between Germany and Poland, for example, or between Germany and Czechoslovakia'. Of this Briand said that Stresemann should be left in no doubt. Chamberlain's comment on this vital point, written from Geneva on 8 June, kept the tone of tired rebuke. He said it hardly required emphasis since the pact could not operate in favour of a state which had defaulted on its legal obligations.[1] But this was precisely what was to happen when France sought to rebuild her eastern alliances in the 1930s.

After these long exchanges between London and Paris the French reply was handed to Stresemann by the French Ambassador in Berlin, M. de Margerie, on 16 June. It accepted the three main British principles: that Germany's entrance into the League was a condition for the 'achievement' of the proposed pact, but not necessarily, as France had argued, for its signature; that the British guarantee could extend beyond the territorial issue only to the arbitration treaties between France and Belgium, on one side, and Germany, on the other; and that the proposed pact could not affect rights and obligations under the League Covenant. The last principle was presumably intended to remind Stresemann that France's insistence on the integrity of the peace treaties was balanced by the opportunity Germany would enjoy as a League Member to plead for their revision under Article 19. None the less, in what was from the French point of view the most significant phrase in the reply, room was left for coercive action, despite the general renunciation of war in the pact, in three cases: in defence of 'treaties in force between the parties', that is, engagements contracted between the parties before the Rhine pact; in defence of the Rhine pact itself; or 'in virtue of the guarantee given to an arbitration treaty by the parties or by any one of them'.[2] By the last phrase France sought to demonstrate that she would not sacrifice her allies to a British guarantee of her eastern frontier.

By this time the mood in Germany had worsened. Despite the advantages the scheme held out by way of bolting the door against further French efforts to enforce the treaties by occupying German land, hopes had been raised by the Anglo-French exchanges that a yet higher price might be exacted for Germany's agreement to the permanent cession of Alsace-Lorraine.

[1] Cmd. 2435, pp. 44–5.   [2] *Ibid.*, pp. 45–51.

On 26 April Paul von Hindenburg had been elected President after the death of Ebert in February. Although this was a reinforcement of the Weimar régime in that the war hero gave his oath to the Republic, Hindenburg was now able to press on Stresemann the doubts of the army about the course of foreign policy. In particular the President urged that Germany should definitely refuse to join the League without some relief in regard to article 16, or at least should use Germany's unequal status, as the only forcibly disarmed Member of the League, to agitate for all-round disarmament. 'I do not meet with deliberate opposition from him,' Stresemann reassured D'Abernon, 'but he is unversed in political affairs.'[1] The effect was that when the Minister replied on 20 July to the French German note he said that some interim solution would have to be found for Germany's special military, economic and geographical position pending the general disarmament to which League Members were committed by the Covenant.[2] Hindenburg also pressed Stresemann to demand the repeal of the War Guilt clause as Germany's price for the acceptance of the western frontier. Stresemann himself had made this demand when he spoke in the Reichstag in the previous year on the legislation required to bring the Dawes plan into operation in Germany. Following Hindenburg's advice he raised the issue again, though not until 26 September when in a note to London he accepted a proposal for a Foreign Ministers' conference to finalise the security pact. But this was largely for home consumption, and on that assumption Chamberlain, replying a few days later, said that it bore no relation to the matter in hand.

The greatest doubts about the pact in Germany, however, were felt by Right-wing Nationalists and army officers anxious as to its effects on Soviet–German relations. The pact, after all, implied a consolidation in western Europe and had distinct anti-Communist overtones; it might reduce German feelings of grievance against the peace of 1919 which united the Republic with Russia as the two great international outcasts. If buttressed by arbitration treaties with Poland, Czechoslovakia and Rumania, it threatened the common interest of Russia and Germany in the weakening of these countries. By giving the successor states more confidence in their relations with Berlin, the scheme might make them more provocative towards Moscow, for which Russia might blame Germany, thus dealing a further blow to Russo-German friendship. Moreover, the

---

[1] D'Abernon, *op. cit.*, III, p. 169.
[2] Misc. No. 9 (1925). Reply of the German Government to the Note handed to Herr Stresemann by the French Ambassador, Cmd. 2468, p. 9.

atmosphere of pacification which might grow out of the pact, together with the economic recovery in Europe which was the condition and also a possible consequence of security, might give a new lease of life to Western capitalism, of which Germany was after all a part, especially if the pact had the backing of the United States.   The Soviet–German connection was based on antagonism between Berlin and the Allies.   Any lessening of the second must weaken the first.

Germany might consider sacrificing the Soviet link in return for a western settlement if she could be sure that the Allies were turning over a new leaf.   It was not easy to be sure in the early months of 1925.   First, there was the Allied decision in January not to terminate the occupation of the Cologne zone for the time being as they alleged that Germany was not fulfilling the treaty.   The only consolation for Stresemann was that this decision was denounced in British political and press circles almost as bitterly as it was throughout Germany.   Then, on 4 June, four months after receiving the report of the Inter-Allied Commission of Control on the state of German disarmament, the Allies sent their note to Berlin specifying Germany's shortcomings.   This created a disagreeable background for the receipt of the French statement of 16 June on the security pact. The note of 4 June argued that the German defaults 'would in the aggregate enable the German Government eventually to reconstitute an army modelled on the principles of a nation in arms' and went on to say that the present breaches of the treaty were the most serious but not the only items on the German crime sheet.[1]   Paris had insisted on the publication of the note against British advice.

On top of this, four days later, on 8 June, a scare was caused by a false report from Geneva, circulated by the French news agency Havas, that Chamberlain and Briand had agreed that the pact should after all be a unilateral arrangement between Britain and France against Germany, and that if the eastern allies of France became the objects of 'manifest aggression' France should have authority to pass through the demilitarised zone to come to their assistance.[2]   Baldwin denied the truth of this piece of French wishful thinking in reply to a private notice question in the House of Commons on 10 June, but the event did not make Stresemann's advocacy of the pact in Germany any easier.[3]   Nor did the French assist him by agreeing to reduce the period of twelve months for the evacuation of the

[1] Germany No. 2 (1925), Cmd. 2429, p. 3.
[2] D'Abernon, op. cit., III, p. 167, n. 1.
[3] 184 H.C. Deb. 5s. Col. 1988.

Ruhr, fixed at the London Reparations Conference in August the previous year. German opinion did not see how negotiations supposed to recognise German equality with the Allies could proceed with French troops still in the Ruhr and the 'sanction' towns of Düsseldorf, Duisburg and Ruhrort, occupied as far back as March 1921.

Stresemann's reply of 20 July to the French note was therefore stiff and angry, disappointing London, which had done so much to talk France into an accommodating mood. The Foreign Minister, looking over his shoulder at domestic opinion, objected to the meaning which could be read into the French note that the Allies meant to use the pact to sanctify the régime of 1919 for all time. He hoped for some lightening of the occupation as a result of the pact, and he strongly contended that France's reservation of her power to come to the aid of her allies in the east meant that France alone was to be the judge of Germany's performance in relation to her arbitration treaties with those states. That, said Stresemann, contrasted markedly with the procedure under the League for testing the guilt of an aggressor.[1] All this could be relied upon to read well in London.

But such angry words reflected the mood of the moment. France did evacuate the Ruhr in August, as she had undertaken. In the same month Chamberlain was dealing with Briand on the meaning of the word 'immediate', as applied to the implementation of the guarantee, which had been used in the French note of 16 June. In these talks the celebrated distinction, later embodied in the Locarno agreements, was adopted between flagrant aggression, in which event the parties would be committed to take immediate action, and such lesser. infringements of the pact as would merely justify reference as a first step to diplomacy, the League Council or some other method of peaceful adjustment. The next stage in the negotiations, the actual drafting of the treaty, required collaboration with the Germans on a continuous basis, preferably outside the highly charged political atmosphere in which the three-cornered exchanges had been carried on hitherto. Chamberlain's expedient for this, reflecting the business mentality which British Ministers had urged in Allied relations with Germany from the beginning, was a meeting of legal experts of the five Powers to assemble in London in September and to work on the basis of a preliminary outline of the pact already drawn up by Sir Cecil Hurst, the Foreign Office's chief legal adviser, and M. Fromageot, representing France. Stresemann con-

[1] Cmd. 2468, p. 8.

sented and sent the foremost legal adviser in the Wilhelm-
strasse, Dr. Gaus, to London. M. Rollin acted for Belgium
and Mussolini indicated possible Italian participation when he
asked M. Pilotti to sit with the group in London. Briand and
Chamberlain werc so satisfied with the progress made by the
jurists after a week's work that when the two met in mid-September in Geneva for the Sixth League Assembly they were
able to issue an invitation to Germany to send Stresemann to
a Foreign Ministers' conference to meet in Locarno. This
culmination of so many months of delicate negotiation came
when the curtain was raised at Locarno on 5 October. The
various agreements, already far advanced in draft when the
conference began, were initialled on the 16th, Austen Chamberlain's birthday, and signed in London on 1 December.

III

The core of the Locarno documents was the treaty of mutual
guarantee binding Belgium, Britain, France, Germany and
Italy severally and collectively to uphold the territorial *status
quo* resulting from the Belgian–German and Franco-German
frontiers laid down at Versailles and the demilitarisation of the
Rhineland stipulated in articles 42 and 43 of the Versailles
Treaty. Next, by article 2, Germany and Belgium and Germany and France respectively undertook never to attack, invade or make war on one another except in self-defence, or in
the event of a flagrant breach of articles 42 and 43 of the Versailles Treaty which constituted an unprovoked act of aggression and rendered immediate action necessary owing to the
assembly of armed forces in the demilitarised zone, or in pursuit of obligations under the League Covenant. These three
Powers further pledged themselves, by article 3, to settle disputes peacefully, either by diplomacy, arbitration (in the case
of disputes 'as to their respective rights') or conciliation by
means of the League Council or of a specially appointed commission. The detailed arrangements for these specific settlements were laid down in arbitration conventions signed by
Germany and Belgium and Germany and France on the same
day as the treaty of guarantee but separate from it.

The procedure for bringing the guarantee into effect applied
the distinction already referred to between the two degrees of
gravity of the offence. A signatory might complain of a *mere*
violation of the undertaking not to attack another signatory in
article 2 or of a *mere* breach of the Versailles articles 42 and 43.
It could do so by bringing the matter before the League Council and if the Council found that the complaint was proper it

would inform all the signatories, each of whom would be severally bound (that is, regardless of what others did) to come immediately to the assistance of the injured country.   But if there was a *flagrant* violation of article 2 or a *flagrant* breach of articles 42 and 43, each signatory would be automatically bound to come to the immediate assistance of the victim without awaiting a report from the Council.   In that case, however, the state rendering the assistance would first have to satisfy itself that the violation or breach constituted an unprovoked act of aggression and that immediate action was necessary either owing to the crossing of a frontier, an outbreak of fighting or an assembly of armed forces in the demilitarised zone.   In addition the parties gave the same undertaking immediately to come to the assistance of the injured party if either Belgium, France or Germany broke the arbitration conventions they had signed and resorted to hostilities or violated the demilitarised status of the Rhineland.   This meant that Britain and Italy, who were not parties to the arbitration conventions signed with Germany, became guarantors of those signed by the other three.   But they were only obliged to take action where a breach of these conventions was accompanied by a flagrant breach of the non-aggression undertaking of the guarantee pact or of the demilitarised régime.   In other cases, as for instance if the arbitration convention was broken without a resort to hostilities, the matter was to come before the League Council and the parties were bound to accept the Council's report as they were for other contentious issues placed before the League.[1]

In the end, then, it was a distinctively British conception of the agreements which prevailed.   Chamberlain succeeded in limiting the British commitment to the territorial *status quo* in the west and to the guarantee of the arbitration conventions between the three Powers in so far as a violation of the latter involved unprovoked aggression or military movements into the demilitarised zone.   To bolt the door against recurrent British involvement in French quarrels with Germany, the violation had to be a 'flagrant' one, Britain herself being in every case the judge, and had to constitute 'unprovoked aggression', the definition of which was again left to Britain.   Even in the most blatant case of an infringement of the pact, like the sudden re-occupation of the Rhineland which actually occurred on 7 March 1936, Britain was not bound to act independently unless she was satisfied that the breach was an unprovoked act of aggression and that immediate action was necessary to pro-

[1] Misc. No. 11 (1925). Final Protocol of the Locarno Conference, 1925, Cmd. 2525.

tect the *status quo*. By the same limitation of the guarantee, of course, France was herself protected against pressures in Britain for assisting Germany should France ever again determine to teach Germany a lesson as she had done in 1923.

But the most important respect in which France bowed to Britain in the negotiation of the Locarno agreements was that on which she had been most insistent during the exchanges of the summer, that is, her right to come to the assistance of Poland and Czechoslovakia, if they were at war with Germany, without being prevented by the Locarno system of guarantees. Under the pact as embodied in the final protocol of 16 October France could only enter Germany from the west to help her allies if she had herself been attacked by Germany, or if Germany, now to be admitted into the League, had been pronounced an aggressor in the sense of article 16 of the Covenant, or if under article 15 (7) of the Covenant the Council had failed to reach an agreed report on the dispute and League Members were therefore at liberty to act as they thought fit.   In all other cases if France attacked Germany from the west she might herself, by article 2 of the pact, be declared an aggressor and therefore subject to sanctions by Belgium, Britain and Italy.   It is true that on the same day on which the pact was signed Germany entered into parallel arbitration conventions with Poland and Czechoslovakia: these were some assurance of Germany's neighbourly intentions towards these allies of France.   But if Germany should ever attack them in violation of the arbitration agreements the Rhine pact might prove a serious handicap to France's efforts to assist them.   France had fought against this danger from the moment she received Stresemann's suggestion on 9 February.

The Locarno accords are generally believed to have had psychological results in symbolising the ending of the cold war between victor and vanquished in western Europe, marking, as Chamberlain said, the real dividing line between war and peace.   They helped to provide an atmosphere in which, for the first time since 1918, if not since 1906, people in western Europe could plan for the future without the shadow of a new Franco-German conflict over their lives.   The agreements, said Ramsay MacDonald, no warm friend of the Rhine pact, wrought a 'miraculous change' of psychology on the Continent; Couéism, he found, was being practised on a large scale.[1] Europe had nearly frozen to death in 1918 and again in 1923. Now the sun was returning and softer winds were blowing to herald the high summer of Franco-German reconciliation

[1] 188 H.C. Deb. 5s. Col. 435 (18 November 1925).

reached at the Thoiry meeting of Briand and Stresemann in 1926. The Locarno meetings were, of course, not so much the cause of this new tide in European affairs as one of its consequences. The economic revival of Europe towards the end of 1924, assisted by the stabilisation of the German mark and the revaluation of the French franc at one-fifth of its pre-war value in 1925, were perhaps the real foundation of the political *détente*. France and Germany required to fortify their economic revival with draughts of American capital; they stood little chance of doing so while the murderous feud between them continued. This was possibly the most persuasive argument used by Stresemann to overcome German distaste for bending the neck freely to the Versailles solution in the west, and by Briand to overcome French resistance to accepting Germany back into respectable society.

Compared with these psychological effects the real contribution to security of the Locarno agreements was small. The guarantee Britain gave to peaceful settlements between France and Germany was effective so long as there was no serious prospect of it ever being called upon. No businesslike military dispositions could be planned by any British General Staff on the assumption that Britain might have to fight with Germany against France or with France against Germany. Military arrangements of such contradictory character cannot be planned in advance, nor is there any evidence that any such arrangements were made. What Locarno did, if it had any practical effect on military security, was to rule out military conversations with France of the kind that Briand had vainly pleaded for at Cannes. As it was impossible for British military staffs to concert with German staffs in the event of war with France and at the same time with French staffs in the event of war with Germany, no military planning took place with either.

Considering the misgivings voiced against the pact as an entangling alliance before its negotiation, it is remarkable how far Chamberlain succeeded in keeping Britain's hands free. Few could disagree when he said in the ratification debate on 18 November that he did not think the obligations of the country 'could be more narrowly circumscribed to the conditions under which we have a vital national interest'.[1] Each guarantor remained the judge of whether the circumstances had arisen bringing the guarantee into operation. Although in practice there would probably be consultation between the Powers should an appropriate case occur, Britain, Chamberlain said, would by no means be bound to take the same view

[1] 188 H.C. Deb. 5s. Col. 429.

as the others.   Even in the extreme case in which unprovoked aggression of the most flagrant character had taken place, Britain had ensured that the issue should still come before the Council, even after the guarantee had been honoured, and that the Council's report should be binding.   This meant that even after a British Government had decided to come to the assistance of an injured party it could still honourably desist, if the Council, on which Britain would always have a vote, decided otherwise.   But in such a case, so defined, Britain would probably have been at war even under the old order before Locarno.

The real British gains from Locarno were of a negative character.   First, as D'Abernon had foreseen, barriers were placed in the way of the consolidation of the Soviet–German alliance.   Chamberlain repeatedly denied in the House on 18 November that the government hoped to form a league against Russia.   But it must have been considered a satisfying aspect of the pact that Germany was apparently returning to respectable company.   The Under-Secretary of State for the Colonies, Ormsby-Gore, in a speech at Manchester eight days after the signing of the Locarno Protocol said that 'the significance of Locarno was tremendous.   It meant that, as far as Germany was concerned, it was detached from Russia and was throwing in its lot with the Western Powers.'[1]   Moreover, the Locarno agreements avoided the payment of any price by Britain for European security other than the lowest possible one.   In only one respect did the pact commit Britain more than she was already committed and that was to come to the immediate assistance, with all the qualifications already mentioned, to a signatory against which a military re-occupation of the Rhineland was directed.   By the Versailles Treaty she was merely committed to regard such a threat to demilitarisation as a 'hostile act'.   Otherwise the commitment to assist France in the event of aggression from across the Rhine was, as Poincaré told Lloyd George three years previously, implicit in the facts of Britain's position and really required no written form to be given to it. Austen Chamberlain had told the League Council in March, when he rejected the Geneva Protocol, that the arrangement Britain preferred was 'special arrangements to meet special needs'.   The Locarno pact, however, had no successor; the special arrangement remained singular; Britain had gone as far as she would by way of commitments against aggression. This was the basis of the Opposition's amendment to Chamberlain's motion for the approval of the ratification of the agreements on 18 November.

[1] Quoted in *The Times*, 26 October 1925.

The amendment regretted that the Treaty of Mutual Guarantee, though a distinct achievement, was apparently not intended to lead to further steps, such as disarmament and the admission of Russia into the League. Lloyd George, without supporting the Labour amendment, spoke of Locarno as a peak from which other peaks should be conquered; he wanted similar security pacts for the Balkans, presumably with the same British guarantee. But the government had not fought so hard against enlargement of commitments before the signature at Locarno only to find the road open to still wider involvements. Chamberlain argued that Locarno paved the way to disarmament by creating a mood of confidence all the way round, but that the initiative towards disarmament should now be taken by others since, after the Washington Conference, it was land armaments which presented the greatest problem and Britain was never a land power. As for wider security arrangements, it was time, in the Cabinet's opinion, to rest on the oars and see how the new spirit in European affairs developed. Besides, Locarno had shown the dangerous implications for Empire unity inherent in the new division of responsibilities for foreign policy as between Britain and the Dominions. It had not proved possible throughout these negotiations on the pact either to call an Imperial Conference so as to get a common view on European security, or to persuade the Dominions to accede to the Locarno accords as they shaped themselves between the European Powers. By article 9 of the Treaty of Mutual Guarantee it was left open to them, and to India, to adhere later if they wished. But it seemed unwise, while the constitutional position of the Dominions and the problem of Empire unity on foreign policy were still unsettled, to embark on even wider commitments.

There was another negative virtue which Locarno had for Britain; it added one more obstacle against further unilateral French acts of force against Germany. It was perhaps this aspect of Locarno which, when all is said, most recommended it to Radical and Left-wing opinion in Britain. The pact was defensive and multilateral; it was therefore a break with the one-sided alliances in which the French Government had consistently sought to trap Britain. It also placed fetters on France herself. So long as the demilitarisation of the Rhineland was guaranteed by Britain any further incursion into the Ruhr or any French attempt to bring military assistance to her eastern allies from the west was not merely illegal but tantamount to war with Britain. Chamberlain made this brutally clear while Stresemann was still considering the French reply on

16 June, possibly to assist the Foreign Minister's thoughts. He had been asked whether the pact gave France the right to march through German territory. 'It is only when the League has exhausted all methods of conciliation, has found them unavailing and invites all its member nations to render what assistance they can to succour the injured and protect him against the aggressor, that any question of the right to march across another nation's territory can arise,' was Chamberlain's reply. MacDonald pressed the point: 'supposing that there is no decision under article 16 of the Covenant?' To which Chamberlain replied that there was no right in that case to march through anyone else's territory.[1]

These negative virtues of the pact for Britain had their positive aspect when looked at from Berlin. No doubt the suggestion that Germany came to Locarno as a free and equal negotiator, to conclude a treaty she herself had initiated, was a pretence. It was belied by the fact that, at Locarno, Germany was resigning part of her sovereignty over part of her soil, the demilitarised Rhineland, and in perpetuity; that the left-bank of the Rhine and the bridgeheads of the river were still under foreign occupation and would remain so for a further ten years (though it was agreed at Locarno that the Cologne zone would be freed and the régime in the occupied Rhineland modified so as to give more power to the local German administrations); and that the obligation to pay reparations from her national wealth remained. Nevertheless, no one could doubt, after Locarno, that Germany's road to rehabilitation had begun. Soon Germany would sit as a permanent member of the League Council on the basis of a compromise formula agreed at Locarno which interpreted League membership as 'loyal and effective' co-operation in support of the Covenant and in resistance to acts of aggression to an extent 'compatible with (a Member's) military situation . . . and geographical position'.[2] To this German rehabilitation Britain had made a decisive contribution, partly through instinctive sympathy with the defeated, partly from the wish to be left in peace, partly from the illusion that France and Germany were equals as between whom Britain had to hold the scales, and that, if from anywhere, the real danger to peace came from France and her allies. And thus:

> *The winning cause the Gods espouse*
> *The losing Cato.*

[1] 185 H.C. Deb. 5s. Col. 1658 (24 June 1925).
[2] Cmd. 2525, pp. 55–7.

While this illusion held British opinion in its grip Germany need not fear an Anglo-French combination against her, save in the most blatant case of German aggression, which no sensible German Government would attempt unless it were strong enough to despise such a combination even if it were formed.

But it is wrong to speak of Locarno as merely a springboard for Hitler. The question is not whether Britain, in taking up Stresemann's suggestion of January, had made the fatal decision to come down on the side of German revival, but whether the British public really understood that pacts have real, as well as moral, implications. The Versailles Treaty had been signed by a British Government which almost at once mentally repudiated some of its basic provisions. The same might happen to Locarno. What had seemed a vital interest in 1919, the alliance with France, had come to seem provocation to Germany in 1925. What seemed equally vital, at least to British Ministers who saw Locarno, not as a form of Couéism, but as a certain relation of real political and military forces, might come to seem an affront to common decency in 1936. The British desire for 'business as usual' in 1925 had a common-sense flavour about it. But politics are not everywhere run by men whose footrule is the profit and loss account.

CHAPTER XI

NEW FORCES IN THE FAR EAST

I

In both Europe and the Far East after the First World War the defeat of Germany and Russia's collapse imposed on Britain a reassessment of policies. In Europe British policy was balanced between the readmission of Germany into the concert of Powers and efforts to satisfy, at least symbolically, the fears of France. In the Far East, however, Germany disappeared from the scene. Her rights in Shantung passed at the peace conference to Japan, her island colonies in the Pacific were divided as mandates between Japan, Australia and New Zealand, her naval strength no longer counted. This eclipse was an aspect of the general decline of Europe in Far Eastern affairs which the war accelerated. Britain and France also found their positions weakened in the postwar decade, France owing to the security problem in Europe, Britain on account of domestic worries, the pressures of nationalism in other parts of the world and the new role of the United States. Russia, on the other hand, though revolution and reconstruction provided her with no more than a watching brief in East Asia, still remained almost as much a Far Eastern Power as she was a European.

By the Li-Lobanov secret treaty with China in 1896 Russia had secured the right to build the Chinese Eastern Railway cutting across the great Manchurian salient to Vladivostok and shortening the distance from European Russia to the Pacific by 570 miles, together with rights of administration over the land required to build, operate and construct the railway. Two years later the Russian Minister for War, General Kuropatkin, persuaded the Tsar to secure a twenty-five year lease of the Liao-tung peninsula, which the Powers had collectively forced Japan to disgorge after her defeat of China in 1895, in order to construct a southern branch of the Chinese Eastern Railway linking it with Port Arthur. These Russian penetrations into China moved the British Government to enter into an agreement with Germany on 16 October 1900 to help defend each other's interests against a third Power. Germany insisted, however, that the agreement did not apply to Manchuria, where Russian designs were most evident and, in the search

273

for an ally in the Far East following the isolation of Britain during the Boer War, Lord Salisbury signed a treaty of alliance with Japan on 20 January 1902.

The treaty ensured British neutrality in the ensuing Russo-Japanese War of 1904–5 and warned France, now united with Russia by her alliance of 1891–2, against going to her ally's assistance since Britain was now bound to join Japan in the event of war with two other Powers. The total Japanese victory over Russia was as much a surprise in London as elsewhere. The result, however, was to consolidate Japanese paramountcy in Korea, formally annexed in 1910, to secure for Japan the Russian lease of the Liao-tung peninsula and Port Arthur, the South Manchuria Railway from Changchun to Port Arthur and the southern part of the island of Sakhalin. In secret treaties entered into with Russia from 1907 until 1916 Japan secured recognition of her dominant interests in south Manchuria while granting similar recognition to Russia in the northern half.[1] With these gains, and with China torn apart by seemingly endless civil war, Japan became the undisputed dominant local Power after the Russian Revolution. By 1919 she was not merely the heir to Germany's rights in China and her possessions in the Pacific north of the equator, but, as an unwearied partner in the Allied intervention in Siberia, the chief potential beneficiary if Russia split apart.

This advance in Japan's power was not disturbing to the British; Japan, similar in its island character to Britain, tended to be regarded as a stabilising force which might serve to prevent Soviet Communism from penetrating China, where the national revolution against the Manchus of 1911–12 was still far from having resulted in a firm central government. Britain continued to support the conservative régime of President Yuan Shi-kai in Peking though its authority had been seriously affected when it accepted the Japanese Twenty-one Demands in 1915, the purport of which was to make China a Japanese protectorate.[2] As a result the more radical group of the Chinese nationalist coalition, the Kuomintang, led by Dr. Sun Yat-sen, had seceded and formed a separate régime in Canton with nationalist pretensions hostile to European rights in China. Japan, as well as being a *point d'appui* against the anti-foreignism of the Chinese revolution, was also regarded in London as a counterpoise to the United States, now, after Germany's defeat,

[1] For an account see E. B. Price, *The Russo-Japanese Treaties of 1907–1916 concerning Manchuria and Mongolia*, Baltimore, 1933.
[2] The text of the Twenty-one Demands is printed in T. E. la Fargue, *China and the World War*, pp. 241–3.

Britain's only naval rival. Though Anglo-American naval competition, which began with President Wilson's Naval Appropriation Act of 1916, was never considered in Britain a possible cause of conflict, the link with Japan, now the world's third naval power, was a useful asset to Britain in the settlement of postwar naval questions with Washington. Moreover, at the end of the war Japan had all the characteristics of a conservatively democratic state. Her sudden accession to the inner circle of Great Powers, with a permanent seat on the League Council, gave her a strong inducement to maintain good relations with the European allies. The war itself represented the victory of liberal democratic forces in the world, reflected in the ascendancy of the moderate Japanese political forces led by the Minseito, or Liberal, party which held office during most of the 1920s. The world-wide postwar economic strains also served to make Japanese politicians circumspect and fearful that gains in exports during the war, when European industry was otherwise occupied, might be thrown away by reckless foreign policies.

II

British policy in the Far East during the nineteenth century had been mainly governed by commercial considerations, in particular the massive attractions of the Chinese market. Commercial considerations led to the two principles of the Open Door, an axiom of British policy in China long before the United States Secretary of State, John Hay, drew up his famous notes in 1899, and of the administrative and territorial integrity of China. With the coming of policies of exclusiveness, pursued by France in south-west China, Russia in Manchuria and Germany in Shantung, the British attitude changed. Britain began to regard participation in the Battle of Concessions as necessary if she was not to be squeezed out, to mark out the Yangtze basin as the special sphere for British investments, to acquire her own lease of a naval base, which she did at Weihaiwei in 1899. The aim in China, as with that other 'sick man', Turkey, was to slacken the pace of disintegration while securing a share in the spoils appropriate to the scale of British interests. Salisbury described the policy in frank terms in May 1898:

> Of course, it is not to be supposed that any one nation of the living nations will be allowed to have the profitable monopoly of curing or cutting up these unfortunate patients, and the controversy is as to who shall have the privilege of doing so, and in what measure he shall do it. . . . Undoubtedly

we shall not allow England to be at a disadvantage in any rearrangement that may take place.[1]

After 1918, despite the threat to Chinese integrity implicit in Japan's Twenty-one Demands of 1915, competition for concessions and privileges in China relaxed. With unrest in all parts of the world stretching British resources to the full, the hope in London was that the Chinese revolution would find some point of stability permitting the revival of British trade and investment.

The uncertain element in the situation was the attitude of the United States, with whom all British destinies were now indissolubly linked. The striking feature of American policy after 1918 was its political detachment from Europe and the Middle East and its continuing concern with events in the Pacific and East Asia. The basis of American policy was the safeguarding of China's integrity coupled with the maintenance of the Open Door, behind which lay the paternalistic regard for China developed over many years of American missionary and educational activity. Japan was conceived, owing to the Twenty-one Demands and the loudly voiced aims of such organisations as the Black Dragon Society, as the chief threat to Chinese integrity. Secretary of State Lansing had entered into an agreement with the leader of the wartime Japanese mission to the United States, Viscount Ishii, in November 1917 which recognised Japan's 'special interests' in China owing to her propinquity to the mainland, while Japan on her side affirmed the principles of the Open Door and the integrity of China.[2] But the American Government could not agree with Japan on the interpretation of the agreement; Lansing held that the Japanese interests referred to were no more than treaty rights, while Ishii argued that they bore more far-reaching political and economic connotations. American fears of Japanese aims were heightened by the Japanese role in the inter-Allied expedition to Siberia in the summer of 1918, to which Wilson consented only with extreme reluctance, the force sent to Siberia by Japan being absurdly out of proportion to that of the other Allies.[3] Wilson's suspicions of Japan were reflected in his stubborn opposition to the cession of German properties in Shantung and colonies in the Pacific to Japan at the peace conference.[4]

[1] Quoted in P. Joseph, *Foreign Diplomacy in China, 1894–1900*, London, 1928, p. 317.
[2] *F.R.U.S., 1917*, pp. 264–5.　　　　[3] See above, Chapter IV, pp. 70–2.
[4] An American writer suggested that it may have been on this ground that the Versailles Treaty received its death blow in the Senate; *Foreign Affairs*, June 1923, pp. 9, 23.

THE FAR EAST, 1919–39

Since the United States did not ratify the Versailles Treaty she could not invalidate the cession of German rights in Shantung to Japan. The position taken by Charles Evans Hughes, however, who became Secretary of State in the Harding administration which entered office in March 1921, was that American rights in the disposal of Germany's former colonies could not be bargained away by the Allies. An agreement was eventually reached with the Japanese at Washington in November 1921 which safeguarded American rights in all Pacific islands under Japanese mandate.[1] The encroachments of Japanese power in the Pacific, however, intensified American fears that Japan's naval strength might be used in the issue of immigration into the western coastlands of the American continent. By the 'Gentlemen's Agreement' of 1907 Japan had consented to limit the issue of passports to the United States to selected groups of her nationals, in which labourers were not included. The agreement had never worked without friction and, with the economic difficulties of postwar Japan, seemed to be a subterfuge for the transfer of more of Japan's surplus population to North America. The American Government retaliated with the Immigration Act of 1924 which definitely excluded further Japanese settlers and was passed to the tune of declarations calling into question the good faith of the Japanese authorities in the matter of the 1907 agreement.

President Harding repeated the American refusal to join the League in his inaugural address in March 1921. He could hardly afford, however, to take up such an Olympian position in Far Eastern affairs, in which he began to work actively for the winding up of the Anglo-Japanese alliance. Any arrangement between two countries the relations of both of which with the United States were far from good was bound to look suspicious in Washington. Added to which was the slightly absurd naval competition between Britain and the United States. The First Lord of the Admiralty, Lord Lee of Fareham, in a speech at the Society of Naval Architects on 16 March 1921, conceded without apparent alarm the principle of parity with the American navy.

We see the Naval Committee of the United States [he said] is laying down the principle that America shall maintain a navy at least equal to that of any other Power. That is a claim of equality which this country has never accepted in the past and never would accept save in connection with

---

[1] United States Treaties, 111, p. 2723.

a great English-speaking nation which sprang from our loins and must ever hold special place in our regard and confidence.[1]

As was explained in the House of Commons on the following day by the Parliamentary Secretary to the Admiralty, this was no new recognition of parity but had been expressed the previous year by Lee's predecessor at the Admiralty, Walter Long, in his speech on the Naval Estimates.[2] The Lee speech was followed in April by talks between the First Lord and Adolph Ochs, the publisher of the *New York Times*, who enjoyed Harding's confidence, which included a breakfast with the Prime Minister, Lloyd George. In these conversations the British Ministers made known their readiness for an understanding with the United States on the basis of naval parity which would have the advantage for Britain of alleviating the economic strain of competitive shipbuilding and of allowing the British fleet to be concentrated nearer home while the United States fleet patrolled the Pacific.[3] Nevertheless, so long as the British alliance with Japan remained the United States could never be sure that the British fleet, even if no greater than the American, might not be used in a sense contrary to American policies. The risk of the alliance dragging Britain into war against the United States was so remote that it could be discounted. But this did not exclude the possibility of circumstances arising in which the alliance might operate as an instrument against American views even if no force were used.[4] In any event, these were real American fears. Hughes even went as far as to tell the British Ambassador in Washington, Sir Auckland Geddes, in June 1921 that the British alliance with Japan might come in as a handy weapon for Anglophobes during the perennial debates in Congress on the Irish question.[5] With Britain so much out of favour with American opinion it it was hard to decide whether this was intended as a hint to Britain to drop her Japanese friends or settle with the Irish nationalists, or both.

For the British Government the case for ending the Japanese alliance and the case for preserving it were equally strong. 'Friendly co-operation with the United States,' Lloyd George told the Imperial Conference in London in June 1921, 'is for

---

[1] Quoted in *The Times*, 17 March 1921.
[2] 139 H.C. Deb. 5s. Cols. 1766–7 (17 March 1921).
[3] E. J. Young, *Powerful America*, New York, 1936, pp. 49–50.
[4] S. F. Bemis (ed.), *The American Secretaries of State and their Diplomacy*, Vol X, New York, 1930, p. 242.
[5] A. W. Griswold, *The Far Eastern Policy of the United States*, p. 281.

us a cardinal principle,' and this did not over-state the truth.[1] Apart from sentimental and cultural affinities, there were a hundred reasons why British sacrifices for American goodwill were worth making. No scheme of European or world security could be drawn up while a firm American commitment was not forthcoming. Nor could it be taken for granted that in any future conflict the safety of the British Empire, even of Britain herself, could be assured without American assistance. The role which Britain hoped America would play in European recovery and the settlement of war debt and reparation problems has already been explained in a previous chapter. On every ground British statesmen could afford to miss no chance of satisfying American grievances. On this account Britain had insisted, when the alliance with Japan was renewed in July 1911, on the insertion of article 4, which released her from any obligation to go to Japan's aid against a country with which Britain had a treaty of arbitration. Since an arbitration treaty had just been negotiated with the United States, the new article was intended as an intimation to Washington that the alliance was not directed against America. In the event the arbitration treaty failed to attain Senatorial ratification, but an Anglo-American Peace Commission treaty signed in 1914 did become effective and the British Government let it be known that they considered this as falling within the reservation in article 4 of the revised alliance with Japan.

On the other side were equally strong arguments against the abandonment of the alliance, which had served Britain well during the war. British Ministers feared involvement in racial controversies; they saw nothing to gain from a racial conflict between East and West which might seal off the Orient from Western trade and influence. British delegates at the 1919 peace conference could not vote for the Japanese proposal for a racial equality clause in the League Covenant or, when this was rejected, for a reference in the preamble to equality of treatment of all nationals. To do so would have been intolerable to the Dominions and hence Lord Cecil, like Wilson, abstained. Nevertheless, the British wish was to spare Japan every possible racial humiliation and the alliance was in Japanese eyes a token of racial equality. To cast the alliance away after it had served its purpose of providing Britain with a friend against her now defeated enemies in the Far East would be to destroy Britain's influence in Japan and perhaps drive her along the road of militarism and exclusiveness at the very moment when liberal

[1] Imperial Conference, 1921, Summary of Proceedings and Documents, Cmd. 1474, p. 13.

forces were gaining ground. The consequence might also be to ruin the prospects of naval disarmament to which British opinion attached such importance. The British Ambassador in Tokyo, Sir Charles Eliot, wrote to Balfour in November 1921 that the military leaders in Japan were divided in their attitude to disarmament, the Navy being in favour and the Army opposed. Japanese public opinion in general, he reported, would welcome the tax reductions flowing from an arms moratorium, but never at the cost of Japan's 'mission in Asia'.[1] But if Japanese goodwill was indispensable to disarmament, and goodwill could not be secured without the continuing assurance that Japan had an important part to play in the world, it was also valuable to the British Empire with its millions of Asian subjects. Any suggestion of British sympathy towards a White Man's pact against Japan, since 1905 the widely accepted leader in East Asia, would be destructive of Britain's position in a multiracial Empire. 'Our foreign policy,' said Lloyd George, 'can never range itself in any sense upon the difference of race and civilisation between East and West. It would be fatal to the Empire.'[2]

As between these fairly balanced arguments the two circumstances which determined the Cabinet to bring the Japanese alliance to an end were the need for a pause in the arms race and the influence of Canada on Imperial policy. The former demanded agreement with the United States, the only serious question being whether domestic pressures for a disarmament agreement might force the Harding administration to negotiate without Britain having to sacrifice her Japanese ally. These pressures had the effect of securing the introduction into the Senate by Senator Borah on 14 December 1920 of a resolution calling on the President to invite Britain and Japan to agree with the United States on annual reductions in naval building plans for a period of five years.[3] The resolution was passed with only four negative votes and was accepted by Harding and mentioned approvingly in his inaugural address when he entered the White House the following March. In early June, however, possibly in order to take advantage of the objections to the continuance of the Anglo-Japanese alliance voiced at the Imperial Conference which opened in London on 20 June, Hughes told the British Ambassador in Washington that Britain must understand the American point of view generally on Far Eastern affairs if the standstill agreement on Anglo-American

[1] Blanche Dugdale, *Arthur James Balfour*, II, pp. 322–3.
[2] Cmd. 1474, p. 13.
[3] Congressional Record, CX, Part I, p. 310.

naval parity which Lord Lee's speech in March had foreshadowed was to be realised. 'If it were true,' Hughes told
Geddes, 'that the policies of Great Britain in the Far East were
like our own there should be co-operation between Britain and
the United States and it should be possible for the United
States to find complete support on the part of Great Britain
for their maintenance and execution.'[1] For a country which
had deliberately withdrawn from the labour of maintaining
peace in Europe and the Middle East this was exacting language. At the opening of the Imperial Conference in June the
Lloyd George Cabinet were therefore still not convinced that
American co-operation in the Far East was sufficiently dependable to justify dropping the Japanese alliance. The moment of decision, however, was quickly approaching. The
alliance was in a state of suspended animation after Curzon
had declared to the League Secretary-General on 8 July of the
previous year that if the alliance continued after July 1921 it
would be in a form more consistent with the League Covenant.
The Lord Chancellor, when questioned by the Imperial Conference, considered the declaration did not constitute denunciation in a legal sense, but it was evidently tantamount to it in
effect.[2] Nevertheless, Geddes told Hughes as late as 23 June
1921 that the alliance, which after its one-year renewal in 1920
would expire on 13 July, would probably be given artificial
respiration for another twelve months.[3]

The second and conclusive argument against the alliance
came in the powerful defence of the American case by the
leader of the Canadian delegation at the Imperial Conference,
the Prime Minister Arthur Meighen. From February 1921
Meighen had been pressing Lloyd George for a British Empire
conference with the United States to which China and Japan
would be invited. At the Imperial Conference in June he
argued the case for ending the link with Japan as a purely bilateral arrangement in the face of united opposition from the
British, Australian and New Zealand representatives, receiving
only partial support from Smuts of South Africa, who considered that alliances like that of 1902 belonged to the outmoded diplomacy of pre-League days. Apart from her common security interest with the United States, Canada shared
the same fear of immigration from the Orient into the western
coasts of North America, the same dread, in perhaps even
stronger form, of British influence being thrown on Japan's

[1] Griswold, *op. cit.*, p. 281.
[2] 144 H.C. Deb. 5s. Col. 916 (11 July 1921).
[3] Griswold, *ibid.*, p. 280.

side in disputes arising out of the immigration issue. During racial unrest in British Columbia before 1914 a friendly United States to the south had been of great assistance to the Canadian authorities; on one occasion, in 1908, the Canadian Commissioner for Labour and Immigration, Mackenzie King, had publicly thanked Theodore Roosevelt for sending the United States fleet to the Pacific. Meighen's object at the conference in 1921 was therefore either to secure simply the lapse of the Anglo-Japanese alliance, or, if that failed, to try to get discussions opened between London and Washington for the replacement of the alliance by an arrangement between all the Pacific Powers to rule out every risk of Britain ever taking Japan's side against North American states.

Meighen was strongly opposed by Hughes of Australia and Massey of New Zealand, both fearing that in any future war involving the Pacific British naval power would be unable to protect their countries without Japanese assistance or at least neutrality, and that in such an emergency United States help might not come, or might come too late. They also feared that Japan, angered by the dropping of a twenty-year-old alliance with one of the greatest Powers of the West, might revenge herself on her southern neighbours, while the United States, seeing the Japanese population problem relieved by Australia's open spaces, might be reluctant to side with the two British Dominions. However, as the argument for and against the alliance continued at the conference it was Hughes who was eventually isolated and compelled to admit defeat. This was partly because of the skill and persistence with which Meighen deployed his case, partly because intimations were received from Washington, while the issue was still in doubt in London, that the United States favoured some broadening of the alliance to make room for the United States.[1]

There followed a not untypical diplomatic comedy. Lloyd George, who enjoyed Curzon's forced changes of position, now told the Foreign Secretary to outline to the Imperial Conference a procedure for an international meeting on the Far East to include the United States, after having instructed him to defend the Japanese alliance at the opening of the Conference. The Prime Minister then entered a race with Harding to be the first with the announcement that a conference of the Powers on the Far East was in the offing, neither President nor Prime Minister wanting to give the appearance of having his hand

[1] Meighen's role at the Imperial Conference is described in 'Canada, the Anglo-Japanese Alliance and the Washington Conference', by J. B. Brebner, *Political Science Quarterly*, March 1935, pp. 45–58; CAB 23/26. 56 (21).

forced by the other. Lloyd George told the House of Commons on 7 July that he was awaiting replies from the United States, Japan and China to inquiries about a conference and would give further news on the following Monday, 11 July.[1] He was, however, beaten to the post by Harding, who, on the morning of that day, authorised a press release stating that he was sounding the European and Far Eastern Powers concerned on a conference. The Prime Minister made a similar announcement later in the day in answer to a question in the House.[2] As if to underline the American position that it was Britain who was seeking United States agreement to end the naval arms race, rather than the United States asking Britain to scrap the alliance with Japan, Harding refused to agree to a conference anywhere outside the United States; in this way any charge of having been captured, like Wilson, by European politicians in their own capitals would be avoided. Consequently when the Washington Conference on disarmament and problems of the Far East and the Pacific at length formally opened on 11 November it was evident that it was the United States which was the ascendant Power, Britain having almost the role of a suppliant.

The British delegation was to have been led by Lloyd George but the Prime Minister was occupied with Irish troubles and Balfour, who had played a dominant role in the formation of the Japanese alliance in 1902, took his place. Balfour, whose now fragile loftiness seemed symbolic of Britain herself, carried with him the definite agreement of the Cabinet to merge the Japanese alliance into a wider understanding.[3] In this way the most important object of the Harding administration had been attained before the Conference began. For this they had a price to pay, their consent to a naval holiday and hence to the surrender of the ambition to excel Britain at sea. However, the strongest doubts existed in the United States whether the latter was in any case a sensible object.[4]

III

The American initiative was maintained at the opening of the Conference by Secretary of State Hughes when he astounded the delegates (representing, besides the United States, the four Allied Powers, Britain, France, Italy and Japan, and the invited

---

[1] 144 H.C. Deb. 5s. Col. 621.
[2] *Ibid.*, Cols. 914–18.
[3] Dugdale, *op. cit.*, II, pp. 319–20.
[4] The U.S. Naval Appropriation Bill, which became law on 12 July, the day following Harding's press release, included as an appendix the Borah resolution on naval disarmament.

states of Belgium, China, the Netherlands and Portugal) by his proposal, firstly that all capital ship-building programmes, actual and projected, should be abandoned, and secondly that further reductions should be effected in old ships on the basis of parity as between Britain and the United States in capital ships, 30 per cent of their combined strength for Japan and 17.5 per cent each for France and Italy. Hughes then went on to break all the rules of diplomatic etiquette by detailing the reductions these principles implied. The total of capital ships condemned to the breaker's yard in this speech was nearly 2 million tons in the case of these three Powers alone, or nearly 40 per cent of existing capital ship tonnage. No wonder Hughes was described as having achieved more than all the sea battles in history.[1] It required all Balfour's conviction that the folly of a naval arms race with the United States must be averted at all costs to override the British seamen, led by Lord Beatty, who listened like a row of indignant bulldogs.[2] The American Advisory Committee assisting Hughes, however, was unable to agree on the total abolition of the submarine, but favoured legal restrictions of the size of submarines and the introduction of stricter rules covering their use in wartime against merchant ships. This would have suited Britain; Lord Lee, the First Lord, was naturally a total abolitionist, but would willingly settle for less. The strongest objection to any agreement on submarines, however, came from France, already shocked by the Hughes proposal that she should be reduced to Italy's level as a naval Power. The French Prime Minister, Briand, had to impose the capital ship ratio on his naval spokesman, Admiral le Bon, from afar after his return to Paris, but was unwilling to extend the standstill programme at the ratios proposed to what he called 'defensive' weapons, in which group he included submarines. Britain, on her side, could not agree to disarmament of smaller ships than capital vessels, that is, battleships and aircraft carriers, if submarines were excluded.

The resulting Five-Power Naval Treaty signed on 6 February 1922 by Britain, France, Italy, Japan and the United States therefore provided that, after scrapping and the completion of ships then building, the United States was permitted to retain 525,850 tons in capital ships, the British Empire 558,950 tons, Japan 301,320 tons and France and Italy 221,170 tons and 182,800 tons respectively. Replacements were to be effected on approximately the same scale. A ten-year holiday in the further construction of capital ships was to be held but

[1] CAB 21/218. W.D.C. 12.
[2] See memorandum by Naval Staff, October 1921; CAB 21/218. 277–B.

the only restriction on ships other than the capital class was that cruisers were not to exceed 10,000 tons and their guns were not to be in excess of 8-inch calibre.   Since many naval authorities considered that the great capital ship had had its day the exclusion of other types of vessels considerably weakened the force of the treaty.

The inferiority accorded to Japan in the Naval Treaty was not wholly unwelcome in that country owing to the strain of naval building throughout the year.   It was estimated that by 1921 the Navy was absorbing on the average one-third of the total budgetary expenditure.[1]   None the less Japanese agreement had to be paid for.   The most important and fateful concession to Japan was the insertion into the treaty of article 19, which provided for maintaining the *status quo* in naval bases and fortifications in the insular possessions of the contracting Powers in the Pacific.   Exceptions were made, the most important being Singapore and Hawaii, with its naval stronghold at Pearl Harbor, but the effect of the provision was to neutralise Guam, the Pago-Pago islands, the Philippines, the Aleutians and Hong Kong, while Japan on her side agreed not to strengthen the defences of Formosa or of the Ryukyu island group.   Taken in conjunction with the agreed naval ratios, which meant that in any future conflict the Japanese navy could only be defeated with a confident margin if British and American naval forces acted together and could be concentrated in the Pacific, the standstill agreement on bases implied that Hawaii, some four thousand miles away, was the nearest place from which naval force could be mustered against the Japanese home islands if war came.   With Japan's ability to re-fuel and re-equip her fleet from her home bases, which were excluded from the agreement, she had little to fear from an attack from the only two naval rivals she had.   It is not surprising that at Washington a Japanese diplomat told a member of the British team that the alliance had at least been given a splendid funeral.[2]

Britain did not realise the hope, which Balfour strongly expressed to Hughes, of having the United States simply added to the alliance, making it trilateral.[3]   This suggested too much of an entangling alliance for American taste.   On the other hand, the Japanese objected to dilution of the alliance through the addition of other states which might be inferior to themselves in world stature.   This combination of circumstances made

---

[1]   *The New Cambridge Modern History*, XII, Cambridge, 1960, p. 434.
[2]   Treaty Series No. 5 (1924), Cmd. 2036.
[3]   CAB 21/218. File No. 31/F/5. W.D.C. 13.

possible the acceptance of Hughes' proposal that France should
be brought into a new arrangement, partly in order to counter-
act her feeling of grievance with the naval ratios.   The result
was the Four-Power Pacific Treaty agreed on 10 December
and signed on the 13th.[1]   Between this and the Anglo-Japanese
alliance, now formally abrogated, with its pledge of mutual
assistance, there was little to compare.   The treaty took the
simple form of undertakings to respect each other's rights in their
'insular possessions and insular dominions in the region of the
Pacific Ocean', to confer together in the event of a dispute
arising on any Pacific question which was not settled by ordinary diplomacy and to consult if any signatory should be
threatened by the aggressive action of any other Power on a
Pacific issue.   The duration of the treaty was fixed at ten years.
After the actual signing of the treaty the Japanese Foreign
Minister, Baron Shidehara, pressed for the exclusion of the
Japanese home islands from the provisions of the treaty, presumably on grounds of national pride, although the treaty as it
stood offered Japan a pledge of respect for her territorial integrity which she was not called on to reciprocate.   Balfour was
at first unwilling to agree since the effect would be to impose
on the Pacific Dominions an unequal status which Japan refused to accept for herself.   But he and Secretary Hughes at
last consented.[2]

The Japanese were no more energetic than the Europeans
or the Americans in demanding the same respect for China's
national status as they required for their own.   In the Japanese mind China played a double role, that of a junior partner
in the development of Asia and that of a protégé.   The latter
was also the role assigned to China in the American mind and
Hughes was active in securing from all the Powers at Washington an endorsement of the American principles of the Open
Door and the equality of opportunity in China in terms of
which this role was conceived.   Hughes' four principles for the
future treatment of China were accordingly laid down in a
nine-Power treaty, the only agreement signed at Washington
by all the states represented, article 1 of which pledged the
signatories to:

1. Respect the sovereignty, the independence, and the
territorial and administrative integrity of China;

---

[1] Treaty Series No. 6 (1924), Cmd. 2037.
[2] For the text of the Japanese declaration see Misc. No. 1 (1922). Conference on
Limitation of Armaments, Cmd. 1627, pp. 41–2. Also J. Chal Vinson, 'The drafting
of the Four-Power Treaty of the Washington Conference', *Journal of Modern History*,
XXV, No. 1, pp. 40–7 (March 1953).

   2. Provide the fullest and most unembarrassed opportunity to China to develop and maintain for herself an effective and stable government;

   3. Use their influence for the purpose of effectually establishing and maintaining the principle of equal opportunity for the commerce and industry of all nations throughout the territory of China;

   4. To refrain from taking advantage of conditions in China in order to seek special rights or privileges which would abridge the rights of subjects or citizens of friendly states, and from countenancing action inimical to the security of such states.[1]

China promised to do nothing to hinder the carrying out of these principles and in particular not to grant exclusive rights or spheres of interest or impose discrimination on grounds of nationality on persons using her railways or other transit facilities. The treaty was, however, more of a self-denying ordinance on the part of the other eight Powers in their future relations with China than a compact between all nine. In order to complete this aspect of the treaty Britain joined the United States in compelling Japan to disgorge her gains of 1919 from China. Balfour and Hughes virtually stood over Baron Shidehara until he agreed to withdraw that portion of the Twenty-one Demands referring to the control of Chinese Government policy, evacuate Japanese troops from Shantung, sell to China the railway there which Germany formerly owned, and surrender the economic privileges in the province won by Japan at the Paris Peace Conference.[2]

   At the same time, although Soviet Russia had no representative at the Washington Conference, Shidehara gave a pledge that Japan would withdraw the troops she had maintained in Siberia since the 1918 intervention and restore the northern part of Sakhalin to Russia.[3] The Japanese delegation considered that these efforts to remove American suspicions were well worth the sacrifice of the gains from China at Versailles, all the more so since China would still remain open to economic penetration from Japan, the only industrialised nation of the Far East. The general atmosphere of renunciation in relation to China at Washington also helped. Britain made her contribution by agreeing to give up her lease of the naval base at Weihaiwei, though the negotiation of facilities for British naval vessels at the port continued to vex Sino-British

[1] Treaty Series No. 42 (1925), Cmd. 2517.
[2] *D.B.F.P.*, Second Series, VIII, p. 766, No. 629, n. 1; CAB 30/14/1. No. 37.
[3] Cmd. 1627, pp. 70–6.

relations throughout the twenties.[1] This British offer restored to China full control, in theory at least, over the Shantung peninusula.

The Washington Conference was acclaimed in Britain and the United States as having arrested the spiral of naval competition which threatened to get out of hand in the immediate postwar years. Hughes said that 'we are taking perhaps the greatest forward step in history to establish the reign of peace.'[2] In Britain it was estimated that the financial saving effected would be £10 million for each of the years immediately after the conference, a cause for congratulation in an age of deflationary monetary policies.[3] As the one truly effective disarmament conference of the inter-war period Washington was judged a 'brilliant success' by a British authority on disarmament.[4] Public opinion in the Anglo-Saxon countries was little concerned with the strategic invulnerability Japan had gained through the suspension of naval fortifications in the Pacific, and only after the experience of Japan's later policy towards China was regret felt in Britain that, by abandoning the alliance, the means of moderating Japanese policy had been cast away. The British connection could never be as important to the United States in the Far East as it was to Japan, and hence American governments had less inducement than the Japanese to take pains to satisfy British wishes. It remains speculative, however, whether and to what extent the alliance, had it been prolonged, would have enabled Britain to control Japanese policy after the world depression of 1931–3. The mere fact that Britain was in a position in 1921 where she had to jettison the alliance at America's behest showed the Japanese who was calling the tune in the Far East.

While the Washington agreements registered a five-Power ratio in capital ships at a less dangerous level than that towards which naval rivalry was tending, the forces making for these ratios were already at work long before November and might have had the same practical outcome without the Conference. In both Britain and the United States strong public pressure was working to slacken the arms race and in Japan civilian influences were for the time being in the ascendant. The same pressure was thrown against more money being spent on naval bases; the first Labour Government in Britain suspended

---

[1] Ibid., pp. 77–88.

[2] M. J. Pusey, Charles Evans Hughes, New York, 1951, II, pp. 488–90.

[3] 151 H.C. Deb. 5s. Col. 836 (6 March 1922). Neville Chamberlain on the financial results of the Conference.

[4] Philip Noel-Baker, The Private Manufacture of Armaments, London, 1936, pp. 523–4.

work on the Singapore base in 1924 even though the base was excluded from the Washington naval treaty, and the resumption under the Conservatives in 1925 was not energetic.[1] Above all, after the great stalemate naval battles in the First World War and the coming of air power, doubts existed as to the value of the massive and slow Ironclads which figured in the arms race of pre-1914.

The real significance of the Washington agreements was political rather than naval. The Conference marked the end of Britain's supremacy and monopoly of moderating influence as between the external Powers with interests in the Far East. Central to that role was the Anglo-Japanese alliance which gave Britain a voice in the policy of the most active and wealthy local Power, Japan, while allowing her to keep the bulk of her fleet disengaged for other purposes. The rise of the United States to world status, foreshadowed by Theodore Roosevelt's intervention at the close of the Russo-Japanese war in 1905, meant that in the final resort British policy had to be agreeable to Washington in order to succeed. This in its turn required the merging of the alliance into wider agreements on the *status quo*, mutual respect for rights in the area and the integrity of China. Yet these undertakings were little more than verbal expressions of principle. No sanctions were provided, no pledges of assistance given. It remained to be seen whether the issuing of general principles was enough.

IV

The nine-Power treaty failed to bring about the peaceful China, well-disposed towards Britain, which Balfour was seeking at the Conference.[2] The reason for this was that the 'effective and stable' government in China which the treaty signatories were bound to help her form and maintain proved not to be within her power to create. For at least six years after the signing of the treaty China was a chaos of warring factions in which the main conflict, between the Kuomintang camp at Canton and the coalition of warlords based on Peking, was complicated by groups of independent provincial condottieri, now in alliance with one or other of the main contestants, now playing a lone hand. It was precisely the decline of firm central government in the second half of the nineteenth century which had led to the complex of unequal treaties, foreign

---

[1] For MacDonald's announcement on the Singapore base, see 171 H.C. Deb. 5s. Col. 319 (18 March 1924). For the Conservative decision to resume work on the base, see 180 H.C. Deb. 5s. Cols. 175–6 (11 February 1925).

[2] G. E. Hubbard, *British Far Eastern Policy*, p. 35.

concessions, settlements and extraterritorial rights which in theory the Washington principles were supposed to remove. Now the demand of the Chinese nationalists for the full restoration of China's sovereignty, which had been conceded in principle at Washington, was made virtually impossible to grant owing to the political chaos in China which the national revolution brought with it. This was strikingly shown in October 1925, when the conference to raise the Chinese tariff in order to provide more revenue for the government at length met in Peking, on Chinese insistence, in accordance with the nine-Power Washington treaty on China's tariffs.[1] The conference was soon made wholly unreal by the deteriorating political situation in the country and was compelled to disband in the following July since the Chinese delegation virtually ceased to exist owing to the civil war.

Britain was still the country with the greatest economic and commercial stake in China, the foremost representative of Western capitalism and hence the chief target in the campaign against external imperialism of the Chinese nationalists. The problem was at one and the same time to protect British interests and nationals thickly distributed in the various foreign enclaves in China, chiefly in the Yangtze valley, and to negotiate the inevitable revision in the status of foreigners in the country, while trying to ensure that a China released from eighty-year-old servitudes should not fall under the influence of any other country hostile to Britain. These aims required a mixture of firmness, liberality and sensitivity to the shifting balance of political power in China. The British Foreign Secretary mostly concerned with this revision in Western status in China, Austen Chamberlain, said of his approach to the question that 'we do not disguise from ourselves the inconveniences and difficulties of the moment, but we are thinking of our relations with China for the next hundred years'.[2] Despite the formidable handicaps, more success was achieved in this policy than in British relations with any other non-European country with the exception of Kemalist Turkey.

The Power most likely to take Britain's place in China, and that of the West generally, was Soviet Russia. The postwar conflict between Britain and Russia in Asia, though less dangerous than before 1914 owing to the military eclipse of Russia during the war, was intensified by the Bolsheviks' verbal disavowal of territorial greed, their astute use of many of the war-time

---

[1] Treaty Series No. 43 (1925), Cmd. 2518.
[2] In a speech at Birmingham, 29 January 1927, reported in *The Times*, 30 January 1927.

slogans coined by the Allied Powers and the revolutionary upsurge in Asia after 1918. Soviet efforts to bring the new Turkey to Russia's side had been foiled by Curzon at the Lausanne Conference. Two years later the Locarno pact weakened the link between Russia and Weimar Germany and seemed, in Russian eyes, to mark the gathering of Western capitalist forces against Sovietism. The inference drawn by the Bolsheviks was that their ties with the nationalist revolution in China must be made all the stronger. The instrument of this policy, Michael Borodin, was sent as political adviser to the Kuomintang régime in Canton at the invitation of Sun Yat-sen in 1924 and along with him a military mission under Marshal Galen. Once in China Borodin served to inflame the xenophobia of the nationalists, with Britain as the chief victim, and fought with the Right of the Kuomintang for the prize of shaping the future of the Chinese revolution. As the Kuomintang's power ranged northwards in 1926 and 1927 it was in any case inevitable that the full force of anti-foreign violence should fall on the dense mass of British interests in the Yangtze basin. But this did not make it less necessary for the British authorities to break the influence of Moscow on the Kuomintang leaders.

The campaign against Britain began in the spring of 1925 with the formation of militant trade unions in the southern areas of China under Kuomintang control, strikes in foreign firms and attacks on British property by mobs organised by the Kuomintang Left wing and the Chinese Communist Party. On 30 May a strike in a Japanese cotton factory in Shanghai led to riots in which British police officers opened fire killing 12 Chinese and injuring 17.[1] The unrest then spread to Hankow and Kiukiang, where there were substantial British settlements under the régime of extraterritoriality, and the crisis reached its height in Canton, the Kuomintang seat of power, towards the end of June, when British and French forces opened fire on a Chinese mob from Shameen island, which is separated from Canton by a creek. According to the British account Chinese soldiers began with a volley of gunshot towards the Europeans on the island; nevertheless 37 Chinese were killed and 70 wounded.[2] This was the beginning of a long and bitter anti-British boycott and strike, Hong Kong being in a state of seige on the land side. The strike did not end until October. British trade with China suffered. Whereas between 250 and 300 million square yards of British cottons were exported annually to China before the

[1] Sir Charles Petrie, *Sir Austen Chamberlain*, II, p. 361.
[2] China No. 1 (1926), Cmd. 2636.

troubles, the figure fell to 173 million square yards in 1925, imports from Japan being the chief beneficiaries.

This was a foretaste of what was to come in 1927. The theatre of unrest in that year was the Yangtze valley in which the great river was almost an international highway, with British businesses and residents massed in its many ports as in the British Isles themselves. The Northern Military Expedition, launched by Chiang Kai-shek in May 1926, apparently with the object of uniting the Right and Left wings of the Kuomintang, reached the triangular conurbation of Hankow–Hanyang–Wuchang before the end of August; the nationalist forces were in possession of the cities by October and thus dominated the Yangtze. Incidents on the river followed when British-owned steamers were commandeered by Chinese troops, resulting in retaliatory action by British gunboats and answering barricades from Chinese soldiers stationed on the river banks. Anti-British movements finally reached a crescendo in January 1927 with the invasion of the British concession at Hankow by a Chinese mob on 4 and 5 January and the overrunning of the concession at Kiukiang, further down the river, on the 6th and 7th. The conflagration then enveloped Nanking in March. Only in 1928, with the advance of Kuomintang forces towards the northern provinces surrounding Peking, was the force of nationalist violence against the British position in central China relaxed. As the storm receded, the Japanese felt the impact of Chinese anti-foreignism in Shantung, sacred to the Chinese as the birthplace of Confucius.

In dealing with the situation Chamberlain's position was delicate on two accounts. In 1921 China had concluded treaties based on reciprocal recognition of equal rights with Austria, Germany and Hungary and with Soviet Russia on the same basis in May 1924. The Nationalists assumed that blunt pressure would secure the same results from other beneficiaries of the old régime. The traditional British defence against such tactics, 'gun-boat diplomacy', was ruled out, except in extreme emergencies, by a watchful Opposition at Westminster, the new code of the League, of which China was a member, and the principles signed at Washington. To which was added the difficulty that the solidarity of the external Powers, which had broken Chinese resistance during the Boxer rising in 1900 and many other outbursts against the West, could no longer be counted on. During the troubles of 1925–7 Japan, who wished to trade her rights in China proper in return for recognition of her position in Manchuria, stood aloof and there was little support from the United States, the progenitor of the Washington principles. Britain was therefore obliged to follow a dual policy: that of reserving force for the really critical occasions, the definition of which had to be left largely to the authorities on the spot, while taking the lead among the Washington Powers in a forward-looking attitude towards the Chinese problem.

The element of force in this policy was represented by the government's decision in January 1927 to organise a British Defence Force for the protection of the international settlement at Shanghai. This was to consist of three brigades of troops dispatched from Britain, the Mediterranean bases and India. In a statement sent to the League Secretary-General on 8 February the government said that the sole reason for the dispatch of the force was the determination not to allow the Hankow and Kiukiang incidents to be repeated at Shanghai.[1] The Foreign Secretary told the House of Commons on 10 February that the contingent was intended for the protection of British nationals only and that units from further afield than India would not be disembarked at Shanghai except in a great emergency, but would concentrate at Hong Kong.[2] The Kuomintang Foreign Minister, Eugene Chen, protested against the decision as an 'act of coercion' and held up his signature of the agreement on the concessions at Hankow and Kiukiang which he was negotiating with the British envoy, O'Malley. Nevertheless, the effect of the decision to send the force was to hold the position and calm nerves at Shanghai. In this action the United States joined by issuing a statement on 4 February calling on the warring Chinese factions to exclude the city from the area of their operations and by landing a detachment of marines from Manila. Neither the Americans nor the Japanese, however, took part in the military cordon thrown round the international settlement at Shanghai by the British forces. The cordon further exasperated the Chinese since it trespassed on Chinese-controlled territory outside the settlement, but this did not prevent the signing of the agreements on Hankow and Kiukiang by Chen and O'Malley on 19 and 20 February respectively. These agreements handed over the British concessions to Sino-British Councils while in return the Chinese undertook to settle outstanding questions with foreign Powers by negotiation and agreement.[3] An announcement to this effect was made by Chamberlain in the Commons on 21 February.[4]

[1] L.N.O.J., 8th Year No. 3, March 1927, pp. 292-3.
[2] 202 H.C. Deb. 5s. Col. 327.
[3] China No. 3 (1927), Cmd. 2869.
[4] 202 H.C. Deb. 5s. Cols. 1367-70.

If other Powers were lukewarm during the attacks on British rights and property, they were possibly even more so in regard to the second element in British policy, the controlled acceleration of China's release from all restrictions under the unequal treaties.   At the conference on Chinese tariffs which began in Peking in October 1925 the British delegates argued against any extension of foreign control of Chinese customs; in particular they criticised the American proposal for foreign control of the surtax provided for in article 3 of the nine-Power Washington tariff treaty, which the Americans now felt should be used to offset the decline in revenues due to the civil war in China.   In a memorandum to the United States Government on 28 May 1926, shortly before the winding up of the conference, the British Government argued, in their new vein of accommodation towards China, that:

> Any failure to implement the Washington treaty might create a very dangerous situation and H.M. Government therefore hold the view that if any reasonably satisfactory assurances are given by the Chinese Government as to the use which it proposes to make of the new resources, the Powers should accept such assurances, abstain from any attempt to impose control or exact guarantees and forthwith authorise the level of the surtax.[1]

The difficulty was that the intended recipient of the new revenues was the northern coalition of warlords, together with Chang Tso-lin, the *de facto* ruler of Manchuria, who were already fighting a losing battle with Kuomintang forces from the south. The Chinese dilemma thus made its appearance again: external Powers would have to make some sacrifice of their privileges in the interest of stable government in China and yet so long as it was uncertain which government to back it was impossible to know to whom the privileges were to be surrendered.

The same dilemma appeared in the work of the international commission on Chinese extraterritoriality which met in January 1926, in accordance with a resolution of the Washington Conference of 10 December 1921, to examine the Chinese legal system and the problems of extraterritorial rights which had been a feature of Chinese life since the first agreement giving foreign consular jurisdiction, signed with Britain at Nanking in August 1842.[2]   By the time the commission met the continuous disorder in Chinese politics since 1911 had prevented the implementation of the judicial reforms promulgated by the Imperial Government in 1907.   The result was that in 1926

---

[1] *The Times*, 28 December 1926.   [2] Cmd. 1627, pp. 53–4.

there were only 139 reformed courts in China, of which only 91 were courts of first instance; only 74 modern prisons had been built, as compared with 1,622 prisons which still stood from days before reform and in which execution by manual strangulation was by no means uncommon.[1] Since it was unthinkable that states with highly developed judicial processes and modern penal systems should entrust their nationals to the unreformed practices of Chinese law, the commission limited itself to making a set of recommendations for Chinese legal reform, the improvement of the judicial and prison system and more efficient administration of justice. The Chinese Government replied by denouncing her extraterritorial agreements with such countries as were unable to retaliate effectively, Belgium, France and Japan.

The impasse resulting from the failure of the tariff conference and the inconclusive work of the extraterritorial commission was hard for Britain to bear since she had most to lose from the resulting Chinese resentment. The British Government therefore determined to take the initiative in hastening a settlement between the Chinese nationalists and the West. They were assisted in this by a serious deterioration in the relations between the Right wing and the moderates in the Kuomintang, on one side, and the Soviet-influenced groups on the other. For the Kuomintang, Soviet help was useful in the struggle against internal rivals and so was the Soviet military mission under Marshal Galen which, by providing instructors for the Whampoa military academy, founded in June 1924, helped form a nursery of Nationalist officers who overwhelmed the northern Tuchuns three years later. But it soon became evident that Russia was seeking to use Borodin in order to embroil the Kuomintang Right wing with Britain; Borodin's haste in putting himself at the head of the mass movement against the British concession at Hankow in January 1927 was a symptom of this. Whatever Britain's sins, she was showing more readiness to negotiate revision of the unequal treaties than any other Power, and was clearly bidding for an equitable arrangement with whatever authorities established themselves in China so as to allow normal trade and investment to be carried on. The danger that attacks on the foreigner might decline into social revolution dismayed the solid bourgeoisie of the Kuomintang. They saw themselves building a strong, independent China; they had no taste for revolutionary socialism.

Tension between the Soviet mission at Canton and the Kuo-

[1] China No. 3 (1926). Report of the Commission on Extra-territoriality in China, Cmd. 2774.

mintang Right began soon after Sun Yat-sen's death in March 1925, but did not become serious until Chiang Kai-shek, the Nationalist Commander-in-Chief, set out to curb the influence of the Chinese Communists. In May 1926, on the eve of the launching of the Northern Military Expedition, he persuaded the Kuomintang to impose restrictions on the Communists within the party. When the seat of the Kuomintang was moved to Great Hankow in the autumn, marking the first stage of the success of the Northern Expedition, the British Minister in Peking, Sir Miles Lampson, was instructed to open talks with the régime, one object of this move being to take advantage of the widening rift between Right and Left in the Kuomintang. The talks were opened with Eugene Chen on 8 December and continued for nine days. By this time it was evident that the northern coalition was in the throes of dissolution, its failure being reflected in the ending of the tariff conference in the summer. The diplomatic missions of the Powers remained at Peking for the time being, however, and it was there on 18 December that O'Malley, in charge of the British mission, issued a memorandum on British policy to the representatives of the Washington Powers while Lampson was still on his way back to Peking. The memorandum was followed by British statements to Chen in Hankow on 27 January and to Dr. Wellington Koo, the Foreign Minister of the moribund Northern Coalition, in Peking on 28 January These statements, which were in effect concrete applications of the principles of the memorandum, set forth detailed proposals for modifying or surrendering the judicial, fiscal and administrative privileges enjoyed by foreign Powers in China.[1]

The December memorandum was an integral part of the British policy of accepting Chinese independence as the basis of future relations with the outside Powers and at the same time weaning the Kuomintang away from Soviet influence. It frankly recognised that the hopes expressed in the Washington accords of a strong central government in China were premature and that fair treatment of foreign rights had to be sought from whatever authorities were able to establish themselves in Chinese territory. The process of coming to terms with *de facto* authorities must involve dilutions of foreign rights, but there was little point in protesting over minor matters, the memorandum said, provided there was some measure of united action where really vital interests were at stake. The effect of a policy of making piecemeal arrangements with the powers-that-be in China would be that, after the prolonged period of

[1] For the text of the statements see *The Times*, 3 February 1927.

uncertainty was over, treaty revision, the essential object of
Chinese nationalism, would be already far advanced when the
time came for dealing with a Central Chinese Government
such as was contemplated in the Washington agreements.
Britain therefore proposed a declaration by the Washington
Powers which would show that they were 'prepared to consider in a sympathetic spirit any reasonable proposals that the
Chinese authorities, wherever situated, may make, even if
contrary to strict interpretation of treaty rights, in return for
fair and considerate treatment of foreign interests by them'.[1]

Notwithstanding its pragmatic appearance, the December
memorandum had a listless reception from the more important
Washington Powers, though the smaller countries reacted more
favourably.   France, according to a semi-official statement on
28 December, proposed to take no action; the Japanese position was the same.   The cold response from the United States
may have been due to a feeling of embarrassment that Britain
was taking the lead in the traditional American policy of defence of Chinese rights and also to offence at the suggestion in
the British memorandum that United States insistence on
foreign control of the Chinese surtax was due to pressure from
American bankers.   There was also a feeling in these three
countries that Britain, who was the chief focus of Chinese hostility, sought to put herself right with the Chinese by an appeasement policy and wanted other countries to pay part of
the price.   But this lack of support by the Washington Powers
did not discourage Chamberlain.   'The present system,' he
said in a speech at Birmingham on 29 January 1927, 'is anti-
quated.   It is unsuited to the conditions of today and it no
longer provides the necessary security and protection for the
peaceful avocations of our merchants.'[2]   Despite strong protests from British residents in China against an alleged policy
of 'scuttle' at Hankow and Kiukiang, the Foreign Secretary
intended to persist.

Though unrewarded by a common policy between the Powers
Chamberlain received some return for the December memorandum in the form of increasing strife between the Kuomintang Right and the Chinese supporters of the Russian
connection, which had up till then been stilled by the successful
military advance on the Yangtze.   The quarrel was resumed
in the spring of 1927, the first round ending in the temporary
defeat of Chiang Kai-shek, who was deposed from his position
as Commander-in-Chief on 17 April by Left-wing factions of the

[1] *The Times*, 28 December 1926.
[2] Quoted in *The Times*, 30 January 1927.

Kuomintang which formed a government at Hankow. The Right then formed a rival authority of their own at Nanking and this received considerable accessions of strength as a result of Chiang Kai-shek's victory over the Communists at Shanghai and the gradual spread of Right-wing influence along the southern coasts. The success of the Right was assisted by the shock administered to Chinese opinion by revelations of Russian designs on China by the Peking authorities, which raided Soviet agencies in the city and captured documents many of which were highly injurious to Chinese national pride. The next step came in June at Hankow, where a Hindu member of the Central Executive Committee of the Comintern disclosed that Borodin had received new instructions from Moscow wholly reversing the previous basis of his co-operation with the Chinese Nationalists. According to Borodin's new brief, his programme was to include the promotion of confiscation of the land in favour of the peasantry, changes in the structure of the Kuomintang so as to secure the dominance of the Chinese Communists, and the formation of a Red Army. The Hankow authorities at once began a purge of the Communists, proclaimed martial law and dismissed Borodin and the Russian mission. Hankow was then reconciled with Nanking and, with the creation of a reformed government at Nanking on 20 September, the Kuomintang was finally rid of Soviet influence. The defeat of a Communist attempt to invade Canton and set up a Soviet-style régime there in December then led to a breach between the Northern Coalition in Peking and Moscow. On 13 December Chiang Kai-shek made his contribution by ordering all Soviet consulates in territory under Kuomintang jurisdiction to be closed despite Moscow's protest that this was a violation of the 1924 treaty between Russia and the Peking Government.

The following year, 1928, saw the victory of Kuomintang forces over the Northern Tuchuns when Yen Hsi-shan took Peking on behalf of the Nanking régime on 8 June and the Manchurian warlord, Chang Tso-lin, withdrew towards Mukden on the fateful journey which ended with his death by an explosion on the Peking–Mukden railway line. By September the civil war was over for the time being, though the three south-western provinces, Szechwan, Kweichow and Yunnan, remained only in loose allegiance to Nanking. When on 10 October the Nanking régime was at last reconstructed with a new constitution the way seemed open to the general treaty revision which was the consistent aim of British policy. A suitable atmosphere for this had been created by the marked absence of anti-foreign demonstrations during the occupation of Peking by Kuomintang forces and by the efforts of the Nanking Foreign Minister, T. V. Soong, to put China's economy in order after the civil war. The question of tariff autonomy was soon settled by a treaty with the United States signed by Soong and the United States Minister, MacMurray, on 25 July and a similar treaty with Britain on 20 December. By the end of 1928 China had received tariff autonomy from eleven of the fifteen Powers to which she was still bound by unequal treaties and on 5 December her new autonomous tariff was announced at Nanking. Only Japan, whose forces had clashed with those of Chiang Kai-shek in Shantung in May, refused to accept the Chinese note on tariff autonomy, though she said she would not oppose it. Extraterritoriality, however, which had been excluded from the British and American revision treaties, proved to be a far harder nut to crack.

Thus far six Powers had refused to surrender their extraterritorial rights, Brazil, Britain, France, the Netherlands, Norway and the United States. To these the new Foreign Minister at Nanking, C. T. Wang, addressed a note on 27 April 1929 urging that steps should be taken, in view of the judicial reforms set in train by the Nanking régime, for China to assume jurisdiction over the nationals of all countries in her territory.[1] The British reply of 10 August, drawn up after long and close collaboration with the other Powers, pointed out that before these wishes could be met reforms embodying Western legal principles must become a 'living reality' in China.[2] The reply then placed the onus of making proposals on the Chinese. The American note was somewhat stiffer in tone.[3] By this time, however, extraterritoriality, with its overtones of national inferiority, had become an intense issue with Chinese public opinion and demands were being expressed for making New Year's Day, 1930, the beginning of a new régime of exclusive Chinese jurisdiction. The Foreign Secretary in the second British Labour Government, Arthur Henderson, realised that Nanking was being carried by public opinion further than it could possibly wish to go, in view of the immense complexities of the extraterritorial question. In order to save its face he agreed in a note of 20 December that 1 January should be the date 'from which the process of the gradual abolition of extraterritoriality should be regarded as having commenced in principle', but he insisted that only negotiations held in a

[1] D.B.F.P., Second Series, VIII, pp. 27–9.
[2] Ibid., pp. 130–3.
[3] F.R.U.S., 1929, II, pp. 596–9.

'friendly and unprejudiced' atmosphere would result in agreement on methods for abolishing extraterritoriality 'by gradual and progressive stages'.[1]

Henderson's aim was to allow the Chinese the satisfaction of naming the day without in fact surrendering any of the rights in China which Britain enjoyed. Note of this position was taken by the Chinese Government in a Mandate issued on 28 December which merely enjoined all foreigners enjoying extraterritorial rights to abide by the laws promulgated by the local and central authorities in China. No obligation appeared to be placed on the Chinese authorities to enforce these laws in Chinese courts if in the event the Mandate was not complied with.[2] It was on this assumption that Henderson (contrary to the advice of Lampson, who believed that the British position would be stronger if the talks were held in London) agreed to open negotiations in Nanking on the whole subject of extraterritorial rights.[3] Henry Stimson, the American Secretary of State, consented to join in this procedure and in January 1930 talks were opened in Nanking by C. T. Wang and Miles Lampson, in the case of British rights, and in Washington by the Chinese Minister, Dr. C. C. Wu, and State Department officials, in the case of American rights. These discussions carried on intermittently until China was engulfed in war with Japan; a final settlement was not reached until 1943.

During these years Britain was almost alone in the campaign for piecemeal revision of foreign rights in China for the purpose of taking the venom out of the anti-foreignism aroused by revolution and civil war. Some regret was felt in London that Britain no longer had the support of Japan, in view of the abrogation of the alliance in 1922. When Count Uchida came to Europe to sign the Pact of Paris on Japan's behalf in 1928 faintly wishful rumours circulated that a renewal of the alliance was discussed at the Foreign Office. These were denied by implication by Chamberlain in the House on 28 November, though he did say that Britain and Japan had 'larger interests' in China than the other Washington Powers and would remain in close contact through their Ministers in Peking.[4] The Shantung affair in the summer of 1928, however, showed that Japan was far too permanently committed to her 'special position' in north China to join fully with Britain in a policy of accommodation towards the Chinese Nationalists. Moreover,

---

[1] China No. 1 (1930), Cmd. 3480, pp. 3–4.
[2] *Ibid.*, p.5.
[3] *D.B.F.P.*, Second Series, VIII, p. 240; Cmd. 3480, pp. 5–6.
[4] 223 H.C. Deb. 5s. Col. 395.

the protection of Japanese interests in Manchuria, which had no parallel in British interests anywhere in China, was coming to be Tokyo's dominant concern, for which it was prepared to sacrifice many of its former common interests with Britain.   In a British Foreign Office paper written on 8 January 1930 it was said of Japan that:

> She is prepared to utilise the surrender of extraterritoriality in reaching a bargain with the Chinese for the protection of her special interests, especially in Manchuria. . . . In these circumstances we can never count on the support of Japan, though it may sometimes suit her convenience to work with us.[1]

On the other hand, the United States, though informed with strong traditional protectiveness towards China, tended to demand one principle, China's integrity, at one time, and another, defence of foreign rights, at another: an attitude equally at variance with British policy.   Britain was compelled to watch events, limiting herself to sheltering her interests from the storm wherever possible.

[1] *D.B.F.P.*, Second Series, VIII, p. 25.

CHAPTER XII

BRITAIN AND SOVIET COMMUNISM

I

WITHOUT the impetus of a strong, or headstrong, personality such as Lloyd George, who resigned in October 1922, British policy towards Russia seemed unable to surmount the barrier of revulsion against Communism. Nor were the trading prospects sufficient to launch a movement to mend the lines to Moscow. As far as the Russians were concerned, fear of a French attack after the Ruhr occupation and preoccupation with preparations for the Communist fiasco in Germany in September 1923 lessened the incentives for improved relations with Britain. But this position changed at the beginning of 1924. The failure of German Communism once more depressed the influence of the revolutionary element in the Soviet leadership; the Allies' decision in March 1923 to recognise the Lithuanian seizure of Memel, and thus accept the existing eastern frontier of Poland, without consulting Moscow showed that without diplomatic recognition questions affecting her interests would continue to be settled above Russia's head. With the easement of political tensions in Europe following the German decision to end passive resistance in the Ruhr in September 1923 Soviet Ministers again began to look to Britain for recognition. Already on 30 November 1923 Mussolini had signified Italy's willingness to grant *de jure* recognition as soon as the talks for a revision of the Soviet-Italian commercial treaty of 1921 were complete. There was a reasonable prospect that Britain would wish to take the lead from Italy if she meant to move at all.

In Britain, too, the early months of 1924 favoured recognition. Curzon was no longer lord of the Foreign Office. The head of the first Labour Government, formed in January, Ramsay MacDonald, had intimated his readiness for recognition during the election campaign and repeated this in a speech at the Albert Hall on 9 January, after his election victory, though he hesitated about sending the recognition note long enough to underline his lack of sympathy for Communism.[1] The business community in Britain too was beginning to have somewhat more faith in the Soviet economy. In August 1923

[1] R. W. Lyman, *The First Labour Government, 1924*, p. 185.

a delegation of British businessmen, including representatives of 80 engineering firms, had visited Russia, returning with a favourable opinion of recognition.[1]   Nevertheless, the long and tortuous negotiations with Russia on outstanding Anglo-Soviet differences which followed, occupying most of the life of the MacDonald Government, showed that whenever relations between the two countries began to move into smoother waters irreconcilable forces on either side were always available to turn them back.

On the Soviet side, the Communist authorities acclaimed MacDonald's *de jure* recognition note of 1 February as the effect of a widespread demand of the British working class which had imposed itself upon the generally hostile leaders of the Labour Party.[2]   Soviet leaders did very little to conceal their contempt for the new British Ministers or to help them against deep-rooted anti-Russian feelings in Britain, expressed in the common allegation that the Labour Party was largely financed by Moscow and in the refusal of King George V to accept a Soviet Ambassador at the Court of St. James since he would be the agent of regicides.[3]   When it became clear that MacDonald was making a settlement of the old questions of war debts and compensation for nationalised property the condition for signing the proposed general treaty to follow recognition, Litvinov launched an attack in *Pravda* on 14 February in which he denounced 'the Western illusion' that they could 'exact a price for recognition'.   This tone was repeated when the two Anglo-Soviet treaties, a commercial treaty and a general treaty, which issued from the negotiations, were signed on 8 August.   The Soviet tendency to represent the general treaty as having imposed a loan to Russia on the British Government because of their inability to deny the stability of the Soviet régime played straight into the hands of hardened opponents of Russia in Britain.   These, including *The Times*, wilfully misrepresented the treaty as forcing British taxpayers' money into Bolshevik pockets.

On the British side, hostility towards Russia on the Right was fanned by the indifferent support given to the negotiations of the two treaties by the Prime Minister.   After putting in an appearance at the opening of the talks on 14 April, when he pointedly distinguished between the Russian and the British

[1] E. H. Carr, *A History of Soviet Russia, IV, The Interregnum, 1923–1924*, p. 245.
[2] See the resolution passed by the Second Congress of Soviets of the U.S.S.R. on 2 February as printed in *Soviet Russia and the West, 1920–1927*, by X. J. Eudin and H. H. Fisher, p. 233. Also Chicherin's statement on the British recognition as reported in the *Manchester Guardian*, 4 February 1924.
[3] Harold Nicolson, *King George the Fifth: His Life and Reign*, p. 385.

brands of socialism, MacDonald left them in the hands of his
Under-Secretary, Ponsonby, who was torn between Foreign
Office officials nursed in the Curzon tradition and backbench
Labour M.P.s who openly took a hand in the proceedings when
deadlock intervened on 5 August and twice got the talks going
again.[1]   The action of these diplomatic interlopers, principally
George Lansbury, E. D. Morel, A. A. Purcell and R. C.Wallhead,
provided material for Right-wing criticism of the resulting treaties as the offspring of backstairs intrigue.   In an atmosphere in
which a Conservative M.P. could seriously speak of the London
poor as hopelessly drunk with gin bought by Moscow gold these
diplomatic *faux pas* were irrelevantly swept into the campaign
against the treaties.   MacDonald could be excused for not
keeping the thread of negotiations in his own hands since he
was at this time preparing for a more important gathering in
London, the Reparations Conference which opened in August to
launch the Dawes plan.   But he had kept the Foreign Secre-
taryship to himself when the Cabinet was formed and was
therefore directly responsible for the negotiation and defence
of the agreements.

   The Premier knew long before the conference began that the
strong Russian delegation which turned up in London in April
with Rakovsky as their leader would require a government
loan or loan guarantee before they would agree to the general
settlement of claims on which MacDonald, like Lloyd George
before him, insisted.   But it was not until 26 July that Ponsonby wired Rakovsky, who was on his way back to Russia, that
in view of the Soviet delegation's failure to raise a loan in the
City the government would offer a guarantee.   This delay was
not for the purpose of getting the Russians to raise their bids;
the Prime Minister had simply not made up his mind.[2]   The
circumstances moreover in which the conference was allowed
to meet on 14 April, when the dominant item in the British
Press was an unrealistic memorandum sent to the government
by a bankers' group, suggested that MacDonald was not unwilling to let the conference die between the irresistible force of
the City and the immovable Russians.   The bankers' stipulations could not have been drafted as a serious basis for discussion.   They included a demand that Russia should recognise
her public and private debts, no mention being made of Soviet
counter-claims for damage suffered during Allied intervention;
should make arrangements for the 'equitable restitution of
private property'; establish a proper Russian civil code and

---

[1] See the interesting account by E. D. Morel in *Forward*, 23 August 1924.
[2] H. H. Tiltman, *James Ramsay MacDonald*, London, 1930, p. 180.

independent courts of law; undertake not to indulge in further confiscation of private property; allow foreign traders to deal freely with private firms in Russia; and pledge herself once again to stop all propaganda subversive of Western social systems. Rakovsky's comment was that 'our answer is a categorical "never!" '.[1]

Since the bankers' memorandum was not matched by any public statement of realistic British policies by MacDonald the inference was that he was content to let the talks drift. This impression was confirmed by the fact that the intervention by eighteen Labour M.P.s when the talks finally broke down on 5 August resulted in the acceptance by the Russians of a third Foreign Office formula, but it did so by proposing only the slightest change of wording in the draft general treaty. Had the government considered an agreement important, it could hardly have been beyond MacDonald's powers to make these suggestions himself considering his able leadership of the Dawes conference.[2]

The general treaty as it stood in draft form in the early hours of 5 August, when Ponsonby declared the talks suspended after nineteen hours of continuous debate, was intended as the forthcoming general treaty referred to in the preamble of the trade agreement of 1921. But it postponed for future settlement almost all the issues in question. The basic conflict, between the Soviet demand for a scaling down of the British claims and the British refusal of a loan guarantee unless the claims issue was settled, was never resolved. Claims by British holders of bonds issued by the Tsarist Government and municipalities were relegated to a later agreement, which had to be accepted by holders of bonds to the value of one-half of the total value claimed. The later agreement was also to cover inter-governmental claims, including Tsarist war debts and Soviet counter-claims arising out of British intervention in Russia. Six assessors, three appointed by each side, were to determine the size of a lump sum to be paid to the British Government, in view of the 'admitted preponderance of British claims', to cover the balance of claims on either side for damage suffered between 1 August 1914 and the date of the entry into force of the treaty. As for British claims in respect of properties in Russia which had fallen within the scope of Soviet nationalisation decrees, Russia was to negotiate later with the organisations representing British claimants on the basis of 'just compensation'. Only after these various claims had been settled was the amount and terms

[1] Quoted in the *Manchester Guardian*, 26 April 1924.
[2] See above, Chapter VII.

of a government guarantee of a loan to Russia to be specified and Parliamentary approval sought.[1] It was on the contentious issue of 'just compensation' in article 12 of the draft that deadlock came. All that the Labour M.P.'s intervention succeeded in doing was to insert among the provisions of this future agreement the words 'an agreed settlement of property claims other than those directly settled by the Government of the U.S.S.R.'.[2] The effect was to emphasise even more that the loan guarantee could not even be contemplated until the property claims had been met to the satisfaction of both sides.

Of the two treaties which emerged from these lengthy negotiations, the commercial treaty was largely uncontentious. It gave Britain most-favoured-nation treatment in trade with Russia, extended to Soviet trade the British Export Credits Guarantee scheme and accorded diplomatic immunity to certain members of the Soviet trade mission in London, their exact identity to be determined later.[3] It was, however, the general treaty which became the focus of attack which revealed British political prejudice in one of its most ignorant forms. In defending the treaty MacDonald did little to clarify the issues so as to guide public opinion. He kept away from the House on 6 August when the treaties were first discussed, being heavily engaged with the Reparations Conference. When he appeared on the next day it was merely to answer the technical question, for which the Opposition demanded a reply from the Prime Minister, whether the treaties could be signed without the approval of the House. On this he took the unusual view that signature merely implied that the government were willing to put treaties before the Commons for rejection or acceptance.[4]

Criticism of the general treaty ranged from disappointment that it left all the burning issues to be settled later to attack on the arrangement as a pact between British and Russian 'Reds' for the ruination of respectable business and the British taxpayer. The most influential critic of the treaty on the first score, Lloyd George, in fact became the willing or unwilling head of an opposition to any dealings with the Bolsheviks which finally helped destroy the Labour Government. Basing himself on the true but unhelpful thesis that the treaty was 'a contract in which the space for every essential figure is left blank',[5] Lloyd George appeared to oppose any loan to Russia, and by

[1] Russia No. 3 (1924), Cmd. 2253.
[2] Russia No. 4 (1924), Cmd. 2260.
[3] Russia No. 5 (1924), Cmd. 2261.
[4] 176 H.C. Deb. 5s. Col. 3138 (7 August 1924).
[5] 176 H.C. Deb. 5s. Col. 3034 (6 August 1924).

concentrating on the question of the loan gave the impression that the loan was the first, instead of the last, step in the further process of negotiation envisaged in the treaty. The word 'fake', which he used to describe the postponement of the vital issues in the treaty, thus came to be attached to almost any bond which could be made with the Russians. Lloyd George's advocacy, coupled with the general climate of opinion in Britain, was such that when the Parliamentary Liberal Party, on whose support MacDonald depended, met to discuss the treaties on 1 October only two Liberal M.P.s came out in their favour. Asquith's voice was on the other side. He had kept a long silence until 22 September, when he characterised the treaties as 'crude experiments in amateur diplomacy'; thereafter he opposed the loan, though at the Liberal meeting on 1 October he approved some features of the treaties. A week later, when the Labour Government fell on the issue of the withdrawal of the prosecution in the Campbell case, only a handful of Liberal M.P.s voted with MacDonald.

From any angle Lloyd George's position was incomprehensible. As Prime Minister he had been a persistent advocate of coming to terms with the Bolsheviks when they were far more revolutionary than they were in 1924. The general treaty negotiated by Ponsonby and Rakovsky followed the same lines as Lloyd George's 1921 trade agreement in deferring the claims question to a later agreement. There was no question of any money passing from the British to the Soviet governments, and even the proposed British guarantee against the interest and sinking fund of a Russian loan in the City was not to be framed in specific terms, nor was Parliamentary approval to be sought, until British bond-holders owning 50 per cent of outstanding claims against Russia were satisfied with the terms they were offered. Lloyd George was in fact criticising the treaty on mutually incompatible grounds; if it was, as he complained, a 'sham' in that it settled nothing there was no case for saying that the government were committing themselves to throwing good money after bad into Soviet pockets.

But these distinctions were lost to sight in the general assault on the treaty from strong Russophobe elements in Parliament and the Press and the debate degenerated into a noisy free-for-all. The atmosphere was ripe for the 'Zinoviev letter' scare which dominated the election campaign in October and sealed the fate of the Labour Government. MacDonald came to be caricatured by his opponents as a friend of the murderous Bolsheviks, whereas the truth was that if he had been able to repress his own aversion for them he might have managed the negotiations so as to secure a better treaty. He would certainly have defended the treaty more effectively.

The 'Zinoviev letter' more properly concerns British domestic politics than foreign policy. It did, however, show how relations with Russia were entangled with British suspicions that a party of the Left was unfit to govern because of its imagined associations with Bolshevism. The authenticity of the letter, which purported to be an instruction dated 15 September from the Third International to the British Communist Party on subversive activities in Britain and which fell into the hands of the Foreign Office and the Press during the general election campaign in October, was never established.[1] A Cabinet committee set up by the succeeding Conservative administration admitted that the original letter was never in the Foreign Office, though they insisted that the letter was genuine[2]. An investigating committee established by the T.U.C., which visited Russia to make inquiries, concluded that the document was a forgery. Certain details of the letter were clearly erroneous, in particular the heading 'Third Communist International', which could not have been used by the Comintern as there had never been a previous Communist International.[3] The person to whom the letter was supposed to be addressed, McManus, also appeared as a signatory. When the Soviet Government, in replying on 25 October to the British note of protest on the 24th, proposed an investigation in order to establish the facts, the British reply of 21 November ignored the offer.[4] Rakovsky, now Chargé d'Affaires in London, repeated the proposal on 28 November and the new Conservative Foreign Secretary, Austen Chamberlain, parried by saying that one of the four sources from whom copies of the letter had been received was still in Russia and his safety might be compromised by a public inquiry. On 21 December Rakovsky offered the man in question full permission to leave Soviet territory, but Chamberlain did not pursue the matter further.[5] British Ministers, moreover, frankly argued that it was immaterial whether this particular letter was genuine or not; the fact was that its purport was in keeping with the general policy of the Third International, which was undoubtedly linked with the Soviet Government.

The 'Zinoviev letter' could not but harm those who were

[1] For the text of the letter see Cmd. 2895 (1927), pp. 30–2.
[2] *The Times*, 5 November 1924; also J. D. Gregory, *On the Edge of Diplomacy*, London, 1928, p. 216.
[3] See Rakovsky's comment, *The Times*, 25 October 1924.
[4] Cmd. 2895, pp. 32–3.
[5] Degras, *op. cit.*, I, pp. 480–2.

seeking in Britain to work out terms of co-existence with Russia. In the nature of things these were well represented in the Labour party, and yet responsible Labour leaders like Mac-Donald knew that the chief hope for Labour as a force in British politics rested on its power to throw off its revolutionary associations and take on the guise of a respectable, reformist party. It is possible that when MacDonald received the copy of the letter sent to him by the Foreign Office at Manchester on 16 October he saw in it an opportunity to publicise his hostility towards Bolshevism, without realising that, whatever happened, the letter would damage Labour's credit with British opinion. When he returned the Foreign Office's draft note of protest to Rakovsky on 24 October he gave no definite instruction that it should be dispatched; Sir Eyre Crowe, the permanent head of the Foreign Office, not attaching much importance to the fact that MacDonald had omitted to initial the draft, sent it off without confirming that the Prime Minister really wished it to go. Thus, without awaiting approval from the Prime Minister, a strong letter of protest was sent to Rakovsky the same evening and copies were distributed to the Press before the Soviet reply had been received.[1] In any case, a version of the 'Zinoviev letter' from a source which was never disclosed appeared in the *Daily Mail* on the following day, 25 October. One possibility is that Eyre Crowe, fearing an early disclosure by the Press, used MacDonald's general coldness towards Russia to get the protest off to Rakovsky since he wanted the Prime Minister to have an opportunity of finally clearing his name of allegations that he was a Communist.[2] It is significant that no copy of the 'Zinoviev letter' was sent either to Ponsonby, who had been responsible for the negotiations with the Soviets, or to Haldane, who, as Lord Chancellor, was chiefly concerned with subversion in the Forces, before the whole story was publicised.

II

With MacDonald's fall and the formation of the second Baldwin Government the hostility of the Conservative towards Russia could be given official standing. The instrument of this new wave of antagonism, Austen Chamberlain, resisted his Russophobe backbenchers with little more success than Mac-Donald had resisted his Russophile backbenchers. In a letter to Rakovsky on 21 November conveying the government's refusal to ratify the general and commercial treaties signed on 8

[1] Lord Strang, *Home and Abroad*, pp. 55–8.
[2] L. MacNeill Weir, *The Tragedy of Ramsay MacDonald*, London, 1938, p. 191.

August Chamberlain refused to discuss the alleged errors in the 'Zinoviev letter' pointed out by Rakovsky in his reply to the protest of 24 October. 'The information in the possession of H.M. Government,' Chamberlain darkly wrote, 'leaves no doubt whatsoever in their mind of the authenticity of M. Zinoviev's letter and H.M. Government are therefore not prepared to discuss the letter.' The Soviet Government were advised to 'weigh carefully' the consequences of ignoring Mac-Donald's insistence in the protest of 24 October that the Comintern and the Soviet Government were the same group under different names.[1] In a talk with Rakovsky on 6 January 1925, before the Soviet envoy left on a visit to Moscow, Chamberlain maintained the same refusal to discuss the letter. 'Our proofs were absolute,' he said, and if Rakovsky attempted to deny them, 'I could only confront him with a formal and absolute denial of the truth of his statements'. After denying Soviet allegations that Britain had brought pressure to bear on the Albanian Government of Fan Noli to withdraw the Russian mission from Tirana and was preventing the Baltic banks from giving credits to Russia, Chamberlain replied to Rakovsky's request for an extension of trade facilities and British export credits schemes to Russia by saying that she must deserve them by her actions.[2]

On Rakovsky's return to London in March Chamberlain had a further interview with him on 1 April. After the customary complaints about Russia's non-fulfilment of the political conditions of the 1921 trade agreement and accusations of Soviet incitements to the Chinese Government to disown their obligations to foreign Powers, the Foreign Secretary made clear that no further negotiations with the Soviets were in prospect until they had discharged the agreements they had already signed.[3] At a final meeting with Rakovsky on 5 November, before the Chargé d'Affaires left London for the last time, Chamberlain said that Russia had more need of Britain than Britain had of Russia (with which Rakovsky seemed to agree) and should therefore cease her 'hostile activities'.[4]

By this time, however, a new element was entering into the situation, namely the efforts of Britain, France and Germany to construct a security arrangement for western Europe to complement the settlement of the reparations problem at the Dawes Plan Conference in August 1924. The Locarno accords, concluded on 16 October 1925, which consummated this movement represented a distinct isolation of Russia and weakened

[1] Cmd. 2895, pp. 34–5.   [2] *Ibid.*, pp. 35–6.
[3] *Ibid.*, pp. 37–9.   [4] *Ibid.*, pp. 39–41.

her tie with Weimar Germany. The latter consequence
might have been far more serious for Russia had her Berlin
Treaty with Germany, published in April 1926, not revived,
though in paler form, the Rapallo agreement.   In an interview
given in Berlin on 4 October, the day before the opening of the
Locarno Conference, Chicherin characterised the proposed
security pact, Germany's impending entry into the League and
the 'statement concerning the defence of Germany against attack by France' as 'just an interlude before the big act directed
against the peoples of Asia and their friends', the most notable
among the latter being of course Soviet Russia.[1]   Stresemann
realised the importance of keeping on friendly terms with Russia; he had agreed in talks with Chicherin in Berlin before the
German delegation left for Locarno that any action against
Russia by the League under articles 16 and 17 of the Covenant
would require Germany's consent, and presumably this would
not be readily given so long as the Soviet connection remained
useful to Berlin.[2]   Nevertheless, Chamberlain's policy of working Germany into a west European security pact could not fail
to arouse the deepest suspicion in people as fearful of encirclement as the Russians.   Litvinov, in an interview given to
Izvestia on 4 January 1925, described 'English envoys in almost
all the countries of the West and the East' as 'initiators of hostile
policies towards the U.S.S.R. and a permanent source of false
information about our state'.[3]   In a similar vein, Chicherin,
in a report to the third Soviet Congress on 14 May said that
until Britain ceased her intrigue and came to negotiated terms
international affairs would never be stable.   The case, he
added significantly, was different with France, 'because we do
not encounter France everywhere in our path.'[4]

It is doubtful whether Chamberlain's primary interest at
Locarno was to injure Russia.   To argue that it was is to
assign too large a place to Russia in British external relations
at this time.   As we have seen in a previous chapter, Locarno
had the great advantage for Britain of satisfying French security
fears at a relatively low cost and at the same time of reintro-
ducing Germany to European diplomacy.   That this arrangement had the additional attraction in British eyes of serving to
weaken the tie between Berlin and Moscow is also beyond
reasonable doubt.   Chamberlain's envoy in Berlin, D'Abernon, perhaps the real father of Locarno, had been active since
Rapallo in weaning Germany away from Russia.   Chamberlain himself sought to dissuade the French from developing

[1] Degras, *op. cit.*, II, pp. 58–9.   [2] *Ibid.*, p. 106.
[3] Degras, *op. cit.*, I, p. 481.   [4] Degras, *op. cit.*, II, p. 41.

new relations with Russia. The Herriot Cabinet, formed in June, proceeded to recognise the Soviets on 28 October, immediately after the 'Zinoviev letter' convulsion in Britain. One of Chamberlain's first foreign journeys on becoming Foreign Secretary in November therefore took him to Paris to see Herriot to try to agree on common Anglo-French policies towards Russia. By consenting not to carry their relations with Russia further for the moment the French Government seemed at these talks to pay the price for a British guarantee of their frontier with Germany at Locarno. Moreover, on 10 May 1925 there appeared in the *New York World* a copy of an alleged British Foreign Office paper purporting to represent official British views on European security. A summary of the document had appeared in the *Chicago Tribune* four days previously. The sentence in the paper which was singled out as typifying British attitudes towards Locarno stated that it was 'in spite of Russia, perhaps even because of Russia, that a policy of security must be framed'. Chamberlain was questioned about the document in the House on 11 May and gave an answer which could hardly be interpreted as other than an admission that it was genuine.[1] Nevertheless, the opposition which British diplomacy was thus presenting to Russia in Europe hardly extended to basing European security arrangements solely on the conception of an anti-Soviet front. The idea that the Locarno Powers were concerting a definite plan for an aggressive attack on Russia was more plausible in Communist cells than in the light of day.

Locarno did nothing to improve Anglo-Soviet relations, nor did the industrial troubles in Britain in the following year. The nine days' General Strike, which was declared on 3 May 1926 in sympathy with the miners' strike which had begun on 30 April and which was to last seven months, aroused intense alarm, especially in Conservative circles, about Soviet interference with the workers of Britain. The acclaim given to the two strikes by the official Soviet Press was bad enough; the funds voted by Soviet trade unions for the support of families of the strikers, though in the tradition of trade union solidarity, provided a graphic example of the exceptional character of relations with Soviet Russia. The Home Secretary, Joynson-Hicks, one of the strongest critics of Russia in the Conservative Party, at first carefully avoided implicating the Soviet Government in the dispatch of the money in the House on 10 June, but on being pressed by MacDonald he threw caution to the winds and said that the Soviet Ministers were responsible.[2] This was

[1] 183 H.C. Deb. 5s. Col. 1455.   [2] 196 *ibid.*, Col. 1676.

strongly denied by the Soviet Chargé d'Affaires on 12 June, when it was asserted that the Soviet Government 'could not interfere with the right of the Russian trade unions to dispose of funds belonging to them'. A British note of protest drew forth a swift Soviet reply on the same lines.[1] Austen Chamberlain, realising that the Home Secretary's ardour had carried him too far, intervened in the House on 14 June to admit that there was no evidence that the Soviet Government was the source of the money, although the Finance Minister had authorised the transfer of the payments.[2] Joynson-Hicks then withdrew his allegations in the House on 17 June and merely argued that the All-Russian Central Council of Trade Unions, from which the funds had come, and the Soviet Government were both run from a 'single controlling authority'.[3] The government then came out with their collection of documents on 24 June which purported to provide proof of Soviet complicity in the strike and were said to have been seized when the offices of the British Communist Party were raided the previous October.[4] Chamberlain explained the government's case in the House on 25 June and was followed by a Narkomindel statement two days later which protested that no single Soviet action had been in conflict with the 1921 agreement.[5] There, as in so many other angry Anglo-Soviet exchanges, the matter rested.

The effect of the dispute over the British strikes was to harden, rather than diversify, differences with Russia. This was shown in the talks between Chamberlain and the new Soviet Chargé d'Affaires, Rosengolz, early in July. Rosengolz had approached the Foreign Secretary for a 'general settlement of the questions outstanding between us' and Chamberlain re-stated the familiar argument that Russia's record in regard to the 1921 agreement did not warrant the making of fresh settlements. The Chargé d'Affaires was told that Russia must agree to base a settlement on the two points, first, that by international law a government inherited the obligations as well as the rights of its predecessors, and secondly that Britain could give neither a loan nor a loan guarantee. That Chamberlain's supporters in the Commons were straining at the leash to break with Moscow was clear from the Foreign Secretary's almost desperate appeal to Russia 'to find a means of controlling the anti-British activities of the Third International'. He desired *if possible* to avoid a rupture, although 'we had tolerated from the Soviet authorities a course of conduct which we had never tolerated

[1] *The Times*, 16 June 1926. [2] 196 H.C. Deb. 5s. Col. 1956.
[3] *Ibid.*, Cols. 2466–8. [4] *Communist Papers*, Cmd. 2682 (1926).
[5] Degras, *op. cit.*, II, pp. 120–3.

from the Tsarist Governments of Russia even at the times of most strained relations'.[1]

The government were once more on the brink of severing relations with Russia. That they did not do so in 1926 may have been due to the fact that, after the Berlin Treaty in April and the talks in Paris during the first six months of 1926 between French and Soviet officials on a debt settlement, the Cabinet felt that Russia might not be alone in a quarrel with Britain. With the coming of 1927, however, and British exasperation with Chinese attacks on British rights in the Yangtze basin the movement towards a breach gathered strength. It was evident that Chamberlain was being precipitated towards a breach, though he sought to postpone it as long as possible. On 23 February 1927 the Foreign Secretary, without much obvious conviction, introduced a new theme of complaint in a note to Rosengolz, namely the 'public utterances in defamation of Great Britain' by such Soviet figures as Voroshilov, Unschlicht, Kamenev, Bukharin, Rykov, Karakhan and Semashko. These he said, were infringements of the undertaking given by Russia in June 1923, after the Curzon ultimatum.[2] In a temperate reply on 26 February Litvinov argued that no Anglo-Soviet agreement had ever restricted the right of free speech within the frontiers of the Soviet Union, and had no difficulty in citing speeches by Birkenhead, Churchill, Joynson-Hicks, Hoare and Worthington-Evans not inferior in venom to any produced on the other side. The British Government, Litvinov went on, 'periodically hurls at the Soviet Government general accusations in the form of base assertions, refusing even to discuss them', and at the same time 'avoids the settlement of mutual claims and grievances either by the diplomatic channels or by means of special conferences, commissions or delegations'.[3]

When these exchanges were discussed in the House of Commons on 3 March the Conservative M.P. who had negotiated the 1921 agreement, Sir Robert Horne, claimed that Britain had everything to gain and little to lose by a diplomatic rupture with Russia. Germany and the United States, he said, were both doing more trade with Russia than Britain, less than £6 million worth of British goods having been sold in Russia the previous year, and yet it was Britain who was singled out in Soviet propaganda campaigns and whose interests were the special target of Soviet machinations. Horne went as far as to argue that Britain was committed to a breach since if one did

---

[1] Cmd. 2895, pp. 42–5. Italics as in original minute of the conversations.
[2] Russia No. 1 (1927), Cmd. 2822, pp. 2–6.
[3] *Ibid.*, pp. 20–5.

not come soon people would think that her threats were all bluff.[1]   The figures of British trade with Russia which he gave, however, were disputed by Lloyd George, who now swung round to Russia's defence and censured the government for making individual attacks on Soviet Ministers, which he said had never happened before since the 1921 agreement.[2]   But it was clear from the Foreign Secretary's speech that the government had already decided on the break; the only question was when and on what pretext.

Chamberlain said that a breach had not been decided earlier because it might have strengthened the 'unfounded rumours' that Britain was organising a coalition against Russia.   But that the government were casting about for a suitable occasion to sever relations became clear when Chamberlain said that 'to act before we have given time for evidence to become clear would have disturbed the European situation'.[3]   What this meant was indicated by the form which the collection of the 'evidence' referred to by Chamberlain took, namely the raiding of the Arcos Trade Agency at 49 Moorgate, London, on 12 May 1927 on a warrant issue under the Official Secrets Act.   This was sufficiently like the raiding of the Soviet trade mission in Berlin by German police on 3 May 1924 to suggest that the British Government preferred, if possible, to keep in step with German anti-Soviet measures.   Moreover, the Soviet Embassy in Peking had been raided by the Peking authorities on 6 April, a month before the Arcos raid, with the usual harvest of incriminating documents.   With these respectable precedents to hand, the Arcos raid could not fail to command some international sympathy.

As a pretext for the diplomatic rupture which Chamberlain notified to Rosengolz on 27 May the Arcos raid had many unsatisfactory features about it.   A considerable amount of damage was done to both institutions lodged in 'Soviet House', Moorgate, that is, the official Soviet trade agency, which enjoyed a measure of diplomatic immunity under the trade agreement, and Arcos Limited, which was actually a British-registered private limited liability company.   The Home Secretary, Joynson-Hicks, said in the Commons on 13 May that he could not distinguish between the rooms occupied at the Moorgate premises by the two organisations respectively.[4]   On 19 May he said it was not proposed to offer compensation for this damage.[5]   Officials of the Soviet trade delegation were

---

[1] 203 H.C. Deb. 5s. Col. 616.   [2] Ibid., Col. 639.
[3] Ibid., Col. 631.   [4] 206 H.C. Deb. 5s. Cols. 796–7.
[5] Ibid., Col. 1343.

not allowed to attend the seizure or inspection of documents belonging to them, nor were they given an inventory of papers taken away. The actual documents, the recovery of which was the ostensible purpose of the raid, two papers allegedly stolen from the British Armed Forces by Soviet agents, were never found. Moreover, although the case against Soviet House was that it was the headquarters and nerve centre for espionage in Britain, no criminal charge was ever brought even though the cipher clerk employed by Arcos, Anton Miller, who was described by the Home Secretary as one of the leaders of the spy organisation, was taken and held in custody for some time by the police. The explanation given by Joynson-Hicks for this omission to prosecute was that the authorities now had a list of Soviet agents and knew on whom to pounce in the event of war.[1] Above all, the documents said to have been captured in the Arcos raid and later printed in a White Paper were of trivial character, not all justifying the sensational title of the publication, 'Documents illustrating the hostile activities of the Soviet Government and the Third International against Great Britain'.[2] Lloyd George said of the White Paper in the debate on the rupture on 26 May that 'it is really rather a ridiculous document . . . an extravaganza of incredible nonsense'.[3] He did, however, consider that the evidence, taken as a whole, justified the break.

Efforts were made by speakers in the Commons debate who doubted the wisdom of the Arcos raid to dissociate Austen Chamberlain from the affair. Though he himself deprecated these efforts, he could hardly have gone into the enterprise willingly, especially at a time when Stalin, now consolidating his power, seemed bent upon subordinating the revolutionary fervour of the Communist cause to defence of the national interests of the Soviet Union. Chamberlain must particularly have regretted the fact that the raid came on the day after the Midland Bank had agreed to open a credit of £10 million in Russia's favour, an event which might have helped pave the way towards more amicable relations with Russia. According to Joynson-Hicks, Chamberlain asked him whether he would have ordered the raid had the circumstances been the same but if another country but Russia had been involved. When the Home Secretary said that he would, Chamberlain's answer was, 'very well then, raid it'.[4] This sounds as though it was said with resignation.

[1] 206 H.C. Deb. 5s. Col. 2301 (26 May 1927).
[2] Russia No. 2 (1927), Cmd. 2874.   [3] 206 H.C. Deb. 5s. Col. 2221.
[4] 206 H.C. Deb. 5s. Cols. 2302–3 (26 May 1927).

Chamberlain notified the diplomatic rupture to Rosengolz on 26 May, the day of the Commons debate, justifying it on the ground that Arcos and the Soviet trade delegation had been engaged in espionage and anti-British propaganda even after the British note of 23 February asking for assurances that these activities would cease.   The government therefore considered themselves free from all obligations under the agreement of 1921, asked for the recall of Khinchuk, the head of the Soviet trade mission, and his staff and declared that existing diplomatic relations were suspended.[1]   It is, however, interesting to see that Arcos was permitted to remain and carry on business, provided its employees observed the laws of the country and 'confined themselves to legitimate commerce', despite its alleged function as a front for espionage and subversion.   This dispensation seemed to imply that the Cabinet were anxious to assuage anti-Russian feelings in the country by a dramatic symbolic gesture and yet to avoid damage to commerce with Russia as far as possible in the process.

III

The Soviet authorities felt the inconvenience of the break to a far greater extent than the British Government.   Indeed it was this which mainly justified the rupture on the British side. The breach was a setback to the Soviet campaign for diplomatic recognition, which was not complete in 1927, even in Europe, to say nothing of the United States.   In addition, since Russia normally had a substantial trade balance with Britain in her favour, Britain being an even more important customer than Germany for Russia's exports, the rupture, by making British trade with Russia more difficult, injured Soviet efforts to acquire foreign exchange vital to economic growth.[2] The fact that the Conservative Government tried to rally diplomatic support abroad for their decision was a further irritant the rupture imposed on Russia.   Nevertheless, in spite of Russia's strong desire on these grounds to repair the breach, the Soviet Government were not prepared to go far in humbling themselves.   When the British Prime Minister, Baldwin, tentatively invited overtures from Moscow in his Guildhall speech on 9 November, Rykov, speaking at a session of the Ukrainian

[1] Cmd. 2895, pp. 69–70.
[2] In 1927, the year of the break, Britain bought goods from Russia (some of which were for re-export, though this does not affect the point) to the value of £21,051,000, as compared with £25,322,000 in 1925 and £24,130,000 in 1926. She sold goods to the value of £4,508,000 to Russia in 1927, as compared with £6,239,000 and £5,858,000 in 1925 and 1926 respectively.   Board of Trade. Statistical Abstract for the United Kingdom, 1913–29, Cmd. 3767 (1931).

Communist Party Congress at Kharkhov two weeks later, returned a dusty answer.[1]   Britain, he said, must take the initiative in restoring the relations she had herself destroyed and
could not hope to make a resumption conditional on the Soviet
Government assuming responsibility for the Comintern or the
Communist trade union International.   Similarly, when Litvinov had an hour's talk with Chamberlain at a League meeting on disarmament in Geneva on 5 December he was prepared
to make no concession on the issue of the activities of the Third
International, although he said Russia was ready to make a
new declaration of official abstention from propaganda and to
discontinue the work of the Tashkent School against British
rule in India.[2]   Chamberlain, so Litvinov reported to the
Central Executive Committee of the Russian Communist Party
twelve months later, merely wanted to talk about the past and
seemed mainly concerned with the possibility of a general election in Britain, at which the decision to break with Russia
would have to be justified.[3]

An important factor in Soviet stiffness was undoubtedly the
general revision of foreign policy which was going forwards in
Moscow as one consequence of Stalin's final victory over Trotsky in 1927.   Though the world missionary aims of Soviet
Communism were not renounced and Stalin's difference with
Trotsky, in so far as it concerned foreign relations, was more a
matter of timing and emphasis than of ultimate goals, Stalin's
efforts to place the defence of Soviet state interests above the
world revolutionary struggle were bound to encounter resistance among his still powerful colleagues.   Hence, the bringing
under control of world revolutionary proselytism, on which
Britain and other capitalist states insisted, was not easy.   At a
joint meeting of the Central Committee and the Central Control Commission of the Soviet Communist Party on 1 August
1927 Stalin laid down his characteristic axiom that 'he is an
internationalist who unhesitatingly, unconditionally and without vacillation is ready to defend the U.S.S.R. . . . it is impossible
to defend and advance this movement (that is, world Communism) unless the U.S.S.R. is defended.'[4]   Stalin admitted in the
Central Committee in July of the following year that the programme he had based on these definitions had been criticised
in 'some Comintern circles' as 'too nationalistic'.   He therefore turned the attack on the Comintern and asked 'what would
the programme of the Comintern be worth, if while dealing

[1] *The Times*, 10 November and 26 November 1927.
[2] *The Times*, 6 December 1927.   [3] Degras, *op. cit.*, II, pp. 350–1.
[4] Degras, *ibid.*, p. 243.

with the world proletarian revolution, it ignored the basic question of the character and tasks of the proletarian revolution in the U.S.S.R., of its obligations to the proletarians of all countries, of the obligations of the proletarians of all countries towards the proletarian dictatorship of the U.S.S.R.?'[1]

The corollary of Stalin's inversion of the normal usage of the word 'international' was that the greatest danger to the proletarian revolution was world war arising from the conflicts between the capitalist states, a war in which the first target of capitalist aggression would be the home of proletarian revolution, the Soviet Union.   It followed that, as Chicherin put it in a statement in August 1928, 'to put an end to war is one of basic aims of Soviet policy'.[2]   This implied Soviet support for complete disarmament, a network of non-aggression pacts with the states of eastern Europe and Soviet signature of the Pact of Paris for the renunciation of war in 1928.   The last measure did not arise from any Soviet assumption that lofty declarations could eradicate the basic evil of capitalism, war, but, as Rykov said at the fifth Soviet Congress in May 1929, the Soviets accepted the Pact because it might 'even if in the slightest degree only, make the psychological preparations for war more difficult'.[3]

These indications of a change in the Soviet attitude towards world revolution, though Soviet attacks on Britain as the chief capitalist foe were not remitted, somewhat eased the tasks of the second Labour Government in Britain, formed on 7 June 1929, in resuming diplomatic contact.   On both sides residues of former attitudes remained active.   Arthur Henderson, the new Foreign Secretary, was sensitive enough to British opinion about Russia and to the distinctly colder feelings of the Labour Party towards Moscow in 1929 as compared with 1924 not to let slip an opportunity of using the offer of resumed relations to win concessions of the matters in dispute.   When the Soviet Ambassador in Paris, Dovgalevsky, crossed to London in July to discuss procedures for resuming relations Henderson told him that Parliament was in recess and that the three months before Parliamentary approval could be given for the resumption of relations should be spent in reaching agreement on the issues dividing the two countries.[4]   When this news reached Moscow Dovgalevsky was recalled and the Soviet authorities threatened to take the question before the Central Executive Committee of the Soviet Communist Party and there the Soviet position would be made clear 'once and for all'.   Had this threat been

---

carried out Stalin's critics might have had their say and decla-
mations of Britain would have ruined the atmosphere.   The
Cabinet therefore had no alternative but to give way and after
talks between Henderson and Dovgalevsky in London at the
end of September a protocol was signed on 3 October which
accepted the Soviet demand that the resumption of relations
must be the first step.[1]   Litvinov let it be known that Russia
would maintain her stand on this even if it meant no relations
with Britain during the Labour Government.[2]

The only concession to Britain in the Henderson–Dovgalevsky
talks was a curious arrangement under which Russia agreed
to 'confirm' article 16 of the unratified and hence entirely invalid treaty of 1924 pledging both sides to refrain from propaganda.[3]   As for the outstanding issues in dispute, negotiations
were to begin after the resumption of relations on a commercial
treaty 'and allied questions', claims and counter-claims,
fisheries and the question of which previous Anglo-Soviet
treaties were to remain in force.   A general treaty on the lines
of the abortive arrangement of 1924 was to be drawn up to
embody agreement on these points.   Despite strong Conservative criticism the Henderson–Dovgalevsky talks and the October
protocol were endorsed by the Commons on 5 November.   As
a special concession to Britain, Russia agreed that Ambassadors
should not actually be appointed until after the protocol had
been approved.   Thus it was not until 20 December that M.
Sokolnikov presented his credentials as the first fully-fledged
Soviet Ambassador in London.   Sir Esmond Ovey did likewise for Britain in Moscow on the following day.[4]   As they did
so notes were exchanged between the two Ambassadors and
Henderson and Litvinov respectively which confirmed article
16 of the 1924 agreement.[5]

Litvinov, reporting to the Soviet Communist Party Executive
Committee, described the resumption of relations as a 'considerable item on the credit side'.[6]   For Russia it certainly was.
Soviet export sales in Britain in 1930, the first full year after the
resumption, were valued at £34,235,000 as compared with
£21,576,000 in 1928, the first full year after the break.[7]   In
the early 1930s Britain was taking almost a third of Russia's
exports where Germany took only some 16 per cent and the

---

[1] Russia No. 1 (1929), Cmd. 3418.   [2] Louis Fischer, *op. cit.*, II, p. 818.
[3] Russia No. 4 (1924), Cmd. 2260.   [4] *D.B.F.P.*, Second Series, VII, pp. 62–4.
[5] Treaty Series No. 2 (1930), Cmd. 3467.
[6] The Royal Institute of International Affairs, *Documents on International Affairs,
1929*, p. 214.
[7] Statistical Abstract for the United Kingdom, Cmd. 4233 (1934), pp.
318–21.

United States only 3 per cent.[1] British sales in Russia were not much more than one-fifth of purchases (£6,771,000 worth in 1930 and £7,291,000 in 1931), although Sokolnikov said in the December following the resumption that between October and November almost £4 million in Soviet orders had been placed in Britain, almost three times the corresponding figure for 1928.[2] Unfortunately the chief types of British products required under the first Soviet Five-year Plan, that is, metallurgical products, machinery and machine tools, electrical and chemical goods, tractors and agricultural machinery, were of no interest to the most depressed British export businesses. In any case, this expanding Anglo-Soviet trade was hard hit by the depression of 1931–2. Moreover, the depression in itself tended to arouse all the old antagonisms, all the more so in that the early years of the Soviet Five-year Plan brought mass trials in Russia of alleged saboteurs who in their confessions detailed every kind of capitalist plot against Soviet security and society.

A temporary Anglo-Soviet trade agreement was signed on 16 April after talks between Henderson and Sokolnikov and between officials of the two sides at the Board of Trade.[3] Conversations on the old problem of debts which began in October, however, were no more fruitful than all previous debates on this question. The general climate was far from favourable. Pathological fears of encirclement remained in Russia, so much so that when Ovey talked with Litvinov in February he found him in a state of complete alarm about some old charge made by Lord Parmoor in the Lords.[4] In Moscow in November there was held a trial of the so-called 'Industrial Party' on charges of sabotage in the interest of certain external Powers, chiefly France and to a less extent Britain; allegations were also made that a British firm, the Union Cold Storage Company, which operated in Russia, had conspired with the defendants to disorganise the supply of food in the Soviet Union.[5] Exchanges between Ovey and Litvinov, who had now been Soviet Foreign Minister since July, dragged on until a final conversation on 24 December without much of real consequence being achieved. Meanwhile, the worsening trade position of the Western countries was producing charges against the Soviet Union of 'dumping' her surplus products on heavily saturated Western markets. France took the lead in the movement to apply reprisals against Soviet trade, while the system of Im-

[1] Max Beloff, *The Foreign Policy of Soviet Russia*, I, p. 35.
[2] *The Times*, 21 December 1929.
[3] Treaty Series No. 19 (1930), Cmd. 3552.
[4] *D.B.F.P.*, Second Series, VII, pp. 100–2.
[5] On the 'Industrial Trial' see *D.B.F.P.*, *ibid.*, pp. 184–9.

perial preference created by the Ottawa agreements of 1932 forced Britain too to cut down Soviet imports, which had been steadily on the increase. Article 21 of the agreement signed with Canada at Ottawa committed Britain to prevent the goods of a third party entering the country if their price was 'maintained by State action' and if they jeopardised the Ottawa agreements. Acting under this article the government gave Russia six months' notice of denunciation of the temporary trade agreement.[1]

Negotiations for a new agreement were started and then suspended by Britain on 20 March 1933 as a result of one of those bizarre occurrences which so often crossed the path of Anglo-Soviet affairs. This was the arrest and trial in Russia of six engineers employed by Metropolitan-Vickers, who had entered into several contracts to supply heavy electrical equipment to the Soviet Union, on charges of spying and 'wrecking activities'. At the beginning of April, since the old trade agreement would lapse on 17 April and negotiations for a new one were in suspense, the government were authorised by Parliament to prohibit all imports from Russia. On 19 April, the day after the end of the Vickers trial and the sentencing of five out of the six defendants of British nationality, this authority was applied against two-thirds of the normal British imports from Russia.[2] The Soviets replied with an embargo of British goods. At the end of June, however, conversations took place at the World Economic Conference in London between Sir John Simon, now Foreign Secretary in the National Government, and Litvinov, with the result that on 1 July the two British defendants at the Vickers trial, MacDonald and Thornton, who had been sentenced to terms of two and three years' imprisonment respectively, were released and the trade restrictions on both sides removed.[3]

Negotiations for the trade agreement which had been envisaged as far back as October 1929 were re-opened on 10 July 1933 and reflected the same tough bargaining of the previous four years, with eventual British acceptance of an increasingly strong Soviet position. In the talks, which continued to the end of the year without result, the British side attempted to insert a clause which would permit Britain to apply an embargo on Soviet imports if a charge of 'dumping' against Russia was satisfactorily made out in future. As a result of Soviet resistance,

---

[1] Imperial Economic Conference at Ottawa, 1932, Cmd. 4174, App. I, pp. 22 3.
[2] *The Times*, 20 April 1933. The sentences were light and were clearly influenced by the desire to avoid trouble with Britain. For details of the trial see Lord Strang, *Home and Abroad*, Chapter III.
[3] *D.B.F.P.*, Second Series, VII, pp. 567–76.

the most which could be gained was a provision for negotiations as and when allegations of 'dumping' were made during
the life of the agreement.   On this basis the treaty was eventually signed on 16 February 1934 and approved by the House
of Commons without a division on 1 March.[1]   Britain remained
in the forefront of Russia's customers in the 1930s, her purchases
rising from 16.6 per cent of Russia's exports in 1934 to 23.5
per cent in 1935 and 32.7 per cent in 1937, while she supplied
between a fifth and a sixth of Russia's external needs.[2]   But it
should be remembered that these proportions must be read
against the general decline of world trade in the 1930s.   Whereas Britain imported some £34 million worth of Russian goods
in 1930, Soviet imports had fallen to £17 million in 1933 and
1934.[3]   Where she had sold £7 million worth of goods to the
Soviets in 1930, out of a total export sale of £570 million, in
1934 she sold only £3,640,000 worth to Russia, out of a total
export sale of less than £400 million.[4]

By the time the trade agreement was signed the international
position of the Soviet Union had strikingly changed.   From
being a pariah nation, a friend of the enemies of the existing
international order, she was fast becoming a support of the
status quo.   Though this meant a radical revision of Russia's
foreign alignments, especially a weakening in her relations with
Germany as Hitler's programme gradually came to light after
his accession to the Chancellorship in January 1933, the British
Government were not impatient to move to Russia's side.
The initiative in getting Russia admitted into the League in
September 1934 was naturally taken by France.   Simon told
the House in July that the government would welcome Russia
into the League if she applied.[5]   Privately he wrote to Neville
Chamberlain on 7 August that he would like to make British
approval of the candidature dependent upon Russia's fulfilment
of some conditions, especially the stopping of Communist propaganda.   'We can certainly intimate that if she is going to
join the Club at Geneva,' Simon wrote, in the language of Pall
Mall, 'we expect her to behave according to the best traditions
of the best clubs.'[6]   The fact that one of the first international
acts of the Roosevelt administration in the United States, which
assumed office in March 1933, was to grant *de jure* recognition

[1] Treaty Series No. 11 (1934), Cmd. 4567.
[2] Beloff, *op. cit.*, I, p. 111.
[3] Board of Trade. Statistical Abstract for the United Kingdom, Cmd. 4801 (1935),
pp. 330–3; Statistical Abstract, Cmd. 5144 (1936), pp. 350–2.
[4] Cmd. 5144, pp. 358–61.
[5] 292 H.C. Deb. Cols. 694–5 (13 July 1934).
[6] *D.B.F.P.*, Second Series, VII, p. 711, n. 1.

to the Soviet Union, made it all the easier to accept Russia at Geneva. At the same time, the British notion of the League as the means of international appeasement, which made Soviet membership acceptable, prevented Russia's entry into the League being conceived in Britain, as it was in many quarters in France, as the first step towards an armed coalition of *status quo* Powers.

Britain had always looked askance at French efforts to build a defensive ring fence along Germany's eastern borders. She had sympathised with German discontent with the peace settlement in the east. Now Russia, after her long attack on Britain as one of the leading imperialist Powers at Versailles, was helping that eastern *glacis* to solidify and at the same time reaching out towards France in the west. After signing non-aggression pacts with Finland, Latvia and Estonia between January and May 1932, and prolonging her pact with Lithuania in May 1931, Russia signed a non-aggression pact with Poland in July 1932 and then entered into a similar pact with Poland's ally and the most determined former enemy of Soviet Communism, France, on 29 November 1932. Although in May 1933, after Hitler had been at the helm in Germany for more than three months, the Soviet Government exchanged with Berlin ratifications of the protocols bringing into effect the Soviet–German non-aggression pact of 1926 and a conciliation convention signed in 1929, Nazi aspirations in the east were already becoming evident. Soviet delegates at the World Economic Conference in June 1933 heard the German Minister for Economic Affairs, Hugenberg, demand that Germany be given a mandate to use her 'constructive and creative energies' to 'reorganise' Russia. Though Litvinov was said to have regarded this statement as a 'joke' Russia notified Berlin that she considered the Hugenberg statement a breach of the Berlin Treaty of 1926.[1]

British Right-wing opinion was by no means out of sympathy with the German revival under Hitler, at least in his 'legality' phase, as declarations by Lords Londonderry, Rothermere and Lothian showed. This sympathy also extended to Liberal leaders, notably Lloyd George, and to such Labour spokesmen as had been revisionist since 1919 and always regarded France and her East European allies as the greatest menace to peace in Europe. To these groups Russia's accession to the League was gratifying in varying degree, but less so than Germany's departure was regrettable. The position of the government was to try to keep the lines open to both countries, even though to do so meant running the risk of falling into the widening gulf

[1] *The Times*, 17 June 1933.

between the two states. Simon was due to visit Hitler in March 1935 for the first important personal exchanges with the Chancellor. The visit was put off on the German side when it was announced that Eden, at that time Lord Privy Seal, would be holding talks in Moscow at approximately the same time. The proposed Simon visit caused almost equal coldness in Moscow. Eventually Hitler relented and both visits took place. Eden's talks with Stalin, Molotov and Litvinov in Moscow between 27 and 31 March issued in a communiqué in which emphasis was laid on the promotion of a European system of collective security and represented the closest contact Britain formed with Russia before the Anglo-Soviet Treaty of May 1942.[1] The visits symbolised the British tendency to try to keep the Powers in step with each other while refusing to agree that any country need, over a long period, remain an implacable enemy. But equally important was the fact that the senior Minister, Simon, accompanied Eden to Berlin, while Eden alone went on to Moscow.

This did not merely reflect the greater power status of Germany in British eyes. It meant that Germany, as at Locarno, was still regarded as 'one of us', a part of Western civilisation, an element of the West, without whose co-operation stability in Europe was impossible in the long run and who, if the worst came to the worst, would always stand in line against any bursting of its banks by Soviet Communism in the East. If there is any doubt about this distinction drawn by British Ministers between Russia and Germany it is useful to compare the angry notes addressed from London to Moscow throughout the period dealt with in this chapter, when the subject-matter was no more than allegations of Soviet misdoings, with the almost congratulatory words addressed to Nazi Germany by Simon in the House of Commons on 21 March 1935, only five days after Hitler had declared his intention to set aside Part V of the Versailles Treaty.

> The object of British policy has been . . . to help bring this great state back into the councils and comity of Europe on terms which are just to her and which are fair and secure for all of us, so that she, with her great talents and resources may contribute with a full sense of equal status and dignity to the task which every good European who wants peace has got to share, and that is the task of sustaining and strengthening general peace by good relations and by agreement and by co-operation between neighbours.[2]

[1] *The Times*, 2 April 1935.   [2] 299 H.C. Deb. 5s. Col. 1409.

CHAPTER XIII

DISARMAMENT: THE NAVAL ASPECT

I

THE majority of British people, having ensured their national independence during the First World War by force of arms, emerged from the conflict deeply convinced of the futility and waste of modern war machines and committed, in the words of article 8 of the League Covenant, to the reduction of armaments 'to the lowest point consistent with national safety and the enforcement by common action of international obligations'. This view was not uniformly shared by the politicians. It is doubtful whether more than a minority of the Conservative Party ever really thought that disarmament by international agreement was possible, and this scepticism extended to Rightwing newspapers and the leading military and naval experts. Winston Churchill said in the House of Commons six months before the World Disarmament Conference in 1932 met that 'nothing has been achieved by all these conferences that have been held and by all the immense amount of pressures of argument and eloquence which has been applied'. He regarded the approaching meeting at Geneva as an event which might, by weakening the French Army:

> Let the boundless deep
> Down upon far-off cities while they dance—
> Or dream.[1]

The sceptics remained on the defensive however, until the last years of the peace. The fact that the inter-war period of British foreign policy coincided with the rise of the Labour Party, with its deep-seated mistrust of great armaments, from a minority faction to a competitor with the traditional rulers of the country meant that the Right was compelled to profess sympathy for disarmament if it was to hold its own with its rivals.

There were many reasons for the appeal of disarmament to British opinion, despite the failure of multilateral disarmament at The Hague conferences of 1899 and 1907. Foremost among them was the belief, the truth of which was never seriously questioned, that war had come in 1914 as a result of the slithering into the abyss of European coalitions (into which Britain

[1] 254 H.C. Deb. 5s. Cols. 956, 963 (29 June 1931).

had been unfortunately drawn) through the dead weight of their massive armaments. Unlike the French or Belgians, the British had not had to defend their soil against foreign armies during the conflict; on the contrary, they had watched their sons churned to pulp in distant battlefields. It was natural to conclude that, without the war machines which had decimated British youth in 1914–18, the holocaust could have been averted, or at least reduced to a human scale. Besides, standing armies had been regarded in Britain as allies of despotism since the time of Cromwell. It was hard to conceive them as other than threats to the liberties which Englishmen saw in Lockean terms of individual versus state, whereas in French eyes the nation in arms had served since 1789 as the defence against native aristocracies in league with foreign Powers. Moreover, the long economic depression of the 1920s was attributed by every economist of note to the burden of government spending, including military budgets. As it happened, this diagnosis was mistaken, but it accorded with the ordinary person's assumption that a nation's economic difficulties, like an individual's, could only be overcome by bringing expenditure into line with income. Added to these factors making disarmament an article of faith in Britain was the tacit belief, which underlay all British foreign policy between the wars, that the quarrels of European nations, from which the need for great armaments arose, derived to a large extent from imaginary causes.

Wise men might deplore the expenditure of resources on war machines, but they knew the almost insuperable difficulties of securing, and policing when secured, international agreements for the reduction of arms. They had all been stated by a British Foreign Secretary, Castlereagh, with superb succinctness a century before in reply to the disarmament proposals of Alexander I of Russia:

> Although a complete and perfect understanding on this subject among all the leading Powers, regulating the amount of their respective forces, would certainly be the most perfect basis on which a general disarmament could rest, yet it is impossible not to perceive that the settlement of a scale of forces for so many Powers, under such different circumstances as to their relative means, frontiers, positions and faculties for rearming, presents a very complicated question for negotiation; that the means of preserving a system, if once created, are not without their difficulties, liable as all states are to partial necessities for an increase of force; and

it is further to be considered that on this, as on many subjects of a jealous character, in attempting to do too much, difficulties are rather brought into view than made to disappear.[1]

Time has certainly not diminished these difficulties. What a disarmament agreement requires is that, for a pre-arranged period, the armed forces of the parties should be stabilised at an agreed level proportionate to the defence needs of each of them. But in the way of achieving this are two obstacles, one material, the other psychological, which experience has never yet found a means of surmounting. The material difficulty is that the elements in one nation's military strength, which are by no means limited to the size and weapons of its military forces, are never exactly comparable to those of another. One country may have a secure geographical position but owing to an ageing population or improvements in speed of transport may be losing this advantage year by year; another may be sited in a traditional centre of conflict yet by reason of its man-power or natural frontiers may be relatively immune to attack provided its neighbours do not unite against it. The arms requirements of two such states are almost bound to be differently assessed by each, especially since the political situation, local and general, and the efficiency of weapons of various kinds are in a constant state of change. Even if an agreement can be hammered out between them to cover a certain period, it must be so stuffed with 'escape' clauses to allow for such changes as virtually to be robbed of all meaning, and all the problems of comparative assessment will present themselves again when the agreement comes up for revision. Difficulties of this kind, which are posed for two states, are multiplied over and again when the object is to attain a general disarmament treaty covering all or most of the nations of the world. Paradoxically, those states which find it easiest to reach agreement tend to be those whose mutual political relations are already such that no agreement is necessary, and, if an agreement is nevertheless reached, it may handicap them in dealing with their common rivals with whom agreement is not possible.

The subjective difficulty is perhaps even greater. Armaments, in so far as their growth is not due to bureaucratic inertia or prestige rivalry, are calculated provisions against hypothetical attack. Estimates of the dangers of such attack are bound to be subjective, however, though they may be based on the material circumstances confronting the state concerned. The outsider may consider these fears groundless, exaggerated,

[1] C. K. Webster, *The Foreign Policy of Castlereagh, 1815–1822*, London 1925, p. 98.

or possibly less than the material position of the state warrants. But he can only fully understand them by putting himself in the shoes of the state concerned and in the last resort this can only be done by the people and government of that state, who have to live with their own situation. No state will allow an assessment of the perils on which its policy decisions are based to be made by the outsider, and certainly not by those states from which it feels it has reason to fear attack. Disarmament has therefore to proceed through comparisons of inherently dissimilar provisions to meet fears which in themselves are, if not wholly impossible to compare one with another, at least sufficiently unlike to make the task of comparing them infinitely arduous and, as Castlereagh foresaw, productive of positive ill-will between the parties which may not have existed before. Hence, as Sir John Simon once put it, there was at the Lausanne Reparations Conference in 1932 a feeling that 'something *must* be done', whereas at the concurrent Geneva disarmament conference the atmosphere was that 'something *ought* to be done'.[1] These difficulties facing disarmament are not hypothetical. They were experienced in all negotiations in which Britain took part in the inter-war period.[2] Though it is arguable that in a more settled period of international relations or with statesmen of greater faith or publics more steadfast they could have been overcome, no British politician of moderate intelligence could have been unaware of them from the moment when the effort to disarm multilaterally began to be made within the League. There was also a difficulty which had made Britain less influential in disarmament negotiations than the strength of the disarmament movement in the country really justified, namely that when the Disarmament Conference finally met in February 1932 both Conservative and Labour Governments had already gone far to reduce British armaments below pre-war levels, a policy which had not been followed by other states with the exception of the Powers forcibly disarmed in 1919.

A full statement comparing military spending by Britain and other leading Powers was made in the Commons by MacDonald, then Labour Prime Minister, in June 1931. This showed that the British Navy had cost £51.5 million in 1914 (or £76 million at current prices), as compared with £56 million in 1924–5 and £52.4 million in 1930. The United States, with due allowance for the roughness of international comparisons, had spent £30 million on the Navy in 1914 (£42 million at 1931

---

[1] 268 H.C. Deb. 5s. Col. 1248 (12 July 1932).
[2] The World Disarmament Conference of 1932 is referred to in Chapter XV, below.

prices), £70 million in 1924 and £78 million in 1930. The British Army, which had cost £28.8 million in 1914, or £40 million at current prices, cost £39 million in 1931, whereas since 1925 spending on the French Army had increased by £20.8 million, on the Italian by £15.4 million and on the American by £15.68 million. British air power had also been allowed to lag behind, so that by 1931 Britain had 800 first-line aircraft, only a half of which were available for home defence, while the estimated figure for France was 1,300.[1] The consequence was that at the Conference in 1932 Britain was in effect asking other states to disarm, while being herself almost militarily incapable of assisting them against attack if they did, even had British public or Parliamentary opinion been ready to promise assistance. She was, moreover, obliged to incur the odium of opposing proposals for flat-rate reductions, such as the Hoover plan, since they made no allowance for reductions already effected. Sir Herbert Samuel told American and French delegates at a meeting on the Hoover proposals at Geneva in June 1932 that the British military budget had fallen by almost one-fifth in the seven years preceding the Conference.[2]

Nevertheless, the attempt to secure world agreement on disarmament had to be made. The undertaking to make it was incumbent on Britain and her wartime allies by reason of the League Covenant and the preamble to Part V of the Versailles Treaty in which the disarmament of Germany (and correspondingly of the other defeated Powers in the other peace treaties) was supposed 'to render possible the initiation of a general limitation of armaments of all nations'. Although in reply to the repeated German claim that Part V was conditional upon general disarmament and was invalid in the absence of such disarmament the Allies had pointed out that the phrase did no more than commit them to open negotiations on general disarmament, it was clear that they were obliged to take some steps in the matter. It was commonly agreed in Britain that the preamble went even further than that. In May 1930 Churchill said in the House of Commons that it obliged the Allies to disarm and the First Lord of the Admiralty, A. V. Alexander, agreed with this interpretation 'if they are to expect the nations who were treated as the vanquished to continue in a state of disarmament'.[3] Moreover, it soon became clear that an appearance of seriousness about disarmament, to say no more, was virtually a condition of government in postwar

[1] 254 ibid., Cols. 910–14 (29 June 1931).
[2] D.B.F.P., Second Series, III, p. 556.
[3] 238 H.C. Deb. 5s. Col. 2191 (15 May 1930).

Britain. Beginnings had to be made, whatever the obstacles. At the same time, the main lines of British foreign and defence policy as prescribed by the general international situation had to be carried on. Much of the resulting story of British disarmament policy turned upon this attempt both to meet the general foreign policy needs of the times, which would have existed had there been no disarmament movement, and to satisfy mounting public pressures to solve the disarmament problem.

II

The first of these needs was to come to some agreement with the chief interested Powers, that is, the United States, Japan, France and Italy, on the size and composition of fleets and, if possible, to use the relative lack of British interest in land armaments to secure agreement of the European states with British naval policy. Economic considerations alone made an approach to these states urgent since the financial burden of building and maintaining great ships threatened to get out of hand with the increase in their size and armaments. Britain could never contemplate total naval disarmament; that was ruled out by the dependence of the home islands on overseas supplies, the vast and scattered character of the Empire and the need to keep shipyards fed with orders since whole British communities were dependent on them. But if an agreement limiting naval building could be reached, especially with the United States and Japan, which allowed these responsibilities to be discharged, the development of increasingly massive ships could be controlled, the naval ambitions and mutual rivalry of France and Italy curbed and the public demand for assurances that disarmament was going forward satisfied. These aims were to some extent realised by the five-Power naval treaty signed at Washington in February 1922 an account of which has been given in a previous chapter.[1] Success at Washington had, however, depended upon Britain having something to offer in exchange for American agreement to parity, namely the prospect of a liquidation of the Anglo-Japanese alliance, and when the British Government sought an extension of the Washington ratios from battle fleets to auxiliary vessels they could only hope that the same economic factors which were operating on the British side were also effective in America. Britain herself had opposed agreement on ratios for cruiser strengths at Washington since neither France, Italy or the United States would consent to the abolition of the submarine,

----
[1] Chapter XI, pp. 285–6.

a form of defence against the cruiser. Winston Churchill in the Commons in May 1930 read out a Cabinet instruction sent to the leader of the British delegation at the Washington conference, Lord Balfour, insisting that if the submarine was not abolished by the treaty Britain must retain complete freedom to build cruisers up to 10,000 tons.[1] The only understanding on cruisers reached at Washington, that they should not exceed 10,000 tons, had itself become highly inconvenient to Britain with the economic stringencies of the middle 1920s since it tended to establish that figure as the standard size for cruisers. This was larger than Britain, with her requirement for a relatively large fleet of cruisers, desired.

The Admiralty's view was that in any general disarmament treaty which carried forward the Washington accords from battle fleets to naval forces as a whole ratios similar to those agreed at Washington should be applied to each of the eight or nine major categories of ships, though the ratios need not be the same for each category. The adoption of this principle would clearly tend to handicap any country which sought to exceed Britain in naval power since it would be compelled to distribute its allowance of tonnage under an arms limitation treaty throughout the categories which Britain, with her large and varied naval force, considered desirable. When in March 1927 this policy was expounded by Viscount Cecil at the third session of the Preparatory Commission appointed by the League Council in 1925 it seemed to enjoy the support of the United States delegate, Hugh Gibson, but collided frontally with the French doctrine of limitation, not by category, but by total tonnage. France, Paul-Boncour told the Commission on 5 April, demanded freedom to transfer units of the total permitted tonnage from one category to another since a relatively minor naval Power must have flexibility to concentrate on forms of defence required by the changing character of warfare. He did, however, propose a compromise by which such transfers would have to be notified to the League Secretariat at least one year before the portion of the tonnage to be transferred was laid down, but this proved unacceptable to Britain and the third session of the Commission closed with deadlock on the issue.[2] Cecil, the only political figure of prominence in the British delegation, thereupon resigned from the Conservative Government on the ground that the Cabinet had rejected three different compromises suggested by the delegation although these compromises, according to Cecil, had a good chance of

[1] 238 H.C. Deb. 5s. Col. 2099 (15 May 1930).
[2] Misc. No. 6 (1928), Cmd. 3211, pp. 9–15.

acceptance and the Cabinet had been warned that refusal would
mean the breakdown of the conference.[1]

Since the United States seemed more inclined to the British
viewpoint than the continental states in the Preparatory Commission, the British Government welcomed an invitation from
President Coolidge to a conference with American representatives at Geneva in the summer of 1927 in the hope that a prior
Anglo-American agreement would have the effect of moving
the French. The British contended all along that if the United
States persisted in the ambitious naval programme contemplated in 1916 Britain would have to follow suit, not so much
on account of fear of American superiority as such, but in order
to keep ahead of lesser naval Powers which might take as their
standard the American, rather than the British, scale of building. The fact that France, who saw no prospect of agreement
with Britain on the category issue, and Italy, who determined
to keep abreast of France at sea, decided not to accept Coolidge's
invitation seemed to improve the prospects of coming to terms
with these two states later, since a firm basis of naval parity
with Washington would have been laid. The fifth signatory
of the Washington accords, Japan, having made herself
well-nigh impregnable to naval attack by the 1922 treaty,
had a distinct interest in a limit being set to Anglo-American
naval rivalry and inclined towards the more conservative
theory of category limitation favoured by the *status quo* Power,
Britain.

Despite these promising omens, however, it soon became
clear when the conference opened on 20 June that the British
Government had seriously underestimated American determination to insist on the right to build heavy cruisers more
suited to the needs of continental defence than the large fleet
of lighter cruisers preferred by Britain, and hence to compel
Britain either to increase her naval budgets or to reduce her
light cruiser strength below safety levels. The British plan,
unfolded by the First Lord of the Admiralty, W. C. Bridgeman,
at the opening session of the Geneva conference, contemplated
limitations in the size and armaments of all categories of naval
vessels and extensions of their life. The outstanding feature
of the British proposal, however, was the insistence that the
Washington ratio of 5–5–3 for Britain, the United States and
Japan should be applied to 10,000-ton cruisers carrying 8-inch
guns, while 7,500-ton cruisers and below, carrying 6-inch guns,
were only to be limited later. Bridgeman frankly admitted
that this division of cruisers into two categories, the category

<hr>

[1] See Cecil's letter to *The Times*, 19 March 1928.

of giant cruisers favoured by the United States to be subject
to parity at once, while the category of smaller vessels preferred
by Britain was left unrestricted, was based on the fact that 'a
number of small cruisers are of vital necessity to an Empire
whose widely scattered parts are divided from each other by
seas and oceans and whose most populous parts are dependent
for their daily bread on sea-borne trade'.[1]   The argument of
Empire, however, was the one least likely to impress the Americans and, with their thoughts mainly bent on mainland security,
their delegation agreed to accept no compromise on the principle of freedom, within any agreed limitation on cruiser
strength as a whole, to devote all their allowance of tonnage to
the heaviest and most powerfully armed class of vessel.   These
differences were played out to the tune of severe acrimony on
both sides and when the conference broke up in August it was
evident that the two states were more widely divided than before.   One consequence was that in November of the following
year a bill for increased naval construction was submitted to
Congress by the Administration.

Hence when the Preparatory Commission resumed for its
fifth session in March 1928 considerable pessimism existed as
to whether a draft disarmament convention could ever be
drawn up to provide a basis for the long-awaited general disarmament conference.   The Italian and American delegates
were dubious about continuing talks in the Commission until
more progress had been attained between the major Powers.
There then intervened a cryptic reference by the French delegate, Count Clauzel, to 'useful conversations' which were continuing between the technical experts, which he hoped would
issue in 'some final settlement' as soon as possible.   It appeared
that he was referring to talks between the French Naval Chief
of Staff, Vice-Admiral Violette, and the British naval representative, Vice-Admiral Kelly, which had been initiated after
Austen Chamberlain had met Briand, the French Foreign
Minister, in Geneva on 9 March, a week before the Commission's session began, to discuss the deadlock between the British
and French viewpoints.   Chamberlain, it soon became known,
had introduced a new British Admiralty plan for reducing the
naval categories from nine to six and for permitting limited
transfers of tonnage from higher to lower categories.   This he
invited Briand to support in return for British acquiescence in
the long-standing French refusal to include trained reserves,
which the French conscription system provided in large

---

[1] Geneva Conference for the Limitation of Naval Armaments, Cmd. 2964 (1927),
p. 15.

numbers, among the effectives to be limited under the land disarmament provisions of the draft convention.

The six-category British scheme was not acceptable to France, but the expert talks continued while the Commission marked time and, after the British Government had agreed to reduce the categories to four and to exclude submarines for coastal defence of 600 tons and under, a final Anglo-French compromise was announced at the end of July. The understanding with respect to trained reserves was naturally not included in the published text of the compromise, but leakages in the French Press left no doubt that it was part of the bargain and aroused suspicion of the existence of even more sinister agreements. The essence of the published compromise, to which other states were ingenuously invited to adhere, was, however, in itself sufficiently startling. This was that the naval limitations to be covered by the draft disarmament convention should embrace four classes of ships: capital ships of over 10,000 tons armed with guns of more than 8-inch calibre; aircraft carriers of over 10,000 tons; other surface vessels of 10,000 tons and below with guns of between 6-inch and 8-inch calibre; and submarines of over 600 tons. Since the Washington Conference had dealt with the first two categories for the five Powers which signed the treaty of 1922, it was proposed that the forthcoming disarmament conference should merely extend the Washington restrictions to non-signatory states and should then fix the total tonnage possessed by all naval Powers for each of the last two categories.[1]

The Anglo-French compromise required little examination to show that it secured precisely what Britain had been striving to attain since 1922, with the exception of the total abolition of submarines. Since the war British naval policy had rested on the assumption that war with the United States, the main champion of the heavy cruiser, was unthinkable; nevertheless the Admiralty illogically feared the American fleet of heavily armed cruisers and it was against these that the Violette–Kelly plan struck. Britain, on the other hand, would be free under the compromise to build as many 6-inch cruisers, which suited her needs, as she wished. Not surprisingly, the compromise was acidly rejected by Washington in a note of 28 September, which described it as even more objectionable than the plan Britain presented to the abortive Geneva conference in 1927. The United States Government continued to insist on the principle of fixing a total tonnage for all cruisers while veering to-

[1] For the text of the Anglo-French compromise see Misc. No. 6 (1928), Cmd. 3211, pp. 27–8.

wards the old French 'transactional' proposal for allowing for a certain shift in the percentage of tonnage allotted to each of the three categories.[1]   Italian reactions were no more enthusiastic, the argument being that limitation by total tonnage was more equitable for the smaller naval Powers.   The chief feature of the Italian reply to the invitation to adhere to the compromise, however, was a repetition of the standard contention that any form of limitation would be agreeable to Rome provided that as a result Italian armaments were not inferior to those of any other continental state, or in other words to those of France.[2]

The compromise also had a cold reception in Germany, where it was correctly read as implying a British concession to France in the matter of land forces.[3]   Since Germany was prohibited by the peace treaty from training her youth by a system of conscription, as Britain herself had insisted in 1919, she was vitally interested in continued British opposition to the exclusion of trained reserves from limitations on land forces. The Anglo-French compromise was strongly criticised on precisely the same ground in Britain, where such radical newspapers as the *Manchester Guardian* quoted from incautious articles in the French Press which spoke of the compromise as putting Britain in France's pocket.[4]   Only the Japanese had a fair word to say for the compromise and it passed from serious international debate, leaving behind only the impression that British principles were always for sale if the price was high enough.

III

The Anglo-American breach, which had been opened by the failure of the Geneva naval conference in 1927 and widened by the Anglo-French compromise, now took a surprising turn for the better with the accession of Herbert Hoover to the White House in March 1929.   A more flexible mood was at once communicated to American disarmament policy.   This was reflected in a notable statement by the American disarmament representative, Gibson, at the sixth session of the Preparatory Commission on 22 April, when he appeared to fall in with British theory of limitation by category and agreed to consider methods of naval limitation besides merely restricting tonnage, both of which were moves in the direction of British anxiety to curtail the larger classes of cruisers.[5]   In the same

[1] Cmd. 3211, pp. 34–8.   [2] *Ibid.*, pp. 39–43.   [3] *Ibid.*, p. 29.
[4] *Manchester Guardian Weekly*, 3 and 24 August 1928.
[5] *D.B.F.P.*, Second Series, I, pp. 4–5.

speech Gibson announced that his government would no longer oppose the determination of the continental states, meaning France and her allies, to have trained reserves excluded and this made possible an agreement in the Commission in favour of exclusion on 27 April, although in the teeth of opposition from the German delegate, Count Bernstorff. A month later the Commission went a step further and adopted on second reading an entire group of articles of the draft disarmament convention and the prospects for summoning a world conference markedly improved. Gibson's statement of 22 April, with its loosening effect on the Anglo-American deadlock, was welcomed by Lord Cushendun, the chief British delegate on disarmament, at the Preparatory Commission on the same day, and 'noted with much interest' by Austen Chamberlain in the Commons on 24 April.[1] As a further gesture towards Britain, Hoover made the significant statement on 7 May that a 'rational yardstick' had to be found for measuring parity between British and American fleets, and this again seemed to acknowledge the British claim that if the United States was bent upon constructing heavily armed cruisers she must agree to limit their numbers. On 2 June the President made known that the naval estimates for the coming financial year, which made provision for the first five of the fifteen cruisers envisaged in the United States Naval Bill enacted on 13 February 1929, were being held back in the expectation of a naval disarmament agreement.

There was therefore a certain parallel between the position of Ramsay MacDonald, when he formed his second Labour Government on 8 June 1929, and his position when he had previously become Prime Minister in 1924.[2] At both times the movement of international affairs was being held up, by the reparations issue in 1924 and by the disarmament deadlock in 1929, though in the former case the issue had lain largely between Britain and France whereas in 1929 it was British and American differences which caused the trouble. At both times the solvent of the difficulties initially came from Washington and the American who had played such a notable role in settling the reparations crisis in 1924, General Dawes, now by a trick of fate came to London on 14 June as the American Ambassador. Moreover, just as the solution of the reparations problem in 1924 had already begun to appear, with the replacement of Poincaré by Herriot as French Prime Minister, before MacDonald formed his first Labour Government, so in

---

[1] VIth Sess. Minutes, p. 5; 227 H.C. Deb. 5s. Col. 856.
[2] A. J. Toynbee, *Survey of International Affairs, 1929*, pp. 3–5.

1929 the disarmament impasse was already resolving itself, thanks to President Hoover's initiative, before he formed his second.

In discussions with Dawes and Gibson during the first days of his new administration MacDonald's object was agreement with the United States on a basis of parity, but parity calculated in terms of a 'yardstick' which took fully into account the three factors of displacement, guns and age of vessels.[1] His fear was that unless some precise ratio was formulated before the five Washington Powers met again in accordance with the treaty to revise the 1922 accords Japan would base the claim she was making for 70 per cent of the world's largest cruiser fleet on the rising American estimates, thus placing Britain in an impossible position.[2] In a memorandum issued after the talks on 29 July the two British desiderata, that is, parity in combatant strength to be reached by categories and agreement on a 'yardstick' to measure parity based on all the factors in the effectiveness of a vessel, seemed to be accepted, but, as Dawes told the Prime Minister on 4 September, naval staff in Washington then raised difficulties about British proposals for translating these principles into figures.[3] The Admiralty had suggested 15 8-inch cruisers for Britain and 18 for the United States. If Japan maintained her demand for 70 per cent of the American cruiser fleet, this would giver her an average of 12.6 8-inch cruisers, which would be satisfactory for Britain. But the American Naval Board were now demanding 23 cruisers of the largest armaments, which meant that Japan would raise her stake to 16, more, that is, than the British fleet. The Naval Board finally agreed to reduce their figure to 21, which, together with an allowance of tonnage in the 6-inch class, would give them an aggregate cruiser tonnage of 315,000 tons, but further than this they would not go. Hoover wrote to MacDonald on 17 September that Britain was proposing for herself an aggregate of 339,000 tons (since she had a much larger fleet of lighter cruisers than the American) and hence in effect America was only claiming an increase in gun calibre of 2-inch on 60,000 tons.[4] When the British Government, at Hoover's suggestion, issued invitations to the other four Washington Powers to a conference in London in January 1930 to extend the 1922 limitations to other classes of vessels, the President was at that moment giving it as his final word that unless the British

---

[1] *D.B.F.P.*, Second Series, I, pp. 8–10.
[2] See MacDonald's statements in the House, 229 H.C. Deb. 5s. Cols. 65–6 (2 July 1929); 230 *ibid.*, Cols. 1305–6 (24 July 1929).
[3] *D.B.F.P.*, Second Series, I, pp. 68–9.
[4] *Ibid.*, pp. 87–90.

tonnage figure was reduced to something like 300,000 tons the United States could make no concession over 8-inch guns.[1] To such ungracious huckstering had prestige rivalry reduced the democratic pair.

When MacDonald visited the United States between 4 and 10 October, being the first British Prime Minister to do so while in office, he found Hoover and his naval advisers no more inclined to make concessions on heavy cruisers. Moreover, he was confronted with new proposals which had evidently not been raised in the discussions with Dawes in England.[2] There was, first, Hoover's strong advocacy of a much more extensive scrapping of large battleships; despite Admiralty doubts about the value of these vessels in the postwar period, MacDonald's advisers were almost as shocked by this talk as British naval officers had been in 1921, when they heard Harding condemn their precious ships to the scrapyard by the thousand ton. In addition, the American team wanted to widen the talks so as to include matters traditionally close to the American heart, such as the ending of the construction of further British naval bases in the Western Hemisphere, new rules on the immunity of private property at sea in time of war, and the exclusion of foodstuffs from blockade. MacDonald understood these propositions as having their origin in Congress rather than the Administration, agreed to consider them but undertook no further commitment either then or later.[3] Perhaps the most serious effect of the Washington visit, however, which the striking impact of MacDonald's personality on the American public served only to heighten, was the suspicion it aroused in the other three Washington Powers, France, Italy and Japan. The Prime Minister in speeches in the Commons on 2 and 24 July and at Lossiemouth on 29 August did his utmost to deny that his new intimacy with the Hoover Administration represented an exclusive Anglo-American alliance. Nevertheless, the American visit produced the same suspicion of British intrigue, though with far less reason this time, as the Anglo-French accord of the previous year. French, Italian and Japanese attitudes after the visit showed that Hoover's belief, never shared by MacDonald, that if Britain and the United States came to terms with each other the three lesser naval Powers would follow, was misplaced.

The Japanese position, as disclosed to MacDonald by the

---

[1] *Ibid.*, pp. 91–2.   [2] *Ibid.*, p. 106 *et seq.*
[3] See MacDonald's report on his visit to the United States and Canada given to the House of Commons on 5 November 1929; 231 H.C. Deb. 5s. Cols. 885–8 and Col. 894.

Japanese Ambassador in London, Matsudaira, in November was not entirely hostile to the partial Anglo-American accord, though Japan's remote position in the Pacific induced her to prefer much more far-reaching restrictions on aircraft carriers, while she had no sympathy with the Anglo-American plea for the abolition of submarines. Matsudaira made quite clear, however, that there was to be no withdrawal from the Japanese demand for 70 per cent of the cruiser strength of Britain or the United States, whichever was the stronger Power.[1] Mac-Donald told the Ambassador in a talk on 9 December that Japan already had 74 per cent of British 8-inch cruiser strength, but this was of little consequence since it was the United States that Japan had most to fear from, American opinion being more hostile towards her than British.[2]

The chief hurdle to be overcome, however, if the Anglo-American agreement on principles was to be accepted by all five Washington Powers, was the bitter naval conflict between France and Italy which had its basis in the clash of policies and aspirations of these two states in south-east Europe and north-west Africa, where both countries had been struggling for hegemony throughout the 1920s. Mussolini's Government referred to the long Italian coastline, the shortage of natural harbours, which demanded a varied and flexible naval defence force, and Italy's exposed position in the Mediterranean, surrounded by risks of hostile incursions through the Turkish Straits, the Suez Canal and the neck of water at Gibraltar. The French, equally acquainted with geography, advertised their three coasts and their extensive overseas possessions (which Italians were unfortunately aware that naval power had won as well as protected) as implying superior defensive requirements to those of Italy. The only two issues on which Paris and Rome agreed set them against the Anglo-Saxon Powers, namely that the submarine was the poor man's equivalent of the battleship and that any extension of the Washington ratios to auxiliary vessels would underline their inferiority in the table of Powers which they were only too anxious to forget. As MacDonald explained to Parliament after the London conference in 1930, Britain belonged to the continental group dominated by France and Italy since by the Locarno agreements and less formal undertakings she was involved with them in the European balance of power. At the same time, she was a member of the 'high-seas group' of which the other members were the United States and Japan. Her policy must therefore be to maintain a rationally

[1] *D.B.F.P.*, Second Series, I, pp. 156–7.
[2] *Ibid.*, pp. 162–3.

computed equality with the United States at a level low enough
to keep Japan in check, while attempting to moderate the
struggle over equality between France and Italy.[1]

As might have been expected, the shadow of the French-
Italian conflict overhung the London naval conference which
met in January and eventually prevented these two states from
signing Part III of the resulting treaty which set forth the agreed
ratios for auxiliary vessels.   The agreement between Britain,
the United States and Japan which formed the substance of this
Part was announced by MacDonald in the House on 10 April[2]
and embodied two major concessions by Washington and Tokyo
respectively, to which the prevailing economic depression no
doubt made its contribution.   On the American side, the Naval
Board agreed to reduce their demand for 8-inch cruisers from
21 to 18; this was by way of reply to the British Admiralty's
decision to scale down their requirements of cruisers from 70
to 50 provided there was an 'adequate' number of new ships in
the lower figure.   The effect of the American offer was to reduce the aggregate tonnage difference between the two fleets
to 12,000 in Britain's favour, which she was permitted to
transfer from one class of cruiser to another.   The American
delegation also had little difficulty in consenting to a British
proposal for reaching the Washington limits for capital ships
within 18 months of the ratification of the London treaty, rather
than by 1936, when the earlier treaty expired.   But they
stirred considerable hostility in British naval circles by refusing
to scale down the maximum size of battleships, as Britain proposed.   The other major concession which made agreement
possible among the 'high seas' signatories was the Japanese
decision, formulated in talks during March between Senator
Reed of the American delegation and Ambassador Matsudaira,
to reduce their demand for a 70 per cent ratio in 8-inch cruiser
strength to one of 60 per cent provided that the larger ratio was
accepted for the other category of vessels covered by the treaty.
The Japanese delegation was also active throughout the conference in support of the British argument for reducing the size
and fire-power of ships of every kind, and in this the relative
immunity of the Japanese islands from naval attack by the
Western Powers, unless they possessed vessels of the greatest
range and striking capacity, clearly played a part.

Since the British Government considered that they stood to
gain from these concessions by their 'high-seas' partners, it
might have been expected that they themselves would have

[1] 238 H.C. Deb. 5s. Cols. 2088-9 (15 May 1930).
[2] 237 H.C. Deb. 5s. Col. 2473.

gone further by way of dissuading France from the heavy naval programme she had embarked upon, which made her signature (and that of Italy) of the London naval ratios impossible. In an able memorandum to the other four Powers of 21 December 1929 the French Government disclosed a naval building programme which would bring the aggregate French fleet to 721,000 tons by 1936, as compared with its existing strength of 423,000 tons. The French claimed that they could only reduce this programme and accept the kind of ratio for auxiliary vessels which the Anglo-Saxon states were suggesting for them if a mutual guarantee and non-aggression pact were signed by the Mediterranean Powers, including Britain. The British reply of 12 January showed a marked lack of interest in the proposed pact, and it was notable that the political framework in which the Anglo-Saxon Powers desired to set the naval conference was the Pact of Paris of 1928, with no machinery of enforcement, rather than the League Covenant, which in any event the French wanted strengthening before they abandoned any particle of their military strength. When the French position was developed before the conference on 12 February the proportions of the naval building programme were even more alarming; the aggregate tonnage to be built by 1936 had now increased by 4,000 tons. On 13 March revised figures were issued, showing a much larger figure for the existing French fleet and somewhat lower prospective totals for 1936. But French statistics, revised or unrevised, did nothing to lessen Italian determination to do at least as well, and the effect of this was to make France the fulcrum of the conference.

The Tardieu Government were willing to scale down their naval undertakings on one or other of two conditions: if Italy would consent to a permanent over-all French superiority of at least 200,000 tons or if France's proposal for a Mediterranean security pact on the model of Locarno were accepted. The Fascist Grand Council in Rome decided on 19 March to confirm the position of its delegation in London that nothing less than parity with France would satisfy, which closed the door on Tardieu's first condition. The Mediterranean Locarno, on the other hand, depended almost entirely upon Britain and while MacDonald was prepared, and even anxious, for some kind of consultative arrangement within the framework of the Pact of Paris, even this was conditional upon United States agreement and participation. When the same proposal was made by France two years later MacDonald told the American delegation at the disarmament conference that the Cabinet 'was unanimously convinced that we could not give such a further assurance for entering into additional commitments involving the possibility of military or naval responsibilities in the event of Continental war'.[1]   That was exactly how matters stood in 1930.   There was a brief moment at the end of March when, with American encouragement, British and French agreement seemed possible on a formula assuring France that the sanctions provisions of article 16 of the Covenant would be interpreted in emergencies in a Gallic sense.   Wind of the talks reached the isolationist House of Commons, however, and the Prime Minister was compelled to assure M.P.s on 1 April and again through Henderson on the 7th that nothing was intended beyond the Covenant as formerly understood.[2]   In so doing he removed all hope that France would submit her naval programme to limitation and the abstention of France, and therefore of Italy, from the ratios agreement could have been foreseen the moment MacDonald's statement was made.   What was less easy to forecast, though the circumstances were the same, was that France's refusal to surrender her weapons except in return for organised security would nullify all efforts for general disarmament.

IV

When the five-Power Naval Treaty was signed on 22 April all the parties agreed to a five-year 'holiday' in the construction of capital ships, the regulation of the conditions of submarine warfare (British and American pleas for the abolition of the submarine having failed), and the limitation of the tonnage and gun calibre of submarines.   These agreements formed Parts I, II, IV and V of the treaty.   French and Italian policies, as we have seen, prevented the vital Part III from being signed by more than Britain, the United States and Japan.   A Franco-Italian agreement, of infinitely complex character, did seem to have been reached in February 1931, but by April this too had passed into limbo.   The effect of Part III was that Britain, the United States and Japan would scrap 5, 3 and 1 of their battleships respectively by 1933 (instead of 1936, as provided in the Washington treaty) and would observe the 1922 tonnage ratios (the Japanese ratio, as already stated, being dealt with separately) for the following four categories of auxiliary vessels: 8-inch gun cruisers, 6-inch gun cruisers, destroyers and submarines.   Article 21 embodied the safeguarding or 'escalator' clause on which Britain had insisted in view of the risks involved in the '50-cruiser principle': this permitted the con-

[1] *D.B.F.P.*, Second Series, III, p. 516.
[2] 237 H.C. Deb. 5s. Cols. 1072–3; *ibid.*, Cols. 1752–6.

tracting parties to increase their tonnage in the agreed categories in the event of unforeseen growth in the naval strength of states not signatory to Part III.[1] Britain ratified the treaty on 1 August and it came into force on 1 January 1931.

MacDonald's defence of the agreement was that it put a stop to battleship replacement, thus allowing time for the future of the battleship to be reconsidered, reduced the number of capital ships and limited the tonnage of auxiliary craft among the 'high seas' signatories.[2] The economic effect of this was stressed by the First Lord of the Admiralty in a speech at Sheffield on 11 April, when he said that the settlement would save Britain between £60 and £70 million during the following six years.[3] Even more important than the financial savings, said the government's White Paper issued on 15 April, which explained British aims and the results of the conference, was the 'elimination of competitive building in cruisers and auxiliary craft between the British Commonwealth, the United States and Japan, with all that this implies in the mutual improvement of their political relations'.[4] The short-lived character of this improvement, however, at least as far as relations between the two Western Powers and Japan were concerned, was evident from the bitter criticism of the agreement by Right-wing Japanese and the Japanese attack on Manchuria only nine months after the treaty came into effect. The agreement was also sharply criticised by Conservative spokesmen and naval authorities in Britain, Churchill leading the attack on the treaty in the Commons on 15 May and Earls Jellicoe and Beatty in the Lords on 8 May and 1 July. The argument of the critics was that Britain had definitely surrendered primacy at sea to the United States, that she would be left inadequately defended in time of war and that the 91,000 tons replacement figure permitted to Britain would make it impossible to maintain even the inadequate fleet of 50 cruisers unless many of them were over-age vessels.[5]

The strength of Conservative hostility to the London naval treaty was shown by Baldwin's motion on 2 June to appoint a select committee to examine the agreement. This was defeated on a 282–201 vote,[6] but the succeeding and largely

---

[1] League of Nations: Treaty Series, Vol. CXII, pp. 65–91.

[2] 238 H.C. Deb. 5s. Cols. 2085–96 (15 May 1930).

[3] *The Times*, 12 April 1930, p. 11.

[4] Misc. No. 8 (1930). Memorandum on the results of the London Naval Conference, Cmd. 3547.

[5] 77 H.L. Deb. 5s. Cols. 458–66 (8 May); 78 *ibid.*, Cols. 186–201 (1 July). 238 H.C. Deb. 5s. Cols. 2098–2114 (15 May).

[6] 239 H.C. Deb. 5s. Col. 1791.

Conservative National Government, which initiated rearmament in 1935 after the failure of the world disarmament conference, complained with some reason that the treaty placed Britain at a disadvantage in the arms race by preventing her from replacing her capital ships until after the end of 1936.[1] This must be the normal and paradoxical effect of partial disarmament measures, especially as between a limited number of states whose political relations are already good enough to make an agreement possible at all. There was thus some point in Churchill's observation that 'we spend an enormous proportion of our naval effort upon maintaining battle fleets at parity with countries we have long ago ruled out of all military consideration, thus depriving ourselves of the power of making provisions against the real dangers which are advancing upon us'.[2] The London naval treaty undoubtedly ended the uneconomic and slightly ridiculous Anglo-American naval arms race, softened conflict between the United States and Japan over restrictions imposed upon Japanese immigration into America and perhaps took the dangerous edge from the tensions arising out of British Commonwealth attitudes towards Japanese immigrants.[3] But it did much less than the government claimed to advance the great problem of world disarmament with which the League Preparatory Commission had been wrestling for almost five years when the London naval treaty was signed. Some supporters of the National Government in the early 1930s argued that the treaty had the effect of weakening British bargaining power at the disarmament conference. If this was so, it is an illustration of the curious truth that one of the motives for refusing to disarm may be the desire to use one's influence to the best effect in the cause of world disarmament.

The London Treaty can be regarded as the last act in the settlement of Pacific questions which had begun at Washington in 1921. In the background of the naval settlement in 1930 between the three Pacific Powers was the four-Power treaty for political consultation signed at Washington along with the naval agreement, and this in 1930 was still considered adequate to provide the stability which makes disarmament possible. The world disarmament convention which the Preparatory Commission was charged to draft, on the other hand, had to be launched amid an essentially European tension, representing the struggle of Germany to throw off the fetters of Versailles in

---

[1] Statement Relating to Defence, 1936, Cmd. 5107, p. 9.
[2] 254 H.C. Deb. 5s. Col. 958 (29 June 1931).
[3] A. J. Toynbee, *Survey of International Affairs*, 1930, p. 1.

face of the opposition of France and her allies. Despite every effort of draftmanship and persuasion, a formula to reconcile these claims, such as the Washington Conference found in 1922 (though largely by deferring the issue), continued to elude the statesmen. Moreover, the Washington and London naval conferences dealt with naval strength the components of which are more easily compared than the complex elements in total national military power, with which the Preparatory Commission and the Disarmament Conference had to deal. Again, owing to the size and costliness of modern warships, evasions of a naval disarmament agreement are often not difficult to detect. Above all, the impetus towards the naval agreements came chiefly from the prevailing economic creed of retrenchment of government spending as the road to recovery. By the early 1930s, when the world Disarmament Conference was in its throes, this doctrine was at last beginning to be questioned by New Dealers in the United States and Nazis in Germany. Had the Disarmament Conference not had to contend with the shocking discovery of the 1930s that nationalism can be indulged in at an economic profit in terms of full employment it might have shared some of the success of the two great naval conferences. Since it lived, or perhaps existed, at the point of collision of Great Power policies and in a less kindly climate of economic thought, its failure, by leading to a general arms race which placed in jeopardy states which had gone to the limit in unilateral disarmament, wiped out many of the gains of Washington and London.

CHAPTER XIV

THE MANCHURIAN QUESTION

I

WHILE China was groping towards unity as a modern state, external Powers such as Britain which had enjoyed a privileged position in the country for almost a century had little alternative but to negotiate for the orderly liquidation of their old rights in the hope that a reformed and fully sovereign China would welcome foreign trade and investment on the same non-discriminating basis which Britain and the United States had sought when China was still a semi-colonial country. In 1928, when the Nanking Government was established and the economic and financial reconstruction of China began with the assistance of friendly Powers and the League, the road seemed to be leading back to an Open Door China, though without the unequal treaties. This might represent a setback for certain European and American interests, but with a stable and prosperous China what was gained by the resulting demand for foreign goods and loans would probably more than compensate for the loss of imposed privileges. Moreover, in the ten years after the First World War questions other than the Far East occupied the attention of Europe, and increasingly as the decade passed. During the Locarno era the improved political and economic climate in Europe and the extraordinary industrial and financial boom in the United States suggested that prosperity might not, after all, be so dependent upon the opening of markets in the Far East as had been supposed in the Battle of Concessions in China in the late nineteenth century.

This brief summer was dramatically ended by the American stock market crash of 1929 which heralded the world slump, but the notions it brought with it did not suffer a similar fate. Had Keynesian ideas on economic recovery been generally known and adopted it is possible that revival might have been effected through large-scale lending to the economically backward areas, including the Far East, so as to increase their demand for industrial imports. The recipe for recovery in 1932 and 1933, however, was still the orthodox one of cutting government spending and shortening financial sail at home and abroad. Recovery, when it finally began in 1933, therefore, took the form (especially for Britain) primarily of a home-market revival with world trade at a markedly lower level than before the collapse. This meant, especially when combined with the focusing of interest on the world Disarmament Conference which at length met in 1932, the continued contraction of European concern with the Far East. This did not affect the strategical interests of the European Powers, including Britain, since it was in Europe, if anywhere, that it was feared war would break out. Neither Britain nor Europe really accepted Smuts' claim, put forward at the Imperial Conference in 1921, that the problems of the Pacific were 'the world problems of the next fifty years or more'.[1]

For Japan, on the other hand, the situation was wholly different. The two events we have mentioned as having led Britain towards an orderly liquidation of her privileges in China, the establishment of the Nanking Government in 1928 and the domestic economic troubles which reached a climax in 1931, had an entirely contrary effect on that country. In the first place Japan was as deeply involved, by reason of geographical position, in affairs in mainland China as Britain was in affairs in western Europe or the United States in matters within the area of the Monroe Doctrine. The tempestuous unification of China under the Kuomintang threatened, not only the favoured position Japan had built up for herself in north China, Manchuria and Korea as a result of her victories over China in 1895 and Russia ten years later, but the security of her home islands themselves. The threat of a struggle for power between Japan and a reunited China was all the more serious in that, whereas Nationalist China might soon enjoy much the same kind of equality *vis-à-vis* the Western Powers as Chinese Emperors had enjoyed during the first trading contacts with the West at the end of the eighteenth century, Japan could hardly survive as the industrial and heavily populated state she had become without the markets and raw materials to be found in Western countries, especially if, in a struggle for power with China, the doors of the mainland were closed to her.

Yet events had shown that if ever the West had difficulties of its own or was for any reason provoked against Japan, Japanese trade and livelihood would at once suffer. To Japanese emigrants the wealth of the West, and especially of North America, was denied; this was no grave handicap since emigration from Japan was never a serious contribution to the relief of population pressure, but it symbolised Japan's dependence on Western goodwill. When the economy of the West collapsed

[1] Cmd. 1474 (1921), p. 25.

in 1929 and sank into the trough in 1931, Japanese exports were the first to be cut. The catastrophic fall in the price and volume of Japanese raw silk exports to the United States during the depression was tantamount to the ruin of Japanese farming, which had come to depend for the margin between life and death on the silk trade.[1] Japanese access to raw materials in Western and Western-controlled territories was not, of course, threatened in the same way, but these could only be purchased by sales of Japanese goods in Western markets whose purchasing power was already weakened by the depression.

If under these conditions of dependency on the West Japan was ever to be engaged in conflict with China, the scales would be heavily weighted against her. China's population was at least six times as great as Japan's and, though far less industrially skilled than the Japanese, would probably absorb Western techniques with the same remarkable speed, especially since Chinese culture was the original basis of Japanese culture and the inventiveness of the Chinese had historically been the equal of that of any other people. The Chinese had no admiration for Japan, which they tended to despise as a country of uncivilised imitators, and the anti-Japanese boycotts of the 1920s in China showed the terrible force of national hatred in a country as large as China. The rapid spread of national consciousness in the Chinese was such that, whereas the war with Japan in 1894–5 was unheard of in most of the myriad villages of China, during the troubles of 1925–7 every attack on a foreign concession was acclaimed throughout the country as a national victory. On every account therefore the prospect that Japan might repeat her victory of 1895 receded year by year. Moreover, if a war to the finish were to be fought between Japan and China, Japan would probably be without allies, whereas China, especially after the Kuomintang's breach with Moscow, could always rely on the friendly attitude of the United States, if not its positive help. Japan had lost her only considerable ally, Britain, and in any case Britain tried to remain on friendly terms only in order to curb the Japanese militarists; if the militarists did return to power, as they must in a national struggle with China, this final link with Britain would disappear. Japan had won some gains at the Washington Conference, chiefly the removal of the threat of naval sanctions from the Western Powers, but these would of little comfort in a single-handed conflict with China. Otherwise Washington represented the isolation of Japan.

To make the outlook more sombre for Japan, the return of

[1] Freda Utley, *Japan's Feet of Clay*, London, 1936, p. 9.

China to unity and strength under the Kuomintang was paralleled by the developing power of Soviet Russia, Japan's other leading rival in Asia. It is significant that Japan's attack on China in 1894 came immediately after the formation of the Franco-Russian alliance and the opening of the Trans-Siberian railway, which brought Tsarist troops to the Amur river province on Japan's doorstep. In much the same way Japan's conquest of Manchuria in 1931–2 had its stimulus in the concentration of Soviet energies on the internal development of Russia and the double-tracking of the Trans-Siberian, completed in 1931. For Russia, the effect of the dismissal of Borodin's team in China in 1927 was to signalise the defeat of world revolution as an immediate object of policy and to vindicate the goal of Socialism in One Country. There followed the initiation of the First Five-year plan in 1928 and this, despite the economic disarray in the capitalist world, was showing results by 1931.

For Japan the implications of the growth in Soviet power, however gradual, were three, of which the second and third were by far the most grave. In the first place a strong Soviet Russia would inevitably tend to reverse the predominant position Japan obtained for herself in Manchuria and Korea by her defeat of Russia in 1905. By 1931 Japan owned and protected with her own forces the South Manchuria Railway which dominated the Liaotung peninsula with its naval base, Port Arthur. It would have required a restraint on the part of Russia for which there was no warrant in history, if, blocked in Europe by the Locarno accords and the Franco-German *rapprochement* of the late 1920s, she did not use her developing strength to challenge Japan for the control of Port Arthur, known as 'sacred Russian soil' to both Tsarist and Soviet navies. If a Russian navy were ever established at Port Arthur with the economic power generated by the Five-year Plans behind it, Japan's position would be as precarious as it has become since the Second World War.

But such an event could not occur without some issue to the growing Sino-Soviet frictions after 1927. One possibility, the second implication for Japan of Russia's new position, was that Russia might overthrow China in a war arising from conflicts in Manchuria. That she intended to stand no interference from China with her position was clearly shown in 1929, when she taught Chang Hsueh-liang, the ruler of Manchuria, a sharp lesson for tampering with her rights in the Chinese Eastern Railway and forced him to accept a settlement favourable to herself. But, with a China free from internal strife and

with Manchuria united with China through Chang's acceptance of the Kuomintang flag in Manchuria, it was by no means
clear that Russia would always enjoy such easy victories. If
Soviet power were to be thrust from Manchuria, a country as
large as France and Germany combined, or if there were to be
an understanding between Russia and China, based on the
recognition of Soviet influence in Outer Mongolia and of Kuomintang rule in Manchuria, this would present Japan with a
third prospect, possibly the most bleak of all. Her hopes of
undisturbed enjoyment of the mineral and forest wealth of
Manchuria, promising release from dependence on Western
caprice and prospects for Japanese youth, many of whom despaired of any future on the poverty-stricken farms at home,
would be gone for ever. The Far East would lie under unchallenged Chinese control, with Japan forced to accept the
terms that were offered.

The moment chosen by Japan to exploit a largely bogus
'incident' on the South Manchuria Railway on the night of 18
September 1931 in order to bring all Manchuria under control
has always been recognised as highly propitious in that Western
Powers were fully occupied with domestic problems. Britain
was temporarily paralysed by the financial crisis which ruined
the Labour Government and, at one desperate moment, cast
doubt even on the reliability of the armed forces. The announcement of Britain's departure from the Gold Standard
and of the Mukden incident all but coincided; during October,
when Japanese troops strengthened their grip in one Manchurian city after another, Britain passed through one of the most
contentious General Elections in her history. The stunned
mood of the United States at the sudden ending of their golden
era of prosperity closed eyes and ears to events outside the
smitten country. The risk therefore that the Western Powers,
which had not even stood together in defence of their nationals'
rights in China against the Nationalists, would join at such a
moment and take the swift action required to stop the almost
unopposed Japanese conquest of faraway Manchuria, or would
jointly invade that country and bring down the puppet state of
Manchukuo erected by Japan after the conquest, was so remote
that it could be discounted.

In any event, the decision to strike did not rest with the
civilian government in Tokyo calculating the risks, but with
the army on the spot, which had a long-prepared plan for
Manchuria. This opinion was reached in a careful analysis
by the British Ambassador in Tokyo, Lindley, sent to the caretaker Foreign Secretary in the new National Government,

Lord Reading, on 1 October.[1] Japanese government since the restoration of the Emperor in 1868 had always, despite the democratic façade, been a balance of power between the military, supported by that group of financial and business interests which stood to gain from policies like the Twenty-one Demands, and the civilian elements which saw a more promising future for Japan in political stability and the peaceful economic penetration of China. During most of the 1920s the latter group, represented in the Liberal (Minseito) party, led by Baron Shidehara, had prevailed and nursed Japan through the period of reconstruction after the great earthquake of 1923. The power of the Army and Navy remained, however, within a constitution outwardly modelled on European democratic forms. The balance swung to the Right with the premiership of Baron Tanaka from 1927 to 1929, who set as the foreign policy of the Conservative (Seiyukai) party the messianic imperialism of the Tanaka Memorial, a lineal descendant of the Twenty-one Demands, in 1927. Even after the return to office of the Minseito party in 1929 the power of the ultra-chauvinists, flourishing in secret patriotic societies whose principle was government by assassination, was shown in the murder of the Prime Minister, Hamaguchi, on his return from the Geneva Naval Conference in 1930 and that of several other politicians who had offended.

With such an uneasy balance of forces at home, the Kwantung Army, led by masterless men like General Doihara and Major Tada, became a state within the state, though its ostensible purpose was merely to protect the South Manchuria Railway. Securely connected with business groups in Japan which looked to Manchuria and north China to solve the problems created by the farm crisis and the shrinkage of world trade, it was free to perform acts of force which, if successful, would provide a career open to the talents for young officers who refused to return to the farms, or, if unsuccessful, would throw discredit mainly on the Tokyo civilian government. The army leaders in Manchuria were probably too ignorant of the world outside to understand the timeliness of their action of 18 September. The spirit behind their decision, however, echoed the thoughts of the militarists and the Right in Japan itself, as they contemplated the larger movement of affairs in the Far East. For them the Mukden incident was timely in that it caught the West unawares. But it was timely in the more vital sense that unless Japan acted soon the whole balance of forces would in all likelihood begin to swing against her.

[1] *D.B.F.P.*, Second Series, VIII, pp. 698–702.

Our legions are brimfull, our cause is ripe:
The enemy increaseth every day,
We, at the height, are ready to decline.

The immediate collapse of all Chinese resistance in Manchuria, to the accompaniment of vain appeals from Nanking to the League of Nations, completed the rout of the Japanese Liberals and the Shidehara régime dropped from history in December 1931. Ten years earlier the British Government considered that hostile Western attitudes towards Japan would weaken the tendencies led by Shidehara. Now, paradoxically, Western passivity and the distaste of the British National Government for any action which might offend the Japanese during the Manchurian affair pushed Japanese democracy beneath waters from which it did not emerge until 1945.

The Japanese fear of a change in the balance of forces in the Far East to Japan's disadvantage was obscured from Western eyes by the immediate situation in Manchuria, which was being discovered by Western publics for the first time. To most people in the West, with their idea of states as integral entities dealing with each other across definite frontiers, it came as a surprise to learn that Manchuria, formally under Chinese sovereignty, was ruled by an overlord not appointed by the Chinese Government who relied mainly on his own skill and resources to survive, and was the subject of international agreements giving Russia and Japan rights akin to those of a sovereign in the country. Just as in 1936 it was hard for liberal-minded people in Britain to deny sovereignty over the Rhineland to Germany, so it was difficult, except for the more naïve who thought of China and Japan as wholly independent and separate states, not to agree that Japan had a position in Manchuria which might have to be defended by measures entirely improper for a foreign government to take in a completely independent country. Britain herself had prepared to take similar measures in Shanghai in 1927. Japan's rights in Manchuria, centred on the South Manchuria Railway, which, like all railways in barely developed countries, was more a form of local government than a medium of transport, are too well known to require description here. They were summed up in the report of the Lytton Commission sent by the League Council to investigate the local position in the words,

> This summary of the long list of Japan's rights shows clearly the exceptional character of the political, economic and legal relations created between that country and China in Manchuria. There is probably nowhere in the world an exact

parallel to this situation, no example of a country enjoying in the territory of a neighbouring state such extensive economic and administrative privileges.[1]

This complex of Japanese rights was threatened by Chinese nationalism in much the same way as British rights in the Yangtze valley and at Canton and Shanghai had been threatened only a few years before. The form in which this threat appeared, however, was not that of attacks by students and the newly organised Chinese workers, as in the campaign against British concessions, but the building by the Chinese of lines parallel to and competitive with the South Manchuria Railway in violation of an agreement of 1905 with Japan. The effect of this, especially in the atmosphere of tension arising from clashes in Manchuria between the Chinese and Korean settlers under Japanese protection, was to outflank the S.M.R. and cut it off from the carrying trade essential to its life. The Japanese could hardly adopt in reply the British policy of retreating from territorial rights and hoping for continued trade with an equal and fully sovereign China because their interest in China was not primarily commercial, although 40 per cent of Japan's foreign trade was with China. Japan's interest in Manchuria was in the first instance political and strategical. Defeat in Manchuria would be for Japan the equivalent of the occupation of the Low Countries by Napoleon or the Kaiser for Britain. But because the Lytton Commission dealt essentially with the local situation the Manchurian crisis was discussed in Europe and the United States as though it were chiefly a question of the protection of foreign rights in China and how far force was warranted in defending them. This prevented critics of Japan from understanding the larger political considerations behind her action and it confused her sympathisers as to the meaning of 18 September until Japanese power was firmly established over the whole of Manchuria and it was too late to do anything about it.

II

When the Manchurian crisis began the British economic connection with the country was slight. Its population of some 30 millions provided no market for British goods to compare with central and south China. In any case, when the Japanese sponsored state of Manchukuo was created in February 1932, thus ending the fiction that the only object of the operations was

[1] *Report of the Commission of Inquiry.* League of Nations Publication No. C. 663. M. 330, VII, Chapter III, Part 1.

to defend the S.M.R., the Japanese Government repeatedly assured Britain that Open Door principles would be respected. In April it was reported that British trade had been affected, though not seriously.[1] In July Eden, then Under-Secretary of State for Foreign Affairs, told the House that the Japanese assurances had been accepted and that no complaints had been received about trade discrimination against foreigners in Manchuria.[2] British investments in Manchuria were also on a minor scale and according to Eden no estimate of their size was possible. The chief British investment was the £1 million of British money sunk in the construction of the Peking–Mukden railway and secured on the Manchurian customs revenues collected at Dairen.[3] When the customs and excise administration office was seized by the Manchukuo authorities in June 1932 Britain 'expressed the hope' in Tokyo that foreign interests would not be affected.[4] In practice during the crisis the proceeds from Manchurian customs collected at Dairen were quietly remitted to Nanking less a proportion to cover the upkeep of the new régime; this was naturally in accord with the wish of the Japanese authorities to avoid alienating foreign states during their consolidation of the conquest of the country. But so long as this attitude continued the British Government felt that no intervention on behalf of its traders and investors was called for. In any case, as Sir John Simon, the Foreign Secretary put it, 'H.M. Government's interest in the territorial status of Manchuria is infinitely less than their interest in maintaining cordial relations with Japan'.[5]

The Government's position was strikingly different in regard to the serious hostilities which broke out in Shanghai on 28 January 1932 as a result of tensions between Chinese and Japanese residents in the Chapei quarter of the city and the Chinese boycott of Japanese goods which had begun in the previous June. As Simon explained, the government 'lost no time' in making urgent representations to both sides.[6] Before evening on 29 January Britain had sent a sharp note to Japan protesting against the Chapei attack and called on the United States to do likewise. H.M.S. *Berwick* was sent from Hong Kong with a battalion of infantry and one of artillery, and naval forces in the area were strengthened all the way round. British proposals

[1] 264 H.C. Deb. 5s. Col. 1385 (19 April 1932).
[2] 268 *ibid.*, Col. 416 (6 July 1932).
[3] 260 H.C. Deb. 5s. Col. 2080 (10 December 1931); E. M. Gull, in *British Economic Interests in the Far East*, gives a figure of £3 – £4 million for British interests in Manchuria before September 1931.
[4] 267 *ibid.*, Col. 2020 (30 June 1932).
[5] *D.B.F.P.*, Second Series, IX, p. 31.
[6] 261 H.C. Deb. 5s. Cols. 17–18 (2 February 1932).

consisting of five points were sent to Nanking and Tokyo. With the renewal of fighting in Shanghai in February after the Chinese rejection of a Japanese ultimatum of the 19th the British Minister at Nanking, Lampson, joined his American, French and Italian colleagues in strong protests to both sides. Britain also played a leading part in the settlement of the Shanghai crisis. The difference between British policies in the two situations, Manchuria, where local British interests were not extensive, and Shanghai, which was the heart of British commercial interests in China, was accounted for by Simon when he said in the adjournment debate in the House on 22 February that the government were:

> in a very special degree charged with the protection and defence of British interests and there is no part of the world in which it can be said with more complete truth than in the Far East that British interests are summed up in the words 'Peace and Trade.'[1]

When China was considered, as it tended to be in the Foreign Office, not as an independent country with a reliable central government, but a chaos of centrifugal forces making settled trade all but impossible, Peace and Trade seemed to depend, in Shanghai, on pacifying the belligerents and, in Manchuria, on refraining from embarrassing the Japanese. It was with this conception of China that Lindley, the Ambassador in Tokyo, had written to Reading immediately after the Mukden incident in September that:

> In considering the Chinese appeal H.M.G. will no doubt give due weight both to the fact that the Chinese have followed a most exasperating policy in Manchuria, where they have ... attempted to undermine the Japanese position, which after all rests largely on treaty rights, and to the obvious probability that Japanese action in Manchuria will react favourably on British interests in China.[2]

Local British interests were therefore the strongest motive governing British policy in China. There were, however, legal obligations to be heeded. Those arising from the League Covenant were most conspicuous in article 10, with its commitment to respect and preserve as against external aggression the existing territorial integrity and political independence of all Members of the League, which included both China and

---

[1] 262 H.C. Deb. 5s. Col. 182 (22 February 1932). British commercial interests in Shanghai were estimated in 1927 to be worth over £63 million; *D.B.F.P.*, Second Series, IX, p. 288.

[2] *D.B.F.P.*, Second Series, VIII, p. 667.

Japan.   Austen Chamberlain had twice stated on behalf of the
Baldwin Government in July 1928 that Britain recognised
Manchuria as a part of China.[1]   Eden said in February 1932
that this was accepted by the National Government, although
the Foreign Secretary, Simon, insisted that in the government's
view the S.M.R. and the land on which it stood were Japanese
property and that Japan was entitled to defend them against
the 'ill-organised Chinese banditry' prevalent in the neighbour-
hood.[2]   However, it was doubtful what exactly was the force
of article 10 considering the various interpretative resolutions
which had diluted it in the early years of the League and the
unwillingness of both Conservative and Labour Governments,
when the Draft Treaty of Mutual Assistance and the Geneva
Protocol were under discussion, to undertake general obligations
to defend the *status quo*.

If action was to be taken under article 10 it had to be agreed
that aggression on the part of Japan had taken place against
Chinese independence and integrity.   The government never
accepted this since they assumed in the first phase of the crisis,
from the September 'incident' to the formation of the Manchukuo régime, that only the defence of the railway was involved.   When this assumption was shown to be false by the
creation of Manchukuo, the government argued that this was
merely one of the Chinese splinter régimes which had risen and
fallen in Manchuria as well as other parts of China since the
collapse of the Manchu dynasty.[3]   This argument in its turn
became equally untenable, but by this time the speed with
which Japan's purpose in Manchuria was effected made any
action under article 10, had it been contemplated, seem like
an effort from a great distance to reverse a secure *fait accompli*,
rather than restraint applied by the world community against
patent aggression.   The swift transition of the Japanese action,
from defence of a railway line to the conquest of a country,
came as a surprise to everybody.   Strang, at the British Embassy in Moscow, was told by Leo Karakhan, the Soviet Vice-
Commissar in charge of Eastern and Far Eastern affairs, in
October that the Soviet Government were convinced that the
Japanese would not extend the area of their operations from
the region of the S.M.R. and had 'no fear whatsoever' that they
would occupy Harbin.[4]

As it happened, the Manchurian dispute came before the

[1] 219 H.C. Deb. 5s. Col. 2637 (13 July); 220 *ibid.*, Col. 1835 (30 July).
[2] 261 *ibid.*, Cols. 479–80 (8 February); 260 *ibid.*, Col. 467 (25 November 1931).
[3] Eden, 262 *ibid.*, Cols. 361–2 (22 February 1932).
[4] *D.B.F.P.*, Second Series, VIII, pp. 697–8.

League not in the form of an appeal to article 10, but as a Chinese request for consideration of the issue under article 11, by which Assembly or Council could be enjoined, at the request of any Member, to examine 'any circumstance whatever affecting international relations' which threatened to disturb international peace 'or the good understanding between nations upon which peace depends'. The Chinese delegation at the League Council, before which the crisis was brought on 22 September, was anxious not to have the question considered as a case of war, since they feared that this would give Japan belligerent rights in the whole of China. Hence at no stage of the dispute did they refer to article 16, stipulating the application of sanctions by Member-states in the event of an illegal resort to war. But, since no state of war was admitted to exist by either party, it was difficult to see how 'aggression', within the meaning of article 10, had occurred. The Manchurian affair in fact contradicted all the principal assumptions on which the League Covenant was based and in particular the idea that the typical situation which the international community would have to face, when the Covenant was invoked, would be a frontal attack by the armed forces of one state across the borders of another, with the rights and wrongs of the case clear from the outset. Above all, dealing with the Manchurian crisis demanded co-operation with the United States and thus exposed Wilson's failure to secure American membership of the League in its most vulnerable form. 'Our general conclusion,' ran the report of a committee of the League Council appointed to consider measures if Japanese forces refused to withdraw to the railway zone, 'is that it would be very difficult to take any action, whether under articles 10, 11, 15 or 16, unless the United States were at any rate benevolently neutral. Indeed any action which sought to exert moral pressure on Japan would require, to be effective, the active participation of America.'[1] Yet it was soon evident that neither was America in the mood for any effective measure of restraint on Japan, nor did the Pact of Paris or the Nine-Power Treaty of Washington require her to do more than express concern, consult and warn.

The then Secretary of State, Henry L. Stimson, though a warm admirer of the Chinese nationalist revolution and a firm adherent of the Rule of Law in international affairs, was at first anxious not to offend the Japanese and in doing so to weaken the liberal forces then in office in that country. When appealed to by the League Secretary-General, Sir Eric Drummond, on the applicability of the Pact of Paris to the dispute,

[1] *D.B.F.P.*, *Second Series*, VIII, p, 800.

he considered that 'it would be wise to avoid action which might excite nationalistic feeling in Japan in support of the military and against Shidehara'.[1] He opposed the appointment by the League of a neutral commission of inquiry on the ground that the civilian elements in Japan should be left to bring the position under control themselves.[2] The utmost to which Stimson was able to go was to issue to Japan and China the celebrated note of 7 January 1932 stating that no American recognition would be afforded to *de facto* situations or agreements impairing the rights of American citizens, the Open Door principle, or the Pact of Paris of 1928 for the renunciation of war as an instrument of national policy. Believing that the note's moral effect would be enhanced if a similar position were taken by a number of nations, he appealed to Britain and other League Members to do likewise. But the Stimson note was acknowledged to be, in the Secretary's own words, a 'substitute for sanctions'; it was intended to close all further discussion and no American reply was sent to the Japanese answer to the note.[3] The British Government agreed to the incorporation of the non-recognition principle, though in weaker form, in the League Assembly resolution of March 1932, which Stimson approved. But, given that Japan's grip on Manchuria was not likely to be relaxed by appeals to her sense of responsibility before world opinion, the question arose whether moral attitudes without material restraints did not do more harm than good. British politicians felt that America had been mainly responsible for the destruction of the Anglo-Japanese alliance, which had served as a channel of Western influence on Japanese policy; that she had been far from consistent in supporting Britain in the conflict with Chinese nationalism in the 1920s; and that Washington, without having the economic stake in China which Britain had, was seeking to embroil London with Tokyo while warning that American help could not be relied on, either in Europe or the Far East, if trouble should come. So trenchant a critic of appeasement as Winston Churchill wrote that the British Government could hardly be blamed 'if they did not seek a prominent role at the side of the United States in the Far East without any hope of corresponding American support in Europe'.[4]

This feeling of grievance in London against the United States explains the brusque treatment by the British Government of American proposals on the crisis, so inconsistent with

---

[1] Henry L. Stimson, *The Far Eastern Crisis*, p. 42.
[2] W. W. Willoughby, *The Sino-Japanese Controversy and the League of Nations*, p. 67.
[3] Stimson, *op. cit.*, pp. 92, 133.   [4] *The Second World War*, I, p. 68.

the British policy since the war of seeking common action with Washington at every point, and their unwillingness to form a united front with America. The communiqué issued by the Foreign Office and published in the Press on 11 January referring to the Stimson non-recognition note was drawn up by Sir V. Wellesley and initialled by Simon; it merely brushed aside the Secretary's appeal for a similar British note on the ground that it was unnecessary in view of repeated Japanese assurances as to the Open Door in Manchuria.[1] Eden spoke on the same lines in the House a month later, when he said that in view of the assurances given by Japan that she had no territorial ambitions in Manchuria and that she would respect the Open Door, there was no need for a British note on the American lines.[2] In the United States these statements not only sounded like a rebuff to Stimson, who had to face persistent charges from American opinion that he was overreaching himself, but also seemed proof that Britain was only interested in commercial profit and not in great world principles. On 17 February Simon was asked in the House by Seymour Cocks whether, in view of Japan's obvious invasion of Chinese territory, he would approach the United States, together with France, Germany and Italy, with a view to concerted action. The Foreign Secretary replied that the question was a matter for the League Powers, of whom Britain was only one, though she was acting in close concert with the United States.[3] In the following week he refused, when pressed, to add anything to this.[4]

These ill-mannered rebuffs to Washington, coupled with the government's dogged refusal to question in any way the sincerity of Japanese assurances, can only be ascribed to irritation with the American habit of invoking high-sounding principles without offering much in the way of practical assistance. The seeds of this irritation were laid in the first vital month or six weeks of the crisis, after which the damage was irreparable. During the second series of meetings of the League Council beginning on 14 October, after the bombing of Chinchow, near the border with China proper, the United States were invited to send a representative to sit with the Council in discussions on the application of the Pact of Paris to the situation. Hoover agreed to do so and on 16 October sent his Consul-General in Geneva, Prentiss Gilbert, to sit with the Council. After a formal opening statement, however, in which he described

---

[1] *D.B.F.P.*, Second Series, IX, p. 102; also Sir J. T. Pratt, *War and Politics in China*, London, 1943, pp. 226–7, 274–6.
[2] 262 H.C. Deb. 5s. Col. 360 (24 February 1932).
[3] 261 H.C. Deb. 5s. Col. 1613 (17 February 1932).
[4] 262 *ibid.*, Cols. 17–18 (22 February).

himself as authorised only to discuss a possible application of the Pact of Paris of 1928, the American played no further part in the Council's proceedings and withdrew from his temporary seat, mainly on account of criticism in the American Press, on 24 October.[1]　When the Council moved to Paris for its critical meeting on 16 November, when it was faced with an unblushing Japanese defiance of the Council's resolution on the withdrawal of Japanese forces to the railway zone, the American Ambassador in London, General Dawes, was sent to Paris to hold himself in readiness, but was left to decide for himself whether he should attend the Council.[2]　He resolved to remain in his quarters. On 19 November, when the news came of the fall of Tsitsihar, the capital of the northernmost province of Manchuria, Heilungkiang, General Dawes was asked whether he could define the American position in view of an impending appeal under article 15 which might involve sanctions.　Dawes could give no commitment.　Stimson explains the position in perhaps the most revealing passage in his memoirs.

On our part we manifestly could give no such commitment. Our Congress was not in session and there was no statutory authority under which the Executive could impose economic sanctions.　Furthermore, it was quite unlikely that any such authority would be granted by the Congress. . . . Under such circumstances manifestly we could not commit ourselves to the imposition of sanctions.　On the other hand, if the League of Nations desired to proceed under articles 15 and 16 of the Covenant and themselves to impose such sanctions, we were anxious not to discourage them or to put any obstacles or dangers in their path.[3]

In view of this American position and the ensuing lack of means available to the League for the forceful restraint of Japan, the British view was that the alternative policy, conciliation, was not consistent with public denunciations of one or other of the parties.

III

Throughout the crisis, from 18 September until 31 May 1933, when the Tangku Truce was signed creating a demilitarised zone of 5,000 square miles between Chinese and Japanese forces, it was clear that sanctions would never be seriously contemplated by Britain if they involved the risk of real conflict with Japan.　The use of military force on the substantial scale required to be effective and with no assurance of help from the

---

[1] Willoughby, *op. cit.*, p. 103.　　[2] Stimson, *op. cit.*, pp. 75–6.
[3] Stimson, *op. cit.*, pp. 76–7.

only country whose help was indispensable, the United States, would certainly have been intolerable to British public opinion, especially in view of the high probability of defeat, at least as far as the immediate object of freeing Manchuria from Japan's grasp was concerned.

The most forward advocates in the British Parliament of energetic action against Japan deliberately excluded the use of force. The first M.P. to call for action, the Liberal Geoffrey Mander, did not do so until 11 November when he denied that physical force would be necessary; economic, financial and moral pressure, he said, would be sufficient to compel Japan to realise that 'war is not going to be permitted to break out again'.[1] Since Japan did not in any case agree that a war was in progress it is perhaps unlikely that her mind would have been changed in this way even if the sanctions referred to could be generally applied, which, as we have seen, was doubtful. The leader of the Opposition, George Lansbury, while recognising the crisis as a challenge to the whole international order, went no further on 25 November, when he raised the question on the adjournment, than proposing a change 'in the long run' in British relations with countries which refused to honour international obligations.[2] On 17 February Seymour Cocks spoke of the withdrawal of Ambassadors and the severance of trade with Japan as the kind of action which Britain could take in company with other Powers.[3] In a foreign affairs debate on 31 October 1932 Attlee, moving a Labour motion which called for 'immediate, universal and substantial reduction of armaments on the basis of equality for all nations and the maintenance of Covenant principles by support for the Lytton Commission report', offered no specific proposals for sanctions; he merely suggested that Britain should give a 'bold lead' to the League and went on to urge the scaling down of armaments to the level imposed on Germany by the Versailles Treaty.[4] Attlee's belief that the 'masses of Japan' would effectively support a British lead on such terms seemed to betray some misunderstanding of the nature of the Japanese political system and the forces behind Japan's foreign policy.

Curiously enough, the trade embargo on which the Opposition insisted most strongly, that involving the supply of arms to the aggressor, was required by Lansbury to apply to both sides.[5] Advantage was quickly taken by Simon of this trap into which Lansbury's pacifism had led him when the Foreign Secretary

[1] 259 H.C. Deb. 5s. Cols. 201–2.   [2] 260 *ibid.*, Col. 464.
[3] 261 *ibid.*, Col. 1613.   [4] 270 H.C. Deb. 5s. Cols. 532–3.
[5] 275 *ibid.*, Col. 46 (27 February 1933).

announced in the House on 27 February 1933 that he had made inconclusive inquiries into the prospects for an international embargo on arms after Japan had refused to accept the report of the committee of 19 appointed by the League Assembly to consider the Lytton Report.   He then said that the Government had decided to prohibit the issue of licences for the export either to Japan or China of articles covered by the Arms Export Prohibition Order of 1931.[1]   This decision was approved by Mander, the most energetic Parliamentary champion of action against Japan who again disapproved of force; 'there are methods,' he said, 'which are far more effective and far less dangerous'.[2]   This attitude of the Opposition, together with the absence of any recommendation of compulsive measures in the Lytton Report, seemed to absolve the government from further effort to answer the insoluble question of what force to use and where to apply it.

The same was true in almost equal measure for trade and financial restraints on Japan.   The government could no doubt have been much more active, both in Geneva and Washington, in pressing for some general embargo on trade with Japan, had they really been determined to bring her to a halt. Considering the heavy dependence of that country on foreign raw materials and the sale of her products abroad, such a blockade might at least have forced her to offer guarantees that her assault on Chinese integrity was now ended.   But, quite apart from the question whether Britain and other League Members were really prepared to stop exporting to a country which not even the Lytton Commission had declared to be an aggressor and at a time when one of their chief anxieties was losses on foreign trade account, the first condition of any such blockade was American neutrality and, if possible, participation.   While Stimson might have been strong enough to secure the former, the Hoover administration was in no position to enforce the latter.   Simon told the Commons in announcing the arms embargo on 27 February 1933 that United States co-operation in this had been sought for but not attained, one reason being the lack of authority in the American Government at the time over the export of arms.[3]   The cessation of trade with Japan unilaterally by Britain and perhaps a few of the smaller countries, with no appreciable effect on her Manchurian policy so long as the United States possessed one-third of Japan's trade, would have been regarded as a strange contribution to solving the economic crisis which the National Government had been given a 'doctor's mandate' to tackle.

[1] 275 *ibid.*, Col. 59.   [2] *Ibid.*, Col. 116.   [3] *Ibid.*, Col. 56.

British policy, as Simon said, was 'clear, consistent and straightforward' at least in rejecting a sanctions programme and in following through the assumption that a Japan satisfied in Asia would be less troublesome in other regions of the Pacific.[1] This was the path of conciliation which British governments had always pursued in the League of Nations and seemed inevitable in the first phase of the dispute, when the issue appeared merely to be one of the safety of Japanese lives and property. Simon said on 30 November 1931, when it was becoming increasingly difficult to believe that that was the whole story, that the government were anxious 'to avoid re-course to sanctions either in the present or in any other dispute which may be brought before the League and for this reason they are concentrating along with other members of the Council on finding a solution by conciliation'.[2] Hence, considering the issue almost wholly in legal terms, Britain led the Council in holding that its resolutions under article 11 must be unanimous, which meant giving a veto to both China and Japan. In the government's view the Council's resolution of 24 October 1931 calling on Japan to complete the withdrawal of troops to the railway zone before the next meeting of the Council on 16 November was not binding since the Japanese delegate had not consented to it. At the same time British delegates were telling the Chinese at Geneva 'to maintain an absolutely correct attitude'.[3]

Britain was a prime mover in the appointment of the Com-mission of Inquiry by the Council in December 1931, since this was entirely consistent with the British view that conciliation had to be based on strictly impartial appreciations of the facts. The Report of the Commission, published in October 1932, came as an evident relief to the government since it emphasised that the facts of the situation in Manchuria were not as simple as the more enthusiastic advocates of collective security sup-posed. By this time, however, the Minseito Cabinet in Japan had disappeared, the Manchukuo régime was firmly established and the government in Tokyo were already considering their next move in China. The adoption of the principles of the Lytton Report by the League Assembly and the British deter-mination to go no further than the Report, and in particular not to revive the sanctions issue, were in effect confessions of the failure of a British conciliation policy for which there was, how-ever, no feasible alternative. Had the Manchurian dispute been

---

[1] *Ibid.*, Col. 50 (27 February 1933).
[2] 260 H.C. Deb. 5s. Col. 737.
[3] *D.B.F.P.*, Second Series, VIII, p. 772.

confined to the S.M.R. question with the parties otherwise well disposed towards each other, conciliation might have worked. But where two nationalisms were in conflict no middle position could be sought by a League Council no member of which, other than Japan and China themselves, was able or willing to do more than look at the facts and deliver a verdict.

What mainly exposed British policy, not as conspiratorial, as has often been claimed, but as effete and incapable of inspiring confidence was the remarkable credulousness on which it seemed to be based, and the impression it gave of permanently suspended judgment and fear of taking up a position lest a leisurely process of inquiry going on somewhere else might be affected. Almost every Japanese profession on the subject of Manchuria seemed to be unquestioningly accepted by government spokesmen, who thus could not avoid creating for themselves in the eyes of the world an image of naïveté which bordered on collusion with Japan. In this they were consistently encouraged by the British Ambassador in Tokyo, Lindley, who described Japanese assurances as 'completely genuine'.[1] Whenever reports were mentioned in Parliament of events which threw doubt on these professions, the standard reply was that no news had arrived through official channels and Japan should not be troubled with questions about unfounded rumours. Possibly the government felt, or had been assured by Japan, that such total lack of suspicion would serve to ingratiate Britain with Japan and thus improve the position of British businessmen in the new Manchuria. If so, they were singularly disillusioned by the announcement of the Greater East Asia Co-prosperity Sphere by Japan a few years later, from which Western capitalism was to be brutally excluded. The British were not alone, however, in their surprise; Stimson later reflected on the crisis that 'few observers then expected that Japanese forces and government would develop such a complete disregard of treaty obligations or world opinion'.[2]

Accompanying this strange British credulousness was the judicial impartiality of the Foreign Secretary, Sir John Simon, who appeared to regard the whole transaction rather as a proceeding taking place in the Royal Courts of Justice in the Strand. The object of the exercise, in his view, was to arrive at a certain legal truth, the best means to that end being the total suspension of judgment and action until the court had declared its findings. What to do with the verdict when given, or how to prevent the situation deteriorating while the jury was out, did not seem to occupy his thoughts, save in a negative

[1] *D.B.F.P.*, Second Series, VIII, p. 701.   [2] *The Far Eastern Crisis*, p. 51.

sense. 'It would be quite improper for anyone,' he said in the House on 22 February 1932, 'to attempt to pronounce a partial or interim judgment in a matter when everything depends on the report which will have to be made by the League, recognised on both sides as proceeding from a complete sense of impartiality.'[1] To expect a report on the position to fulfil such high requirements was almost to damn it in advance. Moreover, when the Lytton Report appeared in October, the government firmly refused to be drawn into commenting on it until the Japanese had had their six weeks in which to express their opinion to the League Council. 'It is not fair and it is not right,' Simon said on 10 November, 'after you have promised to listen to and to read the observations of one of the parties to pronounce a judgment before you have seen them.'[2]

The scrupulous respect of this honest lawyer, quite untutored in world politics, for fair play and judicial impartiality might have been more impressive had there been any indication that it would be followed, after judgment was given, by action biased in favour of the verdict. But such action was never in sight, and hence the sense of anti-climax was all the more devastating when at length, after Circumlocution Office methods of inquiry and patient hearings of all sides, the Foreign Secretary declared that that was the end of the story. As he frankly said in the Commons debate on the Lytton Report on 27 February 1933:

> I think I am myself enough of a pacifist to take the view that, however we handle this matter, I do not intend my own country to get into trouble about it. . . . There is one great difference between 1914 and now and it is this: in no circumstances will this Government authorise this country to be party to this struggle.[3]

Considering that this had been the government's position from the outset—as early as December 1931 Simon had minuted on a Foreign Office memorandum 'no one proposes that we should pick a quarrel with Japan'[4]—it is not easy to see exactly what the long process of inquiry had been for, except to enlighten historians as to the facts in the Manchurian case. It may, however, be argued that the curious naïveté shown by the government and their apparent inability to see the direction in which Sino-Japanese relations were moving did more to inform the dictators in the 1930s of the British state of mind than the government's actual failure to act.

[1] 262 H.C. Deb. 5s. Col. 183.   [2] 270 H.C. Deb. 5s. Col. 537.
[3] 275 *ibid.*, Cols. 58–9.   [4] *D.B.F.P.*, Second Series, IX, p. 33.

CHAPTER XV

THE WORLD REARMS

I

WHEN the long-prepared world disarmament conference[1] met in Geneva on 2 February 1932 the political setting was unfavourable in every respect except for the fervent desire of the peoples of the world for an effective conclusion to the conference, as shown by the mass of petitions which strained the conference tables. On the morning of the opening session Japanese bombs were falling on Chapei and the first meeting of the conference had to be postponed to allow the League Council to review events in the Far East. The conference also met almost at the nadir of the world economic depression which had been shaking men's belief in the future since the Wall Street crash eighteen months before. While the depression supplied some inducement to cut spending on armaments, it also evoked a nervous, introverted attitude among the major countries, especially Britain and the United States, making them even more hesitant than before about commitments to schemes of international security which the 1920s had shown to be the indispensable condition of disarmament. But it was in Germany, whose impatience the conference was partly intended to satisfy, that the political situation had most seriously worsened, and this despite the Allied evacuation of the Rhineland on 30 June 1930, almost five years before the date fixed by the Versailles Treaty.

At the Reichstag elections in September 1930 the rival Communist and National Socialist parties had made notable gains at the expense of the constitutional groups, the Nazis winning 107 seats out of a total of 577 as compared with 12 out of 491 Reichstag seats at the previous elections. This shift towards extremes forced on the German representative on the Preparatory Commission, Count Bernstorff, a more hostile attitude towards the draft convention drawn up by the Commission, and especially towards article 53, with its insistence on the sanctity of existing treaties. The German Minister of Defence described the draft convention as 'anything but a suitable basis for the work of the conference'. The British Foreign Office

[1] The official title was 'Conference for the Reduction and Limitation of Armaments.'

concluded that a 'good deal will have to be done for (the Germans) in the direction of equality before we can hope to bring them into line'.[1] Another disturbing feature as the Preparatory Commission's labours drew to a close in December 1930 was the alignment of the other two dissatisfied states, Russia and Italy, at Germany's side, though for different reasons. This 'revisionist front' was clearly shown in its successful resistance to the appointment of Benes, the symbol of the successor states, as President of the conference. Russia, like Germany, had an interest in the reduction of the military strength of the Western Powers to inoffensive levels and had promoted the Litvinov proposal for total disarmament, unceremoniously swept aside by the Preparatory Commission in April 1929, with this end in view. Italy found in Germany an ally in her struggle for parity with France, with whom her relations on the eve of the conference were said by her Foreign Minister, Count Grandi, to be 'worse than at any previous time'.[2] The effect of this revisionist collaboration was to make France more determined than ever to maintain her three principles: no disarmament without security guarantees; no disarmament without effective supervision; and no revision of treaties.

As though these discouragements were not enough, the conference President, Arthur Henderson, who had been British Foreign Secretary when the Preparatory Commission ended its labours, was now a private individual after the Labour party's *débâcle* in 1931. This change of role assured him greater impartiality in the eyes of the delegates, but the events of 1931 could not but arouse distaste in Henderson's mind for the titular head of the British delegation, MacDonald, and other Ministers of the National Government. When to all this was added the uncertainty of the impending French and German elections, delegates who heard Benes privately say that a 'less opportune moment for the conference could not be conceived' could hardly disagree.[3] But there is such a thing as the force of events. No country could suggest postponing the conference; everyone wished to make a start before the reparations conference met at Lausanne in June. Public opinion was impatient, Germany even more so.

The draft disarmament convention, after five years' labour in the Preparatory Commission, reflected a wide measure of agreement on general principles, such as the limitation of effectives, budgetary controls for land war materials, the

---

[1] *D.B.F.P.*, Second Series, III, p. 459.
[2] *Ibid.*, p. 463.
[3] *Ibid.*, p. 500.

extension of the principles of the London naval conference and the banning of chemical and bacteriological warfare.[1] The basic issues which had run like hardened arteries through the Preparatory Commission's discussions, however, the question of reserves, of security machinery to replace the abandoned armaments and the means of supervising the convention, were never resolved. On these issues Britain, with some backing from the United States, found herself automatically ranged against France and the acquiescent band of France's clients. The draft was therefore never used as the basis of the conference. Instead the Powers produced their own plans, tailored to their own requirements, and their mutual incompatibility at points which looked to the layman like matters of detail but were in fact decisive was at once apparent. The French plan was circulated before British representatives had time to examine the contents of their brief-cases; it was, as feared, an uncompromising marriage of an international police force with compulsory arbitration, and the union was plainly intended as indissoluble.[2] Simon remarked that Britain would adopt a 'benevolent attitude' but only towards 'particular local arrangements likely to increase security in particular areas'.[3] Mac-Donald wanted to 'strengthen the expression and influence of international opinion' rather than talk about a world police force.[4] Italy had no sympathy for the French plan, while Litvinov pleaded once more for wholesale disarmament. Then came Simon's considered statement on the French proposals on 22 April, after an Easter recess in which Hitler had polled 13 million votes in an unsuccessful bid for the Presidency. This was essentially a plea for qualitative disarmament based upon the abolition of 'offensive' weapons, though with some slight provision for internationalisation of armed forces mainly intended for French eyes.

Clearly the only condition on which France would or could agree to the abandonment of weapons denied to the Germans in 1919, which was Simon's answer to the question of inequality of treatment posed by Germany, was a new German undertaking to keep the peace, underwritten by a British or, if possible, an Anglo-American guarantee. Unfortunately the more the movement towards the Right in Germany continued the less willing the French were to lower their terms. The crux seemed reached on 24 April when the German Chancellor, Brüning, made his way to Geneva to wrest from the conference a form of

---

[1] For the text of the draft convention see *Documents on International Affairs, 1931*, published by the Royal Institute of International Affairs, London, 1932, pp. 18–39.
[2] *D.B.F.P.*, Second Series, III, p. 506.   [3] *Ibid.*, pp. 509–10.   [4] *Ibid.*, p. 517.

words relating to German equality which might enable him to steal the thunder of the Nazis. Increased National Socialist gains in municipal elections in Prussia, Bavaria, Württemberg, Anhalt and Hamburg in early April suggested that if Brüning could bring some such concession back from Geneva the Nazis could safely be offered a post or two in the Cabinet on terms which would emasculate them. Discussions were held at Geneva on 26 April between MacDonald, Secretary of State Stimson and the Chancellor concerning a new arrangement to replace the hated Part V of the Versailles Treaty which would legalise Germany's possession of weapons denied to her by the Treaty while firmly limiting her strength. The French Prime Minister, Tardieu, was invited to join the talks and seemed within an ace of doing so when the French Ambassador in Berlin was told by the Defence Minister, the time-serving von Schleicher, that Brüning's days as Chancellor were numbered. This forecast turned out to be correct when, on the last day of May, Hindenburg summoned the unpredictable von Papen to replace Brüning. MacDonald was at once criticised in Britain for the collapse of this delicate structure of hopes, in that he refrained from attempting to force the hand of the French by publicising Brüning's offer of German arms limitations and thus saving the Weimar Republic's last staunch leader. Events were, however, moving fast of their own accord in Germany, Brüning himself having been kept in office in the summer of 1931 only through the announcement of the Hoover moratorium on war debts and reparations. Moreover, the French had shown themselves too firm throughout the disarmament discussions of the previous decade to be stampeded into accepting German claims without a greater instalment of security than the April talks envisaged. Tardieu exclaimed that Germany had already exceeded the military limits set by Part V of the Treaty. Who could trust her to observe new limits once she became stronger?[1]

Meanwhile, British efforts to secure agreement on the abolition of offensive weapons were meeting with all the expected difficulties. The British Chiefs of Staffs themselves advised the Cabinet on the impossibility of distinguishing between defensive and offensive weapons.[2] Nevertheless, since the distinction, if it could be made, might help resolve the Franco-German dilemma, its feasibility was upheld, at least until prolonged discussion in the Land and Naval Commissions of the conference during April showed that a weapon's offensiveness depends, not on its character, but on the circumstances in which

[1] *D.B.F.P.*, Second Series, III, p. 512.   [2] *Ibid.*, Second Series, V, p. 249.

it is used, and these cannot be defined in advance in a disarmament treaty. The British delegation was then driven by the logic of its demand for the abolition of military aircraft, as offensive weapons, to require the internationalisation of all civil aircraft, which for obvious reasons could not be effected by a disarmament conference. Since the attempt to dissuade Germany from seeking offensive weapons by illegalising them was thus frustrated, an alternative approach was tried by MacDonald at the Lausanne Conference which met in June 1932 to reach a final reparations settlement. MacDonald first suggested to Herriot, now French Premier after Tardieu's fall, a 'clean slate' abolition of war debts and reparations, and, when this failed, sought agreement on the abrogation of the 'war guilt' clause of the Versailles Treaty and the precise delimitation of the scale of rearmament to be conceded to Germany, while Germany on her side would make one final reparation payment. At the Lausanne meetings MacDonald's formula was accepted in principle by Herriot and von Papen, but mutterings at once began in both France and Germany and Herriot was obliged to retract. The final declaration issued from Lausanne on 9 July therefore made no allusion to the German claims with regard to war guilt and equality of arms.[1] MacDonald was further censured by German opinion for refusing to make a purely British statement on either of the two issues.

The Prime Minister's reasons for reticence, when he had gone to such lengths to secure French acceptance of the German claims, seemed to lie in his need for French support against the Hoover disarmament proposals which the President instructed Gibson to read out at the General Commission of the conference on 22 June. The Hoover plan, behind which was rising irritation in the United States at the failure of the Geneva conference to 'cut through the brush', focused upon a one-third cut in land forces, except for police personnel, together with the abolition of all tanks, large mobile guns and air bombardment, the reduction of the Washington tonnages for capital ships by one-third and of agreed levels in other categories by one-quarter, and an all-round reduction of cruiser strengths by one-quarter, these cuts to be based on the London naval treaty figures.[2] Baldwin made clear, not without embarrassment, in the Commons on 7 July that the American proposals would make the British Army, already insignificant for a Great Power, incapable of fulfilling its imperial responsibilities: that the Navy could not be further reduced; that light tanks of less than

---

[1] Misc. No. 7 (1932). Final Act of the Lausanne Conference, Cmd. 4126, p. 5.
[2] D.B.F.P., Second Series, III, pp. 606–8.

20 tons were most inoffensive; and that bombing from the air
had its uses on the margins of Empire.[1] The Hoover plan thus
had the surprising effect of putting Britain on the side of France,
whose army was so sacred that guns from the Crimean war,
preserved as public relics, could not be scrapped without an
outcry in Paris. Japan, too, objected, while the German and
Soviet welcome to the Hoover principles widened the gulf between the revisionists and the Entente. The Anglo-French
alliance, thus revived by Hoover, was further strengthened on
13 July when Simon announced a strange device attached to
the Entente banner, namely an accord, signed in Paris that
morning, pledging the two countries to 'exchange views with
one another with complete candour concerning, and to keep
each other mutually informed of, any question coming to
their notice similar in origin to that now so happily settled at
Lausanne which may effect the European régime'.[2]

By the summer of 1932, after six months' talk, the disarmament conference had made no headway with the central
dilemma that a European security system must be forged strong
enough, and soon enough, to contain the German demand for
equality, or France and her partners would refuse to cut their
forces by man or gun. Summarising the position in the House in
July Simon referred to a comprehensive resolution he intended
to submit to the conference welcoming the 'interconnectedness'
inspiring the Hoover proposals, while rejecting the proposals,
listing a dozen propositions 'which we believe we can get
the conference to accept', and inviting the Powers especially
interested in the reduction of effectives or naval disaramament
to get together and do what they could.[3] The resolution
carried at Geneva at the summer adjournment against German
and Soviet opposition was based on this outline and showed
that the only definite commitment undertaken by those who
voted for it was the renunciation of chemical and bacteriological warfare, which had already been declared illegal by
the Geneva convention of 1925. 'A more wholesale admission
of failure and incompetence it would be difficult to find,' a
British authority on disarmament wrote of the Simon resolution.[4] Disappointment was at once voiced by the German
delegate, Nadolny, who told the General Commission on 22
July that his government 'could not undertake to continue its
collaboration if a satisfactory solution on this point'—that is,
the demand for *Gleichberechtigung*—'which for Germany is a

---

[1] 268 H.C. Deb. 5s. Cols. 624–9; Misc. No. 6 (1932), Cmd. 4122.
[2] 268 H.C. Deb. 5s. Col. 1374.   [3] 268 H.C. Deb. 5s. Col. 1249 (12 July 1932).
[4] John W. Wheeler-Bennett, *The Disarmament Deadlock*, p. 55.

decisive one, is not reached by the time the conference resumes its work'.[1]

It was, however, incumbent upon Britain not to allow the conference to be shattered between the Berlin hammer and the Paris anvil. What British compromises had effected in Franco-German affairs time and again since the war they might effect again. MacDonald accordingly issued an invitation on 4 October to France, Germany and Italy to meet with him for an exchange of views on the German claim. These discussions were held in Geneva during the last months of the year, despite Germany's reluctance to have it thought that she was being dragged back to the conference by the rear door. Their development, however, served only to bring more fully into view the rock on which the vessel of disarmament was foundering. The French position, as disclosed by Paul-Boncour at the disarmament conference on 4 November, was that any acceptance of the German claim for equality of rights would be impossible for France save on the basis of the French disarmament plan, and the minimum requirements of this were effective international control, a European security pact to cover the whole Continent (that is, including the successor states) on the basis of mutual assistance and a guarantee of help in case of need from the United States, and the principle of short-service national armies with limited effectives. The last item was hopefully seized upon by Simon in the Commons on 10 November, when he said that French agreement to a short-service Reichswehr amounted to an 'admission that the Versailles Treaty was not sacrosanct', since the Treaty had imposed a long-service professional army on Germany, which she now found inconvenient.[2] But the most that the Foreign Secretary proposed to ask of Germany, in return for freedom to acquire gradually weapons now prohibited and the acceptance of limits on military strength in the disarmament convention rather than Part V of the treaty, was an undertaking not to resort to force. 'The disregard of such an assurance on the part of anybody,' Simon characteristically went on, 'would mobilise world opinion and domestic opinion to a large extent against the disregard of that assurance.'[3] This weak proposal, which would merely have extended the self-denying ordinance of the Pact of Paris from war to force without providing means of enforcement in the event of resort to either, was advanced again by Simon at Geneva on 17 November.[4] Again it was confronted by the doubting face of France.

[1] *D.B.F.P.*, Second Series, III, p. 589.   [2] 270 H.C. Deb. 5s. Col. 541.
[3] *Ibid.*, Col. 546.   [4] Misc. No. 11 (1932), Cmd. 4189.

The gulf was not bridged by talks between MacDonald and Herriot at Geneva on 3 December, which von Neurath joined, but France found it less and less possible to postpone acceptance of the German claim now that pressure was being applied from Washington, where it was feared that further delay would mean the final break-up of the conference. Hence Paul-Boncour finally agreed to join with MacDonald, Simon, the American delegate Norman Davis, von Neurath and Baron Aloisi on 11 December in a formula which accepted with qualifications the principle of equality of rights 'within a system which would provide security for all nations'.[1] On the basis of this formula Germany returned to the Bureau when it met again on 23 January 1933 and to the plenary conference when it resumed on 2 February. But by the first of these dates Germany had moved a further step towards the gulf and by the second yet another. On 4 December, a week before the signing of the compromise formula, von Schleicher displaced von Papen as Chancellor and the latter resolved to strengthen his position by making peace with the Nazis. The outcome of this alliance was the summoning of Hitler to the Chancellorship on 30 January after a breach between Prussian Junker forces and von Schleicher when the Chancellor during his brief period of office exposed the misuse of government 'Osthilfe' funds to line the pockets of the great landowners. Hitler did not, as legend has it, 'seize' power. He came to office in a constitutional manner after von Schleicher's temerity had made his own position impossible and when von Papen engineered the Nazi leader into power to be, as he supposed, his puppet. But this did not mean that Hitler's accession would not toughen the German attitude at Geneva as Nazi power at home was consolidated.

By the compromise formula of 11 December, for which MacDonald had worked so hard, Germany's acquisition of the weapons denied to her in 1919 was to be gradual, and in any case was dependent upon her inclusion in a general arms limitation which it was the business of the conference to determine. Strictly speaking, if the disarmament convention was never agreed (and the prospects appeared remote at the end of 1932), Germany would still be bound by the military clauses of the Versailles Treaty. But it was the vainest of hopes to suppose that these articles would ever again possess enforceable validity. Germany had struck off the military fetters of Versailles merely by making statements and refusing to attend conferences. As for France, the only result of the declaration could be to

[1] R.I.A., *Documents on International Affairs, 1932*, pp. 233–4.

strengthen her opposition to any disarmament. The 'system of security' which was supposed to justify and render harmless the acceptance of the German claim could not be other than a cheque drawn on an empty bank. Britain had repeatedly made clear that commitments beyond Locarno could not be contemplated and the French, for reasons given in an earlier chapter, were not satisfied with Locarno.[1] It was impossible for Frenchmen to believe, with Simon, in German declarations to refrain from force, all the more so after the accession to the Chancellorship of Hitler, who declared at the inauguration of the Reich Ministry of Propaganda in March 1933, 'I will fight against and extirpate the philosophy of Marxism and also the idea of peace'. The only parties to the December compromise likely to take the renunciation of force seriously were Britain and the United States, and their use of force against the new Germany was now becoming essential to France.

II

The moment for rescuing the disarmament conference therefore seemed already passed when the British Government embarked upon a salvaging operation in March 1933. It has been argued that if this effort had been made earlier, in Bernstorff's or Brüning's day, the conference might have been saved: Germany, before Hitler's arrival would have been more amenable and France might have accepted less far-reaching guarantees of security than she asked for in 1933. It is none the less doubtful whether the slide towards extremism in Germany can primarily be accounted for by the failure of the Western Powers to accept the German claim for equality until the eleventh hour. The Versailles *Diktat*, which every German Foreign Minister was bound to denounce, served rather to focus the teeming resentments of lower-middle-class Germans than act as their cause. No agreement by the Allies to revise this or that article of the treaty could satisfy Germany's discontent with her international position; liquidation of the 1919 servitudes, such as the ending of the Rhineland occupation in 1930 and the closing of the reparations account in 1932, seemed only to concentrate dissatisfaction on other claims. On the other hand, it is improbable that the French would ever have consented to reduce their forces to Germany's level under the Versailles Treaty, or to the revised level contemplated by German politicians, without British, and possibly American, agreement to come to France's assistance and that of her allies in the event of a German attack.

[1] See above, Chapter X.

At no time were Britain and the United States prepared for such agreement. Consultation in cases of breach of the Pact of Paris or the disarmament convention was the utmost to which Britain was willing to go. The most that the United States would promise, said Roosevelt, was that if the European states made a collective effort to resist aggression Washington would do nothing to oppose them, provided it approved the general character of that effort in the first place.[1] Moreover, the British Government's insistence during the Geneva conference upon basing the political conditions of disarmament on the Briand–Kellogg Pact, rather than the sanctions machinery of the Covenant, seemed to imply, first, that British isolationism had if anything increased since the 1920s and, secondly, that Britain was more determined than ever not to enter security arrangements without the United States, as a founder of the Pact of Paris, as her partner. Whereas in 1924, when the Geneva Protocol was under discussion, there were moments when it seemed possible that the Labour Government might commit itself to sanctions based on a general definition of aggression, in 1933 the National Government was too shaken by the economic events in which it had its origins to do more than utter appeals for the peaceful solution of disputes.

All this was made abundantly plain in the disarmament scheme, for which Eden was chiefly responsible, which Mac-Donald presented to the conference on 16 March. As if realising that no amount of advocacy would save the plan, the Prime Minister then immediately left for Rome to discuss Mussolini's proposal for a four-Power pact. The British draft began with a security chapter intended as an alternative to the French plan based upon provision for consultation in the event of breach or threatened breach of the Pact of Paris, though no decision to act could be taken without the concurrence of all the Great Powers. There followed a scheme for the limitation of effectives reckoned by the number of days' duty and with an eight months' maximum period of service for continental armies. Definite though provisional figures were laid down for each state. War material was dealt with on a qualitative basis only, with a maximum weight stipulated for guns. The provisions of the London naval treaty were to be extended to France and Italy and the whole naval position stabilised until the conference met in 1935 to revise the Washington Treaty. Fighting planes were to be limited during the five-year transitional period before the proposed convention came into effect, military and naval aircraft gradually abolished, with

[1] *D.B.F.P.*, Second Series, V, p. 158.

effective supervision of civil aviation, and bombing from the air illegalised 'except for police purposes in outlying regions'. A Permanent Disarmament Commission was to be established with wide powers of inspection and control.[1]

Despite the weakness of the security chapter of the British draft, French criticism was less marked than the extreme German hostility. The German delegate, Nadolny, was violently opposed to the standardisation of continental armies on a short-service basis since the Reichswehr had come to favour the professional army to which she was committed by the Versailles Treaty, though on a six-year basis rather than the twelve years laid down in the Treaty. The standardisation of the Reichswehr, Nadolny said, should be left to the Disarmament Commission. Nor did he agree that such paramilitary formations as the S.S., the S.A. and the Stahlhelm should be counted in Germany's military strength for the purpose of limitation. These statements, which Eden described as 'so preposterous that they would, if known, only produce an explosion of feeling which might be dangerous',[2] were accompanied by highly belligerent measures in Germany. The Nazi Storm Troops were incorporated into the Reich police, thus anticipating the argument that they were part of the new German Army and at the same time violating an Allied decision on the organisation of the German police forces of June 1925.[3] Then, on 11 May, an article by von Neurath appeared in the *Leipziger Illustrierte Zeitung* announcing in plain language Germany's intention to rearm whatever the results of the Geneva conference. Eden at once saw the German delegation at Geneva and said that there could be no German rearmament: 'I said His Majesty's Government were resolutely opposed to it. . . . Recent events in Germany had only served to strengthen this determination.'[4] Two days later, however, von Papen extolled Germany's might in a speech in which he urged German mothers to bear more babies, while the Cabinet in London read a dispatch from the Ambassador in Berlin, Rumbold, which stated that 'even when allowance is made for exaggeration attendant upon a political campaign, enough remains to make it highly probable that rearmament and not disarmament is the aim of the new Germany'. Reviewing the writings of Colonel Hierl, a former Reichswehr officer now appointed to head a new department of the German Ministry of Labour intended to control the

---

[1] For the text of the British plan see Cmd. 4279 (1933).
[2] *D.B.F.P.*, Second Series, V, pp. 210–11.
[3] *Ibid.*, pp. 29–30.
[4] *Ibid.*, p. 224.

Nazi Volunteer Labour Corps, Rumbold wrote: 'what Hierl probably means can be more accurately expressed by the formula: Germany needs peace until she has recovered such strength that no country can challenge her without serious and irksome preparations.'[1]

These alarming intimations were received to the accompaniment of strong criticism in the Commons of Hitler's anti-Jewish measures, and a sharp warning was administered to Berlin by Lord Hailsham in the Lords on 11 May.[2] When this was followed by another from Paul-Boncour the German Chancellor decided that his spokesmen had overstepped the mark. Restraining his normal cataract of words by placing in front of himself a sheet of paper with the phrase 'leise und langsam' ('softly and slowly') written on it, Hitler made a conciliatory speech in the Reichstag on 17 May. This enabled the MacDonald plan to be accepted in principle by the General Commission at Geneva on 7 June and Henderson to go off on a tour of Europe to help things forward during the summer recess. But that the new Germany was in no mood for further argument was apparent on 28 June, marked as a Day of Mourning in the Reich for the signing of the Versailles Treaty. Goebbels told Berliners on that day to be patient for eight years; in that time Germany would be 'turned into a furnace of patriotic national feeling such as the world has never experienced'.[3]

In the aftermath of Hitler's Reichstag speech of 17 May it was just possible to believe that disarmament discussions in the various capitals during the summer were making headway. The compromise which began to emerge was that the supervision system should be tried out during the first phase and the French thus satisfied as to its effectiveness, while the military strength of the armed Powers would be limited but not actually reduced. During this phase the Reichswehr would be permitted to expand to the levels permitted by the convention, though always on a short-service basis. During the second phase disarmament proper would be put into effect without discriminating against any state. Within this scheme was left room for differences of opinion (which did not fail to appear) as to whether disarmament should begin before or after the complete transformation of the Reichswehr. Simon explained the compromise to the conference on the morning of 14 October, but in the afternoon the President, Henderson, announced a bombshell: Hitler had sent notice that Germany was leaving

---

[1] *Ibid.*, pp. 47–55. [2] 87 H.L. Deb. 5s. Cols. 897–9.
[3] *D.B.F.P.*, Second Series, V, p. 389.

the conference at once. A week later he quitted the League as well. These actions received an automatic popular endorsement on 12 November. Six days later the Chancellor, asked for his terms for returning to the conference, obliged by giving them. They included recognition of Germany's right to conscript an army of 300,000 men and possess all the weapons forbidden by the Versailles Treaty which the conference could agree upon as 'defensive' only, the exclusion of Germany's paramilitary organisations from the scope of disarmament, the exemption of civil aviation from supervision, and the return of the Saar to Germany without plebiscite.[1] No conference of fifty-odd states could consider such an application for an overdraft from the makers of the Versailles Treaty, and the Bureau adjourned the conference on 22 November to allow 'parallel and supplementary efforts' to resolve the crisis to be carried on by ordinary diplomacy.

The alarm aroused in France by these German actions was expressed in a note to Berlin on 1 January 1934 which denounced the demands as a breach of the compromise signed by the Powers on 11 December 1932; this, the French said, accepted the claim for equality but only on the basis of the standardisation of continental armies as contemplated in the British plan. The French note then went on to propose a form of the MacDonald principles under which French effectives would be reduced during the first period, no definition of the length of which was offered, while German forces on the basis of a standardised, short-service army slowly increased to meet the French total of effectives. Only during the second period would the Reichswehr come into possession of material denied to it by the Versailles Treaty.[2] Hitler rejoined with a sarcastic note on 19 January which pointed out that the French definition of effectives excluded France's considerable colonial armies and then rejected the proposal to standardise armies and to count 'sporting and educational' bodies among effectives. He did agree, however, to submit these organisations to a form of international inspection provided other signatories of the convention did the same for theirs. But the Chancellor chiefly objected to the French contention that weapons hitherto forbidden to Germany should come into her hands only after an indefinite period of years. That, he said, was both contrary to the principle of non-discrimination and ignored the needs of the expanded Reichswehr envisaged in the French plan.[3]

[1] R.I.I.A., *Documents on International Affairs, 1933*, pp. 328–32.
[2] Misc. No. 3 (1934), Cmd. 4512, pp. 3–8.
[3] Cmd. 4512, pp. 8–15.

When Mussolini saw Simon in Rome on 3 and 4 January he took the resigned view that the German claim to an army of 300,000 men had a 'juridical and moral force' behind it, seeing that the conference had accepted the principle of equality twelve months before and in the meantime France and her allies had shown no readiness to reduce their military effectives. He also doubted the feasibility of the standardisation principle on which the MacDonald plan hinged and German opposition focused.[1] The British Cabinet was loath, however, to accept this pessimism about France and less inclined than the Duce to resignation over German rearmament. In a strongly-argued circular of 29 January they made a further effort by way of offering a series of modifications of the MacDonald plan based on the abolition of 'offensive' weapons and the building of a middle ground between French political conditions and German pressure for weapons to touch and feel. It was first proposed that the security arrangements of the original plan should be extended to include a breach or threatened breach of the disarmament convention itself, if this was reported by the Permanent Commission to be set up to supervise the convention. Next, some compromise should be possible between the figure for effectives contemplated in the original plan for France, Germany, Italy and Poland, that is, 200,000 each, and Hitler's demand for an army numbering 300,000. The principle of army standardisation should be persisted in, though in appropriate cases the eight-month period of service should be extended to one of twelve months. Germany's offer to subject quasi-military formations to supervision should be accepted, and if at the end of two years the Permanent Disarmament Commission had not agreed on the abolition of naval and military aircraft, Germany should no longer be denied the right to have them. Such was the revised British plan.[2]

The replies of Paris and Berlin, like all pronouncements by the two capitals on issues where technical details and political overtones were merged, threw into relief the fundamental conflict. The reply from France, handed to the Foreign Office by her Ambassador in London on 19 March, complained that the illicit rearmament pursued by Germany for many years was entirely inconsistent with the Covenant provision for disarmament within a scheme of general security and saw no reason why this rearmament should be urged as a reason why other states should disarm. France refused to accept Germany's proposed army of 300,000 men or any figure based upon it

[1] *Ibid.*, pp. 15–20.
[2] Misc. No. 2. (1934), Cmd. 4498.

without inquiry into the existing condition of the German army. Finally, the note said, such wide-ranging disarmament measures as those proposed by Britain in her draft convention could only be contemplated if linked with adequate 'guarantees of execution'. The French Government denied that an undertaking to consult in the event of a violation of the convention was 'sufficient to ensure the rectification of an established failure to observe the convention'. They dreaded long discussions with British Ministers on whether Germany had broken the law while the Reichswehr swept over their country. The only framework of security remained the League, to which, they insisted, Germany must return.[1] The German reply of 16 April, based largely upon talks between Hitler and Eden in Berlin on 21 February, seemed more conciliatory when read in isolation from the political background in Germany. New regulations were offered to ensure the non-military character of the S.S. and the S.A., although the note rejected the British proposal that Germany should wait for two further years before being allowed military aircraft. As an alternative, the Chancellor demanded a defensive air force of short-range machines, not including bombers and not exceeding in numbers either 30 per cent of the combined air fleets of Germany's neighbours or 50 per cent of the French Air Force, whichever was the smaller.[2] At the end of March, however, the situation was suddenly transformed by the publication of the military budget adopted by the German authorities for the financial year 1933–4. This showed an increase in military spending of 352 million marks. Along with this went the report that Germany was constructing airfields in the demilitarised zone.

The inquiry addressed by Simon to France on 10 April asking whether she was now ready to accept the revised British plan, as modified by Hitler's proposals, in return for some agreement on the definition of 'guarantees of execution' brought the issue at length to the decisive point. The French were bluntly asked what kind of guarantees they had in mind.[3] By this time the French Government appeared to have lost all hope of a breach in the wall of British reticence on the issue of security. Moreover, the French had begun to ask themselves whether they themselves were ready for action against German breaches of treaty of which they complained. They wanted to avoid another Ruhr; French Army leaders doubted whether their forces were organised for such an operation. France had fallen back on a 'policy of extreme caution', wrote Tyrrell from

---

[1] Misc. No. 5 (1934), Cmd. 4559, pp. 11–15.
[2] Ibid., p. 18.   [3] Ibid., p. 19.

Paris on 19 May; she was opposed to any forceful measures which would 'savour of military adventure'.[1]   In their reply to the British inquiry the French limited themselves to requiring Germany's return to the League before any question arose of signing a disarmament convention.[2]   As it was most unlikely that Hitler, having secured popular endorsement of his decision to leave the League, would agree to return except at the price of substantial concessions by France, this was in effect France's intimation that disarmament had reached the end of the road as far as she was concerned.

When the General Commission of the conference met again to consider these unhappy exchanges it was clear that the two-year struggle over disarmament had come to nothing, if it had not positively sharpened differences between the Powers. Rather than frankly admit defeat, the Commission remitted to sub-commissions four of the outstanding questions, namely regional security pacts, guarantees of execution, air forces and the private manufacture and trade in arms.   It also asked governments to study a Soviet proposal that the conference should become a permanent peace organisation with its primary interest in security rather than disarmament.   But there was no disguising the fact that the real concern of governments would henceforth be the scrutiny, not of disarmament plans, but of the problems presented by the evident decision of Germany to rearm.

For this melancholy result British policy bore some responsibility since it had been actively engaged in efforts to reconcile the conflicting factions.   While British Ministers had been proved correct in their assumption that Germany would come to the conference with 'expectations' of equal treatment, they were not entitled to formulate methods of satisfying these without making a definite offer of assistance to France if the Sorcerer's Apprentice became unmanageable.   The difficulties in the way of making any such offer were formidable, especially the mood of withdrawal which overcame the United States with the Great Depression and the nervous state of British opinion.   But this does not excuse the British failure to come to terms with the European unbalance of power from the moment Germany's claim was satisfied, or even seriously considered.   The effect of this omission was to persuade Hitler that nothing would be done to oppose him until it was too late, to convince the German people that their leader understood his foreign enemies better than they feared, and to drive France

<hr />

[1] *D.B.F.P.*, Second Series, V, p. 269.
[2] Cmd. 4559, pp. 20–2.

into an inertia from which she could not be roused. British Ministers considered their main problem to be the unearthing of a formula to bridge opposing fronts, although the massed forces behind these fronts could not be reconciled by words. To understand why British politicians, with some few exceptions were unable to grasp the nature of the continental forces ranged against each other 'in the state and posture of armed gladiators' we must look at the British psychology of that period, when 'pre-war' at last began to succeed 'post-war'.

III

Germany's intention to rearm, which von Neurath made clear as early as May 1933, followed by the deadlock at the disarmament conference and an intense crisis in Austro-German relations, had immediate repercussions on the European governments. Russia abandoned the revisionist cause and made an alliance with a half-hearted France. Belgium demanded guarantees. Mussolini sought to divert Hitler's ambition from Austria to the Polish Corridor and the East by means of a four-Power pact which he invited Britain, France and Germany to join him in signing.[1]   In Britain the ordinary man was loath to infer that the dream of disarmament was over, and that henceforth British ability to affect the course of affairs in Europe would depend upon the country's weight as an ally—or perhaps an enemy—more than on ingenuity in suggesting a *modus vivendi*. The political parties shared this reluctance, stemming as it did from the 1914–18 catastrophe and the distaste it engendered for all talk of armaments as instruments of policy. The Conservatives, sceptical about the League and disarmament, yet feared the disturbing effects of rearming on industry, feared even more to plunge the country into contentions worse than those from which they considered MacDonald and Baldwin had rescued it in 1931. The Labour Party and the Trade Union movement, though shocked by Hitler's assault on the Jews, the German Left and the unions, continued to believe that the disarmament conference had failed through lack of loyalty to the League and collective security on the part of the 1918 victors. For them unilateral rearmament was a return to the abyss.

The economic depression had its effect. In several leading countries new régimes were forced into power dedicated, or driven by events, to reversing the classical techniques of economic management. This shift towards extremes was accompanied by sharp internal controversies, often by violence. In

[1] *D.B.F.P.*, Second Series, V, pp. 56–7.

Britain, neither the Communist nor Fascist parties substantially benefited from the strains of the economic crisis. For this the country's accumulated wealth and the reserve resources of Commonwealth trading were mainly responsible. But a part was played by the spontaneous solidarity of the British people, matched, not perhaps by much understanding of the nature of their troubles, but certainly by unquestioned assurance that good sense and calm would win in the end. Leaders who emerge at such times are apt to be men personifying unity rather than active improvement, conciliation rather than struggle. Such a man was Stanley Baldwin, who succeeded Ramsay MacDonald as head of the National Government in June 1935 (though he had been effectively Prime Minister since its formation).

Much of Baldwin's character remains unknown; there is no doubt, however, about two elements in it which, though vital to the spell he wrought over British opinion, unfitted him for the period which now opened with the failure of the disarmament conference. One was his measureless horror of war, which he expressed more powerfully than any of his pacifist critics, whose influence he frequently overrated. The phrases he used—'the bomber will always get through', 'war—the most fearful terror and prostitution of man's knowledge that ever was known in the world'—provided catchwords for the pacifist opposition to rearmament while eroding his own will to carry it through. The need to rearm was 'a horrible thing to have to say . . . a terrible conclusion'.[1] The second element was Baldwin's fear of awakening latent forces of conflict which had been unleashed to such terrible effect abroad and which he himself had seen in mild British form during the General Strike in 1926. In 1927 he had appealed for an armistice in industrial strife on the text, 'Give us peace in our time, O Lord', moving trade union leaders on Opposition benches to tears; in 1936 he felt the country's unity momentarily racked by Edward VIII's proposed marriage to Mrs. Simpson. Baldwin flinched away from the striking of attitudes, the challenging of settled opinions, which ran the slightest risk of forcing passionate factions to resist. With this went his aversion for foreign affairs; foreign affairs called for the taking up of positions, however deferred, and, to Baldwin's mind, Britain had been too shaken by the conflicts of the past to face conflict over positions yet. 'There was one thing more than anything I was afraid of,' he said, 'party division on foreign policy.' Alliances against alliances, pacts against pacts, conjured up the spectre of division at home,

[1] 309 H.C. Deb. 5s. Col. 1830 (9 March 1936).

and Baldwin thought he had seen too much of that to want to see more.

One incident above all others touched Baldwin's nerve of anxiety about the country's simple faith in itself, and in him as the personification of itself: the East Fulham by-election in October 1933, the month when Hitler left the disarmament conference. A Conservative majority of 14,500 was turned into a Labour gain of 4,800 by a candidate who expressed his foreign policy in the words: 'I am asking for votes for peace and disarmament; my opponent demands armaments and preparations for war.' The same wish for conciliation which had set Baldwin against the extreme anti-trade unionists in his party in 1927 now led him to let this setback rankle in his mind. A Minister who formed his conclusions on the basis of carefully digested facts of the international situation might have ignored it, considering the towering majority in Parliament enjoyed by the government. Baldwin, whose power rested on his flair for embodying all the elements in the country which yearned for peace in industry and international relations, could not. How could disarmament be right if it troubled the tranquil deeps of the British mind? On 8 March 1934 Baldwin made the government's position clear in the Commons: either there must be an agreed disarmament convention, which in itself would probably require some increase in the British air force, or there must be no inferiority to any country within striking distance. Yet, having reached the logical conclusion, he was anxious to move away from it again, the nightmare of East Fulham before him. His *ennui* with defence matters became notorious. On one occasion, in November 1933, he said in the House with reference to a carefully drafted statement made in the Lords by Londonderry, the Air Minister, which several M.P.s had themselves heard in the gallery, 'To be quite frank, I have not the slightest idea what has been said in another place.'[1] His appointment of Sir Thomas Inskip, then Attorney-General, to co-ordinate defence services in 1936 made the government a laughing-stock. The rumour spread that Baldwin refused to appoint a Minister suited to the post, like Churchill, for fear of provoking Hitler into another embarrassing step. In all this Baldwin seemed to accept the need to rearm. But the results in terms of controversy, in which he would have to play a toilsome, active part, he felt to be intolerable. In 1935 or 1936 Baldwin, a man of peace, might have stepped down, his glory untarnished, to give way to a man of war.[2]

---

[1] 283 H.C. Deb. 5s. Col. 1017 (29 November 1933).
[2] G. M. Young, *Stanley Baldwin*, p. 205.

Churchill likewise could have retired from politics with no injury to his fame in 1945. But statesmen who have led their countries through the furnace generally think there is still work for them to do. Baldwin seemed to think so in 1935.

The government, led by a nominal Prime Minister, Mac-Donald, and a sluggish Lord President of the Council, Baldwin, took the first faltering steps with the Air Estimates presented to Parliament in February 1934.[1] These proposed a five-year expansion programme with the ultimate aim of parity in first-line strength between the major Powers. Spending in 1934, however, was to rise by no more than the gross figure of £527,000 (or a net one of £130,000). On 19 July the government made known their decision to increase appreciably the speed of expansion; 41 new R.A.F. squadrons were now to be added within the five-year period, making a total home defence force of 75 squadrons.[2] At this time Britain was estimated to be fifth in the world list of states for total air strength, with half the number of French machines and four-fifths of the Italian Air Force. German air strength, however, remained the largest uncertainty. Estimates of German strength varied from that of the French Government, at 1,100 planes, to that of the British Embassy in Berlin, which reached the figure of 600. Baldwin, without making clear the source of his figures, told the Commons on 28 November 1934 that:

[Germany's] real strength is not fifty per cent of our strength in Europe today. As for the position this time next year, if she continues to execute her air programme without acceleration and if we continue to carry out at the present approved rate the expansion announced in Parliament in July . . . so far from the German military air force being at least as strong and probably stronger than our own, we estimate that we shall have in Europe a margin—in Europe alone—of nearly fifty per cent.[3]

Baldwin assumed that Hitler would follow the British rate of expansion. When Simon saw Hitler in Berlin on 25 March of the following year, however, the Chancellor coolly told him that Germany had already attained air parity with Britain.[4] Baldwin had to admit that his estimate of the German rate of growth was 'completely wrong'. On 22 May he told the House

[1] Memorandum by the Secretary of State for Air to accompany Air Estimates, 1934, Cmd. 4521.
[2] 292 H.C. Deb. 5s. Cols. 1273–6.
[3] 295 H.C. Deb. 5s. Col. 882.
[4] *D.G.F.P.*, Series C, III, p. 1073.

that his assessment of existing German air strength on which
the November speech had been based was correct, but that
neither he nor any of his advisers 'had any idea of the exact rate
at which production was being, could be and actually was being
speeded up in Germany in the six months between November
and now. We were completely misled.'[1] What followed was
significant. In the state of panic after Hitler's declaration the
Air Council decided to bring forward the date for completing
the programme of 3,800 aircraft envisaged for 1939 to 1937.
Lord Weir, Director of Aircraft Production in the First World
War, was recalled to take this expansion in hand. Weir sur-
veyed the aircraft industry, then wrote a letter to Baldwin
which forced the programme to be scaled down to 1,500 mainly
front-line aircraft by 1937. 'What I always feared has happened,' Weir wrote, 'the technical structure behind our production is too weak to carry such a load as is now to be thrust
upon it.'[2]

In the winter of 1934–5 the government were urged by a
group of officials to bring out a White Paper giving a complete
summary of the Defence position and the reasons which made
rearmament necessary. As the draft developed, voices were
raised in the Cabinet in favour of moderating its tone lest Hitler
be driven to the extremes he had already announced as his object; but not with complete success, since the Chancellor at
once took umbrage when the statement was published on 4
March 1935 and cancelled the visit he had agreed to receive
from Simon and Eden. It did not take him long to relent,
however, as it was clear that the educative function of the White
Paper was intended to be more important than its actual effect
on British rearmament. An insignificant increase of £4 million in Defence expenditure was proposed. The efficiency of
the Navy was to be maintained 'within the limits set by the
Washington and London treaties', despite the fact that Japan
had already given notice of withdrawing from the former agreement. Unspecific references were made to the need for modern-
ising the Army, especially in anti-aircraft weapons, but no
further immediate expansion of the air force beyond that announced in the previous July seemed contemplated.[3] Then,
in the debate on the White Paper on 11 March, Baldwin deprecated cries from Labour of 'Hit Hitler'.[4] Two weeks later
in a speech to Young Conservatives at the Albert Hall he extolled 'careful, steady and balanced judgment', as though

[1] 302 H.C. Deb. 5s. Col. 367.   [2] G. M. Young, op. cit., p. 201.
[3] Statement relating to Defence, Cmd. 4827 (1935).
[4] 299 H. C. Deb. 5s. Cols. 50–1.

urging the public not to be too excited over current developments.[1]

During the talks Simon and Eden had with Hitler in Berlin on 25 and 26 March, nine days after the announcement of conscription in Germany, the Chancellor showed some interest in British proposals for an air pact involving immediate air action against unprovoked attack from the air, a declaration condemning indiscriminate bombardment of civilian targets from the air and restrictions on air armaments, to be embodied in a later convention after the pact was signed. Discussion of an East European and a Central European pact and Germany's return to the League was, however, inconclusive and the only concrete outcome of the talks was Hitler's intimation that he would agree to attend a naval conference in London, at which he would propose limiting the size of the German navy to 35 per cent of the British.[2] On 21 May Hitler made a speech in the Reichstag protesting that he was a man of peace with no intention of breaking Germany's foreign obligations. The suggested Anglo-German naval ratio was brought up again.[3] The effects of the speech were to provoke a chorus of relieved comments in Britain, including a sympathetic letter to *The Times* from the Archbishop of Canterbury; to cause many people to forget the introduction of conscription in Germany in March in defiance of the Versailles Treaty; to make the British White Paper seem overstrained. The ground was prepared for the Anglo-German naval agreement signed in London on 18 June 1935.

The formal motive for the agreement on the British side was the desire to pave the way for the larger naval conference which was to meet later in 1935 on the expiry of the Washington Treaty. More substantially, the Chancellor's suggestion was regarded as a means of securing a pause in German naval construction. On the Führer's side, he had already stated in his political testament that he had no interest in a naval arms race with Britain, the danger of which was that it would leave his rear exposed during the fulfilment of his main policy, expansion eastwards.[4] The essence of the resulting agreement, as approved by the British Chiefs of Staff immediately after the Berlin talks in March, was that German naval strength was to be limited to 35 per cent of British Commonwealth forces on a basis of limitation by category. Germany reserved the right

[1] *The Times*, 25 March 1935, p. 9.
[2] *D.G.F.P.*, Series C, III, pp. 1043–80.
[3] *The Speeches of Adolf Hitler*, ed. N. H. Baynes, II, pp. 1218–47.
[4] *Mein Kampf*, Munich, 1932, p. 154.

to parity in submarines, however, though she undertook to limit herself to 45 per cent of Commonwealth submarine strength with provision for this to be increased in emergencies and after consultation. Importance was attached by the British naval chiefs to a provision in the agreement for an exchange of naval information, which held out some slight hope for filling some of the gaps in British intelligence which rearmament had already disclosed.[1]

Although the agreement had the advantage for Britain of helping to control a situation which there was no intention to reverse, the effects abroad were disastrous. Sir Samuel Hoare, disconcerted to find that he was called on to complete the agreement the moment he succeeded Simon as Foreign Secretary in June, sought to delay signature to give time for the French attitude to be ascertained, although Ribbentrop was waiting and the Cabinet were anxious that he should not be deterred by too much protocol. Laval, at this time President of the Council in France, who was in any case embroiled in one of his regular political storms at home, gave Hoare the impression that he had no personal objection to the agreement, though he told Eden that the public outcry would prevent him sending experts to London to prepare for the forthcoming naval conference for a few weeks.[2] The French Press, however, was fluent with complaints: that Britain had broken the Stresa front of April 1935; that, after all its warnings against Hitler's violations of the Versailles Treaty, the British Government had made a pact with him which took his infringement of that Treaty as its starting point; and that, after all, this had been done not only without full consultation with Britain's friends but after unceremoniously pushing them out of the way lest Hitler take offence at their complaints.

The French forgot how difficult they made things for Britain in the early days of the disarmament conference, when an agreement might have been made with the Brüning Government on terms infinitely easier than those which now had to be made with Hitler. They also overlooked the British claim that the naval agreement, by setting a limit to German naval rearmament, still gave France a 30 per cent lead at sea over Germany, and ignored the British reminder that by the exchange of notes embodying the agreement Germany undertook not to exceed the agreed ratio whatever the naval construction of other Powers. None of these assurances affected the general uncertainty as to British purposes which the agreement aroused

[1] Treaty Series No. 22 (1935), Cmd. 4953.
[2] Viscount Templewood, *Nine Troubled Years*, p. 144.

in Europe, especially when it was remembered how a single conciliatory speech by Hitler, like that of 21 May, could stir leaders of British society to a chorus of sympathy. British public attitudes since Hitler's accession had shown alarming variations, from legal rigidity to revisionism, from warnings to Germany to acceptance of her breaches of treaty as facts on which new understandings could be built. The suspicion was bound to remain that Britain either entirely misunderstood the nature of the new Germany or wished to snatch advantage after having given up hope of collective efforts to reverse the movement of events.

The British Government could therefore hardly expect an enthusiastic French response when they issued invitations to the Washington Powers to attend a conference in London on 9 December in accordance with article 23 of the London Naval Treaty of 1930. Japan had withdrawn from the Washington Treaty in December of the previous year, Italy was heavily involved in her Ethiopian adventure and the United States was making the unrealistic suggestion of a one-fifth reduction in the Washington tonnages at a moment when Britain had already raised her projected cruiser fleet from 50 to the original 70 vessels. Baldwin hopefully opened the conference with a restatement of the proposals for qualitative and quantitative disarmament which had formed part of the MacDonald disarmament plan in 1932, but neither France nor Italy was prepared to have even the London naval ratios extended to themselves and the idea of a voluntary declaration limiting construction over the next few years was generally unacceptable. Japan then withdrew her delegation from the conference, though she left observers to watch its progress, after her proposal for a 'common upper limit', another name for parity with Britain and the United States, had been turned down. It remained to gather what fruits of the discussions remained and these proved to be little more than an agreement to notify each other in advance of the construction or acquisition of new ships and to exchange information on their specifications. The value of this as a contribution to disarmament was not apparent, especially as Italy refused to associate herself with the agreement, although the slight degree of naval partnership attained between the signatories, Britain, France and the United States, was not without its uses later. How the old phrases of disarmament talks lingered in the new age was evident in the terms in which the agreement was recommended to Parliament. It was stated, with almost deliberate irony, that 'the agreement should go far to put into effect the hopes expressed by the Prime Minister at

the opening of the Conference that the public mind will be
relieved of the threat of a general race in naval armaments'.[1]

The London naval meetings formed the last chapter in the
story of disarmament. By the time they began in December
the Italo-Ethiopian war had already shown the inadequacy of
the 1935 White Paper to meet the new international situation.
In the previous August, when the danger of Britain being drawn
into the conflict was at its height, the Cabinet decided to
strengthen British forces in Gibraltar, Malta, Aden and Egypt,
only to find their defensive capacity absurdly denuded elsewhere. Moreover, by mid-1935 the full dimensions of the
world arms race were becoming plain even to averted British
eyes. Hitler's announcement of conscription in March was
interpreted as giving Germany a peace-time force of thirty-six
divisions with a strength of 550,000 men. France reintroduced
two-year service and pressed forward with the reinforcing of
her north-eastern fortresses built to take the shock of German
offensives on the pattern of March 1918. The Italian Army,
with almost a million and a quarter men under arms and calling
to the colours still going on, was already on a war footing.
A massive Japanese war budget was envisaged for 1936–7 and
Soviet forces, according to official figures published in January,
had been increased to a total of 1,300,000 men.

In these circumstances the British programme of 'improved
defence' (thus avoiding the displeasing word 'rearmament')
outlined in the Defence White Paper of 1936 was intended as a
drastic acceleration of the 1935 scheme. The main features
were the laying down of the two new capital ships early in 1937,
that is, after the prohibition of new construction under the
1930 treaty had lapsed at the end of 1936, the raising of cruiser
strength from 50 to 70 vessels, the recruiting of four new infantry battalions and the increase of the 1935 target of 1,500
front-line aircraft to approximately 1,750, exclusive of the Fleet
Air Arm. A disturbing feature of the White Paper, however,
was that no firm dates were laid down for the completion of the
programme and also that throughout the survey, despite assurances that all vigour was being applied, it was pointed out
that there was to be no interference with the 'course of normal
trade'.[2] The general impression left by the document was that
the government regarded the international situation as a passing
storm, against which measures unfortunately had to be taken,
rather than a symptom of an epoch in which the weight accorded to a state's voice in affairs was governed by the strength

[1] Misc. No. 2 (1936), Cmd. 5137.
[2] Statement Relating to Defence, Cmd. 5107 (1936), p. 16.

of its military arm and its people's resolve to throw the national economy behind that strength.

When the 1937 Defence survey was published in February the tempo of 'improvement' was seen to be increased. Three further capital ships were to be ordered in 1937–8, the rate of cruiser building was raised from the five of the 1936 White Paper to seven and it was stated that two aircraft carriers had been laid down in 1936, not one as in the White Paper, and that two more were 'probably' to be laid down in 1937. Army recruiting had not, however, made possible the formation of the proposed four new infantry battalions, despite improvements in the conditions of army life, and it was merely reported that two of them would be raised in the near future. Little was said about the Air Force since it was evident that manufacturing capacity was not making the 1936 programme easy to fulfil. The Defence programme was estimated to cost not much less than £1,500 million during the succeeding five years (a figure described as too small in the White Paper for 1938), but the taxpayer was told that he would not have to bear this burden over such a short period.[1] Authority was obtained by the government in February 1937 to issue from the Consolidated Funds sums not exceeding £400 million up to 31 March 1942 as the deferred portion of the bill.[2]

Two questions which remained were, first, whether sufficient drive was being applied from the top, and, second, whether the programme, even if on the scale needed in the circumstances of the day, could be put into effect without that centralisation of the economy which the revisionist states were applying to the task. As to the former problem, Baldwin announced changes in the organisation of Defence in the House on 27 February 1936. The Committee of Imperial Defence, presided over by the Prime Minister, was to remain 'an essential link in all matters of defence', but in July of the previous year, Baldwin said, a new body had been created, the Defence Policy and Requirements Committee, with the Prime Minister in the chair, the object of which was 'to keep the defensive situation as a whole constantly under review so as to ensure that our defence arrangements and our foreign policy are in line, and to advise the Cabinet and Committee of Imperial Defence in the light of the international and financial situation as to any necessary changes in policy or in the defence proposals'.[3] The reasons given for the establishment of the new body sounded ominous

---

[1] Statement Relating to Defence Expenditure, Cmd. 5374 (1937).
[2] Defence Loans. Memorandum on the Proposed Resolution, Cmd. 5368 (1937).
[3] 309 H.C. Deb. 5s. Col. 654.

in the light of Baldwin's notorious boredom with details of defence, which, like the details of disarmament, are often what most matters; they were that pressure of work on the Prime Minister had been increasing in recent years and 'some special assistance in regard to defence matters' was required. Baldwin's statement that the deputy chairman of the new committee would be responsible for the day-to-day control of the reformed defence organisation suggested that he himself would take as little interest in it as he did in the circumstances which made it necessary. The drive which Lloyd George or Beaverbrook would have imparted to rearmament was absent.

More important, however, was the intimation in the White Papers that rearmament was intended to disturb neither established industrial practices, nor the power of the Treasury, nor the settled relations between government and private business. The principal innovation in the 1936 White Paper was the decision to create a new reserve of industrial supply, over and above government munitions factories and the group of firms normally engaged in fulfilling arms orders. This was to consist of a pool of firms which were to be assisted to acquire plant for the manufacture of armaments and given sufficient orders to allow them to train the necessary labour, thus placing them in a state of readiness for emergencies.[1] There was no suggestion, however, of compulsive powers being sought and so long as Ministers failed to strike a note of alarm throughout the country firms on the reserve list could hardly take their role with much seriousness. The apathy of industry in fact symbolised the dilemma of the situation. Rearmament, the government declared, could not be avoided after the failure of the disarmament conference whatever foreign policy was adopted to deal with the resulting situation. Indeed, if a 'collective security' policy were pursued, as urged by the government's Labour and Liberal opponents, the scale of rearmament would probably have to be even greater than that required for a policy of conciliating the dissatisfied. Yet rearmament on the scale of the twentieth century was hardly practicable in a democratic state except on two conditions: that a mental state of urgency be communicated to the population sufficient to overcome the inertia of ordinary peace-time life, and that the traditional notions of government as merely one party to the nation's economic life, rather than its superintendent, be abandoned. The government hoped to attain the level of rearmament needed to restore Britain to a position of account in European affairs, yet without wishing to unsettle

---

[1] Cmd. 5107, p. 17.

'normal' relations between Whitehall on one side and the taxpayer and private industry on the other. In theory, the
government explained, defence policy should go hand in hand
with foreign policy. In practice their inability to satisfy the
two basic conditions of rearmament served to make an inadequate defence policy the master of an indecisive foreign policy.

CHAPTER XVI

THE CONCERT UNREVIVED

I

BRITISH policy since the war, whether Conservative or Labour, had been based, if on any principle at all, on that of the mutual reconciliation of the Great Powers. British Governments considered that by leading the Powers into accepting a *status quo* suitably modified to remove the worst errors of the peace treaties they could avert the division of Europe into armed camps, achieve the disarmament essential to economic recovery and free Britain's hands for the protection of her imperial estate. Germany's resurgence under the Nazis destroyed this policy and opened the road to the collapse of the European system. It did so in two ways. First, Chancellor Hitler was unwilling to accept the status of a partner in a stable European Concert which British policy assigned to him; and his astonishing success in striking off the restrictions of Versailles swept German opinion into agreement with him. Secondly, the reactions of the other two leading European states, France and Italy, to the German revival faced Britain with a choice between alternatives, of which one conflicted with the policy of attempting to reconcile the Powers, while the other imposed on British Ministers a virtual abdication from most of their influence over European affairs. The former choice was that of placing Britain alongside France and Italy in resistance to the German revival; this would have meant the acceptance of 'partial alliances' almost unanimously condemned by British opinion. The second alternative was that of attempting to satisfy the revolutionary régime in Germany with concessions in the hope that it would one day accept its place in the European Concert as Britain envisaged it. As events showed there was hardly a point short of total humiliation towards which this course led.

The head of the Italian Government, Mussolini, had taken a pessimistic view of the disarmament conference from the moment when it became clear that it would give no satisfaction to his demand for naval equality with France. Germany's release from the military fetters of Versailles he regarded as inevitable. A revisionist on doctrinal grounds and as leader of a dissatisfied country, he nevertheless feared Nazi revisionism in respect of the weak buffer state between himself and Germany,

Austria. St. Germain Austria was in no position to take up the cause of the 250,000 Germans in Italian South Tirol. An Austria united with a feverishly rearming Germany would be different, especially if the effect was to encourage Italy's perennial rival across the Adriatic, Yugoslavia. Reconciled to Germany's revival therefore, the Duce sought to divert its consequences to her eastern borders, which were in any case a stronger grievance with German irredentists than the South Tirol. The Polish Corridor, reported the British Ambassador in Rome, Sir Ronald Graham, in March 1933, was in Mussolini's opinion 'one of the most dangerous and pressing questions to be got out of the way'.[1] This belief, together with the Duce's wish to advertise the 'have-not' nations' cause more generally, was the source of his proposal for a pact between the four European Powers, who were to assume a kind of directorate in charge of revision, which he announced in a speech in Turin on 23 October 1932, on the tenth anniversary of the march on Rome.[2]

British reactions to Mussolini's proposal were favourable, firstly on the ground that it was in the tradition of Locarno, the sheet-anchor of British policy in western Europe, secondly because, in the words of Sir John Simon, then Foreign Secretary, such an arrangement 'would tend to eliminate the danger of the formation in Europe of opposing groups and would secure that, as between themselves, the direction and purpose of the policies of the four Powers would be co-ordinated with the primary object of preserving friendly relations and strengthening mutual understanding'.[3] The latter seemed all the more urgent in view of British fears of a collapse of the disarmament conference owing to the intransigent attitudes of France and Germany, the imminence of German rearmament, the failure of the World Economic Conference, and the British desire to bring influence to bear, through Italy, on the developments in Nazi Germany. The British also hoped to incorporate their own disarmament plan, presented to the Geneva conference in March 1933, in the proposed pact, thus ensuring for it some slight possibilities of survival, despite Mussolini's reluctance to have discussion of the pact waterlogged by the old Geneva arguments. Finally, the pact seemed to demand no British commitments beyond Locarno. A device for equilibrating German ambitions with French fears might at last bring the

[1] *D.B.F.P.*, Second Series, V, p. 56.
[2] For the text of the Turin speech see *Scritti e discorsi di Benito Mussolini*, Milan, 1934, VIII, pp. 123–8.
[3] Misc. No. 3 (1933), Cmd. 4342, p. 2.

Powers to sup at the same table without involving Britain in any extra obligations.

The difficulty about the Italian draft of the four-Power pact, as shown to MacDonald and Simon when they visited Rome on 18 and 19 March, was its blunt emphasis on revision of treaties, which seemed to be the pact's major *raison d'être*.[1] The British were not opposed to revision, which had been an article of faith with British opinion almost before the ink had dried on the Versailles Treaty; as Simon told Mussolini, when the Duce harped on the iniquities of the Polish Corridor, the first obligation under the League Covenant was respect for treaties, but the second was to ensure that they were 'not of a perpetual character'.[2] But a pact frankly based on revision would be impossible for France, both on account of her struggle to maintain the Versailles bulwarks against the coming Nazi deluge and on account of her *cortège habituel* of friends among the successor states of eastern Europe. Moreover, did revision mean a return to the 'free-for-all' of pre-1914, with all the hopes of disarmament dashed? It was not difficult for the French Premier, Daladier, and his Foreign Minister, Paul-Boncour, to convince MacDonald and Simon when they talked over the Italian draft in Paris on 21 March, on the British Ministers' homeward journey from Rome, that if 'practical expression' (*portata effettiva*) were given, as Mussolini proposed, to the German demand for equality in armaments if the Geneva conference failed, the effect would be to give Germans an interest in the failure of the conference and hence in a return to the pre-war international chaos.[3]

The greatest danger was that the Italian draft would deepen suspicions between France, if she signed it, and Poland and the Little Entente, and encourage the elements in these countries which wished to break the French connection and come to terms with the new Germany. At the Anglo-French talks in Paris on 21 March and in later exchanges with Czech, Rumanian and Yugoslav representatives in Geneva it was agreed that no revision would be recommended by the four Powers under the pact except with the unanimous consent of all. This undertaking was sufficient for the Little Entente states but did not appease Poland, whose mistrust of France found expression in a revolutionary non-aggression agreement with Germany in the following January. Nevertheless, the 'agreement of understanding and co-operation' between the four

---

[1] The original Italian draft is printed in Francesco Salta, *Il Patto Mussolini*, Milan, 1933, pp. 175–6.
[2] *D.B.F.P.*, Second Series, VI, p. 73.   [3] *Ibid.*, p. 93.

Powers, eventually signed on 7 June, was a pale reflection of Mussolini's original intention, its significance lying in its defeat of his revisionism rather than in its embodiment of it. The agreement merely cited the revisionist article 19 of the League Covenant without removing its voluntarist character; even this was balanced by references to articles 10 and 16, with their principles of respect for territorial integrity and political independence and their provision for sanctions in the event of war being waged in breach of Covenant obligations. In its final form the four-Power pact symbolised the central theme of European affairs: the strains of Germany's revival on the 1919 system.[1]

Germany's attitude to the pact changed from approval of its revisionist spirit to sullen dissent once French influence had been brought to bear. Hitler at first spoke of Mussolini's initiative in a Reichstag speech on 23 March as a 'broad-minded and far-seeing attempt to secure a powerful and consistent development of the whole of European policy'.[2] As the pact was diluted, German frigidity grew.[3] At length the Chancellor, undecided whether to sign the final version, agreed with his Minister of Defence, von Blomberg, that it committed him to nothing and to that extent was not unhelpful for the Führer's policy of showing general co-operativeness while Germany was still weak, but without tying his hands. The next attempt to meet the security problem, however, came from France and, so far from legalising revision, sought to bind Germany to respect her eastern borders as closely as she had been bound at Locarno to respect her western. For this reason the German Chancellor firmly set his face against it. What was more surprising was that he had the support of Poland in doing so, and, with some qualifications, of Britain as well.

The author of this optimistic French policy, already unsuccessfully tried during the Locarno negotiations in 1925, was Louis Barthou, who had become Foreign Minister in the Cabinet formed by Doumergue after the Paris riots of 6 February 1934. By the time the Doumergue Ministry had taken office France had already made a start on expedients for containing the German war machine. On 18 May 1933 the Chamber of Deputies had approved a Franco-Soviet non-aggression pact, hopefully intended as a prelude to the revival of the military alliance with Russia of the 1890s, by the massive majority of 520 to none. With the drawing together of Poland

---

[1] The text of the agreement is printed in Cmd. 4342, pp. 6–10.
[2] *The Speeches*, ed., N. H. Baynes, II, p. 1018.
[3] *D.G.F.P.*, Series C, I, pp. 248–50.

and Germany, partly as a result of the hostile Polish reactions to the four-Power pact, the stage was set for more imaginative French efforts to check Germany.   Barthou was persuaded by Doumergue and Tardieu at a Cabinet meeting on 17 April to break with Britain on the policy of seeking a controlled form of German rearmament and to announce, in reply to British inquiries as to the precise guarantees France sought, that the search for an understanding on German rearmament at Geneva had ended as far as France was concerned.[1]   The French note, by seeming to take responsibility for extinguishing the flickering hopes at Geneva, created the worst possible atmosphere for Barthou's next step, which came at the end of June, especially in British circles.   The Foreign Minister's proposal was for a regional pact to cover eastern Europe, on the model of Locarno but buttressed with mutual Franco-Soviet guarantees which gave the proposal a decided anti-German appearance.   Its provisions fell into two parts.   The first pledged the proposed signatories, the three Baltic states, Czechoslovakia, Finland, Germany and Russia, to consult together in the event of an attack or threatened attack on any one of them whether by another signatory or by any other state.   The second part of the draft applied only to France and Russia.   Russia would undertake the same obligations within the Locarno treaty system as Britain and Italy, but only with respect to France;   she would not be committed to defend Germany in the event of a French attack on Germany in the west.   France on her side would give Russia the same assistance as the signatories of the first part of the agreement extended to one another, when this was required under article 15 or 16 of the League Covenant. France would thus be assured of Soviet help against German aggression in the west, while Russia would receive the additional promise of French assistance against Germany in the east.[2]

The British Government, true to the traditional feeling of detachment in regard to eastern Europe, showed merely mild interest in the Barthou scheme.   If it succeeded, it might contribute to removing bad blood between the Powers which was the leading object of British policy;   more directly, it might deter France from a thoroughgoing military alliance with Russia.   But British Ministers felt that they had little to lose from its failure.   Their main interest in the pact was that it might help restore German membership of the League, which Hitler had quitted the previous October since, as we have seen,

[1] André François-Poncet, *The Fateful Years*, London, 1949, p. 123. For the French note of 17 April see Misc. No. 5 (1934), Cmd. 4559, pp. 20–2.
[2] Misc. No. 3 (1936), Cmd. 5143, pp. 7–8.

the French obligations under the pact were to come into operation in accordance with the League Covenant. This was impossible, however, unless the British took up the obvious German objections to the French outline of the pact. This they
did in talks with the leading French Ministers in London on 11
and 12 July, when they pointed out that if the pact was to stand
any chance of serious consideration in Berlin its provisions must
be made reciprocal, that is, Russia must become a Locarno
guarantor in respect of Germany as well as of France, and
France must agree to come to Germany's assistance, as well as
Russia's, in the event of an attack or threatened attack within
the meaning of the first part of the French draft.[1] When the
French accepted these modifications—which in themselves
exposed the unreality of the whole proposal in the prevailing
political conditions—the British endorsed the draft and agreed
to press Poland and Germany to accept it. Simon made clear
in the Commons on 13 July that the British attitude was that of
'benevolent well-wishers and not of actual contracting parties'.[2]

The Poles, however, remained opposed to the idea of an
eastern pact. The Polish authorities felt more afraid of Stalin
than of Hitler; the notion of Soviet forces entering Polish territory to help repel a hypothetical German attack seemed like
dashing one's brains out to relieve a headache. Lacking
Polish support the pact was a non-starter, though it lingered
for two years more on the European agenda, and Hitler's rejection, delivered on 10 September, was little more than the
dernier coup de mort. In his statement the Chancellor exploited
Germany's alleged inability, as a disarmed state, to fill any
serious role in schemes of mutual military assistance and echoed
British aversion for military commitments in a passage depre-
cating 'extensive new obligations'. Hitler's effort to model his
non possumus on British lines was also apparent in the Chancellor's reference to the attempts made in the 1920s to strengthen
the League machinery by schemes of mutual aid, which, as
Austen Chamberlain had said of the Geneva Protocol, 'multiplied occasions of conflict rather than reduced them'. British
politicians fervently believed this; they were therefore disposed
to accept the conclusions of the German note, namely that
security in eastern Europe was more effectively secured by a
series of bilateral non-aggression pacts on the lines of the Ger-
man-Polish Treaty of January 1934.[3]

Germany, a friendly Poland now between herself and Russia

[1] Cmd. 5143, p. 8.
[2] 292 H.C. Deb. 5s. Col. 697.
[3] For the text of the German note see *F.R.U.S., 1934*, I, pp. 510–16.

and intense mutual mistrust existing between Moscow and Paris, saw little to be gained from extending the Locarno guarantees to her eastern borders. Her situation demanded the greatest caution. The repercussions of the Roehm purge in June had not yet faded, while the Chancellor's meeting with a wary Mussolini in Venice during the same month convinced him that he must walk with care. When the Austrian Nazis made an unsuccessful attempt to seize power in July, murdering Chancellor Dollfuss in the process, alarm in the European capitals held Germany in check. With two Italian divisions sent up to the Brenner Pass and the issue of statements in defence of Austrian independence by Britain and France on 26 July, this was no time for Germany to enter commitments in eastern Europe, the development of which could not be foreseen.

The failure of the eastern Locarno made Barthou all the more anxious to strengthen French ties with the Soviet state, now emerging as a *status quo* Power as a result of the military revival of Germany and the assumption by Japan of a blatantly expansionist policy in China. Through French influence Russia was admitted into the League of Nations with a permanent seat on the Council on 18 September, Britain following unenthusiastically in support, and the French and Soviet Governments cast about for something to erect amid the ruins of the eastern pact. The most they were able to achieve was a Franco-Soviet protocol signed on 5 December, which pledged the two countries to enter into no arrangements with third parties which might compromise the preparation and conclusion of an eastern Locarno.[1] Thereafter these endeavours tended to mark time. Meanwhile, to offset the defection of Poland from France's east European alliance system, the French Foreign Minister was seeking a wider framework for the containment of Germany by consolidating French defensive relations with the countries of south-east Europe. In June, even before Poland's rejection of the eastern pact was known, Barthou was in Belgrade, striving to act as an honest broker between Yugoslavia and Italy in the hope that both countries could be won over to France's side.

These efforts came to nothing with the murder of Barthou himself, together with King Alexander of Yugoslavia, in Marseilles on 9 October, at the beginning of the king's state visit to France. The assassin was a Croatian nationalist allegedly trained in Italy and, some said, suborned to do the murders by the Italian Government.[2] The consequence was a move-

[1] Cmd. 5143, pp. 14–15.
[2] Gaetano Salvemini, *Prelude to World War II*, London, 1953, pp. 168–9.

ment of Yugoslav policy in Germany's direction, symbolised by the accession to the Regency on his nephew Peter's behalf of Prince Paul, a strong admirer of Germany and the Hitler régime. A month after the Marseilles tragedy the Doumergue Government in France fell and a new ministry was formed under Flandin with Pierre Laval in charge of foreign affairs. Laval, intensely hostile to Soviet Communism and a champion of Franco-Italian *rapprochement*, remained the dominant force in French foreign policy until his resignation in January 1936.

France had thus by now succumbed to a double failure. She had failed to prevent German rearmament or engender effective opposition to the re-introduction of conscription in Germany; British and French reactions to Hitler's promulgation of a law on 16 March 1933 for the formation of a conscript army of twelve corps with thirty-six divisions took the form merely of a verbal protest at the League Council and France was left in what the American Ambassador in Paris, Straus, described as 'despair and smouldering resentment' at Britain's refusal to take the matter further.[1]   More importantly, France had failed to resuscitate her old system for the containment of Germany.   The Franco-Soviet Alliance, at length signed on 2 May 1935 when postponement was no longer possible, bore no comparison with the pre-1914 system, strong mistrust on both sides serving to keep it on a purely formal basis.[2]   The succession of Soviet treason trials following the murder of Kirov in 1934 deepened French Right-wing disgust with the Soviet connection, while the connection itself drove wedges between France and her old friends in eastern Europe, especially Poland. The greatest value of the Soviet pact for France was not in fact international at all, but lay in the abandonment by the French Communists of resistance to rearmament.   It is true that during this period France was able to improve her relations with Rome, as Barthou had himself hoped, and Mussolini in speeches on 18 March and 6 October encouraged French Ministers to look further in his direction.   Unfortunately, when Laval sought to take advantage of these offers by a visit to Rome on 5–7 January, the effect was to present Britain with a painful choice between conniving at Italian aggression in Africa in order to please France and supporting the League against Mussolini at the risk of ruining the Franco-Italian accords.   Altogether, wherever the French looked for support friends seemed available only at the cost of making more enemies.

---

[1] *F.R.U.S., 1935*, II, p. 305.
[2] For the text of the alliance see *L'Europe Nouvelle* (Documents Supplement No. 16), 8 June 1935.

These French hardships created little sympathy in Britain. With respect to Barthou's proposal for an eastern pact, for example, the American Ambassador in Berlin, Dodd, said of the British attitude that:

> They are only interested in a very secondary degree them-selves in the pact: their advocacy of it presumably relieving them for the time being of the perennial French pressure for guarantees of security.   They would have indirectly bene-fited had the pact turned out to be a success and they are no worse off by reason of its rejection.[1]

Old British suspicions of the French security system lingered, though the system was now in shreds.   Vansittart, the Perma-nent Under-Secretary of State at the Foreign Office, considered that, above everything else, Britain should stand by France, but his political chief, Simon, laboured to manœuvre Germany back into the European system; this, he knew, meant the ac-ceptance of the German case against the 'inequalities' of Ver-sailles.   Writing to King George V two weeks before a vital meeting with the French in London in February 1935 to con-sider the next stage in organising European security, Simon explained that:

> The point which Sir John has been pressing is that the practical choice is between a Germany which continues to rearm without any regulation or agreement and a Germany which, through getting a recognition of its rights and some modification of the Peace Treaties, enters into the comity of nations and contributes, in this and other ways, to European stability.   As between these courses, there can be no doubt which is the wiser.[2]

Simon and the rest of the Cabinet would not exert them-selves much on behalf of French proposals and were quick to express alarm when these looked as if they might involve France in situations from which the British might have to extract her. Thus, when MacDonald and Simon met French and Italian Ministers at the Stresa conference in April 1935 they pressed Laval to say whether the impending Franco-Soviet pact of mutual assistance contained anything which might involve France in war with Germany and hence drag Britain, through her Locarno obligations, into the quarrel.[3]   Assurances were given by the French Government, although not until the eve

---

[1] *F.R.U.S., 1934*, I, pp. 509–10.
[2] Harold Nicolson, *King George V. His Life and Reign*, p. 522.
[3] Cmd. 5143, pp. 25–6.

of the signature of the pact on 2 May. Hence, when Hitler at once raised the question whether the pact did not undermine the Locarno treaties, British politicians suspected that French security policies had only succeeded in creating the dangers they were meant to avert.

On their visit to Berlin in March Simon and Eden brought up the proposal for an eastern Locarno and a similar pact for central Europe, as they had previously agreed with the French, only to find that the Chancellor considered the former undesirable and the latter unnecessary; Hitler's attitude was that the Reich could only sign bilateral non-aggression pacts, which she was willing to do with all the countries named by France except Lithuania, with whom the Memel dispute was still unsettled.[1] For a moment, and as a tactic for weakening the Stresa 'front', Hitler went a step further when, as reported by Simon at the Stresa meeting, he authorised his Foreign Minister, von Neurath, to tell the British that he agreed to a general non-aggression pact between the east European countries even if some of the signatories concluded agreements for military assistance between themselves, provided such agreements were embodied in separate documents and were understood as not involving Germany.[2] However, when Simon tried to induce the German Ambassador in London, von Hoesch, to come down to details after the Stresa conferees had returned home, there was no inclination on the German side to do so.[3]

Sir Samuel Hoare, who succeeded Simon as Foreign Secretary in June when the latter was acknowledged even by Conservatives as increasingly out of touch with affairs, was more sympathetic towards French designs for an eastern pact. He told M.P.s on 1 August that he regarded it as 'one of the cardinal factors in the field of European progress'.[4] By this time France had a new lever for securing British support for the eastern pact, namely her insistence that any agreement in western Europe for mutual assistance against unprovoked air attack, such as the British now keenly desired, must be conditional on the conclusion of the eastern pact. Since London was perhaps of all European cities the most vulnerable to aerial bombardment, the idea of an air pact to supplement Locarno was winning increasing support in Britain, especially since Ministers had heard from the Chancellor's lips in March that Germany had achieved parity with Britain in front-line aircraft and intended to take the lead if the Soviet air force increased in strength. In his Reichstag speech on 21 May Hitler

---

[1] 300 H.C. Deb. 5s. Cols. 983–6 (9 April 1935).   [2] Cmd. 5143, pp. 24–5.
[3] *Ibid.*, pp. 30–1.   [4] 304 H.C. Deb. 5s. Col. 2962.

stated his willingness to enter into an air convention 'to supplement the Locarno pact' and 'to enter upon discussions regarding this matter'.[1] Immediately on taking up his post at the Foreign Office, however, Hoare discovered that German protests against the Franco-Soviet treaty were reducing the prospects for the eastern pact and, since France was adamant that the two must be taken together, for the air convention as well. As though this was not enough, France now began to introduce a new condition into talks on the air pact in stipulating that before they could begin Germany must agree to the principle of bilateral agreements, as for instance between Britain and France, within the framework of the air convention; the idea seemed to be that in this way France would have a first priority, so to say, on British assistance to any country which came under air attack in western Europe.

These two French demands, that an air pact must be conditional on the conclusion of an eastern Locarno, and that it must not exclude bilateral agreements within its framework, provided Hitler with an opening, at first to refuse to carry the talks further until after the Nazi party congress in Nuremburg in September, and then, as disclosed in an interview with the British Ambassador in Berlin, Phipps, on 13 December, to take up the position that the Franco-Soviet alliance had rendered all further discussion pointless.[2] In the New Year the Chancellor modified his stand by saying that the Franco-Soviet pact only ruled discussion of the limitation of air forces in western Europe out of court. By this time, however, a new factor had appeared, namely the Italian invasion of Abyssinia. This gave the German Government a more conclusive opportunity to defer consideration of all the schemes for European security on which two years of diplomacy had been spent and on behalf of which British Ministers had tacitly agreed to make no difficulties about German rearmament. This opportunity was seized when, in February 1936, the German Chargé d'Affaires in London, Prince Bismarck, told the Under-Secretary of State for Foreign Affairs, Cranborne, that discussion of the air pact was 'obviously not practicable' while the Italo-Abyssinian dispute was in progress.[3]

Italy's conflict with Abyssinia, besides supplying the *coup de grâce* to the crumbling Anglo-French–Italian 'front' based on the Stresa conference of April 1935, thus gave Germany the pretext for withdrawing from talks on European security. Moreover, the fact that Mussolini's action became the leading theme of debate in the second half of 1935 meant that Ger-

---

[1] *The Speeches*, II, p. 1242. [2] Cmd. 5143, pp. 61–2. [3] *Ibid.*, pp. 65–7.

many's reintegration into schemes of European security quietly slipped into the background. Yet the hope that this reintegration would be achieved was the driving force behind British policy since the Nazis assumed power in Germany. Once the Abyssinian struggle had enabled Germany to reject British pleas that she should return to the 'comity of nations', there were few real cards left in Britain's hands to play. The idea of joining with France and Russia in military alliance seemed in British eyes to consummate the division of Europe which the clash of French and German policies had threatened since the disarmament conference opened. At the same time it was becoming clear that the Nazi régime's show of interest in British promptings towards a long-term settlement had a way of fading during long exchanges in which first one difficulty, then another, was raised.

II

During the conflict which began in December 1934 with an engagement between Abyssinian and Italian forces at Wal Wal, a watering place in disputed territory between Abyssinia and Italian Somaliland, and culminated in the Italian invasion of Abyssinia on 3 October 1935 it became evident how ill-adjusted was the League Covenant, on which British policy was ostensibly based, to prevailing international facts. In theory, League members, of whom Britain was by all accounts the natural leader, had little alternative but to come to the assistance of Abyssinia, whose League membership dated from 1923. Italian complaints, set forth in a statement to the League Council on 4 September 1935, cited the 'insecurity of frontiers in north-east Africa', the alleged non-fulfilment by Abyssinia of her obligations to suppress slavery and the traffic in arms which she assumed when she entered the League, and the 'disturbed internal situation in Abyssinia', which was supposed to make impossible the carrying out of treaties on the status of foreigners and Italian economic interests.[1] There was little doubt, however, that the October invasion, preceded as it had been over many months by the dispatch of some quarter of a million Italian troops to Eritrea, portended an attempt to bring the whole of Abyssinia under Roman control for the same reasons as have inspired empire builders throughout history. Marshal de Bono, whom Mussolini placed in charge of the Italian campaign, later revealed that as early as the autumn of 1933 the Duce 'was definitely of the opinion that the matter would have to be settled not later than 1936'. 'You don't

[1] L.N.O.J., 16th Year, No. 11, November 1935, pp. 1355–67.

think me too old?' de Bono asked, to which the Duce replied: 'No, because we mustn't lose time,'[1]

The Fascist régime was therefore in the peculiar position of committing precisely the kind of offence which the League was designed to stop and of having precisely the kind of economy the League sanctions system was capable of crippling without having to resort to warlike measures. Yet in the event the League's action against Italy, in which the British Government, contrary to the convictions of most of its members, served as the main source of inspiration, was a total failure. Italian opinion rallied round Mussolini. Abyssinia was forced under the yoke and the League Powers were compelled to accept the fact by denying to the Emperor, Haile Selassie, the right of representation in Geneva. To complete the *débâcle*, after the winding up of sanctions in July 1936 the League no longer counted in European affairs. The part it played in the Rhineland and Spanish civil war crises only emphasised its ineffectiveness. It was not consulted during the Czech and Polish crises which preceded the war of 1939. To appreciate how this came about it is necessary to look, not merely at the policy of 'half-measures' pursued by British and French politicians, but at the lack of alignment between the League structure and the political crisis it was supposed to control.

In the first place, the offending country, Italy, was a member of the League Council and had been one of the four allied Powers which shaped the League Covenant in 1919. She was a guarantor of the Rhineland pact of 1925, an arrangement most British politicians regarded as the only effective relic of the guarantee system proposed by Woodrow Wilson. Italy had in Africa colonial and economic interests of much the same kind as those of her allies of 1919, all of which went back to days before the League existed. Eritrea had been formed out of scattered areas under Italian occupation by the nationalist Premier, Francesco Crispi, in the 1880s; Crispi's Treaty of Uccialli with the Emperor Menelik of Abyssinia in 1890 made Abyssinia momentarily an Italian protectorate. Before the end of the century Somaliland had been turned into a more lasting protectorate. After Italy's advance into the eastern plains of Abyssinia had been disastrously checked by defeat at Adowa in 1896 she had seen Britain virtually annex the Sudan in 1898 and Britain and France agree in 1904 to respect their predominance in Egypt and Morocco respectively. When France's position in Morocco was recognised by Germany after the Agadir crisis in 1911, in return for substantial transfers

[1] Emilio de Bono, *Anno XIII*, London, 1937, p. 13.

of French Congo territory to Berlin, Italy replied by taking Tripoli, the only section of the north African coastline not yet occupied by European Powers. It was in the hope of extending these African possessions, acquired when European conquests in Africa were the order of the day, that Italy left the Central Powers in 1915 and joined the Entente. But this hope was disappointed.

The Entente Powers, so Italians thought after the war, had not fulfilled the promises of compensation in Africa made to Italy when she joined the Allied side in 1915. Fed by Lloyd George with expectations in regard to Asia Minor, she was disappointed with the Lausanne treaty in July 1923, which ended these hopes, except for the cession of the Dodecanese, which Italy had in any case ruled on a *de facto* basis since 1912. When, by a treaty signed in London on 15 July 1924, Britain handed over a strip of Kenya on the right bank of the Juba river the Fascists considered this an insulting scrap from a plutocrat's table; it did nothing to remove the Italian impression that territorial give-and-take in Africa, without regard to the high-minded ideals of the League, was still a rule of European diplomacy.[1] Thus, Italy found herself after the war a founder member of a League which appeared to renounce old-fashioned imperialism, although other League members had extended their empires considerably as a result of the war, yet which offered little in the way of remedy for her economic difficulties. Nor had the economic problems of the early 1930s found any easy solutions in the League. It could of course be argued in reply that, even if all this were true, Abyssinia offered an exceedingly poor prospect for removing these dissatisfactions, and that, by alienating large sections of world opinion by her brutal attack on that country, Italy was only adding to her problems. Unfortunately, Italy in the 1930s was governed by the kind of régime which existed through having whipped up a brand of resentful militarism which could hardly take account of such considerations.

On the other hand, the League Covenant, apart from its virtual silence about economic disasters such as afflicted the world in the 1930s, seemed to bind states to take action against some of the less dangerous threats to peace while encouraging them to remain passive in the face of greater threats. Drawn up at the end of a war which had begun with Great Power attacks on Belgium and Serbia, the Covenant naturally focused upon armed aggression against another state and in doing so tended to ignore the fact that peace may sometimes be mortally

[1] Treaty Series No. 29 (1925), Cmd. 2427.

affected even without the armed crossing of frontiers. The momentous changes which altered the balance of forces on which European peace rested in those years, especially the re-arming of Germany, were not such as automatically to bring the League machinery into action. Indeed, the implicit in-sistence in the Covenant on the equality of states and the reference in its preamble to 'open, just and honourable rela-tions between nations' seemed to many almost arguments con-doning Germany's rearmament since they clashed with the retributive principles of the peace treaties; while the Cove-nant's principle of 'scrupulous respect for all treaty obligations' was balanced by the revisionist article 19 and, in the view of many League supporters, had already been violated by the Allies when they, or rather France, refused to disarm down to Germany's level. The only effective reply League members could make to German rearmament, once the conference had proved a failure, was either rearmament on their own side or the formation of a counter-grouping against Germany, or both. The former, so far from being expressly required by the Covenant, was to some extent discouraged by the emphatic stress on disarmament in article 8; the latter, when weakly attempted at the Stresa conference in April 1935, appeared to not a few League enthusiasts merely as a return to alliance-politics which were supposedly submerged in the League system.

Of the two solitary Great Powers on whom League action depended in 1935, Britain and France, the latter had the strongest reasons for not wishing to offend Italy. Indeed, perhaps the most important reason for Mussolini's decision to subdue Abyssinia in the autumn of 1935 was that France under Laval had resolved to make an understanding with Italy the substitute both for her old east European system, which, with German rearmament, was now in ruins, and for her abortive eastern Locarno. In the absence of any definite British com-mitment beyond the Locarno pact, French Ministers considered that the only way of dealing with Germany was with Italian support, or at least an improvement in Franco-Italian relations sufficient to enable French forces to be concentrated on the frontier with Germany. Neither possibility was likely if Mussolini was so divided from the other League Powers that he had to seek an ally in Berlin. As an additional factor, the security of French communications in the Mediterranean, essential to the movement of French colonial forces from North Africa to meet a German attack at home, could not be provided for short of coming to terms with Mussolini, whose theme of the Mediterranean as a Roman lake was more than a rhetorical flourish.

With the failure of Barthou's efforts to tie Germany's hands by an eastern Locarno and to bring south-eastern Europe into a containment system opposed to Germany, French energies under Laval definitely turned towards strengthening the tie with Italy, some foundations for which had already been laid by Barthou before his murder. Laval's visit to Rome on 5–7 January 1935 represented a forceful, though ill-considered, attempt to consolidate Franco-Italian relations on the basis of French acquiescence in Italian economic, if not political, aims in Abyssinia, in return for Italian support for France in Europe, especially in opposition to further German assaults on the treaty régime. Doubt still surrounds the precise meaning of the verbal assurances which passed between the two men in Rome, but it is clear that neither the communiqué, published on 7 January, nor the secret protocol which became known after the Second World War, tells the full story. It is most unlikely that Mussolini would have agreed, as announced, to liquidate Italian privileges in Tunisia in France's favour by 1945 merely in exchange for 110,000 square miles of the Sahara Desert and 2,500 of the 34,500 shares of the Addis Ababa–Djibuti railway which the French Government owned. What he received in addition was almost certainly, if only in the form of a silent nod, a French *désistement* in regard, not only to Italian economic penetration of Abyssinia, but to some form of military action as well, in so far as Italian plans for this were formulated in precise shape at this date.[1]

It has been alleged that this tacit portion of the Franco-Italian agreement was expressly communicated to the British Government by the Italians, with an invitation that Britain should endorse it, three weeks after Laval left Rome.[2] However this may be, British Ministers certainly gave their blessing to Laval's Rome journey when they met him and his Premier, Flandin, in London at the beginning of February. In a statement issued at the end of these meetings a British welcome was recorded to the declaration 'by which the French and Italian Governments have asserted their intention to develop the traditional friendship which unites the two nations' and the British Government were associated 'with the intention of the French

[1] For the relevant documents and an explanatory note see *The Middle East Journal*, 15, No. 1, Winter 1961, pp. 69–78.
[2] Gaetano Salvemini (*Prelude to World War II*, pp. 177, 185) implies that when the Rome agreements were handed to the British by the Italian Embassy in London on 29 January French agreement to give Italy a free *political* hand in Abyssinia was also made known.

and Italian Governments to collaborate in a spirit of mutual
trust in the maintenance of peace'.[1] Thus it was clear when
the British, French and Italian Ministers met at Stresa two
months later, that their agreement to oppose 'any unilateral
repudiation of treaties which may endanger the peace of Europe'
was understood by the French and Italians, and probably by
the British too, to exclude Africa.[2] Conversations about the
state of affairs in that continent seem to have taken place
between the African experts attached to the three delegations—
there was little point in their being present otherwise—but,
according to Eden, then Minister for League of Nations affairs,
in the House of Commons in October, there were no official
discussions between the heads of delegations.[3] This was despite the fact that Mussolini's intentions in regard to Abyssinia
were already notorious. The most likely explanation is the
one given by Viscount Templewood, then Sir Samuel Hoare,
namely that the British were unwilling to force a delicate issue
which might break the Allied front.[4] This is in line with the
remark made by Simon, who accompanied MacDonald to
Stresa, in a letter to George V towards the end of February,
when he said that:

> Italy is at present occupied with the Abyssinian question,
> as to which Sir John greatly fears that a serious outcome is
> probable. But it must be handled in a way which will not
> adversely affect Anglo-Italian relations.[5]

Whatever the British reasons for this surprising silence at Stresa,
the French could hardly interpret it except as the price to be
paid for Italian support in Europe.

This conclusion drawn by French opinion was a powerful
factor affecting the British position as the crisis developed. The
fact that British politicians had almost unanimously opposed,
even derided, French appeals for stronger British commitments
against Germany meant that they had neither moral nor logical
ground for resisting France's efforts in 1935 to find friends
where she could. There could of course be no question of
Britain taking on Italy, if war came between that country and
Abyssinia, without close French support. This was the burden
of most of the advice Hoare received when he relieved Simon
at the Foreign Office in June. Churchill, summoned to give
his counsel in August, said that the Foreign Secretary

---

[1] Misc. No. 1 (1935), Cmd. 4798, p. 2.
[2] As reported in *The Times*, 15 April 1935.
[3] 305 H.C. Deb. 5s. Col. 214 (23 October).
[4] Templewood, *op. cit.*, p. 156.
[5] Nicolson, *op. cit.*, p. 528.

was justified in going as far with the League of Nations against Italy as he could carry France; but I added that he ought not to put any pressure upon France because of her military convention with Italy and her German preoccupation; and that in the circumstances I did not expect that France would go very far.[1]

It was abundantly clear that no British naval action of consequence could be staged in the Mediterranean or Red Sea without French support or at least benign neutrality. Yet, in the light of the French Government's determination to avoid offending Italy, there was considerable doubt whether French ports would be open to British naval vessels if fighting were to break out in the Mediterranean.

The primary British interest, on the other hand, was that of keeping negotiations going between the disputing states since, apart from the disastrous effect of fighting in Africa on the general European situation British colonies in East Africa must also be adversely affected.   The precedent of the Fashoda crisis of 1898 was much in the minds of British officials; that earlier conflict of colonial policies had been settled by quiet diplomacy, and there seemed no reason why the same method should not be used to tide over the present quarrel.   Accordingly the British Government took the foremost part in negotiations between the three major Powers concerned, looking towards a peaceable solution; these took place in Paris between 16 and 18 August.   The French made clear their desire to remain in the background, lest their motives to be misinterpreted in Rome.   They did, however, join with Britain in urging on the two disputing states a plan of assistance to Abyssinia, to be given by the three Powers collectively, particular regard being paid to the Abyssinian interests of Italy.   These recommendations were rejected by the Italian Government, which insisted on the unconditional annexation to Italy of all the non-Amharic territories of Abyssinia and an Italian mandate over the rest of the country.   The Paris talks were therefore adjourned on 18 August, leaving Britain for the moment with no alternative but a League sanctions policy if Abyssinia were attacked.[2]

III

Locally there were no fundamental British interests in Abyssinia to the defence of which Abyssinian independence was

[1] Winston S. Churchill, *The Second World War*, I, *The Gathering Storm*, p. 132.
[2] See Eden's report to the League Council; L.N.O.J., November 1935, pp. 1133–4.

essential. This the Italians were relieved to hear when their agents, having access to the British Embassy in Rome, secretly photographed a copy of the report of an inter-departmental committee under the chairmanship of Sir John Maffey, which the British Government set up in March; this came to the conclusion that there was nothing for Britain to worry about in any form of Italian predominance in Abyssinia.[1] The most serious British concern centred upon the security of the area around Lake Tsana, from which some of the headwaters of the Nile spring. This interest had been expressed in a tripartite agreement between Britain, France and Italy concluded on 13 December 1906, which defined the spheres of interest of the three Powers in Abyssinia and in particular recognised Italy's special claim to large tracts of the country, thus laying a basis for the Italian pretensions of the 1930s.[2] In an exchange of notes between Britain and Italy at Rome in December 1925 this semi-protectorate status of Abyssinia was given still further definition; the agreement bound Italy to support the British Government in obtaining a concession to undertake the conservancy of the waters of Lake Tsana, while Britain was to support Italy in her application for a concession to construct a railway linking Abyssinia with Italian Somaliland. Britain also agreed 'to recognise an exclusive Italian economic influence in the west of Abyssinia and in the whole of the territory to be covered by the above-mentioned railway'.[3] Not surprisingly, the Abyssinian Government protested to the League Council against this agreement. The British and Italian reply was that Abyssinia was still free to decide whether she would grant the concessions, which Britain and Italy were free to make and to support each other in making.[4]

By the old axioms of old diplomacy, in which Ministers and officials of all the Powers concerned had been reared, these local interests should have encouraged the British Government to come to terms with Italy, the advancing Power in East Africa, on the principle that a state with minor interests in a foreign territory must sooner or later make its peace with the dominant local authority. If Italy was really bent upon reducing Abyssinia and could not be deterred short of war, which no British politician at the time dared contemplate, there

---

[1] An Italian translation of the Maffey Report was published in the *Giornale d'Italia* on 20 February 1936 and a translation of this appeared in *The Times* on the same day.
[2] *Nouveau Recueil Général de Traités*, ed. by Felix Stoerk, 35, Leipzig, 1908, pp. 556–62.
[3] Treaty Series No. 16 (1926), Cmd. 2680.
[4] L.N.O.J., November 1926, pp. 1517–27.

was much to be said for reaching an arrangement with the Italians to secure the Lake Tsana interests, and certainly for avoiding doing anything which might make it more difficult to reach an agreement later on. On the other hand, if, as most British military advisers expected, the Italian army failed to make good their conquest of the country and a compromise settlement was reached with the Emperor, the conflict must be allowed to run its course before British Ministers could know to whom they should apply for the protection of their interests.

There was in addition the well-established British stake in the Sudan and Egypt and in the security of communications through the Suez Canal and the Red Sea. Many of the strongest supporters of League sanctions against Italy after the invasion began in October feared that if Mussolini was not foiled in Abyssinia he would go on to challenge the whole British position in all these areas. As against this, it seemed a sounder assumption that the premiss on which Italian policy had been based since 1870, namely that Italy must never be engaged in war with British naval power, would deter the Duce from such reckless courses. Many British Ministers nevertheless feared, or professed to fear, that if Mussolini met with serious opposition from the League he would be swept into some desperate act against, say, the British Fleet at Malta rather than suffer a reverse in Abyssinia which would almost certainly shatter the Fascist régime. This seems in retrospect most unlikely, but there was enough of a panic about it in London for five cruisers and some smaller craft to be ordered to Gibraltar and the main fleet to be withdrawn from Malta, which was without anti-aircraft defences, to Alexandria.[1]

As against these reasons for a policy of cautious accommodation towards the Italian dictator stood the fact of British membership of the League of Nations and the bearing of this on contemporary British opinion. On the face of it, once Italian troops moved the government had no alternative to using the sanctions machinery to try to bring aggression to a halt. The report by the League Council on 7 October came down without hesitation on Abyssinia's side and, on any strict interpretation of the Covenant, Britain was obliged, by article 16, automatically to apply economic and financial sanctions without waiting to see what other states would do.[2] In 1931, when Japan had attacked Manchuria, the sanctions machinery had never been invoked, Japan had avoided condemnation by the League for aggression, and British pursuit of a conciliation policy had a certain reasonable basis in the confusion about

[1] Templewood, *op. cit.*, p. 163.   [2] L.N.O.J., November 1935, p. 1225.

Manchuria's exact legal status. In 1935, when an interruption of trade with Italy was in any case easier for exporting countries to bear in view of the economic revival, Italy's flagrant action left little room for prevarication over sanctions. Moreover, Britain had in Anthony Eden a staunch champion of sanctions, whatever the rest of the government might think.

Abyssinia, it is true, was admitted into the League in September 1923 on certain conditions, notably that slavery and the traffic in arms should be suppressed in accordance with established international practice.[1] These obligations Italy claimed had not been fulfilled, and the question arose whether Britain and France were free to regard Abyssinia as a guaranteed state within the meaning of article 10 so long as any doubt existed as to the basis of her League membership. There was the further question whether the Covenant obligations could be rigorously adhered to in respect to a country whose borders were as fluid as those of Abyssinia. This consideration tended to give point to the French argument that if Italian forces could not be driven out of Abyssinia without war, for which neither Britain nor France was prepared, the alternative was to see if that country could not be given the kind of shape which would be easier for League Powers to defend in future.

With these reservations the British Government were bound by the Covenant to act against Italy, though, on the testimony of Duff Cooper, then a junior Minister, almost every member of the Cabinet was reluctant to do so on the ground that British forces were in no state to face the risk of war.[2] But they were also compelled by an intense, though short-lived, surge of public opinion to make some show of action. It is a matter of some difficulty to explain why British opinion in 1935 was so firm in its demand for the enforcement of sanctions against Italy while Germany's far more dangerous breaches of treaties tended to be condoned. Undoubtedly feelings of guilt played an important part; guilt in relation to the Versailles Treaty, the blame for which Italy shared with Britain and France; guilt in regard to European imperialism in Africa, the Italian version of empire not even having behind it the excuse that rule by a democratic Power is more beneficial to a native population than government by local tyrants; possibly also guilt in respect of breaches of the Covenant by other states, which could not be so strikingly demonstrated or, it seemed, so easily redressed as Mussolini's war in Abyssinia. Fear of

---

[1] L.N.O.J., Special Supplement No. 13, Records of the Fourth Assembly, Plenary Meetings, Geneva, 1923, p. 125.

[2] Viscount Norwich, *Old Men Forget*, pp. 193–4.

war also played its part as it did in most British reactions to foreign policy issues at this time; sanctions were considered capable of bringing all aggression to a halt (though no British Minister, except perhaps Eden, could agree) without action having to be taken in Europe, so close to one's doorstep and with so many combustible materials lying about. Fear of war also accounted for the implicit premiss on which British sanctionist opinion was generally based, namely that an economic blockade would suffice without force having to be used, and that sanctions should not be pressed to a point where force had to be used. Neither in Britain nor in any of the Dominions was it seriously suggested that Abyssinia was worth a war.

It is true that in the so-called 'Peace Ballot' organised by a 'National Declaration Committee' under Viscount Cecil's chairmanship in June 1934, before Italy's Abyssinian aims were public knowledge, the results of which were published twelve months later, no less than six and three-quarter millions out of the eleven and a half million people questioned approved, not merely continuing British support for the League and for economic sanctions in cases of breaches of the Covenant, but for military measures, if necessary, 'if a nation insists on attacking another'. It is one thing, however, to support military sanctions 'by the other nations' against a particular nation in the abstract, and quite another to agree to take up arms oneself against an actual nation making war in the concrete. It is possible that, once the risks of a military conflict with Italy over sanctions were known, the millions who voted for forceful sanctions in the 'Peace Ballot' would personally have volunteered for the Services or voted for higher Service Estimates when the specific question was put. As it happened, the Ballot was not framed in specific terms and therefore the light it throws on the British public attitude in the actual crisis of October 1935 is inconclusive. What is clear is that when Baldwin told a meeting during the General Election held in the midst of the crisis that 'there will be no great armaments' the military sanctionists of the 'Peace Ballot' do not appear to have risen to ask how, in that case, the policy they had voted for could be carried out.

Whatever the basis for the massive British approval for League action against Mussolini, there is no doubt that the government were forced to take account of it and to give an appearance of complying with it. Their reactions to the Ballot were described by Lord Cecil when he wrote in a conclusion to the 'Official History' of the Ballot, without seeming to grasp the full implications of his words:

Can we say that British policy has been in any degree assisted by our efforts? I think we certainly can. Since the Ballot was started there can be no doubt that a great change has come over the tone of public statements about the League.[1]

None of these public statements, however, made it any less necessary to sound Italy behind the scenes as to her possible acceptance of compensations which might deter her from plunging into an enterprise which would compel British Ministers to honour their inconvenient undertakings. With this in mind, the Cabinet, at the instance of Hoare, the Foreign Secretary, and the Permanent Under-Secretary of State at the Foreign Office, Vansittart, the leading British exponent of the Stresa 'front', decided to send Eden to Rome at the end of June. The choice was an unfortunate one in view of Eden's speeches in defence of the Covenant at Geneva and his well-known aversion to the Fascist régime in Italy. To make matters worse, the offer which Eden carried with him, namely that Abyssinia should be given a strip of British Somaliland as an outlet to the sea, making in return substantial territorial concessions to Italy, caused a storm in Britain when it was disclosed to a Sunday newspaper by a Parliamentary Private Secretary. In any case, the Duce told Eden in an angry interview that the French had promised him a free hand in Abyssinia. Eden's rejoinder that this was intended merely in an economic sense did not accord with Mussolini's account of the January talks in Rome with Laval.[2] The question after the failure of the Eden mission was how far the French were prepared to go in furtherance of the sanctions policy accepted by the bulk of British opinion. France's attitude towards sanctions was the principal uncertainty at a decisive Cabinet meeting in London on 24 August. 'Our line,' Hoare wrote to Chamberlain a few days before this meeting, 'I am sure is to keep in step with the French and, whether now or at Geneva, to act with them.'[3] In what seemed an effort to stiffen the French if Mussolini should go to extremities, the Cabinet's decision on the 24th was 'to uphold the obligations of Britain under the treaties and the League of Nations Covenant'. Churchill records having heard this decision with alarm; he wrote to Hoare on the following day that Britain had only a half of Italy's strength in modern cruisers and destroyers and less than a half in modern submarines.[4]

[1] Dame Adelaide Livingstone, *The Peace Ballot. The Official History*, London, 1935, p. 61.
[2] The Earl of Avon, *Facing the Dictators*, pp. 221–5.
[3] Keith Feiling, *The Life of Neville Chamberlain*, p. 267.
[4] *The Second World War*, I, p. 133.

But the Cabinet's formula was wholly ambiguous, and no doubt intentionally so. In the traditional British understanding of the Covenant, which had actuated every government since the war, the resolution applied just as much to British obligations to bring the parties to a reasonable compromise by negotiation as to the use of forceful restraints against Italy should she invade Abyssinia; possibly more so. However, the mounting tide of British support for firm League action took little account of these fine distinctions and was evidently sweeping the government behind the idea of the League as a coercive machine at a faster pace than most of its members wished.

The same was true of the reception accorded to Hoare's 'revivalist appeal' at the League Assembly on 11 September, when the Foreign Secretary made the forthright statement that:

> in conformity with its precise and explicit obligations the League stands, and my country stands with it, for the collective maintenance of the Covenant in its entirety, and particularly for steady and collective resistance to all acts of unprovoked aggression.

The rapturous welcome accorded by League delegates to these words took Hoare by surprise.[1]   The explanation was that, in the highly charged atmosphere of Geneva, the Foreign Secretary's audience overlooked the stress laid in the speech on the qualification 'collective', which Hoare was careful to repeat. For all who knew the diplomatic circumstances, the implication was clear: that if France could not go along with her Britain must watch her step.   The speech, according to its author's later account, was most carefully prepared and the vital reservation in it, which seemed to the British Cabinet the merest commonsense, completely lost on the audience.   What Assembly delegations did not know was that, before mounting the rostrum, Hoare had had thorough talks with Laval in which he had learned the force of French objections to any League measure which ran the slightest risk of war.   Laval said that his Ambassador in Rome, Chambrun, had given a more optimistic report on Mussolini's readiness to negotiate than the British representative, Lord Perth.   It was apparently on the basis of French information that the two Ministers agreed that 'patient and cautious negotiation' in keeping with the Paris proposals of August should be attempted in order to keep Italy on the Allied side and that if a united front was needed at Geneva against anybody it was against Germany.   Hoare recalls that 'we both

[1] Templewood, op. cit., pp. 169–70.

excluded the idea of war with Italy as too dangerous and doubled-edged for the future of Europe'.[1]

IV

The search for an understanding continued. A Committee of Five had been appointed by the League Council on 6 September to try to find a basis of negotiation between the Italian and Abyssinian viewpoints; this worked under the impulse of British and French anxiety for a formula generous enough to Italy to dispel the gathering war clouds. On the 18th a 'note' issued from the Committee's labours which set forth a comprehensive scheme of League supervision and control for Abyssinia; in this the British and French representatives secured the insertion of an offer by themselves to continue to search for a peaceful settlement and in particular 'to facilitate territorial adjustments between Italy and Abyssinia by offering Abyssinia, if necessary, certain sacrifices in the region of the Somaliland coasts'.[2] This proposal for an Abyssinian outlet to the sea proved acceptable to the Addis Ababa authorities when submitted to the disputing states at the end of September, but was turned down by Mussolini, though not so decisively as to deter further efforts. Britain and France therefore clung to the phrase 'territorial adjustments' in the Committee of Five's 'note' as giving them authority from the League to propose compensations to Italy at Abyssinia's expense which might at one and the same time save the Duce's face and extricate them from a sanctions policy in which they had no confidence and which they felt to be disastrous in its effects on the European situation. It was on this understanding of the British and French positions that the Italian Army moved across the Abyssinian frontier on 3 October.

The League's reply was commendable in speed, ambiguous in purport. On 7 October the Council adopted its Committee's report which arraigned Italy for violating article 12 of the Covenant.[3] Three days later the Sixteenth League Assembly voted in agreement with the Council, only four member-states out of a total of fifty-four dissenting. A Co-ordination Committee representing the fifty sanctionist states was then appointed for the implementation of article 16 and this worked through a smaller sub-committee of eighteen states for the examination of details of the sanctions policy and the submission of proposals. The entry into force of a policy of eco-

---

[1] Templewood, *op. cit.*, p. 168.
[2] Ethiopia No. 1 (1935), Cmd. 5044, p. 6; L.N.O.J., November 1935, pp. 1620–7.
[3] L.N.O.J., November 1935, p. 1225.

nomic sanctions against Italy, on a strictly cautious basis, was fixed for 18 November.[1]   Meanwhile, the British and French Governments were even more anxiously pursuing their efforts to secure League approval for their search for a negotiated settlement.   Statements were made by British and French delegates at the second meeting of the sub-committee of eighteen on 2 November after which the chairman, M. de Vasconcellos of Portugal, made the decisive summing up:

> Certain suggestions have been made that the great workers in the cause of peace should continue their action within the framework of the League.   It is the committee's duty to take note of these suggestions, in the certainty that the League itself will encourage these countries in their activities. ... The League Assembly and Council have declared that the door of conciliation will always remain wide open.[2]

This statement was entirely satisfactory to the British Government since it seemed to commit the League itself to the same 'double line' that they were pursuing.

At the British General Election in November the crisis in Africa was not the most important issue; that was still unemployment, the means test, the depressed areas and similar questions.   Nevertheless, the government availed themselves of the widespread enthusiasm for the League by advertising Eden's work at Geneva and their own loyalty to the Covenant generally.   'We shall continue to do all in our power'—ran Baldwin's election manifesto—'to uphold the Covenant and to maintain and increase the efficiency of the League.   In the present unhappy dispute between Italy and Abyssinia there will be no wavering in the policy we have hitherto pursued.' That policy was not spelled out in detail but that it meant going no further than a reluctant France was evident before the election campaign began, when the government complied with a French refusal to close the Suez Canal to Italy on the ground that this would be tantamount to a declaration of war against Mussolini.   While the election campaign was in progress British representatives at Geneva were actively discouraging the Canadians from pressing for the inclusion of oil and oil products in the sanctions list approved by the Co-ordination Committee.   The main reason behind these efforts was that an oil sanction, by striking in the most direct way at Italian military operations which, in the British view, would have the greatest difficulty in subduing the Abyssinian highlands, would

[1] *Ibid.*, Special Supplement No. 138, Geneva, 1935, pp. 113–14.
[2] *Ibid.*, Special Supplement No. 146, Geneva, 1936, p. 12.

goad Mussolini into some desperate act capable of engendering the war which British and French policy most sought to avoid. As long as the Duce was not driven to extremes by sanctions, the mounting costs of the Abyssinian campaign would, it was hoped, force him to accept some solution which left more manageable domains for the Emperor to rule. Alternatively, the French, after a period of mild and harmless sanctions, might withdraw openly from a League policy, thus allowing Britain to do likewise without incurring the charge of betraying the League; thus Hoare and Neville Chamberlain explained the possibilities to L. S. Amery shortly before the election.[1]   Hence, on the basis of a policy of sanctions coupled with conciliation, the emphasis on each of these elements to vary in accordance with the development of the general situation and of French attitudes, the government won the election on 14 November with the massive, though reduced, majority of 247 seats over all its opponents in the House of Commons.

The pursuit of a negotiated settlement had entered a more concrete phase even before the election, when the Foreign Office expert on East African affairs, Sir Maurice Peterson, had been sent to Paris to try to frame the outline of a compromise with his opposite number at the Quai d'Orsay, St. Quentin.   The timetable for these talks was largely set by the fact that the sub-committee of eighteen at Geneva had agreed to debate the oil sanction on 11 December and the British Cabinet was facing the possibility of having to come out into the open against it; the Italian Ambassador in Paris, Cerruti, had made brutally clear to the French Government that cutting off Italy's oil would mean war.   The British and French hope therefore was that the expert talks in Paris might result in some arrangement which could be endorsed by the League's Committee of Five, in accordance with the authority the two governments had received in September to pursue a negotiated settlement, and then presented to Abyssinia and Italy as the views of the League.

During this brief interval left for compromise Hoare agreed to join in the Paris talks on his way to a holiday in Geneva; he was in a poor state of health after his long struggle piloting the Government of India Bill through the Commons and had had several fainting fits at the Foreign Office. For what ensued in Paris his low physical condition perhaps bore some responsibility; 'it may be,' he wrote later, 'that I was so pulled down by overwork that my judgment was out of gear.'[2]   The Foreign Secretary had with him little in the way of guidance

---

[1] L. S. Amery, *My Political Life*, III, p. 174.   [2] Templewood, *op. cit.*, p. 178.

from the Cabinet; according to the Premier, Baldwin, there was an 'absence of liaison' between Paris and London during the second vital day of the talks.[1] The government, Neville Chamberlain reported, thought that no detailed proposals needed to be worked out, merely enough of an outline to discourage an oil sanction while the possibility of a negotiated settlement existed.[2] In Paris, however, Hoare at once found himself under the greatest pressure. His British assistants were Vansittart, anxious to wind up the Abyssinian affair lest it damage beyond repair the Anglo-French front against Germany, and Sir George Clerk, the Ambassador in Paris, who had little strength against the Quai d'Orsay. Above all, Laval, who persuaded Hoare to stay a day longer than he intended so as to finalise the arrangement, insisted that the agreement should go much further than the Peterson–St. Quentin recommendations since the military situation in Abyssinia had been going in Italy's favour while the experts had been examining maps and drafting proposals in Paris. As a clinching argument he gave the British to understand that a French mobilisation at short notice could not be counted on if the worst should happen.

The Hoare–Laval plan hatched under these conditions is too well known to require much recapitulation. Its main gist was an Abyssinian outlet to the sea, substantial territorial compensation to Italy in Tigre and in the east and south-east of Abyssinia and a zone in the south and south-west in which Italy would have the monopoly of economic development under a form of League control.[3] The proposals received little serious consideration. When they were leaked to the Paris Press after Hoare had gone on to Geneva there was an immediate storm of disapproval in Britain. The effect was that Baldwin, who at first accepted the plan, telling Hoare when the Foreign Secretary was in bed with a broken nose after a fall on the ice in Switzerland that 'we all stand together', realised that he would have to sacrifice both Hoare and the plan if he was to save the government. At a meeting of the Foreign Affairs Committee of Conservative M.P.s Austen Chamberlain made an indignant speech denouncing this 'betrayal of the League' and the Whips reported that there might be a revolt of government supporters in the House.[4] Baldwin complied, but his tactical manœuvre, the act of a master politician who knew

[1] 307 H.C. Deb. 5s. Cols. 2031–2 (19 December 1935).
[2] Feiling, *op. cit.*, p. 274.
[3] For details of the plan see L.N.O.J., January 1936, pp. 40–1; Cmd. 5044.
[4] Amery, *op. cit.*, III, p. 184.

the strength of British sympathy for a Minister who frankly admits his mistakes, had the effect of leaving the situation as it was before, except that the hopes of a negotiated solution were now ended. The plan, the Prime Minister told the Commons in a debate on the affair on 19 December, was 'absolutely and completely dead'; it had no successor.[1] Since the Hoare–Laval proposals had been rejected by all the parties concerned —by Abyssinia, the British public, Mussolini, who, as it now appears, might have accepted the plan as a basis for agreement had Baldwin not disowned it, and, formally at least, by the British Government—no alternative remained except that the conquest of Abyssinia should be pursued to the bitter end.[2]

The concluding stages form a melancholy page. The question of an oil sanction was remitted to an expert committee of the League which reported in February that it could be effective if generally applied and if the United States, instead of exporting three times the former quantity of oil to Italy, reduced her sales to pre-1935 figures.[3] Eden told the House of Commons on 24 February that the report was under study by the government but not much more than a week later, on 3 March, he was agreeing with the French in Geneva on an indefinite postponement of consideration of the oil sanction. By this time the final Italian offensives in Abyssinia were in operation and on 5 May Italian troops entered Addis Ababa, where the annexation of the country to the Italian Empire was proclaimed. The Emperor, Haile Selassie, had left Abyssinia for his long exile two days before. A month later Hoare was back in the Cabinet, this time as First Lord of the Admiralty, though a similar resurrection was not to be the lot of Laval, who had resigned in January. A few days after Hoare's return to the Cabinet, that is on 10 June, Neville Chamberlain was describing the continuance of sanctions as the 'very midsummer of madness' at a meeting of the 1900 Club. The phrase—it could now be used with impunity since the tides of British public opinion had moved from the African crisis to the affairs of King Edward VIII—put the world on notice as to the impending withdrawal of British support for sanctions; accordingly on 6 July the Co-ordination Committee was obliged to recommend the abandonment of this first and final

[1] 307 H.C. Deb. 5s. Col. 2035.

[2] The Secretary-General of the Italian Foreign Office, Raffaele Guariglia, later testified to the Duce's favourable attitude to the Hoare–Laval plan; La Diplomatie Difficile, tr. par Louis Bonalumi, pp. 66–9. L. S. Amery, op. cit., p. 184, writes that Mussolini telephoned his Ambassador in London, Count Grandi, on 18 December, saying that he accepted the plan, but Grandi waited before passing on this information until Hoare's resignation was confirmed.

[3] L.N.O.J., Special Supplement No. 148, Geneva, 1936, pp. 64–7.

experiment in restraint of aggression by the League.[1] But Chamberlain's speech was of even wider import, signifying Britain's departure even from the pretence of support for the League sanctions system in general. Included in this statement was the decisive passage:

> Is it not apparent that the policy of sanctions involves, I do not say war, but a risk of war? . . . is it not also apparent from what has happened that, in the presence of such a risk nations cannot be relied upon to proceed to the last extremity unless their vital interests are threatened? That being so, does it not suggest that it might be wiser to explore the possibilities of localising the danger spots of the world . . . by means of regional arrangements, which could be approved by the League, but which should be guaranteed only by those nations whose interests are vitally concerned with those danger zones?[2]

The Italian subjugation of Abyssinia was a classic-type aggression more characteristic of the nineteenth than the twentieth century. As such it shocked opinion in the democratic states, or at least that part of it which had come to believe that the world had turned over a new leaf in 1919. It was carried into effect by the ruthless exploitation of Western techniques against a primitive and practically defenceless people which outraged liberal opinion already ashamed of European rule over 'lesser breeds without the law'. Yet Italy's action, though it may have encouraged the more hotheaded militarists in Germany and Japan, did not in itself make her a greater danger to world peace. By pinning down substantial Italian forces in Africa and consuming substantial portions of the Italian budget it probably made her less so. For Britain and France, however, the crisis was nevertheless a disaster of the first magnitude. It went far to destroy whatever confidence they had in each other and dug yet deeper the gulf of mistrust between their peoples and their governments and between both countries and Soviet Russia. It split Britain and France irremediably from Italy, now to become a pawn of the Reich, and showed them before the world's eyes as 'willing to wound and yet afraid to strike', dubious as allies and inconsiderable as enemies. By far the most far-reaching effect of Abyssinia's eclipse, however, was on the general European situation and the attempts to deal with the German problem, to which we must now return.

---

[1] L.N.O.J., Special Supplement No. 149, Geneva, 1936, p. 63.
[2] *The Times*, 11 June 1935.

CHAPTER XVII

THE GERMAN RESURGENCE

I

OF all the European Powers Germany was the only one to profit from the war in Abyssinia; Italy certainly gained little of real value.   The League was now shown to be powerless in the face of any determined opponent, and with the nullification of the League went the undermining of the whole international legal system, including the Versailles Treaty.   The original guardians of Versailles, Britain, France and Italy, had fallen out among themselves and their quarrel gave Hitler an opening, which he was not slow to take, to put off discussions of a west European air pact, which Britain had been urging, together with other arrangements for restoring the unity of the European Powers as a prelude to Germany's return to the League.   The Chancellor made clear to the French Ambassador in Berlin early in December 1935 that there was no future for the air pact so long as the war in Africa continued.[1]   His Foreign Minister, von Neurath, made a similar statement to the British Ambassador, Phipps, in January.[2]   Since France had made her agreement to the air pact conditional on the conclusion of an eastern Locarno the effect was to defer the latter to the remote future.   This was satisfactory to the German authorities since they had no desire to tie their hands with either arrangement.

Mussolini's embroilment with the League Powers also helped Germany in another sense, namely to persuade British opinion that, once her claim to equality had been effectively admitted, she was an essentially conservative Power and hence that her campaign against Versailles, so far from arousing alarm, should be regarded as the necessary preliminary to her assumption of a stabilising role in Europe.   This was the note struck with increasing insistence by the German Chancellor throughout 1935.   The impression he strove to create was that by comparison with the firebrand Mussolini he was himself merely seeking to rectify certain legal disabilities under the peace treaties.   The result was that by March 1936, when German troops marched into the demilitarised Rhineland, Britain was

---

[1] Cmd. 5143, p. 60.   [2] *Ibid.*, pp. 63–4.

passing through a wave of pro-German feeling which smoothed the path of the Rhineland *coup*.

This campaign for the winning of British support had seriously begun with Hitler's Reichstag speech of 21 May 1935, when his object seemed to be to drown the alarm created by his repudiation of the military clauses of the Versailles Treaty in offers of new international agreements especially attractive to British ears. These offers included new collective security arrangements in western Europe 'provided suitable recognition was paid to the revision of obsolete treaties', an air convention to supplement the Locarno pact, the limitation of the German navy to 35 per cent of the British, the abolition of heavy weapons of war and the limitation of the tonnage and armament of naval vessels. The significant statement in this speech that Germany's continuing respect for the demilitarisation of the Rhineland was a 'burden' which was not made easier for the Reich to bear by the behaviour of other countries tended to receive little attention in Britain.[1] In any event all these tenders of new security arrangements, on which British interest was keenly focused, led to nothing when taken up by the British Government. The object which they were evidently intended to serve, namely to convince British opinion that Germany's breach of treaties was merely a struggle up to a plateau of contentment, was served by the mere fact that British Ministers clung so hopefully to them.

With the deepening of the Abyssinian crisis Germany's effort to represent herself as an essentially pacific and law-abiding nation increased. When in a note to the other Locarno Powers on 25 May the German Government raised the question whether the Franco-Soviet treaty signed on 2 May was compatible with the Rhineland pact and received a positive answer, this was submissively accepted, it being merely hinted that the matter would be raised again 'in the framework of other negotiations'. These complaisant gestures were repeated as Britain and France felt the strains of the conflict in Abyssinia on their mutual relations. Von Neurath, visiting London in January 1936, told Eden that no serious differences separated Germany from Britain and France although his government still maintained that the Franco-Soviet pact had ruined the prospects for a west European air pact.[2] Hitler then carried the campaign of reassurance a striking step forwards when, in an interview with Bertrand de Jouvenel published in the *Paris-Midi* on 28 February, he said 'the notion of hostility between

[1] *The Speeches*, II, pp. 1218–47.
[2] Cmd. 5143, pp. 64–5.

France and Germany was absurd' and that 'our people are in no way hereditary enemies'. The Chancellor's appeal in this interview for a *rapprochement* with France if she would abandon her Soviet ally, coupled with the warning that otherwise the Franco-Soviet alliance 'would create a new situation', seemed a direct bid for French Right-wing support, as well perhaps as a reminder to Britain that if she really wished to reduce the developing division in Europe she should direct her efforts against France's Soviet pact.

The British Government earnestly pursued these German gestures as one possible fruit of the breach with Italy. Discussions intended to bring Germany down to concrete terms continued into the spring of 1936; Britain pressed for a start to be made with talks on the air pact and aerial disarmament while Germany replied with protests that she was being encircled and gave the Italo-Abyssinian dispute and the Franco-Soviet pact as reasons for postponing the issue. At the beginning of March some semblance of a common Anglo-French strategy appeared in the form of a joint effort to compel Germany to negotiate, a measure which may have precipitated the impending blow in the Rhineland. On 2 March the French Ambassador in Berlin, François-Poncet, had an interview with Hitler to ask the meaning of the *Paris-Midi* article, and in particular to inquire whether the Chancellor had anything concrete in mind. The reply he received was that the interview had been given ten days before the French Chamber ratified the Franco-Soviet pact, though it was published on the day after ratification, and that the French action had changed the whole situation.[1] Four days later Eden saw the German Ambassador in London and asked point blank whether the German Government were prepared for practical steps to be made with the air pact.[2] Having said in reply that he would have an important declaration to make to the British Foreign Secretary on the following day, 7 March, the Ambassador was as good as his word. The answer from Germany, however, turned out to be the not wholly unexpected one that she had on that day restored her full sovereignty over the Rhineland on the ground that the political basis, if not the legal, of the Locarno agreements had been destroyed by the Franco-Soviet pact.[3]

There was very little doubt that the Franco-Soviet treaty had provided the pretext rather than the cause of Germany's action, which had been an ambition of German policy since the demilitarisation of the Rhineland in 1919. How little the treaty justified the *coup* was apparent from the fact that the

[1] Cmd. 5143, pp. 71–2.   [2] *Ibid.*, pp. 72–5.   [3] *Ibid.*, pp. 76–9.

latter was as much a threat to Belgium as to France, since more than half of the demilitarised zone ran along the Belgian frontier, and yet Belgium had signed no pact with Soviet Russia. The truth was that, for one with Hitler's insight into changing political relations, the European situation had developed as a result of the Italo-Abyssinian dispute in such a way that the *coup* could be perpetrated with impunity. What was no doubt far more difficult to foresee was that the same technique which had served when conscription was re-introduced in Germany in the previous year—consisting of promises of good behaviour to follow hard on the heels of sudden breaches of treaty—would work again when used in the second half of the German note on the Rhineland of 7 March. This time the promises included demilitarised zones on both sides of the Belgian-German and Franco-German frontiers, a 25-year non-aggression pact with France and Belgium, a west European air pact, non-aggression treaties with Germany's eastern neighbours, and Germany's return to the League of Nations provided that the question of her full legal equality and of the separation of the League Covenant from the Versailles Treaty was 'clarified through friendly negotiations'.[1] No explanation was provided as to how new agreements with Germany on these lines could be regarded as any more secure than those she was now violating. Nevertheless, in the absence of any effective means of reversing Germany's action there was little that Britain or France could do except look into these offers seriously, or at least give some impression of doing so.

The illegality of Hitler's action was beyond dispute; it was, in Eden's words, 'a severe blow at the principle of the sanctity of treaties which underlies the whole structure of international relations'.[2] By sending forces into the Rhineland Germany had after all infringed not merely articles 42 and 43 of the Versailles Treaty, which British opinion had always regarded as 'imposed' and hence of doubtful validity, but article 4 of the 'voluntary' Locarno agreement, the bed-rock of British relations with western Europe, with its provisions for the compulsory judicial settlement of legal disputes between signatories. Hitler himself, so Eden said, had accepted the British distinction between 'imposed' and 'voluntary' treaties, considering Locarno as an example of the latter, in his talks with Simon and Eden in Berlin in March 1935.[3] Now, not merely was this distinction repudiated, but in a note of 31 March in reply

---

[1] Germany No. 1 (1936), Cmd. 5118.
[2] 309 H.C. Deb. 5s. Col. 1812 (9 March).
[3] *Ibid.*, Col. 1810.

to protests against the *coup* from the other Locarno states the German Government appeared to argue that any treaty signed by Germany which in her eyes was not based on the principle of 'equality' was as invalid as Versailles.[1]

The immediate question, however, was whether the re-occupation of the Rhineland could be regarded as a 'flagrant breach' of the Locarno pact within the meaning of article 3 of the treaty, such that immediate action was necessary to restore the position. In this event, Italy, the joint guarantor of the *status quo* with Britain under the Locarno agreements, could hardly be expected to play her part in view of the closing stages of the Abyssinian campaign having only just begun. But in any case the British Government were satisfied that there was no immediate threat to Belgium and France which required coercive action under the Rhineland pact. Indeed, the masterly nature of Hitler's action lay in the fact that it did not at once suggest the kind of open threat to Belgium or France which might have compelled Britain to act. It turned the balance of power against all three countries in a far more insidious way.

Given that military action did not seem to be called for in defence of France or Belgium, it remained open to debate whether there were any sanctions to hand which might restore the *status quo*. This question was the subject of anxious exchanges between the French Prime Minister, Flandin, and British Ministers when they met in London on 11 and 12 March. Flandin, inverting the position France had held during the Abyssinian crisis, argued that if Britain and France preserved a firm front Germany would yield and withdraw her forces, or alternatively that if Britain were unwilling to act she should at least allow France a free hand to thrust German forces back across the Rhine. The British reply was that Britain could not afford to run the risk of war; Baldwin told Flandin that even 'if there is one chance in a hundred that war would follow from your police operation I have not the right to commit England. . . . England is not in a state to go to war'.[2] Neville Chamberlain, echoing British fears of the lengths to which desperate dictators might go that had animated the Cabinet during the Abyssinian crisis, refused to accept Flandin's account of how a 'mad dictator' would react when forcibly opposed.[3] This British reluctance to challenge Germany gave

---

[1] Misc. No. 6 (1936), Cmd. 5175, pp. 4–12.
[2] Winston S. Churchill, *The Second World War*, I, p. 154; the Earl of Avon, *Facing the Dictators*, pp. 343, 353.
[3] Iain Macleod, *Neville Chamberlain*, p. 190.

Flandin no lever for fighting against the forces in his Cabinet and especially among his military advisers who favoured a similar policy to that of the British. They had not forgotten the lessons of the French entry into the Ruhr in 1923, which showed the severe practical limits to the use of force in another country in time of peace as a means of compelling that country to do one's will. To the argument, which we know now to have been stronger than it seemed at the time, that if the Nazi régime was taught a sharp lesson it would submit or fall, they replied that no one would be sure that this was so, and that France could no more engage German forces on German territory without British support than Britain could throw the Italian army out of Abyssinia without French support.

By arguments of this kind Anglo-French agreement was soon reached not to attempt military measures against Germany. The French, with Belgian support, then pressed for economic and financial sanctions at meetings with the British Ministers in Paris, despite their recent agreement with the British not to proceed with an oil sanction against Italy. But the British opposed even this form of restraint and in this they had the backing of every important section of public opinion behind them. The point was forcefully stated by the Labour Opposition spokesman on foreign affairs, Hugh Dalton, in a Commons debate on the situation on 26 March when he said that:

> it is only right to say bluntly and frankly that public opinion in this country would not support, and certainly the Labour Party would not support, the taking of military sanctions or even of economic sanctions against Germany at this time, in order to put German troops out of the Rhineland.[1]

As Dalton later explained in his memoirs, 'it was the practically unanimous view of the Labour Party and of a vast majority of the British people at the time that we could not apply sanctions to Germany over the Rhineland'.[2]

The assumptions behind these British reactions appeared to be, firstly, that a government's actions within its own frontiers are internal affairs which can hardly affect its international position and, secondly, that until Germany had had her sovereignty fully restored to her she would remain one of the aggrieved Powers and therefore unable to contribute to the mutual security arrangements which British policy was constantly seeking. It was on this ground that Eden considered sanctions to be out of the question since they would destroy that 'basis of confidence' essential to Germany's entry into such

[1] 310 H.C. Deb. 5s. Col. 1454.   [2] *The Fateful Years*, p. 88.

schemes. Explaining British disagreement with French and Belgian appeals for progressive economic and financial sanctions to compel a German withdrawal from the Rhineland zone, Eden said that his task had been 'to create an atmosphere of confidence in which these negotiations can take place'.[1] Moreover, the feeling in British circles that the Versailles Treaty, which British opinion tended to regard as the chief source of the trouble in the postwar world, was now revised in those clauses against which Germany had a reasonable grievance strengthened the view that only after the reoccupation of the Rhineland could a genuine reconciliation between the Powers be realised. These ideas the German Chancellor was quick to seize upon, his strategy from first to last being hinged upon securing the sympathies of Britain. In his note to the other Locarno Powers of 24 March, sent in reply to their protest note of 19 March, he described his Rhineland action as providing for Germany 'the necessary conditions under which she could become a party to a new agreement for a clear and reasonable organisation of peace in Europe'.[2] There were few leading politicians in Britain who required more concrete evidence of German good faith before such assurances could be accepted. In the House of Commons Austen Chamberlain was alone in chiding M.P.s for searching for reassuring words among Hitler's repertoire. 'You can find plenty,' Chamberlain said, 'All we want is reassuring facts. . . . All the facts are forceful; only the words are reassuring.'[3]

The British position therefore, as stated by *The Times* in an optimistic leader on 9 March and by Eden in the House on the same day, was that, in the Foreign Secretary's words, 'if peace is to be secured there is a manifest duty to rebuild'—to rebuild, that is, amid the rubble of the Locarno treaties. Britain took the lead in securing agreement among the Locarno Powers (minus Germany) on 19 March that, after Hitler's one-sided breach of obligations had been suitably deplored, he should be invited to do three things: to submit his argument that the Franco-Soviet pact was inconsistent with the Locarno treaties to the Permanent Court at the Hague; to suspend the fortification of the demilitarised zone; and to agree to the stationing of an international force in the zone for an interim period.[4] A German rejoinder on 24 March rejected these proposals as allegedly based on the principle of discrimination 'which is intolerable for a great nation' and as representing a 'further

---

[1] 310 H.C. Deb. 5s. Col. 1440 (26 March); Avon, *op. cit.*, pp. 355–9.
[2] Cmd. 5175, p. 2.   [3] 310 H.C. Deb. 5s. Col. 1486 (26 March).
[4] Germany No. 2 (1936), Cmd. 5134.

attempt once more to deny Germany's rights of equality with other states'.[1]   A more considered reply came from Berlin at the end of the month;   this began by arguing that the Locarno treaty could not be regarded as a 'voluntary' agreement since no Great Power would renounce sovereignty over its own terri-tory without being forced to do so, and then answered the three points raised by the protesting states.   Germany, the note said, could not submit the issue of the compatibility of the Franco-Soviet pact with the Locarno agreements to the Permanent Court since judges could not be expected to pronounce upon the vital 'political aspects' of the case;   nor could Germany agree to suspend the fortification of the zone, though German troops would not be moved nearer to the French and Belgian frontiers than they were, nor would they be increased, 'pro-vided the Belgian and French Governments acted similarly'. The Locarno Powers' proposal for an international force for the Rhineland was largely ignored except that the German Government agreed to a commission representing the five Locarno Powers with authority to supervise the limitation of forces in western Europe which Germany was proposing and to report breaches of the forces limitation agreement to the states concerned.

The main body of the German note, however, was charac-teristically occupied with a long recapitulation of former pro-posals for reducing tension.   These included Germany's return to the League 'in the expectation that, within a reasonable time and by means of friendly negotiations, the question of colonial equality of rights as well as that of the separation of the Covenant of the League of Nations from its basis in the Treaty of Versailles setting will be cleared up';   the discussion of a twenty-five-year non-aggression or security pact between Bel-gium and France, on one side, and Germany on the other, with Britain and Italy once more acting as guarantors;   an air pact 'to supplement and reinforce these security agreements';   and an international conference to prohibit the use of inhumane weapons in warfare.[2]   When disagreements sprang up between Britain and the French and Belgian Governments on the atti-tude to be taken up towards these proposals, France and Bel-gium protesting that conciliation had gone far enough while the British maintained that they could in no event go further than staff talks with their allies as a symbol of future military restraints on Germany, Eden secured the adoption of a com-promise in the form of a list of questions to be addressed to the

[1] Cmd. 5175, pp. 2–4.
[2] *Ibid.*, pp. 4–12.

German Chancellor designed to clarify his proposals. The inquiry was drawn up and dispatched, only to be ignored by the Führer. By November Eden was admitting in a debate on the Address that 'important divergencies' still existed between all the Powers.[1] It was now abundantly clear that the offers of future German co-operativeness in the note of 31 March had been intended merely to help remove the sour taste left by the Rhineland *coup* and if necessary save the faces of the injured countries.

The consequences of the reoccupation of the Rhineland were in the first place to worsen the strategical position of all the countries which had reason to fear the German resurgence and, in particular, to divide France from her eastern allies by placing a German force, if only of token strength at the outset, along the eastern border of France. Referring to Hitler's progressive strengthening of his Rhineland defences from the moment when the *coup* occurred, Churchill said in the Commons in April that:

> The moment those fortifications are completed and in proportion as they are completed, the whole aspect of Middle Europe is changed and the whole outlook, which is also important, of Middle Europe is changed—the position of the Baltic States, of Poland and of Czechoslovakia, with which must be associated Yugoslavia, Rumania, Austria and some other countries. All these countries are affected very deeply the moment that this great work of construction is completed.[2]

But, secondly and of more immediate importance, Hitler's action consolidated the division of forces which might have been ranged against him had the Italo-Abyssinian conflict, which gave him his opportunity, never occurred. Whereas before the Italian army embarked on the Abyssinian campaign there was a prospect that Germany, still in the very early days of rearmament, might have been forced to accept British and French demands that she bind herself more securely to respect the *status quo*, after the Abyssinian catastrophe she not only had nothing to fear from the Stresa Powers, but was able to strengthen her western defences so as to render the Stresa 'front' powerless even if it could be revived.

II

Two courses were now open to the British Government: either to press on with forging a system for containing Germany despite the demoralized state of its potential members, or to try

---

[1] 317 H.C. Deb. 5s. Col. 279 (5 November).
[2] 310 H.C. Deb. 5s. Cols. 2485–6 (6 April).

to come to some agreement with Germany directly which might place an effective limit to her ambitions. Some slight attempt was made to achieve the former in the face of the strongest public and Parliamentary distaste for anything suggestive of 'exclusive alliances'. When the Government agreed to General Staff talks with Belgium, France and Italy on 19 March 'with a view to arranging the technical conditions on which the obligations which are binding on them could be carried out in case of unprovoked aggression', there was an immediate outcry in Parliament, compounded of bitter memories of the staff talks with France of pre-1914 and horror at the idea of forming a police force with the arch-criminal, Mussolini. 'This country will not support an exclusive Anglo-French military alliance— we may take that for granted,' Dalton said in the Commons on 26 March.[1] The Liberal Opposition leader, Sir Archibald Sinclair, considered that 'what we want to be certain about is that our status as a mediator has not been forfeited, and that we are not now regarded by France and Belgium as pledge-bound allies'.[2] Lloyd George contended that 'the moment you give a military convention, power at a time of crisis passes from the government to the military'.[3] Even Churchill, for all his respect for France as the main pillar of security in Europe, opposed an alliance with the French 'without first an earnest effort to persevere in the other policy, namely the establishment of real collective security under the League of Nations and of the reign of law and respect for international law throughout Europe'.[4] The Ministers therefore encountered no opposition when they assured the House that staff talks with France and Belgium would not be allowed to develop into political commitments until much more was clear about Germany's future intentions. 'I do not believe that at this time,' Eden said, 'we shall contribute to a solution of our difficulties by fashioning our foreign policy exclusively on that of any foreign country, but rather by seeking to understand the difficulties that exist in each and attempting to contrive a common meeting-place. That is our whole objective'.[5] True to this attitude, the staff talks continued for but a few days and were resumed, this time with France only, merely on the eve of war in 1939.

The sequel for Belgium and France was significant. On 14 October King Leopold III told the Belgian Cabinet that 'we must follow a policy exclusively and entirely Belgian. That policy must aim at placing us outside any dispute of our

[1] 310 H.C. Deb. 5s. Col. 1452.　　[2] *Ibid.*, Cols. 1464–5.
[3] *Ibid.*, Col. 1479.　　[4] *Ibid.*, Cols. 1528–9.
[5] *Ibid.*, Col. 1448.

neighbours.'[1]   As a result of British and French inquiries into
the practical bearing of this statement King Leopold visited
London in March 1937, and his Prime Minister did the same a
month later, with the object of reducing Belgium's commitments
under the Locarno pact without affecting the British and
French pledges to Belgium.   On 24 April, as an outcome of
these visits, an Anglo-French declaration was issued which released Belgium from her Locarno obligations; she would henceforward defend her frontiers against invasion or the attempt to
use her territory for aggression against other states but would
no longer be an active Locarno Power.   Britain and France,
however, on their side renewed their Locarno pledges and the
promises of assistance they had given to Belgium on 19 March
in the immediate aftermath of the Rhineland *coup*.[2]

France thus found her north-eastern frontier, the key to invasion from Germany, suddenly plunged into uncertainty.
Moreover, she had now had new and even graver reasons for
internal dissension and new threats to her security as a result of
the civil war in Spain which broke out in July 1936.   The
effect of these hammer blows was to make France more than
usually reliant upon Britain and more than usually willing to
see where British efforts to come to terms with Germany would
lead.

III

The Spanish civil war, which began with an uprising of
army chiefs under General Francisco Franco in Spanish Morocco on 17 July 1936, was a striking illustration of how in the
1930s affairs were evidently moving in favour of the two Fascist
Powers, Germany and Italy, and this because a succession of
issues was presented to the democratic states, each highly
dangerous to them yet on each of which there were strong
reasons for taking no positive action.   In the Italo-Abyssinian
conflict it was unwise, as Churchill repeatedly pointed out,
though only after the event, for Britain and France to involve
themselves too deeply in disputes with Italy while future relations with Germany were still in doubt.   When the Rhineland *coup* took place in March 1936 no British politician suggested that Germany's action should be forcibly reversed,
though it was a considerable act of faith to believe that Hitler
had any interest in British efforts to stabilise the position.   In
the same way, the balance of advantage was distinctly on the
side of attempting to secure agreement between the Powers on

---

[1] R.I.I.A., *Documents on International Affairs, 1936*, pp. 223–7.
[2] Belgium No. 1 (1937), Cmd. 5437.

a non-intervention policy in Spain, so long as there was any hope that the agreement would be generally respected. It is far from certain, in retrospect, that the Fascist states served their own best interests when they deliberately frustrated the non-intervention agreement, though German troops did indeed acquire some training in *Blitzkrieg* on Spanish battlefields; the General Franco they helped make master of Spain not only placed Spanish interests before those of the general Fascist cause in Europe, but had relatively little difficulty in resisting Axis pressure to join the war on their side after the collapse of France in 1940. However, this does not affect the fact that the moral reverse imposed on the democracies by the defeat of the Republican cause in Spain was at the time a serious one.

British critics of the non-intervention policy, few in number at the outset but increasing as the fiasco of non-intervention became apparent, argued that Britain of all countries had the strongest interest in the survival of the Spanish Republic. This interest was in the first place naval, though British imports of iron ore from Spain for purposes of rearmament were a close second in importance. Italian pretensions to mastery of the Mediterranean were growing and had not been lessened by the evident British fears of an engagement with the Italian Navy during the Abyssinian crisis. By March 1936, when a new agreement was signed for Italian loans of up to 25 million gold francs to Albania, that country had become to all intents an Italian client state, thus bolting the door against any hostile access to Italy's Adriatic coastline from the Mediterranean. Italy's fortification of the rocky island of Pantelleria in 1935, in the narrow neck of the Mediterranean, was a thorn in the side of the British fleet at Malta, while Mussolini's declaration in a speech in Milan in November 1936 that the Mediterranean was a matter of life and death for Italy whereas it was only a 'short-cut' for Britain indicated his general attitude. If Italy, now a junior partner of Germany's, could establish herself in the Spanish Balearic Islands as her price for helping Franco into power, if she could do the same in the Canary islands, from which her submarines might harass British shipping in the Atlantic in time of war while a friendly Franco threatened Gibraltar from the rear, a naval menace would be created for Britain of first-class importance.

The insurgents in Spain, with their Fascist allies in Germany and Italy, were no less a threat to France. Aside from the consequences of an anti-French régime in Spain for France's access to her Arab possessions in the Middle East and through the Straits to her Soviet ally, it had always been essential to

France's European defences that she should be free to draw upon military reinforcements across the Mediterranean from North Africa. With the tightening of the German–Italian axis, Mussolini's power to dominate routes across the Mediterranean from his base in the Balearics and also perhaps from Spanish Morocco would surely undermine this source of French strength, while a pro-Axis Franco on both sides of the Strait of Gibraltar might make it difficult for Britain to help France break this Italian blockade. Moreover, any shift in the balance of naval power in the Mediterranean of this magnitude was likely to have the most discouraging effects on every friend of France in east and south-east Europe, if they were not already thoroughly disillusioned as a result of the Rhineland *débâcle*. With Germany feverishly strengthening the Rhineland defences, Italy unleashed in the Mediterranean and forces hostile to France swelling beyond the Pyrenees, France was in a fair way to becoming encircled.

The strategic implications for Britain and France of a Nationalist victory in Spain were aggravated by the probable economic consequences. About 80 per cent of the foreign capital invested in Spain was either British or French, the largest concentrations being in the country's considerable mineral wealth.[1] This gave British and French businessmen a disposition to favour a Nationalist success since they assumed that the Nationalists would be more indulgent towards foreign property owners. The British and French Governments, however, had to bear in mind the fact that the insurgents, if they succeeded, would in all likelihood make arrangements to divert Spanish mineral ores to Germany, now anxious to conserve her American dollars, in return for German assistance during the civil war. By cutting off mineral supplies to the democracies Franco would also be able to repay some of the massive help he had had from Mussolini, who would thus be in the happy position of being able to turn the economic sanctions weapon against the very countries which had used it against him during his war in Abyssinia.

Some of the most vital British interests would therefore be jeopardised by a Nationalist success. Nevertheless, once the fighting in Spain had started and spread with lightning speed to the whole peninsula, the dangers of British involvement in the conflict seemed to be even greater. In the long history of civil conflict in Spain the general British policy had been to allow the sale of arms to the recognised government of the day, but the Spanish struggle of the 1930s, as it appeared to British

---

[1] Elizabeth Monroe, *The Mediterranean in Politics*, London, 1939, p. 222, n. 1.

policy makers, was unique in that it was an aspect or projection of an ideological war which was threatening to tear every European country apart. The almost instinctive revulsion felt by British politicians against wars of faith, as distinct from wars of interest, drove them—with varying degrees of confidence in the good faith of other states—towards non-intervention. The most convincing argument on the other side was that the Spanish Government was, after all, the lawful authority, that it had been properly elected and was by no means Communist-dominated, and that it had every right to ask for and receive arms from abroad in order to defeat a revolt fed, if not instigated, from outside. There was no denying, however, that none of this constituted a legal obligation on other states to provide the arms; they had to make their own decision about that after an assessment of the probable gains and losses to themselves.

The British Government were strongly influenced by Conservative Party sympathy with the Right-wing and clerical forces in Spain which provided Franco with much of his support. The French Ambassador in London, Corbin, reported to Leon Blum, then French Prime Minister, that there was 'strong pro-rebel feeling in the British Cabinet'.[1] Government supporters less partial towards the Franco side felt that the two Spanish factions were equally hostile to the Parliamentary system as understood in Britain and should be allowed to destroy each other, after which Britain could perhaps intervene with offers of help in reconstruction. Sir Samuel Hoare, in his new post as First Lord of the Admiralty, is credited with having expressed the hope for a war 'in the course of which fascists and bolshevists would kill each other off'.[2] In either case, the kind of alarm which had been aroused in British Conservative circles by the Leninist revolution in Russia twenty years before now tended to be revived by the Spanish Government, even though the latter included neither Socialists nor Communists until the Franco revolt was well under way, and although the reforms it had announced since its assumption of office in February 1936 were of the mildest character. Moreover, above and beyond these reactions to the Spanish conflict in official British quarters, there was also the recognition that the traditional British attitude to civil wars, since at least the French Revolution in 1789, was that they were of no concern to Britain unless accompanied by a distinct threat to the balance of power and British security. Had it been assumed that Franco's protectors, Germany and

---

[1] Pierre Cot, *Triumph of Treason*, p. 339.
[2] Quoted in 'France and Non-Intervention in Spain, July–August, 1936', by Geoffrey Warner, *International Affairs*, London, April 1962, p. 205.

Italy, were already Britain's potential enemies in a future war, this principle would have seemed to justify British intervention on the side of the Spanish Government. The British Ministers, however, were far from admitting that a point had been reached when lines of this kind must be drawn. In this they undoubtedly had the support of the majority of British opinion.

The Spanish civil war, like the other main issues dealt with in this chapter, occurred at a moment when the British Government were engaged in efforts to reach a general European settlement capable of maintaining security and of preventing one-sided breaches of treaties. Only in the autumn of 1936, when the non-intervention agreement was already in force, did signs appear that this policy was failing. If the bid for general European agreement were to fail, the government reasoned, there would be little profit in having acquired heavy commitments in Spain since the main conflict would lie with Germany. On the other hand, so long as there was hope of a general settlement with the dictators, they could hardly be regarded as enemies in a war which had already begun. It is true that when direct attacks were made on British ships in the Mediterranean by 'pirate' submarines the government lost no time in calling a conference at Nyon in September 1937. This was wholly effective; Britain and France agreed to sink at sight any submarine found in suspicious circumstances; the smaller states undertook to do the same in their own territorial waters, and even Italy, who at first refused to have anything to do with the agreement, changed her mind when she saw it was effective and applied for admission to the anti-submarine patrol, which was granted on 21 September. But the 'pirate' submarine question was regarded by the British Government as a wholly different issue, which had to be resolved by different methods, from that of support for one side or the other in the Spanish conflict.

By far the most important consideration for the British Cabinet was not whether the struggle was one between 'Democracy' and 'Fascism'—for there were the greatest difficulties in understanding what these words meant in the Spanish context —but whether British public opinion would support a government which saw it in those ideological terms and which came down on the side of 'Democracy'. Issues involving a clear threat to British security, the Empire or British world communications could be relied upon to unite public opinion, though in the prevailing dislike for strong military action even these would have to be presented in the starkest terms if such action was to win support. The doctrinal question, so the government thought, could be relied upon to divide opinion. For this reason Viscount Cranborne, the Under-Secretary of State at the Foreign Office, repeated Castlereagh's words on the meaning for Britain of the Spanish civil conflict of his own day when he said:

> In this country at all times, but especially at the present juncture, when the whole energy of the state is required to unite reasonable men in defence of our existing institutions ... it is of the greatest moment that the public sentiment should not be distracted or divided by an unnecessary interference of the Government in events passing abroad over which they have no, or at best very imperfect means of control.[1]

The Spanish conflict thus excited in its liveliest form the old fear of British Ministers of being dragged into war over a foreign quarrel, not immediately related to British or Imperial security, a quarrel in which the Dominions and the United States lost no time in declaring their strict neutrality and which threatened to throw the British people into the same state of angry division which characterised almost every other country in Europe.

The dangerous effects on unity at home of support for ideological causes abroad were clearly illustrated by the divisions in the French Government on the question whether the Spanish Republicans' appeal for arms, issued before the Franco rebellion began, should be complied with.[2] The French Popular Front Government formed by Leon Blum on 5 June was a coalition of Radicals and Socialists, depending on the support of seventy Communist Deputies. Blum himself, with the agreement of his Air Minister, Pierre Cot, felt no doubt about the need to help a like-minded Spanish Government and made immediate arrangements for the dispatch of ammunition and bombers. Ranged against these two Ministers was Daladier, the Minister of Defence, with the Foreign Minister, Yvon Delbos, who argued that to answer the Spanish appeal was inevitably to widen the conflict into a general war engulfing Europe. Moreover, France herself since the Paris riots of February 1934 had steered an uncertain course along the brink of civil war; if war began in Europe as a result of France's embroilment with Germany and Italy over Spain, Daladier and Delbos maintained, there could be no assurance that French Right-wing and Fascist bodies such as the Cagoulards would not turn their arms against the government. Hoisted in this

[1] 319 H.C. Deb. 5s. Col. 165 (19 January 1937).
[2] Hugh Thomas, *The Spanish Civil War*, pp. 213–14.

way between the two risks, that of splitting his own followers
by agreeing with Britain on a non-intervention policy and that
of driving the French Right and the Catholics into revolt
against his government, Blum came down with a tortured
conscience on the side of attempting to keep aloof from the
Spanish struggle.   After agonised debate the French Cabinet
endorsed the non-intervention policy on 2 August.

Eden maintained in the House of Commons on 29 October,
when the initiation of the non-intervention agreement at the
end of August was debated, that the suggestion had come from
France.[1]   Though this was perhaps formally correct, there is
no doubt that the strongest British pressure was applied on the
French Cabinet during the decisive days at the end of July.
On 23 and 24 July, while the Spanish appeal for arms was still
under consideration in Paris, Blum and Delbos were in London
for an Anglo-Belgian–French meeting on the problems arising
out of Hitler's Rhineland *coup*.   There British alarm was voiced
at the possibility that the French might help the Spanish Government, although Spain was not on the agenda.   After hearing
from Blum that he intended to meet the Spanish request for
arms, Eden is reported to have said: 'that's your affair.   I
simply ask you one thing—please be careful.'[2]   Later, according to Alvarez del Vayo, subsequently Foreign Minister in
the Spanish Republican Government, Britain warned Delbos
through her Ambassador in Paris, Sir George Clerk, that if
France found herself in conflict with Germany as a result of
having sold war *matériel* to the Spanish Government, England
would regard herself as released from the Locarno obligations
and would not come to help.[3]   This warning seems a rather
unlikely one, but that the British threw their weight into the
scales while the French were making up their minds is beyond
doubt.   At the same time, British fears of the ideological conflict in Spain spreading so as to envelop all Europe in flames had
their native parallels in France.

There was a further argument in favour of non-intervention.
This was that the external supporters of Franco, Germany,
Italy and Portugal, were in a stronger position—the first two
because of their rearmament, Portugal because of its contiguity
with Spain—to help him than the democracies were to help the
government and therefore that if non-intervention were abandoned and arms supplied freely to both sides the Nationalists

---

[1] 316 H.C. Deb. 5s. Cols. 40, 42.   The account given in Eden's memoirs (*Facing
the Dictators*, pp. 401–3) is over-simplified.
[2] *Les événements survenus en France de 1933 à 1945: Rapport*, Paris, 1951, I, p. 216.
[3] J. Alvarez del Vayo, *Freedom's Battle*, London, 1940, pp. 69–70.

would profit more than the Republicans. Eden told the Commons that 'there is not in this country an immediate surplus of arms ready for export, and whatever our policy might have been had there been no non-intervention, a supply from this country could not have had an important bearing on the result'.[1] In some respects this was disingenuous. The scale of Axis aid to Franco, especially from Italy, who eventually had 50,000 of her own troops in Spain, was such that it could not have been easily increased; nor did Hitler and Mussolini wish Franco to have too easy a victory.[2] The argument also presupposed far more sympathy with the Republican régime in British governing circles than in fact existed. Nevertheless, it is far from certain that open intervention by all the Powers, each group stimulating the other to increase assistance to its protégés, would have made the outcome more favourable for the Spanish Government or the struggle less tragic for the Spanish people.

There were thus the strongest grounds for non-intervention at the outset. The Trades Union Congress adopted a General Council resolution in support moved by Ernest Bevin at Plymouth on 10 September by 3 million votes to 50,000. Bevin pointed out that 'our whole policy is dependent on the effectiveness of the agreement. If it is ineffective we are under a pledge to call together the parties to reconsider it'.[3] A month later the annual conference of the Labour party at Edinburgh similarly decided by 1,836,000 votes to 519,000, despite strong criticism from the floor, to support the government, though this was made conditional on the non-intervention policy being loyally carried out and charges by the Spanish Government of breaches of the agreement being immediately investigated.[4] The real issue arose once it became clear that Germany, Italy and Russia showed that they had no intention of observing the agreement and that the assistance they gave to one side or other in the civil war would be governed solely by their estimate of what profit they were likely to derive for themselves. By 7 December Eden was telling the House of Commons that 5,000 German troops had landed at Cadiz in violation of the agreement, that large numbers of Italian troops were in Majorca and that many Soviet and other foreign soldiers were fighting on the government side in Madrid.[5] On 18 December the

[1] 316 H.C. Deb. 5s. Col. 44 (29 October 1936).
[2] Hugh Thomas, *op. cit.*, pp. 611–14, on German and Italian attitudes towards Franco.
[3] Trades Union Congress, 68th Annual Report, Plymouth, 1936, p. 387.
[4] Report on the 36th Annual Conference of the Labour Party, Edinburgh, 1936, p. 181.
[5] 318 H.C. Deb. 5s. Col. 1616.

Foreign Secretary intervened in a Christmas adjournment debate with the admission that:

> I wish to be frank with the House on this subject. Non-intervention has not realised our expectations. Neither in the speed with which the agreement was negotiated nor in the manner in which it has been observed since have we, who joined the French in initiating it, any cause for satisfaction.[1]

The government were active in proposing expedients to close the loop-holes in the non-intervention agreement, especially by placing obstacles in the way of private assistance reaching one side or another in Spain from Britain in the hope that this would encourage the other parties to the non-intervention agreement to do the same. The Merchant Shipping (Carriage of Munitions to Spain) Bill was introduced into the House of Commons at the end of November to illegalise the export of arms to Spain in British ships; the government went out of its way to draw public attention to the Foreign Enlistment Act of 1870 which prohibited the recruitment of British subjects for service in foreign wars. Eventually, in February 1937 and largely as a result of British and French initiative, the Non-Intervention Committee agreed to the general prohibition of service in Spain by nationals of parties to the agreement. Britain also played the foremost role in the creation of machinery for supervising the agreement. As a result, when the two Spanish factions objected to the stationing of observation posts on Spanish frontiers or in Spanish ports, the Committee agreed on the posting of observers outside Spanish territory and national waters. By the Committee's resolution of 8 March eight international organisations were set up for purposes of supervision. The most important of these was a naval patrol shared by Britain, France, Germany and Italy; this had no right of visit and search, but could merely report suspected breaches of the agreement to the governments concerned. This had the effect of swelling the main activity of the Committee, the exchange of complaints and counter-complaints across the table. In any event Germany and Italy withdrew from the naval patrol after the bombing of the German patrol vessel, the *Deutschland*, by Spanish Republican forces.

None of these expedients proved to be of much avail. By the time the faulty observation procedure was in operation the Fascist Powers and Russia had already sent as many troops to Spain as they intended and had little difficulty in evading the control procedure to the extent required to keep these forces

[1] *Ibid.*, Col. 2853.

supplied. The question then arose whether Britain should not honourably withdraw from an agreement for which there was much to be said at the outset but which had clearly become a cloak under which every considerable country except the democracies felt free to help their friends in Spain. The British Labour Opposition had no doubt what the answer to this should be. Less than a month after the Labour Party conference at Edinburgh the National Council of Labour convened a meeting of the Labour and Trade Union Internationals and this adopted a unanimous resolution which said that since Germany and Italy were openly supporting the rebels Britain and France should press for an international agreement restoring complete commercial freedom to Republican Spain. This decision was endorsed without dissent by the three executives of the British Labour Party on 28 October.[1] It was, however, noticeable that the Labour Movement seemed to have no proposal to make in the event that the Axis Powers increased their aid to Franco in the same proportion as aid from the democracies went to the Republic under the Labour resolution. 'When it came to action,' writes the biographer of Ernest Bevin, one of the leading figures in this change of policy,

> what—short of direct intervention by the British and French Governments—had Labour to propose? The Left might convince itself that a determined stand on non-intervention would call Hitler's and Mussolini's bluff, or that freedom to purchase arms would allow the Spanish Government to match the supplies pouring in from Italy and Germany; but if Hitler and Mussolini proved not to be bluffing and increased their intervention on Franco's side, was the Labour Party prepared to run the risk of a general war? The plain answer was No.[2]

The reply given by the Prime Minister, Baldwin, to criticism of the non-intervention agreement was that a 'dam which leaks is better than no dam at all', and that it might be possible to repair the leaks. It was not long before this hope was shown to be unfounded. Moreover, the 'leaks' proved to be almost wholly in General Franco's favour, though this seemed mainly due to the Soviet Government's reluctance to commit itself too deeply in a distant enterprise while the dangers in the Far East loomed so near. A point was thus reached in the early summer of 1937 when the entire basis of British support for the non-intervention agreement was being called into question. That

---

[1] Hugh Dalton, *The Fateful Years*, p. 105.
[2] Alan Bullock, *The Life and Times of Ernest Bevin*, I, London, 1960, p. 595.

the government did not seriously re-examine its Spanish policy as the Opposition required was to a large extent due to a wholly new factor, namely the supplanting of Baldwin as Prime Minister by the energetic and masterful Neville Chamberlain in May 1937. Concluding that the only solution to Europe's difficulties lay in a systematic effort to come to terms with the country which held the key to that solution, Germany, Chamberlain saw in Italy an indirect route to agreement with Berlin. 'If only we could get on terms with Germany,' he wrote, 'I would not care a rap for Musso.'[1] An exploratory mission to Berlin by Lord Halifax in November 1936 had, however, produced no result and a British invitation to the German Foreign Minister, von Neurath, to visit London at the end of June was turned down after a torpedo attack on the German cruiser *Leipzig* off Oran, allegedly by Spanish Republican forces.[2] The senior partner in the Axis thus being deaf, the Prime Minister decided to bid for the ear of the junior.

Chamberlain's Italian policy made him reluctant either to press Mussolini too hard in the matter of breaches of the non-intervention agreement or to make the comprehensive settlement he sought conditional upon an Italian withdrawal from Spain. For these reasons the Spanish struggle began to take on the appearance in Chamberlain's eyes of an increasingly irrelevant side-show as compared with the main business of the day. It was yet another example of events which favoured, or seemed in retrospect to favour, the dissatisfied Powers, yet in which the old Allied Powers, Britain and France, appeared, in the early stages at least, to profit from passivity and the avoidance of any strong position while their efforts for a wider European settlement went forward.

IV

In the twenty-three years of British foreign policy covered in this book the events described in this and the previous chapters formed perhaps the most decisive instalment, to which the remaining months before the outbreak of war in 1939 were a supplement. This is apparent when we compare the British position when Mussolini proposed his four-Power pact in October 1932 with what it was when Chamberlain assumed the Premiership in June 1937. At the earlier date the Weimar Republic still survived in Germany; the disarmament conference was far from having failed, though the basic clash

---

[1] Feiling, *op. cit.*, p. 335.
[2] Sir Nevile Henderson, *The Failure of a Mission*, pp. 68–9.

of Franco-German policies which ruined it was unresolved; the French Army was the strongest military force in Europe and there was little doubt that Britain and France together held an easy mastery over the European scene. When Chamberlain became Prime Minister in 1937 the Nazi régime in Germany had turned that country into the most formidable military machine the world had ever seen in peace; Germany had made Italy her servant and destroyed all the restraints imposed by the Allies in 1919 after a long and cruel war; the Rhineland was under arms, splitting France from her east European allies; in Spain the two Fascist Powers were openly hoisting into power another Fascist, or at least anti-democratic, régime, with grave implications for the balance of power in the Mediterranean; the democratic states had been shown as divided and irresolute, giving no sign that they would resist even the most direct challenges to their existence. To understand how war came in 1939 then, it is necessary to consider, not so much the Czech crisis and Munich conference in 1938, on which most controversy has turned, but the crucial changes which had taken place before Chamberlain took office, though, as a leading Minister, he had made his contribution to them. By June 1937 most of the really important foundations of Munich had already been laid.

Perhaps the most significant factor in this drastic reversal in the fortunes of the democratic states was their underlying inferiority *vis-à-vis* Germany in the ratio of European forces. Germany in 1914–18 had come within an ace of defeating the combined forces of Britain, France, Russia and the United States single-handed. Russia she had laid low; the French she had maimed so grievously that by all military logic they should have come out of the war on the losing side. Once German rearmament under Hitler began the Reich had in its hands potential superiority in Europe, there being no effective co-operation between Soviet Russia and the United States, on one side, and Britain and France, on the other, while Italy was alienated from the democratic states through the disappointment of hopes with which she had joined them in 1915. The surprising thing is not that this potential superiority of German strength should have turned the balance of forces in Germany's favour in the mid-1930s, but that it did not show itself as dramatically as it might. The memory of 1918, which in fact was almost a victory for Germany, was still strong enough in German minds to cause doubt whether the Reich could defy the democracies and still survive. This was especially noticeable during the Rhineland crisis in March

1936, when most of Hitler's lieutenants in power feared immediate and crushing reprisals from Britain and France.

But this leaves open the question of how Germany was allowed to reassert her potential strength by rearmament, or why German disarmament under the Versailles Treaty was not accepted as a basis for general disarmament during the Geneva conference. For this much responsibility lies with British policy-makers and the British public. The main ideas on which these, with different shades of emphasis, based themselves at the beginning of this period were at once traditional and revolutionary. The traditional part was the belief that there was after all, a European 'system' or 'concert', in the maintenance of which all Powers had an interest and to which any Power which had rebelled against the 'system' should be encouraged to return by a suitable removal of its grievances. The revolutionary idea was that all countries had learned such a lesson in the First World War that they would never proceed again to a point where war might become inevitable, though a 'mad dictator', unless carefully nursed, might precipitate a war which nobody wanted. In normal times—if 'norms' exist in international affairs—these two ideas may run together; the nihilistic political movements which took Europe by storm in the 1930s destroyed any compatibility that there was between them. The German and Italian youth under their respective dictator's spell were not interested in a European Concert, except one in which they could decide the programme. As for the risk of war serving as a deterrent to them, the mere fact that the British and, after March 1936, the French as well had ruled out war as a solution to almost any international problem robbed this risk of all significance.

In a sense therefore the National Government's so-called 'appeasement' policy was an attempt to fill a vacuum created by the falsification of the ideas on which British policy was based. But it is as well to remember that these ideas were shared by all sections of British opinion, however varied their doctrinal trappings. As we have seen in this chapter, no considerable section of British opinion opposed the efforts to restore Germany to the 'comity of nations' until the hopelessness of those attempts had become abundantly clear; nor did any important section agree that war should be risked in any of the issues dealt with in this chapter, although all these issues together shifted the balance of forces so much against the democracies that what they did after 1937 was of comparatively little account. And yet the error in these British assumptions was not primarily intellectual but moral. It was because of British convictions that the Versailles Treaty was morally wrong that German repudiation of the treaty was accepted before it was voiced; it was because of a British refusal to believe that men could be so wicked as to wish for war that the dictators' professions of good conduct in the future were credited. The nemesis which awaited such moral miscalculations was not perhaps so much the war which inevitably followed in 1939 but the creation of a mental hiatus in which the victims were uncertain what they were to believe in.

CHAPTER XVIII

JAPAN'S CHALLENGE IN ASIA

WHILE the European situation was moving to the dictators' advantage, forces in Japan which strove to reduce China to a dependency were rising in strength. The British Government's critics in Parliament argued that Hitler and Mussolini were encouraged by the immunity enjoyed by Japan in her Manchurian conquest, and that stronger British action in 1931 (which few if any of the critics had in fact proposed) would have made later threats to peace in Europe easier to handle. The reverse argument was also tenable, namely that the Japanese Army was able to penetrate North China in 1935 because Europe was occupied with the Italian attack on Abyssinia and Hitler's subsequent breaches of the Versailles Treaty. What was clear, however, was that when, after failing to persuade the Chinese to acquiesce in Japan's hegemony in East Asia, the Japanese were impelled to subjugate China, British policy was limited to efforts to influence them rather than offer forceful opposition. As against the Japanese navy, freed from the limitations of the Washington Naval Treaty of 1922 after Japan's denunciation of that agreement came into effect in December 1936, Britain could only send a main fleet to the Far East if French naval support was assured and a clear superiority existed over Germany in European waters, neither of which conditions was wholly effective. Moreover, once Italy had been alienated from Britain as a result of the League sanctions policy in 1935 and the Spanish civil war had broken out, the question of sending adequate naval forces to control Japan became academic. The real question was whether an accommodation could be reached with the Japanese authorities, in Tokyo or in the field in China, which would safeguard at least some of Britain's Far Eastern aims while leaving her free to deal with threats in Europe which were already demanding all her strength.

I

The general objects of British policy were clear. The 'broad basis of English policy in China' was defined by Sir Samuel Hoare shortly after becoming Foreign Secretary in June 1935 as 'the maintenance of the principle of the Open

Door, coupled with the full recovery of China's right to control her own destinies'.[1] In practice this meant the fulfilment of the Nine-Power Treaty of Washington of February 1922, with its pledge of respect for China's sovereignty, independence and territorial and administrative integrity; the averting of a full-scale Sino-Japanese conflict which must fall heavily upon British trading and financial interests in China; and helping China to attain national unity with a central government well disposed towards the West and gradually released from extra-territorial restrictions in accordance with the British memorandum of December 1926.[2] These aims depended in the final resort upon what the Japanese were really seeking in China; even as late as the outbreak of Sino-Japanese hostilities on a national scale in 1937 the answer was never entirely clear.

Was Japan merely attempting to impose order on the warring Chinese factions and in that sense serving the interests of all foreign Powers? Many British politicians thought so during and immediately after the Manchurian crisis. Britain herself had often to take the strongest action to defend property, nationals and settlements during the Chinese civil war. In February 1932 British warships on the Yangtze had had to open fire over thirty times in four years to defend British life and property.[3] Japan's action in Manchuria in 1931, in many British eyes, fell into the same category. Sir Austen Chamberlain, who had dealt with the impact of the Chinese civil war on British interests in the 1920s, said of Japanese policy in Manchuria:

> If there is any excuse, and I think there was some excuse, to be made for the course of action taken by Japan, it was to be found partly in the disorganisation of the Government of China and its inability to give protection and satisfaction, and partly in the provocation which China had given and was giving at that moment.[4]

In a discussion in the Commons on the Lytton Report on Manchuria a year later the Foreign Secretary, Sir John Simon, returned to the point.

> But you do a grave injustice . . . if you do not admit that the case of Japan was one which involved many complications, that she has in fact had very severe trials to put up with, that she has been dealing with a neighbour who has been

[1] 304 H.C. Deb. 5s. Col. 523 (11 July).
[2] See above, Chapter XI, pp. 297–8.
[3] 262 H.C. Deb. 5s. Col. 789 (29 February 1932).
[4] 263 H.C. Deb. 5s. Col. 915 (22 March 1932).

very difficult to deal with and that her situation, apparently
her lawful situation, in Manchuria, is something quite exceptional in the history of the world.[1]

There were moreover grounds for thinking that a Manchuria
under Japanese influence might serve as a wedge between
China and Russia, and hence prevent a Sino-Soviet alliance
such as had seemed so formidable to British policy-makers at
the time of Marshal Galen's mission to China.

The Manchurian 'incident' culminated, as few in Europe
foresaw, in the formation of a Japanese-controlled puppet state
which the Japanese Government recognised as independent in
September 1932, and in which Japanese industrial and commercial monopolies were quickly organised to the exclusion of
third countries.   In accordance with the non-recognition principle laid down by Secretary of State Stimson in January 1932,
Britain took a leading role at the special League Assembly which
in February 1933 adopted the Lytton Report but went little
beyond committing League Members not to accord recognition to the new state of Manchukuo.   However, the British
Government made clear their opposition to further League
action so long as the United States remained inactive.   In May
1933 Baldwin, Lord President of the Council, turned down a
suggestion that Britain should ask for a special meeting of the
League Assembly after reports of a Japanese advance south of
the Great Wall of China.[2]   Eighteen months later Britain
virtually acquiesced in Manchuria as an exclusive Japanese
preserve when agreement was given to a request by a local
Japanese Army commander that British troops stationed in the
Peiping area under the 'Boxer' protocol of 1901 should not
exercise north of the Great Wall.[3]

Nevertheless, in the pause effected by the Tangku truce of
31 May 1933, which provided for the withdrawal of Japanese
forces north of the wall and the formation of a neutralised zone
between Chinese and Japanese Army units, Japanese opinion
was at variance with itself as to what the next step should be.
There was no disagreement that 'special relations' must always
exist with China, or in blunter language that Japan's influence
in China must always exceed that of any other Power; that
Japan had a mission to restore law and order in China; that
the economic development of North China with Japanese
capital would lessen Japan's dependency on Western markets
and raw materials.   But little agreement existed as to whether

[1] 275 *Ibid.*, Col. 53 (27 February 1933).
[2] 277 *Ibid.*, Cols. 821–2 (3 May).
[3] 293 *Ibid.*, Col. 620 (5 November 1934).

these aims were to be achieved merely by creating semi-autonomous régimes in North China run by traditionally-minded Chinese who feared the radicalism of the Kuomintang and the Communists; or whether the Chinese Central Government's power would have to be broken by a full-scale invasion of the country, an invasion which might, at worst, provoke intervention from the outside in China's defence, or, at best, destroy the profitable markets Japanese exporters were building up for themselves in South-East Asia to compensate for the markets lost in China through the action of their own militarists.[1] Japan spoke with at least two voices; it was never clear which would prevail.

In March 1934 the 'forward school' seemed to have won the upper hand with the promulgation of the notorious 'Amau declaration' in which the Foreign Ministry stated that Japan had sole responsibility for peace in the Far East, and that she opposed any efforts on the part of China to seek foreign assistance against Japan and even any technical, financial or military assistance by a third party or parties to China. On the face of it, the statement seemed in the tradition of Japan's famous Twenty-one Demands addressed to China in 1915 and the 'Tanaka memorial' of 1927. But it could as easily be interpreted as an expression of alarm lest the current League of Nations proposals for financial and economic aid for China were intended to exclude Japanese participation.[2]

Simon's reaction to the Amau statement was to assume that it was inspired, not by any monopolistic Japanese aims in China, but by 'apprehensions of dangers to peace, to good relations between China and Japan and to the integrity of China'. He therefore asked Lindley, the British Ambassador in Tokyo, to make a 'friendly communication' to the Japanese government assuring them that they had nothing to fear from Britain.[3] On 30 April Simon reported to the Commons that Hirota, the Japanese Foreign Minister, had told Lindley that Japan would observe the Nine-Power Treaty and 'attached great importance' to the Open Door. Simon considered this reply 'reasonably clear' and the government were 'content to leave that particular question where it is'.[4] Amau, the Japanese Foreign Office spokesman who had issued the declaration, was reprimanded

---

[1] See E. M. Gull, *British Economic Interests in the Far East*, p. 135.

[2] At the international war crimes trial in Tokyo in 1946 Kazue Kuwashima, Director of the Bureau of Asiatic Affairs in the Foreign Office in 1934, said that the Office was concerned about a reported League Secretariat scheme of Chinese economic reconstruction which would have this effect. International Military Tribunal for the Far East, *Record*, pp. 29484–7.

[3] 288 H.C. Deb. 5s. Cols. 1368–9 (23 April).

[4] 289 *Ibid.*, Cols. 13–14.

by Hirota but not dismissed from his post. Simon later disclosed that Hirota had added a postscript to his reply to the
effect that 'Japan opposed any activity in China prejudicial
to peace and order', but this phrase had apparently been included only in the Japanese reply to a United States inquiry
on the subject of the Amau declaration, a copy of which had
been sent to the British Ambassador.[1] Nevertheless, there was
little Britain could do but press on with the policy, strongly
urged by Lindley, of avoiding any confrontation with Japan for
fear of weakening the hands of the more moderate Japanese in
their conflict with the extremists. Hoare, succeeding Simon
as Foreign Secretary in June 1935, considered that 'the best he
could hope for' was to avoid frontal crises with the Japanese
'until we were strong enough to overcome them.'[2]

The consolidation of Japanese power in North China and
Inner Mongolia continued without it being clear how far this
was with the acquiescence of the authorities in Tokyo, or
whether the latter could effectively deal with remonstrances
from other states against it. In June 1935 the Japanese army
leaders in North China secured the withdrawal of Chinese
forces from Chahar by the Chin-Doihara Agreement and a
Mongolian secessionist régime was organised in North Chahar
which claimed sovereignty over Suihuan and Ninghsia. Later
the same month an agreement between General Umezu, Chief
of Staff of the Japanese army in North China, and General Ho
Ying-chin, chairman of the Peiping Military Council, provided
for the retirement of Chinese forces from Hopei. In September
the notorious General Tada, commanding Japanese forces in
North China, was pressing for the formation of a new political
régime in North China independent of the Chinese Government
at Nanking; by the end of the year the Nanking authorities had
gone some distance to meet him by agreeing to the establishment of the Hopei–Chahar Political Council under General
Sung Cheh-yuan, a régime which the Japanese hoped, though
in this they were to be disappointed, would prove obedient to
their will. Meanwhile, the Japanese Government were taking
advantage of what appeared to be a Soviet decision *reculer pour
mieux sauter* by purchasing from Russia the Chinese Eastern
Railway running diagonally across the Manchurian salient.
In December Hoare admitted his regret that 'events should
have taken place which . . . lend colour to the belief that Japanese influence is being exerted to shape Chinese internal political developments and administrative arrangements'.[3] With a

---

[1] *Ibid.*, 289, Col. 711 (7 May).   [2] Templewood, *Nine Troubled Years*, p. 135.
[3] 307 H.C. Deb. 5s. Col. 338 (5 December 1935).

rare exhibition of Anglo-American accord, the State Department put forth a reminder, milder in tone, but to much the same effect. 'This Government,' stated Cordell Hull, 'adheres to the provisions of the treaties to which it is a party and continues to bespeak respect by all nations for the provision of treaties solemnly entered into.'[1] This, after all, was an American act of co-operation with the Hoare of the sanctionist period, before the agreement with Laval over Abyssinia.

If in 1935 the prospects for a term being set to the Japanese advance in North China looked discouraging in London, 1936 saw a deterioration in Japan's position and it seemed once more possible that she could be cajoled into accepting some limitation of her ambitions. Chinese resistance stiffened, especially after the victory in November of provincial forces under General Fu Tso-yi over an attempted invasion of Suiyuan by troops led by Prince Teh with the help of units of the Japanese Kwantung Army. A month later came the Sian affair, when forces of Marshal Chang Hsueh-liang kidnapped Generalissimo Chiang Kai-shek and demanded an alliance with the Communists against the Japanese, the incident being followed by an apparent *détente* against Japan between the principal Chinese factions. At the same time, China's economic position was improving, the effect partly of a mission to the Far East of Sir Frederick Leith-Ross, the economic adviser to the British Government, and partly of a series of loans for Chinese railway construction by Britain, Germany, France and Belgium. China's financial crisis, reflected in the depletion of monetary reserves and the violent appreciation of her currency in foreign exchange markets caused by the purchase of world silver supplies by the United States Treasury in accordance with the American Silver Purchase Act of June 1934, was brought under control. In November a Chinese Government decree was issued nationalising silver and establishing an inconvertible paper currency. This stimulated a revival of trade and industry; for the first time for many years the Chinese were able to seek capital abroad for industrial development.

Another cause of alarm for Japan was the strengthening of Russia's position in 1936, reviving Soviet pressure on Manchuria. In March a mutual assistance pact was signed between the Soviets and the Mongolian People's Republic, a challenge to Japanese aspirations for a 'pan-Mongolian state under Japanese tutelage. Meanwhile, negotiations between Tokyo and Moscow for a boundary agreement in Manchuria remained deadlocked. In consequence, the demands of the Japanese

[1] *F.R.U.S., Japan, 1931–1941*, I, pp. 240–1.

army leaders for strengthening ties with Nazi Germany became more insistent.   Talks had been taking place in Berlin since the autumn of 1935 between Ribbentrop and the Japanese Chargé d'Affaires, General Oshima, a firm admirer of the Nazi régime, but the Japanese Foreign Ministry had succeeded in opposing any exclusive engagement with Germany and attempts were made, without success, to secure wider Western support for an anti-Communist pact.   Shigeru Yoshida, after his appointment as Ambassador to London, sounded the British Government on their attitude towards the proposed pact but the British response was cold.   The same reaction met the Japanese Chargé d'Affaires at The Hague when he approached the Netherlands Government concerning measures to combat Communist influence in the East Indies.   The result was that when the Anti-Comintern Pact between Japan and Germany was finally signed in October 1936 neither side in the Japanese dispute about the pact had had their way.   Japanese Ministers, while fearing involvement in German disagreements with the democracies, had to agree to a pact more limited in membership than they wished.   Japanese militarists, admiring Germany's garrison state, had to forego a military alliance with Hitler and rest content merely with the foundation for a later alliance.

These changing Japanese fortunes were regarded with watchful anxiety in London.   Japan had left the League of Nations in protest against the adoption of the Lytton Report in March 1933.   At talks in London between the representatives of the Washington Naval Treaty Powers in the autumn of 1934 the Japanese made clear that they would agree to no naval disarmament treaty to replace the 1922 treaty and the London Naval Treaty of 1930 unless the principle of a 'common upper limit' of naval tonnage, which would have replaced the Washington ratios with equality as between the chief Naval Powers, was accepted.   Simon took advantage of the talks to sound the chief Japanese delegate, Matsudaira, on Japanese policy generally, asking about the Japanese attitude towards the integrity of China, entirely apart from the question of Manchukuo; he received in return 'no satisfactory or clear-cut reply'.[1]   Since Britain and the United States could not compromise with the Japanese claim for parity, the Japanese Government gave notice of intention to terminate the Washington Naval Treaty on 29 December 1934.   At the naval conference which met in London in December 1935 to frame a treaty to replace the two naval agreements which would lapse in December 1936 the Japanese repeated their claim for a common upper limit and,

[1] *F.R.U.S.*, *op. cit.*, pp. 267–8.

when this was again refused, withdrew from the talks on 15 January 1936.[1] Japan declined the invitation to adhere to the London Naval Treaty signed by the remaining Powers on 25 March 1936, the most important item in which was an undertaking to limit battleship guns to 14-inch calibre. This refusal meant that the restriction never came into force as between the signatories; hence the effect of Japan's decision to quit the Washington naval system was to accelerate the naval arms race and at the same time to rule out the qualitative control of naval armaments.

While this failure to limit the expansion of Japanese naval power was taking place, the British were confronted with a further challenge from Japan in China which threatened to undermine the whole British economic position in that country. This was the massive smuggling of goods and silver in and out of China which the Japanese military authorities in North China seemed either to be encouraging, as a means of ruining the Chinese economy, or at least shutting their eyes to. British trade in North China was affected and heavy losses inflicted on the Chinese Customs, on the service of which foreign loans to China were secured. Since China was at this time seeking foreign capital for reconstruction, this threat to her Customs control could eventually undermine her economy. The British Government announced in June 1936 that 2 million Chinese dollars were estimated as having been lost to the Customs authorities within three weeks.[2] Later in 1936 Eden, then Foreign Secretary, reported that British protests against smuggling were having some effect, but shortly before the outbreak of the Sino-Japanese conflict in 1937 the situation was as serious as ever and the Japanese authorities in Tokyo were telling the British Embassy that smuggling was inevitable in view of the unreasonably high Chinese tariffs.[3]

In these years of increasing Japanese control in Inner Mongolia and North China preceding the Sino-Japanese hostilities of 1937 the British Government adhered to the view stated by Simon in an adjournment debate in the Commons on 18 May 1934, when he said that Britain, as a signatory of the Nine-Power Treaty of 1922, was committed to respect Chinese sovereignty, independence and territorial and administrative integrity, but that there was no question of any obligation to preserve those rights.[4] If Britain took action in defence of the Nine-Power Treaty it would clearly have to be in company with

[1] See above, Chapter XV, pp. 391–2.
[2] 314 H.C. Deb. 5s. Col. 10 (29 June 1936).
[3] 324 *Ibid.*, Col. 9 (24 May 1937).   [4] 289 *Ibid.*, Col. 2102.

other signatories, but there was no evidence that any of these regarded themselves as committed to take action or were disposed to act. Certainly the United States Government, in view of the strength of its isolationist public opinion, intended to avoid any joint action with Britain in the developing situation. After conferring in January 1936 with his representative at the London naval talks, Norman Davis, Cordell Hull concluded:

> The question that presented itself was whether and to what extent there could be suitable arrangements by the law-abiding nations to arrest the rapidly developing plans of military aggression. But our government, we knew, was obliged virtually to ignore this method of preserving the peace for the patent reason that public opinion was, in majority, militantly and almost violently against our entering any such joint undertakings.[1]

While Hull speaks repeatedly in his *Memoirs* of having realised from the outset the aims of Japanese militarists in China, he could do little but follow the advice given by his envoy in Tokyo, Joseph Grew, that the hands of the civilian elements in the Japanese Government should not be weakened by any suggestion that the United States was participating in coalitions hostile to Japan.

American fear of involvement in war was symbolised by the neutrality legislation then occupying President and Congress. The first of the Neutrality Acts, passed by Congress on 31 August 1935, authorised the President to embargo the sale of weapons or the making of private loans or credits to nations which he declared to be in a state of war, and to prohibit Americans travelling in belligerent vessels. When discussions began in 1936 for revision of the Act, a new proposal, the Pittman–Reynolds Bill, sought to extend the embargo to raw materials, but the opposition was too strong and the Bill was abandoned in favour of one strengthening the existing Act. The new Act made it incumbent upon the President to forbid the sale of arms if he found a state of war existing and provided for the automatic extension of the embargo to other states subsequently involved in the conflict. Under this law, which became operative on 1 May 1937, if the President found a state of war to exist, the export of arms, ammunition and implements of war to the belligerents became illegal, as did the transport in American vessels of war implements to belligerent states and the travelling of Americans in belligerent vessels. No distinction was drawn

---

[1] *The Memoirs*, I, p. 455.

in the Acts between aggressors and their victims, and this virtually ruled out American co-operation with the League Powers in imposing economic sanctions against an aggressor state. Moreover, the Acts permitted an aggressor to buy raw materials in the United States provided he could pay for them in cash and possessed the necessary shipping to bring them home.

Another factor in the position of the United States which operated against any effort to organise a common Anglo-American front against Japanese attacks on foreign rights in China was that the United States, unlike Britain, had a far greater economic stake in Japan than in China. Since 1914 American trade with and investments in Japan had been growing much more quickly than her Chinese economic interests. In 1936 the United States sold $204 million worth of her goods to Japan and bought $171 million worth of Japanese goods, the figures for China being $55 million and $83 million respectively. Japan in the mid-1930s was America's third best customer and the United States Japan's best customer, China ranking well below Japan in both respects. As for America's foreign investments, only 6 per cent of these were in the Far East in the 1930s, and in this group $387 million worth were in Japan and only $132 million in China. While Britain owned over a third of total foreign investments in China, only 6 per cent was American-owned. 'In view of these figures,' an American historian wrote in 1938, 'it would have been a gratuitous calculation that rated the Open Door in China an American national interest of vital importance.'[1] American officials were deeply troubled by the breakdown of the Washington treaty system in the Far East, but they realised, like Theodore Roosevelt thirty years before, that the Open Door and the territorial integrity of China were not ideals for which the American people would fight.

Shortly after Neville Chamberlain succeeded Baldwin as Premier in May 1937 a British attempt was made to come to terms with Japan in order to stabilise the position in China and obtain concrete guarantees for the defence of foreign interests. On 25 June Eden told the Commons that conversations with the Japanese Ambassador, Yoshida, had suggested that 'it may be possible at a very early date to begin the examination of concrete proposals'.[2] One suggestion, initiated by the Australian Prime Minister, Lyons, at the Imperial Conference held in London in May 1937, was a non-aggression pact in the Far East which would commit Japan to respect the territory of

---

[1] A. Whitney Griswold, *The Far Eastern Policy of the United States*, pp. 469–70.
[2] 325 H.C. Deb. 5s. Col. 1602.

British colonial possessions and of the two Dominions, Australia and New Zealand. Clearly no such project could be proceeded with without American support, and Chamberlain accordingly wrote to Cordell Hull in June emphasising the need for containing the position in the Far East in view of the risk of Britain being engaged militarily in Europe and the Far East at the same time. The two concrete possibilities Chamberlain suggested were an 'early exchange of views on possible Anglo-American–Japanese arrangements to put our relations on a harmonious footing' and an amendment of neutrality legislation to enable the United States Government to distinguish between aggressors and victims of aggression in the event that such arrangements broke down. Hull's reply was negative on both points. New neutrality legislation, he pointed out, had just been passed by Congress and was not likely to be changed so soon, although under the existing laws some latitude was accorded to the President to favour victims of aggression. As for American participation in schemes of security in the Far East, Hull went on, this would be quite contrary to traditional American policy. The most the Secretary of State could promise Chamberlain was 'consultations between and among the Powers most interested, followed by procedure on parallel lines and concurrently'.[1] Not even this limited co-operation, as we shall see, was always forthcoming from the American Government. The whole project of an Anglo-American–Japanese pact, however, was rendered abortive by the Marco Polo Bridge incident and its sequel in July. The Foreign Secretary stated on 21 July that the talks with Japan would not open so long as the present situation in North China persisted.[2]

II

The British reaction to the outbreak of fighting on a far more intensive scale between Chinese and Japanese forces in the Peiping area following the clash at the Marco Polo Bridge near Lukouchiao on 7 July 1937 was to seek to co-ordinate policy with the United States and to avoid being led into any isolated step as a result of resolutions at the League. The American Government expressed its attitude on 16 July when Cordell Hull issued a statement embodying a list of principles to govern international relations. Hull made these generalities applicable to the Far East in a supplementary statement a month later; they were accepted by sixty nations, including Germany, Italy and Japan, but seemed to shed little light on what the United States was prepared to do in the developing military

¹ Hull, op. cit., I, pp. 531–2.   ² 326 H.C. Deb. 5s. Col. 2182.

situation in China.[1] On 20 July Eden wrote to Lindsay, the British Ambassador in Washington, suggesting a joint Anglo-American approach to Japan and China urging the suspension of hostilities and the acceptance of Anglo-American mediation. At the same time he told Bingham, the American Ambassador in London, that Britain could not act alone.[2] Hull objected to Eden's proposal on the ground that it gave the impression that the Western nations were bringing pressure to bear on Japan, whereas they should act impartially in the conflict; that any joint action should be taken by all nations with interests in the Far East and not by two or three; and that isolationists in the United States would be antagonised by suggestions of joint action with Britain.[3] At the same time Hull was offended by the tendency of the British to publicise their proposals for intervention in the crisis, leaving the inference to be drawn that it was up to the United States to join in.[4] Bingham himself appeared to be quite out of line with his chief when he spoke to Eden on 21 July of a possible Anglo-American embargo on trade with Japan. The State Department at once made clear that the two countries must 'each in its own way' urge Japan and China to maintain peace. In any event, when Eden at a Cabinet meeting passed to Chamberlain Bingham's suggestion of an embargo, the Prime Minister objected that 'it smacked very much of sanctions'.[5]

These exchanges with Washington showed that action by the League must serve to keep in touch with America rather than separate her from the League Powers. After the fiasco of sanctions against Italy there seemed little prospect of effective action originating in Geneva. As Eden pointed out in the House of Commons on 28 July, the most important Powers involved in the situation, the United States and Japan, were not League members.[6] Hence, when in mid-September the League Assembly considered two Chinese statements 'on Japanese aggression in China' and the Chinese invocation of articles 10, 11, and 17 of the Covenant, British efforts were directed towards aligning the League with the United States through the consultative machinery of the Nine-Power Treaty of 1922. On 6 October, after discussion in the League's Far Eastern Advisory Committee, created when the Assembly adopted the Lytton Report on Manchuria in February 1933, the Assembly agreed to two reports by the Committee; one declared that '*prima*

[1] *F.R.U.S., Japan, 1931–1941*, I, pp. 325–6, 355–7.
[2] The Earl of Avon, *Facing the Dictators*, p. 531.
[3] Hull, *op. cit.*, I, p. 538.   [4] Hull, *op. cit.*, I, p. 539.
[5] Avon, *op. cit.*, p. 532.   [6] 326 H.C. Deb. 5s. Cols. 3067–8.

facie the events described constitute a breach by Japan of her obligations towards China and towards other states under these treaties', while the other merely stated that 'further efforts must be made to secure the restoration of peace by agreement' and that the Assembly should recommend the parties to the Nine-Power Treaty to consult, as provided in article 7 of the treaty.[1]

On the day before the Assembly took this action two events occurred which showed how careful the United States Government had to be not to outrun its own public opinion by participating in collective efforts to keep the peace. The first was President Roosevelt's famous 'quarantine speech' in Chicago in which he inserted, apparently without consulting his advisers, the view that the United States could not stand out of such collective efforts.

> War is a contagion (the passage ran), whether it be declared or undeclared. It can engulf states and peoples remote from the original scene of hostilities. We are determined to keep out of war, yet we cannot insure ourselves against the disastrous effects of war and the dangers of involvement. We are adopting such measures as will minimise our risk of involvement, but we cannot have complete protection in a world of disorder in which confidence and security have broken down.[2]

The other event was a reply from the State Department, which was not privy to Roosevelt's 'quarantine' proposal, to a further effort by Eden in favour of joint Anglo-American intervention in the crisis. Eden had wanted some form of joint economic boycott of Japan but his draft was diluted by Chamberlain to include the phrase that Britain was 'not convinced that economic action would be effective'. To this the State Department returned a reply 'replete with emollient phrases' on the same day as the 'quarantine' address.[3] On the next day, however, when the American isolationist press was fulminating against Roosevelt, the State Department announced that 'the conclusions of this Government are in general accord with those of the Assembly of the League of Nations.'[4]

That the President had definitely retracted from his exposed position in the Chicago speech was evident in his broadcast 'fireside chat' on October 12, when he said that the purpose of

[1] League of Nations Documents, A 78, 1937, VII, and A 80, 1937, VII, Geneva, 5 October 1937.
[2] Department of State, *Press Releases*, 9 October 1937, p. 275.
[3] Avon, *op. cit.*, p. 534.
[4] Department of State, *Press Releases*, 9 October 1937, p. 284.

the conference of the Nine-Power Treaty signatories, for which Britain was issuing the invitations, would be to 'seek by agreement a solution to the present situation in China', on which Eden commented that there was little prospect of that.[1] Eden was convinced by this time that economic pressure against Japan could not seriously be considered. In a note to Washington on 19 October he said that the alternatives were to use the coming conference to express moral condemnation of Japan, to help China, or to apply economic pressure against Japan. The first two courses, he thought, were likely to be ineffective, but sanctions would create difficulties unless supplemented by arrangements for mutual military assistance among the countries applying them.[2] The American reply was given to Lindsay by Assistant Secretary of State Hugh R. Wilson, who said that sanctions were not within the conference's terms of reference. Roosevelt and Hull feared that if the United States took the lead in proposing sanctions she would attract Japan's hostility. In these circumstances the British and French Governments took the position that at the conference, which it was arranged would meet at Brussels on 3 November, they would go as far as the United States but no further.[3]

Eden, in an eve-of-the-conference talk with Roosevelt's delegate to Brussels, Norman Davis, repeated that Britain could take no action in the Far East without full American cooperation while the strained conditions continued in Europe but was willing to join the United States in direct pressures on Japan.[4] Davis explained that American public opinion excluded any strong action against Japan, but that Roosevelt feared a total collapse of British power in the Far East and was seeking some action to prevent it. Ideally, the President hoped for the appointment of a small committee to keep the crisis under continuing review, but considered that even if the conference was a total failure it would have served to educate American public opinion. Davis's opening statement at the Brussels talks on 3 November, however, showed that for the present American action was confined to urging pacific settlement; the problems underlying Sino-Japanese relations, he said, 'must be solved on a basis that is fair to each and acceptable to both'.[5] Two days later Davis was telling Eden that if her present search for an agreed settlement failed the United States would refuse to buy Japanese goods and, since Britain and the United States took 75 per cent of Japan's exports

---

[1] Avon, *op. cit.*, p. 535. [2] Hull, *op. cit.*, p. 550.
[3] Hull, p. 551. [4] Avon, p. 537; Hull, p. 553.
[5] Department of State, *Press Releases*, 6 November 1937, p. 352.

between them, this would constitute an effective sanction if Britain participated as well. Eden replied that there were two kinds of sanctions, the ineffective and provocative and the effective and dangerous, and that if effective sanctions were in contemplation the risk of war would have to be faced. Chamberlain told Eden, when the Foreign Secretary returned to London in the course of the Brussels conference, that 'on no account will I impose a sanction' and on 12 November the American Under-Secretary of State informed Lindsay that Davis had 'gone too far' in saying that the United States might refuse Japan credits or recognition of her conquests. The most the American Government expected from Brussels, Welles said, was the creation of a standing committee to examine future possibilities.[1]

Since Japan made clear her intention not to co-operate in any way with the states represented at Brussels, the results of their labours were even more negative than those of the League a month before. On 15 November the conference adopted a declaration stating that there was 'no warrant in law for the use of armed force by a country for the purpose of intervening in the internal régime of another country'; it then continued that, since Japan had refused to attend the conference, the states represented at Brussels could only be invited to consider 'what is to be their common attitude in a situation where one party to an international treaty maintains, against the views of all the other parties, that the action which it has taken does not come within the scope of that treaty and sets aside provisions of the treaty which the other parties hold to be operative in the circumstances'. The final report of the conference, issued on 24 November, declared that its terms of reference could not be carried out in so far as these referred to entering into discussion with Japan; the conference was therefore suspending its meetings 'in order to allow time for the participating governments to exchange views and further explore methods by which a just settlement of the dispute may be attained'.[2]

III

It remained for states with interests in China to defend them as best they might in a spreading but still undeclared war. By the end of 1937 Japanese armies dominated the five northern provinces of Chahar, Suiyuan, Hopei, Shansi and Shantung. Chinese forces had been evicted from these areas, though they had escaped total destruction. Japan's advance was mainly

---

[1] Avon, op. cit., pp. 539–40.
[2] Department of State, Press Releases, 27 November 1937, p. 396.

confined to the principal railway lines and waterways, the intervening spaces still harbouring Chinese military formations which continued to menace the invader's communications. Plunging into a quest for total victory which continually eluded them, Japanese forces had little respect for foreigners who stood in their way, and once they mastered a province or city they proceeded to justify their efforts in the eyes of public opinion at home by discriminations against foreign enterprise in the interest of their own traders and businessmen. British diplomacy was henceforward fully occupied with remonstrances to the Japanese Government concerning inroads into British rights in China. In the more serious incidents, as when two British Embassy cars proceeding from Nanking to Shanghai in August 1937 were machine-gunned by Japanese planes and the British Ambassador to China, Sir Hugh Knatchbull-Hugessen, was seriously injured or when, in December, British naval vessels, including the *Ladybird*, were attacked by Japanese aircraft off the Port of Wuhu, apologies and compensation were sought and received. But for the most part the Japanese authorities excused the repeated interference with the thickly massed British trading and commercial interests throughout China as the inevitable incidents of war. At no time was it easy to establish how far these actions represented a calculated Japanese policy of driving the British from China or merely the zeal or carelessness of local Japanese military and naval forces.

The British Government hoped for a common Anglo-American approach when British and American warships were attacked by Japanese air forces in the Yangtze on 12 December, resulting in the sinking of the American gun-boat *Panay* with heavy casualties. But even in this case the British and American notes of protest had to be sent separately to avoid inflaming American isolationist opinion by any suggestion of joint action. After a preliminary apology to Britain on 14 December, a comprehensive Japanese reply on 28 December declared that the attack was unintentional. A British note in reply on 31 December expressed satisfaction with this explanation while asking to be informed of measures to prevent the recurrence of such incidents and their 'effective application'. The American note asked that the Emperor be informed of the strength of American feeling, while the Japanese reply on 24 December reiterated the claim that the attack was unintentional, gave assurances against repetition and stated that the offenders had been dealt with 'according to the law'. The Japanese Government expressed the 'fervent hope' that friendly relations between Japan and the United States would not be affected by 'this unfortunate affair'. The importance of the incident was that it seemed to strengthen, rather than undermine, the American belief that they would obtain greater satisfaction from Tokyo if they avoided entanglement with the far vaster network of British interests in China. The American historian Griswold commented that 'in obtaining satisfaction as it did, the United States was undoubtedly assisted by the fact that it had kept free of hostile coalitions and coercive enterprise and could approach Japan with an ironclad claim admitting of no political suspicions'.[1]

The *Panay* incident, however, had its outcome in a limited measure of Anglo-American naval co-operation. As soon as the attack in the Yangtze occurred Eden proposed an Anglo-American naval display to warn the Japanese. Roosevelt demurred but then saw Lindsay on 16 December and suggested staff conversations with Britain as in 1916-17, promising to send a naval officer to London for the purpose. The officer chosen, Captain Ingersoll, arrived in London on New Year's Day, 1938, but insisted that the question was merely one of technical co-operation for the time being, and that only after the technical aspects had been fully explored would it be possible to consider political implications. Early in January, however, Lindsay was able to tell Eden that three United States cruisers would be visiting Singapore and that American naval manœuvres in the Pacific would be advanced two or three months so as to begin in February. Roosevelt parried Eden's offer of eight or nine capital and other ships for a joint naval display by replying that all British ships were required in Europe.[2]

The year then opening was one of the most intense strain on the British position in the Far East owing to the crowding dangers in Europe. The Czech crisis and the Anglo-French agreement to Germany's demands at the Munich conference in September stimulated the Japanese military authorities to spread the war in China and cut off the Chinese from all supplies from the outside world. On 12 October 30,000 Japanese troops were landed in and around Bias Bay, 50 miles north-east of the Pearl River, on which the port of Canton lay. Canton fell to a Japanese advance guard on 21 October and four days later Hankow, to which the Central Chinese Government had withdrawn after the fall of Nanking, was occupied by the Japanese. So that, when the military campaigns came to an end that year, the Japanese were in control of most of the chief cities of China and most of her railway and river communications, including China's main channels for contact with the

---

[1] *Op. cit.*, p. 463.   [2] Avon, *op. cit.*, pp. 544-6.

outside world, through which flowed her foreign trade and supplies of war equipment from abroad. The Chinese Government had been forced to make its home in Chungking, some 1,400 miles from the coast.

Japan's domestic economic difficulties were nevertheless mounting, causing her to hasten all the more rapidly along the road of welding together her Asian conquests to form a single economic whole. The total Japanese human and material resources were placed under government control by the National Mobilisation Act which passed the Diet in March 1938, and a bias was given to the development of heavy industries at the expense of light as a means of speeding the war effort. The consequent fall in exports to markets outside the yen bloc necessitated strict control of foreign exchange and the limiting of imports from the non-yen world to the essential minimum. These developments gave point to the arguments of the militarists who had always favoured the creation of a tripartite grouping of Japan, China and Manchuria in which an increasing share of Japan's foreign economic needs could be met. For such a policy to succeed the early ending of Chinese resistance was essential, as was also the positive co-operation of the Chinese in the programme, and as far as possible that of external Powers with interests in China as well. Thus, by the end of 1938 the success of Japan's policy had come to depend upon overcoming Chinese resistance, greatly increasing the tempo of industrial development in Manchuria and North China, and bullying or cajoling external countries, principally Britain, into accepting a contraction of their privileges in China.

For these reasons Sir Robert Craigie, the British Ambassador in Tokyo, obtained little satisfaction from his efforts in the summer of 1938 to persuade the Japanese Foreign Minister, Ugaki, to reach agreements for respecting British rights in China and reducing interference with British interests. On this gamble he urged the government in London to stake much. On August 22 he deprecated a proposed British initiative in favour of a collective approach to Japan calling on her to suppress the bombing of civilian settlements from the air, of which there had been many deplorable examples during the military operations in China; in Craigie's view:

Violent criticism of Japan and hints of economic pressure do infinite harm because they undermine the position of our friends and are discussed by our enemies as either bluff or derogatory to Japan's dignity. Action such as preliminary steps towards economic retaliation would of course produce an impression but, in the present mad-dog temper of these people, it would be infinitely dangerous and should permanently only be contemplated when all further hope of slow advance along present lines has been abandoned.[1]

By the end of October, however, Craigie was sending Lord Halifax, Eden's successor after the latter's resignation as Foreign Secretary in February, a copy of the letter he had handed to the Japanese Vice-Foreign Minister stating that Japan had failed to meet the British desiderata 'in any single instance of any importance'. 'In spite of all my efforts to impress the Japanese Government with the importance of these issues,' Craigie continued, 'we have in fact received no real satisfaction whatsoever.'[2] The essential fact was that, in the absence of more effective means of pressure, there was little that British representatives could do but urge respect for foreign rights on Japan's rulers. Craigie stated the dilemma in the following terms:

> There is a great deal to be said for the application against Japan of really effective sanctions in full co-operation with members of the (League) Council. There is nothing to be said for a purely theoretical or largely ineffectual application, the effects of which must be mischievous in the extreme. Nothing could be better calculated to render irresistible the present trend towards a strengthening of Japan's ties with the totalitarian states. Furthermore, opportunity would be seized by our enemies here to use this as an argument for disrupting our rights in China even more than they are at present.[3]

Strong demands nevertheless continued to be made by the British Parliament and public opinion that help should be extended to China in her hour of need. These pleas had more than a mere eleemosynary basis. If China, despite the remarkable capacity of the country to hold together in the face of invasion owing to its decentralised economy, came to the brink of defeat, there was a distinct possibility that the pro-Japanese elements among China's rulers would have their way and surrender the country to Japan, or alternatively that China would throw in her lot with Russia. Both possibilities might be even more harmful to British interests in China than the present situation. The British Ambassador in China, Sir Archibald Clark-Kerr, taking an opposite viewpoint from Craigie's, re-

---

[1] *D.B.F.P.*, Third Series, VIII, p. 36.
[2] *Ibid.*, p. 170.   [3] *Ibid.*, pp. 108–9.

peatedly warned of an agonising reappraisal of her position on China's part if help from the West was not forthcoming. He complained that he had nothing to offer China: 'I confess that I am feeling parched and barren.'[1] On October 14 he reported that the Munich agreement had shaken British prestige in the Far East. 'The Chinese reaction,' he wrote, 'is that we are entirely self-seeking and have been merely keeping them in play with fair words, throwing them a bone now and again hoping that they would fight long enough to exhaust Japan and so remove a potential danger to ourselves.'[2] Halifax explained in reply that more concrete assistance to China, as for instance the loan asked for by the Chinese Ambassador to London, had always to be measured against the effects on Japan.

This plain fact is [he went on] that Ministers feel unwilling at this moment to take any chance of provoking an incident with Japan which would face us with the choice of climbing down or depleting our forces in European waters, for we are not in a position to defend effectively our interests in the Far East at the moment and this situation is bound to continue until the position in Europe lightens or we are sufficiently rearmed to enable us to maintain a force of ships in Far Eastern waters sufficient to engage the Japanese navy. Any suggeston of help from us to China provokes an uproar in Japan which merely serves to increase the feeling above mentioned.

The position, the melancholy Halifax reflected, 'is not helped in any way by the constant publicity in Parliament, press and elsewhere, for which I fear the Chinese themselves must bear some of the responsibility'.[3]

Parliamentary agitation on China's behalf was nevertheless strong enough to oblige the government to make at least a token offer of help. Early in December 1938 it was decided to include China among the countries to which the Board of Trade was authorised to guarantee exports of up to £10 million in value. In addition a Board of Trade guarantee was provided of up to £500,000 for the purchase of lorries for transporting supplies into China up the Burma Road from Rangoon.[4] This decision was timed to accord with an announcement by the United States Treasury of a credit to China, which Halifax heard on 19 December would probably be for $25 million.[5] On the same day the Foreign Secretary told the Chinese

[1] D.B.F.P., Third Series, VIII, p. 130.   [2] Ibid., pp. 137–8.
[3] Ibid. pp. 142–3.   [4] Ibid., pp. 309–12.
[5] Ibid., pp. 335–6.

Ambassador that a decision would be reached without delay on the Chinese request for a loan similar to the American offer for the purpose of equalising China's foreign exchange rate.[1] Craigie, reporting at the end of the month, said that the news of the credits to China had had a salutary effect since a statement on 22 December by the Japanese Premier, Prince Konoye, explaining Japan's aims in China had been 'politely phrased', though it had hinted that the interests of third Powers would only be respected in China if they 'grasp the meaning of the new East Asia and are willing to act accordingly'.[2]

Chamberlain toyed with the idea that the 'new order' would still leave room for British investments. On 1 November in the Commons he rebutted the Leader of the Opposition's forecast that Japan would refuse to share the economic benefits of her Chinese conquest with other Powers. 'It is quite certain,' Chamberlain said, 'that when the war is over and the reconstruction of China begins, she cannot be reconstructed without some help from this country.'[3] Two days later the Prime Minister saw a dispatch from Craigie on the New Order which seemed to confirm these hopes. Craigie reported a statement of Konoye's of 2 November which began with the contention that 'the Kuomintang Government no longer exists except as a mere local régime' and that Japan would not lay down her arms until that régime was smashed. 'What Japan seeks,' the Konoye statement continued, 'is the establishment of a New Order which will ensure permanent stability in East Asia.' This was to take the form of a 'tripartite relationship of mutual aid and co-ordination between Japan, Manchuria and China'. Craigie considered that Japan's economic difficulties would nevertheless persuade her to make a moderate peace settlement and held out hopes of a British role in the New Order; 'although during hostilities,' he said, 'our respective points of view may be irreconcilable, it is possible to see a point of convergence in the event of an eventual settlement of which we are in a position to approve'.[4] This was in line with Chamberlain's thinking, but it was important to put government critics off the scent. On 9 November the Under-Secretary of State for Foreign Affairs denied that the government were contemplating a deal with Japan and reassured the Commons that 'we could not consider any alterations in the position as laid down in the treaties which have been brought about by unilateral action'.[5]

Chamberlain received little or no encouragement from

[1] Ibid., pp. 336–7.   [2] Ibid., pp. 343–4, 349.
[3] 340 H.C. Deb. 5s. Col. 82.   [4] D.B.F.P., Third Series, VIII, p. 189.
[5] 341 H.C. Deb. 5s. Col. 165.

Tokyo. On 17 November the new Japanese Foreign Minister, Arita, enlarging upon the Konoye statement of 2 November, told Craigie that a 'new situation' had come about, namely the adoption of the plan for a triangular grouping of Japan, China and Manchuria and that 'previous assurances to Britain might no longer be valid'.[1] On the same day Craigie was informed by Shiratori, the spokesman of the Japanese Foreign Office, that the British terms for mediation in the Sino-Japanese dispute were unacceptable and that 'Japan was now in a position to impose what terms she wished on China'. 'Britain,' Shiratori said, 'must resign herself to lose the dominant position she had hitherto held in China; that position would pass to Japan as an Asiatic nation entitled to it by race as well as by conquest.'[2] At the same time the long-drawn-out negotiations between Japan and Germany for a military alliance were causing concern in London. Halifax wrote to Craigie on 18 November that the new plan under contemplation by the Japanese Government envisaged consultation with Germany if either party was involved in a dispute with a third Power and mutual support if either was threatened by a third Power. The effect would be to frustrate all hope of Japanese neutrality in the Far East if Chamberlain's policy of seeking an accord with Germany broke down and war in Europe came. Britain would then have to defend Australia and the Far Eastern dependencies when naval resources would be fully stretched in Europe.[3]

British policy was in a maze in which every path led nowhere. Japan could not be trusted to allow British rights to remain as before once her conquests in China were complete; in any case, British public opinion and the likely reactions from the United States ruled out such a deal with Japan, even if the Japanese agreed to it. The Foreign Office told Craigie on 24 November that the government 'had no intention of allowing themselves to be inveigled into negotiations for a deal with Japan inimical to the rights and interests of China or any other third party'.[4] Chamberlain himself had taken the same strong line when he saw the Japanese Ambassador two days before, saying that 'what we wanted to see was some action by the Japanese Government to give practical proof of their professed wish to respect foreign rights in China'.[5] Yet, in view of the unresponsiveness of the Japanese, the government could not but think that their policy of accommodation with Germany might in some way be used to influence Japan. The Foreign

---

[1] *D.B.F.P.*, Third Series, VIII, pp. 234–6.
[2] *Ibid.*, p. 237.
[3] *Ibid.*, p. 239.
[4] *Ibid.*, pp. 260–1.
[5] *Ibid.*, pp. 262–3.

Office wrote to Craigie on 25 November that the Far East might become a 'not too unpromising field' for a start to be made on Anglo-German co-operation. Britain and Germany, the idea ran, had important common interests in the area: both wanted a peaceful and prosperous China and a Japan saved from an economic collapse of her own making; Germany wanted a strong Japan as an ally against Russia, and for Britain Japan was a valuable market. Despite all evidence to the contrary, the Foreign Office hoped that, as Anglo-German relations became less strained, the United States would join in this Anglo-German co-operation in the Far East.[1] Consistently with this thinking, the United States was told by Lindsay on 1 December that there was no value in retaliatory action against Japan by any government by itself and that 'minor pin-pricks' would only irritate the Japanese without seriously hurting them. 'Nothing short of denouncing the commercial treaty would hurt,' Lindsay said, 'and it was quite a question whether that action might not hurt us more than Japan.'[2]

This pained tergiversation in Britain was brusquely ended when Japan put paid to the idea of negotiating for the defence of British interests in China by a series of statements in which the meaning of the New Order was made plain. The least equivocal of these was given to the foreign press by the Foreign Minister on 19 December. In it the New Order was described as 'a relationship of mutual aid and co-ordination between Japan, Manchuria, and China', signifying 'the creation of solidarity between these three countries for the common purpose of preserving the integrity of East Asia while enabling each nation to maintain its independence and fully to develop its individuality'. 'It is far from Japan's thought,' Arita said, 'to exclude European and American economic interests from East Asia,' but it was 'imperative that the economic activities of other Powers should be subject to certain restrictions dictated by the requirements of national defence and economic security of the countries grouped under the New Order'. Craigie considered it 'impossible to overstate the seriousness of the effect of the realisation of these recently announced policies upon our position *vis-à-vis* the Japanese Government'. If Japan succeeded in creating an all-China puppet government, Craigie reasoned, 'the experience of the Western Powers in Manchuria would be repeated; they would simply be told to address all their grievances to the new régime which would, however, be entirely without power to redress them'. The Ambassador urged 'further and early action to bring it home forcibly to this

---

[1] *Ibid.*, pp. 267–8.   [2] *Ibid.*, pp. 278–9.

country that we are not disposed to look on while the policies envisaged in this statement are translated into action'.[1]

From this moment Craigie's tone changed; abandoning his fear of weakening the hands of moderate Japanese, he asserted that 'the psychological moment for economic pressure has arrived'. 'It is no longer a question of protecting this or that vested or trade interest in China', he wrote on New Year's Day, 1939, 'but of preventing, while there is yet time, the formation in East Asia of a valid economic entity which may have serious repercussions on the credit of every category of Power'.[2] The question still remained, however, by what means Britain was supposed to frustrate the New Order. Halifax, giving the government's reaction to Craigie on 5 January, said that they were 'not prepared to accept or recognise changes of the nature indicated which are brought about by force'; they intended to stand by the Nine-Power Treaty and could not agree to any unilateral modification of its terms. Nevertheless, when it came to practical action, the government could think of little except expressing willingness to consider Japanese proposals for an agreed revision of the Washington Treaty and promising to resume negotiations with a 'fully independent China' for the abolition of extra-territoriality when peace had been restored.[3] These principles were embodied in a British note to Japan on the New Order which Craigie was instructed to present on 14 January.[4]

In his message to Congress on 3 January Roosevelt warned Americans of the dangers threatening their civilisation from the aggressor states and said that there were methods short of war for making their protests effective. Chamberlain welcomed this statement on 5 January as an indication of America's 'vital role'.[5] At the same time, Halifax, fearing that 'China might be tempted to despair and make peace with the Japanese', asked Mallett in Washington to propose a joint Anglo-American currency loan to China.[6] Roosevelt's hesitations returned. He doubted whether there was any constitutional basis on which he could participate in the proposed British loan to China without authority from Congress. The most he could do was to agree to make known his own measures for assisting China, such as the purchase of more Chinese silver, at the same time as the announcement of the British loan.[7] Mallet reported from Washington on 9 February that the American Government

[1] *D.B.F.P.*, Third Series, VIII, pp. 355–8.
[2] *Ibid.*, pp. 362–3.   [3] *Ibid.*, pp. 371–3.
[4] The text of the note was printed in *The Times*, 16 January 1939.
[5] *The Times*, 6 January 1939.
[6] *D.B.F.P.*, Third Series, VIII, pp. 373–4.   [7] *Ibid.*, pp. 384–5.

also feared that the time was not ripe for a policy of direct pressure on Japan, as by a boycott of Japanese imports. The Minister explained that 'any suspicion that our two governments were acting secretly in collusion against Japan might well arouse even greater criticism while Congress is in its present mood of intense criticism of the President'.[1]   Halifax considered that 'our aim must be active Anglo-American co-operation wherever possible', but that, so long as Roosevelt's position was uncertain, Britain should not go out of its way to oppose Japan while the Japanese reply to the British note of 14 January was under consideration.   Accordingly, the British delegation at Geneva was instructed to apply the brake on the Chinese so as to avoid 'provocative references' to Japan.   R. A. Butler reported from Geneva on 19 January that, in furtherance of this policy, Britain had joined France in resisting the extension of a resolution on Japan's New Order so as to include the establishment of a committee for co-ordinating effective counter-measures.[2]

European developments in the spring of 1939 had their effects.   The German occupation of Bohemia on 15 March put new heart into the pro-Nazi group in the Japanese Government, causing them to press more strongly for a military pact with Berlin.   Craigie's talks with Arita on 29 March left him with the impression that the notion of such a pact had revived, after its virtual abandonment, owing to the effect on the Japanese army of the 'irresistible power displayed by Germany in the Czech *coup*'.[3]   The government had also to consider the effects on Japan of the Anglo-French efforts during the summer to conclude a mutual defence pact with the Soviet Union.   Assurances were given to Japan that the talks with Russia were limited to Europe, though they could be extended to cover the Far East if circumstances justified it.   The overriding consideration was that Japan should not be precipitated into declaring war against Britain when the now almost inevitable conflict in Europe erupted and while the United States was still pledged to isolation.   Hence, assistance to China had to be governed by calculations as to whether such help would be useful for strengthening China as an ally should Japan, in the end, join Germany in war against the democracies; or whether it would tip the scales against those Japanese who strove to remain neutral in a European conflict.   Halifax explained the position to Clark-Kerr after his talks with the Chinese Ambassador on 27 March:

[1] *D.B.F.P.*, Third Series, VIII, pp. 447–51.
[2] *Ibid.*, p. 408.   [3] *Ibid.*, p. 536.

So long as Japan remains neutral, even malevolently neutral, we shall do everything possible to prevent her siding with the enemy Power. To that extent we shall be compelled to avoid too open a collaboration with the Chinese Government in their struggle with the Japanese . . . if on the other hand Japan becomes a declared enemy we shall want to assist the Chinese, so far as we can, in their struggle with the Japanese and obtain from them any help which they give us in return

Halifax added the important point:

arrangements with the Chinese Government could only be made in the light of conditions existing at the time, and it is clear that the Chinese proposals could only come into consideration once we were sure that Japan would be actively opposed to us.[1]

The extreme isolation of the British position was manifest. At Geneva in May the Chinese were insisting upon a small committee being set up for co-ordinating economic sanctions against Japan, the main brunt of which, the Foreign Office noted on 9 May, would fall on Britain, leaving her more exposed than ever to the retaliatory action which Japan could always take against British interests in China in the guise of security measures in areas of military operations.[2] The government were repeatedly told by critics in both Houses of Parliament that the United States would take part in the proposed co-ordinating committee at Geneva, but Lindsay, when asked for an opinion, commented on 19 May on the 'absurdity' of expecting the American Government to join the League Committee when Congress was framing legislation to make neutrality more effective.[3] The Ambassador added on the following day that the State Department, so far from wanting an invitation to join the committee, was asking Britain to prevent the Chinese Government from 'making a fool of itself' as the Department did not believe that any agreement on sanctions could be obtained.[4] Grew, in Tokyo, proposed to go on leave during the summer and was wholly against a common Anglo-American policy during the emergency period.[5] Craigie suspected that, at this moment of intense pressure on Britain, the Japanese were attempting to drive a wedge between Britain and the United States by according lenient treatment

---

[1] *D.B.F.P.*, Third Series, IX, pp. 5–7.
[2] *Ibid.*, p. 47, n. 3.
[3] *Ibid.*, p. 86.   [4] *Ibid.*, p. 90.   [5] *Ibid.*, pp. 102–3.

to the latter, while allowing the full attack on foreign rights in China to fall on Britain.[1] Halifax disagreed with this view, believing that interference with foreign interests in China was the sporadic work of Japanese soldiers and sailors not subject to more than the partial control of the government. He was, however, dispirited with the American attitude. 'I think we must accustom ourselves to take an isolated step forward,' he wrote to Craigie, 'and it may be that this will in the end prove to be the most efficacious means for encouraging the United States to follow, for they have always in the past shown a marked disposition to help those who help themselves.'[2]

The 'isolated step forward' which Halifax chose to take in the form of challenging the Japanese in Tientsin was not matched by help from the United States until it had met with the sharpest rebuff from Japan. The Tientsin crisis of the summer, when the British Concession was blockaded until a final settlement was reached on 12 June 1940 and British nationals passing in and out of the Concession were subjected to undignified searches by Japanese guards, arose from a Japanese demand for the handing over of four Chinese charged with conspiracy to murder a pro-Japanese bank official. The background of the issue was the sustained anti-British campaign conducted by the Japanese authorities in North China, focused on the charge that Britain was harbouring Chinese guerillas in the Concession and was seeking to disrupt the economy of North China by refusing to recognise the Japanese-controlled currency and hand over the silver reserves deposited in the Concession by the national Chinese banks. Halifax entered the dispute in a conciliatory spirit. On 28 April he wrote to Broadmead, the British Consul in Shanghai, that 'for safety of our interests we shall have to take more drastic measures to prevent the use of the Concession for political activities'.[3] Evidently, however, he began to feel that the campaign against Britain would have to be resisted at some point, however threatening the situation in Europe, unless there was to be a complete British withdrawal from China. The Foreign Secretary outlined to Shigemitsu, the Japanese Ambassador, on 19 May 'the whole series of interferences with British rights in China, which seemed to indicate the beginning of a concerted drive against our interests there'.[4] Accordingly, the Foreign Office instructed the British authorities in Tientsin on 22 May that since, in the British view, the evidence against the four men was inadequate, they should be kept *incommunicado*, but that if, in future, the Consul-General, Jamieson, was satis-

[1] *D.B.F.P.*, Third Series, IX, pp.107–8. [2] *Ibid.*, p. 120.
[3] *Ibid.*, p. 29. [4] *Ibid.*, pp. 86–8.

fied that political offenders were implicated in terrorist activities they should be handed over to the Japanese.[1] Jamieson feared reprisals against the Concession and on 2 June asked for authority to hand the men over; 'it seems inevitable,' he wrote, 'that the men will have to be handed over if we are to avoid the natural consequences of our failure to do so.'[2] Craigie backed Jamieson by stressing to Halifax that if a show-down had to come with Japan it should not come on this particular issue.[3] Halifax nevertheless confirmed to Jamieson on 5 June that the four men were not to be handed over.[4] The distraught Jamieson then pointed out that neither he himself nor the municipal authorities in Tientsin had the right to refuse the execution of warrants for arrest issued by the Tientsin District Court. Jamieson's own view and that of other leading members of the Tientsin Concession was that the Japanese were 'legally and morally justified in their demands'.[5] Whereupon Halifax moved a step back by agreeing to the establishment of a committee of 'independent and reputable persons' to consider whether a *prima facie* case existed against the men.[6] Craigie replied to the Foreign Secretary on 14 June that the Japanese were wholly opposed to the idea of an independent committee, that they demanded the men forthwith and warned that if they were not handed over reprisals would be applied against the Concession the exact nature of which it would be left to the Japanese military authorities on the spot to decide.[7]

Halifax, realising too late the trap into which his Western legal attitudes had led him, urgently asked Lindsay in Washington to approach the American Government for its good offices in the dispute.[8] But the long-sustained American fear of seeming to be aligned with Britain against the Japanese operated to the last. Only after the Tientsin crisis was temporarily resolved by a formula agreed between Foreign Minister Arita and Craigie on 24 July did the United States act on the 26th by cancelling its commercial treaty with Japan, a move too late to influence the Tokyo negotiations. By the Craigie–Arita formula Britain recognised the 'actual situation in China', admitted the special needs of the Japanese forces in respect to the safeguarding of their own security and the maintenance of public order in the regions under their control and undertook not to countenance acts prejudicial to these needs. According to Chamberlain in the Commons on 31 July, the formula was

[1] *D.B.F.P.*, Third Series, IX, pp. 97–8. [2] *Ibid.*, pp. 125–6.
[2] *Ibid.*, p. 127. [4] *Ibid.*, p. 133.
[3] *Ibid.*, pp. 159–61. [6] *Ibid.*, p. 162.
[4] *Ibid.*, pp. 170–1. [8] *Ibid.*, p. 165.

a 'statement of fact', denoting no change in British policy.[1] It was supplemented by a final agreement on 12 June 1940 which secured for Japan a measure of British co-operation in the suppression of terrorist activities, but went a considerable way to safeguarding the rights of the Chinese Government in Chungking in the matter of rival currencies and the fate of the Tientsin silver stocks. Nevertheless, these agreements, by accepting the legitimacy of Japanese military operations in China, legalised the limitation of foreign rights which British policy had sedulously sought to avoid since the outbreak of Sino-Japanese hostilities in July 1937.

The Craigie–Arita agreements thus brought a temporary stability while underlining the fact that, denied naval power to bring to bear on Japan, denied the possibility of joint action with the United States, the British position was almost wholly at the discretion of the kind of attitudes which the Japanese could be induced by diplomatic pressure alone to adopt. The situation was somewhat eased by the Nazi–Soviet Pact of August 1939, which profoundly shocked Japanese opinion and momentarily destroyed the Anti-Comintern agreements; the Nazi–Soviet pact meant that Japan could no longer count upon German support in any clash with Russia. Nevertheless, Britain's weakness, symbolised by her inability to reply effectively to the Soviet–German attack on Poland in September and the Nazi conquest of Western Europe in 1940, left the Japanese to conclude that Germany would probably win the war. For the time being, however, they considered that, as Germany seemed likely to emerge victorious they should not weaken themselves by war with Britain and the United States but should press on with the creation of the New Order in Asia in relative isolation from Europe.

IV

It is unnecessary to examine in detail the final stages of British policy in the Far East before war came between Japan and the democracies in December 1941. While the outbreak of war in Europe in September 1939 had no radical effect on Far Eastern affairs, it committed Britain more than ever to a quiescent policy, seeking above all to confirm Japan's neutrality while affording all possible assistance to China to keep her in the field. It remained more true than ever that when Japan put forward demands on Britain which she was prepared to back to the full extent of her power, as in the Tientsin dispute in the summer of 1939, Britain had little alternative but to draw

[1] 350 H.C. Deb. 5s. Col. 2025.

back. This occurred, to the horror of China's friends, when the British Government were compelled to close the Burma Road, which brought supplies to China from the Indian Ocean, for three months in the later summer and autumn of 1940, after the Japanese had prevented the Chinese obtaining supplies through French Indo-China when France collapsed. It is significant that, just as an American gesture of support for Britain came immediately after the conclusion of the Craigie–Arita agreement of 24 July 1939, so only after Britain was forced to close the Burma Road on 18 June 1940 did Roosevelt restrict the purchase of Japanese war materials in the United States. In both cases the American timing was unfortunate.

What mainly stands out in this record is the disproportion between the vast British interests in China, together with the commitment which Britain shared with the other signatories of the Washington Treaty to respect the independence and integrity of China, and the actual resources at the disposal of British Ministers. The two crucial circumstances were the decision of the Admiralty that proposals for stationing a fleet at Singapore were beyond present and likely means, and the remote distance from Europe at which the Japanese operated against Chinese forces and foreign rights.[1] Coupled with this was the fact that Britain was acting alone, or almost alone. The United States Government were well enough aware of the nature of Japan's challenge to peace in the Far East; but on each occasion when joint, or even parallel, action with Britain was suggested, the aversion of Congress and American public opinion to 'ganging up' with Britain, and its accompanying risk of American involvement in war, was strong enough to prevent it.

To this must be added the continuous interaction between the Far Eastern crisis and concurrent developments in Europe. Ironically, the two means of dealing with the threat from the European dictators which were open to the British Government both required a conciliatory attitude towards Japan. Resistance to the dictators, certainly during the Czech crisis of 1938, was unthinkable without an understanding with Japan which left Britain and France free to deal with the consequences of opposing Hitler. This was the justification for Craigie's talks with Ugaki in the summer of 1938. On the other hand, the policy of redressing Germany's grievances, which formed the basis of Chamberlain's approach to the European crisis, was naturally regarded as having its counterpart in a parallel effort

---

[1] See the Admiralty's view of the Fitzmaurice proposals for stationing a main fleet in the Far East: *D.B.F.P.*, Third Series, VIII, Appendix I, pp. 542–50.

to reach accommodations with Japan, on whom Chamberlain thought that Germany would have far more influence than Britain and France could hope to exert. When by March 1939 Chamberlain's German policy was seen to have failed, the government could still not despair of suitable arrangements being reached with Tokyo since, much as Japan's extremists admired Germany's military force and diplomatic success, the one thing on which they seemed to agree with the moderates was that Japan must be kept out of European entanglements. In every way, a premium seemed to be placed on talking with the Japanese rather than on organising a forceful coalition against them.

These considerations explain the extraordinary dilemmas confronting British policy-makers. They could not forcefully obstruct Japanese interference with British rights, except in a purely verbal sense, since, as the Craigie–Arita talks in the summer of 1939 showed, such obstruction could in the last resort only be maintained by force; and force Britain was in no position to apply, except on the wholly unrealistic condition that the United States was at her side. But if Japan was to be persuaded to respect British rights, British 'sincerity' in accepting Japanese aims in East Asia had to be established in Japanese eyes. This meant, notwithstanding the strongest pressures of opinion in Britain to the contrary, restraint upon assistance to China and discouragement of Chinese efforts to secure demonstrations against Japan at the League of Nations which provoked the Japanese without restraining them. But here again there was a risk of going too far. If, owing to a negative attitude on the part of the democracies, Chinese resistance collapsed and Japan was wholly free to impose her terms in East Asia, British interests in China would be even harder to defend, and Japan would be at liberty to turn her attention to British possessions in South and South-East Asia and towards Australia and New Zealand. Alternatively, China might throw in her lot with Russia, which again might prove even more destructive of British interests in China than the Sino-Japanese conflict. Against which was the risk that more open British support for China might drive Japan to conclude the long-awaited military alliance with Germany, with results fatal to the hopes of preventing the division of the world into armed camps which continued to inspire British Ministers to the last. These various dilemmas would have been easier to resolve if Britain had had naval power in the area or if Roosevelt had been backed by American public opinion. But the situation had so developed that neither condition was fulfilled.

CHAPTER XIX

MAN OF PEACE

THE last two years of British foreign policy before the outbreak of war in 1939 were inevitably bound up with the personality and outlook of Neville Chamberlain, who increasingly dominated it after his appointment as Prime Minister on 28 May 1937. Chamberlain's political career had until that moment been spent mainly in home affairs; he had been a reforming Minister of Health in Baldwin's second government between 1924 and 1929 and a Chancellor of the Exchequer for six years in the National Government formed in 1931. From 1934, however, he had been increasingly concerned with the inner circle of Ministers who decided foreign policy.[1] While anxious that government spending should not interfere with the process of economic recovery, he had played an important part in the shaping of the Defence White Papers of 1935 and 1936, and wished to fight the general election in 1935 on the Defence issue. His views on international affairs were consistent with the main lines of British thinking. Chamberlain did not invent 'appeasement'. He carried it to its logical conclusion and showed, unwittingly, that in a violent world the rationalist assumptions of British politicians were out of place.

Chamberlain's beliefs were close to those of most British public men and the great bulk of public opinion of his day. They were that war was the ultimate evil which almost any price was worth paying to avoid; that war must never be embarked upon unless the supreme issues of national and Imperial survival were clearly at stake; that it was inconceivable that any foreign government could, with eyes open, plunge Europe into war again. Chamberlain assumed that peace depended in the last resort on understanding between the Great Powers, based on recognition of their common interests, and especially between the two greatest Powers, Britain and Germany. He had little respect for politically unstable France, almost none for Italy. Russia he believed to be a spent force after the great purges which began in 1936; the Soviet ideology he abhorred, though there is little to support the allegation that he deliberately sought to turn Hitler's ambitions eastwards. He had

[1] Sir Keith Feiling, *The Life of Neville Chamberlain*, p. 245.

formed an unfavourable view of the United States' attitude
to its international responsibilities at the World Economic Conference in London in 1933, which Roosevelt torpedoed by
refusing to stabilise the dollar. The American Government
appeared to him as prevented at all critical junctures from
playing a helpful role in European security by its isolationist
public opinion; 'it is always best and safest,' he once said, 'to
count on nothing from the Americans but words.'[1] This left
Britain and Germany as the sole effective Powers, and since
war between them would almost certainly destroy all that
Chamberlain held dear, as well as bring suffering on the heads
of many millions in many countries, his course must be to remove one by one the obstacles to Anglo-German understanding.
These were of two kinds: the injustices remaining from the
Versailles settlement, which few Englishmen defended, and
the residue of mistrust in the minds of both people.

Chamberlain had little or no admiration for the Nazi system,
which he more than once characterised as an unspeakable
horror. But he considered that the concentration of supreme
power in Germany in one man's hands facilitated the comprehensive settlement with Germany which he sought, provided
contact could be made with that one man without interference
from subordinates. Like many other British politicians, Chamberlain looked upon the ideologies of foreign statesmen either
as irrelevant to the settlement of practical differences or as a
kind of smokescreen which would disappear as opportunities
for profitable agreements came into view. He took comparatively little account of the internal depravity of the Fascist
régimes, but this was consistent with the traditional British rule
that domestic and foreign affairs should be kept in separate
compartments. Chamberlain's central article of faith was that
no foreign ruler, whatever he may have written in his political
testament, could wilfully seek the mastery of Europe which
must bring him into conflict, and ultimately war, with Britain
and France. Because of the utter folly of any such course, he
needed far more evidence than would convince the averagely
objective person that any modern government could commit
it. Nevertheless, in Chamberlain's view, unsettled business
between democracies and dictatorships could catapult both
into war which neither desired. The purpose of policy must
therefore be a step-by-step settlement of this business. In the
nature of things, the major concessions in the early stages of
building confidence must be made by the democracies. But
this was only because the democracies had saddled Europe with

[1] Feiling, *op. cit.*, p. 325.

a peace settlement which was bound to evoke passionate resistance from the Powers defeated in 1918.

To this enterprise Chamberlain brought great assets and vices which were the reverse of the assets. He was courageous, energetic, dedicated, austere. No one could doubt that his hatred of war was deeply felt, or that he would exert himself to the utmost in efforts to avert it. His mind was lucid, logical, tenacious, capable of seeing the drift of an argument or implication of a proposal with lightning speed. He was persuasive, with an incisive, dry style of speaking bare of artifice and sentiment. These qualities gave him unchallenged leadership of the Conservative Party until at least his return from Munich. On the other side of the medal were his impatience and ruthlessness, his intolerance of opposition and readiness to sweep aside methods and men standing in his way. As his desire to come to grips across the table with the dictators grew, so did his faith in his own power to turn them into reasonable men who would honour their cheques. Without the daily criticism of colleagues whose ability he could genuinely respect, he became credulous and naïve, believing that, when Hitler assumed a benignant air as a convenient tactic, he himself had wrought this change and that henceforth the Führer was a man to be trusted. For these faults in Chamberlain the Baldwin era bore some responsibility. Opportunities missed in those locust years, Chamberlain thought, must be made good by a forced march towards Anglo-German *rapprochement*. Those who advised caution must be swept aside.

I

One of these was Anthony Eden. The quarrel between Chamberlain and Eden which culminated in the Foreign Secretary's resignation on 20 February 1938 was in one sense a product of a British system in which the Foreign Secretary occupies, with the Chancellor of the Exchequer, the next most important Cabinet position after the Prime Minister, and Prime Minister and Foreign Secretary share responsibility for foreign policy. If the Premier is content to leave the main lines of policy to the Foreign Secretary, as was Baldwin, no problem arises. But this must be a rare situation in the twentieth century and some degree of friction between the two men is unavoidable. There was an undeclared war between Lloyd George and Curzon; Eden himself was to disagree on many vital matters with Winston Churchill in the wartime and postwar governments. It would have been remarkable had two Ministers with the positive views of foreign policy held by

Chamberlain and Eden been able to work together in critical times without disagreement. Chamberlain's sense of the urgency of a settlement with Germany made him impatient with Eden's provisos and qualifications. Eden's awareness of the rule of law collapsing in Europe while Franklin Roosevelt wrestled with his isolationists made him feel that Chamberlain was undermining the final bastions of order.

When the break finally came in February 1938 over the proposed Anglo-Italian conversations in Rome, Chamberlain claimed, in his letter accepting Eden's resignation, that the difference was solely one of timing.[1] Eden contended that the talks should not begin until Mussolini had made some progress in carrying out the British formula for the withdrawal of 'volunteers' from Spain, which he had accepted in principle. Chamberlain's reply was that the Italian Government were saying that they had a choice between settling their differences with Britain and coming to terms with Germany, and that if Britain did not seize the opportunity for talks in Rome, Mussolini must inevitably move to Germany's side. The effect of his doing so would be to frustrate the Prime Minister's object of seeking to ease the two dictators apart. It was, from Chamberlain's point of view, electorally expedient to state the issue in these terms. The Prime Minister also tried to soften the political impact of Eden's departure by having it put about that the Foreign Secretary's health prevented him from continuing.[2]

There were, however, as Eden claimed, more fundamental differences of outlook and method. Eden was aggrieved that Britain should always have to go cap in hand when the dictators called, and should be told, if she asked for assurances that the dictators would respect their undertakings before another round of talks began, that she was wrecking the prospects for a settlement. He deeply mistrusted Mussolini after the sanctions fiasco and was loath to believe that sound business could be done with no regard to principles of international conduct. Above all, lacking Chamberlain's sharply conceived conception of a comprehensive settlement of outstanding issues leading up to a permanent understanding with the dictators, Eden could not agree that the Duce's words should be accepted at face value without concrete evidence as to the trustworthiness of the Italian leader.

The two men had equally sharp differences over President Roosevelt's proposal for a wide-ranging conference on general international issues which he had launched in January. Since

[1] The Earl of Avon, *Facing the Dictators*, pp. 596–7.
[2] *Ibid.*, pp. 584–5.

the proposal was communicated in confidence to Britain, Eden was able to do no more than hint at the issue in his resignation speech in the Commons on 21 February. He would in fact have preferred to break with Chamberlain on the Roosevelt proposal but could not do so owing to the confidential nature of the President's message.[1] The episode showed, however, that if the Premier was credulous in relation to the dictators, so was Eden in relation to Roosevelt's power to render effective assistance.

The President had been urged in the previous October by his Under-Secretary of State, Sumner Welles, to summon a world conference to reach agreement on the basic principles of international relations. Roosevelt eventually opted in favour of calling the Diplomatic Corps in Washington to a meeting at the White House on Armistice Day, 1937, where they were to hear a Presidential message on the need for world agreement on principles for conducting international affairs, a system of world economic justice and suitable revisions of treaties. Somewhat surprisingly, the proposal was condemned as 'illogical and impossible' by Roosevelt's Secretary of State, Cordell Hull, and was then diluted by Sumner Welles until it took the form of a suggestion that the United States should join with nine of the smaller countries in a conference to work on problems of world disarmament, equal access to the world's raw materials and the laws of warfare. The proposals which emerged from this conference were then to be set before other nations. It was to be firmly insisted, however, that there could be no question of any political involvement of the United States in the conference's conclusions. Hull approved the plan on these lines provided the British Government were privately sounded on the idea before invitations were issued, and if they gave whole-hearted support. The message was sent to London on 11 January with a strong recommendation from the British Ambassador in Washington, Lindsay, that it be favourably considered. A reply was required before 17 January.[2]

Chamberlain regarded Roosevelt's hands as tied by isolationist opinion, which he thought would prevent any practical American co-operation in arrangements to hold the European situation in check. That opinion had violently reacted against Roosevelt's 'quarantine' speech in October and had ruled out any strong American stand at the Brussels conference on the Sino-Japanese conflict a month later. The Prime Minister

[1] *Ibid.*, p. 565.
[2] William L. Langer and S. Everett Gleason, *The Challenge to Isolation*, pp. 22–6; Hull, *Memoirs*, I, pp. 547–8, 573, 579–81.

anticipated from the Roosevelt proposal a wide-ranging debate on general principles which could not be agreeable to the dictators, and which might interfere with the dealings he had in mind to do with them. Without consulting Eden, then on holiday in the South of France, Chamberlain gave what Sumner Welles called a 'douche of cold water' to the President's suggestion on 13 January, expressing in his reply the fear that it might cut across the impending negotiations in Europe. Eden, urged to return home at once by Cadogan at the Foreign Office, realised on reading the telegrams during his return journey that Chamberlain's reply would have a depressing effect on the efforts he himself had been making to secure naval co-operation with the United States in the Far East, all the more so as Chamberlain had indicated in his reply that Britain was contemplating *de jure* recognition of the Italian conquest of Ethiopia. On reaching London, the Foreign Secretary talked Chamberlain into sending two further telegrams to the White House intended to soften the impression left by his first reply; in these it was pointed out that the impending recognition of Italian Ethiopia was only designed as part of a general settlement of accounts with Italy, and that furthermore Chamberlain was now able to support the Roosevelt initiative.[1]

By this time, however, Roosevelt, after sanctioning a counterblast from Hull against the whole idea of recognising Mussolini's work in Ethiopia, was beginning to have second thoughts about the idea of a conference. At first he said he would defer his proposal until after Hitler's speech on 20 February; in the end it was never made. The most to be hoped for from the President's plan was that it might have edged the American public one step closer to co-operation with the European democracies. As against this was to be set the almost certain prospect of a general, indeterminate examination of world problems which could not touch the concrete issues in dispute between the democracies and the revisionist Powers.

The conclusions of the American historians, Langer and Gleason, on the Roosevelt initiative are that

> Mr. Roosevelt and his advisers sympathised with the British and wished them well in whatever efforts they felt constrained to make in the direction of peaceful adjustment, but there was never any question of approving or supporting their specific policy and certainly no thought of discussing any political or military commitment in connection with it.

[1] Avon, *op. cit.*, pp. 564–5.

Under the circumstances, these writers believe, Hitler was perfectly safe in discounting the influence of the United States.[1]
So presumably was Chamberlain.

These points at issue between Chamberlain and Eden were
rendered the more difficult to overcome by the Prime Minister's
distaste for Foreign Office protocol and his search for more
direct methods of making contact with the dictators.   His aide
in this heretical diplomacy, Sir Horace Wilson, was actually
the Government's Chief Industrial Adviser, and had favourably
impressed Chamberlain, as Chancellor of the Exchequer, when
both attended the Ottawa conference in 1932.   Wilson was
reprimanded by Eden, after Chamberlain took over the
Premiership, for interfering in foreign affairs which he did not
understand; Sir Horace retaliated by warning Eden's friends
that they would find advancement difficult if they supported
the Foreign Secretary in this conflict.[2]   Chamberlain also
offended Eden's professionalism by resorting to unofficial
agents to make contacts with the dictators.   Notorious among
them were his sister-in-law, Lady Chamberlain, who, though
contrary to the Prime Minister's wish, revealed his letters to
her to the Italian Foreign Minister, Count Ciano, during her
holidays in Rome; and Sir Joseph Ball, an official of the Conservative Central Office, who was employed to make arrangements with the Italian Ambassador, Count Grandi, to see
Chamberlain.[3]   Back-bench Labour M.P.s had played a somewhat similar role as interlopers in diplomacy during the negotiations with Soviet Russia in 1924, and the argument for by-
passing the Foreign Office had always been paraded by radical
critics of the old school of foreign policy.   But to a specialist
in foreign affairs like Eden, this could not but seem an eruption
of amateurs into the operating theatre.   To crown Chamberlain's short-cuts in achieving results, the Prime Minister committed inexcusable breaches of political manners, as for instance at a meeting with Grandi at 10, Downing Street, on
18 February, which Eden attended, when he appeared to draw
the Ambassador on to make points against Eden's reservations
about opening the Anglo-Italian conversations in Rome before
the question of Italian troops in Spain had been settled.
Grandi's account of the interview is no doubt coloured by his
wish to show Ciano what an effective envoy he was.   But that
Chamberlain showed unveiled sympathy for Grandi's catalogue
of grievances against the Foreign Office is evident from his

    [1] *Op. cit.*, p. 32.   [2] Avon, *op. cit.*, p. 595.
    [3] Viscount Templewood, *Nine Troubled Years*, p. 278; Iain Macleod, *Neville
Chamberlain*, pp. 218–20.

attack on Eden when the first part of the interview was over and Grandi had withdrawn. 'Anthony, you have missed chance after chance,' Chamberlain protested, 'you simply cannot go on like this.'[1]

The fact remains, however, that on most of the major issues of Chamberlain's foreign policy Eden disagreed only to the extent of wanting more tangible evidence of Mussolini's good faith before going further. Eden had never proposed forceful resistance to Hitler's reoccupation of the Rhineland and had resisted Flandin's demand for economic sanctions; his attitude towards the Spanish civil war was for all practical purposes identical to that of the Prime Minister; he was not even opposed to *de jure* recognition of Italy's conquest of Ethiopia, provided this was in return for guarantees of Mussolini's good behaviour in Europe; he had no fault to find with Chamberlain's position on the Far Eastern conflict; he agreed in a half-convinced way to the general strategy of attempting to reach a lasting settlement with the dictators. Eden too, despite his enthusiasm for League sanctions against Mussolini, shared Chamberlain's contempt for the idea often expressed on the opposite benches in Parliament that it was enough to summon the League to dispose of any international difficulty. He once told Opposition speakers in the House that if the League were called to intervene in the Spanish civil war, as they proposed, it would be found that many League members wanted Franco to win. Moreover, if Chamberlain was autocratic, Eden was by no means self-effacing; he did not co-operate easily if his views were not accepted. A striking instance of this was given in June 1935, when Hoare was appointed Foreign Secretary in succession to Simon, and Eden threatened to resign from the government because he had been passed over, although by every test he was junior to Hoare. Nevertheless, Eden's refusal in February 1938 to run at the beck and call of the dictators might, if upheld, have averted the humiliating genuflections towards Hitler which Chamberlain's policy brought him to before the year was out.

Eden's successor at the Foreign Office, Lord Halifax, was a member of the inner circle of Ministers with which Chamberlain now began to surround himself and which he used to consolidate his grip on the Cabinet. The others were the former Foreign Secretaries, Hoare and Simon.[2] The Foreign Office

[1] Galeazzo Ciano, *L'Europa verso la catastrofe*, pp. 249–78; Avon, p. 582.
[2] Viscount Templewood records the 'Big Four' meetings as having begun on 10 September 1938, but it is clear that the group had begun to take shape before this; Templewood, *op. cit.*, p. 301.

lost its Parliamentary allies of Eden, Cranborne, the Under-
Secretary of State, and J. P. L. Thomas, Eden's Parliamentary
Private Secretary, who both resigned with Eden on 20 February.
Halifax's membership of the House of Lords gave Chamberlain
undivided control of defence of his foreign policy in the Commons; there his combative qualities developed and his opinions became more entrenched as a result of daily exchanges
with the Opposition.[1]

Halifax, through genuine agreement with Chamberlain's
aims, proved himself a pliant servant of the Prime Minister—
in the remaining phases of British policy before the war Halifax
wrote documents which Chamberlain in effect dictated—although, we have seen, his stolid moral sense could drive him
to sullen resistance to totalitarian demands, as in the Tientsin
crisis in the summer of 1939. He had equally well co-operated
with Eden, during the latter's occasional absences from the
Foreign Office, and had ably assisted Eden at the conference of
the Locarno Powers in London in the immediate aftermath of
Hitler's Rhineland coup. He respected Eden, shared his mistrust of Hoare, and had tried hard to work out a compromise
formula to avoid Eden's resignation at the last minute.[2]

Halifax had already made one inconclusive excursion into
dealing with the dictators in November 1937, when, during
Eden's absence at the Brussels conference on the Far East but
with Eden's qualified approval, he had visited Goering's Hun-
ting Exhibition in Berlin and talked with Hitler at Berchtesgaden on 19 November.[3] The talk was desultory and no indications of agreement emerged; Hitler had said that immediate
negotiations with Britain were not necessary, but that if Britain
really wished to improve her relations with Germany she could
make a start by satisfying the Reich's colonial claims.[4] When
Halifax returned and told Chamberlain about the talks, the
Prime Minister was not deterred by their sterile character.
With Eden out of the way, he braced himself for the supreme
task of forging a settlement with Germany. Almost every subsequent event was, or to a less persistent man might have been,
discouraging.

II

On Sunday, 20 February, when the Cabinet was holding
the second of its two meetings to consider the rift between
Chamberlain and Eden, Hitler announced in a speech in the

---

[1] Templewood, op. cit., p. 281.   [2] Avon, pp. 383, 591.
[3] The Earl of Halifax, Fulness of Days, London, 1957, p. 184.
[4] D.G.F.P., Series D, I, pp. 55–71; Halifax, op. cit., pp. 188–90.

Reichstag his intention to protect the 10 million Germans 'who live in the states adjoining our frontiers'. The Chancellor called for a peaceful solution, but threatened violence if force were used by others in the settlement of this problem.[1] Since 6½ million of the ten lived in Austria and the remaining 3½ million in Czechoslovakia, the next two items in the Nazi programme were clearly marked out.

The omens were altogether favourable for a German move to annex Austria. France, who had vetoed the proposed Austro-German customs union in 1930, had made known to the German Government through the German press correspondent Friedrich Sieburg in November 1937 that she 'had no essential objection to a further assimilation of certain of Austria's domestic institutions with Germany's, though she could naturally not declare her disinterestedness in territorial changes'.[2] Italy, who had sent two divisions to the Brenner frontier to warn Germany at the time of the assassination by Austrian Nazis of Chancellor Dolfuss in July 1934, was now busily digesting her Ethiopian conquest and heavily engaged in Spain. In effect the Spanish civil war consolidated the bond between Hitler and Mussolini which had grown out of the Duce's resentment at British and French attitudes during his war against the Negus.[3] When Dolfuss's successor, Kurt von Schuschnigg, met Mussolini in Venice in April 1937 he was told that times had changed and Italy could no longer support him against Germany.[4] Similarly, Grandi, when asked by Chamberlain at the 10, Downing Street meeting on 18 February 1938 whether he thought the Stresa front could be revived for the purpose of defending Austria, replied that he had no instructions on the matter.[5] As for the British attitude to Austria, Eden disclosed to the German and Italian Ambassadors in London that at an Anglo-French conference at 10, Downing Street, from 28 to 30 November 1937, at which a report was given on Halifax's visit to Germany, the British Ministers had told the French that 'the question of Austria was of much greater interest to Italy than to England', and that people in England 'realised that a closer connection between Germany and Austria would have to come some time'. All they wished was that a solution by force should be avoided.[6] At the same time, Hitler knew, when he made his declaration of 20 February, that if Chamberlain were to carry out his project of coming to terms with Italy the effect

[1] *The Speeches of Adolf Hitler*, ed. by N. H. Baynes, II, pp. 1404–6.
[2] *D.G.F.P.*, Series D, I, pp. 81–4.
[3] Alan Bullock, *Hitler: a Study in Tyranny*, pp. 318–20.
[4] G. E. R. Gedye, *Fallen Bastions*, pp. 209–11.
[5] Avon, *op. cit.*, pp. 581, 617. [6] *D.G.F.P.*, Series D, I, pp. 88–90.

might be to make any absorption of Austria harder to accomplish. If he could move in time against Austria with Mussolini's acquiescence, an Anglo-Italian agreement, such as was eventually signed in Rome on 16 April 1938, would be robbed of much of its force.

Nevertheless, Hitler was not preparing for any immediate military annexation of Austria, as the highly inefficient manner in which the German army finally moved into Austria in March showed. The Chancellor found to his surprise that he could achieve the *Anschluss* without firing a shot.[1] The central factor was the deteriorating situation in Austria since the Austro-German *modus vivendi* had been signed by Hitler's envoy, von Papen, and Schuschnigg in Vienna on 11 July 1936, which had committed the Austrian Government to accept the legitimacy of Nazism in Austria while Hitler acknowledged Austrian independence. On 25 January 1938 the Vienna police seized the headquarters of the 'Committee of Seven', which had been appointed under the 1936 agreement to bring about a reconciliation between the Austrian Nazis and the Chancellor's own party, the Fatherland Front. At the same time the Nazi leader, Tavs, was arrested. Tavs, so documents seized in the raid showed, was in possession of a plan for provoking large-scale unrest in Austria on the supposition that Hitler would be compelled to invade once Schuschnigg began to retaliate against the Austrian Nazis. But this was a difficult moment for Hitler: he was in conflict with his Minister of War, von Blomberg, and his Commander-in-Chief, General von Fritsch, both of whom he dismissed at the end of January, after which he assumed supreme command of the Reich armed forces together with the War Ministry on 4 February. Schuschnigg took advantage of this diversion in Germany to call a Cabinet and press through measures for stronger action against the Nazis. As a price of doing so, however, the Chancellor was forced to offer a Cabinet post to the covert Nazi (or, as he was generally known, the *betont Nationaler*) Seyss-Inquart. The German Ambassador to Vienna, von Papen, heard of this development and, although he himself had been unexpectedly relieved of his post by Hitler on 4 February, hurried to Berchtesgaden on the 5th and told the Führer that Schuschnigg was ripe for making concessions and that a summons to the Berghaus would in all probability bring the Chancellor to his knees. As a reward for this advice, von Papen was sent back to Vienna and Schuschnigg obeyed the summons to see Hitler, having already promised Seyss-Inquart that the post of Minister

[1] Jürgen Gehl, *Austria, Germany and the Anschluss, 1931–38*, p. 194.

of Interior with Public Security was waiting for him, and a second Cabinet seat for the extreme Nationalists, as soon as acts of violence ceased.

At the Berchtesgaden meeting on 12 February Hitler had three of his generals with him. Schuschnigg, spending the 'worst day of his life', confirmed the promises he had already made to Seyss-Inquart; that is, two Cabinet posts for the Opposition, the recognition of Nazism as a possible ideology for Austria, a gradual amnesty for Nazis under arrest, military co-operation between Austria and Germany, and more posts in national and local government service for the National Opposition. Hitler then added further demands, giving Schuschnigg three days in which to comply. These included the appointment of a Nazi, Glaise-Horstenau, to be the Minister of Armed Forces, the exchange of Austrian with German Army officers, regular Austro-German General Staff conferences, and the assimilation of the Austrian and German economic systems. The first and last of these demands were, however, later dropped.[1] On 15 February the Austrian Government duly complied, Seyss-Inquart moved to the Ministry of Interior with the Austrian police under his control, and a general amnesty was proclaimed for those who prior to 15 February had broken the law in the pursuance of political objects. Britain and France protested against the extreme brutality with which Schuschnigg had been treated at Berchtesgaden, but received no satisfaction from Ribbentrop.[2]

The Austrian Chancellor's protest was more disastrously effective. On the evening of 9 March Schuschnigg announced a plebiscite to take place the following Sunday, 13 March, in which the Austrian people were asked to cast their votes 'for a free and German, independent and social, for a Christian, united Austria; for peace and work and the equality of all who acknowledge their faith in our people and Fatherland'. The voting age in this exercise in democracy by acclamation was fixed at 24, so as to exclude many of the younger Nazis, and no alternative was allowed to the plebiscite slogan. Hitler, who recognised the power of plebiscites to silence opposition, understood the significance of the weapon when used against him; the effect of Schuschnigg's referendum must have been to undermine the whole basis of the claim on which Hitler's foreign policy was based, namely that Germans abroad were yearning to return to the Reich. Glaise-Horstenau was sent to Vienna on 11 March and gave the Führer's order for the postponement

---

[1] *D.G.F.P.*, Series D, I, pp. 513–15, 515–17.
[2] *Ibid.*, pp. 529–31, 532–3.

of the plebiscite to Seyss-Inquart for communication to Schuschnigg. The Chancellor at first agreed to resign, so that the referendum should not appear to be a vote of confidence in him, then cancelled the plebiscite, only to find that President Miklas was being asked to appoint Seyss-Inquart to the Chancellorship. After protests and refusals, the President at length gave way and Hitler withdrew his orders to his troops to march. The news then came to Berlin that Miklas had not appointed Seyss-Inquart as Chancellor. Hitler telephoned Mussolini asking for his understanding, then made the decision to set his troops in motion on 12 March. He himself appeared at his mother's grave at Linz on 13 March. The Austrian bastion was down.

Britain was under no obligation to act in defence of Austrian independence. Halifax told Schuschnigg when the Chancellor was faced with his fatal decision on 11 March that the British Government 'could not take the responsibility of advising the Chancellor to take any course of action which might expose his country to dangers to which His Majesty's Government are unwilling to guarantee protection'.[1] The most Britain was obliged to do, Chamberlain told the House of Commons on 14 March, was to consult with Italy and France if any action was taken threatening Austrian independence. This obligation arose from the Anglo-French–Italian agreements of February and September 1934, and the Stresa agreement of April 1935.[2] Consultations were duly held. Mussolini, as indicated by his Press statement of 14 March, was satisfied with the assurances he had received from Hitler that the 1919 Brenner frontier was unaffected. As it happened, in France there was no government, the Chautemps Cabinet having fallen on 10 March, and the Foreign Minister in the caretaker government, Delbos, could do no more than warn the German Ambassador, Welczeck, that such incidents as the German march into Austria could lead to war. Anglo-French exchanges resulted in agreement that only force could have reversed the *Anschluss* and that there was no question of force being used. Corbin, the French Ambassador, saw Foreign Office officials on the morning of 14 March and tried to secure a reference in Chamberlain's afternoon statement in the Commons indicating how Britain would react in the event of a German attack on Czechoslovakia. The Prime Minister doubted whether he could help in this.[3] The most the British and French Governments could do was to protest, and the force of the British protest was

---

[1] *D.B.F.P.*, Third Series, I, p. 13.   [2] 333 H.C. Deb. 5s. Cols. 45–52.
[3] *Ibid.*, pp. 50–1.

THE TROUBLED GIANT

weakened by Sir Nevile Henderson's description, in the presence of his German hosts, of Schuschnigg's decision to hold the plebiscite as 'ill-conceived and ill-prepared folly'. For this he received a reprimand from Halifax, not for the first or last time.[1]

The German reply was to deny that there had been any ultimatum from Berlin to the Austrian Chancellor and to assert that 'the form of relations between the Reich and Austria can only be regarded as an internal affair of the German people which is no concern of third Powers'. Sitting at lunch with Austrian Nazis at Linz on 13 March Hitler said: 'England has sent me a protest. I would have understood a declaration of war; to a protest I shall not even reply.'[2] The sole crumb of comfort for Britain and France was a statement made to Mastny, the Czech Minister in Berlin, by Goering that 'Austrian developments would have no detrimental influence on Czech–German relations'. Goering added the words, for all they were worth: 'Ich gebe Ihnen mein Ehrenwort.' In a second statement the Field-Marshal repeated the assurance on Hitler's behalf and undertook that German forces would be withdrawn 15 kms from the Czech frontier.[3] The Reich Foreign Minister, von Neurath, repeated this assurance to Mastny on 13 March.[4] The Czechs had merely to consider the strategical results of the *Anschluss* for their country, now left like a tongue projecting from the wolf's mouth, to take the measure of these undertakings. The most important reason for their being given was probably to deter any Czech intervention on Austria's behalf.

It was not so much the principle of the *Anschluss* which shocked British Ministers as the brutal way in which it was executed. If Hitler had been able to unify the two countries by agreement with a browbeaten Schuschnigg, the British Government would probably have given their blessing, though the consequences for the European balance of power would have been the same. It was the manner in which the act was done which momentarily disturbed feelings. Chamberlain exclaimed that it was 'an exceedingly serious situation', when news of the German ultimatum to Austria was broken to a luncheon party at 10, Downing Street, in honour of Ribbentrop, when retiring from the German Embassy in London to become the Reich Foreign Minister.[5] When German troops invaded

[1] *Ibid.*, p. 25.
[2] Franz Langoth, *Kampf um Österreich*, Wels, 1951, pp. 239–42.
[3] *Le livre jaune français; documents diplomatiques, 1938–39*, pp. 2–6.
[4] *Europäische Politik, 1933–38, im Spiegel der Prager Akten*, ed. Fritz Berber, pp. 94–5.
[5] Joachim von Ribbentrop, *Zwischen London und Moskau*, pp. 133–6; *D.G.F.P.*, Series D, I, pp. 273–5.

Austria, Halifax paced his office muttering: 'Horrible! Horrible! I never thought they would do it!'[1]

In Britain there had always been a sentimental conviction on both Left and Right that the veto placed by the peace conference in 1919 on a union of Germany with Austria had been a mistake. This echoed the views of the Foreign Office during the First World War that an Austria stripped of its subject nations and joined to Germany would put the brake on militaristic tendencies in Berlin, as well as place restraints on the smaller East European states which were to emerge from the peace conference. It was therefore not surprising that when Halifax talked with Hitler at Berchtesgaden in November 1937 he should have spoken of the revision of Austria's position, along with the redress of Germany's grievances against Danzig and Czechoslovakia, as inevitable. Britain, Halifax said, was only interested in seeing that any changes should be effected by peaceful methods. If Hitler was sincere in replying to Halifax that he hoped that the Austro-German agreement of July 1936 would suffice to remove all difficulties, and it was essential to Chamberlain's policy to believe that he was, the British Government had no objection to a close union of Austria with Germany, always provided she was not forcibly incorporated into the Reich.[2] Chamberlain, reflecting on Halifax's talk with Hitler, concluded that Britain should give assurances not to oppose Germany provided she obtained her ends in Eastern Europe peacefully.[3]

How closely bound together the Austrian and Czech questions were was apparent in a long talk which Sir Nevile Henderson had with Hitler and Ribbentrop, covering the whole field of Anglo-German relations, in Berlin on 3 March, a week before the *Anschluss*. Henderson's theme was 'tranquillity' in Europe, which he said could be secured by an arms limitation agreement and by 'appeasement in Czechoslovakia and Austria'. Britain, the Ambassador said, was not yet in a position to assess the Austro-German agreements concluded at Berchtesgaden on 12 February, but the latest developments had caused concern in many quarters, 'which must unavoidably hamper a general settlement'. Hitler's reply was that Britain had no right to interfere in German relations with other countries in Central Europe and that he would not allow third countries to influence the way in which he sought his major objective, 'the prevention of injustice to millions of Germans'.

Hitler then seemed to suggest to Henderson that the Austrians

[1] A. C. Johnson, *Viscount Halifax*, London, 1941, p. 456.
[2] *D.G.F.P.*, Series D, I, pp. 62–4.   [3] Feiling, *op. cit.*, pp. 332–3.

should be asked their views in a plebiscite, but quickly retracted when pressed by the Ambassador, confining himself to a re-statement of the general principle that the right of self-determination must be granted to the Austrians and the Sudeten Germans. If 'explosions' were to occur from within Austria and Czechoslovakia, the Führer went on, Germany would not remain neutral but would 'act with lightning speed'. Ribbentrop then referred to complaints against German pressure on Austria which the British Minister in Vienna had made to von Papen; these Ribbentrop and Hitler represented as incitements to Chancellor Schuschnigg not to honour the Berchtesgaden agreements. In reply Henderson made one of his customary attempts to curry favour with the German leaders by saying that the British Minister did not necessarily reflect the viewpoint of the British Government and that he himself had often expressed opinions in favour of an Austrian *Anschluss* with Germany. The interview as a whole, like Halifax's talk with Hitler in the previous November, suggested no concrete possibilities of Anglo-German agreement. The only definite proposal which Henderson took with him to the meeting namely that Germany should participate in a new international administration for the Congo Basin as a possible solution of the colonial problem, incited Hitler to ask why Britain did not simply restore the colonies which the Allies had seized from Germany in 1919. But he did not wish to press his colonial demands.[1] Hitler believed in extending the area covered by the German flag in Europe, not in Africa.

III

Since the immediate effect of the Austrian *coup* was to leave Czechoslovakia's southern flank exposed, the British Government had to define their attitude in the event of a German move to fulfil Hitler's undertaking to secure justice for the remaining $3\frac{1}{2}$ million Germans on the Reich frontiers, those living in the Sudeten fringe of Bohemia. Czechoslovakia itself was a far more formidable military proposition to overcome than Austria. The Czech army was strong; inroads into the country even from the south were not easy. Benes, the Czech President, told a British journalist on 18 March: 'unlike Austria, we will fight. We shall be massacred, but we will fight.'[2] France was bound by her 1925 treaty with Czechoslovakia to come to her assistance against unprovoked aggression, although the likeli-

---

[1] Sir Nevile Henderson, *Failure of Mission*, pp. 113–18; *D.G.F.P.*, Series D, I, pp. 236–8.
[2] *D.B.F.P.*, Third Series, I, p. 75, n. 2.

hood was, following the pattern of the *Anschluss*, that a German move against Czechoslovakia would not come in that form. Delbos, holding the French Foreign Ministry between the Chautemps and Daladier Cabinets in early March, confined himself to the statement that the Franco-Czech treaty would come into force in the event of armed intervention by Germany into Czechoslovakia, but he did not specify the form which French assistance might take. French intervention would depend upon 'the gravity of the facts'.[1]

Russia too was under treaty obligation, by an agreement signed on 16 May 1935, to come to Czechoslovakia's aid in the event of aggression, although she was not bound to do so until France was actually engaged in that country's defence. The problem as far as Russia was concerned was whether she was capable of effective military action after the purges in the upper reaches of the Soviet High Command in 1936 and 1937. These, according to Lord Chilston, the British Ambassador in Moscow, reporting to London on 19 April, had affected 65 per cent of senior Red Army officers. The opinion of Chilston's Military Attaché, Colonel Firebrace, was that the Soviet Army, while equal to a defensive war within Soviet frontiers, could not carry the war into the enemy's territory without running the risk of endangering the régime. 'It would be contrary to reason,' Firebrace went on, 'for the rulers of the country to involve the Soviet Union in war unless vital national interests were involved.' Chilston added his own view that the Soviet Union 'must for the time being be counted out of European politics in so far as the exercise of a decisive influence one way or the other is concerned'.[2] Moreover, Russia was without a common border with Czechoslovakia. Her troops must pass through either an intensely hostile Poland or an only slightly less hostile Rumania; if, as seemed likely, her assistance to the threatened country was to take the form of an air strike against German cities, her bombers would have to utilise Rumanian air space and information conflicted throughout the Czech crisis whether the necessary authority would be given. Litvinov, the Soviet Foreign Minister, could only say in a Press statement issued in Moscow on 17 March that 'means would be found' of assisting Czechoslovakia despite the lack of a common frontier. He added the chilling news that, if the crisis arose, Russia would look in the first instance to the League machinery.[3] It was easy to envisage the delays this suggested while German tanks rolled into Bohemia.

[1] *D.B.F.P.*, Third Series, I, p. 83.   [2] *Ibid.*, pp. 161–5.
[3] R.I.I.A., *Documents on International Affairs, 1938*, I, pp. 314–15.

Britain had no direct commitment to defend the Czechs except the already much diluted obligation to preserve their territorial integrity and independence under article 10 of the League Covenant. Halifax had already stated, in the aftermath of the *Anschluss*, that the League was 'no practical advantage' in the Austrian question and that the only result of involving it in such situations was to expose it to open humiliation.[1] Identical considerations were considered to apply in the Czech crisis. Nor was there any direct British obligation to fight alongside France except when, under the still valid Locarno agreement, France was the subject of flagrant aggression, the kind of action Hitler would have every inducement to avoid in settling the Czech problem. There was never any doubt, however, that Britain could not stand aside from a Franco-German fight to the finish, which must before long involve British security. The French insisted that since this was clearly the position the sooner Britain said so the better. This was, however, precisely the kind of statement British governments had persistently avoided making since 1919. It was intensely unpopular in Parliament. It ran the risk, British Ministers thought, of handing over the basic question of war and peace to Paris, and ultimately, in view of the Franco-Czech pact, to Prague. To establish such a commitment moreover was to plunge into that very situation of two armed camps in Europe which Chamberlain's whole policy was expressly designed to avoid.

British commitments were reviewed in the light of the post-*Anschluss* situation and conclusions reached which Halifax explained to the French Government on 22 March. The Cabinet's starting point was a speech made by Eden when Foreign Secretary at Leamington on 20 November 1936 which defined (or left undefined) the circumstances in which Britain would assist victims of aggression when it was proper to do so under the League Covenant. Such a case, Eden said, *may* include Czechoslovakia, but he continued: 'I use the word "may" deliberately since in such an instance there is no automatic obligation to take military action . . . it is moreover right that this should be so for nations cannot be expected to incur automatic obligations save for areas where their vital interests are concerned.' Britain, Halifax went on, would certainly come to France's assistance under the Locarno treaties against unprovoked aggression; she was proposing technical conversations at an early date between the British and French air staffs to provide for the fulfilment of this undertaking. But the British 'could not add to these obligations'. Halifax re-

[1] *D.B.F.P.*, Third Series, I, p. 32.

minded the French that in the talks with Chautemps and Delbos in London in November 1937 following Halifax's visit to Germany Chamberlain had explained that Britain 'could certainly not go as far as to state what her action might be in the event of an attack on Czechoslovakia by Germany'. But the British Ministers insisted that once war broke out formal commitments would be of little account. Uncommitted countries would sooner or later be drawn in for the defence of their security.[1]

The French were not satisfied. Corbin, the French Ambassador, saw Halifax again on the following day and pressed him to join with France in making a 'very firm declaration' to avert German dominance in Central Europe. The Foreign Secretary on his side saw little point in warning Germany against intervention in the Czech situation since the Reich had so far not openly intervened in the conflict between the Czech Government and the Sudeten German Party, and had declared no intention to take action. He also doubted whether Britain and France could enforce such a warning; British military plans, for defence and offence, were not sufficiently far advanced.[2] The fact was that on 10 March, the day before the fatal ultimatum was handed to Schuschnigg in Vienna, the British War Minister, Leslie Hore-Belisha, had placed Britain's continental commitments last among the calls upon the British Army in his first Estimates speech in the House of Commons. The three principal objectives of military planning, the Cabinet had agreed, were the defence of the home islands against invasion, the safeguarding of the sea routes between Britain and her foreign sources of food and raw materials, and the security of oversea territories. Assistance to Britain's continental allies came fourth in the list, and the pace of rearmament barely sufficed for adequate provision for the first three needs.[3] Halifax accordingly told Corbin that he could 'intelligently anticipate' the decision the Cabinet would come to about the statement Chamberlain was to make in the Commons on the following day, 24 March; they would almost certainly conclude that the state of British public opinion and the attitude of Commonwealth Governments ruled out any enlargement of British commitments, but that, in the sacred formula, 'the inexorable drive of facts, once a war started, might be expected to be so strong that it was hard to say what country might not become involved'.[4]

---

[1] *D.B.F.P.*, Third Series, I, p. 85.
[2] *Ibid.*, pp. 85–6, 90–1, 150–1.
[3] R. J. Minney *The Private Papers of Hore-Belisha*, p. 87.
[4] *D.B.F.P.*, Third Series, I, pp. 88–90.

British Ministers at the Cabinet meeting before Chamberlain's major speech on foreign policy on 24 March took a pessimistic view of the military position. Czechoslovakia's situation, they recognised, had been gravely weakened by the *Anschluss*. The information to hand about the state of Czech armed forces was not encouraging. Mason-Macfarlane, the British Military Attaché in Berlin, reported his doubts whether the Czech army could withstand the Germans for a 'very considerable time', and Poland and Hungary might march with Germany against Prague in order to settle their own minority claims.[1] There was little hope that military assistance afforded by the two pledged countries, France and Russia, even if both honoured their obligations, could prevent the Germans overrunning Czechoslovakia. The restitution of the Czech state would have to await the conclusion of a victorious campaign against Germany by those who had taken up arms in Czechoslovakia's defence.

Britain was in no position to contribute forces at the outset of the conflict for hastening the end of a war which was bound to be long and costly. Within a few days of the Cabinet meeting the Chiefs of Staff were to report that Britain was quite unprepared for war and that time must be gained for re-armament.[2] Nor was it easy to see exactly how the French could assist Czechoslovakia, apart from throwing their troops against passive German defences on the left bank of the Rhine, where it was expected that Germany would enjoy air superiority. Moreover, British Ministers recognised that after the *Anschluss* Germany was in control of Czechoslovakia's only effective access to the outside world. Merely by an economic stranglehold she could bring Czechoslovakia to her knees without using military force. If Britain were to strengthen her undertakings to France or issue warnings to Germany Hitler might be tempted to realise his objects by economic means alone. The Cabinet felt that their conclusion must be that, apart from giving a general warning that if war broke out Britain could hardly avoid being involved at some stage, Britain and France should for the present do everthing to persuade the Czechs to remove the causes of friction with the Sudeten Germans and try to achieve a solution short of the actual seccssion of the Sudetenland.[3]

This assessment of the position was repeated by Chamberlain

[1] *D.B.F.P.*, Third Series, I, pp. 271–2.
[2] Lieut. Commander P. K. Kemp, *Key to Victory: the Triumph of British Sea Power in World War II*, Boston, 1957, p. 26.
[3] *D.B.F.P.*, Third Series, I, p. 86.

in the Commons in the afternoon after the Cabinet discussion, when he defined British commitments in a manner to which he adhered throughout the crisis. The government, Chamberlain said, could give no advance guarantee of military help to France if she were involved in war with Germany in fulfilment of her pledge to Czechoslovakia, nor to Czechoslovakia to prevent forcible interference with her independence and integrity, since this would remove Britain's decision for peace or war out of her own hands. 'This position,' Chamberlain said, 'is not one that His Majesty's Government can see their way to accept in relation to an area where their vital interests are not concerned in the same degree as they are in the case of France and Belgium: it is certainly not the position that results from the Covenant.' But, the Prime Minister went on, in these matters legal obligations alone were not involved: no one could foresee what changes the pressure of facts would effect if fighting began.

In that event it would be well within the bounds of possibility that other countries, besides those which were parties to the original dispute, would almost immediately become involved. This is especially true in the case of two countries, like Great Britain and France, with long associations of friendship, with interests closely interwoven, devoted to the same ideals of democratic liberty and determined to uphold them.[1]

This was as far as the government would go, and whenever the French asked what the British would do when the blow fell they were referred to the statement of 24 March.

On the same day on which Chamberlain spoke Halifax saw the Soviet Ambassador, Maisky, and told him that Britain was rejecting a Soviet proposal for a conference of interested governments to consider methods of checking aggression. The British objection was that Germany, whose attitude to the European security problem Chamberlain most wished to influence, would not be represented at the discussions as Russia envisaged them; in any case Britain wanted to keep the handling of the situation at the level of conciliation, holding all suggestion of compulsion well in the background. Halifax said that a 'conference only attended by some of the European Powers and designed less to secure the settlement of outstanding problems than to organise concerted action against aggression would not necessarily, in the view of His Majesty's Government, have such a favourable effect upon the prospects of European peace'.[2]

[1] 333 H.C. Deb. 5s. Cols. 1399–1407.   [2] *D.B.F.P.*, Third Series, I, p. 101.

In this way began the long process of bringing pressure to bear on the Czechs, directly and through France, to come to an agreement with the Sudeten Germans, the assumption being that Hitler, as he told Halifax at the Berchtesgaden meeting in November 1937, would rest content with an autonomous Sudetenland within existing Czech frontiers, but free from what British Ministers had come to regard as genuine grievances. The problem was to avoid the appearance of direct British intervention in what was still ostensibly an internal Czechoslovakian question. The 'inner Cabinet' cast about for means of securing a Czech invitation to London to offer its good offices. By good fortune, on 14 March, the day of Chamberlain's Commons statement on the Austrian situation, the Czech Minister in London, Jan Masaryk, wrote to Hoare, then Home Secretary, asking for 'direct, blunt, concrete advice' on whether the Czechs should make concessions. He received in reply on the 25th Hoare's counsel, 'speaking as an old friend', that the Czech Government should ask Britain and France for their good offices.[1] The Czechs, however, showed no haste to do so.

British Ministers feared that an incident might occur on the Czech-German border, especially in view of the mood of elation prevailing among the Sudeten Germans after the *Anschluss* and that Reich forces might be sent to settle it. The nearer this danger approached, the greater the urgency of bringing home to the Czechs and their French supporters the necessity for a peaceful settlement, which must involve Czech concessions. Halifax wrote to Phipps, the British Ambassador in Paris, on 11 April that:

> unless the French and Czech Governments can be brought to face the realities of the present position, it is to be feared that the Czech Government will not realise the necessity of making drastic concessions to the German minority, but will content themselves with superficial measures . . . which will no longer meet the case, while the French Government for their part will fail to appreciate the necessity of using their undoubted influence in Prague to promote a supreme effort on the part of the Czech Government to find a solution of the problem on the settlement of which the continued existence of Czechoslovakia as an independent state within her present borders will depend.[2]

The Foreign Secretary followed this up on the next day with a message to the British Minister in Prague, Basil Newton, in

---

[1] Templewood, *op. cit.*, pp. 292–5; *D.B.F.P.*, Third Series, I, pp. 113–14.
[2] *D.B.F.P.*, Third Series, I, pp. 140–3.

which he urged that the aim of the Czech Government must be direct negotiations with Henlein, the Sudeten leader, 'covering the whole field of the problem and having as their object a comprehensive and lasting settlement'. The British and French should keep the pressure up on the Czechs in this sense, then watch developments closely and be ready 'at the appropriate time and in the appropriate manner to use their influence to direct and secure a settlement'.[1]

The breadth of the gap between the Sudeten German demands and the utmost which Benes and his colleagues felt able to offer was made clear when, on 19 April, Newton reported home on the Czech Government's carefully considered proposals for solving the minority problem. These consisted of no more than a new statute of minorities (the Czechs refused to accept the term 'nationalities'), new language regulations, the devotion of a fixed proportion of the national budget to minority uses, and the appointment of public servants from the minority groups in accordance with a population index.[2] Five days later Henlein replied with a speech at the Kurhaus in Carlsbad at the annual general meeting of the Sudeten German Party (S.P.D.). His requirements were: full equality of status between Czechs and Germans; a guarantee of this equality by the recognition of the Sudeten Germans as constituting a 'legal personality'; the definition and recognition of German regions within the state; full self-government for these regions; legal protection for every citizen living outside the region of his own nationality; the removal of injustices inflicted on the Sudeten Germans since 1918 and reparation for damages suffered thereby; German officials for German regions; full liberty to profess the German nationality (*Volkstum*) and the German political philosophy.[3] The Carlsbad programme did not precisely amount to secession of the Sudeten areas, but it was a demand that Czechoslovakia should no longer be recognised as an integral state.

In face of the deadlock presented by these proposals and counter-proposals Daladier and Bonnet, Prime Minister and Foreign Minister respectively in the new French Government formed on 10 April, came to London to review the position with Chamberlain and his closest colleagues at 10, Downing Street, on 28 and 29 April. Chamberlain significantly opened the talks by proposing that Anglo-French military co-operation be

[1] *Ibid.*, pp. 149–50.
[2] The composition of Czechoslovakia's population according to the 1930 census was as follows; Czechs, 7,477,000; Germans, 3,210,000; Slovaks, 2,309,000; Magyars, 691,000; Ruthenians, 549,000; Poles, 81,000.
[3] *D.B.F.P.*, Third Series, I, pp. 182–6.

taken first. This reflected his view that the political solution
of the Czech problem must depend on the military realities,
which he regarded as unfavourable. Daladier, on the contrary, fearing that the Sudeten Germans' grievances were only
significant as an element in Hitler's wider design to subjugate
Europe, believed that Anglo-French military arrangements
should be made to square with the necessities arising from this
assessment of German political aims. He nevertheless accepted
Chamberlain's proposal on the order of the agenda and in
doing so agreed that Britain should take the lead in the forthcoming struggle.

As far as the staff talks were concerned, Chamberlain reminded the meeting that these had been provided for in the
Anglo-French agreement of 19 March 1936 which followed
Hitler's reoccupation of the Rhineland.[1] He insisted, however,
that they were not to give rise to any political undertaking or
obligation regarding the organisation of national defence. The
first British military commitment, Chamberlain said, was home
defence and therefore any British assistance to France must
chiefly be by sea and air. Britain could only hope to send two
army divisions to France in the event of war and these would
not necessarily be motorised for modern war. Consequently,
Chamberlain went on, there was no need for army staff talks,
nor for naval talks either since effective naval co-operation
could easily be arranged after the actual outbreak of hostilities. The Prime Minister was satisfied with air staff talks alone
for the time being. He wished to create the least possible
alarm in Germany and feared that Anglo-French naval co-
operation would drive Italy closer to Germany's side.

At the afternoon session on the 28th Daladier pressed for an
altogether more vigorous approach to the question, proposing
the motorisation of the two British divisions earmarked for
continental service and calling for army and navy staff talks
as well as those agreed for the air. Chamberlain at length
grudgingly consented to contacts between the Army staffs and
the respective Military Attachés to decide the arrangements in
case British forces should go to France. But the utmost to
which he would go in the matter of naval talks was that agreement to hold them should be recorded, but that effect should
only be given to the principle of these talks 'as opportunity
offered'. Chamberlain wanted to see what came of Hitler's
proposed visit to Rome before going further.

Chamberlain's hesitant attitude towards military co-opera-

[1] Germany No. 2 (1936), Cmd. 5134; Misc. No. 4 (1936), Cmd. 5149; see above,
p. 435.

tion with the French reflected, and at the same time reinforced, his gloomy view of the prospects of helping Czechoslovakia against a determined German assault. A month before he had written in a private letter,

> You have only to look at the map to see that nothing that France and we could do could possibly save Czechoslovakia from being overrun by the Germans if they wanted to do it ... therefore we could not help Czechoslovakia—she would simply be a pretext for going to war with Germany. That we could not think of unless we had a reasonable prospect of being able to beat her to her knees in a reasonable time and of that I see no sign.[1]

Halifax sustained the same argument to the French on 29 March. 'If the German Government determined to take hostile steps against the Czech state,' Halifax said, 'it would be impossible in the present military situation to prevent these steps from achieving immediate success.' The Czech state could not be re-established, if war came, for a long time. Hence, Halifax urged, the British and French should set themselves two tasks: to impress on the Germans not to impose a solution by force, and to convince the Czechs that this might be the last chance for a negotiated settlement.

Daladier saw the situation differently. Germany's policy was to destroy the equilibrium of Europe; 'war could only be avoided,' Daladier considered, 'if the British and French made their determination quite clear to maintain the peace of Europe by respecting the rights and liberties of independent peoples.' He did not agree that Britain, France and Czechoslovakia were powerless to act. The Czech peacetime army was 180,000 and could soon be enlarged to 500,000. If Britain and France took action, Poland and Rumania might change their equivocal attitude to Czechoslovakia's fate; the Soviet air force was the strongest in Europe and Russia's potential resources were great. Chamberlain retorted that Daladier's talk of threats was bluff; Britain and France were not strong enough to make victory certain. British public opinion would not allow the government to run the risk of war under such conditions. Chamberlain also doubted whether Hitler wanted to destroy Czechoslovakia since Henlein had shown in his Carlsbad speech that he was not asking for an *Anschluss*.

The question which concerned the French was what Britain would do if both countries joined in putting pressure on Benes to go to the limit in concessions to Henlein and if Czechoslovakia

[1] Macleod, *op. cit.*, p. 224.

was nevertheless attacked by Germany. Chamberlain, despite his insistence that joint pressure be applied in Prague, was still unable to go beyond his Commons statement on 24 March in reply to this question. With that the French had to be satisfied. The next issue was how the negotiations in Prague should be accelerated. Halifax wanted a direct approach to Hitler to use his influence with the Henleinists. Daladier and Bonnet could not agree to the negotiations being taken out of the hands of the Czechs. Chamberlain then put forward a compromise solution; Britain would tell the Führer that she was doing her best to find a solution and that an Anglo-French approach was being made to the Czechs with the object of securing the maximum concessions for the Sudeten Germans; at the same time Hitler would be asked to make his own proposals known. At the end of all this was to come a carefully contrived warning. If no agreement was reached in the Czech–Sudeten German negotiations, the British could say with a clear conscience that they had done their best, and if in those circumstances the Germans resorted to force, they must remember that the French had their obligations to Czechoslovakia and that Britain could not guarantee to remain neutral.[1] On the basis of this formula, the Anglo-French talks came to an end. Chamberlain wrote two days afterwards: 'fortunately, the papers have no hint of how near we came to a break over Czechoslovakia'.[2]

Halifax saw Masaryk on 2 May to tell him the conclusions of the Anglo-French talks. If a settlement of the minorities question was to be reached, Halifax said, the Czech Government would have to be prepared to go a very long way. The Minister replied that Benes was willing to go a very long way indeed.[3] Henderson was likewise told the results of the talks on 4 May and was asked to inquire of the Germans the lines of settlement they favoured. It was significant, however, that the warning agreed to in the Anglo-French talks as to the consequences if Germany had recourse to force was relegated to the second stage of the approach to Germany in Halifax's message to Henderson.[4] Halifax explained that Britain did not wish to convey the warning 'unless and until it is really necessary'. The government's problem, he went on, was 'to ride the line between giving our blessing to anything that the Germans propose and sponsoring at Berlin some plan that Benes might submit to us.'[5]

[1] D.B.F.P., Third Series, I, pp. 198–233.   [2] Feiling, op. cit., p. 353.
[3] D.B.F.P., Third Series, I, pp. 235–8.   [4] Ibid., pp. 243–5.
[5] Ibid., pp. 253–5.

First reactions from Prague and Berlin to the British and French *démarche* were the reverse of encouraging. In Berlin the Political Director of the Foreign Ministry replied to Henderson on 7 May, since Ribbentrop was accompanying Hitler on his visit to Rome, saying that the matter was one for direct negotiation between Henlein and the Czechs; this was an argument the Germans were very soon to abandon.[1] On the following day Krofta, the Czech Foreign Minister, told Newton that he, like the French, did not take so bleak a view of the military position as the British and that he was not optimistic about the prospects of satisfying Henlein.[2] Newton himself reported two days later, after talking with the German Minister in Prague, Eisenlohr, that Henlein would probably prove insatiable. 'My intuitive impression from his general attitude,' Newton wrote of Eisenlohr, 'was that the Sudeten German Party might continue indefinitely to extract from the Czech Government the maximum concessions obtainable under whatever pressure could be applied and that then, however favourable the position achieved might be, they would feel perfectly free to secede and break up the Czech state if it suited their purpose and that of the German Reich to do so.'[3] This conflicted with the opinion given by Henderson on 6 May when he wrote to Halifax that 'both Hitler and Henlein are moderates compared to many of their followers and Benes's sole hope in my opinion and in the interests of his country is to make a maximum offer that these two cannot well decline it'.[4] But it was towards Newton's more pessimistic view that Chamberlain inclined. A few days after he had read these dispatches the American and Canadian newspapers were filled with reports of an indiscreet 'off the record' statement the Prime Minister had made to correspondents at one of the notorious Clivedenset parties of the period at Lady Astor's to the effect that Czechoslovakia could not continue in its present form and that the integrity of Czechoslovakia 'within adjusted boundaries' should be guaranteed by a four-Power pact. The report of this anticipation of the eventual Munich agreement was 'broadly, if not in detail, correct'.[5]

The two lines the British Government were pursuing in Berlin and Prague respectively rested on the curious assumption that they could be kept separate, and that the Czechs and Germans could be prevented from hearing what British representatives were saying to each. 'While we are emphasising

[1] Henderson, *op. cit.*, p. 132; *D.B.F.P.*, Third Series, I, p. 260.
[2] *Ibid.*, pp. 265–71.   [3] *Ibid.*, pp. 277–80.   [4] *Ibid.*, pp. 257–8.
[5] Macleod, *op. cit.*, pp. 231–2. *New York Times*, 15 May 1938.

in Prague the weakness of the military situation,' Halifax explained to Henderson on 11 May, 'we hope to make the German Government think long before doing anything likely to break the peace.'[1] It could, however, be inferred from the line of argument used by Ribbentrop, now returned from Rome, when talking with Henderson on 7 and 11 May, that he was aware of Newton's messages to the Czechs. The German Foreign Minister expressed scepticism concerning Benes's desire for a comprehensive settlement, about which the British Ambassador had always been doubtful; he then alleged that Hitler would be virtually compelled to take immediate action if things were allowed to drift, and added that Germany would be 'saturated' once the Sudeten question was settled, only the colonial problem remaining between Britain and Germany.[2] Ribbentrop's menaces were, as always, faithfully echoed in Henderson's advice to Halifax; 'disagreeable though it may be,' the Ambassador wrote on 14 May, 'I am nevertheless convinced that in the interests not only of European peace but of the existence of Czechoslovakia a serious effort should be made to compound with Germany while there is yet time.' Hitler, Henderson was quite clear, was determined to restore the Sudeten Germans to the homeland (though they had in fact never been part of Germany since its reunification in 1871) and 'only a successful war will prevent or delay the realisation of his aims'.[3] This was the conclusion which Chamberlain had himself reached, as the Prime Minister's statement now being reported in the translantic press showed. Yet it seemed to conflict with the assurances which Henlein gave to Churchill, Sir Archibald Sinclair, the leader of the Liberal Opposition, together with other Parliamentarians, and to Robert Vansittart, when he talked with them on 13 May on a visit to London. Henlein represented his object as being no more than local autonomy for the Sudeten Germans so that they could settle their local affairs through their own organs of administration, a kind of federal devolution on national lines.[4] The force of the Sudeten leader's personal charm was such that even Vansittart considered him to be a reasonable man. No one in London imagined that Hitler had appointed Henlein his 'viceroy' as early as 28 March and that in return Henlein had promised that 'we must always demand so much that we can never be satisfied'.[5]

[1] *D.B.F.P.*, Third Series, I, pp. 281–2.
[2] *Ibid.*, pp. 284–7; *D.G.F.P.*, Series D, II, pp. 261–2, 269–71.
[3] *D.B.F.P.*, Third Series, I, pp. 294–7.
[4] *Ibid.*, pp. 297–9; Winston S. Churchill, *The Gathering Storm*, p. 223.
[5] *D.G.F.P.*, Series D, II, p. 198.

The momentum of the crisis was passing beyond the control of all the parties, including the German authorities, who sought to influence it. Bonnet told Halifax in Geneva on 12 May, when the two Ministers were attending a meeting of the League Council, that Britain must intensify her pressure on Czechoslovakia 'to save France from the cruel dilemma of dishonouring her agreements or becoming involved in war'.[1] Yet in Prague resistance was stiffening among Czech public opinion to making further concessions to the Henleinists. On 17 May a manifesto signed by several hundred Czech intellectuals was published, calling on all citizens to maintain their unity and traditions of freedom and democracy.[2] The Czech authorities were perplexed, wrote Newton, how to deal with the incidents which were now a daily occurrence in the Sudeten areas after the local elections; if they imposed law and order the Germans might intervene to save their nationals, and yet if they failed to maintain order this in itself might provide the Germans with grounds for intervention.[3] That German forces would cross the frontier if the tension passed beyond a certain point there could be no doubt. On 19 May Henderson sent to London alarming reports on German troop movements in Southern Silesia and northern Austria, adding that Germany would fight if incidents involving bloodshed occurred in Czechoslovakia.[4] Two days later information was in the hands of the Czech authorities that the German 7th and 17th infantry divisions were moving towards the Czech frontiers in Bavaria and the crucial decision was taken to put into force the Defence Act which permitted the government to call one class and certain army specialists to the colours. At this time Henlein was in Austria, where he had gone on the 19th. On returning on 23 May he declared that he would hold no negotiations with the Czech authorities so long as peace and order in the Sudeten areas and the constitutional rights of the Germans were not upheld.

War, it seemed, was but a hair's breadth away. Ribbentrop bluntly told Henderson on 20 May that Germany could not wait much longer; if the Czech provocations continued, Germany's 75 million people 'would act as one man'.[5] When pressed by Henderson to use his influence with Henlein to get him to resume negotiations, the Foreign Minister refused and said it was for the British to use their influence with Benes.[6] On the following day, Henderson had another interview with

[1] D.B.F.P., Third Series, I, p. 299, n. 2.
[2] Ibid., pp. 309–10.
[3] Ibid., p. 320.
[4] Ibid., pp. 317–18.
[5] Ibid., pp. 329–30.
[6] Ibid., pp. 334–5.

Ribbentrop to make the same request, but this time he brought with him the strongest warning which Chamberlain allowed to have uttered throughout the crisis. 'We could not foresee the results,' Henderson was instructed to say, 'if force were resorted to and there could be no guarantee that Britain would stand aside.' Though panic-stricken at the possibility of having to fight with Communists as his only allies, Bonnet told a press conference in Paris that France would certainly respect her treaty obligations with Czechoslovakia in the event of German aggression.[1]

These unexpected warnings astounded Hitler and his associates, considering that it was on the Czech side that the most forward military moves were made. But, combined with the evident determination of the Czechs to resist attack, they were effective in securing a standstill in the German military preparations. Hitler retired in fury and humiliation to Obersalzberg, where he kept himself aloof for five days. Nevertheless, Halifax saw fit to advise the French through Phipps that they should not read too much in the stern line Britain had taken in Berlin.

> If the French Government were to assume [Halifax wrote] that H.M. Government would at once take joint action with them to preserve Czechoslovakia against German aggression, it is only fair to warn them that our statements do not warrant any such assumption. In the view of H.M. Government the military situation is such that France and England, even with such assistance as might be expected from Russia, would not be in a position to prevent Germany overrunning Czechoslovakia.

The only result of Anglo-French military assistance in the Czech's cause, Halifax gloomily concluded, would be a European war, 'the outcome of which, so far as could be foreseen at the moment, would be at least doubtful'.[2]

The lesson drawn from the May crisis by Chamberlain and his close colleagues was thus, not that the Nazi leader would be restrained by a firm stand against him, but that everything must be done to avoid a repetition of the crisis since next time the outcome would be far more unpleasant.

---

[1] *D.B.F.P.*, Third Series, I, p. 340. Henderson, *op. cit.*, pp. 135–7; *F.R.U.S.* 1938, I, pp. 512–15.
[2] *D.B.F.P.*, Third Series, I, p. 347.

CHAPTER XX

THE RIM OF CHAOS

I

MINISTERS in London felt that the breathing space provided by the May crisis should be used for two purposes; to remove the resentment the crisis had left in the Reich in the hope that the Germans would use their influence to moderate Henlein's demands, and to liquidate the deadlock in the talks on the minorities question in Prague by impressing on the Czechs the consequences if no agreement was reached. To further the first of these objects, Halifax saw the German Ambassador, von Dirksen, and explained the care that had been taken in the preparation of the statements on the crisis made in Parliament by Chamberlain and himself on 23 May in order to protect them from any charge of partiality.[1] As for gingering up the Czechs, the Foreign Secretary talked with Masaryk, who was about to leave for consultations in Prague, on 25 May and stressed the urgency of putting the time gained by the crisis to good use. Taking his cue from Sir Nevile Henderson's description of Hitler as a man barely able to hold his extremists in check, a judgment almost exactly the reverse of the truth, Halifax said that the German Chancellor might have to capitulate to the intransigents at home if another incident occurred like the shooting of two Sudeten German motor cyclists at Eger in the Sudetenland during the tension at the week-end.

But the deadlock in Prague persisted. The Sudeten leaders contended that negotiations could not be resumed after the week-end crisis until the Czech military measures had been revoked; the Czechs retorted that cancellation of the military measures would merely touch off the crisis again. Meanwhile, indignation soared among the Sudeten Germans as their districts increasingly took on the appearance of an occupied country. Halifax saw the extent of the British commitment to find a solution; he confessed to Newton on 31 May his fears of a catastrophic sequel if a settlement were delayed. Pressure on the Czechs was getting nowhere; Newton even believed that the army in Czechoslovakia might wrest power from Benes if the British and French pressed too hard.[2] Once the Prague talks were resumed, the sticking point seemed to be the Sudeten

[1] *D.B.F.P.*, Third Series, I, pp. 369–71. [2] *Ibid.*, pp. 442–4.

511

demand for their own national Parliament, or Volkstag, which Benes naturally considered was intended to split the Czech state territorially. Halifax wrote to Newton on 8 June that the Czech Government should not close their minds entirely to the idea of a Volkstag. Henlein, he felt, had made a good impression even on critics of the Nazis during his visit to London, and had even seemed to retreat from the Carlsbad programme.[1] Halifax hinted, through Phipps, that the French should join in getting the Czechs to accept Henlein's ideas as a basis for discussion.[2]

It was natural for British Ministers to wonder whether the French were doing as much as they had promised to press the Czechs to come to terms with Henlein, however hard that may be. Bonnet, so Phipps wrote home early in June, had seen Osusky, the Czech Minister in Paris, on the eve of his return to Prague for a visit and told him to warn Benes that the French attitude to their obligations might change if the Czechs were unreasonable. Halifax was on the whole satisfied with this statement, but did not think it sufficiently precise, exactly the objection the French had always raised against British forecasts of their probable action if war came in Europe. Halifax accordingly made the extraordinary request to the French through Phipps that they should let him know exactly what they were saying to the Czechs.[3] This was not the only turn of the screw on France which the Foreign Secretary now gave. On 17 June he told Phipps that the British Cabinet were doubtful whether a solution of the minority question by itself would remove all risk of war.

The 'root of the difficulty', British Ministers were beginning to think, was the undertaking of assistance which Czechoslovakia had received from France and Russia. Halifax explained to Phipps that he had been turning over in his mind possible 'readjustments' in Czechoslovakia's external relations which, 'by reducing what Germany professes to regard as provocative elements in the Czech system of treaties, should tend to promote stability in Central Europe and lessen the chances of France being called upon to fulfil her obligations to Czechoslovakia in possibly unfavourable circumstances'. Halifax blandly continued:

The easiest and least disturbing course would be to 'remodel' Czechoslovakia's relations so that Czechoslovakia

[1] Ibid., pp. 453–4.
[2] The Ministry for Foreign Affairs, Czechoslovak Republic and U.S.S.R., New Documents on the History of Munich, pp. 49–50.
[3] D.B.F.P., Third Series, I, pp. 495–6.

would not be bound to assist Russia and France in the event of a German attack, Germany would undertake not to infringe Czech integrity but to assist Czechoslovakia if attacked, and Czechoslovakia would pledge herself not to use her territory for aggression against other states as a passage or base of operations.[1]

This was a new refinement in the theory of conciliating the aggrieved; it meant asking him whether he would like concessions which would immensely strengthen his position before he himself had formally proposed them. Bonnet delayed his comment until 10 August, then merely said that the question was inopportune.[2]

The minority problem remained the immediate one; and the time was approaching when Britain would have to make some positive move to prevent an irreversible step being taken to precipitate the conflict which British policy was dedicated to avoiding. The idea that a mediator with administrative experience and knowledge of minority questions might be dispatched to Prague had been mooted in the Foreign Office, and Chamberlain and Halifax were attracted by it, provided Czechs and Germans agreed. The problem was that of the right moment for putting the proposal into effect. Newton thought that this would not come until the Czech–Sudeten German negotiations had reached a point at which it was clear that they were not going to succeed, and Halifax agreed with this. That point was not far off. Newton summed up the Czech Government's memorandum of 23 June, which listed their objections to the Sudeten demands, by saying that 'both sides approach the question from fundamentally opposed points of view'. The Czech Government still hoped to run the state as a single unit on the basis of individual citizens, whereas the Sudeten Germans were clearly aiming at severing it into separate national units, which would allow them to manage their affairs on National Socialist lines.[3] Newton was accordingly unable to extract from Benes any grounds for hope that an agreed solution was possible. He reported to London the ominous news that the Czech Government might have no option but to introduce in Parliament in mid-July measures representing the maximum which they could give.[4] Halifax considered that this would be disastrous as it would suggest that negotiations with Henlein were at an end; he preferred that the Parliamentary measures should cover merely the items which had

[1] Ibid., pp. 496–8. [2] D.B.F.P., Third Series, II, pp. 71–4.
[3] Ibid., I, pp. 510–11. [4] Ibid., pp. 525–6.

been agreed with the Sudeten Germans during the negotiations.[1] On 14 July, however, all hope of getting the reforms, in whatever shape, on the Czech Statute book fell to the ground when the Cabinet in Prague refused to accept Prime Minister Hodza's proposals which had been so many agonizing weeks in preparation.

The time for mediation, it seemed, had now arrived. Newton came to the conclusion, after a two-and-a-half hour talk with Benes on 16 July, that the outlook for a definitive agreement with the minority leaders was poor; sharp disagreements divided the Czech Cabinet and the Parliamentary committee dealing with the Sudeten demands on the question of the powers of the provincial diets and the proposed *curiae*, or committees of national deputies within the diets which would have sole power to legislate in matters affecting the nationality concerned[2]. Henderson reported two days later that preparations were afoot in Germany for some *coup* before the Nazi Rally at Nuremberg in September, although he regarded these as bluff designed to secure results in Prague.[3] However interpreted, the prospects looked dark for the autumn, when the harvest would be gathered in and the Nuremberg meetings would whip the Germans into hysteria. Two events in particular combined to convince the British Ministers that no time should be lost in forcing the Prague talks to a finish through the agency of a British mediator. One was the Czech Government's decision to bring their proposals before Parliament in a take-it-or-leave-it fashion without giving the Sudeten Germans the opportunity to bring forward points of objection. This procedure Halifax thought indefensible and likely only to entrench the two parties in their positions.[4] The other was a visit to London by Captain Wiedemann, an envoy of Hitler, for a talk with the Foreign Secretary on 18 July.

Ostensibly the aim of the Wiedemann visit was to test the ground for a later visit by Goering to discuss Anglo-German relations in all their aspects. In reality, the object seemed to be to nourish British faith in Hitler's wish for better relations and to strengthen the assumption that he would prefer to have the Sudeten problem settled peacefully. Hitler, Wiedemann said, was well disposed towards Britain but felt he had been rebuffed; it was evident, for instance, that Lord Halifax had taken no concrete proposals with him to Germany in November 1937. Wiedemann then gave 'binding assurances' that Germany was planning no forcible action against Czechoslovakia

[1] *D.B.F.P.*, Third Series, I, pp. 563–5. [2] *Ibid.*, pp. 569–73.
[3] *Ibid.*, pp. 580–1. [4] *Ibid.*, pp. 581–3.

and had no intention of resorting to any such action. Hitler, Wiedemann went on, wanted a comprehensive settlement of the Sudeten question by peaceful means, but incidents might occur which he could not overlook. Halifax in reply said that the proposed Goering visit was desirable in principle, provided the ground was carefully prepared beforehand. Nevertheless, the chief obstacle to better Anglo-German relations, Halifax pointed out, remained Czechoslovakia and the prospects for a peaceful settlement would be much improved if Germany could declare her intention of co-operating in a peaceful solution.[1] That intention was never expressly stated by Captain Wiedemann; it is hard to see what would have been the practical consequences if it were. But the Wiedemann visit and the imminence of an open breach between the negotiating parties in Prague left no room for delaying the British mediation proposal.

II

The mediation mission, which Lord Runciman had now accepted on condition that all the parties concerned agreed, was discussed on Halifax's visit to Paris when the king and queen went to the French capital on 19 and 20 July. Halifax emphasised to a querulous Daladier and sceptical Bonnet that the British accepted no responsibility for the Runciman report: 'our responsibility,' he said, 'would begin and end with finding him and with turning him loose at Prague to make the best that he could of the business.' Meanwhile, Britain and France, the French Ministers were persuaded, should bring all pressure to bear on Benes to prevent him bringing the full nationalities statute before the Czech Parliament on 25 July, as the President intended, since this would inevitably have the effect of hardening the position. Halifax also made use of the talks with the French to reduce still more the hope of Britain going to war on the Czechs' behalf; he revealed that before leaving for Paris he had talked with the Aga Khan, who had stressed the fact that Britain could make no commitment involving the British Empire in war. 'The same would be the position in South Africa,' the Foreign Secretary added.[2]

Benes's first reaction to the Runciman mission proposal, when Newton told him of it on 20 July, was one of intense shock. He protested that it infringed Czechoslovakia's sovereignty; it might touch off a political crisis and force the government's resignation.[3] Hodza, to whom Newton put the mediation proposal on the next day, retorted that it meant putting the

---

[1] *D.B.F.P.*, Third Series, I, pp. 584–9.
[2] *Ibid.*, p. 602.   [3] *Ibid.*, pp. 600–1.

Czech Government on the same level as the Sudeten parties. He agreed to consult the Cabinet, however, and after two days of discussion the Czechs agreed to accept the Runciman mission, thus giving colour to the fiction that they had asked for it.[1] On 26 July Chamberlain told the House of Commons of two valuable results he expected from the mission; it would inform world opinion of the real facts of the case and 'issues which have appeared intractable would prove under the influence of the mediator to be less obstinate than we thought'.[2] The main purpose of the mission, however, as Halifax explained to Henderson, was to try to prevent a breakdown in the negotiations in Prague.[3] Henderson himself thought the mission would fail as the Sudeten leaders would not accept a purely national Czech state; but it might serve as a further means of bringing pressure to bear on the Czechs despite the fact that Runciman was supposed to be independent of instructions from the British Government. To Henderson the Czechs were a 'pig-headed race' and Benes 'not the least pig-headed among them'.[4] The influence which the Ambassador had over the Foreign Secretary found its reflection in Halifax's own statement on the mission in the House of Lords on 27 July, from which he omitted a warning to Germany on the lines of that of 21 May, which he had intended to give, and substituted a request that Germany should play its part, as Henderson advised. 'Since we are pressing the Czech Government to be generous and conciliatory,' the wording ran, 'we confidently count on Germany to give similar advice when she may, with a view to avoiding a deadlock the consequences of which may be incalculable.'[5]

Runciman arrived in Prague on 3 August with no sign of interest in the mission's objects from Berlin. The Reich Foreign Minister, Ribbentrop, first complained that news of the mission had been leaked to the Press before the German authorities had heard of the proposal from Henderson, and then not inaccurately claimed that it was an entirely British affair. On 28 July, while Halifax was writing to Ribbentrop expressing regret at this non co-operative attitude, Henderson sent serious news home; rumours were afoot in Berlin of a German test mobilisation to be held on 15 August, the plan being to hold manœuvres in East Prussia and Silesia. Hard on the heels of this message came a communiqué issued by the

1 Ibid., p. 620.   2 338 H.C. Deb. 5s. Cols. 2957-8.
3 D.B.F.P., Third Series, II, pp. 3-4.
4 Ibid., pp. 10-12; Henderson, op. cit., pp. 141-2.
5 110 H.L. Deb. 5s. Col. 1284.

official German news agency D.N.B. on 30 July which forbade
access to western Germany to all foreign Military Attachés.
According to Henderson, the Military Attachés had been told
that the new decree applied to parts of the Bavarian–Czech
border and to practically all Germany between the Oder and
the Polish frontier.[1] On 3 August, while the Runciman party
was arriving in Prague, the German Government made known
their intention to bring seven or eight divisions in the Reich
and all their forces in Austria to full strength by September.
Henderson interpreted these moves as a 'mixture of bluff and
real menace'; they were a warning to Britain to get results from
Benes and an indication that the question must be settled by
September.[2] But the wide publicity given to these measures
suggested that Hitler was mainly interested in their psychological effects.

Henderson's Military Attaché, Colonel Mason-Macfarlane,
advised the British Government that the situation was 'fraught
with dangerous possibilities'. He was reasonably certain that
the German Army had no desire to take action against Czechoslovakia, but 'the possibility that the Government may have
intentions in this respect is becoming much greater and they
are forcing the army to take steps which may well produce a
crisis or alternatively put them in a position in which they will
feel that the cards are so favourable that they can and should
start the game'.[3] Henderson followed this up by advising
Halifax on 4 August that although he still thought it was an
open question whether Hitler had made up his mind irrevocably
to use force against the Czechs that autumn, 'the possibility
that he may do so has now become more real'.[4] Henderson
was convinced that while Hitler did not want war, he would
be compelled to fight if a peaceful settlement on the basis of
self-determination for the Sudeten Germans broke down. 'Just
as I was convinced years ago,' he wrote to Halifax on 6 August,
'that Austria must inevitably come into Germany sooner or
later, so I am convinced that the Sudetens must do so in the
end.'[5] Halifax had now come round to the same viewpoint.
Writing to Henderson from York the previous day he had made
clear that, 'like you, I have no intention of going to war over
Czechoslovakia if I can avoid it'. To fight a war, he wrote,
for one, two or three years to protect or re-create something that
you know you cannot directly protect and probably could never
re-create 'did not make sense'.[6] Here again, the point was

[1] *D.B.F.P.*, Third Series, II, p. 27.
[2] *Ibid.*, pp. 39–40.
[3] *Ibid.*, pp. 42–5.
[4] *Ibid.*, p. 46.
[5] *Ibid.*, pp. 58–60.
[6] *Ibid.*, pp. 75–6.

made, as it was increasingly by British Ministers throughout the crisis, that even if they succeeded in defeating Germany in a war fought on Czechoslovakia's behalf they probably would not restore the Czech state of 1919.

Runciman's first report to Halifax, sent on 10 August, indicated how widely separated the two sides were. The mission had in fact met its first obstacle with the refusal of the Sudeten leaders to negotiate with a specially appointed Czech Parliament committee of six deputies and their insistence on dealing with the government. The Czech attitude in response to these complaints was steadily hardening, Newton reported on 17 August.[1] Halifax had up to this stage been content with merely being informed by Runciman of the state of affairs in Prague so as to maintain the fiction of being a detached observer of the mediation proceedings. Now he stepped into the ring with advice. On 18 August he wrote to discourage the mediator from submitting an independent reform scheme of his own as this would have the effect of apportioning blame between the adversaries and would lead the party which accepted the scheme to expect that they would have British support. At the same time the Foreign Secretary urgently questioned Runciman as to whether he could produce results before the Nazi rally in September.[2] The reply was discouraging, but the negotiations somehow stumbled on. Runciman was even able to report on 23 August that the two sides had moved closer together. The Czechs had drawn up a comprehensive list of the points they were willing to concede to the Sudeten Germans and the question, as the mediator saw it, was whether Benes was willing 'to do the large thing' and clinch the agreement.[3]

Halifax exerted himself in making appeals to Germany to help create a better atmosphere. On 11 August he wrote to Hitler asking him to modify his recent military measures; he feared that the Czechs might take precautionary measures and this would be bound to have adverse effects on the Runciman mission.[4] This appeal the German Foreign Office refused to accept on the ground, as Woermann, the Under-Secretary of State, explained, that the British protest had been broadcast by Radio Luxemburg on that day, 13 August, before Hitler had received Halifax's letter.[5] Woermann was particularly outraged by the form taken by the British protest. The British note had been sent to Hitler, not through the Foreign Ministry,

[1] *D.B.F.P.*, Third Series, II, p. 100.
[2] *Ibid.*, pp. 111–15.
[3] *Ibid.*, p. 142.
[4] *Ibid.*, pp. 78–80; *D.G.F.P.*, Series D, II, pp. 549–51.
[5] *D.B.F.P.*, Third Series, II, pp. 92–3.

but through the Reich Minister, Lammers, and a copy had gone to the Foreign Ministry only after Lammers had received the note.[1] Lammers wrote to Ribbentrop on 17 August that Hitler proposed to take no action on the British protest but would discuss it further with Ribbentrop.[2] The Foreign Minister's reply to Halifax was sent on 21 August and merely stated that there could not possibly be any discussion with the British about internal military measures. At the same time Ribbentrop said that Germany could not co-operate with the Runciman mission 'which came about without German participation'. The effect of British efforts, Ribbentrop claimed, was merely to strengthen the Czechs in their 'intransigence and aggressiveness'; the attitude of Prague, he said, was the only real obstacle to a settlement.[3] On the same day as this cold retort was received in London, Henderson gave Halifax the even more chilling news that his Military Attaché had heard that in the previous week Hitler had told his generals that Czechoslovakia must be attacked at the end of September and that the German mobilisation must be complete by 15 September.[4] Events were surging to their critical point.

Halifax, as he told the French Chargé d'Affaires, Cambon, on 25 August, thought that the right policy in the circumstances was 'to keep Germany guessing'. Hence, in reply to Cambon's request for further British warnings to Germany, the British refused to go beyond Chamberlain's statement of 24 March, even though they saw the situation in as grave a light as the French and believed that Hitler would in all probability resort to force against the Czechs by the end of September if an agreed solution was not reached.[5] Chamberlain's aide, Sir Horace Wilson, however, did not believe in keeping Germany guessing; he spelled out the British attitude without concealment to Theodor Kordt, the German Chargé d'Affaires in London, a few days before Halifax's talk with Cambon. Provided Hitler confined himself to peaceful methods, Wilson said, he could have virtually what he wanted in east and south-east Europe. According to Kordt's account, Wilson regarded a peaceful settlement of the Sudeten question as the prerequisite of a wider Anglo-German understanding, the effect of which would be to give Germany predominance over all eastern Europe.

Britain and Germany [Kordt reported Wilson as having said] were in fact the two countries in which the greatest

[1] D.G.F.P., Series D, II, pp. 551–3; Henderson, op. cit., p. 144.
[2] D.G.F.P., Series D, II, pp. 576–7.
[3] D.B.F.P., Third Series, II, pp. 127–9; D.G.F.P., Series D, II, pp. 599–601.
[4] D.B.F.P., Third Series, II, pp. 125–6.   [5] Ibid., pp. 158–60.

order reigned and which were the best governed. Both were built up on the principle of human relationship. The reverse of this, Bolshevism, meant anarchy and barbarism. It would be the height of folly if these two leading white races were to exterminate each other in war. Bolshevism would be the only gainer thereby.

Wilson went on to say that 'a constructive solution of the Czech question by peaceful means would pave the way for Germany to exercise large-scale policy in the south-east . . . neither had Britain any intention of opposing a development of Germany's economy in a south-easterly direction. Her only wish was that she should not be debarred from trade there'.[1]

This may well have been a highly coloured version of the official British attitude as Wilson interpreted it. The sketch of British opinion as given by Baron von Welck, the Secretary of Legation at the German Embassy in London, after talking with Baron Hahn, a member of the office of the official German news agency, D.N.B., in London, was probably closer to the truth. Hahn said that the British Government were prepared to exact the most far-reaching sacrifices from Czechoslovakia if only Germany adhered to peaceful methods. The British Government and people had no interest in Czechoslovakia other than that the affair should not end in Germany using force. Hahn knew for certain, he said, that Chamberlain had an 'intense desire' to begin conversations with Germany as soon as possible. If the Anglo-German talks were satisfactory, France would join on Britain's side and Italy on Germany's, or so Chamberlain hoped.[2]

A special Cabinet meeting held in London on 30 August faced a situation depressing in the extreme. All information to hand pointed to Hitler's determination to move. Germany as a whole, Mason-Macfarlane had reported from Berlin in the previous week, was convinced that Hitler had decided to force a solution of the Czech problem before the year's end. Britain must make up her mind at once, he said, whether she was prepared to fight Germany on general principles but with a possibly unsound case, the Sudeten issue, as the one occasion for fighting.[3] From Campbell in Paris came the Military Attaché's assessment of the French view. Colonel Gauche, head of the French Second (Intelligence) Bureau, had told him that the French were 'convinced beyond any possible doubt that the German army was in process of mobilisation'. Militarily

[1] D.G.F.P., Series D, II, pp. 606–9.
[2] Ibid., pp. 621–2.
[3] D.B.F.P., Third Series, II, pp. 161–3.

speaking, Gauche said, Germany was ready for immediate war against Czechoslovakia and the German Government were still under the impression that neither Britain nor France would fight to save that country.[1] When the Cabinet met on the 30th Henderson, recalled from Berlin to take part in the discussion, rehearsed his well-known view that Hitler would 'reluctantly' be compelled to move unless the Czechs capitulated, at least to the extent of accepting the Carlsbad programme in full. Henderson prophesied that Hitler would make an unpleasant statement at the Nuremberg rally, possibly demanding a plebiscite.[2] Hore-Belisha, present at the Cabinet meeting in his capacity as Minister for War, recorded afterwards that 'he was against any threat being made that we would declare war if Germany attacked Czechoslovakia unless there was an overwhelming public demand first, and on the facts no such overwhelming public demand exists'. 'I am alarmed at what it means for the Army,' Hore-Belisha went on, 'All we could do at the outset would be to provide a force of two divisions which would be inadequately equipped for offensive operations ... we cannot at present put an army into the field large enough to have any decisive effect'. Having concentrated on the air defence of Great Britain, the country was less prepared than in 1914 to send a force to France.[3]

The Cabinet, Kordt reported, felt that the Czech proposals were reasonably close to the Carlsbad programme, but that it was still an open question whether Henlein would reject them, in which case he would be going beyond his previous demands.[4] It was in these circumstances that Chamberlain conceived the idea of a personal visit to Hitler. Of the Cabinet, only Halifax, Hoare and Simon were let into the secret prior to its being announced on 14 September.[5] Henderson, however, was sounded either before or immediately after the Cabinet meeting on the 30th; he approved on the ground that it might induce Hitler to cancel his decision to invade Czechoslovakia if he had already made it. Until the afternoon of 13 September Chamberlain considered that the plan might be put into operation on or about 17 September.

In the meantime the heat must be increased in Prague in order to secure results capable of convincing Hitler that a peaceful solution was possible. In view of the rumours that Benes intended to go back on his seven concessions, which had provided the only ray of hope at the special Cabinet meeting in

[1] Ibid., pp. 190–1.   [2] Ibid., pp. 195–6.
[3] R. J. Minney, The Private Papers of Leslie Hore-Belisha, p. 138.
[4] D.G.F.P., Series D, II, pp. 661–2.   [5] Minney, op. cit., p. 139.

London on the 30th, Newton was instructed by Halifax that the Czechs must reach a comprehensive settlement with the Sudeten leaders without delay since Hitler must have a diplomatic success.[1] Benes, so Runciman reported to Halifax on 1 September, had made a bad impression on the British mission by hanging back after his seven proposals had been accepted by the Sudeten leaders, although Runciman agreed that Benes had some reason for doing so as the Sudeten Germans seemed to regard the proposals merely as a bridge for re-opening negotiations rather than as substantive offers in their own right.[2] The situation worsened with an unsatisfactory meeting on 2 September between the President and the Sudeten spokesmen at which the latter practically rejected Benes's proposals and produced an entirely new memorandum containing counter-proposals.[3] Newton saw Benes on the following day, went once more over the difficult situation Czechoslovakia would be placed in if war came, and pleaded with the President to go to the limit in making concessions, not even stopping short of the Carlsbad programme if that would make a settlement possible.[4] This pressure was sufficient to evoke a new scheme of reform from Benes on 6 September which amounted to self-administration on a territorial basis for the nationalities of the Czech state.

III

The strategical balance of forces as the *Parteitag* at Nuremberg on 5 September approached was not improving for Czechoslovakia and her allies. The French Ambassador in London saw Halifax on 31 August and expressed the French fear of an Italian attack on French possessions in North Africa and even from Franco Spain if France were engaged in defence of Czechoslovakia; consequently, the French Government wanted the Czech problem solved and believed the key lay in Berlin. France, Corbin said, wanted to take action in Berlin whether alone or jointly with Britain.[5] Phipps wrote from the Paris Embassy on 6 September that Litvinov, the Soviet Foreign Minister, had told the French that if Germany attacked Czechoslovakia Russia would take no action until France had begun to fulfil her obligations to Prague; she would then bring the matter before the League of Nations. To add to this chilling news, the French had been told that Rumania, despite recent reports to the contrary, would not after all allow Soviet planes to fly over her territory on their way to assist Czecho-

---

[1] *D.B.F.P.*, Third Series, II, pp. 195–6.
[2] *Ibid.*, pp. 198–9.
[3] *Ibid.*, p. 215.   [4] *Ibid.*, pp. 226–7.   [5] *Ibid.*, pp. 196–8.

slovakia.[1] Chilston, the British Ambassador in Moscow, had equally discouraging reports to make; he saw Potyemkin, the Soviet Deputy Foreign Minister, on 8 September and was reminded that Russia had no obligation to intervene until France was actually engaged; Potyemkin doubted whether France was in a position to make an immediate or powerful move.[2] Czechoslovakia, on the other hand, seemed to be in better military shape than the Great Powers who were debating whether they could assist her. According to Stronge, the British Military Attaché in Prague, writing on 8 September, while Czech forces were numerically much inferior to the Germans, 'there was no material reason why they should not put up a really protracted resistance single-handed'.[3]

Strong nerves were needed as the Nuremberg rally approached. The Sudeten Germans seemed bent on organising incidents in Czechoslovakia which would give Hitler a decent opportunity to intervene. On 8 September, the day after Hodza had handed to the Sudeten leader Kundt the so-called Fourth Plan, which went a long way to meet the Carlsbad demands, an incident occurred which once more deadlocked negotiations. A delegation of Sudeten deputies arrived in Mahrich-Ostrau, ostensibly with the object of visiting some Germans imprisoned for gun running. A dispute broke out between the delegation and Czech policemen which ended in the beating up of a Sudeten deputy. Despite conflicting reports of how the incident actually began, British consuls on the spot considered that it had been deliberately staged by the Germans.[4] The British Cabinet nevertheless looked upon the new Czech proposals as offering a good basis for discussion and contemplated a press statement by the Prime Minister stating that a peaceful solution was possible, the object being to deter Hitler from irretrievably committing himself when he spoke at Nuremberg. This plan was seriously undermined by a *Times* leading article on 7 September which appeared to let the cat out of the bag as far as the government's thinking was concerned. The fatal words ran as follows:

It might be worth while for the Czech Government to consider whether they should exclude altogether the project which has found favour in some quarters, of making Czechoslovakia a more homogeneous state by the secession of that fringe of alien populations which are contiguous to the nation

[1] *D.B.F.P.*, Third Series, II, pp. 255–6.   [2] *Ibid.*, p. 266.
[3] *Ibid.*, pp. 258–9.   [4] *Ibid.*, p. 265, n. 1.

with which they are united by race. . . . The advantages to Czechoslovakia of becoming a homogeneous state might conceivably outweigh the obvious disadvantages of losing the Sudeten German district of the borderland.

The Foreign Office promptly issued a denial that the article had any official support, though it followed the lines of Chamberlain's reported remarks of early May. 'The Foreign Office went up through the roof,' wrote the editor of *The Times*, Geoffrey Dawson: 'not so, however, the Foreign Secretary who came and lunched with me at the Traveller's and had a long talk.'[1] *The Times* returned to the theme of secession in a less pronounced form on the following day under the heading 'The Threat of Force'. Runciman considered that the articles added to his difficulties, which were already great enough.[2]

In the eyes of German observers in Britain, the country's temper was stiffening from day to day in the early days of September. The Counsellor of Legation at the German Embassy, Selzam, reported on the 10th that the whole of the British Press, including even *The Times*, left no doubt that Britain could not remain neutral if Germany acted by force.[3] Kordt, writing two days later, spoke of a complete change in British public opinion since the end of August. A T.U.C. resolution adopted at Blackpool on 7 September called for collective defence against aggression and urged the government to leave no doubt that they would unite with the French and Soviet Governments to resist any attack on Czechoslovakia. Attlee, Churchill and Eden gave their full support to any strong measures which Chamberlain decided and there was virtually no opposition to the Prime Minister. The American Ambassador, Joseph Kennedy, remarked to Selzam that there was 'a new glint in Neville Chamberlain's eyes, in those of Sir S. Hoare and of the others which I have never noticed before. This time they mean business.' According to Kordt, the British had the feeling that they had American sympathy. Halifax had been careful to keep Roosevelt informed of every detail of British policy throughout the crisis, and of the British naval and military measures taken at the beginning of September. Roosevelt in return had made known through Kennedy (so Kordt's account ran) that Britain could depend on American support if she became involved in war. Feeling in the United States had never been so anti-German.[4] But this was much exag-

---

[1] Sir Evelyn Wrench, *Geoffrey Dawson and Our Times*, pp. 371–2.
[2] *D.B.F.P.*, Third Series, II, p. 271, n. 1.
[3] *D.G.F.P.*, Series D, II, pp. 734–5.
[4] *Ibid.*, pp. 742–3.

gerated. Roosevelt was compelled on 9 September to describe press talk that the United States was joining Britain and France in a 'stop Hitler bloc' as 'one hundred per cent wrong'. Very little of this new British spirit showed itself in Halifax's attitude. He saw Corbin on 9 September and flatly told him that the British public and Government were loath to fight on account of German aggression against Czechoslovakia. 'To fight a European war,' the Foreign Secretary said, 'for something that you could not in fact protect and did not expect to restore was a course which must deserve serious thought before it was undertaken.' If Hitler demanded a plebiscite in his Nuremberg speech, Halifax went on, most people would think it unreasonable to embark on a European war to prevent people voting on their future position. To Corbin's protest that the issue was not only one of Czechoslovakia and that if this aggression were allowed to succeed, France's turn would come next, Halifax retorted that this was really an argument in favour o' a certain war now against the possibility of war, perhaps in more unfavourable conditions, later. 'With that argument,' Halifax said, 'I have never been able to feel any sympathy.'[1] To Henderson, however, in accordance with the now accepted principle of using different voices in different places, the Foreign Secretary wrote a message for Ribbentrop on the following day in which the new Czech proposals were recommended as offering a basis for discussion and the warning was given that if force were used and the Czech Government asked for help, the French would be bound to help, and this would result in a conflict from which Britain would not stand aside.[2] Henderson, commenting from Nuremberg, where he had gone for the Nazi rally, considered that such a message would 'drive Hitler straight off the deep end'.[3] The inner Cabinet of four in London agreed and it was never sent.[4]

On the eve of Hitler's Nuremberg speech on 12 September when, if ever, precise words of deterrence were in order, Halifax was as vague as ever in advising Phipps in Paris as to British policy in the event of a military *dénouement* to the crisis. Bonnet had asked Phipps 'as a friend' what answer Britain would give to France if France said she was going to march and wished to know whether Britain would march with her. Phipps interpreted the question as meaning that Bonnet was 'desperately anxious for a possible way out of this without being obliged to

[1] *D.G.F.P.*, Series D, II, p. 732; *D.B.F.P.*, Third Series, II, pp. 275–7.
[2] *Ibid.*, pp. 277–8.
[3] *Ibid.*, p. 280.
[4] Viscount Templewood, *Nine Troubled Years*, p. 301; Duff Cooper, *Old Men Forget*, pp. 226–7.

fight'. The answer Phipps gave was not intended to stiffen Bonnet's nerve; it was that the question could not be dealt with 'in advance and without reference to the nature of the German aggression'.[1] Armed with this reply, Bonnet was able to tell the British delegation in Geneva on 11 September that France could not fight Germany, Spain and an Italy which in all probability would enter the war on Germany's side. Poland, Bonnet said, would remain neutral in a Czech–German conflict and would resist the passage of Soviet troops. A French declaration of war in these circumstances, the Foreign Minister said, would be like 'jumping from the Eiffel tower', and France proposed to do nothing of the kind.[2] Halifax endorsed the reply Phipps had given to Bonnet when he wrote to the Ambassador on 12 September; the Foreign Minister's question, he said, though plain in form, 'could not be dissociated from the circumstances in which it might be posed, which are necessarily at this stage completely hypothetical'. Apart from the fact that the Dominions would have to be consulted, the British, Halifax said, were unable 'to make precise statements of the character of their future action, or the time at which it would be taken, in circumstances that they cannot at present foresee'.[3] This refusal to be specific was all the more remarkable in that it was now common knowledge that Germany meant to settle the Czech question by the end of the year, if not by the end of September.

The precise circumstances in which force might have to be used defined themselves more sharply on the very day when Halifax was writing these words. At Eger and Carlsbad in the Sudetenland the police opened fire on crowds listening to an open-air broadcast of Hitler's Nuremberg speech, resulting in six deaths and the serious wounding of twenty more; as usual, reports conflicted on the extent of provocation. Martial law was at once introduced into the affected districts, covering Eger and Falkenau, two of the hard cores of Sudeten German extremism. Events were moving back to the May crisis but at a graver level. Panic seems to have seized Bonnet at these developments. He wrote to Runciman earnestly begging him to state his intention to bring out a plan to bridge the conflicting parties in Czechoslovakia; 'the whole question of peace and war may only be a matter of minutes,' Bonnet exclaimed.[4] Phipps described the Foreign Minister as seeming 'completely to have lost his nerve and to be ready for any solution to avoid

---

[1] *D.B.F.P.*, Third Series, II, p. 303, n. 1.
[2] *Ibid.*, pp. 293–4.   [3] *Ibid.*, p. 303.
[4] *Ibid.*, pp. 305–6.

war.'[1]   In a talk with Bonnet on 13 September Phipps found him relieved to hear British denials that they were automatically bound to come to France's assistance if she went to war, since these were useful with 'certain bellicose French Ministers'. Bonnet confided to the Ambassador on the following day that France would agree to any form of settlement if only war could be averted: 'we cannot sacrifice ten million men to prevent $3\frac{1}{2}$ million Sudetens joining the Reich'.   In the final resort and as a means of avoiding German aggression, Bonnet told Phipps, the French were agreeable to a plebiscite on whether the Sudetenland should be inside or outside Czechoslovakia.   The French, Bonnet said, could certainly not count on Russia. Her Foreign Minister, Litvinov, had told Bonnet at Geneva on 11 September that the Soviets would consult the League Council in the event of German aggression and that there was no question of Soviet military action until the Council had obtained Rumania's consent to the passage of Soviet troops and aircraft.[2]

Daladier was only one degree less despondent.   He had been instructed by Gamelin, his Chief of Staff, that France could only make bloody frontal attacks against German fortifications while the Luftwaffe dominated the skies; that Czechoslovakia could not be defended; and that France could expect little initial help from Britain or Russia.[3]   Without waiting for the situation to worsen, the French Premier had Phipps dispatch an urgent message to Chamberlain on 13 September proposing an immediate disclosure of the Runciman report and the summoning of a three-Power conference, from which the Czechs and Russians would presumably be excluded, to agree on a peaceful settlement as called for by Hitler in his Nuremberg speech.[4]   Hitler had in fact given no hint in the Nuremberg address that his army would be given its marching orders if the Czechs failed to satisfy him.   But it was, Henderson commented, a reasonable inference from the speech that 'if the Czech Government cannot or will not give satisfaction, war will ensue whatever the consequences'.[5]

IV

This was the moment, it seemed to Chamberlain, for making his personal approach to Hitler, the object being to convince

---

[1] *Ibid.*, p. 309.
[2] *Ibid.*, p. 323; Georges Bonnet, *Défense de la Paix*, I, *De Washington au Quai d'Orsay*, pp. 198–200.
[3] Bonnet, *op. cit.*, I, pp. 176–80, 225; General Gamelin, *Servir*, II, pp. 341–2, 344–7.
[4] *D.B.F.P.*, Third Series, II, pp. 313–14; *F.R.U.S.*, 1938, I, pp. 594–6.
[5] *D.B.F.P.*, Third Series, II, pp. 306–7.

the Chancellor that the Sudeten grievances could be redressed without the need for force and that the Czech Government would carry into effect any arrangements reached by peaceful negotiations. The Prime Minister had arranged that his plan should come as a thunder-clap; afterwards he wrote with delight that Hitler was 'struck all of a heap' on receiving the proposal that Chamberlain should fly to Germany to search for a peaceful solution.[1] As for the French, the Czechs and even the British Cabinet, they were informed only after all arrangements had been made and Hitler had agreed. The proposal ran great risks. It was demeaning for a man of 69 to fly backwards and forwards between colleagues and allies on one side and a German leader twenty years his junior on the other. But Chamberlain insisted that prestige should not stand in the way of any expedient to ward off the unbearable catastrophe of war. More importantly, the flight to Berchtesgaden directly engaged Britain in the crisis and focused on her the question whether it was to be resolved by negotiation or force. Henceforward, with France following lamely behind, with Russia for all practical purposes excluded by Chamberlain's own decision, the conflict was a face-to-face one between Britain and Germany. But this was merely bringing into the open an element in the situation which had been present from the outset.

Chamberlain took with him to Berchtesgaden on 15 September two questions, neither of which was clearly answered. One was whether a peaceful settlement of the Czech question along the lines of self-determination for the Sudetenland would serve as a prelude to an Anglo-German understanding to place peace in Europe on a stable basis. The other was whether Hitler's claims against Czechoslovakia represented genuine national grievances or a design to include the Czechs with the Austrians as prisoners in the Reich. To obtain an answer to the first question, Chamberlain proposed taking Anglo-German relations first and postponing discussion of the Czech problem until the next day. The Chancellor would have none of this; 300 Sudeten Germans, he claimed, had been killed and the situation brooked no delay. Chamberlain was shocked that Hitler could believe these stories, not suspecting that it was irrelevant to Hitler's aims whether he believed them or not, but he realised that the situation was even more serious than Henderson had led him to think. The general Anglo-German issue, which in Chamberlain's mind was the whole *raison d'être* of his German journey, was never reached until Hitler ejaculated his formal 'ja, ja' to Chamberlain's invitation to sign the

[1] Feiling, *op. cit.*, p. 363.

Anglo-German declaration at the close of the Munich conference at the end of the month.

As for Chamberlain's second question, that concerning the future security of Czechoslovakia, Chamberlain had to be content with Hitler's declaration that he was merely seeking justice for his compatriots and had no desire to annex 'a lot of Czechs'. Nevertheless, Czechoslovakia must break her ties with Moscow, the Chancellor insisted; the Soviet–Czech pact was a 'spear in Germany's side'. On the immediate issue of the Sudeten minority, Britain must agree to the principle of secession of districts with a population German to the extent of 50 per cent and over, or Hitler would settle the matter by force. Chamberlain's reply was that he himself had no objection to secession but that he would have to consult his colleagues and allies. Would Hitler agree to keep his military machine in check until Chamberlain returned to Germany again with the results of these consultations? Hitler said he would, but warned that his hands might be forced if incidents occurred in Czechoslovakia. On the question, however, of how far a settlement of the Sudeten question on the terms demanded by Germany would lay the basis for a definite pacification in Europe, for which alone the Czech sacrifice would be worth making, Chamberlain was forced to return with little more than hope.[1]

Two Cabinet meetings were held on the 17th to hear an account of the Berchtesgaden talks. Chamberlain insisted that it was a question of accepting the self-determination principle or fighting, and although no formal conclusions were reached by Ministers, the case for fighting seemed unconvincing. The Prime Minister's only considerable critic, Duff Cooper, First Lord of the Admiralty, believed, according to balance of power principles, that there would be no peace in Europe so long as Nazism remained. But even he was loath to run the risk of war while there was a possibility of avoiding it and considered that war should be postponed in the hope that internal developments against Hitler might occur in Germany.[2] Having grudgingly assented to the principle of the secession of the Sudeten districts, Duff Cooper much weakened his case for resigning over the Munich agreement when it was finally signed.

Chamberlain, when he met Daladier and Bonnet at 10 Downing Street on the next day to review the Berchtesgaden talks, did not disclose that he had conveyed to Hitler his per-

---

[1] *D.B.F.P.*, Third Series, II, pp. 338–41.
[2] Duff Cooper, *op. cit.*, pp. 229–30.

sonal agreement to the principle of secession. He made clear, however, that there was no choice between an immediate secession of the Sudetenland and war, and that if further negotiations were held with Germany they could only concern the manner in which the transfer of the territory to the Reich was to be effected. Daladier, in the cruel dilemma of having to ask a friend to have one of his legs amputated, admitted that the problem facing France was to find some means of avoiding being forced into war in fulfilment of her treaty obligations and at the same time to save as much of Czechoslovakia as was humanly possible. He was, however, aware that raising the principle of self-determination for one national group in the polyglot Czech state was tantamount to sentencing the state itself to death; moreover, once Britain and France committed themselves to the revision of frontiers on the basis of plebiscites, German minorities scattered all over Europe would be demanding ballot boxes. The Downing Street conference concluded, with curious simplicity, that they could confine their agreement merely to secession of the Sudetenland without the status of other minorities into the Czech state being brought into the argument. It was like removing one bad tooth in the hope that this would make the others less noticeable.

On these lines the conference designed its message to Prague. The Czechs were to be told that their vital interests could not be secured without an immediate transfer of the Sudeten areas to the Reich; the areas in question were to be those with a population over 50 per cent German; frontiers were to be adjusted by an international commission which would also deal with exchanges of population; Britain would join in an international guarantee of the new boundaries against unprovoked aggression on condition the Czechs accepted the Anglo-French plan for secession of the German provinces, but in this case the existing treaties which Czechoslovakia had with France and Russia would lapse. It was apparently not thought necessary to inquire what Russia would make of all this. The *démarche* to Prague was to be made at noon on Monday, 19 September to give time for Daladier to obtain his Cabinet's consent that morning. The Czech reply would have to be to hand for Chamberlain to report to Hitler in Germany not later than Wednesday, 21 September.[1]

The expected brief agony took place in Prague. The Czech Cabinet replied to the British and French Ministers, Newton and Lacroix, that they must consult Parliament; they then

---

[1] *D.B.F.P.*, Third Series, II, pp. 373–99; *New Documents on the History of Munich*, pp. 83–5.

invoked the Czech–German Arbitration Treaty of 1926. Halifax sternly rejoined that if this attitude became known it would immediately trigger off a German invasion. Benes replied by taking a step to which only the extreme of desperation could have led him, namely to inquire of the Soviet Foreign Office whether Russia would stand by Czechoslovakia if she resisted and fighting began. To this the standard Soviet reply was returned that Moscow would honour its obligations but only if France played her part; in the circumstances this meant that Czechoslovakia was alone.[1] Newton, together with the French Minister, wrestled with Benes throughout the night of 20–21 September. The President in turn struggled over the problem with Czech party leaders, then refused to accept the Anglo-French terms without a written declaration from Britain and France that they would stand by this country if Germany attacked after he had agreed to secession. Finally Benes had to be satisfied with the expression of a *voeu* that such an undertaking would be given. Newton had made brutally clear that if the proposed terms were rejected Czechoslovakia would have to face Germany alone.

When Chamberlain confronted Hitler for a renewal of the Berchtesgaden talks at Godesberg on the 22nd the Chancellor was evidently a disappointed man. He had never imagined that the Prime Minister would return with agreement to the secession demand; the effect of Chamberlain doing so was to rob the Führer of a military triumph over the Czechs. He could not but regard Chamberlain (so Kirkpatrick, of the Berlin Embassy, who accompanied the Premier, was told by German informants) as an 'impertinent busybody who spoke the ridiculous jargon of an outmoded democracy'.[2] It was this necessity to parade the full *panache* of German military power which compelled Hitler to refuse the Sudeten districts when handed to him by Chamberlain at Godesberg unless the act were done in such a way as to show his contempt for 'the man of peace to the depths of his soul'. The Czechs, Hitler demanded, must begin to evacuate the Sudeten districts not later than 8 a.m. on 26 September; this was given as Hitler's final word to Chamberlain at 10.30 p.m. on 23 September. The German occupation must be complete by the morning of 29 September. Hitler could not accept an international commission to demarcate the frontier; the line of demarcation must be the language frontier and behind this the Czechs must withdraw

---

[1] *Documents and Materials Relating to the Eve of the Second World War*, Moscow, 1948, p. 240; Zdenek Fierlinger, *Ve Sluzbách CSR.* Part I, Prague, 1951. Appendix 3.
[2] Sir Ivone Kirkpatrick, *The Inner Circle*, p. 122.

their army, police and other state organs within the time limit laid down. There would be no right of compensation for property left by the Czechs in the areas to be ceded. In districts where German predominance was in doubt a plebiscite could be held under international supervision and those which voted against Germany would be retroceded to Czechoslovakia; but eligible voters must include all Germans who had been born there even though at the time of the plebiscite they might be resident elsewhere, while the Czechs would be unable to vote. The effect of this schedule of imperatives was to give the maximum amount of Czech territory to Germany, including all the forward fortifications the Czechs had built to defend themselves against a German invasion; to drive the Czechs in panic flight from their lands without being allowed to take with them any of their property or even food for their journey; and to force the whole operation through within the space of a few hours and without benefit of any form of international control.[1]

The following day, 23 September, was spent by Chamberlain and the rest of the British party pursuing desperate thoughts at the St. Petersburg Hotel in Godesberg across the Rhine from the conference rooms at the Hotel Dreesen. In the messages which flowed to and fro across the river the Chancellor adhered to his demand that the Sudetenland must be evacuated by Czech forces and occupied by the Reichswehr within the timetable laid down. The Prime Minister rejoined that this would be condemned as an 'unnecessary display of force', thus suggesting that it was not so much the German proposals themselves to which he took exception, but the effect they would have on the different strands of public opinion which he was trying to win over to the secessionist principle. The Premier at length asked Hitler for a memorandum setting forth his demands so that it could be shown to the Czechs and the French. When Chamberlain received this he threw it down in disgust, calling it an ultimatum; unlike the Germans in 1918 the Czechs were being presented with a *Diktat* before they had had the chance to prove themselves in battle. Hitler made the scornful reply that if Chamberlain looked at the document again he would see it was headed by the word 'memorandum'.[2]

The final discussion, over maps at the Hotel Dreesen, showed a scarcely perceptible softening in Hitler's attitude, reflecting perhaps the misgivings of his generals, the warm welcome given to Chamberlain by the German bystanders, or Hitler's

---

[1] *D.B.F.P.*, Third Series, II, pp. 463–73; *D.G.F.P.*, Series D, II, pp. 870–9.
[2] *D.B.F.P.*, Third Series, II, pp. 478, 482–3, 484–5, 495–6; *D.G.F.P.*, Series D, II, pp. 898–908.

own practice of justifying himself to the utmost before an act of force. Appealing to the weakest point in the Prime Minister's armoury, he spoke of the issue in dispute as a possible turning point in Anglo-German relations; it was the last question remaining open, and thereafter Chamberlain's dream would be ready for realisation. There were also some unimportant changes in the memorandum to which Hitler agreed, describing Chamberlain as the only man to whom he had ever made a concession as he did so.[1] But the memorandum stood in all essentials as his final word. Chamberlain confessed that he would return from Godesberg with a heavy heart; was the recourse to force really worth while when Hitler's objective was already within his grasp? The laying down of a timetable, he repeated, would have a deplorable effect on public opinion, and there was no assurance that the German occupation would be confined to areas of preponderant German population. There was little comfort to be drawn from Hitler's answering comment that although German forces under the plan would be occupying plebiscite areas which might have to be returned to Czechoslovakia after the vote, the plebiscite areas as a whole would include German language islands which would remain in Czech hands, the one set of districts cancelling out the others.[2]

Ministers in London faced the same basic realities after Chamberlain flew home with his report. Three indecisive Cabinet meetings were held at which Duff Cooper and Hore-Belisha pressed for some measures of mobilisation while the Prime Minister dissented.[3] In Chamberlain's mind, if war came it would be fought over the implementation of a principle already agreed among most of the belligerents. The assessment of the military prospects remained unchanged. Czechoslovakia, Chamberlain and his intimates thought, would be overrun after a short and bitter struggle, and since Germany would in all probability simply stand on the defensive at the Siegfried line in the west, it would be up to the allies to take the offensive against her; in effect this meant that the burden would fall on France, who would not receive much support from Britain until Germany was in a position to withdraw her divisions from a defeated Czechoslovakia to use them in the west. In France it was apparent that there was no stomach for the fight. Phipps wrote to Halifax on 24 September that Pierre Cot, the French Air Minister, had been authorised by

[1] Kirkpatrick, *op. cit.*, pp. 120–1.
[2] *D.B.F.P.*, Third Series, II, pp. 499–508.
[3] Duff Cooper, *op. cit.*, pp. 234–7; R. J. Minney, *op. cit.*, pp. 144–7.

Daladier to say that if Germany carried out a *coup de force* against Czechoslovakia France would fulfil her commitments; this statement was given prominence in all the French press. Phipps himself, however, considered that 'all that is best in France is against war, almost at any price'; 'unless we are sure of considerable initial successes,' he continued, 'we shall find that all that is best in France, as well as all that is worst, turn against us and accuse us of egging the French on to fight what must have seemed from the beginning a losing battle'.[1] Phipps's judgment was not confused by pro-German sympathies; he had in fact been moved from the Berlin Embassy to Paris at the beginning of Chamberlain's premiership partly because he was thought too stiff towards the Nazis.

The Soviet attitude, seen from London, remained an enigma, though there was little disposition to probe it. Soviet assistance, it was confidently thought, could not be counted on. Litvinov reiterated to the French that there was no question of Russia acting until France was actually engaged; the action she would then take would be to ask the League Council to apply to Rumania for authority to fly over her territory.[2] Butler, reporting from Geneva on 24 September on talks which he and Earl de la Warr had had with Litvinov, gave a similar account of the Foreign Minister's words; Russia would come to Czechoslovakia's aid if Germany determined on military action and if the French honoured their obligations. Litvinov had spelled this out publicly on the previous day at the League Assembly's Political Committee, when he made clear that the Czech–Soviet pact would only come into operation if the French assisted Czechoslovakia.[3] Litvinov's proposal, made during the Geneva meetings, in favour of a three-Power meeting, preferably in Paris, to show that Czechoslovakia's friends meant business, was considered in London as likely to precipitate an armed conflict before agreement had been reached on exactly how it was to be fought.[4] The conference had already been rejected by Britain and France when put forward earlier in the summer; Litvinov must have known that it probably would be again and that this would relieve the Soviets of any further responsibility.

That the Czechs themselves at no time throughout the crisis made any formal application for Soviet assistance, which the Agrarian Party in the Czech Coalition Government deemed

---

[1] *D.B.F.P.*, Third Series, II, p. 510.
[2] *Ibid.*, p. 489.
[3] *L.N.O.J.*, Special Supplement, 189, pp. 34–5.
[4] *D.B.F.P.*, Third Series, II, pp. 497–8.

hardly less undesirable than a German invasion, showed that Czech–Soviet co-operation, if it came to war with Germany, could never be easy. Broadcasting on the evening of 30 September, when the Munich *débâcle* had occurred, the Czech Minister of propaganda, M. Vavrecka, said:

We had to consider that it would take the Russian Army weeks to come to our aid—perhaps too late, for by that time millions of our men, women and children would have been slaughtered. It was even more important to consider that our war by the side of Soviet Russia would have been not only a fight against Germany but it would have been interpreted as a fight on the side of Bolshevism. And then perhaps all of Europe would have been drawn into the war against us and Russia.[1]

Fierlinger, the Czech Minister to Moscow, was asked by Potyemkin, of the Soviet Foreign Ministry, on 22 September why the Czechs had never asked for unconditional aid by the Soviet Union. Fierlinger replied that it was difficult to consider this, 'in view of the geographical situation'.[2] More important was the fact that for Czechoslovakia to be allied alone with Russia was to become in effect a Soviet satellite.

With this situation before him, Chamberlain seems to have made up his mind, when a second series of meetings was held between British and French leaders in Downing Street on 25 September, that Hitler's terms must after all be accepted, provided some vestige of international control could be secured to avoid the impression of a forcible seizure of the territories. This was what he had told a Cabinet meeting the previous evening.[3] His conclusion was at first strongly resisted by Daladier, who said that Hitler must be asked to go back to his position at Berchtesgaden and that, if he refused, 'each of us would have to do his duty'. Chamberlain and then, in his best court-room manner, Simon, cross-questioned Daladier on how exactly France proposed to take military action if the Godesberg memorandum were rejected and German forces unleashed against Czechoslovakia. With rising irritation at being subjected to this examination when he was without his military advisers, the French Prime Minister replied that France would make bombing raids in Germany, undertake land offensives and not sit inert in the Maginot line, and would work in close co-operation with Russia, who possessed 5,000 planes some of

[1] S. Morrell, *I Saw the Crucifixion*, p. 291.
[2] *New Documents on the History of Munich*, p. 109; for the Soviet attitude in general, see Keith Eubank, *Munich*, pp. 109–14.
[3] Duff Cooper, *op. cit.*, p. 225.

which had been seen to good effect in Spain. Chamberlain explained that the French had to be pressed for answers to these embarrassing questions because the British 'must clearly have before them the circumstances in which they would have to make a decision'. To all intents, however, the decision appeared to have been made; it was only necessary to show the French that it was the inevitable one, as Chamberlain thought.

General Gamelin was then summoned from Paris to explain the military position as the French general staff saw it. France, Gamelin said, could ultimately mobilise five million men and could put a hundred divisions into the field at the outset; with firm discipline France could take the strain of the conflict. The Czechs, too, he thought, could give a good account of themselves, but for only a matter of weeks, not months. But there was little to hope for, the General said, from Soviet land forces owing to the opposition expected from the Poles and Rumania; the most to be expected from Russia was bombing raids on Germany, for which Gamelin thought Rumania would in the event allow Soviet aircraft to pas through her air space.[1] After hearing this surprisingly encouraging report from Gamelin Chamberlain left the full conference for a private talk with Daladier, in which he promised the French Prime Minister that if France had to fight as a result of the present crisis Britain would be at her side and would send an expeditionary force to France, the very undertaking the French had been pressing for for months.[2] In return for this assurance Daladier agreed with Chamberlain that one last effort should be made to persuade Hitler to accept a negotiated transfer of the territory under a measure of international control and with minimum safeguards for Czech rights. Sir Horace Wilson was to carry a letter from Chamberlain to the German Chancellor in which the Anglo-French objections to the Godesberg plan were explained. Hitler was to be asked to agree to a meeting of Czech and German representatives to discuss orderly means of handing over the Sudeten territories.[3]

Simultaneously with Chamberlain's letter and on the authority of Halifax, the Foreign Office issued its famous communiqué, characterised by the Paris newspaper *Matin* as a 'clever lie'; 'if in spite of all the efforts made by the British Prime Minister a German attack is made on Czechoslovakia the immediate result must be that France will be bound to

[1] *D.B.F.P.*, Third Series, II, p. 575, n.1; Bonnet, *op. cit.*, I, pp. 269–70; General Gamelin, *op. cit.*, II.
[2] Templewood, *op. cit.*, p. 315.
[3] *D.B.F.P.*, Third Series, II, pp. 536–42; Cmd. 5847 (1938), pp. 19–20.

come to her assistance and Great Britain and Russia will certainly stand by France'.[1] This was after Halifax had admitted to a Labour Party delegation on 21 September that there had been no contact with Russia for nearly a fortnight, and there is no evidence of any such contacts during and immediately after the Godesberg meetings.[2] The background to the Foreign Office's reference to Russia in the communiqué of 26 September may well have been General Gamelin's statement during his London visit that, notwithstanding the unlikelihood of effective Soviet intervention, Russia was moving thirty divisions as a precaution up to her Western frontier.

The Foreign Office communiqué and the raising of voices in Britain and France against further surrender after Godesberg seemed at first, however, to have little effect on Hitler, except to make him possibly more violent than before. At his first meeting with Wilson to receive Chamberlain's message on 26 September he agreed to a discussion with the Czechs, but only if they accepted his memorandum together with the date 1 October for completing the occupation. The Czechs must make up their minds at once whether they wished to send a representative to Berlin not later than 2 p.m. on 28 September to agree with the Germans on the completion of the take-over. Whatever happened, Hitler told Wilson, by 1 October he would have Czechoslovakia 'where he wanted her' and that if Britain and France decided to strike, he did not care a farthing.[3] At a later meeting with Wilson, Henderson and Kirkpatrick on the same day, following a volcanic tirade in the Berlin *Sportpalast*, the Chancellor shouted that he would 'smash the Czechs', grinding his heel into the carpet as these words were uttered. 'One could see that he was itching to drop a bomb on Prague, to see Benes in flight,' wrote Kirkpatrick.[4] Hitler made clear that he would not depart from his Godesberg memorandum, but said that, if he had to fight the Czechs, he would stand on the defensive on his western front. He repeated over and again that the onus of attacking in the west would lie on Britain and France.[5]

In the late afternoon of 27 September Chamberlain succumbed to Duff Cooper's appeals for the mobilisation of the fleet but refrained from announcing it in a broadcast to the nation that evening in which he spoke with horror of the nightmarish preparations for war on account of a 'quarrel in a far-off

[1] R.I.I.A., *Documents, 1938*, II, p. 261.
[2] Lord Dalton, *The Fateful Years*, p. 188.
[3] *D.B.F.P.*, Third Series, II, pp. 554–7.
[4] Kirkpatrick, *op. cit.*, p. 125.   [5] *D.B.F.P., ibid.*, pp. 563–4.

country'. He told the First Lord that he wished to give the least publicity to the fleet mobilisation.[1] To Benes the Prime Minister wrote that he took no responsibility for giving the Czechs advice concerning Hitler's latest ultimatum, but said that all the information in his hands indicated that German forces would cross the Czech frontier almost at once unless the Czechs accepted the German terms by 2 p.m. on the following day.[2] At the same time Halifax wired to Henderson in Berlin to make one more 'last effort' to persuade the Germans to accept a reasonable scheme of transfer. The British proposal which the Ambassador was to present was that the occupation should take place by stages beginning on 1 October, to be completed by the 10th or at latest the 31st; a commission representing Britain, Germany and Czechoslovakia would make arrangements for securing the Czech evacuation and the Sudetenland would be policed by officers of the British Legion and later by four British battalions pending the entry of German forces.[3] The door seemed not yet entirely closed, as Hitler's final reply to the letter from Chamberlain taken by Sir Horace Wilson showed. The Chancellor answered the complaint that Czechoslovakia would lose a major part of her fortifications, which were situated in the territory to be ceded, by saying that this was an inevitable consequence of the whole transaction, and that if the Czechs were to build new fortifications before the takeover began Germany would have to wait for months, perhaps years. Nevertheless, Hitler held out the bait of a German guarantee for the Czechoslovak rump, despite a highly ambiguous reference to the guarantee in his *Sportpalast* speech of the previous day. His final words were that he left it with Chamberlain to decide whether to continue his efforts to 'bring the Government in Prague to reason at this very last hour'.[4] The impression left by this message was that, while the Chancellor still demanded his triumph, he knew his people preferred it to be a bloodless one, or at least that if war was to come Hitler intended that his final contribution to the diplomatic argument should be a mild one. The mobilisation of the British fleet may have played some part in this decision, as Duff Cooper and Churchill later insisted, though the public announcement of the mobilisation came three hours after Hitler's reply to Wilson.

Chamberlain's response, after receiving Henderson's advice that the Czechs must submit or fight alone, was to reply saying

---

[1] Duff Cooper, *op. cit.*, p. 240.   [2] *D.B.F.P.*, *ibid.*, p. 570.   [3] *Ibid.*, pp. 572–3.
[4] Cmd. 5847, Misc. No. 7 (1938), pp. 21–2; *The Speeches of Adolf Hitler*, II, p. 1526.

that Hitler's letter made him feel certain that Germany could get 'all essentials without war and without delay'. He was ready, he said, to go to Berlin immediately to discuss the transfer arrangements with Hitler and Czech representatives, together, if Hitler wished, with French and Italian leaders. Agreement could be reached within a week, and in reply to the German propaganda point that the Czechs could not be trusted to honour an agreement, Chamberlain assured Hitler that he had no reason to doubt 'the power of the British and French Governments to see that promises are carried out fairly and fully and forthwith'. This message was repeated to Mussolini with the request that Italy should be represented at the proposed conference and that the Duce should use his influence with Hitler to get him to agree to the meeting.[1] Mussolini was genuinely shocked suddenly to learn that war was imminent and at once pressed Hitler through his Ambassador, Attolico, to agree to a conference, which the Chancellor did, provided Mussolini would come in person. From this sprang Hitler's invitation to the British and French Ministers to the Munich meeting, which Chamberlain announced in the House of Commons on 28 September, at the end of a long account of his labours on behalf of a peaceful settlement. His appeal to M.P.s to allow him to go and make what he could of this last effort was met with what Harold Nicolson later described as 'mass hysteria'.[2] The German mobilisation was deferred for twenty-four hours.

When the four-Power conference finally opened at Munich in the afternoon of the 29th Chamberlain had taken no steps to work out a common plan of action with Daladier. This omission was not matched on the Axis side, as was shown when Mussolini produced a memorandum for the conference which had in fact been drawn up in the Reich Foreign Ministry. The agreement which the negotiators at length signed in the early hours of the following day indicated that Hitler had abandoned some of the more offensive of his Godesberg demands. It was these differences between Godesberg and Munich which Chamberlain argued in the four-day debate in the Commons on his return had justified his efforts.[3] The Godesberg memorandum, he contended, had been a one-sided ultimatum, whereas the agreement he had signed at Munich went back to the Anglo-French plan for occupying the territories by stages ending on 10 October, instead of at one fell swoop. In the case of the

---

[1] Cmd. 5848, Misc. No. 8 (1938), pp. 2–3.
[2] Quoted by Sir A. Southby, 339 H.C. Deb. 5s. Col. 115 (3 October 1938).
[3] 339 H.C. Deb. 5s. Cols. 42–4; Macleod, *op. cit.*, p. 253.

fifth and last zone of 'territory of preponderantly German character' the line to be occupied by German forces was to be fixed by an international commission representing the four Munich Powers and Czechoslovakia. The commission was also to define the plebiscite areas, and these were to be occupied, not by German troops, as in the Godesberg plan, but by 'international bodies', which were to remain there until the plebiscite was complete, that is, not later than 30 November. Moreover, the conditions of the evacuation were to be determined by the international commission, instead of the brutal order in the Godesberg memorandum that Czechs wishing to leave the ceded territories should take no furniture, livestock or food with them. A further concession to the Czechs, Chamberlain argued, was the right of option into and out of the provinces to be surrendered; this had to be exercised within six months, after which free movement for Czechs wishing to leave Germany would presumably be ended. As a final step forward from Godesberg, Germany and Italy agreed at Munich to give a guarantee to the new Czechoslovakia, to match the British and French guarantees contemplated in the Anglo-French plan; but this was to be effective only when the question of Polish and Hungarian minorities in Czechoslovakia had been settled.[1]

Yet it was clear from the speed with which the Munich transaction was hurried through that most of these concessions were granted merely for the purpose of easing British and French consciences and giving the two Prime Ministers material for their defence when they returned home. The vagueness of wording in the agreement served to this end. No definition was provided of the term 'installations' in paragraph 2 of the agreement, which the Czechs were committed not to damage during their evacuation; it might refer to the fortifications alone or the weapons and other equipment in them as well. The all-important 'fifth area', referred to in paragraph 4, which was to be 'ascertained' by the international commission and taken over by German forces not later than 10 October, was also left undefined, so that the map attached to the agreement, indicating merely the boundaries of the first four areas, gave a wholly misleading impression of the full extent of Germany's gains. No indication was given as to the areas to be covered by the plebiscite; the matter was simply referred to the international commission, which was charged with organising the poll 'on the conditions of the Saar plebiscite'. This imprecision left Germany free to force an interpretation suitable

---

[1] The text of the Munich agreement is printed in 'Cmd. 5848, pp. 3–6.

to her interests. After all, the Czechs had been wholly excluded from the Munich decisions; the British and French had virtually abdicated from responsibility as the price of a respite; Italy was entirely at Hitler's command. Consequently no international commission representing these four states and Germany could be other than an agent of the Reich. In fact, when the commission began to wrestle with the question of plebiscites and frontiers in early October, the German viewpoint was almost uniformly imposed.[1] So formal in practice was the role of the commission to be in the execution of Munich that no provision was made in the agreement for its voting procedures.

To complete the German triumph, the Munich treaty, as indicated in a separate declaration signed by the four Powers, envisaged further conferences for the mutilation of the rump of Czechoslovakia by committing the four to meet again if the 'problem of the Polish and Hungarian minorities' in the Czech state was not settled within three months by agreement. Since the proposed German guarantee to Czechoslovakia, for what it was worth, could not be operative until this agreement was reached, for at least three months the Czechs would have no insurance cover from Germany for the territory remaining to her. Moreover, if another four-Power conference were held at the end of the three-month period, Germany would be able to threaten the Czechs that unless they settled the minorities question on her own terms there would be no question of a guarantee. In the event, when the British and French Governments raised the question of the guarantee with Germany on 8 February 1939, Hitler delayed his reply for almost a month. He then said that there must first be 'clarification of the internal development of Czechoslovakia and the improvement of that country's relations with surrounding states'.[2] Not surprisingly, the guarantee was never effective.

V

Certain misconceptions must be removed in considering Chamberlain's attitude towards the issues raised by the Munich agreement. First, there is the charge that the Prime Minister, out of sneaking regard for Fascism or hatred of Communism, connived in the rape of Czechoslovakia, as in that of Austria, as a means of diverting Hitler's attention to the east, and that, in general, as a spokesman for Western business interests

---

[1] See Minutes of the Commission, *D.G.F.P.*, Series D, IV, pp. 2–4, 9–15, 22–4, 27–9, 34–5, 41–3, 63–6; also Protocol of 5 October, *ibid.*, pp. 32–3.
[2] *D.B.F.P.*, Third Series, IV, pp. 171–3; see below, pp. 552–4.

he feared Communism more than Hitler.[1] Chamberlain's undoubted aversion for and mistrust of Russia probably led him to underestimate her military strength and readiness to come to Czechoslovakia's assistance. But there is no evidence that his Czech policy formed part of any deliberate plan to turn Germany east; we may be sure that Soviet historians, when they ransacked Nazi archives after Germany's defeat, would have produced such evidence had they found it. Chamberlain's failure energetically to come to terms with Russia over the handling of the Czech question was a blunder big enough almost to rank as premeditated malice. But not quite.

The second myth is that Chamberlain was personally proud of the Munich transaction and regarded Czech dismay as ignorant and contemptible. Fear of war made him willing to believe the most unlikely things, but not this. On returning from Munich he was persuaded by an official, as he moved to a balcony to speak to Downing Street crowds, to compare his achievement with the 'peace with honour' brought back by Disraeli from Germany in 1878. It was a foolish phrase, emitted under emotional stress, at the end of a tiring day, and one which, as he explained in the October debate in the Commons, he later regretted.[2] Nor can Chamberlain be charged, as he has often been, with personal callousness towards the Czechs; for a man of Chamberlain's years to 'yawn continuously' during the final stages at Munich when the agreement of the Czechs had to be obtained is not surprising considering the exacting hours he had passed through; in itself the incident was no evidence of indifference to the Czechs' fate. The most impartial first-hand reports of the Munich Conference describe him as fully sensitive to their feelings. His view was that, although the disaster overtaking them was a terrible one, their sufferings if war came might well be greater; that they must collapse and fall wholly into German hands within a space of weeks; that their sacrifice would involve the lives of many millions more, who would not thank the statesmen for involving them in war to achieve an impossible task. Chamberlain was satisfied that Hitler was not bluffing when he said he would order his war machine into motion if the Sudetenland was not handed over forthwith; what we now know of the Chancellor's war plans shows that this assumption was correct. There were of course active critics of Hitler's war policy in the German

---

[1] For this interpretation, see F. L. Schuman, *Europe on the Eve*, Chaps. IX–XI, and R. W. Van Alstyne, *American Diplomacy in Action*, Stanford University Press, 1944, p. 381, n. 2.

[2] 339 H.C. Deb. 5s. Col. 551 (6 October 1938).

High Command. Ewald von Kleist, an old German conservative, told Churchill and Vansittart of this opposition when he flew to London in August; Theodor Kordt unfolded to Halifax a similar tale in September.[1] But it would have been irresponsible to base policy on the assumption that Hitler's determination to invade Czechoslovakia would have been frustrated by his own generals. The conclusion of Sir John Wheeler-Bennett on the theory that Chamberlain's three flights to Germany saved Hitler from a revolt of his General Staff is that:

There is no evidence but the flimsiest assertion that, had Mr. Chamberlain never gone to Berchtesgaden or to Godesberg or to Munich, the conspirators would have been sufficiently prepared or resolute to strike, and the rapidity with which they snatched at this excuse for inaction is at least an indication of their unreadiness.[2]

The German generals might have grumbled; almost certainly they would have marched.

There is yet a third myth; namely, that Chamberlain was persuaded that the Sudetenland was Hitler's final territorial demand in Europe, and that the Munich agreement had made peace secure. When he said to Halifax, referring to the crowds welcoming his return to Downing Street, 'all this will be over in three months', he was admittedly speaking of the enthusiasm of the moment, rather than the prospects for stability between the Powers in Europe. On balance, he was disposed to trust Hitler, but was fully conscious that his own policy was after all a gamble, on which he had staked everything; he thought it wrong to plunge the world into war until it had been conclusively proved that the gamble was lost. In the bitter hours spent in the hotel at Godesberg he began to see that time was running out for the appeasement policy. On returning from Munich he underlined the need for accelerating rearmament, though this was more to strengthen his hand in future dealings with the dictators than to prepare the country for war. 'If we want to secure a lasting peace,' he said, 'I realise that diplomacy cannot be effective unless the consciousness exists . . . that behind diplomacy is the strength to give effect to it.'[3] To assume that Chamberlain sincerely believed that the declaration on Anglo-German relations which he persuaded Hitler to sign at Munich meant a permanent renunciation of force is to rate him a simple-minded person, for which there is no warrant in his

[1] J. W. Wheeler-Bennett, *The Nemesis of Power*, London, 1953, pp. 410–14; Erich Kordt, *Nicht aus den Akten*, Stuttgart, 1950, pp. 280–1.
[2] Wheeler-Bennett, *op. cit.*, p. 424.
[3] 339 H.C. Deb. 5s. Col. 551 (6 October 1938).

political career.[1]   It is reasonable to suppose that he had two main purposes in mind in asking Hitler to sign the declaration.   One was to help sweeten what was by all accounts a bitter pill for the British to swallow; if there was the remotest chance that the Czech sacrifice would lead to better Anglo-German relations, on which European peace depended, it was worth taking and might justify the Czech contribution, if anything could.   The second purpose was to secure from Hitler a final pledge of peaceful intentions to use with British, and, perhaps even more importantly with American, opinion in the event that Hitler later broke his word.   This is the interpretation of the scrap of paper to which Kirkpatrick inclined.[2]

The central questions which Chamberlain put to himself were whether the democracies could conceivably fight to keep $3\frac{1}{2}$ million Germans in Czechoslovakia when their official spokesmen opted for secession; and whether the democracies could fight to any advantage in the circumstances in which Hitler's attack on Czechoslovakia would be launched.   His answer to each question was a negative.   It is true that on the first issue, that of self-determination for the Sudeten Germans, there was no reason why the British should have felt that moral right was mostly on the German side.   The Czechs notoriously treated their minorities better than any other East European country, though this was not a high standard to set.   The Sudeten Germans were tolerably satisfied with their situation until the agitation from Germany began after 1933.[3]   By no means all the Sudeten Germans wished to enter the Third Reich; the Jews, Socialists and other anti-Nazis regarded it as a torture chamber.   Nevertheless, the Versailles settlement had been ostensibly based on the self-determination principle, which had assumed authority with enlightened democratic opinion, and statesmen had to deal, not with individual Germans, but with the Henleins, Franks and Kundts who spoke in their name. The British Government had, in Runciman's final report of 21 September on his mission, a clear recommendation in favour of secession of the provinces.[4]   Having agreed at the Anglo-French meetings in London on 18 and 19 September that the territories would have to come under German rule (and this reflected the broad band of British opinion), could Britain and France have declared war over the manner in which this transfer was effected?   Chamberlain regarded it as inconceivable

[1] See Eubank, op. cit., pp. 219–21, for a contrary view.
[2] The Inner Circle, p. 130.
[3] J. W. Bruegel, 'German Diplomacy and the Sudeten Question before 1938', International Affairs, July 1961, pp. 323–31.
[4] Cmd. 5847, pp. 3–8.

that millions should suffer death and deprivation through disagreement as to how an act of political justice, as he saw it, was to be effected. It was on this issue of method, not that of the principle of the transfer of the territory, that Duff Cooper resigned; he objected that the transfer was not being carried out 'with some respect to common decency'.[1]

Once the view had been formed that Hitler might, after all, be primarily concerned only with the redress of a wrong, the pessimistic assessment of the military situation formed by Chamberlain followed almost as a matter of course. The question was: what would happen if the Munich terms were rejected and Czechoslovakia was overrun, as British military advisers thought she would be after a few weeks? There would, Chamberlain thought, be little help from Russia. Apart from the generally assumed weakness of the Soviet army and the problem of access for Soviet land forces into Czechoslovakia, Stalin would hardly take on the main brunt of attacking Germany when his rear was exposed to Japan. In the September crisis there was little sign that the Soviet Government were preparing for the possibility of war.[2] The only evidence of serious intentions was a Soviet note to Poland on 23 September warning that any crossing of the Czech frontier by Polish forces would force Russia to denounce the Soviet–Polish Non-Aggression Pact of July 1932 and the reported moving of 30 infantry divisions to the vicinity of Russia's western frontier.[3] At no time was any intimation of Soviet intentions conveyed to Germany. Schulenburg, the German Ambassador in Moscow, advised his government that Russia would do as little as possible if war came, but would try to keep her army intact.[4]

If Russia held aloof, or was unable to engage German forces owing to Polish or Rumanian obstruction, the fighting would have to be done by France, and there was no escaping the drift of the reports available to Chamberlain indicating that France had no stomach for the fight. The French would have to take the offensive, and, apart from British air bombing of Germany, would receive even less assistance from Britain than they had in 1914. France was weaker in 1938 as compared with Germany than she had been in the First World War, when she

[1] Duff Cooper, op. cit., p. 235.
[2] The conclusion of Max Beloff in The Foreign Policy of Soviet Russia is that 'the Soviet record in the Munich crisis will certainly stand up to examination, even though the only diplomatic démarche of which there is indisputable record dealt solely with the secondary menace from Poland. But, had it intended action, the Soviet Government could have gone further in making its position known after Litvinov's speech on 23 September.' II, 1949, pp. 165–6.
[3] Izvestia, 26 September 1938; New Documents on the History of Munich, p. 118.
[4] D.G.F.P., Series D, II, pp. 601–2, 604–5, 629–31.

received three years' help from Russia, and from that war she had emerged only by the skin of her teeth. As Chamberlain saw it, France would batter herself to death against a stonewalling Germany if Hitler's challenge was taken up and war came. There was, thus, not only the risk of defeat for the two democracies, but the knowledge that the risk was being run in defiance of a principle in which most British and French people professed to believe.

As for the United States, her government could do no more than act as observers. After the Godesberg meeting, Roosevelt took up an idea of his Ambassador in Paris, Bullitt, that he should appeal to the leaders of Britain, France, Germany, Italy and Poland to send delegates to The Hague to discuss means of preserving peace and should himself offer to send an American representative. He even considered an offer of American arbitration but changed his mind when his advisers thought otherwise, and on 26 September confined himself to urging Benes, Chamberlain, Daladier and Hitler to pursue their efforts for a 'peaceful, fair and constructive settlement'. This was followed by a second message to Hitler on the 27th suggesting that, if the present negotiations failed, there should be a meeting of the parties in a neutral European city. But no mention was made of sending an American participant and American non-involvement was carefully stressed. Shortly before this the President sent a personal message to Mussolini asking him to help in the continuation of efforts to reach a solution by peaceful means. This message was apparently known to the Italian Foreign Office though not through the American Ambassador, Phillips, who did not deliver it until 4 p.m. on the 28th, shortly before Lord Perth handed in Chamberlain's appeal to Mussolini which led to the Munich conference; it may have played some part in the Duce's decision to use his influence with Hitler, but, if so, it could only have been a marginal one.[1]

Roosevelt was relieved when Chamberlain accepted the invitation to Munich, as is evident from his laconic message, 'Good man', which his London Ambassador, Kennedy, gave the Prime Minister on his behalf. But that this applied merely to the decision to continue negotiations, rather than to Chamberlain's policy at Munich, is evident from Cordell Hull's statement issued when the agreement became known; this recorded the universal sense of relief that war had been avoided, but refused to 'pass upon the merits of the differences to which the four-Power pact signed at Munich yesterday related'. In a

[1] Edward L. Henson, 'Britain, American and the Month of Munich', *International Relations*, April 1962, pp. 299–300.

message to Chamberlain on 5 October, however, the President seemed inclined to the Premier's view that the Munich agreement might serve as a basis for better things: 'I fully share your hope and belief,' he wrote, 'that there exists today the greatest opportunity in years for the establishment of a new order based on justice and on law.' However this may be, the fact remains that the American Government could do little but urge the Powers to settle their differences peacefully.[1]

In taking stock of these elements in the situation the mistake Chamberlain made was to think too much in terms of Czechoslovakia, too little in terms of the wider strategic effects of Nazi control of the Sudeten areas and ultimately of Bohemia. That France's last remaining allies in east and south-east Europe would be outflanked or demoralised by Munich; that Germany would acquire a stranglehold over Czechoslovakia which would put her in a position to master the considerable military and industrial resources of that country including the Skoda armaments industry; that every small state in Europe would, after Munich, realise the necessity of making their peace with Germany; that Stalin would write off the democracies as serious allies; that French morale would take a further plunge downwards: none of this appeared to play a part in Chamberlain's thinking.

But behind this is the greater failure of insight which Chamberlain shared with the great bulk of the British people, not entirely to the discredit of either. Chamberlain could not believe that any European leader could plunge the world into war for any other cause than the sheer imperatives of national survival. That war could bring glory, wealth, position; that it, or the thought of it, could bring satisfaction to resentful people dreaming of the overthrow of established order: this did not make sense to British Ministers. To the last Chamberlain continued to think that Hitler would pause on the rim of chaos and draw back to build with fellow statesmen bulwarks against a return to the abyss. As it happened, these assumptions were false; Hitler, coolly and with eyes open, calmly set out on the road to war. This was a phenomenon British politicians believed had passed with Frederick the Great or Napoleon, or at least the First World War. But since it was impossible to believe that a modern statesman could be so utterly senseless as to want to fight, it followed that a government's word must be taken at its face value when it said it wanted peace. 'The Prime Minister,' Duff Cooper said in the Commons on 3 October,

[1] Langer and Gleason, op. cit., pp. 32–5; Hull, Memoirs, I, pp. 590–6; Peace and War: United States Foreign Policy, 1931–41, Washington, 1943, pp. 39–40.

explaining his resignation as First Lord of the Admiralty in protest against the Munich agreement, 'has believed in addressing Herr Hitler through the language of sweet reasonableness. I have believed that he was more open to the language of the mailed fist.'[1] But no one in civilised England would have applauded a British Government which unleashed the horrors of war before going to the utmost in sweet reasonableness. The dictators were abhorred, but not charged with wanting to soak themselves and their people in blood. At least, in September 1938 that had not been proved beyond all reasonable doubt. What Munich did was to help complete the process of education of the British in the ways of depraved men.

[1] 339 H.C. Deb. 5s. Col. 34.

CHAPTER XXI

THE IDES OF MARCH

I

BRITISH policy during the Czech crisis rested on the assumption that the successor states of East Europe were morally and strategically indefensible so long as they included substantial minorities of German population; and that after territorial amputations had been made to satisfy the national principle more viable units would emerge. The fate of Czechoslovakia after Munich showed this assumption to be unfounded. The tangled pattern of nationalities in eastern Europe was such that once one group of secessionist claims was raised with the backing of force behind it the entire peace settlement of 1919 was brought to ruin. Moreover, the satisfaction of German claims in the Sudetenland ignited all the latent grievances and ambitions of those states east of the Rhine which fancied that they could exploit Czechoslovakia's fall while avoiding Hitler's wrath by refusing to oppose him.

After bowing to Germany at Munich the new Czech Government had to meet the claims of Poland and Hungary, the satisfaction of which was supposed to be a condition of the effective operation of the international guarantee of the revised Czech state which the Munich Powers had agreed. Promptly on 1 October the Czechs were forced to accept a Polish demand for the surrender of Teschen within 24 hours and of other districts on the frontier, including Freistadt, within ten days. Hungary's claims, being more extensive in character, took longer to settle. On 3 October the Czechs refused to comply with Hungarian demands centring upon the Magyar minority in southern Slovakia and proposed a Czech–Hungarian commission to meet at Komarom. The commission met but ran into deadlock following ten days of talk and, after a visit by the Czech Foreign Minister, Chvalkovsky, to Hitler at which assurances of Czechoslovakia's loyal attitude to Germany were conveyed, the problem was handed over for arbitration to the German and Italian Foreign Ministers, Ribbentrop and Ciano, who gave their award at Vienna on 3 November: this recommended the cession to Hungary of 12,400 sq. kms. of Czech territory with a population of 1 million.[1]   Poland, now wishing

[1] *D.B.F.P.*, Third Series, III, pp. 225–6.

to revise her claims upwards in view of these developments, had meanwhile framed further demands for the rectification of her frontier with Czechoslovakia at six points. These were promptly accepted by the Czech Government and final agreement on the Czech–Polish border was reached on 2 November. The effect of these cessions of territory to Germany at Munich and to Poland and Hungary as an immediate consequence of Munich was that Czechoslovakia was reduced to a population of 10 millions and that Czech and Slovak minorities were increased in the neighbouring states despite the whole operation having been defended in terms of national justice. Germany would henceforward include 750,000 Czechs and Slovaks, Hungary more than 398,000 and Poland more than 180,000.[1]

But it was in the work of the international commission created by the Munich agreement that the full subordination of Czechoslovakia to Germany's will was most brutally clear. The first major difference occurred over the statistics to be employed in determining German preponderance in the districts to be ceded to the Reich. The Czech delegate argued for the figures of the 1930 or 1921 census and the German for those of 1910, the last figures favouring Germany because they reflected the position before the exodus of German-speaking people when the Czech state was formed at the end of the war. Despite the British view that it would be grossly unfair to accept the 1910 figures, these were in fact imposed. Henderson, the British representative on the commission, considered that the Czechs 'will be well advised to yield once again to *force majeure* and to endeavour after 10 October to recover certain positions by direct negotiations'.[2] Henderson's attitude towards the international commission was well indicated in a dispatch which he wrote on 7 October which included the passage:

> It would be as unwise as it would be misleading to encourage the Czech Government to believe that they have much to hope for from the International Commission. The question of standard year and the percentage for preponderantly German areas is an instance of this reality. When my French colleague referred the matter to his Government their answer to all intents and purposes was 'do nothing to spoil the effects of Munich'.

Henderson in fact advised the Czechs to avoid recourse to the commission and to reach what agreements they could bilaterally with Germany. 'It is kinder in the end,' he wrote, 'to be

---

[1] *D.G.F.P.*, Series D, IV, pp. 118–27.
[2] *D.B.F.P.*, Third Series, III, pp. 93–4.

absolutely realistic than to encourage false hopes out of excessive sympathy or sensibility.'[1]

Henderson's strongest protest against German tactics in the commission came when the demand was made for plebiscites designed to increase the areas to be handed to the Reich even above those determined by the 1910 figures. At this point he threatened to withdraw from the commission if the demand was maintained.[2] But that this would not have affected the basic realities was made clear when Sir Basil Newton, the British Minister in Prague, told Chvalkovsky and the Czech Commander-in-Chief, General Krejci, on 8 October that if Germany pressed her territorial claims against Czechoslovakia beyond the limits agreed at Munich the Czech Army would be unwise to offer any resistance; with this Chvalkovsky agreed.[3] By 13 October Germany had withdrawn the demand for plebiscites but only in return for a formula to the effect that the line agreed to by the commission on 5 October, based, as Germany demanded, on the 1910 statistics, could be further extended in accordance with article 6 of the Munich agreement. This clause allowed the Germans to claim additional 'minor modifications' of any eventually agreed line and accordingly a German claim was presented on 14 November which involved the transfer of a further 40,000 people to the Reich, almost all of them Czechs. No discussion of this demand was permitted and the Czech authorities were given 48 hours in which to comply.[4] By mid-November the Czechs and Germans had bilaterally agreed to the cession of this, the sixth zone, and the commission was summoned at short notice to ratify the agreement. Ogilvie-Forbes, the British representative on the commission after Henderson's departure from Berlin on leave, was told by the Czechs that they had no alternative but to sign.[5] The final delimitation of the Czech–German frontier was signed in Berlin on 20 November and the acting chairman of the commission, Ritter, asked forthwith for the commission to be dissolved as its work was finished. Ogilvie-Forbes protested and his objection was sustained by the commission on 8 December.[6] But there was no doubt that the commission was wholly without effective power to prevent the transformation of Czechoslovakia into a German satellite. As Ogilvie-Forbes wrote to the Foreign Office in early December, 'all questions arising out of the Munich agreement are being and will be decided at

[1] D.B.F.P., Third Series, III, p. 123.
[2] Ibid., pp. 149–50.
[3] Ibid., pp. 140–1.
[4] D.G.F.P., Series D, IV, pp. 63–6; D.B.F.P., Third Series, III, p. 227.
[5] Ibid., pp. 234–5.   [6] Ibid., p. 242, n. 2.

German Nazi dictation.   The Ambassadors' Conference might well be dead for all the use it is.'[1]

There remained the fate of the international guarantee of Czechoslovakia, a fate which the Poles were to remember when the British proposed a similar guarantee for Poland in August 1939 in the event of the Danzig question being peacefully settled.   Chamberlain minced no words in telling Daladier and Bonnet when he and Halifax met the French Ministers at the Quai d'Orsay on 24 November that for Britain the guarantee had only been in the nature of an extra assurance to the 'somewhat suspicious Czechs' and was less necessary 'now that the Czech position would be one of almost complete safety.'[2] Morally, if not legally, the British guarantee had been in force from the date of the Munich agreement, according to a statement made by the Minister for the Co-ordination of Defence, Sir Thomas Inskip, on 4 October.[3]   But British Ministers were anxious that the guarantee when finally negotiated between the Munich Powers should not be a 'joint and several pledge' under which Britain would be saddled with an obligation to defend Czechoslovakia even if the other signatories stood aside. Halifax explained to the French Ministers at the Quai d'Orsay meeting in November that it rested with Czechoslovakia to follow a policy 'entirely in conformity with Germany's wishes'; if she failed to do so, this would constitute 'a certain element of provocation' to Germany and Britain and France might be forced to intervene on her behalf.   With this argument Daladier was persuaded that Czechoslovakia must be asked to rest content with a joint guarantee which would be ineffective unless all, or a substantial majority, of the guarantors acted together.   This still left the possibility that Germany would refuse to take up the guarantee if Russia was a party, as the Anglo-French plan of 19 September had envisaged.   Chamberlain considered it more desirable to have a German than a Soviet guarantee, if there had to be a choice, and it was agreed that the Czech Government should be asked whether they wished to have a guarantee from the four Munich Powers without mention being made of the possibility of Russia adding a fifth signature.[4]   Chvalkovsky replied to Newton on 11 December that he did not mind what form the guarantee took so long as it was given soon, but he preferred that the Munich Powers should give it in the first instance.[5]

It remained to be seen whether Hitler was still interested in

[1] *D.B.F.P.*, Third Series, III, pp. 379–80.
[2] *Ibid.*, p. 305.   [3] 339 H.C. Deb. 5s. Col. 303.
[4] *Ibid.*, p. 302.   [5] *Ibid.*, pp. 423–4.

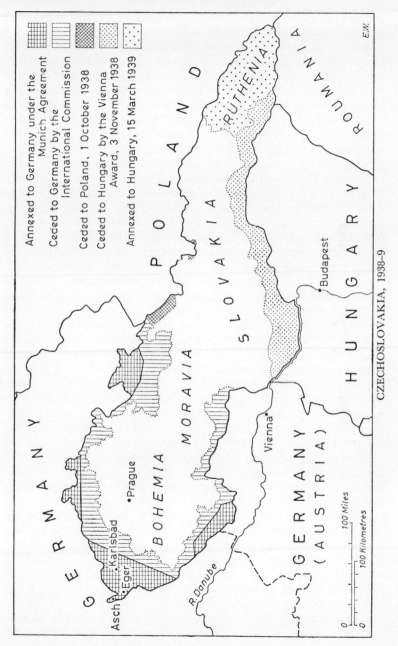

Annexed to Germany under the
    Munich Agreement
Ceded to Germany by the
    International Commission
Ceded to Poland, 1 October 1938
Ceded to Hungary by the Vienna
    Award, 3 November 1938
Annexed to Hungary, 15 March 1939

GERMANY

Asch
Eger
Karlsbad
Prague

BOHEMIA

MORAVIA

R. Danube

GERMANY
(AUSTRIA)

Vienna

POLAND

SLOVAKIA

RUTHENIA

ROUMANIA

HUNGARY

Budapest

100 Miles
100 Kilometres

CZECHOSLOVAKIA, 1938–9

E.W.

the guarantee now that the changes in the Czech frontier had been completed and Czechoslovakia was deprived of her former French and Soviet alliances. British and French notes inquiring into the German attitude were sent on 8 February 1939 and a month elapsed before an answer was given by Ribbentrop to Henderson, who marked his return to Berlin after his leave by telling Hitler at a reception for the Diplomatic Corps on 2 March that Chamberlain was 'still thinking on the lines of Munich'. The British and French declarations in favour of a guarantee to Czechoslovakia, the German Foreign Minister told Henderson, might have the effect of 'accentuating the differences between that country and surrounding states rather than of contributing a factor of appeasement in the area'. The German Government, Ribbentrop went on, thought it necessary 'to await firstly a clarification of the internal development of Czechoslovakia and an improvement of that country's relations with surrounding states before they can make any further definition of their attitude'.[1] When the question of the guarantee was next raised, after the final dismemberment of Czechoslovakia two weeks later, it was evident that there was nothing left to guarantee.

The British Government were little disquieted about the fate of the guarantee because Czechoslovakia was now, as Chamberlain said, 'safe', that is, safely under German control. The guarantee had ostensibly been designed to defend Czechoslovakia against a German attack after the cession of the Sudetenland, but Czechoslovakia now lay so securely in Germany's hand that any such attack was deemed in London to be superfluous; Hitler could obtain all he wanted from Prague without the need to send his forces. As early as 7 October Newton was writing to Halifax that the Prague Government realised 'even though with bitterness, that Czechoslovakia is at the mercy of Germany and must draw the necessary inferences in her foreign policy and in all other ways'.[2] A month later Newton was reporting the growth of Fascist trends in Czechoslovakia as the process of accommodation with Germany forced to the surface men with a similar outlook to that of Germany's leaders.[3] When Chvalkovsky visited Hitler at Munich on 14 October to remove all doubt about Czechoslovakia's submission to the Chancellor's will, he was told that if the Czechs wavered from their new course 'in 24 hours—no, in 8 hours—I will make an end (*mache ich Schluss*)'.[4] A new Czech Government was formed on 1 December designed so as to ensure that this eventuality

[1] *Ibid.*, IV, pp. 86–7, 169, 171–3.   [2] *D.B.F.P.*, Third Series, III, pp. 123–4.
[3] *Ibid.*, pp. 213–18.   [4] *Ibid.*, pp. 221–2.

would never occur. 'No Czech Government today,' commented Newton on the new régime, 'has any option but to submit to German dictation whether in the political or economic field.'[1] But this was not regarded in Berlin as sufficient reason for allowing the pressure on Prague to relax until every shred of 'Benesism' had been expelled. Chvalkovsky was summoned before Hitler again on 21 January, this time in Berlin, and accorded a 40-minute interview in which the Chancellor expounded for 30 minutes continuously his lack of confidence in Czechoslovakia's capacity to eliminate all anti-Nazi and Jewish elements from the country.[2] Before the end of January the Czech Foreign Minister was forced to sign two further agreements symbolising the satellite status of his country: one allowed the Nazi movement full freedom of activity in Czechoslovakia, the other was a railway agreement which gave the Reich facilities for the transport of military supplies through three main routes across Czechoslovakia. 'If Germany wishes to take over the remainder of this country,' Newton reported, 'no power on earth can at present stop her doing so. It is largely a matter of Germany's own convenience whether she occupies Czechoslovakia.'[3]

British Ministers viewed these developments without serious alarm. All this was happening in East Europe and it was a settled principle of Chamberlain's policy that very little could be done to prevent East Europe becoming mainly a German sphere of interest, given that British commercial interests were not excluded and Germany agreed to respect the *status quo* in the West and the general world positions of Britain and France. The line to be followed was close collaboration with France in order to keep western Europe secure and, somewhat inconsistently, not wholly to exclude the Soviet Union lest her assistance be wanted in the future, though the circumstances in which this might be the case were not clearly conceived. Halifax explained his leader's general philosophy to Phipps in Paris on 1 November. Britain and France, Halifax said, must count on German predominance in Central Europe 'for obvious geographical and economic reasons'.

> In these conditions [he continued] it seems to me that Great Britain and France have to uphold their predominant position in western Europe by the maintenance of such armed strength as would render any attack upon them hazardous. They should also firmly maintain their hold on

[1] *Ibid.*, p. 380.
[2] *D.G.F.P.*, Series D, IV, pp. 190–5.
[3] *D.B.F.P.*, Third Series, III, pp. 413–14.

the Mediterranean and the Near East. They should also keep a tight hold on their Colonial Empires and maintain the closest possible ties with the United States.

Halifax admitted that this division of Europe between Germany on one side and Britain and France on the other left the position of Poland and Russia obscure. He had no objection to Poland falling into the German orbit if France, having burned her fingers over Czechoslovakia, decided to drop her alliance with Poland; but he considered that Russia could never ally herself with Germany and had therefore no other choice than that of withdrawing into isolation, which was never in any long run a satisfactory policy, or improving her relations with the Western Powers. To facilitate the latter course, Halifax thought, France should not abandon her ties with Moscow though she should avoid becoming 'entangled' with Russia in a war with Germany while the future was so uncertain. But Halifax's mind, like that of most British politicians, handled more easily the familiar western scene and was at home pondering the hopes of succour from Italy. Mussolini, the government thought, could never be detached from Germany, but Western support, if only arrangements could be made to circumvent French mistrust of Italy and venom against Rome in the British Parliament, could give the Duce greater power of manœuvre and freedom to resume what Halifax called 'the classic Italian role of balancing between Germany and the Western Powers'.[1]

This thinking stemmed, like the Munich agreement, from the assumption that Hitler, with appetite sated in east and south-east Europe, would reciprocate British and French efforts for a long-term understanding with Germany. Hitler did appear to respond as far as France was concerned, but only with the all too obvious purpose of breaking her bond with Britain. When François-Poncet, the French Ambassador to Germany, made his farewell to Hitler at Berchtesgaden on 18 October before leaving for his new post in Rome, he was treated with extreme cordiality and given the highest decoration in Germany.[2] The talk resulted in a Franco-German declaration along the lines of that signed by Hitler and Chamberlain at Munich but embodying a pledge of mutual respect for frontiers.[3] Ribbentrop went to Paris for a two-day visit in December to sign the agreement, engendering suspicions in the British Foreign Office that Bonnet would use the occasion

[1] *D.B.F.P.*, Third Series, III, pp. 251–3.
[2] A. François-Poncet, *Souvenirs d'une ambassade à Berlin*, pp. 340, 343–7.
[3] *Le livre jaune français*, p. 38.

to give the German Foreign Minister a free hand in East Europe, similar to that given in regard to Abyssinia by Laval to Mussolini in Rome in January 1935. Bonnet went as far as to tell Phipps on the day before Ribbentrop's arrival in Paris that he wished 'to loosen the ties that bind France to Russia and Poland', and this in itself made Ribbentrop's journey worth making on Germany's behalf.[1] After the Prague *coup* in March 1939 Weizsäcker, permanent head of the German Foreign Office, noted in a memorandum that Bonnet had stated his *désintéressement* in Czechoslovakia's fate in his talks with Ribbentrop; otherwise, Weizsäcker claimed, Germany would never have consented to the December agreement with France. Hence Germany could not accept the French protest against the occupation of Bohemia.[2]

For Britain, on the other hand, the German Government showed intense hostility, correctly judging her to be the seat from which resistance to German expansion would be organised, if from anywhere. Speaking at Weimar on 6 November, Hitler made a full-scale attack on British 'warmongers', singling out Churchill and Arthur Greenwood for calumny, and uttering no word of praise for all Chamberlain's efforts on behalf of Anglo-German understanding. Rising anti-British sentiment in Germany reached a climax after the murder of the German diplomat, vom Rath, in Paris by a Polish Jew on 7 November, when attempts were made to associate British politicians with the crime. Halifax made a sharp protest against this campaign, which Ogilvie-Forbes handed to Woermann, of the German Foreign Office, on 14 November. In reply Woermann referred to a statement by Goebbels dissociating the German Government from the campaign and undertaking to look into the complaint.[3] The German authorities' intention seemed to be to dangle once more the bait of German friendship before the British Government if they would renounce their rearmament measures and restrain British politicians who were bold enough to criticise Germany. In any event, it was a bitter sequel to the Anglo-German declaration signed at Munich. *The Times'* Berlin correspondent reported Hitler as having told a group of German journalists in mid-November that he ceased to lay any value on friendship with Britain after Munich; Britain was no longer to be treated with consideration by the German Press since she had followed up the Munich

---

[1] *D.B.F.P.*, Third Series, III, p. 397, n. 1.
[2] *D.G.F.P.*, Series D, VI, pp. 20–1. Bonnet in his memoirs denies that any such agreement was reached: *Fin d'une Europe*, p. 38.
[3] *D.B.F.P.*, Third Series, III, pp. 271–2.

declaration by renewed rearmament. 'Britain,' the Chancellor said, 'could not at the same time run with the United States and Nazi Germany as American policy was under the influence of Wall Street and international Jewry.'[1]

A more concrete retort to the British rearmament programme came from Berlin on 10 December when Hitler announced his intention to exercise his option under the Anglo-German Naval Agreement of June 1935 to build submarine tonnage up to the level of that of the British Commonwealth and to increase the armament of German cruisers.[2] How hard Chamberlain was now finding it to please Hitler was evident again when the Premier addressed a Press Association dinner of 13 December and found Dirksen, the German Ambassador, and the corps of German pressmen conspicuously absent owing to some words which it was known in advance that Chamberlain would use in his speech in defence of Baldwin against German press attacks. The Munich agreement, it seemed, had contributed little towards realising Chamberlain's dream of Anglo-German understanding.

II

The question at the opening of the fateful year, 1939, was: in which direction would Germany strike next? Her central situation provided her with a wide choice. Economic strains, shortages of raw materials for her four-year plan, and the pressure at which the wholesale militarisation of the nation were being forced, all, in the view of British advisers, demanded an early attack on one or other of her neighbours. The psychopathic temperament of her Nazi master made this forecast all but a certainty.

The most plausible assessment in Whitehall immediately after Munich was that Hitler would agitate for an independent Ukraine to supply him with the grain and timber he professed to require to achieve immunity from blockade. The British Government had no intention of trying to frustrate any such plan. Their only fear, as Chamberlain told his French colleagues at the Quai d'Orsay meeting on 24 November, was that France might be embroiled in defence of Russia against a German move to wrench the Ukraine free.[3] If an attack were made towards the East, the likelihood was that Britain would have to sit back and watch it happen. Ogilvie-Forbes, speculating in January on German intentions for 1939, said that Britain was powerless to check a German advance to the East;

---

[1] *D.B.F.P.*, Third Series, III, pp. 278–9.   [2] *Ibid.*, pp. 422–3.
[3] *Ibid.*, pp. 306–7.

'*the Pax Britannica*,' he wrote, 'was no longer respected in Central Europe and Britain could no more hope to be the policeman of Europe.' Britain's only hope of keeping out of war, Ogilvie-Forbes went on, was to recognise in good time that 'we cannot guarantee the *status quo* in Central and East Europe', and to exert efforts 'to cultivate and maintain good relations with Field-Marshal Goering and the moderate Nazis with a view to their exercising a restraining influence on the extremists'.[1] But no sooner were these conclusions reached than a new fear came, that of a devastating air strike against Britain, which would account for Germany's professions of warm regard for France, intended to keep the French aloof and indifferent when the blow against Britain fell. Chamberlain had poured out his fears to the French on this score at the Quai d'Orsay meeting on 24 November; he received in return Daladier's assurance that in this case Britain would not be alone, but was unable to answer the French Prime Minister's question whether the British could not make their own contribution to the alliance by giving less priority to home air defence and by preparing to send more than two solitary army divisions, and these unmotorised, to the Continent in the first three weeks of hostilities.[2]

These anxious speculations were given a firmer direction early in January when definite signs appeared that Germany proposed to remain quiescent in the East. On 5 January Colonel Beck, the Polish Foreign Minister, responded to a summons to Berchtesgaden, and the British Foreign Office, trying three days later to piece together evidence of what passed at this meeting, came to the conclusion that Hitler was going slow in the East in order to prepare for an attack in the West. The object of his talk with Beck, the Foreign Office thought, might have been to promise him a stake in the colonies of the Western Powers, to be shared out after Germany's defeat of Britain, France and Holland, as the price of Polish neutrality.[3] This evidence of a German–Polish *détente* appeared confirmed towards the end of January when Ribbentrop paid a two-day visit to Warsaw and spoke in approving terms to the German colony of the Polish–German agreement framed between Hitler and Pilsudski in January 1934. Nor was Hitler in any hostile mood towards the Soviets; the British Ambassador in Moscow, Sir William Seeds, reported on 27 January that a German mission was expected in Moscow in search of timber and manganese led by Schnurre, the head of the Eastern Department of the economic section of the German Foreign Office.[4] The

---

[1] *D.B.F.P.*, Third Series, III, pp. 561–4. [2] *Ibid.*, pp. 288–91.
[3] *Ibid.*, pp. 589–90. [4] *D.B.F.P.*, Third Series, IV, pp. 33–4.

British Cabinet had come to accept the inferences to be drawn from these moves towards the end of January. They now believed, Cadogan explained to Mallet in Washington for the information of the State Department, that while no particular plan may have been decided, the most likely possibility was an invasion of Holland or a sudden air attack on Britain; economic difficulties, the permanent head of the Foreign Office thought, were forcing Germany into external adventures and the retirement from their offices of such men as Dr. Schacht and Captain Wiedemann showed that the more cautious spirits were being forced out.[1]

At the beginning of February the government were compelled to face the possibility of a definite German attack in the West. It was decided that any invasion of Holland should be regarded as a *casus belli* for Britain, provided the Dutch resisted, though the same apparently was not to apply for the time being to an attack on Switzerland. Halifax told the French Ambassador, Corbin, on 28 January of this decision, adding that the government were proposing closer staff talks with France. Corbin replied with a catalogue of complaints about the output of British military equipment and its inadequacy for making a serious British contribution to Western land forces. Britain, Corbin said, concentrated far too much on the production of anti-aircraft guns, and the same complaint was made by Daladier to Phipps on the following day, when the French Prime Minister repeated his customary inquiry as to when conscription was to be introduced in Britain.[2] The replies to British soundings in Holland and Belgium about their intentions in the event of a German attack were discouraging too, but in a different sense, these countries being unwilling to be jostled into a 'peace front' prematurely. Sir Nevile Bland reported from The Hague on 30 January the unwillingness of the Dutch Foreign Minister to believe rumours of a German plan to attack Holland; if invasion did come, the Dutch authorities proposed to inundate the country and would hope to survive the three or four days which were the estimated maximum for their forces' resistance.[3] Sir Robert Clive, giving reactions from Brussels on the following day, said that the King of the Belgians desired peace at almost any price; he was definitely opposed to staff talks with the French as he feared that these would provoke Germany. Writing again on 1 February after talking with the Belgian Foreign Minister, Clive reported that the Belgian Government considered that France had no troops

[1] *F.R.U.S.*, *1939*, I, pp. 3–5.   [2] *D.B.F.P.*, Third Series, IV, p. 50.
[3] *Ibid.*, pp. 52–3.

to spare for the defence of Belgium and in any case could not keep military secrets; hence, although Belgium meant to maintain a policy of independence as long as possible, she wanted no commitments with any other country in carrying out this policy.[1] In these circumstances it was left to Britain and France alone to pledge their strength in defence of western Europe. At the urgent request of the French on 5 February, Chamberlain made his declaration on the 6th in the House of Commons: 'the solidarity of interest, by which France and this country are united, is such that any threat to the vital interests of France from whatever quarter it came must evoke the immediate co-operation of this country'.[2] This statement was understood as implying British support for France if necessary against Italy, though in this case it would be left to France to say whether she wanted help which might have the effect of bringing Germany into the conflict. At the same time the British Government were framing arrangements for closer staff talks with the French and considering Daladier's repeated appeals for the introduction of conscription. By 10 February firm Anglo-French agreements had been reached that any attack on Holland or Switzerland must be regarded as a *casus belli* for both countries and that the closest possible military integration was a matter of urgency.'[3]

These various moves, despite French hesitations over pressing on with the staff talks until the British were more forthcoming over conscription, seemed to have their effect within the month when fears of an imminent German attack in the West subsided in Whitehall as quickly as they had developed. Halifax, writing to Lindsay in Washington at the end of February, when the launching of Nazi forces to overrun the West had been confidently forecast, disagreed with the alarming reports Lindsay reported the State Department as having received about German military plans: Germany, the Foreign Secretary thought, had been impressed by such evidence as the firm attitude France had taken up towards Italian demands, British rearmament, Chamberlain's declaration of Anglo-French solidarity of 6 February, and the recent anti-German tone of American public opinion: there was no reliable information of impending mobilisation in Germany.[4] Lindsay told Sumner Welles that British opinion had swung over to a state of almost unbelievable optimism.[5]

Halifax was evidently not troubled by the thought that

[1] *D.B.F.P.*, Third Series, IV, pp. 66–7. [2] 343 H.C. Deb. 5s. Col. 623.
[3] *Ibid.*, pp. 100–2. [4] *Ibid.*, pp. 159–61.
[5] *F.R.U.S.*, *1939*, I, p. 18.

Hitler might have more sinister business to promote than an attack in the West. Cadogan, on the other hand, after talking with Corbin on 1 February, had noted indications of a possible *rapprochement* between Berlin and Moscow; the straws in the wind were German proposals to convert the anti-Comintern Pact into a military alliance, which would be an assurance to Russia that it was not specifically directed against her, the projected Soviet–German trade talks, and the absence in Hitler's Reichstag speech of 30 January, celebrating his accession to power in 1933, of any reference, abusive or other, to the Soviet Union.[1] The insistent note sounding from Moscow was one of Soviet disbelief in British intentions to stand firm when Hitler struck; this in itself was a clue to Russia's developing policy of remaining aloof from entanglements with the Western Powers, except on the most favourable terms, and hence her availability for suitable arrangements with Germany. Seeds wrote home to much the same effect after a talk with Litvinov on 19 February; 'the Soviet Government and people,' he reported, 'see no sign whatever that France and Great Britain would do anything but continue to capitulate; the Soviet Union would therefore keep aloof, all the more readily as their interests are not directly threatened'.[2] No significant inference, it seems, was drawn by the British Cabinet from this growing Soviet renunciation of the Litvinov thesis of the indivisibility of peace, except the conclusion that the resolute British and French mood should be once more declared. The possibility that Russia and Germany might find common interests seemed too remote to be taken seriously.

An important factor in the British acceptance of a lull towards the end of February was the reassuring reports from Germany of Sir Nevile Henderson, who returned to his post in Berlin on 13 February after a period of leave since mid-October. On the 18th Henderson was stating as his definite impression since his return that Hitler 'does not contemplate any adventures at the moment and that all stories and rumours to the contrary are completely without real foundations'. 'I believe in fact,' Henderson wrote, 'he would like in his heart to return to the fold of comparative respectability.'[3] Ten days later the Ambassador was accounting for the Chancellor's comparatively mild speech of 30 January in terms of his surprise, after a long sojourn in Berchtesgaden, in discovering the poor economic condition of the country: 'I anticipate in the immediate

[1] *D.B.F.P.*, Third Series, IV, pp. 70–1.
[2] *Ibid.*, pp. 123–4.
[3] *Ibid.*, pp. 120–2.

future a period of relative calm' was the conclusion to be drawn.[1] These dispatches were, on the government's admission, an important factor in Chamberlain's decision to issue a *mot d'ordre* to the press on 9 March describing the international situation as 'one to give less cause for anxiety than for some time past'.[2] On the same day Henderson called for sympathetic understanding for Germany and British disinterest in East Europe; 'the best approach to good relations with Germany,' Henderson counselled, 'is along the lines of the avoidance of constant and vexatious interference in matters in which British interests are not directly or vitally involved, and the prospect of British neutrality in the event of Germany being engaged in the East'. 'Hitler prides himself on keeping his word,' the Ambassador added.[3] By a cruel, but not undeserved, irony, this dispatch was received in the Foreign Office on 16 March, the day after Hitler's occupation of Bohemia. Only late on 10 March did Henderson write to suggest that Hitler might be contemplating a move against Czechoslovakia. Sir Orme Sargent acidly minuted in the Foreign Office that this was Henderson's first recognition of the possibility that Hitler might have other adventures in store.[4] Henderson was, however, not recalled for incompetence; he enjoyed the government's trust until the end.

In accordance with Halifax's theory that East Europe was Germany's sphere of interest and western Europe the British and French domain, there was no reason why Britain should have reacted as violently as she did against the German occupation of Bohemia on 15 March, followed by the conversion of Bohemia and Slovakia into protectorates of the Third Reich. The Slovak secessionist crisis arising out of the dismissal of the Tiso Government by the Prague authorities announced on 10 March served as a convenient pretext for Germany's action, but the *coup* did little more than formally register the subordination of Czechoslovakia to Germany's commands which had been increasingly evident since Munich. For Britain and France to intervene would have meant war as surely as it would have done in September 1938. The French were most unlikely to act and it was pointed out in a Foreign Office memorandum two days before the Prague *coup* that Britain 'would have no *locus standi* in taking the initiative' since the proposed guarantee of Czechoslovakia had fallen to the ground.[5] Bonnet and Béranger, the President of the Foreign Affairs Committee

---

[1] *D.B.F.P.*, IV, pp. 163–5.
[2] *The Times*, 10 March.
[3] *Ibid.*, pp. 210–17.
[4] *Ibid.*, p. 218.
[5] *Ibid.*, pp. 238–41.

of the French Senate, told Phipps that the less they interfered in the Czech crisis the better. 'They both remarked,'
Phipps reported, 'that this renewed rift between Czechs and
Slovaks only shows that we nearly went to war last autumn to
boost up a state that was not viable.'[1]

Perhaps the most irritating immediate consequence of
Hitler's action was that the President of the Board of Trade and
the Secretary of the Department of Overseas Trade were about
to visit Berlin to work on the all-important economic aspects of
appeasement and that these visits must now be postponed.
The extinction of Czech independence, however, did not prevent an agreement to control 'unhealthy competition' being
signed on 16 March by the *Reichsgruppe Industrie* and the Federation of British Industries as a result of negotiations conducted
in Düsseldorf.[2]   Hence it was a mild note which Halifax sent
to the German Government immediately before the *coup* of
15 March deploring any action in Central Europe 'which
would be a setback to general confidence, especially when the
Anglo-German economic talks were about to begin'.[3]   Cadogan told Corbin, the French Ambassador, that Britain was not
contemplating a *démarche* to Berlin over German reactions to
the dismissal of the Tiso Cabinet because there was probably
nothing effective Britain could do to prevent the execution of
Germany's plans.   Cadogan agreed that Britain could approach Germany under the Anglo-German declaration signed
at Munich, since this provided for consultations in matters of
common concern; but he foresaw that Germany would reply
that Britain had no interest in Czechoslovakia.   Cadogan
pointed out that Britain was mainly concerned to maintain her
prestige and the melancholy conclusion followed that 'it was
for consideration whether one should not lose more prestige by
attempting to deter Hitler and being flouted by him than by
waiting for the event to happen and then formally drawing
our own conclusions'.[4]

When German troops actually made their entry into
Bohemia on the 15th Halifax adopted a tougher tone with the
German Ambassador, von Dirksen, but again it was more in
sorrow than in anger that he spoke. 'Hitler's move,' the
Foreign Secretary said, 'was in flat contradiction to the spirit
of the Munich agreement.' which had provided for four-Power
consultations in such matters.   'The conclusion which every-

[1] *Ibid.*, p. 243.
[2] *F.R.U.S., 1939*, I, pp. 77–8, giving text of the agreement.
[3] *D.B.F.P.*, Third Series, IV, p. 250; *D.G.F.P.*, Series D, VI, p. 10.
[4] *D.B.F.P.*, Third Series, IV, pp. 266–8.

body in this country and far outside it would draw,' Halifax continued, 'must be that (Germany) had no great desire to establish good relations with this country, that they were prepared to disregard world opinion and were seeking to establish a position in which they could by force dominate Europe and if possible the world.'[1] The fact was that while in theory disinterest in East Europe might seem to justify an attitude of indignant detachment from the Prague *coup*, such a position was by a variety of factors suddenly rendered impossible for the British Government to maintain. The principle of disinterest in Central and East Europe had to be scrapped overnight. Europe could not be artificially divided in such a way that force used in defiance of agreements in one quarter could be viewed indifferently from another.

In the first place, the sheer brutality of Germany's action against a defenceless and subservient Czechoslovakia shocked all but the most cynical of Western observers. Even such an apologist for German policies as Bonnet told Phipps on 15 March that Britain and France could not intervene in any way in this affair, but was 'clearly most disturbed by the unnecessary Nazi brutality and gangster-like methods'. Bonnet remarked repeatedly, said Phipps, that Britain and France had better continue their rearmament as rapidly and as intensively as possible and that their close union was 'more than ever essential'.[2] The Prague affair made it all but impossible for any Munich-type agreement to be signed between the Western Powers and Hitler again.

In the second place, it was now clear beyond doubt that all the small countries of Europe, whether containing German minorities or not, were within the range of Germany's guns and the Führer's wrath; that if Germany willed to subdue them there was nothing that they could do to avoid being turned into German protectorates like Bohemia; and that Britain and France were hardly in a position to offer them any immediate protection though they might be liberated by Britain and France after a war with Germany. Not surprisingly, a form of paralytic alarm seized all the small states of Europe after the Prague *coup*, arising from the realisation that if they made a move to protect themselves they might be signing their own death warrants. Shepherd, the British representative in Danzig, the German port and city in Polish territory which had been placed under League protection in 1919, wrote to Halifax on 15 March that Burckhardt, the League High Commissioner in Danzig, had stopped in Berlin on returning to his post after

---

[1] *D.B.F.P.*, Third Series, IV, pp. 270–2.   [2] *Ibid.*, p. 263.

a period of leave and had heard that Germany intended to occupy the Free City in the following week.[1]   On the day before the Prague *coup* Halifax received the Rumanian Minister in London and was told that if Britain made no move in the Czech crisis the effect would be disastrous for British prestige throughout Central Europe and the Balkans just when it was beginning to recover from the blow dealt to it at Munich. Halifax was advised to give the greatest publicity to the commercial missions Britain was sending to Rumania and to raise at once the British legations in Rumania, Yugoslavia and Greece to embassy status.[2]   On the day following the German entry into Bohemia Orme Sargent saw the Rumanian Minister and received an account of Rumania's plight after the total collapse of Czechoslovakia.   Rumania had had substantial arms contracts in Czechoslovakia which could not now be fulfilled; and she required a £10 million loan to enable her to equip her armed forces adequately.[3]   Events such as these showed that in the absence of a vigorous response to the occupation of Bohemia Britain would be without a friend in Europe.

The third and most powerful inducement for a far stronger reaction to the final extinction of Czech freedom on 15 March than the policy of detachment in East Europe would logically have justified, was the shock and dismay expressed in the House of Commons on that day at Hitler's deliberate decision to press beyond the limits of the national principle in Czechoslovakia. Chamberlain began the adjournment debate with what he later described as a 'cool and objective' account of events in keeping with his unemotional spirit and designed to reduce the temperature.   The statement was ballasted with colourless announcements, such as that the loan scheme for Czechoslovakia, framed after Munich, could not now be proceeded with and that a final judgment on all the details of the Prague *coup* should await further confirmation.   Chamberlain acquitted the government of responsibility for taking any further action, since although the guarantee was still morally if not legally operative, the state which it was intended to protect had ceased to exist with the declaration of Slovak independence.   But he was unrepentant about Munich and could describe the Prague tragedy in no larger terms than 'a shock to confidence when it was beginning to revive'.   Chamberlain said the government would not be deflected by these events from their course, namely pursuit of the methods of discussion rather than

---

[1]   *D.B.F.P.*, Third Series, IV, p. 265.
[2]   *Ibid.*, pp. 283–4.
[3]   *Ibid.*, pp. 284–5.

of force. It was at once obvious that the Prime Minister had seriously misjudged the mood of the House as one speaker after another rose to express alarm and the necessity for immediate action. Eden called for an all-party government as in a time of grave national emergency, Duncan Sandys for an international conference to halt aggression, Viscount Wolmer for the prompt introduction of national service. Only a few back-bench Conservatives echoed the old theme of 1938, that Czechoslovakia was in any case unviable and that Britain should remain free of East European commitments. The sense of release from illusions was well expressed by Godfrey Nicholson when he said,

> We should feel heavy responsibility for our surprise today over what has happened, for our weakness, for our anxiety for the future. I frankly admit that I feel that I, as an M.P., have failed in my duty and that every M.P., without distinction of party, has failed in his duty.

Simon, replying for the government, found himself in a position which no British Minister had occupied since 1919, that of having to defend the policy of the 'free hand' as against the rising support for Sandys' suggestion of a conference of nations to exchange guarantees of the *status quo*. Such a proposal, Simon argued, using the time-hallowed words of British Ministers since the war, would involve Britain in the unprecedented venture of having to defend 'very long and varied frontiers', and would take the choice of peace and war out of the hands of an elected British Government and place it in the hands of a 'whole lot of foreign countries'. For the last time the policy of the 'free hand', on behalf of which Britain had made so many sacrifices of friends and interests since the war, was heard in a British Parliament:

> I doubt whether it is possible in the abstract and without knowledge of the circumstances to pledge this country to the frightful business of modern war, in a whole list of additional cases, when it appears that in most instances it would be impossible to judge the circumstances in the abstract, precisely and definitely, and where, I believe, our duty to our own people requires us to adopt a more cautious policy.

The 'more cautious policy', however, the government were forced, against their better judgment, to abandon as a result of the Commons debate on 15 March.[1]

[1] 345 H.C. Deb. 5s. Cols. 435–564.

III

Parliament and public opinion demanded action; the government provided it. Halifax promptly sent a tough note of protest to Henderson for delivery to the German Government on 17 March, in which Hitler's action was described as a 'complete repudiation of the Munich agreement and a denial of the spirit in which the negotiators of that agreement bound themselves to co-operate for peaceful settlements'.[1] After delivery of the note the Ambassador was ordered home for consultations. The same evening Chamberlain sought to remove the tepid impression left by his Commons statement in a speech to the Unionist Association in Birmingham in which the crucial question was raised: 'is this the last attack upon a small state, or is it . . . a step in the direction of an attempt to dominate the world by force?' Above all, a feverish search was instituted for a European security system aimed at containing Germany at all points of the compass. In the haste to erect a sign reading 'Halt! Major Road Ahead' little consideration was given to the far-reaching political issues raised by this security system, which finally rendered it ineffective. What was wanted was countries to guarantee, as a form of gage thrown down in Hitler's path, and that soon.

On the decisive 17 March, when the government seemed at length to have its mind up on the new course, the first opportunity to demonstrate it came with a statement by the Rumanian Minister, Tilea, to the effect that Germany had demanded a monopoly of Rumania's exports and the restriction of Rumanian industry in Germany's favour in return for which Rumania was to have a German guarantee against aggression. It later transpired that Tilea had been acting on his own responsibility in emitting this appeal for help; the Germans alleged that his motives were fear that his personal fortune would be adversely affected by the German–Rumanian trade negotiations then proceeding in Bucharest. However this may be, the Minister was given a severe reprimand by the Rumanian Foreign Minister, Gafencu, and told to issue an immediate *démenti* to the British Government.[2] By this time, however, Halifax had sounded alarm bells in Paris, Moscow, Warsaw, Ankara, Athens and Belgrade inquiring into the readiness of the authorities in these capitals to join Britain in assisting Rumania without apparently realising that it would be reckless for them to commit themselves to stand in Germany's path

1 R.I.I.A., *Documents, 1939–1946*, I, p. 71.
2 *D.G.F.P.*, Series D, VI, p. 46.

unless it was first clear what exactly Britain intended to do.[1]
Litvinov raised the obvious question when he saw Seeds about
the inquiry on 18 March: did Britain wish the Soviet Union
to engage herself in Rumania's defence while leaving her own
hands free?[2] Campbell, the British Chargé d'Affaires in Paris,
was a given a lesson in diplomacy to somewhat the same effect
by Léger, the head of the French Foreign Office, when he was
told that Britain should not subordinate her own attitude to
the replies she was receiving from other governments about the
Rumanian situation; these governments, Léger pointed out,
would make up their minds in accordance with decisions
reached by Britain and France.[3] To crown the generally unpromising return from this first venture into the realm of collective defence, the Rumanian Foreign Minister told the British
Minister in Bucharest, Sir Reginald Hoare, there was no
truth in Tilea's report of a German ultimatum; the economic
negotiations with Dr. Wohlthat, the Ministerial director for
special duties in the Reich Ministry of Economics, were proceeding normally, Gafencu said, and the tone of the German
negotiators was more conciliatory than before the Prague
coup.[4]

Almost the only positive outcome of the British Government's
efforts was to strike an answering chord, though of doubtful
practical import, in the United States. The American Ambassador, Joseph Kennedy, having heard from Halifax on
17 March the unaccustomed doctrine that states must now 're-
examine their view that people could make themselves secure
by avoiding commitments', told the Foreign Secretary that
Roosevelt had been impressed by recent European events to
the extent of seeing even more clearly the need for revision of
the neutrality laws; he would shortly be calling conferences of
American political leaders to draw up a programme of revision.
Kennedy stated the American attitude to the European situation in a riddle from which at least a grain of comfort could be
extracted; namely that if German aggression took place against
Rumania, the United States would be more ready to act than
if Britain did nothing about Rumania and expected America
to help if Britain was later involved in trouble over aggression
against Greece and Turkey.[5]

The new and dominating problem now entering the picture
with the British Government's change of course was that if
British policy was to commit itself to defending countries even

[1] *D.B.F.P.*, Third Series, IV, pp. 360–1.
[2] *Ibid.*, p. 372.   [3] *Ibid.*, p. 382.
[4] *Ibid.*, pp. 369–70.   [5] *Ibid.*, pp. 364–6, 380.

in East Europe when threatened by Germany, the factor hitherto neglected in British thinking, the Soviet Union, had somehow to be drawn in. Since relations between Rumania and Russia and between Poland and Russia, for historical, territorial, religious and cultural reasons, were as bad as, if not worse than, those between any of these states and Germany, Britain was presented with an element of choice between Russia and the countries immediately within the range of Germany's armaments. To side with Russia meant to run the risk of driving Poland and Rumania into Germany's arms, or at the best of facing them with agonizing decisions which might hamper their effective action in an emergency. To come down on the side of Poland and Rumania meant only, so British Ministers seemed to think, to run the risk of driving Russia into isolation from which it was assumed that she would eventually emerge, in her own good time and in her own interest, in opposition to Germany. It was never seriously considered that she might emerge as a fellow conspirator with Germany against the ruling international system; in any case, the British, according to the American Ambassador, Kennedy, relied on their information that the Russian Air Force was weak and of short range, their Army poor and its industrial backing inadequate, and that 'all the help they could give Poland would be to slip some ammunition'.[1]

The Soviet problem, which remained the continuing theme of British diplomacy until the outbreak of war in September, was at once posed by Litvinov's proposal to Seeds on 19 March of a conference to meet in Bucharest of British, French, Soviet, Polish and Rumanian delegates to consider a programme of common action.[2] Halifax returned a discouraging response when he talked with the Soviet Ambassador, Maisky, who had brought the proposal with him, at the Foreign Office on the same day. Halifax was confident that quick decisions could not be reached at the proposed conference in Bucharest since, for some undisclosed reason, Britain would be unable to send a Minister, and moreover 'to hold such a conference without a certainty that it would be successful was dangerous'. The British Government, Halifax told Maisky, were working on a somewhat similar proposal for making public the solidarity of Britain, France, Russia and Poland, and this would serve both as a 'plain signal of danger to Germany' and a 'rallying point and vitalising force for smaller states'.[3] The proposal, in the

[1] F.R.U.S., 1939, I, p. 99.
[2] D.B.F.P., Third Series, IV, p. 385.
[3] Ibid., pp. 392–3.

shape of a draft declaration by the three Great Powers and Poland, appeared in its final form on the following day and ran: 'we, the undersigned, duly authorised to that effect, hereby declare that, inasmuch as peace and security in Europe may be affected by any action which constitutes a threat to the political independence of any European state, our respective Governments hereby undertake immediately to consult together as to what steps should be taken to offer joint resistance to any such action'.[1] A host of assumptions underlay the declaration: that Russia could find in it a firm assurance that Britain and France would agree to military action, if necessary to repel aggression, when consultations were held; that Germany would be deterred by a mere undertaking of her opponents to consult; that effective co-operation would ever be possible between Poland and Russia as a result of such consultations; and that Poland and Rumania, if the latter consented to be drawn into such a peace front, could openly associate themselves with Russia in the forward line against Nazi Germany.

The unreality of the last of these assumptions was soon made clear. When Bonnet met Halifax at the Foreign Office on 21 March for the purpose of confirming the Anglo-French oral agreement reached in January to regard attacks on Holland, Belgium or Switzerland as attacks on themselves, he described how the Rumanian Ambassador in Paris had explained to him the total unwillingness of his country to be linked in a defence arrangement with Russia; the Rumanian upper classes, he said, were more afraid of Stalin than of Hitler. Bonnet himself thought that the vital thing was to get Poland involved since Russia could not act in co-operation with the Western Powers without Polish agreement.[2] Yet the Poles showed no eagerness to enter agreements except on their own terms and certainly not with Russia as a partner. Colonel Beck was at his most evasive in talking with the British Ambassador, Kennard, about Polish attitudes to the rising dangers in East Europe; he considered a German attack on Rumania most unlikely and although his Vice-Minister for Foreign Affairs took a graver view, he thought Poland was not included in Germany's designs and that a German incursion into Russia or the Ukraine was more probable.[3] The Foreign Minister was most emphatic about Polish difficulties regarding Russia when he dined with Kennard and the visiting British Minister for Overseas Trade, R. S. Hudson, on 22 March. Without being

[1] *D.B.F.P.*, Third Series, IV, pp. 400–1.
[2] *Ibid.*, p. 425.
[3] *Ibid.*, pp. 401–2.

specific, Beck implied that the participation of Russia in the proposed British four-Power declaration would make it practically impossible for Poland to sign, but that Poland might be able to associate herself with Britain and France if Russia were omitted.[1]

Yet the Polish situation was becoming critical with the Lithuanian cession of Memel to the Reich on 22 March and the rapid signature of German treaties with Lithuania, Slovakia and Rumania; a German–Lithuanian treaty including a non-aggression clause was concluded on 22 March, a German treaty of protection with Slovakia on 18 March and a German trade agreement with Rumania on the same day which gave the Reich a large measure of control over all branches of the Rumanian economy.[2]   Halifax accordingly sounded the Polish Ambassador, Count Raczynski, on 24 March concerning a final Polish decision about the proposed British declaration and was told that Hitler would probably regard it as the last straw if Poland were associated with Russia in the declaration. Hence the Polish Government, Raczynski said, had decided to ask Britain 'as an exceptional measure in view of the special circumstances' to give Poland a confidential bilateral understanding to act in the spirit of the proposed declaration.[3]   From this interview stemmed the fatal British decision to guarantee Poland in advance of an agreement with Russia.   Three days later, on 27 March, the government had made up their minds. They regarded Poland as the one strong Power bordering on Germany in the East and as a potentially effective barrier in herself, provided Rumania could be brought into a scheme of common defence as the country most immediately threatened, in the British view, by Germany.   They were preparing, with France, to assist Poland and Rumania if these countries resolved to resist direct or indirect threats to their independence and if they agreed to keep Britain and France informed of developments which threatened their independence.   Poland was to be asked to enter joint defence arrangements with Rumania and to agree to reciprocity to the extent of assisting Britain and France if they opposed German aggression in western Europe or against Yugoslavia.   As for Russia, she was merely to be informed 'at some stage' of these approaches to Warsaw and Bucharest, and her assistance, if only in the form of a benevolent neutrality, would be solicited.   'It is becoming clear,' Halifax wrote to Lindsay for the information of the

---

[1] *Ibid.*, pp. 453–4.
[2] German White Book, 1940, p. 363; *D.G.F.P.*, Series D, VI, pp. 42–5, 91–6.
[3] *D.B.F.P.*, Third Series, IV, pp. 500–3.

State Department, first that 'it is vital to get Poland organised into a peace front against Germany' and secondly that 'our attempts to consolidate the situation will be frustrated if the Soviet Union is openly associated with the initiation of the scheme.'[1]

The government were thus hustled into the unilateral guarantee of Polish independence, which Chamberlain announced in the Commons on 31 March, by rumours of an imminent German attack either on Poland itself or on Rumania, whose defence was considered impossible without Polish support, and by the Polish rejection of a multilateral arrangement including the Soviet Union.[2] A French guarantee was given on the same day. It was an integral, though unpublished, part of the guarantee to Poland that Britain and France should be kept posted on fundamental Polish–German developments since, with the guarantee, the Polish Government now had what the British had always dreaded, the power to commit Britain and France to war through the exercise of their own diplomacy with Germany. It was, however, almost at once evident that the Poles intended to handle their relations with the Reich with the least interference from London or Paris. Kennard reported from Warsaw on 29 March that during the previous fortnight Germany's desiderata had been communicated to the Poles; they included a change in the status of Danzig, a motor road across the Corridor and Poland's adherence to the Anti-Comintern Pact. Kennard was quite unable to extract from the Polish Foreign Ministry any indication of Poland's attitude towards this German *démarche*.[3] When Chamberlain included in his Commons statement on the Polish guarantee an innocuous reference to the desirability of peaceful negotiations between Berlin and Warsaw, Raczynski at once complained to Halifax, expressing his fear of another Munich, seemingly oblivious of the fact that Poland had made her own contribution to the dismemberment of Czechoslovakia.[4] But the Ambassador did not disclose that the Polish Government had in fact replied to the German *démarche* on 26 March and had done so negatively with regard to the first two of the three German demands while preserving silence on the third.[5] Nor did Colonel Beck, when he visited London for talks with British Ministers and officials on 4 April; he denied that exchanges with Germany about

[1] *Ibid.*, pp. 526–30.
[2] 345 H.C. Deb. 5s. Col. 2415.
[3] *D.B.F.P.*, Third Series, IV, p. 543.
[4] *Ibid.*, p. 575.
[5] Polish White Book, *Les relations Polono-Allemandes et Polono-Sovietiques, 1933–1939*, pp. 92–5.

the Corridor had 'passed beyond the stage of conversations' and that negotiations were in progress about Danzig.[1] The British Government later retorted to the German argument that their guarantee had made the Poles obstructive by pointing out that Poland had rejected the German proposals on 26 March whereas the British guarantee was not given until 31 March. But the Poles, as we have seen, were aware as early as 22 March, and certainly by 24 March, that the guarantee was theirs for the asking if they accepted the perfunctory conditions Britain and France were laying down. They knew that they could now afford to take a stronger line with Germany. Joseph Kennedy recorded after a talk with Beck when he was in London in April that he was 'more than happy to have England's support given in the way that it was, i.e. that Poland is the one to determine when England is come to her rescue'.[2]

It was a further British understanding of the guarantee to Poland that it should form part of a wider system of collective security, such as British public opinion was now insistently demanding, and that at some stage Russia should certainly be associated with it. Chamberlain explained his anxieties on this score to Beck when they met in London on 5 April. What people in Britain were asking for, the Prime Minister said, was a banding together of states round Britain and France as a nucleus; the cases of Holland and Belgium as well as Poland and Rumania should be covered, and the system should bring Britain into war if necessary on the principle of defence of the independence of countries within the system, not of protection of the local interests of states which thought they could act defiantly when they had a guarantee from the great Powers. But in reality, the Premier said, a separate guarantee to Poland had emerged which might strike people as selfish. Chamberlain received little satisfaction on this point from Beck, however; the Foreign Minister repeated Polish unwillingness to have Russia brought in on the ground, which British Ministers never thought entirely genuine, that this would only bring the conflict nearer, and although he undertook to open negotiations with Rumania on the issue of joint defence, as Chamberlain insisted, he sounded unhopeful. The chief danger to Rumania, Beck said, came, not from Germany, but from Hungary, and Poland was reluctant to enter into agreements with Bucharest which might drive Hungary into Hitler's arms.

The outcome of Beck's London talks was that the British guarantee was made reciprocal but a permanent treaty was to

[1] D.B.F.P., Third Series, V, pp. 17–18.
[2] F.R.U.S., 1939, I, pp. 113–14.

replace the temporary British undertaking only after certain additional conditions had been settled, including the matter of Polish assistance to Britain and France if they were involved in war in defence of countries in western Europe, which the Polish Government agreed to examine. The Poles, however, gave no undertaking to come to Rumania's help if attacked; they merely agreed to pursue this question in direct talks with the Hungarian and Rumanian Governments.[1] The discussions ended with Beck receiving a further assurance: namely that although Britain would continue to discuss collective defence with Russia, these exchanges must not be regarded as extending Poland's obligations. In other words, Poland would continue to enjoy the right to negative any arrangements with Russia which provided for Soviet–Polish co-operation.

The hope of British Ministers that, even if Soviet–Polish arrangements were unpractical, Poland and Rumania might be brought together through the lever of the British guarantees was soon falsified. The Rumanian Minister in London, Tilea, and the Secretary-General of the Rumanian Foreign Ministry, Cretzianu, who had been sent to London in March because of the feeling in Bucharest that Tilea could not handle the question alone, told Halifax on 10 April that the Rumanian Government did not wish to wait for the outcome of negotiations with the sinuous Colonel Beck before having a British guarantee capable of giving them the heart to stand against Germany's demands. What Rumania was really afraid of, they claimed, was to be presented with a choice between Russia and Germany, or in other words between Bolshevism and Nazification, and any further work on constructing the general defence pact which the British Government were seeking must incline Rumania towards Russia's side.[2] Further pressure for a unilateral British guarantee to Rumania came on 12 April from the Rumanian Foreign Minister, Gafencu, who told Halifax that he would feel fortified when he went to see Hitler on the 18th if he had a British guarantee in his pocket, and from the French, who informed Halifax through Corbin that they definitely intended to give Bucharest a pledge of support whatever the British decided. Corbin saw Halifax with this announcement on 13 April, to be met with the argument that British and French guarantees to Rumania would remove the lever for inducing Poland and Turkey to commit themselves to Rumania's defence as part of the collective scheme on which Britain and France had agreed in principle; besides, Halifax added, with

[1] *D.B.F.P.*, Third Series, V, pp. 1–19, 30–6, 47–9.
[2] *Ibid.*, pp. 74–7.

the Italian annexation of Albania on 7 April, the focus of attention had moved away from Rumania. But Corbin could only say that Daladier's mind was made up; in the circumstances Britain could only follow in the train of French policy. Thus, by 13 April, the British Government had decided in deference to France to give Rumania the guarantee she asked for without awaiting the outcome of the proposed Polish–Rumanian talks and, once more, without consulting Russia. As the British had prophesied to the French, little more was heard of the Polish–Rumanian talks, and yet another wrench was given to the tender plant of co-operation with Russia. Britain had by now switched from the policy of the free hand to a policy of unilateral commitments which went far to ensure that if she was involved in war in Europe it would be with the support of weak rather than strong states.

It is an extraordinary fact that these revolutionary commitments were entered into in the face of the plainest warnings that they could render an association with Russia impossible except on her own terms, and that Stalin, now that Britain and France had thrown down the gage to Hitler in the form of guarantees to Poland and Rumania, would have every inducement to stand aside and allow the impending conflict between the democracies and Germany to run its course to the ruin of both. Stalin had said at the 18th Congress of the Soviet Communist Party in Moscow on 10 March that, while Russia was ready to defend countries threatened by aggression, she had no intention of 'pulling the chestnuts out of the fire' for other people.[1] The fatal separation between Russia and the West, of which this speech was an early warning, began to show itself in Soviet reactions to the British announcement of the Polish guarantee on 31 March. Litvinov complained bitterly to Seeds that by this action Britain had rendered ineffective two proposals on which Russia and the West were working: the Soviet proposal for a conference in Bucharest and Britain's own proposal for a four-Power declaration. Litvinov expressed doubt whether in the event Britain would regard a German attack on Danzig or the Corridor as a threat to Polish independence within the meaning of the guarantee; Russia's safest policy, the Foreign Minister concluded, was to stand aside.[2] Litvinov confessed to an even lower opinion of France; he told Hudson when the Minister for Overseas Trade was in Moscow in early April that France was practically 'done for'; she was 'full of German agents, disaffected and disunited, at

---

[1] *Soviet Documents on Foreign Policy*, ed. Jane Degras, III, pp. 315–22.
[2] *D.B.F.P.*, Third Series, IV, pp. 574–5.

the mercy of certain leading politicians whom he profoundly distrusted'.[1]

Before many days were out Maisky was asking Halifax the obvious question: if Poland and Rumania were making such difficulties about associating with Russia, why did not Britain and France make their pledges of assistance conditional upon Poland and Rumania accepting co-operation with Russia? Halifax replied that the government had thought of this but had decided that if the Soviet association were forced on them they might repudiate it and bolt into the German camp; it was for Russia, Halifax said, to remove the anxieties of the Poles and Rumanians.[2] Seeds in Moscow was adamant about the folly of these countries refusing to accept help without which, if they understood their situation, they would realise they could not survive. They were placing an irresistible temptation before the Soviet Union to sit back and do nothing; there was even a possibility, Seeds wrote on 13 April, that Germany would seek to appease Russia by offers of Bessarabia, parts of eastern Poland, Estonia and Latvia.[3] It would be an ironical fate if Poland and Rumania, having refused offers of Russian help for fear of having to satisfy Soviet territorial claims in the process, were to find themselves overrun by Germany and then compelled to offer these same territories to Russia. Nevertheless, as far as Britain was concerned, the guarantees had now been given and her course was set.

IV

The theme of the peace front had become the major refrain of British policy; but the older *leit-motif* of the harmonisation of the great European Powers continued to sound intermittently as a variation, the two combining to form what Sir Samuel Hoare called the Double Line.[4] The last thing Chamberlain desired was anything in the nature of an ideological war in Europe; the point at issue, he insisted, was one of making clear to Germany how far she could safely go in bending the *status quo* to her will while assuring her that if she observed the rules of peaceful change she could enjoy a generous share of Europe's wealth, a greater share in fact than had ever been her lot before the Nazi revolution. In the Commons on 23 March Chamberlain explained his approach:

I wish to make it clear that there is no desire on the part of His Majesty's Government to stand in the way of any

---

[1] *D.B.F.P.*, Third Series, IV, pp. 584–5.
[2] *Ibid.*, V, pp. 82–4.   [3] *Ibid.*, p. 104.
[4] Viscount Templewood, *Nine Troubled Years*, Chapter XXXIII.

reasonable efforts on the part of Germany to expand her export trade. . . . Nor is the Government anxious to set up in Europe opposing blocks of countries with different ideas about the form of their internal administration.[1]

Consistently with this distaste for ideological divisions, it was natural to assume that Hitler's Axis partner, Mussolini, could be applied to, as in September 1938, to bring the Chancellor to a more accommodating frame of mind, and use was made to this end of the Anglo-Italian agreement based on respect for the *status quo* in the Mediterranean of April 1938, to sign which Chamberlain had broken with his Foreign Secretary, Eden. We must now see how this agreement had fared during and after the Munich crisis. The delay in withdrawing Italian troops from Spain, as Mussolini had promised, had made it impossible to bring the agreement into effect, but on 4 October Count Ciano demanded of the British Ambassador, Lord Perth, a definite statement as to whether Britain wished to make the agreement effective, since a meeting of the Fascist Grand Council was to be held from 6 to 9 October and if there was no answer from London Italian foreign policy would have to change, by which Ciano seemed to mean that ties with Germany would have to be strengthened.[2]   Mussolini had told Chamberlain at the Munich Conference that he meant to withdraw a substantial number of Italians from Spain as he was tired of supporting Franco and Ciano mentioned to Perth a figure of 10,000, which he represented as equivalent to half the total Italian force in Spain, although the British War Office estimated the latter as consisting of 40,000 men.   The question for the British Government was what public and Parliamentary opinion, to say nothing of American opinion, would make of a proposal to consolidate links with Italy by bringing into force an agreement which meant British *de jure* recognition of Mussolini's Abyssinian conquests.   Halifax argued the case for the agreement in a letter to Lindsay in Washington on 27 October: the Spanish civil war, Italian involvement in which had held up the agreement, was no longer a threat to peace in Europe; the agreement might restore to Mussolini some of his freedom of manœuvre and induce him to abandon intrigues against Britain in the Near and Middle East; conversely, if the agreement were allowed to die the Berlin–Rome Axis would be proportionately strengthened.[3]   It remained to be seen whether Mussolini could give some concrete evidence of co-operative-

---

[1] 345 H.C. Deb. 5s. Col. 1462.
[2] *D.B.F.P.*, Third Series, III, pp. 322–3.   [3] *Ibid.*, pp. 343–4.

ness to make the Cabinet's task easier when it came to presenting to Parliament the decision to bring the agreement into force.

In order that Mussolini should be in a position to moderate Hitler's designs it was essential to improve his relations with France. This was a task of the greatest delicacy. The French could be persuaded to join in the appeasement of one dictator when another country was the victim; they were not likely to co-operate in the appeasement of a second when they themselves had to make the sacrifices. By accident or design, Italian anger against France flared up when Chamberlain and Halifax were in the midst of their preparations to visit Rome in January to answer the Italian request to bring the April agreement into effect after the two Ministers had made their peace on the issue with Parliament.[1] On 31 November, at the end of a speech by Ciano in the Chamber of Deputies and in the presence of Mussolini, shouts of 'Tunis', 'Jibuti', 'Corsica' were heard in the Chamber. Perth, reporting on the outbursts on the following day, said that two or three members of the public galleries seemed to have exceeded their instructions and shouted 'Nice' and 'Morocco' although the orders given referred only to Tunis, Jibuti and Corsica.[2] Perth interpreted the incident as implying that 'the feeling has grown in Italy that if the injustices inflicted upon the vanquished by the Peace Treaties are in process of swift revision, how much more ought the injustices suffered by one of the victors at the hands of her own allies to be repaired'.[3] It was impossible for any British observer to have much sympathy for these feelings seeing that Italy had seized Abyssinia with impunity; one British official, Cadogan at the Foreign Office, drew the moral that the Italians thought that the democracies were 'on the run' and that all they had to do was to shout for unjustifiable concessions.[4] In any event, the French were in no mood for concessions; as Daladier and Bonnet told Chamberlain and Halifax when they called at Paris on 10 January on their way to Rome, it would be political suicide for them to speak differently. Chamberlain assured the French that he had no intention of mediating in the Franco-Italian quarrel.[5]

But this did not prevent the Prime Minister probing Italian grievances against France, without however receiving very specific replies, when he talked with Mussolini and Ciano in

[1] 110 H.L. Deb. 5s. Cols. 1621–78; 340 H.C. Deb. 5s. Cols. 207–332; Cmd. 5923 of 1939.
[2] D.B.F.P., Third Series, III, p. 464. [3] Ibid., pp. 496–502.
[4] Ibid., p. 502, n. 2. [5] Ibid., pp. 513–15.

Rome from 11 January until the 13th. Chamberlain expressed puzzlement at the violent Italian objections to the agreement signed with Laval in January 1935, the collapse of which had heralded the present Franco-Italian tension. Mussolini evidently regretted having abandoned his right to protect Italian interests in Tunis as a result of the agreement and claimed that the latter had in any case been invalidated by French opposition to his conquest of Abyssinia despite Laval's alleged consent to this conquest in 1935. But Chamberlain sensed that the French problem was altogether dangerous ground for British Ministers to tread. Mussolini and his Foreign Minister, however, were hardly more forthcoming about the promised withdrawals from Spain; they refused to accept Halifax's denials of the truth of their statements that no Italian planes or artillery had gone to Spain in recent months. Moreover, Chamberlain found little light thrown during his Roman journey on the main question worrying him: what were Hitler's intentions and was there any likelihood that Mussolini had the power to divert him from them if they were aggressive in character?[1]

There the matter rested. By the beginning of April the Franco-Italian dispute seemed to have eased. François-Poncet, who had taken over the French Embassy in Rome after leaving Berlin, was confiding to British officials that the Italian demands in regard to Jibuti and the Suez Canal 'should present no difficulty' and that, as regards Tunis, the Italians would probably be satisfied with some arrangement to safeguard the status of the Italian community.[2] The truth seemed to be that Mussolini had perhaps after all been forced to echo the demands against France which were voiced in the Italian Chamber in December, but then realised the need to climb down as a result of the uncompromising French attitude, Chamberlain's declaration of support for vital French interests in the Commons on 6 February, and Hitler's Prague *coup* of 15 March, the last of which indicated that the Chancellor was more interested in grinding Germany's own axes than in helping to sharpen Italy's. Nevertheless, an Italy thwarted by France, cold-shouldered by Germany and sermonised by Britain could not but look around for an outlet somewhere.

On 20 March, in the immediate aftermath of Hitler's Prague *coup*, Chamberlain tried to cash some of the credit he had tried so hard to build up in Rome by writing a personal appeal to the Duce for an Italian move to allay the newly awakened tension; such a move might be a positive intervention with Germany or the negative one of refraining from any aggressive

[1] *D.B.F.P.*, Third Series, III, pp. 517–21.   [2] *Ibid.*, IV, p. 359.

action against France or Albania in the general disarray created by Germany's action in Czechoslovakia.[1] At the end of March Mussolini's reply came with its clear indication that Italy was still primarily an aggrieved Power and that her grievances were the tap-root of her policy; 'I do not consider I can take the initiative,' was the burden of Mussolini's letter, 'before Italy's rights have been recognised.'[2] Once again, as in 1935, the Duce was demanding his price, in terms of other people's territory, before he would consent to act as a general peacemaker. By 4 April it was evident that Italy proposed to satisfy her needs, this time against Albania, the purpose being, the British Government were informed by their Minister in Durazzo, to be in a position to hold Corfu, which the Italians intended to occupy in the event of a general war in Europe.   Two days later Perth warned Ciano on Halifax's behalf that no action should be taken which might lead to a clash of arms and thus increase the anxieties which at the moment beset Europe; Perth pointed out that both Italy and Britain had recognised the independence of Albania as well as the integrity and inalienability of its frontiers at the Ambassadors' Conference on 9 November 1921.[3] Simultaneously Halifax was asking Phipps to give the French a 'delicate nudge' to accept an offer Ciano had made to Perth to open negotiations on the Franco-Italian dispute; if constructive lines were established between Paris and Rome it might take the heat out of the Mediterranean situation.[4]

On the fateful Good Friday, 7 April, of the Italian landings in Albania Halifax demanded formal assurances from Mussolini that the 'solution of the Italo-Albanian question will take place in such a form as not to provoke a crisis in Anglo-Italian relations or the international situation in general'.[5] Anyone who had closely followed British efforts to convert Italy into a satisfied Power would know what significance to attach to this warning.   Later the same day, in a more peremptory note, Perth was instructed to demand 'the frankest and fullest explanation of the Italian landings on the Albanian cost and the future intentions of the Italian government'.[6] The 1935 situation had repeated itself: Mussolini had embarked on adventures at the moment when Britain was looking to him to help keep Germany within bounds; yet the mere fact that Britain was keen to have this assistance assured Mussolini that he had little to fear from her.

Again as in 1935, though this time with less public demand

[1] *D.B.F.P.*, Third Series, IV, pp. 402–3.	[2] *Ibid.*, pp. 572–4.
[3] *D.B.F.P.*, Third Series, V, p. 125.	[4] *Ibid.*, pp. 126–7.
[5] *Ibid.*, p. 129.	[6] *Ibid.*, p. 131.

for collective action behind them, the British Government had no intention to make war against Italy, which alone would have restored the situation. Halifax announced to Corbin on 8 April that the Cabinet did not even propose denouncing the Anglo-Italian agreement of April 1938, even though this pledged Italy to respect the *status quo* in the Mediterranean, in the hope that the threat of denunciation could later be used to deter further Italian acts of aggression. 'In the long run,' Halifax said, 'the right answer might be found to a tightening of the mutual obligations of support as between ourselves, on the one hand, and Greece and Turkey.'[1] Bonnet and Daladier were then informed by Phipps that Britain was giving assurances of help to Athens in view of reports of an impending Italian attack on Corfu and the French Ministers replied that they too would declare war on Italy if Greek territory were attacked and Britain came to Greece's help.[2] At the same time Mussolini was told that Britain would continue to respect the 1938 agreement with Italy but only in return for assurances about Greece. These were given by the Italian Chargé d'Affaires at Athens to the Greek Prime Minister on 10 April in the form of a declaration that 'Fascist Italy confirms that it is her intention to respect in the most absolute manner the territorial and insular integrity of Greece.'[3] Perth was also able to extract from Ciano, as a further *quid pro quo* for British acquiescence in the annexation of Albania, Mussolini's promise that all Italian volunteers would be withdrawn from Spain as soon as Franco's victory parade had been held, and this was anticipated on about 20 April.[4] The government concluded that the 1938 agreement with Italy was proving its value and the refusal to scrap it in a fit of pique after the events of Good Friday was felt to be abundantly justified.

The principal consequence of the Italian attack on Albania, however, like that of Hitler's Prague *coup*, was to accelerate the now quickly gathering momentum of the process of building British-inspired defence arrangements between threatened states. It also played its part in hustling the British Government into making unilateral guarantees in preference to a unified general system of collective defence. The British plan had been to give a pledge to help the Greek Government with all the support in Britain's power if action were taken threatening Greek independence which the Greeks decided to resist by their national forces; but not to extend this guarantee for the time being to Rumania. The guarantee to Rumania, as we have

---

[1] *D.B.F.P.*, Third Series, V, pp. 136–8.   [2] *Ibid.*, p. 148.
[3] *Ibid.*, p. 161.   [4] *Ibid.*, pp. 149–51.

seen, was to be held in reserve as a lever for getting Poland and Turkey committed to take action in defence of the *status quo* in south-east Europe. Halifax inquired of the Turkish Government on 11 April if they could commit themselves to give a similar pledge of assistance to Greece as the British proposed to give since the existing Greco-Turkish treaty only committed Ankara to go to Greece's defence against attack from a Balkan state. The Turkish reply was that they would only consent to pledge themselves to one side in a possible conflict in the Mediterranean if they had a guarantee for their own security.[1] From this sprang the Anglo-Turkish agreement announced in the House of Commons on 12 May; this foreshadowed a later, long-term arrangement in the interest of the national security of both countries and in the meantime pledged both countries to effective co-operation involving all mutual aid and assistance in the event of aggression leading to war in the Mediterranean area.[2] But, while this development was on foot, the French were showing their determination to couple their own pledge to Greece with a similar commitment to Rumania and the British Government were compelled to abandon their plan to keep their guarantee to Rumania in reserve.[3]

Thus, when Chamberlain made his announcement in the Commons on 13 April and Daladier his at a press interview in Paris on the same day, when they dealt with the after-effects of the Albanian aggression for their respective policies, it was seen that the two countries were now committed, separately and without any apparent connection between the two commitments, to defend Greece and Rumania, and that negotiations were on foot for a similar pledge to Turkey.[4] As for Britain, the policy of opposition to undefined commitments had been abandoned with a vengeance, but it had been replaced by a piecemeal system of guarantees, some reciprocal, some unilateral, into which the government had been precipitated by domestic public opinion, French pressures, swiftly changing rumours as to where the next Axis blow would fall and the importuning of leaders of small nations. The peace front was, to all appearances, more like a patchwork quilt than an armoured rampart.

[1] *D.B.F.P.*, Third Series, V, p. 187.
[2] 347 H.C. Deb. 5s. Cols. 952–3.
[3] *D.B.F.P.*, Third Series, V, pp. 183–4, 186, 197.
[4] 346 H.C. Deb. 5s. Col. 13; *Temps*, 14 April 1939.

CHAPTER XXII

LAST DAYS OF EUROPE

I

Through the spring and summer of 1939 British Ministers, like most European politicians, considered that the risk of Russia coming to terms with Nazi Germany need not seriously be taken into account. Russia, they thought, must ultimately be involved in defence of the *status quo* in any general conflict in East Europe even if the problem of associating her with the guaranteed states, Poland and Rumania, could not be surmounted in the remaining months of peace; but her effective contribution could not be considerable. The immediate need seemed to be to impress upon Germany as soon as possible after the Prague *coup* British and French determination to stand by countries likely to be the next victims of Nazism and to develop a resolute if conciliatory frame of mind in those states, especially in Poland and Rumania. This could not be achieved, it was thought, by forcing upon them an alliance with Russia which many of their ruling classes feared as much as they feared a German attack. If the French Right could say in 1936 'better Hitler than Blum', the Polish and Rumanian Right (and there was hardly any other effective political force in those states) could say 'better Hitler than Stalin'. But would Stalin agree to act as an assistant in Anglo-French security schemes, a 'hired labourer', to use Zdanov's expression, standing by to give additional aid if required, while more than half-convinced that Britain and France lacked both resolution and strength to take their share of the German fury when eventually unleashed?

Soviet anxieties on this score were plainly indicated by the proposals for common action which Seeds in Moscow was given on 18 April, after Stalin's plea a month earlier for a conference in Bucharest had already been rejected by Britain in favour of the policy of unilateral guarantees. There were six main items in Russia's April proposals: Britain, France and Russia were to conclude a military aid agreement of five years' duration; the three Powers were to promise to give all aid in their power to all the East European states bordering the Soviet Union; they were also to agree 'in the shortest possible time' on the specific military assistance they were to give under the first two heads; the British guarantee to Poland was to be made specifically operative against Germany, to avoid any suggestion that Russia might be the aggressor; the three signatories were to commit themselves not to make a separate peace after the outbreak of hostilities or enter into negotiations with the aggressors; and they were to seek agreement with Turkey on measures of mutual military assistance.[1]

The British reaction was to recoil from this comprehensive proposal with all its delicate political issues and its implication that Russia was now to be added to the states capable of embroiling Britain in war. The first task, in the Government's opinion, was to make practical arrangements for the safety of the states most directly menaced; only after this stage could Britain consider extending the arrangements to cover countries like the Soviet Union herself, which were not so immediately in danger. Moreover, even though the Turks were fully prepared for joint defence arrangements with Russia, the Poles professed to regard them as highly provocative to Germany and it was imperative in the British view, to maintain Polish 'self-reliance'. Then what was Russia to do? Halifax's reply was that she should follow the British and French example and give unilateral guarantees to the threatened countries, if these wanted her assistance.[2]

The French, so Phipps reported on 24 April, agreed with Britain's objections to the Soviet plan; they were even more confident than the British that Poland would resist even a unilateral Soviet guarantee. But they understood Russia's aversion to being involved in war on Poland's or any other country's behalf without a firm pledge of help from the Western democracies; and they saw no reason, after Poland's behaviour in the Czech crisis, to humour Warsaw. The French Government therefore suggested taking the bull by the horns and making a straightforward offer of a tripartite pact to Russia under which Britain and France would agree to help her and she them if either side was at war in defence of the *status quo* in Central or East Europe.[3] The proposal was easy for the French to make as they already had their 1935 alliance with Russia and their interest in having the German army engaged on the eastern front in any general war was even greater than that of Britain. Nevertheless, it was a suggestion, raised at an early stage of the long negotiations with Russia, which the British would have done well to adopt. What prevented them doing so, according to Halifax, was the thought that the proposal

---

[1] *Soviet Documents*, III, p. 329.
[2] *D.B.F.P.*, Third Series, V, pp. 266–9.
[3] *Ibid.*, pp. 294–5.

must involve at least indirect Soviet assistance to Poland, which the Poles had made abundantly clear they did not want.[1]

Nevertheless, Halifax began to appreciate the force of Soviet fears of being left to bear the brunt of Germany's war machine. In a talk with Gafencu on 25 April, when the Rumanian Foreign Minister was in London during his European tour, the British Minister emphasised the importance of 'keeping the Soviet Union in play', despite Gafencu's protests that Rumania was caught between two fires, the German and the Soviet, and that Rumania's chief interest must be to try to maintain the peace by avoiding giving provocation to Germany through acceptance in advance of Soviet offers of help.   Halifax, seemingly thinking aloud, wondered if Russia would be attracted by a scheme under which she agreed to give help to Rumania or Poland, if these countries expressly desired it, but only after Britain and France were definitely engaged in their defence.[2]   The major considerations actuating the British Government were set out in dispatches to the British envoys in Warsaw and Bucharest three days later.   They comprised four negatives: not to forego the hopes of Soviet help in case of war; not to jeopardise the emerging common front by disregarding the susceptibilities of Poland and Rumania; not to forfeit the sympathy of the world by conniving at the expansion of Soviet influence in East Europe, thus giving a handle to German anti-Communist propaganda; and not to endanger peace by provoking violent action by Germany.   The British Government, in other words, did not regard war as inevitable; the aim of the peace front was to bring Germany to the conference table, not to prepare for war.   In accordance with these principles a British formula was shaped which then went to France for approval before being forwarded to Moscow in reply to the Soviet proposals of 18 April.   In this the initiative was once more to lie with Russia: she was to be called on to make a public declaration of assistance to Britain and France, should this be desired, if these countries were involved in hostilities as a result of 'new obligations accepted on behalf of certain East European countries'.   The latter would not be named in the declaration.[3]

Without showing exceptional insight, French Ministers doubted whether such a formula, with its relegation of Russia to an auxiliary sought only in the most desperate straits, would be acceptable to Stalin.   Maisky was soon describing it to

[1] *D.B.F.P.*, Third Series, pp. 358–9.
[2] *Ibid.*, V, pp. 321–34.
[3] *Ibid.*, pp. 357–8.

Halifax as one of 'various patchwork attempts at strengthening international security' and much less valuable than a 'more comprehensive effort to include all possible points of danger'.[1] The French insisted that it was above all necessary to conclude as rapidly as possible an agreement for Poland and Rumania to receive at least indirect assistance from Russia.[2] The danger of delay was sharply underlined by Hitler's truculent Reichstag speech on 28 April, when he denounced the Anglo-German naval treaty of 1935 and the Anglo-German agreement for the exchange of naval information of 1937, and by the replacement of Litvinov, with his collective security background and greater accessibility to Western diplomats, by Molotov as Soviet Foreign Minister on 3 May. Other sinister indications followed. Sir Percy Loraine, writing from the British Embassy in Rome on 5 May, recounted an 'astonishing theory' of François-Poncet to the effect that Stalin had dismissed Litvinov in order to make an arrangement with Germany which would allow Hitler to attack Poland and retake the Corridor without fear of Soviet interference; on the following day the Foreign Office was in possession of a message from Dr. Goerdeler, a former Mayor of Leipzig, that the German generals had had a 'new and unexpected offer from the Soviet Union which might entirely change the situation'.[3] Halifax's reply to Loraine gave the British interpretation of Litvinov's dismissal:

That Stalin contemplates arrangements with Germany (he wrote) is not obvious: but he may think isolation and complete neutrality (which would favour Germany in practice) preferable to association with the Western Powers if they will not guarantee the Soviet Union against a German attack.[4]

In spite of this reading of Soviet intentions the British Government did not propose favouring Russia with any such guarantee. Their eventual reply, given two days after Litvinov's dismissal, still expected from Russia a public offer to help Britain and France, if desired, should they be in difficulties in attempting to fulfil their obligations in East Europe. Soviet assistance continued to be regarded as a convenience which must in no way embarrass its recipients. As to the Soviet plan of 18 April, it was said to take too little account of practical difficulties and would take too long to negotiate.[5] The stumbling-block, Halifax told Maisky when explaining the British

[1] *D.B.F.P.*, Third Series, V, pp. 373–5.   [2] *Ibid.*, pp. 404–5.
[3] *Ibid.*, pp. 429, 433, n. 2.   [4] *Ibid.*, p. 451.
[5] *Ibid.*, pp. 448–50.

reply, was that the Soviet plan would involve Soviet support
for Poland and Rumania since it was an offer of assistance to
Britain and France when engaged on those countries' behalf,
and 'this is exactly what all our information has led us to believe would cause great embarrassment to these countries'.[1]
The striking feature of the British formula, however, was that it
made no mention of Western assistance to Russia, thus touching
off all the old Soviet fears that Russia would find herself fighting
Germany alone. These fears seemed strengthened when
Molotov asked Seeds after receiving the British note whether
Britain meant to start military conversations with Russia at
once, and received the reply that there was no objection to such
conversations but that a Soviet declaration on the lines proposed
was all that was needed for the present. The Russians drew,
or affected to draw, little comfort from Halifax's reminder that
under the British formula Britain and France would be already
engaged in defence of Poland and Rumania when Soviet help
was applied for and hence Russia need have no reasonable fear
of being left alone.[2] A Tass communiqué published on 10
May drew a caricature of the British plan as seen through Soviet
eyes:

> The Soviet Government must give immediate help to
> Britain and France in case the latter are involved in military
> operations in execution of the obligations assumed by them
> in regard to Poland and Rumania. However, in these coun-
> ter-proposals the English Government does not say anything
> about any help which the Soviet Union must receive from
> France and Great Britain on a basis of reciprocity if the Soviet
> Union is similarly involved in military operations in execu-
> tion of its obligations in regard to these states in East Europe.[3]

The Soviet decision to publicise its own version of the state
of the negotiations was in itself significant. It implied that a
process had already begun on the Soviet side of advertising the
offers the Western democracies were making in case Germany
should wish to better them, and of preparing public opinion at
home for whatever decision the Soviet Government would ultimately make. At the same time, the public statement of the
Soviet case was no doubt designed to increase the pressure of
public opinion in Britain on the Government.

Maisky harped on the question of reciprocity when he saw
Halifax on 11 May, this time referring to the possibility that

[1] *D.B.F.P.*, Third Series, V, pp. 453–4.
[2] *Ibid.*, pp. 469–71, 479–80.
[3] *Soviet Documents*, III, p. 330.

Russia might be engaged in defence of the Baltic states, which were not covered by the British and French guarantees, and hence, under the British formula, could not expect British or French assistance. Halifax admitted that this was so, but pointed out that Russia would similarly not be committed to render assistance if Britain and France were involved against German aggression in western Europe.[1] The demand for reciprocity nevertheless remained the central item in the Soviet rejoinder of 15 May. Britain and France, it was insisted, would not be expressly committed to assist the Soviet Union in the British plan and Russia's north-western frontier with Finland, Estonia and Latvia would be left outside the collective system. Reciprocity would only be secured, in the Soviet view, by a definite pact of mutual assistance between the three Powers, by a joint guarantee of the three to the states of Central and East Europe, including Latvia, Estonia and Finland, and by a concrete three-Power agreement on the form of assistance they were to give each other and the guaranteed states if the emergency arose.[2] Molotov, in explaining these proposals to Seeds, was able to make skilful use of the differences now apparent in the British and French positions. The French, always more sensitive than the British to the importance of an arrangement with Russia if the Anglo-French guarantees to Poland and Rumania were to be made effective, wished to settle at once for a tripartite pact, which Britain regarded as fatal to relations with the guaranteed states. By accident or design Bonnet had allowed the Soviet Ambassador in Paris, Suritz, to see the French draft proposals sent to Britain, in which the Anglo-French divergence was clear to see, and the Soviet Foreign Minister was able to exploit it.

Again, the British Ministers took their time over formulating their reply to these Soviet objections. Halifax explained to Seeds that other interested governments had to be consulted and the matter thrashed out at a Cabinet meeting specially called for 24 May. 'We would rather delay for a few days longer,' Chamberlain said, 'than hastily take a step which might result in the work we have already done crumbling before our very eyes.'[3] The Polish and Rumanian Governments now began to be seriously sounded for the first time on their reactions to a new British formula providing for reciprocity as between the three Powers, Britain, Russia, France, in the event of attack by another Power or their involvement in war in

[1] *D.B.F.P.*, Third Series, V, 528–9.
[2] *Soviet Documents*, III, pp. 330–1.
[3] 347 H.C. Deb. 5s. Col. 1839 (19 May 1939).

defence of a state which had requested their assistance. Halifax sensed that 'we may be approaching a point where we have to choose between some such formula and a breakdown in the negotiations, with all that that might involve'.[1] The new form of words was intently discussed by the Foreign Secretary with Daladier and Bonnet when the three met in Paris on 20 May during Halifax's journey to a League Council meeting in Geneva. Halifax explained his objections to the kind of triple pact providing for straightforward military assistance between the three Powers which the French desired, arguing that it might provoke Germany to violent action and divide opinion in Britain when it was now united behind the government. Daladier said, even so, that he failed to see why Britain should make such difficulties, but he agreed to let Bonnet join Halifax in pressing Maisky in Geneva to accept a new British formula, known as draft E, designed to meet Polish and Rumanian objections to help from Russia. This provided for mutual assistance between the three Powers if one of them was engaged in hostilities defending a state which was the victim of aggression and which had asked for the assistance of that country. Daladier, who had been more successful all along in gauging Soviet reactions, doubted whether even this would please the Russians, but he agreed to give it a try. Two days later at Geneva Maisky confirmed Daladier's doubts; Rumania and Poland, Maisky said, might collapse suddenly or move to Germany's side. What would be the position of the three-Power pact then? Halifax found himself falling back on draft B, which provided for direct mutual assistance between the three and for assistance when one of the three was involved in hostilities through helping another state. 'I think the choice between us is disagreeably plain,' Halifax concluded, 'that is, the breakdown of the negotiations or draft B.'

But another objection came from the Soviet side. The British might have conceded the principle of reciprocity, Maisky agreed in a discussion with Vansittart before the British delegation left for Geneva, but the possibility remained that the states lying between Russia and Germany might become satellites of the Reich, like Czechoslovakia before 15 March, and allow German forces through their territory to attack Russia. Would Britain and France be committed to help in such a case, where there was no question of Russia being attacked on account of the assistance she was rendering to a third state and where there might be doubt whether any definite attack, at least in its early stages, was being mounted

---

[1] D.B.F.P., Third Series, V, pp. 597–8.

by Germany? The British draft would have to be revised to take account of this possibility, but this time in the light of a clearer British appreciation that Russia might after all come to terms with Germany, or alternatively stand clear of a German conflict with the democracies and emerge triumphant as the *tertius gaudens*. Vansittart referred to this possibility in a minute written in the Foreign Office on 22 May. He remembered some words used by General Weygand: 'it was essential if there must be war, to try to involve the Soviet Union in it, otherwise at the end of the war the Soviet Union, with her army intact and England and Germany in ruins, would dominate Europe'.[1] This reasoning was a strong inducement for Britain to make yet a further step towards the Soviet position in the hope of avoiding a Soviet declaration of neutrality if war came.

Hence emerged from the British delegation at Geneva draft F sent to Russia on 25 May. This provided for mutual assistance between Britain, France and Russia when one went to war in defence of another state against aggression and that state had requested its assistance; or, secondly, when one was at war through defending a state which had called for its help to defend its neutrality (this was a limited step to meet Soviet fears of Polish or Rumanian collaboration with Germany); or, thirdly, when one of the three was itself the object of an aggressive attack.[2] To this complex formula was added a link with the League of Nations, the preamble of the draft speaking of 'giving effect to the principle of mutual support against aggression which is embodied in the Covenant of the League of Nations'. This phrase, the British Government argued, was essential to win public support for the pact at home; the idea seemed to be that those who were shocked at the idea of an alliance with Communist Russia might revise their views when they saw that it was being framed under the aegis of Geneva. 'I presume,' said Churchill, 'that all the engagements into which we are entering, or will enter, will be in harmony with the letter and the spirit of the Covenant.'[3]

When Molotov spoke at the Supreme Soviet on 31 May he revealed how conscious the Russians were becoming of being courted by both democratic and Axis Powers. 'The endeavour of the non-aggressive European Powers to attract the U.S.S.R. into collaboration in the cause of resistance to aggression,' the Foreign Minister said, 'has to be acknowledged as one of the

---

[1] *D.B.F.P.*, Third Series, V, p. 639, n. 1.
[2] *Ibid.*, pp. 649–50.
[3] 345 H.C. Deb. 5s. Col. 2498 (3 April 1939).

chief features of modern times.' 'At the same time,' Molotov said, 'while conducting negotiations with England and France we see no necessity for refusing commercial relations with such countries as Germany and Italy.' Trade and credit talks with Germany, Molotov revealed, had been going on since January and though they had been interrupted owing to differences of opinion, they were now likely to be resumed. As to the negotiations with Britain and France, Molotov said, the Western proposals of 25 May envisaged help to the Soviet Union if she were engaged in defence of the countries Britain and France had guaranteed but made no reference to the three analogous countries on Russia's north-western borders, Estonia, Finland and Latvia.[1] This omission was rectified in a new Soviet plan circularised to Britain and France on 2 June. According to this, mutual assistance was to be operative between the three Powers in cases of direct aggression against one or other of the three by a European Power; or when one or other was involved in war as a result of direct aggression by that Power against Belgium, Greece, Turkey, Rumania, Poland, Latvia, Estonia or Finland, or as a result of assistance rendered by one or other of the three to another European state which had requested that assistance in order to resist violations of its neutrality. There was to be agreement in the shortest possible time on the methods, forms and extent of assistance to be afforded in these three cases, and this agreement was to come into force simultaneously with the main agreement. Consultation was to take place where there was a threat of aggression by a European Power and the prohibition of a separate peace by any of the signatories which had figured in the original Soviet plan was repeated.[2]

II

The differences as they now appeared between Soviet thinking and that of Britain and France seemed in certain respects to be narrowing. Britain and France had conceded the principle of reciprocity and mutual assistance against a direct attack. Russia had at least made one step towards defence of the *status quo* in the West by agreeing to assist Britain and France if they were engaged in war through coming to Belgium's defence. The remaining difficulties seemed not beyond the bounds of negotiability. There was the question of the unwilling candidate for a guarantee: that is, a situation in which Germany attacked one of the signatories through a bordering state which,

---

[1] *Soviet Documents*, III, pp. 332–40.
[2] *Ibid.*, pp. 340–1.

having become a satellite of the Reich, did not wish to avail itself of the protection of the three-Power treaty. The British hoped that consultation would be sufficient to take care of such cases.[1] There was the Soviet proposal for naming the guaranteed states in the treaty; to this Britain objected, mindful of the fears of Poland, Rumania and the Baltic states lest they incur Germany's wrath by having their names published in a collective defence treaty signed by the Soviet Union. Furthermore, the list of guaranteed states in the Soviet plan pushed the principle of reciprocity too far in Russia's favour in British opinion; all the states on Russia's western border would be covered whereas some of Britain's and France's neighbours, the Netherlands and Switzerland in particular, were left out of the picture. British Ministers also strongly objected to the idea of the coming into force of the political treaty having to await that of the accompanying military agreement. Military co-operation with Russia was uncharted territory for the Western democracies; if it had to be fully explored first the psychological impact of the peace front on Germany would be rendered ineffective through delay. The outstanding issue, however, was whether pledges of help should be imposed on countries like the Baltic states and Finland which had repeatedly made clear that they wanted no such thing, at least from Russia. Maisky was adamant that they should be imposed in his talks in early June with Halifax. 'The problem of the Baltic states,' he said, 'was the fundamental problem without which the negotiations could not be brought to a successful conclusion . . . if agreement could not be reached on this, it would be very difficult to reach an agreed formula.'[2]

Nevertheless, William Strang, of the Foreign Office, was sent off to Moscow to help argue British reservations on this issue with Seeds, to the tune of complaints from the French, who had resigned the lead in the negotiations to London, that a person of front rank eminence should be sent. Again, the Soviet authorities were quick to make public the state of play, authorising a press communiqué on 16 June recording the Foreign Ministry's adverse reactions to the British and French statements of their positions. On the same day Seeds reported on the Soviet reply. The Soviet Government could not agree to the exclusion of Estonia, Finland and Latvia, which Britain and France proposed; 'they would be unable to reconcile themselves to the position of inequality, humiliating for the Soviet Union'. If the Baltic states could not agree, the Soviet reply

[1] *D.B.F.P.*, Third Series, VI, pp. 3–4.
[2] *Ibid.*, pp. 50–1.

stated, this must mean the abandonment of the whole idea of incorporating guarantees to third states in the agreement. Russia in this case could only offer an undertaking of mutual assistance in the event of a direct attack on one or other of the three signatories.[1] But this would be disastrous for Britain; it would set at nought the entire British purpose in the negotiations, namely to secure a backing of Soviet support, if needed, for the guarantees already to be given to Poland, Rumania, Greece and Turkey. There followed a frantic search to bridge the gap and if verbal dexterity alone had been in question the deed would have been done. Halifax finally came out on 17 June with a wording of article 1 of the draft treaty which pledged mutual support against direct aggression, or in the event of aggression against another European state which menaced the security of one of the signatories (here was an indirect reference to the case of the Baltic states), or where aggression occurred against another European state which one of the contracting parties, with the consent of that state, had undertaken to assist.[2] But the Soviet reply of 22 June was a blank rejection, condemning the new Anglo-French formula as a mere repetition of previous proposals.[3]

Halifax, in extreme puzzlement, sent for Maisky and asked him for an explanation of the Soviet attitude. So far, he said, Britain and France had made all the concessions; they were even considering whether they might agree to naming the eight guaranteed states, though this would have to be in a secret appendix. Russia on her side had yielded not an inch. Did she really want an agreement?[4] The reply came, not from Maisky, but from Seeds, who wrote on 24 June that she probably did if she could obtain 'an international warrant for going to the assistance of the Baltic states even without the assent or contrary to the wishes of the government concerned.' Seeds gave an explanation in terms of Soviet fear of the Baltic states moving into the German orbit and becoming a launching site for German attacks on Russia's security about which she could do nothing until the actual attack came. 'They therefore have it in mind,' he considered, 'to secure our assistance or at least apparent connivance should they ever find it expedient to intervene in the Baltic states . . . on the plea that the government and ruling classes, as distinct from the rest of the population, were about to compound with Germany.'[5]

[1] *Soviet Documents*, III, pp. 349–50.
[2] *D.B.F.P.*, Third Series, VI, 92–3.
[3] *Soviet Documents*, III, p. 351.
[4] *D.B.F.P.*, Third Series, VI, pp. 152–3.
[5] *Ibid.*, pp. 160–3.

Again, the British position was left with no alternative but to move. This time, on 27 June, Halifax agreed to the naming of the states protected by the agreement; the list was to include the Baltic states and Finland, together with the Netherlands, Switzerland and Luxemburg, which did not figure in the Soviet list, but the government preferred the list to be secret and not included in the public treaty. But Halifax insisted that if this far-reaching concession were made no further difficulties must be raised.[1] But more difficulties were raised. When Russia replied on 4 July, apart from objecting to the inclusion of the two Western states, with whom she had no diplomatic relations, she raised the intricate and ultimately crippling question of indirect aggression, which had been lying just beneath the surface since the beginning of the negotiations. Suppose a government succumbed to Germany, not through armed invasion, but by reason of a campaign of brutal threats such as that to which President Hacha was exposed before the fall of Prague? Should Britain, France and Russia have the right to call for each other's help if they found themselves at war with Germany in consequence of having come to the assistance of a country in such a plight? The concept of indirect aggression, with which Western diplomacy was unfamiliar, raised far-ranging difficulties of definition. The Soviet note of 4 July identified it with 'an internal *coup d'état* or reversal of policy in the interests of the aggressor'.[2] Any such definition would confer on a signatory of the proposed pact the licence to interfere in almost any turn of events in a neighbouring state of which it disapproved, and to do so with the connivance of the other two signatories.

The British negotiators now began to realise that the end of the compromises they could reasonably expect to make was in sight. Little or nothing in the way of concessions had so far come from the Soviet side to make the going easier; on the contrary, no sooner had Britain and France given way on some point 'fundamental' to the Soviet Union than they found themselves facing yet another equally 'fundamental' difficulty presented by Moscow. Further concessions were now offered by the West; again it was insisted that these would be the last though more still were yet to come. On 6 July Seeds was instructed that Britain no longer insisted on the inclusion of the Netherlands, Switzerland and Luxemburg in the agreed list of states whose protection was to be a ground for calling in the assistance of the other signatories, but that there must be at least provision for consultation if these Western states were

[1] *Ibid.*, pp. 173–4.   [2] *Ibid.*, pp. 251–2.

victims of attack. Moreover, while Britain, with immense reluctance, now agreed to some definition of indirect aggression
being included, this must not be in article 1, which stated the
basic obligations of mutual assistance between the parties, but
should be attached to the unpublished list of protected states.
In any case, Britain wished to have her own definition of indirect aggression accepted; this was framed to defend the
guaranteed states against undue interference in their internal
affairs and was intended to cover 'action accepted by the state
in question under threat of force by another Power and involving the abandonment by it of its independence and sovereignty'. Seeds was told that if no agreement could be reached
along these lines they would have to fall back on the simple
tripartite treaty, even though the British had long objected to
this as affording them no assurance of Soviet assistance when
they were fulfilling the guarantees they had so hastily assumed
after the Prague *coup*.[1]

The fact was, however, that by this stage Britain could hardly
afford to let the negotiations fail. There would be an uproar
in Parliament, the scene of so many recent confessions of failure
by the government. The Opposition would repeat the charge
they had been making since March that vital allies were being
lost through class prejudices of Ministers. Even apart from
the government's own position, the guarantees to the East
European states could not be made effective, it was now clear,
without Soviet participation. Moreover, if Russia remained
neutral she might well be the only state to profit from the coming war in Europe whichever side was the formal victor, while
if she came in on Germany's side the dice would be loaded
against the prospects of an Anglo-French victory. Nevertheless, the refusal of the East European states to accept help from
the Soviet Union, or to be associated with pacts which gave
Russia the right to send troops into their territory whenever she
disapproved of their domestic politics, remained as strong as
ever. Gripenberg, the Finnish Minister in London, was quite
explicit on this point when he saw Halifax on 5 July.[2] The
Latvian and Estonian Governments were equally adamant in
notes to Britain on 12 and 17 June respectively.[3] Polish and
Rumanian dread of any such arrangement with Russia had
long been notorious. Similarly, in western Europe, the Netherlands Minister saw Halifax on 1 July, telling him that his
government strongly objected to the Powers giving each other

---

[1] *D.B.F.P.*, Third Series, VI, p. 276.
[2] *Ibid.*, pp. 307–8.
[3] *Ibid.*, pp. 48–9, 96.

guarantees affecting Holland's position, and even threatened to publish his statement if the Moscow negotiations in this matter were persisted in.[1] What haunted all the small states of Europe was the spectre of a war of armed ideologies similar to the Spanish conflict on their soil.

In these circumstances the Russians could not but know that they could dictate their own terms to Britain and France without much fear of the talks being broken off while their own negotiations with Germany were proceeding. Molotov told Seeds and the French Ambassador, Naggiar, with the utmost bluntness on 9 July that the Soviet definition of indirect aggression could not be modified and that there was no prospect of a political agreement until an understanding covering specific measures of military co-operation had been framed and signed. As for the British requirement that the Netherlands, Switzerland and Luxemburg be included in the system, the only terms on which Russia could accept this, Molotov said, was that these countries must agree to diplomatic relations with the Soviet Union, and Poland and Turkey must first conclude pacts of military assistance with her. Seeds, who desperately wrote home for instructions after hearing this catalogue of demands, doubted whether even a simple tripartite agreement, to which British Ministers were now clutching as a last expedient, would be acceptable to Russia if the present negotiations failed.[2]

This was the stage in the Moscow exchanges at which Britain and France might have said, with a good conscience, that they had gone as far as they could. They had made six substantial concessions; to cover the Baltic states; to exclude the Netherlands, Switzerland and Luxemburg from the main agreement; to agree, first, to the insertion of a provision regarding indirect aggression and then to a form of words defining this, though the whole enterprise was against Britain's better judgment; to agree, as they were now willing to do, that this definition should be in the main agreement and not in the subsidiary secret list of states; and to accept Molotov's demand for a pledge that the parties should not conclude a separate peace in the event of war breaking out. Two basic differences remained: they arose from the Soviet definition of indirect aggression, which the British regarded as warranting interference in the internal affairs of other states; and from the Soviet demand that the political agreement should be dependent on the treaty for military co-operation. The British view of indirect aggression was that the test must be that the state in question was acting

[1] *D.B.F.P.*, Third Series, VI pp. 226–7.
[2] *Ibid.*, pp. 310–13.

against its will and under threat of force, and that this threat should be such as to compel it to abandon its independence and neutrality; whereas the Soviet definition contended that aggression against a state had occurred if that state began to follow the German political line even when its leaders denied that they were doing so through fear of German military force. It was not necessary, in Russia's view, for the pressure of armed force to be apparent or for the state in question to have lost its independence or neutrality. As for the Soviet demand for the simultaneous entry into force of the political and military agreements, the British objections were, first, that, if this were conceded, the Russians would be able to demand virtually what military conditions they liked, and to threaten that the political agreement, which was what the British and French were seeking in Moscow, would not be signed unless they had their way; and secondly, that Russia would be in possession of British and French military plans before it was known for sure whether she would be their friend or foe. Experience of Soviet negotiating methods so far showed that even if these issues were surmounted by further concessions on the Western side, which must compromise Britain and France in the eyes of sympathisers throughout the world, there was no assurance that further issues of principle would not be raised on the Soviet side.

The French, however, with their responsibility for shouldering the full force of German land strength in case of war, favoured pressing on at whatever cost. Bonnet urgently wrote to Halifax on 19 July of the absolute necessity to conclude the deal with Moscow; he would make no bones about the military agreement or indirect aggression.[1] Strang wrote a report of the negotiations on the following day to almost the same effect; his advice was to accept article 6 of the Soviet draft dealing with the interdependence of the political and military agreements, to send an Anglo-French military mission to Moscow at once and to continue the efforts to reach agreement on article 1 relating to indirect aggression.[2] The Cabinet, with much heart-searching, accepted this advice and on 21 July Halifax indicated his agreement to the opening of military talks but made clear that, on the issue of indirect aggression, he would not be a party to an 'arrangement whereby His Majesty's Government may be placed in the position of becoming accessories to interference in the internal affairs of other states'.[3] If the Russians thought that by holding up agreement in the mili-

---

[1] D.B.F.P., Third Series, VI, pp. 397–8.
[2] Ibid., pp. 422–6.
[3] Ibid., pp. 427–9.

tary talks they could have their way on the political side, the British planned to do the same.

When this decision had been reached, the British side of the mission being entrusted to an Admiral with the Gilbertian name of Sir Reginald Aylmer Ranfurly Plunkett-Ernle-Erle-Drax, the government's attitude was that the mission could afford to take its time while Seeds and the French Ambassador wrestled with Molotov in Moscow on article 1 of the draft. The instructions handed to the British members of the mission were saturated in the deepest gloom in regard to the Soviet Union; they could hardly approach their task with much seriousness when they were told by these directives that, for example, by all the rules of logic the Soviet national transport system ought to break down under the strain of war.[1] Despite urgings from the French that the mission should take the overland route through Germany, this, on Henderson's advice, was considered too provocative to Hitler and General Doumenc, the head of the French section, had a strong aversion to travelling by air.[2] General Ismay, of the Committee of Imperial Defence, thought that the delay of 24 hours or so involved in travel by sea to Leningrad made no difference but that if the French wished to go by train, let them. With such a spirit behind the mission, it might have been prudent not to send it at all. Nevertheless, the British members were informed that in the government's view the Russians probably did desire an agreement since they appreciated that a two-front war would be a serious deterrent to Germany.[3] Later, through French pressure, the British attitude towards the mission changed and the instructions issued at the outset to the British members to go slow were withdrawn.

The political negotiations, confounding British expectations that the contrary would be the case once the military mission had been conceded, marked time. Molotov first refused to issue a joint communiqué stating that the military talks were beginning because the political side of the agreement had made adequate progress, then complained bitterly of a statement made by R. A. Butler in the House of Commons on 31 July, which he represented as charging the Soviet Union with intending to infringe the independence of the Baltic states. After this incident Seeds reported that the Foreign Minister was 'a different man from what he had been at our last interview and I feel our negotiations have suffered a severe set-back'.[4]

[1] *D.B.F.P.*, Third Series, VI, Appendix 5, p. 766.   [2] *Ibid,*, pp. 545–6.
[3] *Ibid.*, p. 764.
[4] *Ibid.*, pp. 570–4.

Molotov thenceforward refused to make suggestions concerning article 1 and allowed Seeds and Naggiar to tie themselves in knots in the vain search to bridge the two conceptions of indirect aggression. When the military talks at length began on 12 August it was at once apparent that the long-standing political issues would wreck them. Seeds wrote on 15 August that he and the French Ambassador agreed that the Soviet representatives had raised 'the fundamental problem on which the military talks will succeed or fail and which has indeed been at the bottom of all our difficulties since the very beginning of the political conversations, namely how to reach any useful agreement with the Soviet Union so long as this country's neighbours maintain a sort of boycott which is only to be broken ... when it is too late'.[1] This issue was nakedly stated by Voroshilov, head of the Soviet delegation at the military talks, when he said on that day that the talks could only continue if the Poles gave the Soviet Union permission to pass through the Wilno Gap and Galicia and the Rumanians allowed Russia to transfer troops through their territory at suitable points.[2] Again, the French were prompt in taking the lead to circumvent the problem; they proposed instructing their Military Attaché in Warsaw to make contact with the Polish General Staff to see if the Soviet demand could be met, while Britain, more tardy than usual in devising expedients of this kind, could merely add that the Rumanians should be asked to send a representative to Warsaw to join the talks. But the Moscow atmosphere was oppressive: Admiral Drax reported the Russians as stating their 'demands' (not 'requests') 'somewhat in the manner of a victorious Power dictating terms to a beaten enemy'. They made it plain, Drax wrote, 'that we have come here as suppliants asking them to give us a treaty of assistance'.[3]

In the end, as in the beginning, the question lay with Poland and her answer, given by Beck to Sir Howard Kennard on 19 August, was negative. Voroshilov was trying to obtain peacefully, Beck said, the Polish land he had tried to obtain by force in the 1920s, though the Foreign Minister did not add that much of it was territory thickly populated by Ukrainians. The most encouraging thing Beck could say was that his negative answer to Russia's demand need not be publicised, and that his attitude might change if war actually broke out and Poland found herself fighting for her life.[4] The French Government decided to exploit these reservations in the Polish reply by

---

[1] *D.B.F.P.*, Third Series, VII, pp. 1–2.
[2] *Ibid.*, pp. 3–5. [3] *Ibid.*, pp. 32–5.
[4] *Ibid.*, pp. 85–6.

telling the Russians that the Poles agreed in principle to the passage of Soviet troops provided that war with Germany had actually broken out. The British, now as exasperated with the Poles as the French, found themselves forced into the same position, though their mendacity was less specific: they merely said that they assumed Poland would have the 'right attitude' in wartime.[1] But these glosses on the truth were unnecessary since Russia and Germany were now in the final stages of negotiating their non-aggression treaty. On 21 August *Pravda* described the commercial agreement signed with Germany two days previously as 'possibly an important step in the question of further improving not only the economic but also the political relations between the U.S.S.R. and Germany'. The proposed Nazi–Soviet non-aggression pact was announced in Moscow later the same day and Marshal Voroshilov said that the military talks were adjourned, if not *sine die*, at least for a long period, since the Soviet officers had important duties to attend to in connection with the autumn manœuvres. He agreed to meet on the following day, however, only to say that he was dissatisfied with the British and French statements about the Polish attitude, that he wanted affirmative replies from the Polish and Rumanian Governments themselves, and that he saw no point in continuing the talks 'until the political situation was clearer'.

Meanwhile, a British protest against the proposed Nazi–Soviet pact was handed by Seeds to Molotov on 22 August: on French advice the instruction to Seeds was later modified so as merely to ask for more information about the pact, but by this time the Ambassador had made the original representation. In reply, Molotov said that he had always charged Britain and France with lack of sincerity; this was nowhere better displayed, he said, than when the Anglo-French military mission arrived in Moscow empty-handed and unable to deal with the fundamental points on which the question of reciprocal assistance depended, namely the passage of Soviet troops through Polish and Rumanian territory.[2] With this final statement the long negotiations for bringing Russia into Western defence arrangements came to their unhappy conclusion. On 23 August Ribbentrop arrived in Moscow to sign with Stalin the agreement, of which the non-aggression pact was published and the arrangement for the partitioning of Poland remained secret. Instructions to the British mission to withdraw were not sent until 25 August.[3]

[1] *D.B.F.P.*, Third Series, VII, pp. 106–8. [2] *Ibid.*, pp. 142–3.
[3] *Ibid.*, p. 224.

It is impossible, with Molotov, to charge Britain and France
with 'lack of sincerity' in the Moscow negotiations. They undoubtedly desired an agreement with Russia; the question was
one of terms, Britain began, and France was unable to dissuade her, by asking Russia to pledge herself to help if necessary
and if wanted. Such a role would have been humiliating and
hazardous for the Soviet Union, coupled as it was with no definite assurance of effective British and French co-operation. An
arrangement of this kind, as Stalin warned, would be equivalent
to expecting Russia to pick other people's chestnuts out of the
fire, especially as Russia had no confidence in France's military
capacity to stand up to Germany and the British military mission in Moscow told Voroshilov that the most Britain could
expect to put into the field against Germany was 'two divisions
now and two later'.[1] Once this initial error on the part of the
British had been corrected and the principle of reciprocity
accepted, the bedrock problem was reached of Soviet insistence
upon intervention in neighbouring states whenever they embarked on policies which she regarded as contrary to her interests, and upon access through Polish and Rumanian territories.
The former Britain was on the brink of accepting and no doubt
would have accepted, provided some decent form of words
could have been devised. The latter neither she nor France
had the means to compel Poland and Rumania to accept.
Poland and Rumania had their guarantees from Britain and
France. Poland was involved in a dispute with Germany over
German minorities in her territory; she, and Rumania too, had
it in their power to commit Britain and France to war, and
hence the two democracies had constantly to appeal to these
countries to refrain from actions likely to provoke Germany.
Britain and France were thus in the position of being suppliants,
not only towards Russia, but towards Poland, and to a less
extent Rumania. It is small wonder that they were without
the means to compel the Poles to accept Russian demands until
it was too late. Of all British politicians of the day only Lloyd
George came near to hinting that the Poles should be presented
with a choice between accepting help from Russia and a termination of the guarantee. This was when he said in the House
of Commons on 3 April,

> If Russia had not been brought into this matter because
> of certain feelings the Poles have that they do not want the
> Russians there, it is for us to declare the conditions, and un-
> less the Poles are prepared to accept the only conditions with

[1] Winston Churchill, *The Second World War*, I, p. 302.

which we can successfully help them, the responsibility must be theirs.[1]

There was in addition the inevitable background of mistrust on both sides. A Conservative Government in Britain could never undertake with ease a revolutionary change in foreign policy in co-operation with a régime Conservatives had always heartily detested and with which a Conservative Government had once broken off diplomatic relations. 'Co-operating with the devil' could be achieved by a Churchill later, but that was in wartime and when there was no alternative. The government in 1939 approached the Russians as the Allies approached them in 1918, as a 'colony of lepers', to use Lloyd George's phrase, with whom one should only do business in extreme emergencies and with full provision for personal disinfection afterwards. Chamberlain's own view of Russia is well known:

> I must confess to the most profound distrust of Russia. I have no belief whatever in her ability to maintain an effective offensive, even if she wanted to. And I distrust her motives, which seem to me to have little connection with our ideas of liberty and to be concerned only with getting everyone up by the ears. Moreover she is both hated and suspected by many of the smaller states, notably by Poland, Rumania, and Finland.[2]

This was written on 26 March, before the negotiations we have described began. The Russian attitude towards the infidels was much the same; moreover, this was their first major negotiation with capitalist Powers, with more implications for good or evil than Genoa or Rapallo in the 1920s, and at all times they wondered, like the Western democracies, whether they were doing the right thing. They had moreover a further cause of mistrust, Munich, giving rise to inevitable debate in Communist ranks as to whether Britain and France could be counted as serious allies in the hour of trial, whether they would not capitulate once more, leaving Russia to shed her blood alone. The clumsy and ill-considered guarantees given by Britain and France after the Prague *coup* were far from being a reassurance.

Above all, the underlying factor in the Moscow negotiations was: who was to take the shock of the German assault if and when Armaggedon was unleashed; who was to emerge from the conflict with the least damage to his national strength?

[1] 345 H.C. Deb. 5s. Col. 2510.
[2] Keith Feiling, *The Life of Neville Chamberlain*, p. 403.

No doubt Britain and France did not deliberately plan to embroil Russia with Germany so as to destroy two enemies at once; such long-range calculations are wholly out of character with the fumbling Anglo-French diplomacy of 1939. But neither did they wish to see Russia stand aloof and extend the reach of Communism in Europe after a ruinous war in which Russia was neutral; to avoid this they were willing to pay a high, but not high enough, price. Equally, on the Soviet side, Stalin had no interest in helping Britain and France out of their difficulties. What he mainly seemed to want was to keep Soviet power intact so as to use it with maximum effect to mould the consequences of the coming war in Europe.

III

The negotiations for a pact with Russia, culminating in Stalin's decision to trade his neutrality for a share in Hitler's Polish spoils, made no fundamental change in British attitudes towards the Polish–German dispute, except perhaps to accelerate the efforts to secure Mussolini's help in bringing home to Germany the consequences of her policy. The British position, as explained by Halifax in a speech at Chatham House on 29 June, comprised two main elements: adherence to the pledge to defend Poland against a clear threat to her independence, though not necessarily her existing borders, and a continuing search for a peaceful resolution of the dispute consistent with Polish independence. The march into Prague had been a setback for the latter object but Halifax was certain that 'once the ice was broken, the British side would go far to reach an adjustment with Germany'.[1]

The fulfilment of these two aims seemed possible during the months leading up to the Nazi–Soviet pact owing to Hitler's evident reluctance to embroil himself with Britain and France so long as there was a risk that Russia might join them in opposing his designs against Poland. Sir Howard Kennard, reporting from Warsaw on 24 February, said that his German colleague, von Moltke, had told him that, although Hitler would ultimately insist on the incorporation of Danzig in the Reich and a corridor through the Corridor, there was no intention to press these demands for the present.[2] With the Polish rejection of German demands on 26 March and the announcement of the British and French guarantees on the 31st, a lull seemed to set in, despite the appearance in Goering's

---

[1] *Documents and materials relating to the eve of the Second World War*, II (Dirksen Papers), p. 128.
[2] *D.B.F.P.*, Third Series, IV, pp. 146–7.

newspaper *National Zeitung* at the end of March of the first German allegations of the ill-treatment of the German minority in Poland. It thus seemed in London that some accommodation might be possible. The French were asked once more on 27 April to mend their fences with Italy in order that Mussolini might feel more inclined to lend his help in Berlin; the British were in a strong position to make this appeal since conscription in Britain, which the French had long urged, had been announced on the previous day. Shortly afterwards Beck was told that the British guarantee would only be operative if Polish independence was clearly threatened and that there would have to be agreement between London and Warsaw to establish that this was the case.[1]

A possible solution, the British Government thought, was hinted at in Hitler's otherwise truculent Reichstag speech on 28 April, when he talked of Danzig becoming a 'free city in the German Reich'. The fact that Danzig was governed by a German Senate which followed the same Nazi doctrines and practices as the Reich made nonsense of German charges that the Danzigers were persecuted by Poland; nevertheless, Danzig was without question a German city and its return to the Reich seemed on the face of it not unjust provided Poland received adequate compensation by way of arrangements for her future security. Halifax discussed with Daladier and Bonnet, when he met them in Paris a week after the Prague *coup*, the possibilities of a plan 'by which the specific character of the Free City might be maintained in the sense that it would not be occupied by German troops'. Danzig, if its return to the Reich were negotiated, would be administered like any other German city and would even be represented in the Reichstag; but it would have a special constitution placed under the guarantee, not of the League, but of a group of Powers such as Germany, France, Britain and Poland. Perhaps the Pope's good offices could be used to get the plan agreed. Daladier thought the proposal 'interesting' but Hitler did not, nor did the Poles; Marshal Smigly-Rydz told the British Ambassador that 'whoever controls Danzig controls our economic life'.[2] Moreover, what was to prevent Germany remilitarising Danzig as she had the Rhineland on the ground that otherwise Germany was being treated as an inferior? Halifax did not explain.

Following their regular cyclical motion, rumours of a German *coup* against Danzig increased in June, together with forecasts that the Chancellor would appear personally in the city on

---

[1] *Ibid.*, V, pp. 401–2.
[2] *D.B.F.P.*, Third Series, V, pp. 608–11; VI, pp. 404–5.

20 July. Halifax appealed to Mussolini on 5 July to intervene to prevent war; there was every possibility of peaceful negotiation, the Foreign Secretary said, but only if the Germans did not regard Danzig as a means for destroying Poland.[1] The Duce was not helpful and it was clear that if it were to come to war he would be on Germany's side, after the signing of the Pact of Steel in May, or at least benevolently neutral.[2] But British Ministers never easily despaired of Mussolini. Chamberlain wrote a strongly worded letter to Daladier on 13 July on the need for a Franco-Italian *détente*, praising him as the strongest Prime Minister France had had in recent times and consequently well placed to make concessions to Italy. The last thing Chamberlain wanted was that when the clash came over Danzig which everybody talked about Mussolini should be feeling aggrieved with France and unwilling to use his influence with Hitler.[3] The Pope too was considered a possible factor in conciliation; he was given the British side of the case, including the readiness to negotiate about Danzig after a decent interval in which tempers on both sides could cool. His Holiness was not, however, asked to take any action and hence no assistance came from that quarter.[4] Nor did it come from France.

At the same time, the British Government made energetic efforts to see if Germany's general economic and colonial aspirations could be met without vital sacrifices of interest on the part of the Western Powers. Halifax, in his Chatham House speech on 29 June, dwelt on the new principle of international accountability for dependent territories. This principle might allow Germany to resume colonial responsibilities through membership of a multi-national mandate system which would avoid the political objections to any redistribution of colonies; Halifax had himself proposed the idea to Hitler in November 1937, receiving, however, only the coldest response. The Secretary for Overseas Trade, R. S. Hudson, developed the theme in discussions with Wohlthat, the Commissioner for the Nazi Four-Year Plan, in London on 20 July, when he proposed a form of Anglo-German economic co-operation in Africa, leading to a scheme for Africa to be administered by the Powers, including Germany, in trust. British public opinion, Hudson said, would never countenance a direct return of German colonies. Hudson also discussed with Wohlthat the broad lines of economic collaboration between Britain, Germany and the United States if existing political difficulties could be settled;

---

[1] *Ibid.*, VI, pp. 257–8.
[3] *Ibid.*, pp. 350–2.
[2] *Ibid.*, pp. 288–90.
[4] *Ibid.*, pp. 290–2.

Hudson thought that Britain and the United States could, for instance, provide some of the capital Wohlthat said Germany needed in order to be able to remit abroad the interest and amortisation on her debts.[1] He later explained that all this was conditional on German disarmament.[2] In two parallel talks which Wohlthat had with Sir Horace Wilson the idea of a delimitation of British and German spheres of interest was discussed, together with a new colonial settlement the outlines of which were left vague, and an Anglo-German non-aggression pact which, according to von Dirksen's report, Wilson had said 'would enable Britain to rid herself of her commitments *vis-à-vis* Poland'. Wilson finished the talks by proposing that Hitler should 'authorize some person to discuss the above-mentioned programme'. The storm of disapproval voiced in the British press, however, when reports of the talks were leaked, notably in the *Daily Telegraph* and *News Chronicle*, ruled out any attempt to carry the matter further.[3]

The Hudson–Wohlthat conversations had an unfortunate outcome. Chamberlain was questioned by irate M.P.s in the House on 24 July and claimed that, although he himself saw no harm in the talks, the Cabinet knew nothing about them, nor did any other Minister but Hudson; the talks did not constitute a proposal for a British loan to Germany.[4] The French, too, took offence at the idea of schemes of economic and colonial collaboration, with their inevitable political overtones, being discussed with German representatives by British Ministers, presumably with some authorisation by the Prime Minister, without themselves being consulted. The German and Italian press wrote the talks off as British attempts to set a price upon other countries' aspirations. What the talks showed, however, was that the British Government were seeking at all costs some means of averting the approaching clash over Danzig.

Realising, as he must have done, that the British could always be counted on to calm the situation whenever it was inconvenient for him to have it deteriorate, Hitler allowed another lull to intervene. In mid-July he summoned Forster, the Gauleiter of Danzig, knowing that Forster would pass the message to the League High Commissioner, Burckhardt, and hence to the British, and told him that he would do nothing to provoke a conflict; he would wait a year, even longer, for a solution. Halifax rose to the occasion by asking the Poles to do nothing

[1] *D.B.F.P.*, Third Series, VI, pp. 407–10.
[2] Interview in *The Daily Express*, 24 July.
[3] *Documents and materials relating to the eve of the Second World War*, II, pp. 67–72; *D.G.F.P.*, Series D, VI, pp. 954, 966–7.
[4] 350 H.C. Deb. 5s. Cols. 1025–8.

to allow incidents to occur in or around Danzig; 'whenever the German Government gave concrete evidence of their willingness to forswear force', he told the approving Henderson, 'we should be willing to meet them half-way'.[1] He was displeased with Beck's reply that he could give no binding pledge in no circumstances to take military action, if challenged by Germany, without consulting the British Embassy in Warsaw, though he would 'do anything possible to let us know if he sees combustion point approaching'.[2] Such was the frame of mind in which Halifax agreed to see the Swedish businessman, Birger Dahlerus, who combined an *entrée* into Nazi ruling circles with a flair for leading the British to hope that a respectable accommodation might be possible.

On 25 July the Foreign Secretary heard from Dahlerus the advice that it would be useful to have a moderate tone in the British press during the next few weeks in order to allow Hitler to make a peaceful speech at the Nuremberg Rally.[3] The interview seemed to have some effect, if not on the British press, then on the government themselves. Halifax evolved the doctrine of a *silence menaçant* to deal with the situation. Writing to Henderson on 28 July he agreed with the Ambassador that warnings to Germany could be overdone; hence Chamberlain when he spoke in the Commons on 31 July and he himself when he addressed the Lords on 3 August would confine themselves to general observations, saying that their position had already been plainly stated and that they had nothing further to add.[4] But, as so often with the Chamberlain Government's efforts to induce congenial responses from Germany by soft words, no answer came from the Reich. Von Dirksen, the German Ambassador in London, in a talk with Sir Horace Wilson on 3 August could think of nothing concrete which Hitler could do to engender the better atmosphere which Britain was describing as the essential preliminary to negotiations over Danzig. Wilson suggested that Hitler might make a conciliatory statement to ease the British Government's position or announce that he was giving home rule to Bohemia or Slovakia; this struck the Ambassador as 'delicate'.[5] Lord Lothian had made a similar proposal, as a basis for restoration of British faith in Chamberlain's policies, to the German agent, Adam von Trott zu Solz, in June but no German reaction came.[6]

---

[1] *D.B.F.P.*, Third Series, VI, pp. 432–3, 441–2.
[2] *Ibid.*, pp. 445–7.   [3] *Ibid.*, pp. 483–4.
[4] *Ibid.*, pp. 529–30.
[5] *Ibid.*, pp. 579–82. *Documents and materials relating to the eve of the Second World War*, II, pp. 117–25.
[6] J. R. M. Butler, *Lord Lothian*, p. 230.

How inconsiderable the control Britain and France had over the development of Polish–German relations on which peace now hung, was evident only a day later, when the Danzig Customs Administration, clearly operating on German instructions, ordered officials at four Polish customs posts not to report for duty in future on the ground that Poland had increased the number of customs administrators as a means of strangling Danzig's economic life. The Polish Government sent the Danzig Senate what the Germans called an ultimatum and the Poles a 'stiff note', and the German Government then intervened for the first time in the long-sustained dispute between Poland and the Danzig authorities. A German note to Warsaw warned that if Poland persisted in its threat to prevent the import of Danzig goods into Poland, which appeared to be the object of Poland's customs policy, Danzig's economic life would be adversely affected and Danzig would retaliate by redirecting its trade. Poland replied to this, on the whole moderate, *démarche* by denying Germany's right to intervene in the dispute and by threatening that German intervention in Poland's measures to protect her rights in Danzig would be regarded as aggression.[1]

This was precisely the situation the British had feared since their guarantee to Poland was given on 31 March. Cadogan, acting an improbable schoolmaster's role, laid down for the Polish Ambassador on 11 August the lines on which Poland should conduct her relations with Germany. Whenever Poland felt she must take the initiative, the lesson ran, she should consult with Britain, as she had not done in the crisis of 4 August.[2] Later Beck explained to Kennard that speedy action was sometimes essential, as in the matter of the customs officials, and Britain could not expect to be consulted in such cases.[3] As far as Germany was concerned, however, Britain proposed to follow the *silence menaçant* principle and take no action, preferring to await the outcome of a visit to be paid by Forster and Burckhardt to Hitler at Berchtesgaden on 11 August.

Hitler's tactics at this encounter, which he knew would be retailed by Burckhardt to London, were clearly to entice Britain out of her commitments to Poland and thus leave the way open for him to settle with Poland without interference from the West. He said little about Danzig, so the High Commissioner told Roger Makins, who went to Basle on behalf of the Foreign

---

[1] Cmd. 6106 (1939), pp. 87–8; German White Book, II, No. 445; Polish White Book, p. 124.
[2] *D.B.F.P.*, Third Series, VI, pp. 679–81.
[3] *Ibid.*, pp. 683–4.

Office to hear the story of the interview from Burckhardt; what he mainly desired was an extraterritorial road through the Corridor, though he knew that the Poles were definitely opposed to this. He could wait about Danzig, provided the Poles kept calm, because he realised that Britain and France 'belonged inseparably together' and he had no wish to provoke their joint resistance unnecessarily. But if the slightest thing happened in Danzig he would hit hard. If it came to war in Europe, he had air superiority over Britain and France, and Russia, in Stalin's phrase, would not pull other people's chestnuts out of the fire. He had to hold in check a country straining at the leash; 'last year my generals were prudent and I had to urge them on. This year I have to hold them back.' But his principal aims were the achievement by Germany of self-sufficiency in grain, which could only come from the East, and in timber, for which Hitler needed but one colony; he had to create a situation in which Germany could live off its own fat and not succumb to blockade. With England he wanted to live in peace; in a section of the interview which the British did not show the French Hitler said he wished to conclude a definitive pact with Britain, guaranteeing all British possessions in the world and laying the basis for lasting collaboration. As a final touch to this appeal to British credulity he told Burck-hardt to ask the British to send an emissary like General Ironside, who had been on a visit to Warsaw, with whom he could talk man to man.[1]

Halifax concluded from this report that Hitler was still un-decided and must be given no excuse for acting intemperately; this meant that the Polish Government must express their willingness to negotiate.[2] Yet Hitler's fair words were not regarded as ground for sending a leading figure to Germany, as the Chancellor proposed; 'we saw no basis,' Cadogan wrote, 'on which a conversation usefully could proceed'.[3] In Britain's eyes the first need was some definite improvement in the Polish–German atmosphere, but appeals by both London and Rome to Germany in this connection were without avail. Halifax wrote to Chamberlain on 19 August giving the information that Count Ciano had been summoned, first to see Ribbentrop at Salzburg, then Hitler himself at Berchtesgaden, to be told that the Chancellor contemplated only a decisive local action against Poland and that Britain and France would remain aloof; hence there was no need for Italy to advise caution since her help would not be required and she could remain neutral.

[1] *D.B.F.P.*, Third Series, VI, pp. 688–98.
[2] *Ibid.*, VII, pp. 6–7.　　　[3] *Ibid.*, p. 32.

Henderson gave self-contradictory advice about the best form of a British approach to Germany, first saying that there should be no repetition of the 21 May incident of the previous year, when Hitler was warned against invading Czechoslovakia, and then proposing that General Ironside be sent to Germany, a move which in the circumstances would almost certainly be interpreted as a warning to Germany. Halifax eventually made up his own mind in favour of a letter from Chamberlain to Hitler recalling the charge that Britain could have done more to avert war in 1914 by making her intentions clear at an early stage and stating that while Britain, along with France, would certainly stand by her obligations to Poland, she welcomed every opportunity for a negotiated settlement.[1]

Chamberlain pondered for three days, then decided to send the letter by Henderson rather than through a special emissary. Since the Nazi–Soviet pact was now on the point of being signed, Chamberlain began by insisting that this agreement would not deter Britain from fulfilling her obligations; he then followed the lines suggested by Halifax. The core of the letter was a plea for a truce to press polemics and incitements, which would create the conditions for holding Polish–German talks. Any agreement resulting from the latter, however, would have to be guaranteed by the Powers, Chamberlain said, and Britain was somewhat deviously described as willing to make 'what contribution she could to the effective operation of the guarantee'.[2] While this message was on its way, Halifax was once more urging Mussolini to support the Prime Minister's letter by any representations within his power to make to Hitler.[3] Both efforts were barren. Hitler's reply on 23 August said that negotiations with Poland were out of the question so long as the Poles felt they could afford to be unreasonable with the British and French guarantees behind them; the Chancellor then threatened to mobilise Germany's armed forces if Britain and France carried out the military measures they had announced. Mussolini, on his side, speaking in great confidence as Hitler's closest ally, saw a prospect for Polish–German negotiations, but only on the basis, which the British could not urge the Poles to accept, of an immediate cession of Danzig to the Reich.[4] The standard broadside of allegations of Polish ill-treatment of Germans was now discharged and, at a second talk with Henderson on 24 August, Hitler said he was ready for war with England: 'better war now when he was 50 rather than 55 or 60'.

[1] *D.B.F.P.*, Third Series, VII, pp. 80–2.   [2] Cmd. 6106, pp. 96–8.
[3] *D.B.F.P.*, Third Series, VII, pp. 144–5.
[4] *Ibid.*, pp. 157–8, 174–6, 186.

Henderson reached the, for him, unprecedented conclusion that 'it is practically hopeless to deal with him', though the Ambassador noted that he himself had 'held from the beginning that the Poles were utterly foolish and unwise'.[1]

Yet Hitler was still evidently angling for British and French neutrality, using for the purpose Dahlerus and his own art of suggesting better things to come after his immediate demand was granted. Goering went to great efforts to secure Dahlerus a seat on the plane to England on 25 August so that he should talk to British Ministers, advising him to herald his arrival by telling British business colleagues with access to the Foreign Office that the 'Boss' (that is, Goering) 'wanted to know if he could sell rubber in London and if the Premier's speech that afternoon ruled out rubber sales'.[2] Goering's proposal, Dahlerus reported to the Foreign Office on his arrival, was that Danzig and the Corridor should be handed to Germany as 'the last revision of the Versailles Treaty that was necessary in Europe'; Britain was to advise the Poles to enter into negotiations on this basis and to send negotiators and advisers to Berlin; in return for her efforts Britain would be left with a free hand in the Far East, though Goering did not say how, after Japan had been alienated against Germany by the Nazi–Soviet pact, Hitler was to persuade Tokyo to co-operate. Halifax told Dahlerus, after a hurried glance at this document, that he thought 'there was a great deal on which we should be quite willing to help'.[3] On the same day Hitler handed what he called his 'large, comprehensive offer' to Henderson; he refused to accept the British conditions for a negotiated settlement with Poland, but 'after the Polish–German question was solved' (that is, after German demands on Poland had been met) Hitler would guarantee, not Poland, but the continued existence of the British Empire, provided Germany's colonial ambitions were satisfied. Moreover, Britain while shirking her own obligations to Poland, would have to respect Germany's obligations to Italy. Once the Polish question was out of the way Hitler would settle down; 'he was by nature an artist, not a politician'. Henderson thought that his offer should be taken seriously: the British Government, he said, should not 'by any off-hand rejection give cause for reasonable bitterness'.[4]

The Cabinet deliberated its reply, but no British Government, the mood of Parliament being what it was, could feel satisfied with any other conditions than a freely negotiated Polish–

[1] *D.B.F.P.*, Third Series, VII, pp. 201–2, 212–13.
[2] *Ibid.*, pp. 194–5.   [3] *Ibid.*, pp. 231–5.
[4] German White Book, III, No. 457; *D.B.F.P.*, Third Series, VII, pp. 227–9, 235.

German settlement with absolute equality between the parties and a guarantee of its terms by the Great Powers. Such conditions could never have appealed to Hitler; nevertheless, even he must take account of critics among his *entourage* of his determination to overrun Poland even at the cost of a general European war. Lochner, of the Associated Press of America, gave the British Embassy in Berlin a horrifying account of a speech given by Hitler to his generals at Obersalzburg on 22 August, which shocked some of his warlords. His decision to attack Poland, he said, had been reached in the spring, and to arrive at an agreement with Stalin in the autumn of 1938.

The attack upon and destruction of Poland [Hitler continued] begins on Saturday, August 26, early . . . the citizens of western Europe must tremble with horror. . . . The 'death-head' formations would be put in front to send women and children of Polish origin to death ruthlessly and without compassion. . . . I experienced those poor worms, Daladier and Chamberlain, in Munich. They will be too cowardly to attack. They cannot go beyond a blockade . . . the opportunity is as favourable as never before. I have but one worry, namely that Chamberlain or some other such pig of a fellow will come at the last moment with proposals or with ratting. He will fly down the stairs even if I shall personally have to trample on his belly in the eyes of the photographers.[1]

But the action planned against Poland for 26 August was suspended, owing, so Lochner informed the Embassy, to the intervention of Hitler's Commander-in-Chief, von Brauchitsch. Von Brauchitsch was alarmed because Italy and Japan objected to article 4 of the Nazi–Soviet pact, which provided that neither party should participate in any grouping of Powers which was either directly or indirectly aimed against the other party; because the Anglo-Polish Treaty making the guarantee of 31 March reciprocal was about to be signed; and because the French mobilisation was proceeding so effectively as to show that the French really meant business.[2]

The expression of these fears no doubt accounted for Hitler's decision to send for Henderson on 25 August and make his 'large, comprehensive offer'. But if the Nazi–Soviet pact had strained German relations with Italy and Japan, the use Hitler was able to make of the prospect of further Anglo-German negotiations threatened to strain British relations with France on the very eve of the German attack on Poland, which, whatever

[1] *D.B.F.P.*, Third Series, VII, pp. 258–60.
[2] *Ibid.*, pp. 316–17.

von Brauchitsch might say, could only be postponed, not abandoned. Receiving the British reply on 29 August, which Henderson had gone to London to bring, with its agreement to take up Anglo-German relations after a freely negotiated Polish–German settlement had been signed and guaranteed, Hitler asked Henderson point-blank if Britain wanted an alliance. Henderson was incautious enough to reply that an alliance was not excluded if events justified it.[1] The extreme danger of such a move, if it were publicised, was at once appreciated at home and Henderson was warned that an alliance was not practical, though a new Anglo-German treaty was; an alliance, the Foreign Office pointed out, 'might create the worst possible impression in the United States and all friendly countries'.[2]

The substantive British demand for direct Polish–German negotiations and for German assurances that Poland's vital interests and independence were not in question seemed at first conceded in Hitler's reply, which Henderson received on the evening of 29 August. But the conditions attached showed that no freely negotiated settlement, such as Britain desired, was possible; they were that, if there was to be a guarantee, Russia must be associated with it, although Poland had successfully resisted British and French efforts to persuade her to accept a Soviet guarantee against Germany, and that Poland must send an emissary to receive the German demands to arrive in Berlin on the next day, 30 August. This procedure the British Government could not advise the Poles to accept; Dahlerus, who talked with Chamberlain and Halifax in the morning and afternoon of 30 August, rang Berlin from London three times but was unable to secure any modification in the German demand and Henderson, too, failed to persuade the Germans to follow the normal procedure and invite the Polish Government through their Ambassador in Berlin to make suggestions for the conduct of the negotiations.[3] Ribbentrop's reply was given to Henderson in the early hours of 31 August, when he read the sixteen German demands 'at top speed'. The remarkable moderation of these was clearly designed to put Germany right with world opinion on the eve of the invasion of Poland; they included the cession of Danzig, a plebiscite in the Corridor after a delay of twelve months and an international commission to supervise the Corridor in the meantime, and guarantees to be exchanged of the rights of German minorities in other parts of Poland and of Poles in Germany. The Foreign Minister

[1] *D.B.F.P.*, Third Series, VII, pp 351–5.
[2] *Ibid.*, p. 354, n. 8.
[3] *Ibid.*, pp. 388–90, 410.

said it was now too late to discuss these demands since a Polish envoy had not arrived in Berlin by midnight, 30 August.[1] There followed frantic British efforts to bring Germans and Poles into contact. Mussolini intervened with a proposal for an international conference, but only after the cession of Danzig to the Reich. Chamberlain dug in his toes about this: 'Danzig seemed to us to be the vital point, the very heart of the dispute, and we could not ask the Poles to give away the main point in advance'.[2] After the statement by the Berlin wireless station at 5.40 a.m. on the fatal 1 September that Poland had refused a settlement and appealed to arms and that Hitler had 'no other choice but to meet force with force', Mussolini tried again, this time with a proposal for an armistice and a conference, but Halifax replied to Rome that this was unthinkable while German troops were on Polish soil.[3] A preliminary warning was given by the British Government to Germany at 5.45 p.m. on 1 September that they would fulfil their obligations to Poland unless Germany suspended her military operations and withdrew their forces from Poland.[4] On the evening of 2 September Chamberlain told a House of Commons in almost open revolt at the agonising delay in declaring war that no German reply had been received to the warning and that the Germans might be considering the Italian proposal for a conference.[5] The French Cabinet were insisting upon more time for the evacuation of their people from the frontier with Germany and the effective mobilisation of their armed forces, whereas the British Admiralty feared that delay would give the German navy time to make its dispositions. Under pressure from Parliament and from Ministers who threatened to strike unless the Polish guarantee was soon honoured, the Prime Minister agreed to hand in the British ultimatum at 9 a.m. on 3 September, timed to expire at 11 a.m.[6] Consistently to the last with the disharmonies between British and French policies which had marked all the inter-war years, Coulondre, the French Ambassador in Berlin, was not instructed until noon, one hour after the expiry of the British ultimatum, to ask for his passports as from 5 p.m.

Thus the British Government pursued the will-o'-the-wisp of a negotiated settlement with Nazi Germany, leading to some ultimate upland of stability, to the last. There is little doubt that if Hitler had been willing to accept a demilitarised Free City of Danzig within the Reich, an extraterritorial corridor

---

[1] Cmd. 6106, pp. 145–6.
[2] *D.B.F.P.*, Third Series, VII, p. 465.
[3] *Ibid.*, pp. 505–6.
[4] Cmd. 6106, p. 168.
[5] 351 H.C. Deb. 5s. Cols. 280–2, 284–5.
[6] Cmd. 6106, p. 175.

through the Corridor, with some international guarantee for Poland's future security, British Ministers would have exerted the strongest pressure on the Poles to accept, and might well have regarded their guarantee inoperative had they refused to negotiate some such terms. Hitler was also assured, if he really wanted it, participation in a scheme for multi-national administration of the African colonies and sympathetic consideration of requests for foreign capital. German policy, however, though this was not known to Britain at the time, was dedicated to the destruction of Poland as a result of the pact with Russia as well as by Hitler's then unknown earlier plans; this could only have been acquiesced in by Britain at the cost of the total alienation of domestic and foreign opinion. Since Munich British and French capacity to fight Germany on the issue of the sanctity of treaties (for it was this, not Poland, which was at stake) had gravely deteriorated; moreover, the policy of unilateral guarantees embarked upon after the Prague *coup* in March had, as we have seen, made Britain and France suppliants at Stalin's door and presented him with a choice. Nevertheless, if the Munich policy could ever be justified, its justification lay in the fact that by September 1939 Britain and France could feel that war, as never before in history, was right. Moreover, no matter how formidable the task of overcoming Germany, their cause must ultimately be that of the world. For what their diplomacy, however grave its shortcomings, had shown was that Hitler was seeking not so much the striking off of Germany's fetters, but the destruction of an international order in which every state had a vital interest.

CHAPTER XXIII

THE FAULT IN OURSELVES

Few will deny today that the twenty-three years of foreign policy traced by this book were among the most unsatisfactory in the long record of the British government. When these years opened, Britain was on a pinnacle of eminence, the centre of the most extensive empire known to history, the *primus inter pares* in an alliance bloodily forging its ascendancy in the greatest war the world had seen. When they closed, her prestige had fallen so low that she was virtually written off by many external sympathisers, especially in the United States, on whom she was now dependent for survival. In areas of the world subject to British rule, such as India and the Middle East, nationalist leaders considered it merely a matter of time before they would be dealing with new masters. The chief object of British policy, peace, had failed and the conflict with Nazi Germany was entered upon in the most unfavourable circumstances and with countries which might have been allies either ranged on the enemy side or hopeful of finding safety in neutrality. British decisions in the 1930s of the greatest moment were condemned as errors of judgment and the relief with which many British people faced war with Germany in 1939 was a measure of their disillusionment with their foreign policy and the men who had made it.

Responsibility for these failures is not unnaturally laid by critics at the door of other people, or of other political parties than those with which the critics indentify themselves. Radical wings of British opinion regard the 'appeasers', especially Neville Chamberlain, as Guilty Men for having misunderstood the Nazi and Fascist threats to peace, and perhaps through subconscious admiration for these régimes, for having conspired to strengthen them against Communist forces in the Europe of the 1930s. If, however, the 'appeasers' were wrong, so was the great bulk of British public opinion which supported them, with more or less enthusiasm, until the last days of peace. Moreover, one at least of the central ideas of men like Baldwin, Simon, Hoare, Chamberlain was not only common to wide areas of British opinion of the day, but even at the present time is not patently unsound. It was that modern war is so hideous and so unpredictable in its outcome, whatever the purposes for which it may be waged, that no shred of doubt must exist that national survival is really at stake before it is unleashed.   What present-day critics of the 'appeasers' tend to forget is that war was regarded by many politically unpartisan people in the 1930s as in every way as destructive as thermonuclear war is regarded today.   Those who in the 1960s would willingly fight a nuclear war in defence of, say, West Berlin are alone entitled to criticise British Ministers who in 1938 refused to make themselves responsible for sentencing millions to death in order to keep the Sudeten Germans in Czechoslovakia.

On the other side, the few present-day defenders of British policy in the thirties are apt to place the blame on contemporary British public opinion, with its predominantly anti-war complexion, and on Labour and Liberal Opposition leaders, who allegedly confused the issues by demanding resistance to the dictators and voting against the government's rearmament measures at one and the same time.   But, just as critics of 'appeasement' draw an unreal distinction between public and Ministerial responsibilities for the failures of those years, so their defenders assume that Ministers were unaffected by the unrealistic thinking of the times.   As this book has sought to show, it was not as though Ministers fully understood the drift of affairs but refrained from telling the truth for fear of being ousted from office.   The fact is that Ministers themselves did not for the most part consider that armaments were the necessary means for deterring the aggrieved Powers.   They found it hard to believe that established European states would deny their peoples the right to secure and healthy lives in the interests of creating the military basis for the redress of their grievances.   'I do not believe,' said Neville Chamberlain in November 1937, 'that such a Government anywhere exists among civilised peoples,' and few, if any, of his colleagues would have disagreed.[1]   Europe, it was felt, had had such a taste of war in 1914-18 that, although it might slide into catastrophe again through the sheer weight of unsettled problems, this could never occur through deliberate intent.   There must be some point at which governments would halt the drift to Armageddon; but they were unlikely to do so through fear of opposing forces, but only through real problems being negotiated away.   In holding these views British Ministers, like the broad band of British opinion, were, in Professor Toynbee's words, 'prematurely humanised'.[2]

The true weakness of British policy lay in the force of certain

---

[1] Neville Chamberlain, *In Search of Peace*, London, 1940, p. 50.
[2] *The World in March, 1939*, ed. by A. J. Toynbee, London, 1952, p. 34.

widely diffused moral and political ideas, pacifist, humanist, bourgeois and eminently unfanatical, rather than in calculated disloyalty to democratic ideals on one side of the political fence or confused Socialist or internationalist notions on the other. But if the analysis is placed in a wider setting, if the whole of our period is taken into account rather than merely the dramatic events of the late 1930s, it is evident how ill-adapted were the entire style and temper of British foreign policy to the international conditions in which it had to operate. In considering this aspect we must think, not so much of individual statesmen or attitudes towards particular countries or issues, but of a whole mental approach to foreign relations.

At risk of over-simplification, and setting aside for the present intermediate bands of opinion between one political extremity and the other, the underlying premises of British thought on foreign policy during our period could be characterised on the following lines. There was, in the first place, a basic conservatism in regard to the prevailing international order appropriate to a wealthy, contented Power, with a larger stake in the external world than it was in fact able to defend, and apprehensive as to the effect on its accumulated interests of violence or revolutionary change almost anywhere. While leaders of the Labour Party, notably Clement Attlee, repeatedly called for a breach with traditional diplomatic practices and the substitution of collective security for the effort to protect national interests by national armaments, the party in fact never expressly proposed reforms in the League Covenant so as to eliminate the principle of national sovereignty. It constantly feared any closer British integration with other states, especially in Europe. Labour and Liberal leaders, at least until March 1936 and in many cases even later, were as nervous as Conservatives of military staff talks with France and Belgium on the ground that they would take the choice of war or peace out of Britain's sovereign hands. The Labour Party front bench moreover was almost as opposed as the National Government to anything in the nature of a Popular Front against the revisionist Powers and remained until the Munich crisis highly suspicious of the Soviet Union. These attitudes suggest that, had the Labour party been in office, it might have wrought no revolutionary change in the characteristic lines of British policy.

The idea of the avoidance of advance commitments and of the preservation, as far as possible, of a free hand for Britain was a striking feature of all significant sectors of British opinion between the wars. We have seen in this book how at every critical juncture British Ministers took fright at the prospect of becoming pledge-bound and at no time, except in the immediate aftermath of the German entry into Bohemia in March 1939, did they find themselves at variance on this with Parliamentary or public opinion. The policy of the free hand bore the prestige of great names like Lord Salisbury; it conjured up the untroubled times of pre-1914; it chimed in with the British conception of politics as a process of unforced growth and development, with which commitment to the *status quo*, as urged by France and other beneficiaries of the 1919 settlement, conflicted; it left Britain free to probe American intentions with respect to peace in Europe and the Far East, free to pursue her wider interests beyond the European perimeter. When the policy of the free hand was abandoned, as at Locarno in 1925 and in the hurried guarantees given to European states after the fall of Prague in March 1939, the abandonment was more apparent than real. As we have seen, the British Government regarded Locarno as effective only so long as Britain was not called upon to honour her cheque; if ever the Franco-German reconciliation which made Locarno possible evaporated, the Rhine pact would have lost its *raison d'être* and Britain would be facing the same threat to the European balance as in August 1914. In much the same way, the 1939 guarantees were never meant as permanent changes in the policy of non-commitment. Their object, as seen in Whitehall, was to induce in Germany a frame of mind essential for negotiating the all-European settlement which would henceforth render unnecessary such departures from the policy of the free hand.

The second element in the long-standing British approach to foreign policy which study of our period makes clear is the tacit assumption that economic issues and considerations are paramount, and that political arguments—those having to do with national power, status and standing, with relations of dominance and submission, and with the ordering of society in accordance with a pre-conceived frame of values—are distractions from the essential work of the market-place and board room. The British, true to the instincts of a trading nation, stubbornly believed that trouble-making foreign governments would lay aside their political ideologies when opportunities for profitable business presented themselves; indeed that these ideologies were only embraced in the first place to appease ignorant local opinion or frighten other countries into coming to the negotiating table. The unconscious acceptance by the British people of certain political dogmas which never needed to be articulated or argued for; the absence in Britain, even in the 1930s, of fundamental political cleavages serious enough to

impair normal processes of government; the tacit agreement
that the alignment of British foreign policy with one or other of
the warring ideologies of the Continent would jeopardise the
social unity which was one of the main sources of British
strength: all these led British Ministers to regard foreign ideologies with a certain unbelief. Surely responsible statesmen
abroad could not wish to ruin the prospects of good business
through indulgence in 'vague and puzzling idealism', as the British Foreign Office described the idea of European Union in
1930. Surely, as Lloyd George imagined in 1922, Lenin really
wanted trade rather than anything so impractical as world revolution. Surely, as Neville Chamberlain believed when he went
to see Hitler at Berchtesgaden in 1938, beneath the Führer's
demagogic façade was a man with a grievance, who, after the
grievance had been attended to, was interested in nothing so
much as the signing of business contracts.

Along with this assumption went another, equally derived
from the economic frame of reference, namely that between
extreme positions, as between buyers' bids and sellers' starting
prices, there is always a middle term to be found if the auction
goes on long enough. The whole *ethos* of the trader is pointless
without the assumption of a hidden middle term. The middle
term implies concessions and counter-concessions; it assumes
an interest in both sides in the maintenance of the market and
the rules of business. It is hard to convince the trader that
those he meets in the market are not there to buy and sell but
to burn down the emporium and build a gladiatorial school.
Even when his illusions are shattered, as they were in 1939, he
will continue to think that fattening the thin Communist, for
example, will turn him into a respectable businessman. And
who, considering the imponderable hazards of the alternative
assumption, can blame him?

These two strands of British thought on international policy
were functions of a quiescent, humanist frame of mind which
suited a sated Power with dependent territories and trading
connections scattered like hostages to fortune in all parts of the
world, and with a vital interest in keeping foreign discontents
restrained and appeased. To these, however, was added a
third element: the social grievances awakened by the First
World War and symbolised by the rise of the Labour party.
We have had occasion to see how much closer the foreign policy
attitudes of the Labour Governments were to those of the Conservatives than is often supposed. Fear of war and great armaments, mistrust of France, at least in the 1920s, aversion for
partial alliances and positive European commitments, dissatis-

faction with the 1919 peace treaties: were all attitudes common to Left and Right in Britain. But there is no question that the bitterness left by the 1914–18 war in the Labour Movement, the repugnance for the international system from which the war had sprung, the sustained *malaise* on the Left with the social order within the country, however understandable these feelings were, handicapped the government, and would have handicapped any Labour Government, in the organisation of a balance of power against the dictator states. The Left, as is now claimed, did indeed demand action against the dictators, but it was often action contrary to the rationale of the existing international system. The example of League sanctions against Italy is crucial. In 1936 it was against the German reoccupation of the Rhineland that action was required by the contemporary logic of the balance of Power. But Hitler's move was not highly offensive to the Left, or to League supporters, since the blow he struck was against the Versailles system which they tended to associate with the discredited international order of the past. It was, however, Mussolini's African venture, owing to its being assimilated with the general imperialist enemy of the radicals, which was placed in the dock, even though the invasion of Abyssinia, while no doubt immoral by any test, was not nearly the threat to the balance of power which Hitler's action in the Rhineland represented. The rise of the Labour Movement thus inhibited the predominantly Conservative Governments of the period from pursuing balance of power practices while failing to convince them that the League of Nations was an effective substitute for the older practices of the international system.

Hence the British approach to foreign policy in our period may be regarded as compounded of three elements, of which two were old and the third a product of the unsparing social criticism released, if not caused, by the First World War. What was required for the success of this political style was a margin of security, a surplus of means over needs, a reserve of time to allow for adjustment to the more barbaric realities of the day, a balance out of which errors and misjudgments caused by good-natured trust in human reasonableness could be compensated. The circumstances of the day unhappily made no allowance for this. Strain was continuous, resources consistently less than needs, the balance of world forces at most times precarious and at some times decisively unfavourable.

This central feature of Britain's international position in the inter-war period went largely unnoticed, largely because the catastrophe of the First World War had riveted attention on something quite different, namely the idea that the traditional international system was for all practical purposes bankrupt and unworthy of further support. The post-1918 international scene, for many influential levels of British opinion, stood permanently frozen

Between two worlds, one dead,
The other powerless to be born.

The fact, however, from which all eyes were averted was that, for the four and half years of the First World War, Germany, with no considerable asistance from her allies, had held the rest of the world at bay, had beaten Russia, had driven France, the military colossus of Europe for more than two centuries, to the end of her tether, and, in 1917, had come within an ace of starving Britain into surrender. It would have required a coalition of all these states, together with the United States, to contain Germany after 1918, even had the Nazis never come to power. But such a coalition was never in sight.

In the years following 1918 Russia was divided from Britain and France by ideological discords; in any case she had to remain on guard against a Japan infinitely more powerful than the Japan which had invaded her Far Eastern provinces in 1918. Between Russia and Germany the peace treaties had created a belt of militarily weak successor states which feared Russia as much as they feared Germany, some of them more so. Any alliance between Russia and the Western democracies aimed at restraining Germany must mean the extinction of the independence of some of these states or the surrender of parts of their territory to the Soviets, and yet the defence of these states was one of the strongest grounds on which a British Government could have justified to its public opinion an active British intervention in the European balance. Italy, Britain's ally in the First World War, was, if not positively on Germany's side, at least alienated from her fellow victors of 1918, and the question which France constantly had to face was whether, if she were embroiled in war with Germany, Italy would not attack her from the south, as was to happen in 1940. The United States Government were if anything more opposed to taking part in the European balance than in 1914 and for all practical purposes could be discounted in the assessment of forces on the European continent. In the Far East China was in a state of chronic civil war and Japan at liberty to embark on building her New Order in East Asia with practically no opposition from the Western Powers. These Powers had on the contrary the strongest interest in reaching private arrangements with her in order to defend privileges in China which they could no longer protect out of their own resources.

The balance of world power was thus potentially unfavourable for Britain and her sole considerable ally, France, from the outset. The most direct means for preventing this potentiality from becoming actual was that the two democracies should ensure that Germany never rearmed or remilitarised the Rhineland. This they could only have done in the final resort by the actual occupation of German territory, but, apart from the unanimous refusal of British opinion to countenance this at any time, France had tried this policy in the Ruhr in 1923 and had disastrously failed. The alternative was to organise and maintain in being a permanent balance of power against Germany such that not even her rearmament or fortification of the Rhineland could have endangered peace. But such a strategy was wholly in conflict with the basic British attitudes of timely intervention from afar to redress piecemeal grievances, of mediation between European Powers of relatively equal weight, of cajoling the Powers back into an assumed latent equilibrium, with politics properly subordinated to economic commonsense. These attitudes, comprising the native British style of foreign policy, thus conflicted with the logic of the international system of the day. At the same time, the diminished resources of Britain after the war tended to harden rather than weaken British foreign policy style, dictating, or seeming to dictate, a technique of striving for composure abroad rather than of framing a counter-balance against Germany. This decline in British resources for foreign policy may be illustrated in three major fields: naval power, economic strength and solvency, and the process of devolution in the Commonwealth.

British naval power, which, at least as a potential deterrent, had played such an important part in the nineteenth-century *Pax Britannica*, came under the severest challenges in the period after 1918. The First World War had shown the vulnerability of the slow-moving battleship to the submarine and the bombing plane, the submarine proving impossible to abolish by international agreement in the disarmament talks of the 1920s and the bomber increasing year by year in speed and accuracy of aim. Moreover, the navy emerged from the war no more than equal in strength to the American and time and energy were spent in securing a standstill in the highly irrelevant Anglo-American naval arms race at the cost of handicapping the development of British fast cruisers. The rift in British and American political attitudes in the Manchurian crisis of 1931 and the Sino-Japanese War which began in July 1937 meant that the navies of these two Powers could not be jointly employed against Japan, which had incidentally gained much immunity from naval attack at the Washington Naval Conference of 1921–22; accordingly Britain found that such naval power as she had would have to be deployed in European rather than Far Eastern waters. Naval power after the First World War could clearly never be used on any substantial scale by Britain except in close co-operation with the United States, and yet the essential political consensus to make that co-operation possible was at all times lacking.

But perhaps the most notable weakness of British naval power in this period was not so much its actual magnitude as compared with that of rivals, as its irrelevance to the task of correcting the strains in the political balance as it then existed. In the 1930s the threat to the balance came in eastern Europe with the Nazi campaign to destroy the newly created states of the Versailles system. British naval power could be no effective restraint on this land-based and land-locked *Drang nach Osten* unless efforts to deter Germany ended in a general war, which it was their chief purpose to avert. On their side, the German Government were able to threaten Britain that her cities would be laid in ashes by air bombardment if she challenged the *Lebensraum* policy and war ensued. But, as it happened, the air defence of Britain was a competitor for British resources with the naval arm and hence, by a curious turn of affairs, the re-equipment of the British navy came in some measure to depend upon the threat of air bombardment being removed through British acquiescence in Hitler's threats to the treaty system. This was evidently consistent with Hitler's own purposes since he angled for a bargain by which the security of the British Isles and the Empire would be guaranteed in return for freedom to pursue his own designs in eastern Europe. For Britain, however, the implication of these facts was that her naval power were both too weak to restrain Hitler's partners, Japan and Italy, at the same time and largely irrelevant to the task of deterring the Führer himself from making the countries between Germany and Russia his pawns.

The economic strains and doctrines of the time were also sources of weakness. Britain, after a short-lived boom due to the supplying of wartime shortages and demands deferred during the conflict, entered the peace with a reserve of unemployed which never fell below a million men. The core of idle manpower was concentrated in areas where old export trades, chiefly coal, cotton and shipbuilding, were heavily localised. These industries were in the position either of having been over-expanded during the First World War or, as in the case of textiles, of having had their traditional markets encroached upon during the war by new, low-cost competitors, especially in the Far East. A thorough-going national plan for redirecting these idle resources to accord with post-war economic trends in the world might have solved the problem of mass unemployment had the economic dogmas of the time permitted it and had there been a prospect of rising effective demand in the world as a whole. Economic doctrine was, however, unfavourable, holding to the deflationary thesis that times of stress are times for reducing Government spending, a remedy which only aggravated the disease; and the long-term world economic depression, culminating in virtual paralysis in 1931–32, was especially severe on countries like Britain which were highly dependent on a vigorous flow of international trade and investment. The intense economic nationalism of the times only increased Britain's problems. New nations created by the 1919 peace settlement not unnaturally sought to build up home industries behind protective tariff walls, and all nations, Britain included, sought an equilibrium in their balance of payments, when the Great Depression struck, by the most painless method to hand, that of discouraging imports. In this climate of shrinking world markets and effective demand, with its accompanying mentality of *sauve qui peut*, Britain could expect to make greater economic losses than any other great Power.

But it was perhaps the psychological effects of this economic experience which most influenced British policy. These strengthened tendencies we have already noted: the distaste for rearmament, which, as a form of Government spending, was regarded as aggravating the economic problem; the fear of external commitments which might have the effect of ranging the nations in armed camps against each other, thus entrenching the trade barriers between them which economic nationalism had built; the grasping at every shred of hope of across-the-board settlements which might close the book of political discord once for all and open that of peaceful trade. Over all British foreign policy during this period, over Lloyd George's and Bonar Law's disagreements with the French on German reparations, over Simon's attitude towards the Japanese in Manchuria, over the approaches of Baldwin and Neville Chamberlain to the dictators, hung the nostalgia for the old world of peaceful trade, with armaments and political feuds finally laid aside. British economic interests, in short, disposed British Ministers to think that other states sought the same world of free and peaceful economic co-operation as themselves; at the same time, these same economic compulsions made it harder to deal with the situation in the event that those assumptions proved to be false.

The third major weakness in Britain's international position derived from the rapidly decreasing cohesion of the British Commonwealth and Empire. In August 1914 the question whether Britain should enter the armed conflict in Europe was debated in Cabinet in the knowledge that, whatever was decided, the Empire would fall into line. Never again was that to be the position. After 1918 every major decision of British policy had to be preceded by an inquiry into the likely attitude of the British Dominions, which had shown their independence in no uncertain way at the Paris Peace Conference, had joined the League of Nations as separate entities and had received their formal certificate of autonomy in the Balfour resolutions of 1926, later embodied in the Statute of Westminster in 1931. Had war between Britain and Turkey broken out in 1922 it is possible that the Dominions would have remained neutral; the Locarno Pact of 1925, British negotiations with Russia on European security in the 1930s, the British guarantees to Poland and other European states in 1939, to mention but a few of the outstanding acts of British policy in this period, left the Dominions, if not unmoved, certainly uncommitted. We have also seen how British fear of political unsettlement in India played a major role in the making of British policy towards Turkey and the Arab states during the reshaping of Near Eastern affairs after 1918. While it is true to say that British Ministers, as during the negotiations on the Geneva Protocol in 1925, were apt to use the hesitations of the self-governing states of the Empire as pretexts for refusing commitments which they had decided to reject on other grounds, the isolationism of these countries undoubtedly served to reinforce British insularity, and at a moment when this insularity was becoming harder to justify. It is possible that a firm announcement by the British Government of the need for active measures to correct the European balance after, say, the introduction of conscription in Germany in 1935 might have enticed the Dominions out of their isolation; but if this German breach of treaty did not seem to the British to threaten their security it could hardly have impressed the Dominions as raising the issue of British independence, on behalf of which they were indeed willing to fight. It should be remembered, in the matter of this relation between the vital interests of Britain and those of the Dominions, that as the independence of these countries grew so did the divergences between their several interests.

South Africa, for example, was stirred to the depths by Mussolini's attack on Abyssinia in 1935 while opinion was but mildly affected in Canada and Australia. The German reoccupation of the Rhineland in 1936 was more significant for Canada than for South Africa; and so on. The problem before Britain was how and when to join issue with dissident states in such a way as to unite all the Dominions with their separate interests behind her. In such a calculation a premium tended to be placed on delay rather than on the over-hasty choice of issues.

Thus while the international situation was lacking in that margin of safety required by the peculiar British style of foreign policy, the country's resources were themselves under intense pressure. It is remarkable, however, how little these limitations on the sinews of policy were understood at the time and now much they have been overlooked since by critics of British policy. In the inter-war period it was commonly believed by both Government and Opposition that it was for Britain to make her decisions and the appropriate consequences would ensue in the international system. We have seen how British Governments, with strange disregard for the world-wide considerations on which British foreign policy is often said to be based, seemed to attach little significance to the fact that after the First World War the European balance, much more that in the Far East, could not be maintained without extra-European help, in particular that of the United States and Russia. While the deeply entrenched isolationism of the former state and the revolutionary crusade pursued by the latter made effective co-operation with either to preserve the European balance all but impossible, British Ministers were not always much disturbed by this fact. Neville Chamberlain, for example, tended to regard Franklin Roosevelt somewhat as a tiresome interloper in his own efforts to reach agreement with Hitler and Mussolini, and neither he nor his predecessors had much confidence in the ability or readiness of Russia to play her part in the European balance. Yet if the First World War, the economic recovery of Europe in the 1920s, the diplomatic ascendancy enjoyed by Germany in the mid-1930s proved anything, it surely was that after 1914 the European equation of forces was no longer a function of European terms alone.

The Government's critics were equally unmindful of Britain's lack of power to stabilise European affairs by her own effort or example. The Opposition in the 1930s talked of collective security but were as reluctant as the Government to enter into hard-and-fast commitments with France or any other *status quo* country. Their attitude towards Russia was at all times warmer than the National Government's, but this, it seems, was more on account of faint ideological sympathies than of strategical considerations. Opposition leaders tended to think that Britain, almost by force of example alone, could lead the world into disarmament and the rational organisation of the world's economic resources. Here indeed was one reason for the failure of the Labour Opposition and Winston Churchill to combine effectively, save for the six months or so immediately preceding the outbreak of war in 1939. Churchill, for all his talk of the League Covenant, really wanted an old-fashioned military alliance among all those threatened by Germany; Attlee considered it enough that Britain should 'give a lead to the world' at Geneva looking towards the utter renunciation of arms and alliances. This same over-estimation of British capacity to influence events has affected critics of British policy since 1939. What these overlook is that although at critical junctures judgment was certainly lacking in British Ministers and contemporary public opinion, even if their wisdom had been flawless the force of circumstances was adverse for the troubled British giant.

If there is any general conclusion to be derived from this record perhaps it is that men at all times, and especially when their country's power is declining relatively to that of others, have a special responsibility to examine and re-examine the things they take for granted about the political world they inhabit. The failure of British policy between the two wars was indeed a failure of resources; but it was more truly a failure of ideas, or rather a failure to adjust ideas born in one age to the requirements of another. The British political mentality has been described by a French historian in the following terms:

> The English only make up their minds to fight when their interests seem absolutely threatened. But then, plunging into the struggle because they feel themselves bound to do so, they apply to it a serious and concentrated passion, an animosity the more tenacious because its motive is so self-regarding. Their history is full of alternations between indifference which makes people think them decadent and a rage which baffles their foes. They are seen, in turn, abandoning or dominating Europe, neglecting the greatest Continental matters and claiming to control even the smallest, turning from peace at any price to war to the death.[1]

In an age of secure British preponderance this attitude was correct; it was rooted in a sense of proportion in recognising

[1] Albert Sorel, *L'Europe et la Révolutiom française*, I, 3rd Edn., Paris, 1893, pp. 340–1.

what was essential for the preservation of the European balance of power.   In an age of strain and trouble, however, when resources are stretched and self-confidence undermined, it left allies uncertain where they stood and prompted international incendiarists to pull the European house down while the British debated whether they had heard a noise.   Detachment and refusal to be involved are permissible when there is a margin available for the making of errors; where the impact of pressures is direct and sharp the risk is run of losing the battle before realising it has begun.

SELECT BIBLIOGRAPHY

The following is a selection of the sources used in writing this book; it does not include British Parliamentary Papers, references to which will be found in the footnotes to the text.

I. DOCUMENTS

Czechoslovak Republic and U.S.S.R., Ministries of Foreign Affairs, *New documents on the history of Munich*, Orbis-Prague, 1958.

J. Degras (ed.), *Soviet documents on foreign policy, 1917–1941*, 3 vols., London, R.I.I.A., 1951–53.

Documents diplomatiques secrets Russes, 1914–1917, tr. by J. Polonsky, Paris, Payot, 1928.

France, Ministère des Affaires Étrangeres, *Documents diplomatiques*, Paris, 1924.

—*Le livre jaune français*, Paris, 1939.

F. A. Golder, *Documents of Russian history, 1914–17*, N.Y., Century, 1927.

A. Hitler, *The speeches*, ed. by N. H. Baynes, 2 vols., London, R.I.I.A., 1942.

H.M.S.O., *Documents on British foreign policy, 1919–39*, ed. by R. Butler and E. L. Woodward, later J. P. T. Bury, London, 1947, continuing.

—*Documents on German foreign policy, 1918–45*, London, 1957, continuing.

—*The trial of German major war criminals. Proceedings of the international Military Tribunal at Nuremberg, 23 vols.*, 1946–51.

The International Military Tribunal for the Far East. *Trial of the major Japanese war criminals, Report*.

Italy, Ministero degli Affari Esteri, *I documenti diplomatici italiani*, 6a serie, 1918–22, Vol. I, Rome, 1956; 7a serie, 1922–35, Vols. I–IV, Rome, 1953–62; 8a serie, 1935–39, Vols. XI and XII, Rome, 1952–53.

P. Mantoux (ed.), *Les délibérations du conseil des quatre*, 2 vols., Paris, Centre national de la recherche scientifique, 1955.

R.I.I.A., *Documents on international affairs*, annual, 1928 to 1939–46 (Vol. I), 14 vols., London, 1929–51.

U.K., Foreign Office, *Documents on the origins of the war, 1898–1914*, ed. by G. P. Gooch and H. Temperley, 11 vols., London, H.M.S.O., 1926–38.

U.K., Public Record Office, War Cabinet Minutes, Cabinet Conclusions, Cabinet Office Papers, Foreign Office Files, December 1916–October 1922.

U.S.A., Department of State, *Foreign relations of the United States*, Washington, D.C.

U.S.S.R., *Documents and papers relating to the eve of the Second World War*, (Dirksen Papers), Moscow, 1948.

II. MEMOIRS AND BIOGRAPHIES

Lord D'Abernon, *An ambassador of peace*, 3 vols., London, Hodder and Stoughton, 1929–30.

P. Aloisi, *Journal*, tr. by M. Vaussard, Paris, Plon, 1957.

L. C. M. S. Amery, *My political life*, 3 vols., London, Hutchinson, 1953–55.

H. H. Asquith, *Memories and reflections*, 2 vols., London, Cassell, 1928.

The Earl of Avon, *Facing the dictators*, London, Cassell, 1962.

J. Beck, *Dernier rapport*, Neuchâtel, Éditions de la Baconière, 1951.

G. E. Bonnet, *Défense de la paix*, 2 vols., Geneva, Bourquin, 1946–48.

Sir G. W. Buchanan, *My mission to Russia*, 2 vols., London. Cassell, 1923.

J. R. M. Butler, *Lord Lothian*, London, Macmillan, 1960.

Sir C. E. Callwell, *Field-Marshal Sir Henry Wilson*, Vol. II, London, Cassell, 1927.

Sir J. A. Chamberlain, *Down the years*, London, Cassell, 1935.

Sir W. S. Churchill, *The world crisis, 1911–23*, 6 vols., London, Thornton Butterworth, 1923–29.

—*The Second World War*, Vol. I, *The gathering storm*, London, Cassell, 1948.

Ciano di Cortellazzo, *L'Europa verso la catastrofe*, Verona, Mondadori, 1948.

A. D. Cooper (Lord Norwich), *Haig*, 2 vols., London, Faber, 1935–36.

—*Old men forget*, London, Hart-Davis, 1953.

P. Cot, *Triumph of treason*, Chicago, N.Y., Ziff-Davies, 1944.

R. Coulondre, *De Staline à Hitler*, Paris, Hachette, 1950.

C. A. Cripps (Lord Parmoor), *A retrospect*, London, Heinemann, 1936.

Lord Dalton, *The fateful years. Memoirs, 1931–45*, London, Muller, 1957.

H. von Dirksen, *Moskau, Tokio, London*, Stuttgart, Kohlhammer, 1949.

W. E. Dodd, *Ambassador Dodd's diary, 1933–38*, New York, Harcourt Brace; London, Gollancz, 1941.

B. E. C. Dugdale, *Arthur James Balfour*, 2 vols., London, Hutchinson, 1936.

L. J. L. Dundas (The Earl of Ronaldshay), *The life of Lord Curzon*, 3 vols., London, Benn, 1928.

Sir K. G. Feiling, *The life of Neville Chamberlain*, London, Macmillan, 1946.

P. É. Flandin, *Politique française, 1919–40*, Paris, Éditions nouvelles, 1947.

A. François-Poncet, *Souvenirs d'une ambassade à Berlin*, Paris, Flammarion, 1946.

M. G. Gamelin, *Servir*, 3 vols., Paris, Plon, 1946–47.

D. Lloyd George, *The truth about the peace treaties*, 2 vols., London, Gollancz, 1938.
—*War memoirs*, 6 vols., London, Nicholson-Watson, 1933–36.

J. C. Grew, *Turbulent era*, 2 vols., Boston, Houghton Mifflin; London, Hammond, 1953.

Viscount Grey, *Twenty-five years*, 2 vols., London, Hodder and Stoughton, 1925.

Raffaele Guariglia, *La diplomatie difficile*, tr. by L. Bonalumi, Paris, Plon, 1955.

Earl Haig, *The private papers of Douglas Haig*, ed. by R. Blake, London, Eyre and Spottiswoode, 1952.

M. A. Hamilton, *Arthur Henderson*, London, Heinemann, 1938.

Sir W. K. Hancock, *Smuts, the sanguine years, 1870–1919*, Cambridge, C.U.P., 1962.

U. von Hassell, *The von Hassel diaries, 1938–44*, London, Hamilton, 1948.

Sir N. M. Henderson, *Failure of a mission*, London, Hodder and Stoughton, 1940.

E. Herriot, *Jadis*, 2 vols., Paris, Flammarion, 1948–52.

C. Hull, *The memoirs of Cordell Hull*, 2 vols., New York, Macmillan; London, Hodder and Stoughton, 1948.

T. Jones, *A diary with letters, 1931–50*, London, O.U.P., 1954.
—*Lloyd George*, London, O.U.P., 1951.

Sir I. A. Kirkpatrick, *The inner circle*, London, Macmillan, 1959.

P. Kleist, *Zwischen Hitler und Stalin*, Bonn, Athenäum-Verlag, 1950.

R. Lansing, *The peace negotiations*, Boston, Houghton Mifflin; London, Constable, 1921.

J. Laroche, *La Pologne de Pilsudski*, Paris, Flammarion, 1953.

Sir R. H. B. Lockhart, *Memoirs of a British agent*, London, Putnam, 1936.

I. N. Macleod, *Neville Chamberlain*, London, Muller, 1961.

D. H. Miller, *My diary at the conference of Paris*, 21 vols., N.Y., privately published, 1924–26.

R. J. Minney, *The private papers of Hore-Belisha*, London, Collins, 1960.

S. G. Millin, *General Smuts*, 2 vols., London, Faber, 1936.

Lord Newton, *Lord Lansdowne*, London, Macmillan, 1929.

Sir H. Nicolson, *Curzon, the last phase*, London, Constable, 1934.

—*King George the Fifth*, London, Constable, 1953.

F. Owen, *Tempestuous Journey*, London, Hutchinson, 1954.

W. H. Page, *Life and letters*, 2 vols., Garden City, N.Y., Doubleday, Page; London, Heinemann, 1923–25.

M. Paléologue, *An ambassador's memoirs*, tr. by F. A. Holt, 3 vols., London, Hutchinson, 1923–25.

F. von Papen, *Memoirs*. tr. by B. Connell, London, Deutsch, 1952.

J. Paul-Boncour, *Entre deux guerres*, 3 vols., Paris, Plon, 1945–46.

Sir C. Petrie, *The life and letters of the Rt. Hon. Sir A. Chamberlain*, Vol. II, London, Cassell, 1940.

J. von Ribbentrop, *Zwischen London und Moskau*, Leoni am Starnberger See, Druffel-Verlag, 1953.

G. A. Riddell, *Lord Riddell's intimate diary of the peace conference*, London, Gollancz, 1933.

C. Seymour (ed.), *The intimate papers of Col. House*, 4 vols., Boston, Houghton Mifflin; London, Benn, 1926–28.

Viscount Simon, *Retrospect*, London, Hutchinson, 1952.

H. W. Steed, *Through thirty years*, London, Heinemann, 1924.

H. L. Stimson, *The Far Eastern crisis*, N. Y. and London, Harper, 1936.

Lord Strang, *Home and abroad*, London, Deutsch, 1956.

G. Stresemann, *Diaries, letters and papers*, ed. by E. Sutton, 3 vols., London, Macmillan, 1935–40.

A. P. G. A. Tardieu, *La paix*, Paris, Payot, 1921.

Viscount Templewood, *Nine troubled years*, London, Collins, 1954.

A. Vallentin, *Stresemann*, London, Constable, 1931.

Sir R. G. Vansittart, *The mist procession*, London, Hutchinson, 1958.

E. von Weizsäcker, *Erinnerungen*, Munich, List, 1950.

Sir J. E. L. Wrench, *Geoffrey Dawson and our times*, London, Hutchinson, 1955.

G. M. Young, *Stanley Baldwin*, London, Hart-Davies, 1952.

III. SECONDARY WORKS—GENERAL

G. M. Carter, *The British Commonwealth and international security*, Toronto, Ryerson Press, 1947.

G. A. Craig and F. Gilbert (eds.), *The diplomats, 1919–39*, Princeton, Princeton University Press, 1953.

M. Gilbert, *The European Powers, 1900–45*, London, Weidenfeld and Nicolson, 1965.

W. McElwee, *Britain's locust years, 1918–40*, London, Faber, 1962.

P. N. S. Mansergh, *Survey of British Commonwealth affairs*, Vol. III, *Problems of external policy, 1931–39*, London, R.I.I.A., 1952.

W. N. Medlicott, *British foreign policy since Versailles*, London, Methuen, 1940.

C. L. Mowat, *Britain between the wars*, London, Methuen, 1962.

S. Pollard, *The development of the British economy*, London, Arnold, 1962.

P. E. G. Renouvin, (ed.), *Histoire des relations internationales*, Vols. VII and VIII, Paris, Hachette, 1957–58.

P. A. Reynolds, *British foreign policy between the wars*, London, Longmans, 1954.

R.I.I.A., *Political and strategic interests of the United Kingdom*, London, 1939.

—*Survey of international affairs*, annual, 1920–23 to 1939, 23 vols., London, 1927 *et seq.*

J. A. Spender, *Between two wars*, London, Cassell, 1943.

Lord Strang, *Britain in world affairs*, New York, Praeger; London, Faber, 1961.

A. J. P. Taylor, *English history, 1914–45*, Oxford, Clarendon Press, 1965.

A. P. Thornton, *The imperial idea and its enemies*, London, Macmillan, 1959.

The history of 'The Times', Vol. IV, London, 1952.

A. J. Toynbee, *The conduct of British Empire foreign relations since the peace settlement*, London, R.I.I.A., 1928.

Sir A. Willert, *Aspects of British foreign policy*, New Haven, Institute of Politics Publications, 1928.

A. Wolfers, *Britain and France between two wars*, New Haven, Yale University Press, 1940.

A. J. Youngson, *The British economy, 1920–57*, London, Allen and Unwin, 1960.

Sir A. E. Zimmern, *The British Commonwealth in the post-war world*, London, O.U.P., 1926.

IV. SECONDARY WORKS—SPECIAL ISSUES

1. *First World War Diplomacy*

R. S. Baker, *Woodrow Wilson and world settlement*, 3 vols., Garden City, N.Y., Doubleday, Page, 1922; London, Heinemann, 1923.

A. Chatelle, *La paix manquée?* Paris, Firmin-Didot, 1936.

C. R. M. F. Cruttwell, *A history of the Great War*, Oxford, Clarendon Press, 1936.

K. Forster, *The failures of peace*, Washington, American Council of Public Affairs, 1941.

O. H. Gankin and H. H. Fisher, *The Bolsheviks and the World War*, London, O.U.P., 1940.

W. W. Gottlieb, *Studies in secret diplomacy during the First World War*, London, Allen and Unwin, 1957.

Paul Guinn, *British strategy and politics, 1914 to 1918*, Oxford, Clarendon Press, 1965.

H. J. T. Johnson, *Vatican diplomacy during the World War*, Oxford, Blackwell, 1933.

W. Millis, *Road to war*, Boston, Mass., Houghton Mifflin, 1935.

A. Pingaud, *Histoire diplomatique de la France pendant la Grande Guerre*, 3 vols., Paris, Alsatia, 1938–40.

H. R. Rudin, *Armistice, 1918*, New Haven, Yale University Press, 1944.

C. Seymour, *American diplomacy during the World War*, Baltimore, Johns Hopkins Press, 1934.

C. J. Smith, *The Russian struggle for power, 1914–17*, N.Y., Philosophical Library, 1956.

L. Stein, *The Balfour declaration*, London, Vallentine, 1961.

C. C. Tansill, *America goes to war*, Boston, Mass., Little, Brown and Co., 1938.

G. Terrail, *Les négociations secrètes et les quatre armistices*, Paris, Librairie Ollendorff, 1919.

M. Toscano, *Guerra diplomatica in Estremo Oriente, 1914–31*, Turin, Einaudi, 1950.

M. Toscano and others, *La politica estera italiana dal 1914 al 1943*, Turin, Edizioni RAI Radiotelevisione Italiana, 1961.

Z. A. B. Zeman, *The break-up of the Habsburg Empire, 1914–18*, London, O.U.P., 1961.

2. *Peacemaking, 1919–23*

R. Albrecht-Carrié, *Italy at the peace conference*, N.Y., Carnegie Endowment for International Peace, 1938.

B. M. Baruch, *The making of the reparation and economic sections of the treaty*, N.Y., Harper, 1920.

P. Birdsall, *Versailles twenty years after*, London, Allen and Unwin, 1941.

S. Bonsal, *Unfinished business*, N.Y., Doubleday; London, Michael Joseph, 1944.

P. M. Burnett, *Reparations at the Paris peace conference*, 2 vols., N.Y., Columbia University Press, 1940.

D. J. Footman, *Civil war in Russia*, London, Faber, 1961.

F. W. Hirst, *The consequences of the war to Great Britain*, London, O.U.P., 1934.

H. N. Howard, *The partition of Turkey*, Norman, University of Oklahoma Press, 1931.

E. Kedourie, *England and the Middle East*, London, Bowes, 1956.

T. Komarnicki, *Rebirth of the Polish Republic*, London, Heinemann, 1957.

B. Ling, *Parliaments and the peace treaty*, unpub. London, Ph.D. thesis, 1938.

A. M. Luckau, *The German delegation at the Paris peace conference*, N.Y., Carnegie Endowment for International Peace, 1941.

F. S. Marston, *The peace conference of 1919*, London, O.U.P., 1944.

R. B. McCallum, *Public opinion and the last peace*, London, O.U.P., 1944.

I. F. D. Morrow and L. M. Sieveking, *The peace settlement in the German–Polish borderlands*, London, R.I.I.A., 1936.

Sir H. Nicolson, *Peacemaking, 1919*, London, Constable, 1933.

H. V. W. Temperley (ed.), *History of the peace conference of Paris*, 6 vols., London, R.I.I.A., 1920–24.

S. P. Tillman, *Anglo-American relations at the Paris peace conference of 1919*, Princeton, Princeton University Press, 1961.

3. *Soviet Communism*

M. Beloff, *The foreign policy of Soviet Russia, 1929–41*, 2 vols., London, O.U.P., 1947.

F. Borkenau, *The Communist International*, London, Faber, 1938.

J. Bunyan, *Intervention, Civil War and Communism in Russia*, Baltimore, Johns Hopkins Press, 1936.

E. H. Carr, *A history of Soviet Russia. The Bolshevik Revolution, 1917–23*, Vols. I and III, London, Macmillan, 1950, 1953.
—*The Interregnum, 1923–24*, London, Macmillan, 1954.
—*Socialism in one country, 1924–26*, Vol. III, Parts I and II, London, Macmillan, 1964.

W. H. Chamberlin, *The Russian Revolution*, 2 vols., New York and London, Macmillan, 1935.

W. P. and Z. K. Coates, *A history of Anglo-Soviet relations*, 2 vols., London, Lawrence and Wishart, 1943–58.

K. W. Davies, *The Soviets at Geneva*, Chambéry, Réunis, 1934.

G. Dimitrov, *The United Front*, London, Lawrence and Wishart, 1938.

X. J. Eudin and H. H. Fisher (eds.), *Soviet Russia and the West, 1920–27*, Stanford, Stanford University Press, 1957.

X. J. Eudin and K. C. North (eds.), *Soviet Russia and the East, 1920–27*, Stanford, Stanford University Press, 1957.

L. Fischer, *The Soviets in world affairs*, 2nd. edn., 2 vols., Princeton, Princeton University Press, 1951.

S. N. Harper (ed.), *The Soviet Union and world problems*, Chicago, University of Chicago Press, 1935.

G. F. Kennan, *Soviet-American relations, 1917–20*, Vol. I, *Russia leaves the war*, Princeton, Princeton University Press; London, Faber, 1956.

R. W. Lyman, *The first Labour government, 1924*, London, Chapman and Hall, 1957.

Sir B. Pares, *The fall of the Russian monarchy*, London, Cape, 1939.

A. U. Pope, *Maxim Litvinoff*, N.Y., Fischer, 1943.

Sir J. W. Wheeler-Bennett, *Brest-Litovsk: the forgotten peace*, London, Macmillan, 1938.

A. S. Whiting, *Soviet policies in China, 1917–24*, N.Y., Columbia University Press, 1954.

4. *Britain, France and Germany*

C. Bergmann, *The history of reparations*, London, Benn, 1927.

H. L. Bretton, *Stresemann and the revision of Versailles*, Stanford, The University Press, 1954.

R. T. Clark, *The fall of the German Republic*, London, Allen and Unwin; New York, Macmillan, 1935.

D. Lloyd George, *The truth about reparations and war debts*, London, Heinemann, 1932.

G. Glasgow, *From Dawes to Locarno*, London, Benn, 1925.

—*MacDonald as diplomatist*, London, Cape, 1924.

W. M. Jordan, *Great Britain, France and the German problem*, London, R.I.I.A., 1943.

W. W. Kulski and M. Potulicki, *Germany: from defeat to conquest, 1913–33*, London, Allen and Unwin, 1945; New York, Macmillan, 1947.

J. R. MacDonald, *The foreign policy of the Labour party*, London, Palmer, 1923.

Sir A. McFadyean, *Reparation reviewed*, London, Benn, 1930.

A. Rosenberg, *A history of the German Republic*, tr. by I. F. D. Morrow and L. M. Sieveking, London, Methuen, 1936.

E. Stern-Rubarth, *Three men tried*, London, Duckworth, 1939.

P. S. Wandycz, *France and her Eastern allies, 1919–25*, Minneapolis, University of Minnesota Press, 1962.

L. Zimmermann, *Deutsche Aussenpolitik in der Ära der Weimarer Republik*, Göttingen, Musterschmidt, 1958.

5. *The League and disarmament*

L. Archimbaud, *La conférence de Washington*, Paris, Payot, 1923.

R. Bassett, *Democracy and foreign policy*, London, The London School of Economics, 1952.

Viscount Cecil, *A great experiment*, London, Cape, 1941.

R. A. Chaput, *Disarmament in British foreign policy*, London, Allen and Unwin, 1935.

J. F. Charvet, *L'influence Britannique dans la Société des Nations*, Paris, Librairie L. Rodstein, 1938.

G. Engely, *The politics of naval disarmament*, London, Williams and Norgate, 1932.

H. Latimer, *Naval disarmament*, London, R.I.I.A., 1930.

D. H. Miller, *The drafting of the Covenant*, 2 vols., N.Y., and London, Putnam, 1928.

P. J. Noel-Baker, *The Geneva protocol*, London, P. S. King, 1925.

J. Schwoebel, *L'Angleterre et la sécurité collective*, Paris, Recueil Sirey, 1938.

H. M. Swanwick, *The extraordinary Assembly*, London, Union of Democratic Control, 1926.

F. P. Walters, *A history of the League of Nations*, London, R.I.I.A., 1952.

Sir J. W. Wheeler-Bennett, *The disarmament deadlock*, London, Routledge, 1934.

B. H. Williams, *The United States and disarmament*, N.Y. and London, McGraw-Hill, 1931.

H. R. Winkler, 'The development of the League of Nations idea in Great Britain, 1914–19', *Journal of Modern History*, June, 1948.

Sir A. E. Zimmern, *The League of Nations and the rule of law*, London, Macmillan, 1936.

6. *The Far East*

C. A. Buss, *War and diplomacy in Eastern Asia*, N.Y., Macmillan, 1941.

Sir R. L. Craigie, *Behind the Japanese mask*, London, Hutchinson, 1946.

A. L. P. Dennis, *The Anglo-Japanese alliance*, Berkeley, University of California Press, 1923.

I. S. Friedman, *British relations with China, 1931–39*, N.Y., Institute of Pacific Relations (I.P.R.), 1940.

M. J. Gayn, *The fight for the Pacific*, New York, Morrow; London, Bodley Head, 1941.

J. C. Grew, *Ten years in Japan*, N.Y., Simon and Schuster, 1944.

A. W. Griswold, *The Far Eastern policy of the United States*, New Haven, Yale University Press, 1938.

E. M. Gull, *British economic interests in the Far East*, London, I.P.R., 1943.

A. N. Holcombe, *The Chinese Revolution*, Cambridge, Mass., Harvard University Press, 1931.

W. L. Holland and K. Mitchell (eds.), *Problems of the Pacific*, Chicago, I.P.R., 1939.

G. E. Hubbard, *British Far Eastern policy*, N.Y., I.P.R., 1943.

G. F. Hudson, *The Far East in world politics*, Oxford, Clarendon Press, 1937.

F. C. Jones, *Japan's New Order in East Asia*, London, O.U.P., 1954.

M. D. Kennedy, *The problem of Japan*, London, Nisbet, 1935.

T. E. La Fargue, *China and the World War*, Palo Alto and London Stanford University Press, 1937.

O. Lattimore, *Manchuria, cradle of conflict*, N.Y., Macmillan, 1932.

D. E. T. Luard, *Britain and China*, London, Chatto and Windus, 1962.

C. Muto, *A short history of Anglo-Japanese relations*, Tokyo, Hokuseido Press, 1936.

Sir J. T. Pratt, *War and politics in China*, London, Cape, 1943.

H. S. Quigley, *Far Eastern war, 1937–41*, Boston, Mass., The World Peace Foundation, 1942.

R.I.I.A., *British Far Eastern policy*, London, 1939.

—*China and Japan*, London, 1941.

M. Royama, *Foreign policy of Japan, 1914–39*, Tokyo, I.P.R., 1941.

T. Takeuchi, *War and diplomacy in the Japanese Empire*, London, Allen and Unwin, 1936.

G. E. Taylor, *The struggle for North China*, N.Y., I.P.R., 1940.

W. W. Willoughby, *Foreign rights and interests in China*, 2 vols., Baltimore, Johns Hopkins Press, 1927.

—*The Sino-Japanese controversy and the League of Nations*, Baltimore, Johns Hopkins Press, 1935.

7. *Britain and the United States*

H. C. Allen, *Great Britain and the United States*, London, Odhams, 1954.

C. A. Beard, *American foreign policy in the making, 1932–40*, New Haven, Yale University Press, 1946.

T. A. Bisson, *American policy in the Far East, 1931–40*, N.Y., I.P.R., 1940.

R. . Buell, *The Washington conference*, N.Y. and London, D. Appleton, 1922.

H. Feis, *The road to Pearl Harbor*, Princeton, Princeton University Press, 1950.

W. L. Langer and S. E. Gleason, *The challenge to isolation, 1937–40*, New York, Harper; London, R.I.I.A., 1952.

B. Rauch, *Roosevelt from Munich to Pearl Harbor*, N.Y., Creative Age Press, 1950.

C. C. Tansill, *Back door to war. The Roosevelt foreign policy, 1933–41*, Chicago, Regnery, 1952.

8. *Britain and the Dictators*

F. J. Berber, *Europäische Politik 1933–38 im Spiegel der Prager Akten*, Essen, Essener Verlag, 1942.

F. Borkenau, *The Spanish cockpit*, London, Faber, 1937.

J. Braunthal, *The tragedy of Austria*, London, Gollancz, 1948.

G. Brook-Shepherd, *Anschluss: the rape of Austria*, London, Macmillan, 1963.

A. L. C. Bullock, *Hitler: a study in tyranny*, London, Odhams, 1952.

E. R. Cameron, *Prologue to appeasement: a study in French foreign policy*, Washington, American Council of Public Affairs, 1942.

P. A. M. van der Esch, *Prelude to war*, The Hague, Nijhoff, 1951.

G. E. R. Gedye, *Fallen bastions*, London, Gollancz, 1939.

G. Gehl, *Austria, Germany and the Anschluss*, London, O.U.P., 1963.

B. Granzow, *A mirror of Nazism*, London, Gollancz, 1964.

'Hispanicus' (ed.), *Foreign intervention in Spain*, Vol. I, London, United Editorial, 1937.

The Marquess of Londonderry, *Ourselves and Germany*, London, Harmondsworth, 1938.

M. H. H. Macartney and P. Cremona, *Italy's foreign and colonial policy, 1914–37*, London, O.U.P., 1938.

Sir L. B. Namier, *Europe in decay*, London, Macmillan, 1950.

K. Schuschnigg, *Austrian requiem*, London, Gollancz, 1947.

R. W. Seton-Watson, *Britain and the Dictators*, Cambridge, C.U.P., 1938.

Prince Starhemberg, *Between Hitler and Mussolini*, London, Hodder and Stoughton, 1942.

H. Thomas, *The Spanish civil war*, London, Eyre and Spottiswoode, 1961.

M. Toscano, *Le Origini del Patto d'Acciaio*, Florence, Sansoni, 1948.

Sir J. W. Wheeler-Bennett, *The nemesis of power*, London, Macmillan, 1953.

E. Wiskemann, *The Rome-Berlin axis*, London, O.U.P., 1949.

9. *The Eve of War*

D. J. Dallin, *Soviet Russia's foreign policy, 1939–42*, New Haven, Yale University Press, 1944.

K. Eubank, *Munich*, Norman, University of Oklahoma Press, 1963.

G. Gafencu, *Prelude to the Russian campaign*, London, Muller, 1945.

M. Gilbert and R. Gott, *The appeasers*, London, Weidenfeld and Nicolson, 1963.

W. Hofer, *War premeditated*, London, Thames and Hudson, 1955.

S. Mackiewicz, *Colonel Beck and his policy*, London, Eyre and Spottiswoode, 1944.

I. M. Maiskii, *Who helped Hitler?* London, Hutchinson, 1964.

W. N. Medlicott, *The coming of war in 1939*, London, Routledge and Kegan Paul, 1963.

S. Morrell, *I saw the crucifixion*, London, Peter Davies, 1939.

Sir L. B. Namier, *Diplomatic prelude*, London, Macmillan, 1948.

L. Noël, *Une ambassade à Varsovie*, Paris, Flammarion, 1946.

H. Ripka, *Munich: before and after*, London, Gollancz, 1939.

F. L. Schuman, *Europe on the eve*, New York, Knopf; London, Hale, 1939.

A. J. P. Taylor, *The origins of the Second World War*, London, Hamilton, 1961.

A. Werth, *France and Munich*, London, Hamilton, New York, Harper, 1939.

Sir J. W. Wheeler-Bennett, *Munich: prologue to tragedy*, London, Macmillan, 1948.

INDEX

Abyssinia, 406–25, 486, 488.
Admiralty, 333, 335, 339, 340, 479.
Adrianople, 140, 155.
Afghanistan, 201–2, 220.
Africa, 407–25, 606, 616.
Aga Khan, 515.
Albania, 13, 311, 437, 576, 581–2.
Alexander, A. V., 331.
Alexander, Greek King, 145.
Allenby, Lord, 12, 128.
Aloisi, Baron, 375.
Alsace-Lorraine: and Allied war aims, 9, 17, 25, 30, 31, 35; at Paris Peace Conference, 99; in Treaty of Frankfurt (1871), 171; Stresemann on, 251.
Amanullah, 201.
Amau Declaration, 453.
Amet, Admiral, 127.
Amery, L. S., 250, 422.
Anatolia, 126, 135, 142, 143, 148, 155.
Anglo-American Guarantee to France (1919), 105–6, 160.
Anglo-German Naval Agreement (1935), 389–91, 558, 587.
Anglo-Japanese Alliance, 15, 274, 278, 280–3, 290.
Anglo-Russian Agreement (1907), 203.
Anglo-Soviet Trade Agreement (1921), 212–14.
Anschluss, 490–6.
Anti-Comintern Pact, 456, 478.
Arabs, 10–13, 34–5, 125, 127–33, 137.
Arcos Trade Agency, 316.
Arita, H., Japanese Foreign Minister, 471.
Armenia: proposed independence, 133, 137, 148; proposed U.S. mandate, 134; by Treaty of Sèvres, 142, 143; by Treaty of Lausanne, 154.

Asquith, H. H., 4, 6, 9, 21–2, 91, 308.
Astor, Lady, 507.
Attlee, C. R., 363, 524, 619.
Australia, 232, 242–3, 283, 460, 480, 628.
Austria: Allied war claims on, 13; peace feelers (1917), 26–9; and Germany (1917), 28; and Bolsheviks, 60; 1934 crisis, 384, 402; Anschluss, 490–6.
Axis, Berlin–Rome, 578.

Baldwin, Stanley; and Lloyd George (1922), 144, 152–3; and Geneva Protocol, 240, 242; and Rhine Pact, 250, 263; and Soviet Russia, 318; and disarmament, 345, 372; and rearmament, 385–95; and Italo-Abyssinian war, 421, 423–4; and Rhineland (1936), 430; and Spanish civil war, 445; and Manchurian crisis, 452; philosophy, 617.
Balearic Is., 437.
Balfour, Lord: in War Cabinet (1916), 22; American mission (1917), 24–5; and Col. House, 31; and Austria (1918), 37; British war aims, 37–8; and Bolsheviks, 56–8: and intervention in Russia, 66–8, 70, 73, 76, 84; on Poland (1919), 109–11; and Chanak crisis, 150; and France, 229; and Rhine Pact, 249; at Washington Conference, 284–8.
Balfour Note (1922), 180–1, 184.
Balkans, 14.
Ball, Sir J., 487.
Baltazzis, Greek Foreign Minister, 147.
Barnes, G. N., 118.
Barthou, L., 399–400, 402–3.
Beatty, Lord, 285, 345.
Beaverbrook, Lord, 394.

Beck, Joseph, 559, 571–2, 573–5, 600, 609.

Belgium: in 1914, 5–6; and Allied war aims, 15, 17, 23; and Ruhr occupation, 189; and Locarno Pact, 265–6; and reoccupation of Rhineland, 429–30, 433, 435–6; and Nazi Germany, 560–1; and British guarantees (1939), 574.

Benckendorff, Count, 11.

Benedict XV, 29.

Benes, E.; and Allies (1918), 72–3; at World Disarmament Conference, 369; and Hitler, 496; in Sudeten German crisis (1938), 506, 515, 522; and Russia, 531.

Bernstorff, Count, 17, 24, 338, 368.

Berthelot, Philippe, 133.

Bessarabia, 25, 59, 577.

Bethmann-Hollweg, Th. von, 28.

Bevin, Ernest, 443, 445.

Bingham, U.S. Ambassador, 461.

Birkenhead, Lord, 76, 96, 150, 198, 249, 250.

Bismarck, Prince, 406.

Black Sea, 126, 143, 153.

Bland, Sir N., 560.

Bliss, General T., 39, 41.

Blomberg, W. von, 399, 491.

Blum, Leon, 441–2.

Bolsheviks, 11, 32, 53, 55–64, 65–90, 198–9.

Bonnet, Georges: in Czech crisis (1938), 503–6, 509, 512–13, 515, 525–7, 529; and Czech guarantee, 552; and Germany, 556–7; and March, 1939, crisis, 563–5; and 1939 guarantee system, 571; and Italy, 579; and Russia, 589–90, 598.

Bono, Marshal de, 407.

Borah, Senator, 281.

Borden, Sir R., 242.

Borodin, M., 202–3, 292, 296, 299.

Bosnia, 25.

Bradbury, Sir J., 185.

Brauchitsch, W. von, 613, 614.

Briand, Aristide: and Turkish settlement, 147–8; and proposed Anglo-French Pact, 225–7; and Rhine Pact, 260–1; and Stresemann, 268; at Washington Conference, 285; and naval disarmament, 335.

Bridgeman, W. C., 334.

British Empire: and intervention in Russia, 77; and League of Nations 231–2; and Rhine Pact, 270; and British public opinion, 440; and Czech crisis (1938), 515; Hitler's assurances on, 612; and British policy, 627–8.

Brockdorff-Rantzau, Col. U. von, 83.

Brüning, H., Chancellor, 370–1.

Bryce, Viscount, 96.

Buchanan, Sir G., 47, 48, 53, 56, 57.

Buckler, W. H., 78.

Buckmaster, Lord, 96–7.

Bullitt, W. C., 81.

Burckhardt, Prof. C. J., 565–6, 607, 609–10.

Burma Road, 479.

Burns, John, 5.

Butler, R. A., 474, 599.

Cadman, Sir J., 133.

Cadogan, Sir A., 486, 560, 562, 564, 579, 609, 610.

Cagoulards, 441.

Calthorpe, Admiral, 127.

Cambon, Paul, 6, 26, 27.

Canada, 151, 232, 242, 282–3, 323, 628.

Cannes Conference, 148, 215, 225–6, 268.

Canton, 299.

Caporetto, battle, 27, 28.

Caucasus, 58–9, 74, 86, 136.

Cecil, Lord Hugh, 109, 118.

Cecil, Lord Robert: and Colonel House, 36; on Allied war aims, 52; and Trotsky, 57; and intervention in Russia, 59, 72–3, 76; and League, 119; and Draft Treaty of Mutual Assistance, 233;

and Japan, 280; and naval disarmament, 333; and 'Peace' Ballot, 417.

Chaikovsky, N., 74, 79.

Chamberlain, Sir Austen: and Turkish settlement, 150; on Geneva Protocol, 244–5; and Rhine Pact, 248–50, 255–70; and Chinese civil war, 291, 293, 298, 301; and Russia, 309, 310–18; and naval disarmament, 335, 338; and Italo-Abyssinian war, 423; and Hitler, 432; on Japan, 451.

Chamberlain, Lady, 487.

Chamberlain, Neville: on Italo-Abyssinian war, 422; on League sanctions, 424–5; on Rhineland crisis (1936), 430; on Italian policy, 446, 377–80; Japanese policy, 460–1, 464, 479–80; aims and policy, 481–3, 617–18; and Eden, 483–8; and Austria, 490, 493, 494; and Czechoslovakia, 500–1, 503–8, 510, 513, 516, 524, 552, 566–7, 606; and Hitler, 521, 527–48, 558, 559, 607, 611–15, 621; and France, 561; and guarantee system (1939), 568–72, 574, 583, 589; and Russia, 603; and Roosevelt, 628.

Chanak, 150, 232.

Chang Hsueh-liang, 351, 455.

Chang Tso-lin, 295, 299.

Charles, Austrian Emperor, 26, 27.

Chen, Eugene, 294, 297.

Chicherin, G., Soviet Foreign Minister: in England (1917), 58; in Russian civil war, 67–8; and President Wilson, 78; and Paris Peace Conference, 79–81; and Russo-Polish war, 87–8; and Curzon, 199–200; and Turkey, 205, 207; and Genoa Conference, 215; and Britain (1923), 222; and Rhine Pact, 312.

China: in First World War, 15; and Tsarist Russia, 273; at Washington Conference, 287–8; civil war, 290–300; extra-territoriality, 295–

302; reconstruction (1928), 348; and Manchurian crisis, 355–66; and Japan (1933–7), 452–5, 460–1; and Britain, 469–80.

Chinese Eastern Railway, 273, 351, 454.

Chiang Kai-shek, 203, 293, 297, 298–9, 300, 455.

Chilston, Lord, 497, 523.

Churchill, Winston: in Cabinet (1914), 4, 5; intervention in Russia, 72, 76, 80; and League, 118; and Turkish settlement, 144, 150; and Greece, 145, 147; and Soviet Russia, 198, 191; and Locarno, 249, 250; on disarmament, 327, 331, 333, 345; and Manchurian crisis, 360; and Baldwin, 386; and Italo-Abyssinian war, 412–13, 418; on occupation of Rhineland, 434–5; and Eden, 483; and Czechoslovakia, 508, 524, 538; and Labour, 629.

Chvalkovsky, F., Czech Foreign Minister, 549, 551, 552, 554–5.

Ciano, Count G., 487, 549, 578, 579, 580, 610.

Cilicia, 129, 130, 136, 146.

Clemenceau, Georges: and Sykes-Picot Agreement, 10; and Fourteen Points, 36; and intervention in Russia, 58–9, 66, 75, 77; at Paris Peace Conference, 97, 99–107, 112; and Syria, 127–9; and Feisal, 130–1.

Clark-Kerr, Sir A., 468–9.

Clerk, Sir G., 423, 442.

Clive, Sir R., 560–1.

Cliveden, 507.

Cocks, Seymour, 363.

Committee of Imperial Defence, 393, 599.

Communist Party (British), 309, 314.

Conservative Party, 235, 327, 345, 384, 439.

Constantine, King, 145, 149.

Constantinople, 9, 25, 136–41, 148, 155.

Coolidge, President, 334.

Corbin, French Ambassador, 439, 493, 499, 525, 560, 575.

Cot, P., 441, 533-4.

Craigie, Sir R., 467-8, 470-1, 472, 473, 474, 477-8, 479.

Craigie-Arita Agreements, 477-9.

Cranborne, Viscount, 406, 441, 489.

Crane, C. R., 128.

Crewe, Lord, 194, 250.

Crispi, F., 408.

Crowe, Sir E., 135, 250, 310.

Cuno, Dr. W., German Chancellor, 183, 250-1.

Curzon, Lord: in War Cabinet, 22; and intervention in Russia, 76, 84-6; and Turkish settlement, 135, 139, 147, 150-1, 152; at Lausanne Conference, 153-8; and Anglo-American Guarantee to France, 160; and France (1920), 164; and Ruhr occupation, 187-9, 194, 195; and Soviet Russia, 199, 207, 210-11, 219-22; and Persia, 302-4; and Anglo-French pact, 224, 227-9; and Japan, 283.

Curzon Line, 87, 199.

Cushendun, Lord, 338.

Cyprus, 158.

Czernin, Count O., 27-8.

Czechoslovakia: at 1919 peace settlement, 111; and France, 267, 400; after Anschluss, 494-5; Sudeten German crisis, 496-548; after Munich, 549-55, 563-5.

Czechs: in Russia (1918), 72-4.

D'Abernon, Lord, 87, 254-5, 269, 312.

Dahlerus, B., 608, 612, 614.

Daladier, E.: and four-Power Pact (1932), 398; and Spanish civil war, 441-2; and Czech crisis (1938), 503-6, 515, 527, 529-30, 534, 535-6, 539; and Czech guarantee, 552; and Britain (1939), 559, 560; and Rumania (1939), 576; and Italy, 579; and Russia, 590; and Danzig, 605.

...atia, 13, 14.

Dalton, Hugh, 431, 435.

Danzig: and allied war aims, 25; at Paris Peace Conference, 111-14, 117-18, 121; and Germany, 495, 565-6, 574, 604-6, 609-10; subject of 1939 negotiations, 611-12, 614-15.

Dardanelles Straits, 125, 126, 137, 140, 142, 148, 153-4.

Davies, David, 49.

Davis, Norman, 375, 458, 463.

Davison, C. F., 221.

Dawes Conference, 189-96.

Dawes, General, 190, 194, 338-9, 362.

Dawes Plan, 194, 223, 305.

Dawson, Geoffrey, 524.

Defence, 388-95, 481.

Defence Policy and Requirements Committee, 393.

Delacroix, Belgian statesman, 173.

Delbos, Yvon, 441-2, 493.

Denikin, General, 75, 76, 85, 86.

Deterding, Sir H., 215.

Dirksen, H. von, 558, 608.

Disarmament: and Anglo-French pact, 226; and League Covenant, 232; and Geneva Protocol, 240; and Locarno, 270; at Washington Conference, 284-6, 289-90; British attitudes to, 327-32; naval (1922-30), 332-47; at world disarmament conference, 368-84, 397; naval (1935-6), 389-92; and Japan, 456-7.

Dmowski, R., 109, 113.

Dodecanese, 13, 409.

Doihara, General, 353.

Dollfuss, Chancellor, 402, 490.

Dominions: and intervention in Russia, 77; and reparations, 94; claim to independence, 116; and Chanak crisis, 150-1; and League 231-2; and Geneva Protocol, 242-4; and Rhine Pact, 270; and Anglo-Japanese alliance, 287; and Spanish civil war, 441; and Czech crisis (1938), 526; effects on British policy, 627.

Doumenc, General, 599.

Doumergue, Gaston, French states-man, 50, 399–400.

Dovgalevsky, Soviet diplomat, 320–1.

Drax, Admiral, 599, 600.

Drummond, Sir E. (Lord Perth), 25, 359, 419, 579, 581, 582.

Dual Monarchy, 35.

Duff Cooper, A., 416, 429, 533, 537, 538, 544, 547–8.

Dukhonin, General, 56–7.

Dunsterville, L. C., 74.

East Fulham by-election, 386.

Eastern Locarno, 399–401, 405.

Eden, Anthony: in Moscow (1935), 326; on Manchuria, 356, 358, 361; and disarmament, 377, 378, 382; in Berlin (1935), 389, 405; on Stresa Front, 412; in Abyssinian crisis (1935), 416, 417, 424; and Rhineland crisis, 429, 431–2, 433–4, 435; and Spanish civil war, 442, 443–4; and Japan, 457, 459, 461, 462, 464, 466; and Chamberlain, 483–9; and Austria, 490; and Czechoslovakia, 498, 524, 567.

Edward VIII, 385.

Egypt, 142, 158, 223, 392, 408, 415.

Eisenlohr, E., German diplomat, 507.

Eliot, Sir C., 281.

Entente, 125.

Eritrea, 13, 407, 408.

Erzerum, 142.

d'Esperey, Franchet, 75.

Estonia, 84, 577, 589, 592, 593, 596.

Exports Credits Guarantee Scheme, 307, 469.

Falkenhayn, General, 1, 19, 46.

Fan Noli, 311.

Federation of British Industries, 564.

Fehrenbach, K., German Chancellor, 169.

Feisal, Emir, 12, 127, 128–9, 130–33.

Ferid Pasha, 144.

Fierlinger, Czech diplomat, 535.

Finland, 84, 589, 592, 593, 595.

Firebrace, Col., 497.

Flandin, P., 403, 411, 430–1.

Fleuriau, French Ambassador, 173, 258.

Foch, Marshal: supreme command, 3; armistice negotiations, 39, 41–2, 45; intervention in Russia, 75, 80; and Rhine, 102–3, 107; and French security, 163–4.

Foreign Office: and reparations (1918), 93; and League Covenant, 118; and Arabs (1919), 128; and Near East, 158; and French security, 249; and Soviet Russia, 306, 309–10, 313; and China, 357; and United States, 361; and Germany, 368–9; and Japan, 471–2; and Austria, 495; and Czechoslovakia, 524; and Poland, 559; and European Union, 621.

Forster, A., German Gauleiter, Danzig, 607, 609.

Four-Power Pact, 377, 384, 397–9, 446.

Fourteen Points, 32–6, 39, 42–4, 94, 116.

France: at war, 2, 623; war aims, 25; armistice (1918), 39–45; and Bolsheviks, 59, 75, 77; at Paris Peace Conference, 95, 99–109, 110; and League (1919), 121; and Turkey, 126, 140–1, 583; and Britain in Near East, 126–33, 136–7, 146, 148, 156–7; security problems, 160–5, 223–4; and reparations, 170–1, 181–9; and Russia, 212–3, 325, 403, 427, 505, 589–601; Anglo-French pact, 224–31; and Locarno, 248–72; and disarmament, 284–6, 332–44, 370–84, 390–2; Eastern Locarno, 398–406, and Italo-Abyssinian war, 410–13, 419–25; and Rhineland occupation, 430–; Spain, 437–8, 441–2; and ...slovakia, 496–7, 509, ... 529–30, 531, 545–6

Britain in Czech crisis, 498–9, 503–6, 512, 515, 529–30, 535–6; and Germany (1938–9), 556–7; British guarantee to, 561; and Poland (1939), 573, 600–1; and Rumania (1939), 576; and Italy (1939), 579–80; and Turkey (1939), 583.

Francis Joseph, Emperor, 26.

Franco, General, 436, 437, 438, 445.

François-Poncet, A., 428, 556, 580.

Franklin-Bouillon Agreement, 141, 146, 152.

Freedom of the Seas, 33–4, 42.

Fritsch, General von, 491.

Gafencu, G., 568, 575, 586.

Galen, Marshal, 292, 296.

Gallipoli, 155.

Gamelin, General, 527, 536, 537.

Gauche, Col., 520–1.

Geddes, Sir A., 279, 282.

General Election: (1918), 4, 91; (1922), 153; (1923), 193; (1931), 352; (1935), 417, 421.

General Strike (1926), 313–4, 385.

Genoa Conference (1922), 210–11, 215–18.

George V, 304.

Germany: in First World War, 1–3, 623; and Belgium (1914), 6; and United States (1917), 17–18, 24; negotiations with Allies (1916–18), 22, 28–30, 32–6; armistice, 39–45; and Bolsheviks (1918), 58–63, 66–7, 69–70; and Paris Peace Conference, 93–116; and Soviet Russia (1920s), 162, 200, 216–7, 269; reparations, 167–71, 173, 175–6; and disarmament, 167–9, 263, 368–84; elections (1920s), 168, (1930), 368; inflation, 179; Rhine Pact, 249–72; ¬d Far East, 273; and Soviet ¬sia (1930s), 325, 559; rearma-380, 382, 387–90, 426–34; ¬nd reoccupation, 426–34; ¬ish civil war, 442–3; 1937, 447–8; Ansch-

luss, 489–95; and Czechoslovakia, 494, 496–548, 549–54, 563–5; and Britain (1930s), 514–15, 519–20, 528–48, 557–8, 558–67, 604–16; and France (1939), 556–7; and Russia (1939), 587, 601.

Gibraltar, 34, 392, 415, 437.

Gibson, H., 333, 337–8.

Gilbert, Prentiss, 361.

Goebbels, J., 379.

Goerdeler, Dr., 587.

Goering, Hermann, 489, 494, 514, 612.

Gold Standard, 352.

Gounaris, Greek statesman, 147.

Gouraud, General, 130, 132, 146.

Grabski, Polish Foreign Minister, 88.

Graham, Sir R., 397.

Grandi, Count, 369, 487–8, 490.

Greater East Asia Co-prosperity Sphere, 366, 470–3.

Greece: in First World War, 3, 14–15; and Turkey, 135, 137, 141–2, 144–50, 152; British guarantee to, 582–3.

Greenwood, A., 557.

Grew, J. C., 157, 458, 475.

Grey, Viscount: outbreak of war (1914), 4, 5, 7, 8; and Allied war aims, 10, 13, 14, 15; and Col. House, 17–18; and President Wilson, 134; and Rhine Pact, 250.

Gripenberg, G. A., Finnish diplomat, 596.

Hahn, Baron, 520.

Haig, Field-Marshal, 2, 3, 21, 40–1, 45, 110.

Haile Selassie, 408, 424.

Hailsham, Lord, 379.

Haldane, Lord, 247, 310.

Halifax, Lord: in Berlin (1936), 446; and Sino-Japanese war, 469–70, 473–4, 475, 476–8; succeeds Eden, 488–9; meets German leaders, November 1937, 489; and Anschluss, 493–5, 498; and Germany, 499, 514–15, 516–18, 519,

525–6, 555–6, 557, 560, 561, 605; and Czechoslovakia (1938), 502, 505–10, 511, 513, 521–2, 536–8, 552, 564–5; and France (1938), 512; and United States (1938), 524; and British guarantee system (1939), 568, 571–2; and Mussolini, 606; and Polish crisis (1939), 607–8, 611, 614.

Hankey, Sir M., 87, 139.

Hankow, 292, 293, 294, 296, 299, 466.

Hanyang, 293.

Harding, President, 278, 281, 284.

Hardinge, Lord, 162, 213, 229.

Hay, John, 275.

Hedjaz, 129, 142.

Henderson, Arthur: and Versailles Treaty, 238; and Geneva Protocol, 241, 247; and China, 300–1; and Soviet Russia, 320–1, 322; and French security, 344; President of Disarmament Conference, 369, 379.

Henderson, Sir Nevile: and Anschluss, 494, 495, 496; and Sudeten German crisis (1938), 506–10, 514, 516, 517, 519, 521, 525, 527; and international commission on Czechoslovakia, 550–1; and Germany (1939), 554, 562–3, 599, 611, 612.

Henlein, K., 503, 507, 508, 509, 512, 521.

Herriot, Edouard: and Dawes Conference, 194; and French security, 235, 237, 240, 250; and Soviet Russia, 313; and disarmament, 372, 375.

Hertling, German statesman, 34.

Herzegovina, 25.

Hicks, Capt., 70.

Hierl, Col., 378–9.

Hindenburg, Paul von, 47, 262.

Hirota, K., Japanese Foreign Minister, 453, 454.

Hitler, Adolf: accession to power, 375; policy, 376, 379; and Locarno, 272; and Russia (1933),

324; meets Simon (1935), 326, 388; and League and Disarmament Conference, 380, 382; rearmament, 387; and arms control talks with Britain, 389–91; 405–6; attitude to Britain, 396; and four-Power Pact, 399; and Austria, 402, 489–96; reoccupation of Rhineland, 426–9, 432; and Franco, 443; and Czechoslovakia (1938), 502, 506, 508, 510, 514–15, 517, 519, 527–32, 537–41, 545; and post-Munich Czechoslovakia, 554–5; and France (1938–9), 556; and Britain (1938–9), 558; and Soviet Russia, 559; eve of war, 562, 563–5, 580, 587, 604, 605, 609–16.

Hoare, Sir Reginald, 569.

Hoare, Sir Samuel: and Anglo-German naval agreement (1935), 390; and Eastern Locarno, 405–6; and Italo-Abyssinian war, 418–20, 422–4; and Spanish civil war, 439; and China, 450–1; and Japan (1935), 454–5; and Eden, 488; and Czechoslovakia, 502, 524; and Dictators, 577; and war, 617.

Hoare–Laval Plan, 422–4.

Hodza, E., 514, 515–16, 523.

Hoffman, General, 63, 172.

Hogarth, Commander, 12.

Hong Kong, 34, 69, 286, 292, 294.

Hoover, President, 337, 338, 339, 340, 361, 371, 372–3.

Hopei–Chahar Political Council, 454.

Hopwood, Sir F., 26.

Hore-Belisha, L., 499, 521, 533.

Horne, Sir R., 182, 315.

House, Colonel: in London (1916), 17; and Balfour mission, (1917), 24–5; mission to Europe (1917), 31–2; in armistice negotiations, 40–4; and intervention in Russia, 71; at Paris Peace Conference, 100, 103–4; break with Wilson, 134.

Howard, Sir E., 65, 113.
Hudson, R. S., 571, 606–7.
Hugenberg Memorandum, 325.
Hughes, W. M., Australian states-
man, 283.
Hughes, Charles Evans: and Wei-
mar Republic, 184–5; and Dawes
Plan, 192, 250; and Anglo-Japan-
ese alliance, 279, 281–2; at
Washington conference, 284–5;
and China (1922), 287–8; on
Washington naval treaty, 289.
Hull, Cordell, 455, 458, 460,
485.
Hungary: and Allies (1917), 25;
Czechoslovakia, 549–50.
Hurst, Sir C., 264.
Hussein, Sherif, 11–12.
Hussein–McMahon correspondence,
11–12.

Imperial Conference: (1921), 147,
279–80, 282–3, 349; (1923), 187.
Imperial War Cabinet, 108, 109,
487–8.
India, 125, 138, 220, 223, 224,
294.
India Office, 138, 139, 158.
Ingersoll, Capt., 466.
Inskip, Sir T., 386, 552.
Iraq, 132, 133, 154–5.
Ireland, 77, 223, 243, 284.
Ironside, General, 610, 611.
Ismay, General, 599.
Ismet Pasha, 155, 156, 159.
Ismid Line, 144.
Italy: Pact of London (1915), 13–
14; peace feelers (1917), 26–7;
and Allies (1918), 35; and inter-
vention in Russia, 77; and Tur-
kish settlement, 137, 140–1, 145;
and Locarno, 265–6; and dis-
armament, 284–6, 341–4, 370;
and Austria, 396–7; invasion of
Abyssinia, 400–25, 622; and
France, 411, 579–80; and Spain,
437–46, 578; and Chamberlain,
484, 578–82; and Munich, 539,
541.

Japan: in First World War, 15;
intervention in Russia, 37, 67,
69–72; and China, 274, 287–8,
300, 349–55, 450, 452–7, 460–1,
472–3, 623; and Britain, 274–5,
280–3, 464–80; and disarmament,
284–6, 334, 339, 342–4, 391, 467–
7; and four-Power Treaty (1922),
286–7; and Manchuria, 349,
358–67; and Soviet Russia, 455–6;
and Germany, 456, 478.
Jellicoe, Admiral, 2, 2, 345.
Joffe, A., 58, 202.
Jouvenel, B. de, 427.
Joynson-Hicks, 313, 314, 316, 317.

Kahr, G. von, Bavarian Prime
Minister, 172.
Kaledin, General, 57, 58.
Kamenev, L., 87–8.
Kapp putsch, 162–3.
Karakhan, L., 202, 358.
Kemal Ataturk, 125, 135–6, 144,
159, 204–5.
Kemp, Admiral, 67.
Kennard, Sir H., 571, 573, 600, 604.
Kennedy, Joseph, 524, 569, 570,
574.
Kenya, 409.
Kerensky, A., 16, 50–1, 53–4, 54–5,
56.
Kerr, Philip (Lord Lothian), 28, 83,
104, 325.
Keynes, J. M., 93, 111, 122.
Kilmarnock, Lord, 161–2, 169, 173.
King, Dr. H. C., 128.
Kirkpatrick, Sir I., 531, 537, 544.
Kiukiang, 292, 293, 294.
Kleist, E. von, 543.
Knatchbull-Hugessen, Sir H., 465.
Knox, Sir A., 47, 53, 56, 63.
Kolchak, Admiral, 74, 76, 82–6, 89.
Konoye, Prince, 470.
Kordt, Th., 519, 521, 524, 543.
Kornilov, General, 53–4.
Krassin, L., Soviet diplomat, 88,
211, 212.
Krofta, Dr. K., Czech Foreign
Minister, 507.

Kühlmann, Baron von, 30, 60, 66.
Kuomintang, 202–3, 292–302, 349, 453.
Kurdistan, 136, 142, 154.

Labour Party: and Versailles Treaty, 121; attitude to militarism, 235, 237; and Soviet Russia (1920s), 304–10; and disarmament, 327, 384, 386; and collective security, 394; and reoccupation of Rhineland, 431; and Spanish civil war, 443, 445; and Russia (1938), 537; policy, 618–19, 621–2, 629.
Ladybird, H.M.S., 465.
Lampson, Sir M., 297, 301, 357.
Lansbury, G., 305, 363.
Lansdowne, Lord, 20, 21, 30–1.
Lansing, R., 70–1, 128, 276.
Latvia, 577, 589, 592, 593, 596.
Lausanne Conference, 125, 153–7, 292.
Lausanne Reparations Conference, 330, 372.
Lausanne Treaty, 126, 409.
Laval, P., 390, 403, 411, 418–19, 423–4, 580.
Law, A. Bonar: in War Cabinet, 22; and armistice (1918), 39; and Russian Revolution, 50–1, 55; and Turkey, 139; and Lloyd George, 144, 152–3; and reparations, 164–5, 184–5; and Germany, 251.
Layton, Sir W., 49.
League of Nations: as Allied war aim, 23, 35–6; at Paris Peace Conference, 106, 116–21; and new order in Europe, 223; Draft Treaty of Mutual Assistance, 232–4; Geneva Protocol, 239–46; and Rhine Pact, 265–7; and Soviet Russia, 324-5; and Manchurian crisis, 357-9; Germany leaves, 380; Japan leaves, 456; and Italo-Abyssinian war, 408–25; and Sino-Japanese war, 461–2.
Lee, Lord, 278–9, 285.
Leith-Ross, Sir F., 455.

Lenin, V. I., 56, 63–4, 65, 81, 90, 208, 209.
Leopold III, 435–6.
Liberal Party, 121, 308, 394, 618.
Libya, 13, 142.
Lichnowsky, Prince, 5.
Lindley, Sir F., 352–3, 357, 366, 453, 454.
Lindsay, Sir R. C., 461, 466, 472, 475, 485, 561.
Lithuania, 303, 572.
Litvinov, Maxim: and Allies (1917–18), 78–9; and British credits, 219; and propaganda, 220; and Britain (1925), 312; (1927), 315, 319; (1929), 321; and Eden (1935), 326; and disarmament, 369–70; and Czech crisis (1938), 497, 522, 527, 534; and negotiations with Britain and France (1939), 562, 569, 576; dismissal, 587.
Lloyd George, David: Liberal Minister (1906–14), 4; War Cabinet, 3, 12; war aims, 16, 22, 31–6; and President Wilson, 19–20; and peace feelers, 26–7; and armistice, 40–3; and Tsarist Russia, 48–9; and Russian Revolution, 50–1, 58, 61, 63–4, 69, 72, 76–82; Russo-Polish war, 87–8; 1918 election, 91; Paris Peace Conference, 92, 93–4, 101, 102–8, 110–14, 119–24; and Turkish settlement, 126–7, 130, 133, 136–53; and German reparations, 165–71, 172–9, 181–3; and Soviet Russia, 209–19, 307–8, 316, 317, 602–3, 621; and Anglo-French Pact, 225–6; and Geneva Protocol, 248; and Rhine Pact, 258, 270; and United States, 279–80; and Japan, 281; and Washington Conference, 283–4; and Nazi Germany, 325; and Curzon, 483; on staff talks with France, 435.
Lloyd-Graeme, Sir P., 219.
Locarno Agreements, 244, 248–72, 311–13, 376, 429–30, 620.

Lockhart, Bruce, 63, 64, 66, 67, 68.
London Naval Conference (1935), 391-2.
London Naval Treaties: (1930), 344-7, 372, 456; (1936) 391-2, 457.
Londonderry, Lord, 325, 386.
Long, Walter, 279.
Ludendorff, General E., 45, 63, 171-2.
Luxemburg, 595, 597.

MacDonald, J. Ramsay: and Russian Revolution, 52; and Dawes Plan, 193, 195-6; and European security, 231, 234-40, 249; and Geneva Protocol, 245-7; and Rhine Pact, 267; and Soviet Russia, 303-11, 313; and disarmament, 330, 338-42, 345, 369, 371, 374, 375, 377; and Mediterranean Locarno, 343-4; on war debts, 372; and rearmament, 387; and four-Power Pact, 398; and Stresa Conference, 404; resignation, 385.
McKenna, R., 20, 190.
McMahon, Sir H., 11.
McNeill, R., 157, 195.
Maffey, Sir J., 414.
Maisky, I., 501, 570, 577, 586, 590, 593.
Makins, R., 609.
Malta, 392, 415, 437.
Maltzan, Ago von, 254-5.
Malleson, General, 75.
Manchester Guardian, 32, 34, 337.
Manchukuo, 352, 355, 358, 365, 452.
Manchuria, 273, 299, 302, 349-67, 451-2.
Mandates system, 122, 126, 131-2.
Mander, G., 363.
Mannerheim, Marshal, 84.
Margerie, de, French Ambassador, 261.
Masaryk, Jan, 502, 506, 511.
Masaryk, T. G., 73.
Mason-Macfarlane, Lieut.-Col., 500, 517, 520.

Massey, V., 283.
Matin, Le, 107, 536.
Matsudaira, T., 341, 342.
Maurice Debate, 91.
Mediterranean, 154, 343, 410-11, 413, 437, 578, 582.
Mehmed IV, 144.
Meighen, A., 282-3.
Meinertzhagen, Col., 129.
Mellon, A. W., 179.
Memel, 303, 572.
Mesopotamia, 12, 128, 129.
Mezes, Dr., 104.
Michaelis, German Chancellor, 28-9.
Middle East: in First World War, 9-14; peace settlement, 125-59.
Milner, Lord, 41, 49, 59, 72, 76, 127-8.
Millerand, Alexandre, 87, 163, 164-5, 167, 169, 194.
Miliukov, Paul, 16.
Molotov, V., 326, 587, 589, 591-2, 597, 599-600, 601, 602.
Monroe Doctrine, 349.
Montagu, E., 76, 138-9.
Montenegro, 23.
Montreux Convention, 125.
Morel, E. D., 305.
Morley, Lord, 5, 6.
Morocco, 142, 408.
Mosul, 10, 133, 153-5.
Mudania Convention, 152.
Mudros armistice, 125, 126-7.
Munich Conference and Agreement, 529, 539-48, 551, 556, 558, 564, 568.
Mussolini, Benito: and Locarno, 265; and Soviet Russia, 303; and four-Power Pact, 377, 396-8; and disarmament, 381; and Abyssinia, 407-8, 410, 415, 418, 420, 424; and Britain, 419; and Britain and France, 421, 422, 426; and Spanish civil war, 437, 438, 443, 484; and Austria, 490, 493; and Munich, 539; and British policy (1939), 556, 578-81, 605, 606, 611, 615.

Nadolny, German diplomat, 373, 378.

Nanking, 293, 299, 356, 466.

National Government, 358, 364, 369, 377, 448.

National Socialists, 368, 371, 375, 378, 396, 482.

Navy: and Geneva Protocol, 237, 247; and Washington Conference, 284–6; and London Naval Treaty (1930), 333–47; and rearmament, 388–92; and Italo-Abyssinian war, 415; and Spanish civil war, 437; and Far East, 450, 479; and France, 504; mobilisation (1938), 538; and foreign policy, 624–5.

Nazi-Soviet Pact, 478, 601, 604, 611–13.

Netherlands, The, 285, 560, 561, 574, 593, 596–7.

Neurath, C. von, 375, 378, 426, 427, 446, 494.

Newton, Sir B., 501, 511, 513, 514, 531, 551, 554, 555.

New Zealand, 232, 242, 283, 460, 480.

Nicholas II, 47–8.

Nicholson, Godfrey, 567.

Nicolson, Harold, 539.

Non-intervention, 437–46.

Noulens, French Ambassador, 54, 69.

Nyon Agreement, 440.

Ochs, A., 279.

Occupation of German territory: at Paris Peace Conference, 103–9, 160; (1920), 164; as sanction, 169–70, 176; Cologne zone (1925), 263; Ruhr, 187–8, 264; termination, 368, 376.

Ogilvie-Forbes, Sir G. A. D., 551–2, 558–9.

Oil supplies, 125, 132–3.

O'Malley, O. St. Clair, 294, 297.

Open Door, 275–6, 348, 356, 360, 361, 450–1, 453.

Orlando, V. E., Italian statesman, 27, 58, 77, 97.

Osusky, S., Czech diplomat, 512.

Ottoman Empire, 125, 137, 204.

Ottowa Conference and Agreements, 323, 487.

Outer Mongolia, 352.

Ovey, Sir E., 321, 322.

Pact of Paris (1928), 320, 343, 360, 362, 377.

Pact of Steel, 606.

Paderewski, President, 113, 114.

Page, Walter H., 18.

Palestine, 10, 12, 31–2, 128, 129, 158.

Panay, U.S.S., 465–6.

Papen, F. von, 375, 378, 491.

Paris Peace Conference, 75–80, 91–124, 128, 131.

Parmoor, Lord, 242, 247.

Paul-Boncour, J., 333, 374, 375, 379, 398.

'Peace Ballot', 417–18.

Permanent Court, 155, 191, 432.

Pershing, General, 45.

Persia, 203–4.

Pétain, Marshal, 45, 50.

Peterson, Sir M., 422.

Petrograd Conference (1917), 49–50.

Phillimore Committee, 36, 117, 118.

Phipps, Sir E., 406, 512, 522, 525–7, 534, 564, 582, 585.

Pichon, French Foreign Minister, 59, 73, 99, 106, 110.

Picot, Georges, 10, 11, 146.

Pilsudski, Marshal, 88.

Poincaré, Raymond: on First World War, 7; peace talks (1917), 26; and Turkish settlement, 148, 151, 152; and reparations, 179, 181–4; and Ruhr, 186–7; and Anglo-French Pact, 226–30; and Cuno offer, 251; resignation, 194.

Poland: and Allied war aims, 25, 31, 35; and Russian civil war, 85; Russo-Polish war, 87–8, 199; at Paris Peace Conference, 109–16; Corridor, 112, 397–8, 574, 604, 610, 612, 614, 615–16; and France, 267, 398; and Germany,

399–401, 609–15; and Czecho-
slovakia, 112, 549–50; and Russia
(1939), 570, 584; British guaran-
tee to, 571–6, 586, 588, 602.
Ponsonby, A., 247, 305, 308, 310.
Port Arthur, 274, 351.
Portugal, 285, 442.
Prinkipo Conference, 79–80.

Raczynski, Count, 572, 573.
Rakovsky, C., Soviet diplomat, 305,
306, 308, 309, 310–11.
Rapallo Treaty, 200, 216–17, 249,
254.
Rath, vom, German diplomat, 557.
Rathenau, Walter, 178.
Reading, Lord, 31, 38, 48, 71.
Rearmament, 387–95.
Redcliffe, Sir P., 87.
Reichswehr, 374, 378, 379, 380, 532.
Reilly, Sidney, 69.
Reparations (German): pre-armis-
tice negotiations on, 42–4; at
Paris Peace Conference, 93–6;
coal deliveries, 161–2, 170; Lon-
don Conference on, 181–7, 230;
Dawes Conference on, 189–92;
proposed abolition, 372; ended,
376.
Reparation Commission, 95, 165,
172–3, 176–8, 182, 184–5, 191.
Revelstoke, Lord, 49.
Rhineland: at Paris Peace Confer-
ence, 92, 102–9, 121; and Anglo-
French Pact, 226, 228; and
Locarno, 251, 255–72; evacuated,
368, 376; remilitarised, 426–34,
447–8, 504, 622.
Ribbentrop, J. von: and Anglo-German naval agreement, 390; and
Japan, 456; and Anschluss, 494–
6; and Czechoslovakia, 508, 509–
10, 516, 549, 554; and France,
556–7; and Poland, 559; and
Russia, 601; on eve of war, 614–15.
Robertson, Sir W., 21, 48.
Robins, R., 63, 64.
Roosevelt, F. D., 324, 377, 462–3,
466, 473, 482, 484–6, 524–5, 546–7.

Roosevelt, Theo., 283, 290.
Rothermere, Lord, 325.
Royal Air Force, 387.
Rozengolz, A., Soviet diplomat,
314–16.
Ruhr: occupation (1920), 162–4;
proposed occupation as sanction,
169–70; occupied (1923), 194–5,
230, evacuation, 263–4; and
French policy, 431, 624.
Rumania: in First World War, 1,
14; and Bolsheviks (1918), 75;
and Straits, 153, 497; and Czech
crisis (1938), 522–3; and Russia,
504, 508; and Britain, 568–9,
571–2, 575–7, 582–3, 588, 602; on
eve of war, 566, 572.
Rumbold, Sir H., 378–9.
Runciman Mission, 515, 516–18,
524, 544.
Russia: in First World War, 2, 46,
50, 58–64; war aims, 7, 9–10, 16;
revolution (1917), 50–1, 55–6;
and Allies (1918–19), 34, 65–90;
Russo-Polish war, 87–8; in Asia,
200–7; and Far East, 202, 273–4,
291–2, 296–7, 299, 351–2, 358,
455–6; and Straits, 126, 153, 205–
6; and Genoa Conference, 215–18;
and Locarno, 252, 262–3, 269,
292; and Britain, 197–8, 212–14,
303–24, 501; and France, and
League, 412; and Spanish civil
war, 444–5; and Czechoslovakia,
497, 522–3, 527, 534–4, 545; and
Germany, 601; on eve of war, 562,
569–71, 572–3, 576–7, 584–604.

Saar, 92, 99–102.
Sadoul, Jacque, 63.
Saint-Aulaire, Count de, 188, 224,
229.
Sakhalin, 288.
Salisbury, Lord, 275–6, 620.
Samuel, Sir Herbert, 331.
Sandys, D., 567.
San Remo Conference, (1920), 131,
133, 141, 146, 165–6.
Sargent, Sir Orme, 563, 566.

Sazonov, S. D., Russian Foreign Minister, 9, 10, 48, 79, 83.
Schacht, Dr., 560.
Schleicher, von, German Defence Minister, 371, 375.
Schlieffen–Moltke plan, 7.
Schubert, Carl von, 255.
Schulenberg, Count F. W. von der, 545.
Schuschnigg, Kurt von, 490–4.
Seeckt, General von, 169,
Seeds, Sir William, 559, 562, 594, 595, 597, 599, 600, 601.
Serbia: in First World War, 1; Allied undertakings to, 14, 17, 23, 25.
Sèvres, Treaty of, 125, 126, 131, 141–3.
Seydoux, French Finance Minister, 182.
Seyss-Inquart, Dr. A., 491–3.
Shanghai, 292, 294, 354, 355, 356–7.
Shidehara, Baron, 287, 288, 353, 354, 360.
Shigemitsu, M., 476.
Shuvayev, Russian War Minister, 48.
Simon, Sir John: and Russia, 323, 324; meets Hitler (1935), 326; on Japan, 356, 358; and Far East, 357; and Manchurian crisis, 363–7; and disarmament, 330, 370, 373, 374, 376, 379, 381, 382; and German air strength, 387; and U.S., 361; and air Locarno, and four-Power Pact, 397–8; and Eastern Locarno, 401; and Stresa Front, 404–5; and Italy, 412; and Manchuria, 451–2; and China, 453, 457; and Czech crisis (1938), 535, (1939), 567; and war, 617.
Simons, Walter, German Foreign Minister, 169, 170, 173, 175–6.
Sinclair, Sir Archibald, 435, 508, 578.
Singapore, 237, 286, 289–90.
Sixte, Prince, 26–7.
Slovakia, 572.
Smigly-Rydz, Marshal, 605.

Smuts, General, 28, 41, 68, 94–5, 111, 121–2, 282, 349.
Smyrna, 15, 135, 136, 137, 140, 142, 149, 154.
Snowden, Philip, 52, 247.
Sokolnikov, 321, 322.
Solf, Dr., German Colonial Secretary, 38.
Somaliland, 13, 407, 414, 418, 420.
Somme, battle, 1, 18.
Sonnino, Baron S., 27, 158.
Soong, T. V., 300.
South Africa, 232, 242, 515, 628.
South Manchuria Railway, 273–4, 351, 352, 353, 354, 355, 358, 366.
Spa Conference (1920), 88, 169–71.
Spain (civil war), 436–46.
Spring-Rice, Sir Cecil, 16, 22.
Stalin, 319–20, 326, 576, 584, 604.
Stimson, H. L., 301, 359–62, 364, 452.
Stinnes, H., 169.
Strang, W., 358, 593, 598.
Stresa Front, 404–5, 412, 493.
Stresemann, G., 189, 193, 249–54, 262, 263, 264–5, 268, 312.
Stronge, Lieut.-Colonel, 423.
Stürmer, B. V., Russian statesman, 48.
Sudan, 142, 408, 415.
Sudeten Germans: at peace settlement (1919), 111; and self-determination claim (1938), 497, 503, 506, 511, 513, 514, 516–18, 522–3, 529–30, 544.
Suez Canal, 415, 421, 580.
Sun Yat-sen, 202, 297.
Supreme Council, 135, 163, 225.
Supreme War Council, 36–7, 43, 71.
Switzerland, 560, 561, 593, 595, 597.
Sykes, Sir M., 10, 11.
Sykes–Picot Agreement, 10–11, 127, 133.

Tada, Major, 353, 454.
Tanaka, Baron, 353.
Tangier, 229.
Tangku Truce, 362, 452.

Tardieu, André, 100, 102, 104-5, 106, 343, 371, 400.
Teschen, 112, 549.
Third International, 200, 209, 219, 220, 309, 314, 317, 319.
Thomas, Albert, 48, 53.
Thomas, J. P. L., 489.
Tientsin, 476-8.
Tilea, V. V., Rumanian diplomat, 568, 575.
Times, The, 36, 56, 81, 152, 304, 432, 523-4, 557.
Tirol, South, 13, 397.
Torretta, Marquess della, 186.
Trans-Siberian Railway, 72, 351.
Treasury, 93.
Trieste, 13.
Tripoli, 409.
Trotsky, Leon, 30, 56-7, 58, 60-1, 61-3, 65, 67, 68, 73, 209, 319.
Trott zu Solz, A. von, 608.
Tsana, Lake, 414, 415.
T.U.C., 309, 443, 524.
Turkey: at war (1914), 9; and Allied war aims, 9-13, 23; peace-making (1919-23), 125-59; and Russia, 204-7; and British guarantee system (1939), 575, 583.

Uchida, Count, 301.
Ugaki, K., Japanese Foreign Minister, 467-8, 479.
Ukraine, 58, 59, 62, 68, 69, 75, 112.
Unemployment, 625-6.
United States: and Allies (1914-16), 16-19; enters war (1917), 24; and Allied war aims, 24-6; at Paris Peace Conference, 93-124; and Turkish settlement, 126, 133-5; ratification of Versailles Treaty, 134-5, 160; war debts, 179; and Dawes Plan, 192-3; and Soviet Russia, 218, 324-5; and Far East, 276-8, 293-4, 359-62; and Britain, 278-80, 283-90, 298, 337-47, 458-9, 460-6, 475-80; and disarmament, 284-6, 334-47; and Spanish civil war, 441; Neutrality Acts, 458-9; and

Japan, 465, 480; and Europe (1930s), 484-7, 623; and Czech crisis (1938-9), 524-5, 546-7, 569.
Upper Silesia, 114, 116, 176, 251, 254.

Vansittart, Sir R., 404, 418, 423, 508, 591.
Vayo, Alvarez del, 442.
Venizelos, E., 15, 135, 141, 145.
Verdun, battle (1916), 1, 19, 46.
Versailles Treaty, 121-4, 134, 135, 167, 172, 223, 226, 228, 253, 265, 272, 288, 326, 331, 346-7, 371, 374, 375, 376, 416, 426, 429, 432, 449, 482-3, 544.
Vickers Trial (1933), 323.
Viviani, R. R., French Foreign Minister, 9.
Voroshilov, Marshal K., 600, 601.
Vorovsky, 79, 206, 207, 221.

Wallhead, R. C., 305.
Wang, C. T., 202, 300-1.
Ward, Col., 69.
War Debts, 179-80, 372.
War Office, 138, 158, 578.
Washington Conference (1921-2), 218, 225, 283-91, 332-3, 347, 350, 451.
Webb, Admiral, 135.
Webster, Captain, 70.
Wedgwood, J., 247.
Weihaiwei, 275, 288.
Weir, Lord, 388.
Weizsäcker, E. von, 557.
Welck, Baron von, 520.
Welles, Sumner, 485, 486.
Wellesley, Sir V., 361.
Wellington Koo, 297.
Westminster Gazette, 34.
Weygand, General, 591.
Wiedemann, Captain, 514-15, 560.
William II, 44, 96-8.
Wilson, Sir Henry, 41, 49, 71-2, 76, 77, 79, 80.
Wilson, Sir Horace, 487, 519-20, 536, 537, 538, 607, 608.

Wilson, Hugh R., 463.

Wilson, Woodrow: attitude to war (1916), 16–18, 19, 22; war aims (1917), 23; and Allies (1917), 25–6, 31–2, 32–9; and armistice (1918), 39–44; and Allied intervention in Russia, 71–2, 76–7, 78, 83; Paris Peace Conference, 94–116; and Turkish settlement, 126, 128, 133–5; and Japan, 280.

Wirth, German Finance Minister, 169, 177, 183.

Wiseman, Sir William, 22, 23, 24, 38.

Woermann, Dr. E., 518–19, 557.

Wohlthat, Dr., 569, 606–7.

Wolmer, Viscount, 567.

World Disarmament Conference, (1932), 347, 368–84.

World Economic Conference, (1933), 323, 325, 397, 482.

Worthington-Evans, Sir L., 150–1.

Wrangel, General, 86.

Wu, C. C., 301.

Yangtze, 275, 291, 293, 315, 355, 451, 465.

Yoshida, S., 456, 459.

Youssouf Kemal Bey, 146.

Yudenich, General, 86.

Yugoslavia, 402–3.

Zinoviev, 201, 209.

'Zinoviev' Letter, 308–11, 313.